POLARIS
RANGER 800• 2010-2014

More information available at Clymer.com

Phone: 805-498-6703

Haynes Publishing Group
Sparkford Nr Yeovil
Somerset BA22 7JJ England

Haynes North America, Inc
859 Lawrence Drive
Newbury Park
California 91320 USA

ISBN-10: 1-62092-177-4
ISBN-13: 978-1-62092-177-7
Library of Congress: 2017951650

Author: Ron Wright
Technical Illustrations: Steve Amos
Cover: Mark Clifford Photography at www.markclifford.com.
2013 Polaris Ranger Crew 800 courtesy of Coyne Powersports, El Centro, California

Special tools provided by Motion Pro (www.motionpro.com) and RV Service Tools (www.rvservicetools.com)

Our thanks to Clawson Motorsports, Fresno, California, for providing the vehicles used for our teardowns and photography in this manual. Thanks also to Russel Cotta Jr. for help with clutch teardown and providing valuable technical information, and Russell Cotta for the spare engine. Special thanks to Jim Parker for help in the shop and for transporting Ranger models back and forth to the shop. We would also like to thank service writers John Guerra and Kevin McGaughey at Clawson Motorsports, Fresno, California, for taking time to answer our questions and also helping with additional research and photography during their busy work schedule.

M293, 6V1, 17-512
ABCDEFGHIJKLMNOPQRST

Common spark plug conditions

NORMAL

Symptoms: Brown to grayish-tan color and slight electrode wear. Correct heat range for engine and operating conditions.

Recommendation: When new spark plugs are installed, replace with plugs of the same heat range.

WORN

Symptoms: Rounded electrodes with a small amount of deposits on the firing end. Normal color. Causes hard starting in damp or cold weather and poor fuel economy.

Recommendation: Plugs have been left in the engine too long. Replace with new plugs of the same heat range. Follow the recommended maintenance schedule.

TOO HOT

Symptoms: Blistered, white insulator, eroded electrode and absence of deposits. Results in shortened plug life.

Recommendation: Check for the correct plug heat range, over-advanced ignition timing, lean fuel mixture, intake manifold vacuum leaks, sticking valves and insufficient engine cooling.

CARBON DEPOSITS

Symptoms: Dry sooty deposits indicate a rich mixture or weak ignition. Causes misfiring, hard starting and hesitation.

Recommendation: Make sure the plug has the correct heat range. Check for a clogged air filter or problem in the fuel system or engine management system. Also check for ignition system problems.

PREIGNITION

Symptoms: Melted electrodes. Insulators are white, but may be dirty due to misfiring or flying debris in the combustion chamber. Can lead to engine damage.

Recommendation: Check for the correct plug heat range, over-advanced ignition timing, lean fuel mixture, insufficient engine cooling and lack of lubrication.

ASH DEPOSITS

Symptoms: Light brown deposits encrusted on the side or center electrodes or both. Derived from oil and/or fuel additives. Excessive amounts may mask the spark, causing misfiring and hesitation during acceleration.

Recommendation: If excessive deposits accumulate over a short time or low mileage, install new valve guide seals to prevent seepage of oil into the combustion chambers. Also try changing gasoline brands.

HIGH SPEED GLAZING

Symptoms: Insulator has yellowish, glazed appearance. Indicates that combustion chamber temperatures have risen suddenly during hard acceleration. Normal deposits melt to form a conductive coating. Causes misfiring at high speeds.

Recommendation: Install new plugs. Consider using a colder plug if driving habits warrant.

OIL DEPOSITS

Symptoms: Oily coating caused by poor oil control. Oil is leaking past worn valve guides or piston rings into the combustion chamber. Causes hard starting, misfiring and hesitation.

Recommendation: Correct the mechanical condition with necessary repairs and install new plugs.

DETONATION

Symptoms: Insulators may be cracked or chipped. Improper gap setting techniques can also result in a fractured insulator tip. Can lead to piston damage.

Recommendation: Make sure the fuel anti-knock values meet engine requirements. Use care when setting the gaps on new plugs. Avoid lugging the engine.

GAP BRIDGING

Symptoms: Combustion deposits lodge between the electrodes. Heavy deposits accumulate and bridge the electrode gap. The plug ceases to fire, resulting in a dead cylinder.

Recommendation: Locate the faulty plug and remove the deposits from between the electrodes.

MECHANICAL DAMAGE

Symptoms: May be caused by a foreign object in the combustion chamber or the piston striking an incorrect reach (too long) plug. Causes a dead cylinder and could result in piston damage.

Recommendation: Repair the mechanical damage. Remove the foreign object from the engine and/or install the correct reach plug.

CONTENTS

NOTES

QUICK REFERENCE DATA

Model: _____ **Year:** _____

Vehicle Identification Number (VIN): _____

Engine Serial Number: _____

Throttle Body Serial Number: _____

TIRE PRESSURE

Tire pressure
  Standard Ranger models
    Front and rear .... 8-12 psi (55-83 kPa)
  Crew models
    Front.. 12 psi (83 kPa)
    Rear... 16 psi (110 kPa)
Tire tread depth (minimum) .... 1/8 in. (3.2 mm)

RECOMMENDED LUBRICANTS AND FLUIDS

Brake fluid.. DOT 4 brake fluid
Coolant
  Type .... Ethylene glycol-based antifreeze and water
  Mixture ratio... 60/40 (antifreeze/distilled water) or as required for freeze protection in operating area
  Capacity
    Standard Ranger models .... 3.25 qts. (3.1 l)
    Crew models .... 6.4 qts. (6.0 l)
Engine oil
  Type .... Polaris PS-4 or similar 4-stroke engine oil
  Capacity .... 2 qt. (1.9L/1900 ml)
Front gearcase
  Type .... Polaris Premium Demand Drive
  Capacity .... 9.0 oz. (266 ml)
Fuel requirement .... 87 octane minimum
Grease nipples... Polaris Premium U-joint Grease
Transmission
  Type .... Polaris AGL Synthetic Gearcase Lubricant
  Capacity .... 33.8 oz. (1000 ml)

SPARK PLUGS

  Type .... Champion RC7YC3
  Electrode gap .... 0.035 inch (0.90 mm)

BATTERY SPECIFICATIONS

Type and capacity
  Stock (conventional battery).. Yuasa YB30L-B, 12V, 30Ah
  Battery upgrade (maintenance-free batteries) .... Yuasa GYZ32HL, YIX30L, YIX30L-BS
Open circuit voltage (static test)
  Yuasa YB30L-B (conventional battery type)................................ 12.7 volts or higher
  Maintenance-free battery type .... 12.8 volts or higher

BULB SPECIFICATIONS

Headlights
    2010 models... 50W x 2
    2011 and later models.. 60/55W x 2
Taillight/brake light assembly
    Type .... LED
        Capacity
            Brake light... 3.1W
            Taillight... 0.3W

FUSES

2010 models
    Accessory.. 15 amp
    ECM .... 15 amp
    EFI .... 15 amp
    Lights .... 15 amp
    Main chassis... 20 amp
    EPS*... 30 amp
2011 and later models
    Accessory.. 20 amp
    Drive .... 20 amp
    ECM .... 20 amp
    EPS*... 30 amp
    Fuel pump... 10 amp
    Lights .... 20 amp
Models equipped with electric power steering (EPS)

WALKER EVANS SHOCK ABSORBER ADJUSTMENT - FRONT AND REAR

Compression adjustment positions
    Standard... 8 clicks out from fully counterclockwise position
    Softest... Adjuster turned fully counterclockwise
    Hardest.. Adjuster turned fully clockwise
Spring preload stock settings
    Front .... 10.75 inches (273 mm)
    Rear .... 10.5 inches (267 mm)

TORQUE SPECIFICATIONS

NOTE

One foot-pound (ft-lb) of torque is equivalent to 12 inch-pounds (in-lbs) of torque. Torque values below approximately 15 ft-lbs are expressed in inch-pounds, because most foot-pound torque wrenches are not accurate at these smaller values.

Item	ft.-lb.	in.-lb.	N.m
Coolant bleed screw			
At thermostat housing	--	70	8
At cylinder head	--	60-80	7-9
Engine oil drain plug	14-18	--	19-24
Front gearcase			
Oil filler plug	8-10	--	11-14
Oil drain plug	8-10	--	11-14
Transmission			
Oil level check plug	10-14	--	14-19
Oil fill plug			
2012 and later models	10-14	--	14-19
Oil drain plug	10-14	--	14-19
Spark plugs	18	--	24
Wheel nuts			
Aluminum (cast) wheels			
2010 models	90	--	122
2011 and later models			
First step (initial torque)	30	--	41
Second step	Turn 90° (1/4-turn)	--	--
Steel wheels	35	--	47

GENERAL INFORMATION

CONTENTS

1 ABOUT THIS MANUAL

The aim of this manual is to help you get the best value from your motorcycle. It can do so in several ways. It can help you decide what work must be done, even if you choose to have it done by a dealer; it provides information and procedures for routine maintenance and servicing; and it offers diagnostic and repair procedures to follow when trouble occurs.

We hope you use the manual to tackle the work yourself. For many simpler jobs, doing it yourself may be quicker than arranging an appointment to get the motorcycle into a dealer and making the trips to leave it and pick it up. More importantly, a lot of money can be saved by avoiding the expense the shop must pass on to you to cover its labor and overhead costs. An added benefit is the sense of satisfaction and accomplishment that you feel after doing the job yourself.

We take great pride in the accuracy of information given in this manual, but motorcycle manufacturers make alterations and design changes during the production run of a particular motorcycle of which they do not inform us. No liability can be accepted by the authors or publishers for loss, damage or injury caused by any errors in, or omissions from, the information given.

Using the manual

The manual is divided into Chapters. Each Chapter is divided into numbered Sections, which are headed in bold type above a horizontal line. Each Section consists of consecutively numbered paragraphs. Specifications are located at the end of each Chapter.

The reference numbers used in illustration captions pinpoint the pertinent Section and the Step within that Section. That is, illustration 3.2 means the illustration refers to Section 3 and Step (or paragraph) 2 within that Section.

Procedures, once described in the text, are not normally repeated. When it's necessary to refer to another Chapter, the reference will be given as Chapter and Section number. Cross references given without use of the word "Chapter" apply to Sections and/or paragraphs in the same Chapter. For example, "see Section 8" means in the same Chapter.

Even though we have prepared this manual with extreme care, neither the publisher nor the author can accept responsibility for any errors in, or omissions from, the information given.

NOTE

A *NOTE* provides information necessary to properly complete a procedure or information which will make the procedure easier to understand.

CAUTION

A *CAUTION* provides a special procedure or special steps which must be taken while completing the procedure where the *CAUTION* is found. Not heeding a Caution can result in damage to the assembly being worked on.

WARNING

A *WARNING* provides a special procedure or special steps which must be taken while completing the procedure where the *WARNING* is found. Not heeding a Warning can result in personal injury.

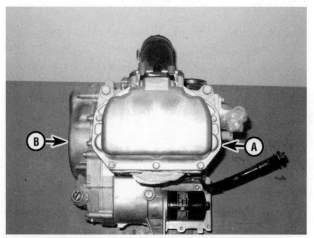

1.13 Engine position reference - PTO (A) and MAG (B) sides

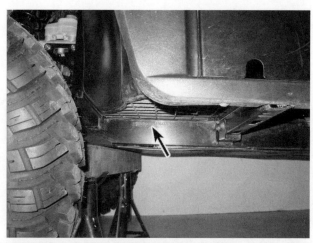

2.3a Stamped frame VIN location for standard Ranger and Crew models - lower front frame rail behind the left-front wheel

Reference to the side of the vehicle

References to the left or right side of the vehicle assume you are sitting on the driver's seat, facing forwards.

References to the side of the engine

The terms PTO and MAG are used when referring to the sides of the engine. PTO refers to the power take off side (clutch side) of the engine. With the engine sitting in the frame, the PTO side is facing the left side of the vehicle. MAG refers to the side of the engine that the flywheel (magneto) is installed on. With the engine sitting in the frame, the MAG side is facing the right side of the vehicle **(see illustration)**.

2.3b VIN decal location for standard Ranger models - frame rail underneath the passenger seat

2 MODEL NAMES AND IDENTIFICATION NUMBERS

1 Polaris uses several names to identify the models covered in this manual. For example, the 2-seat models have been named XP 800, XP 800 EPS, HD 800, 4x4 800 and 4x4 800 EPS. The 4-seat models have been named Crew 800 and Crew 800 EPS. In the interest of clarity, this manual refers to the models as either standard Ranger (2-seat) or Crew (4-seat). When it is necessary to distinguish a model with EPS, it will be identified in the text. Actual model names and their model numbers and engine model numbers are listed in this Chapter's Specifications.

2 The following identification numbers should be kept in a handy place so they are always available when purchasing or ordering parts for your machine. The VIN and engine numbers should be recorded and kept in a safe place so they can be furnished to law enforcement officials in the event of a theft.

3 **See illustrations 2.3a through 2.3c** for VIN stamped and decal number positions.

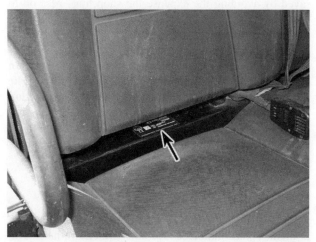

2.3c VIN decal location for Crew models - frame rail underneath the right rear passenger seat

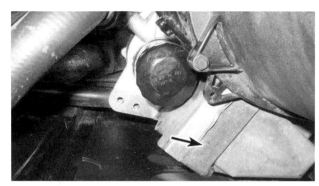

2.4a Stamped engine serial number position on lower crank-case below oil filter

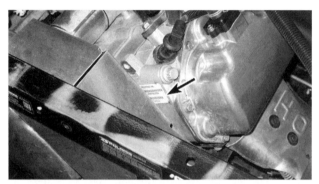

2.4b Engine decal location on cylinder head (2010 models)

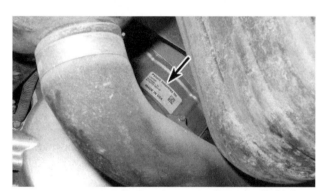

2.4c Engine decal location on cylinder block and located above the alternator cover (2011 and later models)

2.5 Transmission serial number decal location on right side of transmission (arrow)

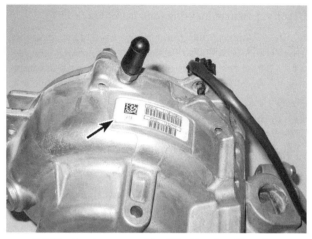

2.6 The front gearcase identification decal location

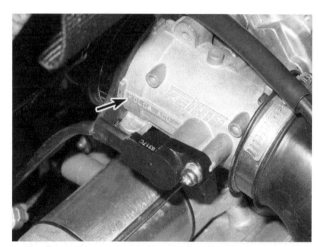

2.7 Throttle body number location (2010 model shown)

4   The engine serial number is stamped on the lower crankcase, below the oil filter (see illustration). On 2010 models, an engine serial number decal is placed on the cylinder head (see illustration). On 2011 and later models, an engine serial number decal is placed on the cylinder block (see illustration).

5   The transmission identification decal is mounted on the right side of the transmission (see illustration). Information on the decal includes serial and model numbers.

6   The front gearcase identification decal is mounted on the top of the housing (see illustration). The decal lists the serial number and the model number.

7   The throttle body number is stamped on the housing (see illustration).

Decoding vehicle identification numbers (VIN)

8   A 17-digit VIN number is used (for example, 4XAVH76A98D000000). It decodes as follows:

4XA - These first three digits, which are always the same, are the world manufacturer identification assigned to Polaris.

V - Body Style

H - Powertrain

76 - engine identification number

A - emissions

9 - check digit (can be either a letter or number)

8 - model year (2008 shown here). For the 2009 model year, the number 9 is used. Starting with 2010 models, letters are used to identify the model year: A (2010), B (2011), C (2012), D (2013) and E (2014).

D - Plant number

000000 - the serial number of the individual machine

9   Once you have found all the identification numbers, record them for reference when buying parts. Since the manufacturers change specifications, parts and vendors (companies that manufacture various components on the machine), providing the ID numbers is the only way to be reasonably sure that you are buying the correct parts.

10   Whenever possible, take the worn part to the dealer so direct comparison with the new component can be made. Along the trail from the manufacturer to the parts shelf, there are numerous places that the part can end up with the wrong number or be listed incorrectly.

11   The two places to purchase new parts for your vehicle - the accessory store and the franchised dealer - differ in the type of parts they carry. While dealers can obtain virtually every part for your vehicle, the accessory dealer is usually limited to normal high wear items such as shock absorbers, tune-up parts, various engine gaskets, cables, brake parts, etc. Rarely will an accessory outlet have major suspension components, cylinders, transmission gears, or cases.

12   Used parts can be obtained for roughly half the price of new ones, but you can't always be sure of what you're getting. Once again, take your worn part to the wrecking

2.14 Replacement key series numbers are identified by the first two numbers on the key

yard for direct comparison. When purchasing parts over the internet, make sure the seller offers a guaranteed return policy in case the condition of the part is not as described, or is simply the wrong part.

13   Whether buying new, used or rebuilt parts, the best course is to deal directly with someone who specializes in parts for your particular make.

Replacement keys

14   Replacement keys can be purchased through a Polaris dealership by using the series number on the original key to identify it. The series number is the first two numbers on the key **(see illustration)**. A dealership will then cross-reference the series number with the correct part number and order the new key. The dealership will then cut the new key by using your original key as a pattern. If you have lost all of the keys or they are damaged and cannot be traced, it will be necessary to purchase a new ignition switch.

NOTES

3   SAFETY FIRST!

1   Professional mechanics are trained in safe working procedures. However enthusiastic you may be about getting on with the job at hand, take the time to ensure that your safety is not put at risk. A moment's lack of attention can result in an accident, as can failure to observe simple precautions.

2   There will always be new ways of having accidents, and the following is not a comprehensive list of all dangers; it is intended rather to make you aware of the risks and to encourage a safe approach to all work you carry out on your bike.

Asbestos

3   Certain friction, insulating, sealing and other products - such as brake pads, clutch linings, gaskets, etc. - contain asbestos. Extreme care must be taken to avoid inhalation of dust from such products since it is hazardous to health. If in doubt, assume that they do contain asbestos.

Fire

4   Remember at all times that gasoline is highly flammable. Never smoke or have any kind of naked flame around, when working on the vehicle. But the risk does not end there - a spark caused by an electrical short-circuit, by two metal surfaces contacting each other, by careless use of tools, or even by static electricity built up in your body under certain conditions, can ignite gasoline vapor, which in a confined space is highly explosive. Never use gasoline as a cleaning solvent. Use an approved safety solvent.

5   Always disconnect the battery ground terminal before working on any part of the fuel or electrical system, and never risk spilling fuel onto a hot engine or exhaust.

6   It is recommended that a fire extinguisher of a type suitable for fuel and electrical fires is kept handy in the garage or workplace at all times. Never try to extinguish a fuel or electrical fire with water.

Fumes

7   Certain fumes are highly toxic and can quickly cause unconsciousness and even death if inhaled to any extent. Gasoline vapor comes into this category, as do the vapors from certain solvents such as trichloroethylene. Any draining or pouring of such volatile fluids should be done in a well ventilated area.

8   When using cleaning fluids and solvents, read the instructions carefully. Never use materials from unmarked containers - they may give off poisonous vapors.

9   Never run the engine of a motor vehicle in an enclosed space such as a garage. Exhaust fumes contain carbon monoxide which is extremely poisonous; if you need to run the engine, always do so in the open air or at least have the rear of the vehicle outside the workplace.

The battery

10   Never cause a spark, or allow a naked light near the vehicle's battery. It will normally be giving off a certain amount of hydrogen gas, which is highly explosive.

11   Always disconnect the battery ground terminal before working on the fuel or electrical systems (except where noted).

12   If possible, loosen the filler plugs or cover when charging the battery from an external source. Do not charge at an excessive rate or the battery may burst.

13   Take care when topping up, cleaning or carrying the battery. The acid electrolyte, even when diluted, is very corrosive and should not be allowed to contact the eyes or skin. Always wear rubber gloves and goggles or a face shield. If you ever need to prepare electrolyte yourself, always add the acid slowly to the water; never add the water to the acid.

Electricity

14   When using an electric power tool, inspection light, etc., always ensure that the appliance is correctly connected to its plug and that, where necessary, it is properly grounded. Do not use such appliances in damp conditions and, again, beware of creating a spark or applying excessive heat in the vicinity of fuel or fuel vapor. Also ensure that the appliances meet national safety standards.

15   A severe electric shock can result from touching certain parts of the electrical system, such as the spark plug wires (secondary leads), when the engine is running or being cranked, particularly if components are damp or the insulation is defective. Where an electronic ignition system is used, the secondary voltage is much higher and could prove fatal.

Remember...

16 **Don't** start the engine without first shifting the transmission into PARK. You must also apply the brake pedal before starting the engine.

17 **Don't** suddenly remove the pressure cap from a hot cooling system - cover it with a cloth and release the pressure gradually first, or you may get scalded by escaping coolant.

18 **Don't** attempt to drain oil until you are wearing suitable gloves to protect your hands and arms. When the oil is hot it can scald you and cause severe burns.

19 **Don't** grasp any part of the engine or exhaust system without first ascertaining that it is cool enough not to burn you.

20 **Don't** allow brake fluid or antifreeze to contact the vehicle's paintwork or plastic components.

21 **Don't** siphon toxic liquids such as fuel, hydraulic fluid or antifreeze by mouth, or allow them to remain on your skin.

22 **Don't** inhale dust - it may be injurious to health (see Step 3).

23 **Don't** allow any spilled oil, antifreeze or grease to remain on the floor - wipe it up right away, before someone slips on it.

24 **Don't** use damaged or ill-fitting wrenches or other tools which may slip and cause injury. These vehicles are equipped with both U.S. Standard and metric fasteners. Make sure to use the correct tool when loosening and tightening fasteners.

25 **Don't** lift a heavy component which may be beyond your capability - get assistance.

26 **Don't** rush to finish a job or take unverified short cuts.

27 **Don't** allow children or animals in or around an unattended vehicle.

28 **Don't** inflate a tire above the recommended pressure. Apart from overstressing the carcass, in extreme cases the tire may blow off forcibly.

29 **Do** ensure that the machine is supported securely at all times and with the wheels blocked to prevent the vehicle from rolling. This is especially important when the machine is blocked up to aid wheel or suspension removal.

30 **Do** take care when attempting to loosen a stubborn nut or bolt. It is generally better to pull on a wrench, rather than push, so that if you slip, you fall away from the vehicle rather than onto it.

31 **Do** wear eye protection when cleaning parts, using compressed air, and using power tools such as drill, sander, bench grinder, etc.

32 **Do** use a barrier cream on your hands prior to undertaking dirty jobs - it will protect your skin from infection as well as making the dirt easier to remove afterwards; but make sure your hands aren't left slippery. Note that long-term contact with used engine oil can be a health hazard.

33 **Do** keep loose clothing (cuffs, ties etc. and long hair) well out of the way of moving mechanical parts.

34 **Do** remove rings, wristwatch, etc., before working on the vehicle - especially the electrical system.

35 **Do** keep your work area tidy - it is only too easy to fall over articles left lying around.

36 **Do** exercise caution when compressing springs for removal or installation. Ensure that the tension is applied and released in a controlled manner, using suitable tools which preclude the possibility of the spring escaping violently.

37 **Do** ensure that any lifting equipment used has a safe working load rating adequate for the job.

38 **Do** get someone to check periodically that all is well, when working alone on the vehicle.

39 **Do** carry out work in a logical sequence and check that everything is correctly assembled and tightened afterwards.

40 **Do** remember that your vehicle's safety affects that of yourself and others. If in doubt on any point, get professional advice.

41 **If** in spite of following these precautions, you are unfortunate enough to injure yourself, seek medical attention as soon as possible.

Handling gasoline safely

42 Gasoline is a volatile flammable liquid and one of the most dangerous items in the shop. Because gasoline is used so often, many people forget that it is hazardous. Only use gasoline as fuel for gasoline internal combustion engines. When working on the vehicle, keep in mind that gasoline is always present in the fuel tank and fuel system. To avoid an accident when working around the fuel system, carefully observe the following:

Never use gasoline to clean parts. See Section 8 for additional information on parts cleaning.

a) *When working on the fuel system, work outside or in a well-ventilated area.*

b) *Do not add fuel to the fuel tank or service the fuel system while the vehicle is near open flames, sparks or where someone is smoking. Gasoline vapor is heavier than air, collects in low areas and is more easily ignited than liquid gasoline.*

c) *Allow the engine to cool completely before working on any fuel system component.*

d) *Do not store gasoline in glass containers. If the glass breaks, an explosion or fire may occur.*

e) *Immediately wipe up spilled gasoline with rags. Store the rags in a metal container with a lid until they can be properly disposed of, or place them outside in a safe place for the fuel to evaporate.*

f) *Do not pour water onto a gasoline fire. Water spreads the fire and makes it more difficult to put out. Use a class B, BC or ABC fire extinguisher to extinguish the fire.*

g) *Always turn off the engine before refueling. Do not spill fuel onto the engine or exhaust system. Do not overfill the fuel tank. Leave an air space at the top of the tank to allow room for the fuel to expand due to temperature fluctuations.*

3.43 Typical labels attached to a new vehicle

Warning Labels

43 The manufacturer has attached several warning labels to the vehicle. These labels contain instructions that are important to safety when servicing and operating the vehicle. Refer to your owner's manual for additional information on the labels. Replacement labels can be ordered through a dealership parts department. Note that the part number is printed on each label **(see illustration)**.

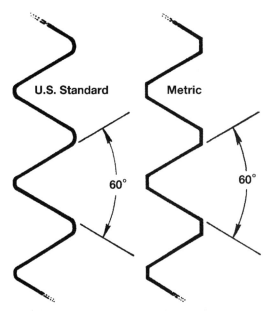

4.6 Standard and metric thread comparision

4   FASTENERS

1   Proper fastener selection and installation is important to ensure the vehicle operates as designed and can be serviced efficiently. The choice of original equipment fasteners is not arrived at by chance. When installing replacement fasteners, make sure they meet the design requirements of the manufacturer.

2   Fasteners are nuts, bolts, studs and screws used to hold two or more parts together. There are a few things to keep in mind when working with fasteners. Almost all of them use a locking device of some type, either a lockwasher, locknut, locking tab or thread adhesive. All threaded fasteners should be clean and straight, with undamaged threads and undamaged corners on the hex head where the wrench fits. Develop the habit of replacing all damaged nuts and bolts with new ones. Special locknuts with nylon or fiber inserts can only be used once. If they are removed, they lose their locking ability and must be replaced with new ones.

3   Rusted nuts and bolts should be treated with a penetrating fluid to ease removal and prevent breakage. Some mechanics use turpentine in a spout-type oil can, which works quite well. After applying the rust penetrant, let it work for a few minutes before trying to loosen the nut or bolt. Badly rusted fasteners may have to be chiseled or sawed off or removed with a special nut breaker, available at tool stores.

4   If a bolt or stud breaks off in an assembly, it can be drilled and removed with a special tool commonly available for this purpose. Most service and machine shops can perform this task, as well as other repair procedures, such as the repair of threaded holes that have been stripped out.

5   Flat washers and lockwashers, when removed from an assembly, should always be replaced exactly as removed. Replace any damaged washers with new ones. Never use a lockwasher on any soft metal surface (such as aluminum), thin sheet metal or plastic.

Fastener sizes

6   The models covered in this manual are equipped with both standard (sometimes called U.S. or SAE) and metric fasteners **(see illustration)**. Therefore, it is important to be able to tell the difference between standard and metric hardware, since they cannot be interchanged.

7   All threaded fasteners, whether standard or metric, are sized according to diameter, thread pitch and length. For example, a standard 1/2 - 13 x 1 bolt is 1/2 inch in diameter, has 13 threads per inch and is 1 inch long. An M12 - 1.75 x 25 metric bolt is 12 mm in diameter, has a thread pitch of 1.75 mm (the distance between threads) and is 25 mm long. The two bolts are nearly identical, and easily confused, but they are not interchangeable.

8   In addition to the differences in diameter, thread pitch and length, metric and standard bolts can also be distinguished by examining the bolt heads. To begin with, the distance across the flats on a standard bolt head is measured in inches, while the same dimension on a metric bolt is sized in millimeters (the same is true for nuts). As a result, a standard wrench should not be used on a metric bolt and a metric wrench should not be used on a standard bolt. Also, most standard bolts have slashes radiating out from the center of the head to denote the grade or strength of the bolt, which is an indication of the amount of torque that can be applied to it. The greater the number of slashes, the greater the strength of the bolt. Grades 2, 5 and 8 are used on models covered in this manual. Metric bolts have a property class (grade) number, rather than a slash, molded into their heads to indicate bolt strength. In this case, the higher the number, the stronger the bolt. Property class numbers 8.8, 9.8 and 10.9 are commonly used on Powersport vehicles.

9   Strength markings can also be used to distinguish standard hex nuts from metric hex nuts. Many standard nuts have dots stamped into one side, while metric nuts are marked with a number. The greater the number of dots, or the higher the number, the greater the strength of the nut.

10   Metric studs are also marked on their ends according to property class (grade). Larger studs are numbered (the same as metric bolts), while smaller studs carry a geometric code to denote grade.

11   It should be noted that many fasteners, especially Grades 0 through 2, have no distinguishing marks on them. When such is the case, the only way to determine whether it is standard or metric is to measure the thread pitch or compare it to a known fastener of the same size.

12   Standard fasteners are often referred to as SAE, as opposed to metric. However, it should be noted that SAE technically refers to a non-metric fine thread fastener only. Coarse thread non-metric fasteners are referred to as USS sizes.

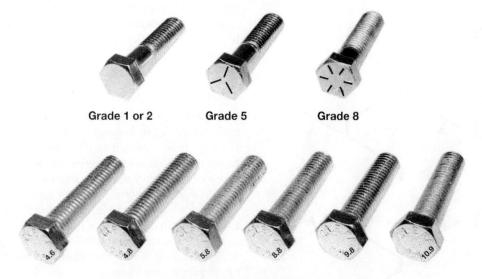

Grade 1 or 2   Grade 5   Grade 8

Bolt strength marking (standard/SAE/USS; bottom - metric)

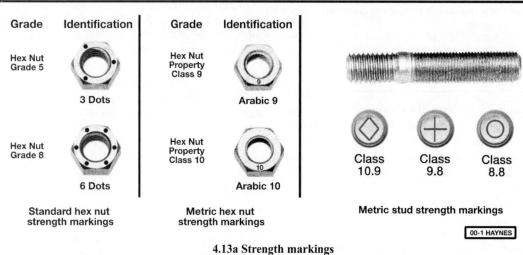

Grade	Identification	Grade	Identification
Hex Nut Grade 5	3 Dots	Hex Nut Property Class 9	Arabic 9
Hex Nut Grade 8	6 Dots	Hex Nut Property Class 10	Arabic 10

Standard hex nut strength markings

Metric hex nut strength markings

Class 10.9   Class 9.8   Class 8.8

Metric stud strength markings

00-1 HAYNES

4.13a Strength markings

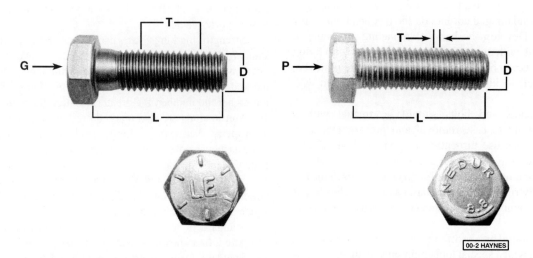

00-2 HAYNES

4.13b Standard (SAE and USS) bolt dimensions/grade marks

G   Grade marks (bolt strength)
L   Length (in inches)
T   Thread pitch (number of threads per inch)
D   Nominal diameter

4.13c Metric bolt dimensions/grade marks

P   Property class (bolt strength)
L   Length (in millimeters)
T   Thread pitch (distance between threads in millimeters)
D   Diameter

4.17 New replacement fasteners with a dry film threadlock patch preapplied to threads

13   Since fasteners of the same size (both standard and metric) may have different strength ratings, be sure to reinstall any bolts, studs or nuts removed from your vehicle in their original locations. Also, when replacing a fastener with a new one, make sure that the new one has a strength rating equal to or greater than the original **(see illustrations)**. Also note that some fasteners used on the models covered in this manual have the designation SP on the screw or bolt head. These are special fasteners and must be replaced with original OEM fasteners with the same designation.

Torque specifications, tightening sequences and procedures

14   Most threaded fasteners should be tightened to a specific torque value (torque is the twisting force applied to a threaded component such as a nut or bolt). Overtightening the fastener can weaken it and cause it to break, while undertightening can cause it to eventually come loose. Bolts, screws and studs, depending on the material they are made of and their thread diameters, have specific torque values, many of which are noted in each Chapter's Specifications. Be sure to follow the torque recommendations closely. For fasteners not assigned a specific torque, a general torque value chart is listed in this Chapter's Specifications. As was previously mentioned, the size and grade of a fastener determine the amount of torque that can safely be applied to it. Specifications for torque are provided in foot-pounds (ft.-lb.), inch-pounds (in.-lb.) and Newton-meters (Nm).

15   The materials used in the manufacture of the vehicle may be subjected to uneven stresses if fasteners are not installed and tightened correctly. Fasteners laid out in a pattern, such as cylinder head bolts, oil pan bolts, differential cover bolts, etc., must be loosened or tightened in sequence to avoid warping the component. This sequence will normally be shown in the appropriate Chapter. If a specific

pattern is not given, the following procedures can be used to prevent warping.

16   Initially, the bolts or nuts should be assembled finger-tight only. Next, they should be tightened one full turn each, in a criss-cross or diagonal pattern. After each one has been tightened one full turn, return to the first one and tighten them all one-half turn, following the same pattern. Finally, tighten each of them one-quarter turn at a time until each fastener has been tightened to the proper torque. To loosen and remove the fasteners, the procedure would be reversed. See Section 8 for additional information.

Self-Locking Fasteners

17   Many of the fasteners used on these vehicles were pre-coated with a dry film threadlock that releases evenly over the threads when the fastener is installed and tightened **(see illustration)**. Normally, these fasteners are designed to be used once, as when they are removed, the threadlock bond between the two thread sets is destroyed. However, when a new fastener is not immediately available and it is necessary to reuse the original fastener, remove the threadlocking compound residue from the threads with a thread chaser or a wire brush or wheel. Then clean the fastener threads with an aerosol electrical cleaner and allow to dry. Before installing the fastener, apply a threadlocking compound to the threads on the original fastener.

Washers

18   The two basic types of washers are plain washers and spring lockwashers. Plain washers are simple discs with a hole to fit a screw or bolt. Spring lockwashers are used to prevent a fastener from working loose. When using a spring lockwasher with a plain washer, position it between the fastener and the plain washer. Washers can be used as spacers and seals or to help distribute fastener load and prevent the fastener from damaging the component. Copper or aluminum plain washers are often used as sealing washers on drain plugs, threaded brake hose fittings and on some engine assembly screws.

19   When replacing washers make sure the replacements meet the original specifications. Thin and/or weaker grade washers can deflect under torque and cause the fastener to loosen. During disassembly, inspect spring lockwashers. If a spring lockwasher is flattened, it is fatigued and must be replaced.

Cotter Pins

20   A cotter pin is a split metal pin inserted into a hole or slot to prevent a fastener from loosening. In certain applications, such as the front and rear axles, the fastener must be secured in this way. For these applications, a cotter pin and castellated (slotted) nut is used.

21   To use a cotter pin, first make sure the diameter is correct for the hole in the fastener. After correctly tightening the fastener and aligning the holes, insert the cotter pin through the hole and bend the ends over the fastener. When

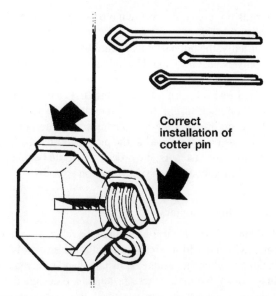

4.21 How to install and lock a cotter pin when used with a castellated nut

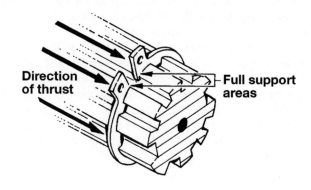

4.23 Various selection of snap rings and E-clips

Internal circlip   Plain Clip

External Clip   E-ring

using a cotter pin with a castellated nut, tighten the nut to the proper torque specification, and if necessary, tighten the nut to align the closest slot in the nut with the fastener hole and install and tighten the cotter pin **(see illustration)**. Unless instructed to do so, never loosen a tightened fastener to align the holes.

22   Cotter pins are available in various diameters and lengths. Measure length from the bottom of the head to the tip of the shortest pin.

Snap Rings and E-clips

23   Snap rings (sometimes called circlips) are circular-shaped metal retaining clips **(see illustration)**. They are required to secure parts and gears in place on parts such as shafts, pins or rods. External type snap rings are used to retain items on shafts. Internal type snap rings secure parts within housing bores. In some applications, in addition to securing the component(s), snap rings of varying thicknesses also determine endplay. These are usually called selective snap rings.

24   The two basic types of snap rings are machined and stamped snap rings. Machined snap rings can be installed in either direction because both faces have sharp edges **(see illustration)**. Stamped snap rings are manufactured with a sharp edge and round edge **(see illustration)**. When installing a stamped snap ring in a thrust application, install the sharp edge facing away from the part producing the thrust.

25   E-clips are used when it is not practical to use a snap ring. Remove E-clips with a flat blade screwdriver by prying between the shaft and E-clip. To install an E-clip, center it over the shaft groove and push or tap it into place.

4.24a Machined snap ring

Direction of thrust   Full support areas

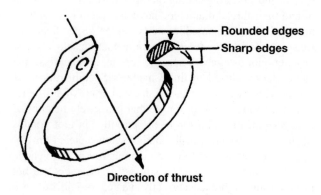

4.24b Stamped snap ring

Rounded edges
Sharp edges

Direction of thrust

4.26 Here a pair of snap ring pliers are used to install a snap ring, while a pair of needle nose pliers are used at the same time to support the snap ring and prevent it from twisting

26   Observe the following when servicing snap rings:

   a) *Wear eye protection when removing and installing snap rings.*
   b) *Remove and install snap rings with snap ring pliers (see Section 6).*
   c) *Before removing a snap ring, mark its outside with a marking pen. If the snap ring is a stamped type, the mark will help identify which side faces out so the new snap ring can be installed facing in the same direction.*
   d) *It is good practice to discard a snap ring after removing it. Snap rings are usually deformed during installation and removal, which weakens them and may cause a failure while under service. This is especially true for smaller snap rings, which can easily twist and distort during removal.*
   e) *Compress or expand snap rings only enough to install them. If overly expanded, they will lose their retaining ability.*
   f) *After installing a snap ring, check it carefully to make sure it is completely seated in its groove.*
   g) *A good way to install a new external snap ring without distorting it is to open the new snap ring with a pair of snap ring pliers while holding the back of the snap ring with a pair of needle nose pliers* **(see illustration)**. *Then hold and slide the snap ring down the shaft and seat it into its groove. This technique can also be used to remove a snap ring from a shaft once it is free from its groove.*

Sales company oil code number

OIL CLASSIFICATION
MA: Designed for high-friction applications
MB: Designed for low-friction applications

5.3 JASCO Certification Label found on oil containers

API SERVICE SYMBOL

Oil classification

When ENERGY CONSERVING is listed in this part of
the label, the oil has demonstrated energy-conserving
properties in standard tests. Do not use ENERGY
CONSERVING classified oil in motorcycle engines.
Instead, look for this API service symbol.

Oil viscosity

5.4 API service symbol found on oil containers

5   SHOP SUPPLIES

Lubricants and Fluids

1   Periodic lubrication helps ensure a long service life for
any type of equipment. Using the correct type of lubricant is
as important as performing the lubrication service, although
in an emergency the wrong type is better than not using
one. The following section describes the types of lubricants
most often required. Make sure to follow the manufacturer's
recommendations (see Chapter 2 Specifications).

Engine oils

2   Engine oil for use in a four-stroke motorcycle engine
is classified by three standards: the Japanese Automobile
Standards Organization (JASO) T 903 certification
standard, the American Petroleum Institute (API) service
classification, and the Society of Automotive Engineers
(SAE) viscosity index.
3   The JASO certification specifies the oil has
passed requirements specified by Japanese motorcycle
manufacturers. The JASO certification label identifies
which of the two separate classifications the oil meets
(see illustration). It also includes a registration number
to indicate that the oil has passed all JASO certification
standards for use in four-stroke motorcycle engines.
4   Two letters are used to indicate the API service
classification. A number or sequence of numbers and letter
(10W-40) identify the oil's SAE viscosity rating. The API
service classification and the SAE viscosity index are not
indications of oil quality (see illustration).
5   Viscosity is an indication of the oil's thickness. Thin
oils have a lower number while thick oils have a higher

number. Engine oils fall into the 0- to 50-weight range for
single-grade oils.
6   Most manufacturers recommend multi-grade oil. These
oils perform efficiently across a wide range of operating
conditions. A W after the first number indicates that the
oil is a multi-grade type and it shows the low-temperature
viscosity.
7   Always use oil with a classification recommended by
the manufacturer. Using oil with a different classification can
cause clutch slippage and engine damage. Do not use oil with
oil additives or oil with graphite or molybdenum additives.
Do not use oil with a diesel specification of CD. Do not use
vegetable, non-detergent or castor-based racing oils.

Greases

8   Grease is lubricating oil with thickening agents added
to it. The National Lubricating Grease Institute (NLGI)
grades grease. Grades range from No. 000 to No. 6, with
No. 6 being the thickest. Typical multipurpose grease is
NLGI No. 2. For specific applications, manufacturers may
recommend a water-resistant type grease or one with an
additive, such as molybdenum disulfide (MoS 2).

Molybdenum oil solution

9   This is a 1:1 mixture of engine oil and molybdenum grease, which is used as an assembly lubricant during engine and chassis assembly to prevent wear and galling during start-up. Mix the solution in a clean container and cover with a removable cap to prevent contamination during storage. Apply the mixture with an acid brush.

Coolant

10   Coolant is a mixture of water and antifreeze used to dissipate engine heat. Ethylene glycol is the most common form of antifreeze used. Check the vehicle manufacturer's recommendations when selecting antifreeze, as most require one specifically designed for use in aluminum engines. These types of antifreeze have additives that inhibit corrosion.

11   Only mix distilled water with antifreeze. Impurities in tap water may damage internal cooling system passages.

Front gearcase and transmission

12   Both drive units have different lubricant requirements and require a different oil. Refer to the oil requirements listed in Chapter 2 Specifications.

Cleaners, Degreasers and Solvents

13   Many chemicals are available to remove oil, grease and other residue from the vehicle. Before using cleaning solvents, consider their uses and disposal methods, particularly if they are not water-soluble. Local ordinances may require special procedures for the disposal of many types of cleaning chemicals.

14   Use brake parts cleaner to clean brake system components when contact with petroleum-based products will damage seals. Brake parts cleaner leaves no residue. Use electrical contact cleaner to clean electrical connections and components without leaving any residue. Carburetor cleaner is a powerful solvent used to remove fuel deposits and varnish from fuel system components. Before using a carburetor cleaner, refer to the manufacturer's recommendations for application and use.

15   Generally, degreasers are strong cleaners used to remove heavy accumulations of grease from engine and frame components.

16   Most solvents are designed to be used with a parts washing cabinet for individual component cleaning. For safety, use only nonflammable or high flash point solvents.

Gasket Sealant

17   Sealants are used in combination with a gasket, seal or occasionally alone. Follow the manufacturer's recommendation when using sealants. Use extreme care when choosing a sealant different from the type originally recommended. Choose sealants based on their resistance to heat, how various fluids may affect them, drying time, and their sealing capabilities.

18   One of the most common sealants is RTV, or room temperature vulcanizing, sealant. This sealant cures at room temperature over a specific time period. This allows the repositioning of components without damaging gaskets.

19   Moisture in the air causes most sealants to cure. Always install the tube cap as soon as possible after applying a sealant. Some sealants have a limited shelf life and will not cure properly if the shelf life has expired.

20   Keep partial tubes sealed and discard them if they have surpassed the expiration date. If there is no expiration date on a sealant tube, use a permanent marker and write the date on the tube when it is first opened. Manufacturers usually specify a shelf life of one year after a container is opened, though it is recommended to contact the sealant manufacturer to confirm shelf life.

Gasket Remover

21   Aerosol gasket remover can help remove stubborn gaskets by speeding up the removal process and prevent damage to the mating surface when scraping gaskets. Most of these products are very caustic, so care must be followed when using them. Follow the gasket remover manufacturer's instructions for use.

22   Depending on gasket thickness and other factors, the gasket remover will not always penetrate completely through the gasket with a single application. This will become evident when you attempt to remove the gasket, as the gasket scraper may only remove the gasket's top layer. When this happens, reapply the gasket remover and repeat until the gasket can be easily removed. Do not force the tool through the gasket as it may damage the gasket surface.

23   To prevent chemical overspray when applying a gasket remover, spray a small amount of gasket remover into a small plastic container and apply it to the gasket surface with an acid brush. If necessary, block off areas with paper towels.

Threadlocking Compound

24   A threadlocking compound is a fluid applied to the threads of fasteners. After tightening the fastener, the fluid dries and becomes a solid filler between the threads. This makes it difficult for the fastener to work loose from vibration or heat expansion and contraction. Some threadlocking compounds also provide a seal against fluid leaks.

25   Before applying threadlocking compound, remove any old compound from both thread areas and clean them with aerosol parts cleaner. Use the compound sparingly. Excess fluid can run into adjoining parts or between gasket surfaces.

26   Threadlocking compounds are available in various strengths, and for different operating temperature and repair applications.

6   TOOLS

1   Most of the procedures in this manual can be carried out with hand tools and test equipment familiar to the home mechanic. Always use the correct tools for the job. Keep tools organized and clean and store them in a tool chest with related tools organized together.

2   Quality tools are essential. The best are constructed of high-strength alloy steel. These tools are light, easy-to-use and resistant to wear. Their working surfaces are devoid of sharp edges and the tools are carefully polished. They have an easy-to-clean finish and are comfortable to use. Quality tools are a good investment.

3   When purchasing tools to perform the procedures covered in this manual, consider the tool's potential frequency of use. If a tool kit is just now being started, consider purchasing a tool set from a quality tool supplier. These sets are available in many tool combinations and offer substantial savings when compared to individually purchased tools. As work experience grows and tasks become more complicated, specialized tools can be added.

4   Some of the procedures in this manual specify special tools. In most cases, the tool is illustrated in use. Well-equipped mechanics may be able to substitute similar tools or fabricate a suitable replacement. However, in some cases, the specialized equipment or expertise may make it impractical for the home mechanic to attempt the procedure. When necessary, such operations are identified in the text with the recommendation to have a dealership or specialist perform the task. It may be less expensive to have a professional perform these jobs, especially when considering the cost of the equipment.

5   The manufacturer's part number is provided for many of the tools mentioned in this manual. These part numbers are correct at the time of original publication. The publisher cannot guarantee the part number of the tools in this manual will be available in the future.

Screwdrivers

6   The two basic types of screwdrivers are the slotted tip (flat blade) and the Phillips tip. These are available in sets that often include an assortment of tip sizes and shaft lengths.

7   As with all tools, use the correct screwdriver. Make sure the size of the tip conforms to the size and shape of the fastener. Use them only for driving screws. Never use a screwdriver for prying or chiseling. Repair or replace worn or damaged screwdrivers. A worn tip may damage the fastener, making it difficult to remove.

8   Phillips-head or cross-head screws are often damaged by incorrectly fitting screwdrivers. Quality Phillips screwdrivers are manufactured with their cross-head tip machined to Phillips Screw Company specifications. Poor quality or damaged Phillips screwdrivers can back out and round over the screw head (camout). Compounding the problem of using poor quality screwdrivers are Phillips-head screws made from weak or soft materials and screws initially installed with air tools.

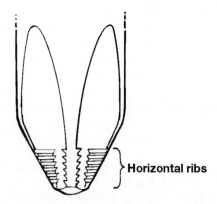

6.9 Horizonal ribs used on ACR Phillips II screwdrivers help prevent camout when loosening and tightening cross-head screws

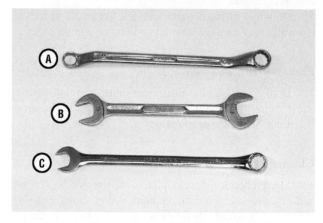

6.11 Several popular wrench designs for performing service work

A   *Box-end wrench*   C   *Combination wrench*
B   *Open-end wrench*

9   The best type of screwdriver to use on Phillips screws is the ACR Phillips II screwdriver, patented by the Phillips Screw Company. ACR stands for the horizontal anti-camout ribs found on the driving faces or flutes of the screwdriver's tip **(see illustration)**. ACR Phillips II screwdrivers were designed as part of a manufacturing drive system to be used with ACR Phillips II screws, but they work well on all common Phillips screws. A number of tool companies offer ACR Phillips II screwdrivers in different tip sizes and interchangeable bits to fit screwdriver bit holders.

10   Another way to prevent camout and increase the grip of a Phillips screwdriver is to apply valve grinding compound or Permatex Screw & Socket Gripper onto the screwdriver tip. After loosening/tightening the screw, clean the screw recess to prevent possible contamination.

Wrenches

11   Wrenches are designed to loosen and tighten fasteners and available in a variety of types and sizes. Open-end, box-end and combination wrenches are commonly used when servicing powersport vehicles **(see illustration)**.

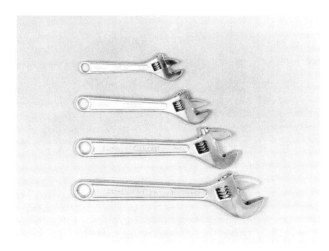

6.16 Adjustable wrenches are available in different sizes

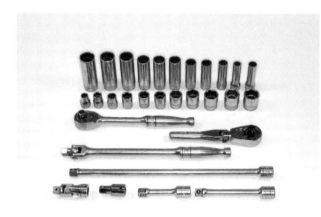

6.17a 3/8 in. socket set

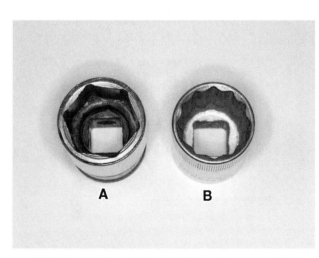

6.17b 6-point (A) and 12-point (B) socket comparision

12 The number stamped on the wrench refers to the distance between the fixed jaws on the tool. It does not refer to the fastener diameter. Always match the wrench to the size of the fastener head. If a wrench is too large, it will round the corners on the fastener, making it harder to remove and tighten.

13 The box-end wrench is designed with either a 6- or 12-point opening. This is the preferred wrench to use when loosening and tightening fasteners as its design allows it to grip the fastener on all sides and reduces the chance of the tool slipping. For stubborn or damaged fasteners, the 6-point provides superior holding ability by contacting the fastener across a wider area at all six edges. For general use, the 12-point works well as it allows the wrench to be removed and reinstalled without moving the handle over such a wide arc. The 12-point opening can be used to turn both hexagonal and square fastener heads.

14 An open-end wrench is fast and works best in areas with limited access. However, it contacts the fastener at only two points, and is subject to slipping under heavy force, especially if the fastener head is soft and/or worn. A box-end wrench is preferred in most instances, especially when breaking loose and applying the final tightness to a fastener.

15 The combination wrench has a box-end on one end, and an open-end on the other. This combination makes a convenient tool, as the box-end can be used to loosen/tighten the fastener and the open-end can be used to quickly remove/install the fastener.

Adjustable wrenches

16 An adjustable wrench has one fixed jaw and one adjustable jaw and can fit nearly any nut or bolt head that has clear access around its entire perimeter **(see illustration)**. However, while useful in some situations, adjustable wrenches should never be used as a substitute for box-end and open-end wrenches. Typically, adjustable wrenches are used to hold a nut or bolt while the other end of the fastener is turned with a socket or wrench. And because adjustable wrenches can only contact the fastener at two points, they are more prone to slipping off a fastener. When using an adjustable wrench, position its solid jaw so that it is the one transmitting the force, and tighten the knurled nut as tight as possible.

Socket wrenches, ratchets and handles

WARNING:

Do not use hand sockets with air or impact tools as they may shatter and cause injury. Always wear eye protection when using air and impact tools.

17 Sockets that attach to a ratchet handle are available in 6-point and 12-point openings and different drive sizes **(see illustrations)**. The drive size indicates the size of the square hole that accepts the ratchet handle - 1/4 in.,

3/8 in., 1/2 in., 3/4 in. and larger. The number stamped on the socket is the size of the work area and must match the fastener head.

18   As with wrenches, a 6-point socket provides superior holding ability, while a 12-point socket needs to be moved only half as far to reposition it on the fastener.

19   Sockets are designated for either hand or impact use. Impact sockets are made of a thicker material for more durability. Compare the size and wall thickness of a 19-mm hand socket and a 19-mm impact socket **(see illustration)**. Use hand sockets with hand-driven attachments. Use impact sockets when using an impact driver or air tool.

20   Various handles are available for sockets. The speed handle is used for fast operation. Flexible ratchet heads in varying lengths allow the socket to be turned with varying force and at odd angles. Extension bars allow the socket setup to reach difficult areas. The ratchet is the most versatile. It allows the user to install or remove the fastener without removing the socket.

21   Sockets combined with any number of drivers make them undoubtedly the fastest, safest and most convenient tool for fastener removal and installation.

Hand impact driver

> *WARNING:*
>
> *Do not use hand sockets with air or impact tools because they may shatter and cause injury. Always wear eye protection when using air and impact tools.*

22   A hand impact driver provides extra force for removing fasteners by converting the impact of a hammer into a turning motion. This makes it possible to remove stubborn fasteners without damaging them. This tool is especially useful when trying to remove screws that cannot be loosened with a screwdriver. Impact drivers and interchangeable bits are available from most tool suppliers **(see illustration)**. When using a socket with an impact driver, make sure the socket is designed for impact use.

Allen wrenches

23   Allen wrenches are used to turn fasteners with hexagonal recesses in the fastener head. These wrenches are available in L-shaped bars, hex sockets, T-handle and ball hex types **(see illustration)**. Allen screws and bolts are sometimes called socket screws and bolts.

Torx tools

24   A Torx fastener head has a 6-point star-shaped pattern, and can be either internal or external. Torx fasteners are identified with a T (internal) or E (external) and a number indicating their drive size. For example, T25 or E10. Tools required to turn Torx fasteners are available in several different types, similar to those found for Allen wrenches (see Step 23). External Torx sockets are also available.

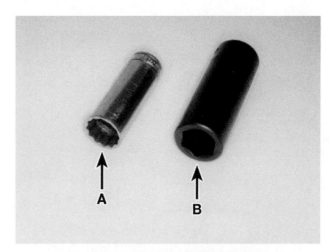

6.19 Hand (A) and impact (B) socket comparision

6.22 Hand impact driver with different interchangeable bits

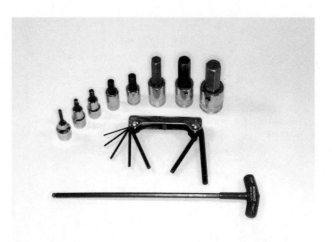

6.23 Several types of tools used to turn Allen screws

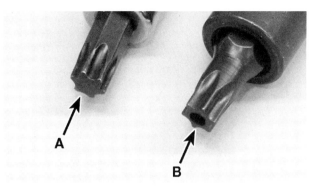

6.24 Regular (A) and security (B) Torx sockets

6.25a Pliers

6.25b Locking pliers

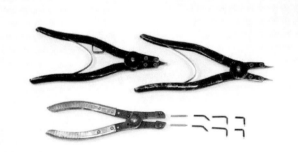

6.26 Snap ring pliers

Internal type security Torx fasteners have a post in the center of their head and require a security driver to turn it. To do this, security drivers are made with a a hole in the center of their head **(see illustration)**.

Pliers

25   Pliers come in a wide range of types and sizes **(see illustration)**. Pliers are useful for holding, cutting, bending, and crimping. Do not use them to turn fasteners unless they are designed to do so. Each design has a specialized function. Slip-joint pliers are general-purpose pliers used for gripping and bending. Diagonal cutting pliers are needed to cut wire and can be used to remove cotter pins. Needlenose pliers are used to hold or bend small objects. Locking pliers hold objects tightly **(see illustration)**. They have many uses ranging from holding two parts together, to gripping the end of a broken stud. Use caution when using locking pliers as the sharp jaws and applied pressure will damage the objects they hold.

Snap ring pliers

> *WARNING:*
> *Snap rings can slip and fly off when removing and installing them. In addition, the snap ring pliers' tips may break. Always wear eye protection when using snap ring pliers.*

26   Snap ring pliers are specialized pliers with tips that fit into the ends of snap rings to remove and install them. Snap ring pliers are available with a fixed action (either internal or external) or are convertible (one tool works on both internal and external snap rings). They may have fixed tips or interchangeable ones of various sizes and angles **(see illustration)**.

Hammers

> *WARNING:*
> *Always wear eye protection when using hammers. Make sure the hammer face is in good condition and the handle is not cracked. Select the correct hammer for the job and make sure to strike the object squarely. Do not use the handle or the side of the hammer to strike an object.*

27   Various types of hammers are available to fit a number of applications. A ball-peen hammer is used to strike another tool, such as a punch or chisel. Soft-faced hammers are required when a metal object must be struck without damaging it. Never use a metal-faced hammer on engine and suspension components; damage will occur in most cases.

Ignition grounding tool

28   Some test procedures in this manual require turning the engine over without starting it. Do not remove the spark plug cap and crank the engine without grounding the plug cap. Doing so may damage the ignition system.

29   An effective way to ground the system is to fabricate a tool using a No. 6 screw, two washers and a length of wire with an alligator clip soldered on one end (see illustration). To use the tool, insert it into the spark plug cap and attach the alligator clip to a known engine ground.

30   This tool is safer to use than a spark plug or spark tester because there is no spark to potentially ignite fuel vapor spraying from an open spark plug hole or leaking fuel component.

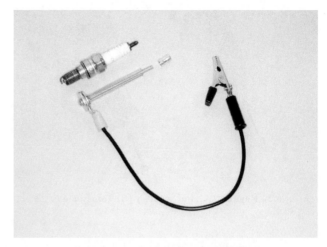

6.29 Shop made ignition grounding tool

Gear holder

> *WARNING:*
>
> *Using a hand-grinder and a cut-off wheel as described here will cause flying particles that can cause permanent eye damage. Do not operate a grinding tool without eye protection.*

31   An inexpensive gear holder can be made by using a small hand-grinder and cut-off wheel to cut a section of gear teeth from a discarded gear. Note that small cut-off wheels wear rapidly, especially when cutting gears and other hardened material. Purchase a sufficient amount of cut-off wheels for the job. If possible, select a gear with a large inside diameter. This will reduce the amount of material that must be cut through the gear to make the gear holder.

32   Mark the number of gear teeth to be removed, then mount the gear in a vise. Cut through the gear with a hand grinder and cut-off wheel at the two marks (see illustrations). If the gear holder is too long after cutting, you can shorten it with a hand grinder and shape it as required to fit your application.

> *WARNING:*
>
> *The gear holder and gear will be hot after cutting them. Allow both parts to cool before handing them.*

6.32a Cutting through a gear with a small hand-grinder and cut-off wheel . . .

Clutch tools

33   Special tools are needed to remove and service the drive and driven clutches. These tools are available from RV Service Tools (www.rvservicetools.com) or from a dealership. Tool numbers are listed in the relevant sections of this chapter. Do not attempt to service a clutch unless all the indicated tools are on hand. The clutch may be damaged if it is serviced without the proper tools. If the tools are unavailable, have the work performed by a dealer service department or other qualified service shop.

6.32b ... results in a small section of gear teeth that can be used as a gear holder

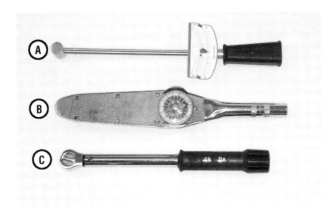

6.34 Torque wrenches

A   Deflecting beam
B   Dial indicator
C   Micrometer or
    audible click

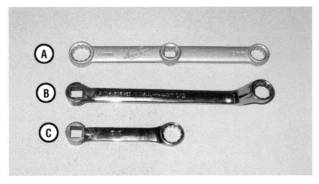

6.35a Torque adapters

A   Aftermarket torque adapter
B   Shop made torque adapter
C   Shop made torque adapter

6.35b Motion Pro Torque Wrench Adapter - allows torquing of fasteners using combination wrench sizes 1/4-3/4 in. (6-19 mm) and Allen wrenches

Torque wrenches

34   Torque wrenches are essential for tightening critical fasteners, like head bolts, flywheel and suspension fasteners. A torque wrench is used with a socket, torque adapter or similar extension to tighten a fastener to a measured torque.

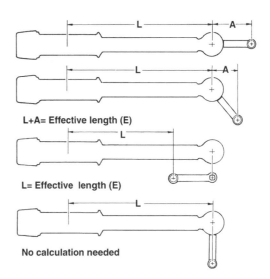

L+A= Effective length (E)

L= Effective length (E)

No calculation needed

6.37a Torque adapter positions and how they affect torque when mounted on a torque wrench

Torque wrenches come in several drive sizes (1/4, 3/8, 1/2 and 3/4) and have various methods of reading the torque value. The drive size indicates the size of the square drive that accepts the socket, adapter or extension. Common methods of reading the torque value are the deflecting beam, the dial indicator and the micrometer or audible click **(see illustration)**. When choosing a torque wrench, consider the torque range, drive size and accuracy. The torque specifications in this manual provide an indication of the range required. A torque wrench is a precision tool that must be properly cared for to remain accurate. Store torque wrenches in cases or separate padded drawers within a toolbox. Follow the manufacturer's instructions for their care and calibration.

Torque adapters

35   Torque adapters, or extensions, extend or reduce the reach of a ratchet, breaker bar and torque wrench and allow the fastener to be loosened or torqued when a normal socket or wrench cannot access the fastener. Specific adapters are required to perform some of the procedures in this manual. These are available from the vehicle manufacturer, aftermarket tool suppliers, or can be fabricated to suit a specific purpose **(see illustrations)**.

36   When you mount a torque adapter onto a torque wrench and it changes the length of the torque wrench (the effective lever length), the torque reading on the wrench will not equal the actual torque applied to the fastener. Before using a torque wrench with this set-up, it is necessary to recalibrate the torque setting on the wrench to compensate for the change of lever length. However, when a torque adapter is mounted at a right angle on the torque wrench, calibration is not required because the length of the torque wrench did not change.

37   To recalculate a torque reading when using a torque adapter, note the examples and formula **(see illustrations)**.

$$TW = \frac{TA \times L}{L + A}$$

TW is the torque setting or dial reading on the wrench.

TA is the torque specification and the actual amount of torque that will be applied to the fastener.

A is the amount that the adapter increases (or in some cases reduces) the effective lever length as measured along the centerline of the torque wrench.

L is the lever length of the wrench as measured from the center of the drive to the center of the grip.

The effective length is the sum of L and A.

Example:

TA = 20 ft.-lb.

A = 3 in.

L = 14 in.

$$TW = \frac{20 \times 14}{14 + 3} = \frac{280}{17} = 16.5 \text{ ft.lb.}$$

In this example, the torque wrench would be set to the recalculated torque value (TW = 16.5 ft.lb.). When using a beam-type wrench, tighten the fastener until the pointer aligns with 16.5 ft.-lb. In this example, although the torque wrench is preset to 16.5 ft.-lb., the actual torque is 20 ft.-lb.

6.37b Formula and example on how to recalculate a torque wrench when a torque adapter extends the length of the torque wrench

7   MEASURING TOOLS

1   The ability to accurately measure components is essential to successfully service many components. Engines, transmissions and other components are manufactured to close tolerances, and obtaining consistently accurate measurements is essential.

2   Each type of measuring instrument is designed to measure a dimension with a certain degree of accuracy and within a certain range. When selecting the measuring tool, make sure it is applicable to the task.

3   As with all tools, measuring tools provide the best results if cared for properly. Improper use can damage the tool and cause inaccurate results. If any measurement is questionable, verify the measurement using another tool.

4   Accurate measurements are only possible if the mechanic possesses a feel for using the tool. Heavy-handed use of measuring tools produces less accurate results. Hold the tool gently by the fingertips so the point at which the tool contacts the object is easily felt. This feel for the equipment will produce more accurate measurements and reduce the risk of damaging the tool or component.

Feeler gauge

5   The feeler, or thickness gauge, is used for measuring the distance between two surfaces **(see illustration)**. A feeler gauge set consists of an assortment of steel strips of graduated thicknesses. Each blade is marked with its thickness. Blades can be of various lengths and angles for different procedures. Wire (round) type gauges are used to measure spark plug gap.

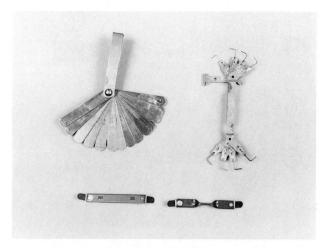

7.5 Feeler gauges

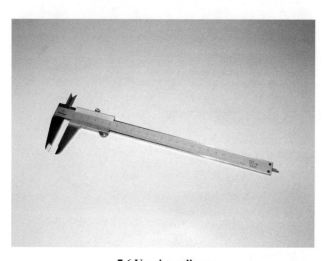

7.6 Vernier caliper

Calipers

6   Calipers are excellent tools for obtaining inside, outside and depth measurements **(see illustration)**. Although not as precise as a micrometer, they allow reasonable precision. Most calipers have a range up to 150 mm (6 in.).

7   Calipers are available in dial, vernier or digital versions. Dial calipers have a dial readout that provides convenient reading. Vernier calipers have marked scales that must be compared to determine the measurement. The digital caliper uses an LCD to show the measurement.

8   Properly maintain the measuring surfaces of the caliper. There must not be any dirt or burrs between the tool and the object being measured. Never force the caliper closed around an object; close the caliper around the highest point so it can be removed with a slight drag. Some calipers require calibration. Always refer to the manufacturer's instructions when using a new or unfamiliar caliper.

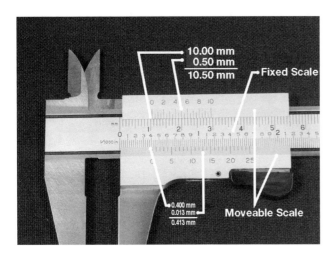

7.9 Example on how to read a metric vernier caliper

7.10 Micrometer used to measure a small hole gauge

9   To begin reading a metric vernier caliper, note that the fixed scale is marked in 1 mm increments. Ten individual lines on the fixed scale equal 10 mm (1 cm). The moveable scale is marked in 0.05 mm (hundredth) increments. To obtain a reading, establish the first number by the location of the 0 line on the moveable scale in relation to the first line to the left on the fixed scale. In this example, the number is 10 mm. To determine the next number, note which of the lines on the movable scale align with a mark on the fixed scale. A number of lines will seem close, but only one will align exactly. In this case, 0.50 mm is the reading to add to the first number. The result of adding 10 mm and 0.50 mm is a measurement of 10.50 mm **(see illustration)**.

Micrometers

10   A micrometer is an instrument designed for linear measurement using the decimal divisions of the inch and meter. While there are many types and styles of micrometers, most of the procedures in this manual call for an outside micrometer. The outside micrometer is used to measure the outside diameter of cylindrical forms and the thicknesses of materials **(see illustration)**.

11   A micrometer's size indicates the minimum and maximum size of a part that it can measure. The usual sizes are 0-1 in. (0-25 mm), 1-2 in. (25-50 mm), 2-3 in. (50-75 mm) and 3-4 in. (75-100 mm).

12   Micrometers that cover a wider range of measurements are available. These use a large frame with interchangeable anvils of various lengths. This type of micrometer offers a cost savings; however, its overall size may make it less convenient.

Adjustment

13   Before using a micrometer, it's important to check its adjustment. First clean the anvil and spindle faces.

14   To check a 0-1 in. (0-25 mm) micrometer, turn the thimble until the spindle contacts the anvil. If the micrometer has a ratchet stop, use it to ensure the proper amount of pressure is applied. If the adjustment is correct, the 0 mark on the thimble will align exactly with the 0 mark on the sleeve line. If the marks do not align the micrometer is out of adjustment. Follow the manufacturer's instructions on how to adjust the micrometer.

15   To check a micrometer larger than 1 in. (25 mm), use the standard gauge supplied with the micrometer. A standard gauge is a steel block, disc or rod that is machined to an exact size. Place the standard gauge between the spindle and anvil to measure its outside diameter or length. If the micrometer has a ratchet stop, use it to ensure the proper amount of pressure is applied. If the adjustment is correct, the 0 mark on the thimble will align exactly with the 0 mark on the sleeve line. If the marks do not align, the micrometer is out of adjustment. Follow the manufacturer's instructions on how to adjust the micrometer.

Care

16   Micrometers are precision instruments and must be used and maintained with great care. Note the following:

   a) *Store micrometers in protective cases or separate padded drawers in a toolbox.*
   b) *When finished with a micrometer and putting it away, make sure the spindle and anvil faces do not contact each other or another object. If they do, temperature changes and corrosion may damage the contact faces.*
   c) *Do not clean a micrometer with compressed air. Dirt forced into the tool will cause wear and damage.*
   d) *Periodically lubricate micrometers to prevent corrosion.*

Reading

17   When using a micrometer, close it around the highest point so it can be removed with a slight drag. This takes a touch feel and can be learned with practice. Numbers are then taken from different scales on the micrometer and added together.

18   For accurate results, properly maintain the measuring surfaces of the micrometer. There cannot be any dirt or burrs between the tool and the measured object. Never force the micrometer closed around an object.

Standard inch micrometer

19   The standard inch micrometer is accurate to one thousandth of an inch (0.001 in.). The sleeve is marked in 0.025 in. increments. Every fourth sleeve mark above the sleeve line is numbered 1, 2, 3, 4, 5, 6, 7, 8, and 9. These numbers indicate 0.100, 0.200, 0.300, and so on. The marks below the sleeve line are spaced 0.025 in. apart. The tapered end of the thimble has 25 lines marked around it. Each mark equals 0.001 in. One complete turn of the thimble will align its zero mark with the first mark on the sleeve or 0.025 in. **(see illustration)**.

20   When reading an inch micrometer, add the number of thousandths of an inch on the sleeve line with the number of thousandths on the thimble **(see illustration)**.

   a) *Find the largest number visible above the sleeve line. Each of these whole numbers equals 0.100 in.*

   b) *Below the sleeve line, count the number of lines visible between the numbered sleeve mark and the edge of the thimble. Each of these sleeve marks equal 0.025 in.*

   c) *Read the thimble mark that aligns with the sleeve line. Each thimble mark equals 0.001 in. Note that if a thimble mark does not align exactly with the sleeve line, estimate the amount between the lines. For accurate readings in ten-thousandths of an inch (0.0001 in.), use a vernier inch micrometer.*

   d) *Add the three readings to determine the overall measurement.*

Metric micrometer

21   The standard metric micrometer is accurate to one one-hundredth of a millimeter. The sleeve line is graduated in millimeter and half millimeter increments. The marks on the upper half of the sleeve line equal 1.00 mm. Each fifth mark above the sleeve line is identified with a number. The number sequence depends on the size of the micrometer. A 0-25 mm micrometer, for example, will have sleeve marks numbered 0 through 25 in 5 mm increments. This numbering sequence continues with larger micrometers. On all metric micrometers, each mark on the lower half of the sleeve (half-millimeter line) equals 0.50 mm. The tapered end of the thimble has 50 lines marked around it. Each mark equals 0.01 mm. One complete turn of the thimble aligns its 0 mark with the first line on the lower half of the sleeve line, or 0.50 mm. **(see illustration)**.

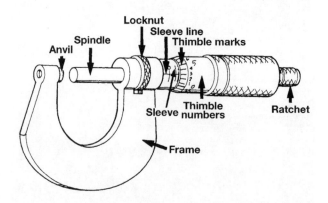

7.19 Standard inch micrometer details

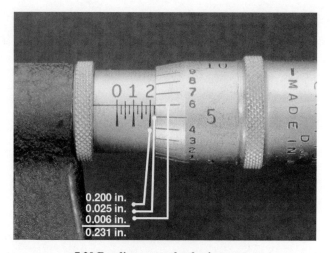

0.200 in.
0.025 in.
0.006 in.
0.231 in.

7.20 Reading a standard micrometer

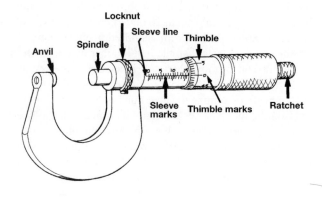

7.21 Metric micrometer details

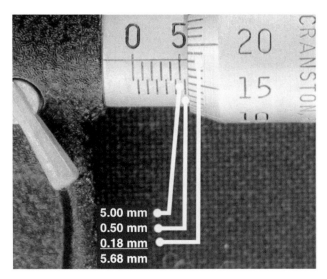

7.22 Reading a metric micrometer

22   When reading a metric micrometer, add the number of millimeters and half-millimeters on the sleeve line to the number of one one-hundredth millimeters on the thimble **(see illustration)**:

   a) *Read the upper half of the sleeve line and count the number of lines visible. Each upper line equals 1 mm.*

   b) *See if the half-millimeter line is visible on the lower sleeve line. If so, add 0.50 mm to the reading. If this line is not visible, do not add 0.50 mm.*

   c) *Read the thimble mark that aligns with the sleeve line. Each thimble mark equals 0.01 mm. Note that if a thimble mark does not align exactly with the sleeve line, estimate the amount between the lines. For accurate readings in two-thousandths of a millimeter (0.002 mm), use a metric vernier micrometer.*

   d) *Add the three readings to determine the overall measurement.*

Telescoping and Small Hole Gauges

23   Use telescoping gauges and small hole gauges to measure bores and holes in component parts. Neither gauge has a scale for direct readings. An outside micrometer must be used to determine the reading.

24   To use a telescoping gauge, select the correct size gauge for the bore **(see illustration)**. Loosen the lock screw on the end of the gauge and compress the moveable posts by hand, then tighten the lock screw. Center the gauge in the bore at the measurement point. With the gauge at a slight angle, loosen the lock screw to allow the posts to slide out and contact the bore wall. Lightly tighten the lock screw, then tilt the gauge in the opposite direction to allow the posts to move inward and conform to the bore diameter. Do not tighten the lock screw so tight that the posts cannot move inward when conforming to the bore as they could damage the bore surface. You should feel a slight resistance as you tilt and remove gauge from the bore. After removing the gauge, measure across the gauge posts with a micrometer to determine the bore inside diameter. Repeat the measurement several times to get a feel for using the gauge and to obtain accurate measurements.

7.24 Telescoping gauge set

7.25 Small hole gauge set

25   To use a small hole gauge, select the correct size gauge for the bore **(see illustration)**. Loosen the lock screw and adjust the gauge so that it can be installed into the bore without any resistance. Tighten the lock screw on the end of the gauge to carefully expand the gauge fingers to the limit within the bore, while slightly tilting it from side to side until you feel a slight resistance. Do not overtighten the gauge; there is no built-in release. Excessive tightening can damage the bore surface and tool. Remove the gauge and measure the outside dimension with a micrometer **(see illustration 7.10)**. Repeat the measurement several times to get a feel for using the gauge and to obtain accurate measurements.

Dial Indicator

26   A dial indicator is a gauge with a dial face and needle used to measure variations in dimensions and movements. Measuring brake rotor runout is a typical use for a dial indicator.

27   Dial indicators are available in various ranges and graduations and with three types of mounting bases: magnetic, clamp or screw-in stud **(see illustration)**.

Cylinder Bore Gauge

28   A cylinder bore gauge is similar to a dial indicator. These typically consist of a dial indicator, handle and different length adapters (anvils) to fit the gauge to various bore sizes. The bore gauge is used to measure bore size, taper and out-of-round. When using a bore gauge, follow the manufacturer's instructions.

7.27 Dial indicator mounted on a magnetic stand

Compression Gauge

29   A compression gauge measures combustion chamber (cylinder) pressure. The gauge adapter is either inserted and held in place or screwed into the spark plug hole to obtain the reading. Disable the engine so it will not start and hold the throttle in the wide-open position when performing a compression test. An engine that does not have adequate compression cannot be properly tuned. Refer to Chapter 1, Section 5 on how to perform a compression check.

Leak-down tester

30   A leak-down tester is installed into the spark plug hole, much like a compression gauge. With the piston positioned at top dead center on its compression stroke, the cylinder is pressurized with compressed air supplied by an air compressor. As air is forced into the cylinder with the valves closed, the rate leakage is measured as a percentage.

31   Used in conjunction with a compression test, which may identify one or more weak cylinders, the leak-down test better determines exactly where the problem lies. A cylinder leak-down can locate problems like a blown head gasket, leaking valves, cracked cylinder heads and walls, and faulty pistons or rings. With the cylinder pressurized, air will leak past the worn or defective parts. By listening for the escaping air, you can tell exactly where it's coming from. Refer to Chapter 1, Section 6 on how to perform a leak-down test

Multimeter

32   A multimeter is an essential tool for electrical system diagnosis **(see illustration)**. The term "multimeter" is used because the meter performs multiple functions: it measures voltage (volts), resistance (ohms) and current (amperes). The meter can be used to check battery voltage and the charging system. Before using a multimeter, read the manufacturer's instructions.

7.32 Digital multimeter

33   Some manufacturers' specifications for electrical components are based on results using a specific test meter. Results may vary if using a meter not recommend by the manufacturer. Such requirements are noted in the text when applicable.

Back-probe pins

34   Back-probing a connector is required when performing voltage and resistance tests at a connector when it is connected into the vehicle's wiring harness. To do this you insert a thin back-probe pin, or simply a pin, into the rear of the connector shell to contact the terminal inside. If a pin is used, you then clip your meter lead to the pin. If you've never back-probed a connector before, it's easy to see that it must be performed carefully to prevent from damaging or distorting the connector, wire and terminal. On most connectors, wires entering the connectors are

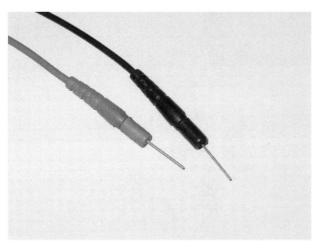

7.35 Back probe pins used with a multimeter

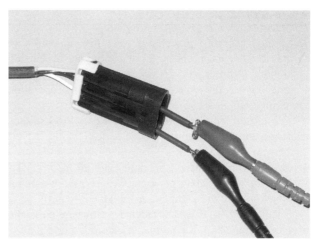

7.40 T-pins shown inserted into a connector with attached ohmmeter leads used to check the resistance of a sensor

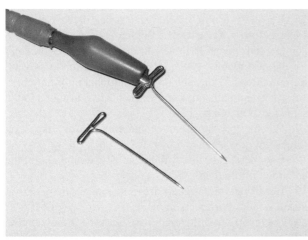

7.36 T-pins are useful for penetrating wires and contacting connector terminals

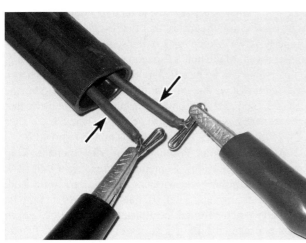

7.38 Note how heat shrink has been applied to these two T-pins

protected by seals. Damaged seals and distortion can lead to a poor connection and corrosion at that terminal later. While back-probe pins come in all styles and names, the term back-probe pin is used generically to represent all types of electrical test pins.

35 Use test leads equipped with back-probe pins **(see illustration)**. These lead ends are smaller than typical test leads and mount onto standard meter leads. Sharpen the lead ends if blunt.

36 If back probe pins are not available, use T-pins available from fabric and craft stores **(see illustration)**. These pins are thin and sharp enough to push through a wire without damaging it, and the T-shaped head makes an ideal connection point for your meter's test leads.

37 To use a back-probe pin when a connector is not disconnected from a component or another connector, slide it alongside the wire and insert it into the seal from behind the connector until it contacts the terminal inside the connector. Make sure not to short circuit the pin by inserting it through two wires.

38 When using back-probe during testing, note they are not insulated and must not contact each other when installed in a circuit or they will short circuit. Position them and the meter test leads carefully during testing. If necessary, you can easily insulate a set of back-probe with heat shrink **(see illustration)**. Another benefit to using heat shrink on a back-probe pin is how the heat shrink can hold the back-probe pin in place against a connector's male terminal during the test.

39 After completing the test, remove the back-probe pin and cover the pin hole in the wire or seal with silicone sealant, making sure the sealant does not contact the connector terminals.

40 Back-probe pins can also be inserted into the front of a connector to contact the terminals when the connector halves have been disconnected for test purposes **(see illustration)**.

8   SERVICE METHODS

1   Many of the procedures in this manual are straightforward and can be performed by anyone reasonably competent with tools. However, consider previous experience carefully before performing any operation involving complicated procedures.

2   When servicing the vehicle, park it on a level surface and apply the parking brake. If necessary, block the wheels so the vehicle cannot roll in either direction.

3   Label all parts for location and mark all mating parts for position. If possible, photograph or draw the number and thickness of any shim as it is removed. Identify parts by placing them in sealed and labeled plastic bags or plastic divided containers. It is possible for carefully laid out parts to become disturbed, making it difficult to reassemble the components correctly without a diagram. See Step 22 for additional information.

4   Label disconnected wires and connectors. Do not rely on memory alone. Note how they are routed and the location of all clips and plastic ties.

5   Protect finished surfaces from physical damage or corrosion. Keep gasoline and other chemicals off painted surfaces.

6   Use penetrating oil on frozen or tight bolts. If it is necessary to use heat, note that heat can warp, melt or affect the temper of parts. Heat also damages the finish of paint and plastics. Refer to Steps 50 through 61 for additional information.

7   To prevent objects or debris from falling into the engine, cover all openings.

8   Read each procedure thoroughly and compare the illustrations to the actual components before starting the procedure. Perform the procedure in sequence.

9   Recommendations are occasionally made to refer service to a dealer service department or specialist. In these cases, the work can be performed more economically by the specialist than by the home mechanic.

10   The term replace means to discard a defective part and replace it with a new part. Overhaul means to remove, disassemble, inspect, measure, repair and/or replace parts as required to recondition an assembly.

11   If special tools are required, have them available before starting the procedure. When special tools are required, they will be described at the beginning of the procedure.

12   When a part is a press fit or requires a special tool for removal, the information or type of tool required to remove the part is identified in the text. Otherwise, if a part is difficult to remove or install, determine the cause before proceeding.

13   Some operations require the use of a hydraulic press. If a press is not available, have these operations performed by a shop equipped with the necessary equipment. Do not use makeshift equipment that may damage the vehicle or cause injury to yourself.

14   Do not direct high-pressure water at the steering assembly, fuel hoses, wheel bearings, suspension and electrical components. The water forces the grease out of

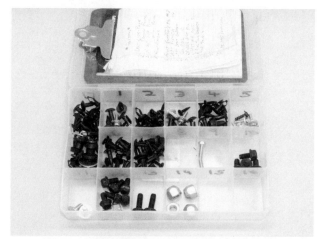

8.22 Compartmented boxes work well for storing fasteners and small parts during service

the bearings and could damage the seals.

15   Repairs are much faster and easier if the vehicle is clean before starting work. Degrease the vehicle with a commercial degreaser; follow the directions on the container for the best results. Clean all parts with cleaning solvent. Refer to Steps 33 through 43 for additional information.

16   Make sure all shims and washers are reinstalled in the same location and position.

17   Whenever rotating parts contact a stationary part, look for a shim or washer.

18   Use new gaskets if there is any doubt about the condition of old ones.

19   If self-locking fasteners are used, replace them. Do not install standard fasteners in place of self-locking ones.

20   Use grease to hold small parts in place if they tend to fall out during assembly. Do not apply grease to electrical or brake components.

Component disassembly

21   Component disassembly should be done with care and purpose to help ensure that the parts go back together properly. Always keep track of the sequence in which parts are removed. Make note of special characteristics or marks on parts that can be installed more than one way, such as a grooved thrust washer on a shaft. It is a good idea to lay the disassembled parts out on a clean surface in the order that they were removed. It may also be helpful to make sketches or take digital photos of components before removal.

22   When removing fasteners from a component, keep track of their locations. Sometimes threading a bolt back in a part, or putting the washers and nut back on a stud, can prevent mix-ups later. If nuts and bolts cannot be returned to their original locations, they should be kept in a compartmented box or a series of small boxes. Plastic boxes and cupcake tins are ideal for this purpose, since each cavity can hold the bolts and nuts from a particular area (fender rivets and screws, engine cover screws, engine mount bolts, etc.). A pan of this type is especially helpful

when working on assemblies with very small parts, such as the valve train, other engine components and body fasteners. The cavities can be numbered with a marking pen to identify the contents (see illustration).

23 Whenever wiring looms, harnesses or connectors are separated, it is a good idea to identify the two halves with numbered pieces of masking tape so they can be easily identified.

Gasket sealing surfaces

24 Throughout any vehicle, gaskets are used to seal the mating surfaces between two parts and keep lubricants, fluids, vacuum or pressure contained in an assembly.

25 Many times these gaskets are coated with a liquid or paste-type gasket sealing compound before assembly. Age, heat and pressure can sometimes cause the two parts to stick together so tightly that they are very difficult to separate. Often, the assembly can be loosened by striking it with a soft-face hammer near the mating surfaces. A regular hammer can be used if a block of wood is placed between the hammer and the part. Do not hammer on parts that could be easily damaged. With any particularly stubborn part, always recheck to make sure that every fastener has been removed.

26 Avoid using a screwdriver or bar to pry apart an assembly, as it can easily mar the gasket sealing surfaces of the parts, which must remain smooth.

27 After the parts are separated, the old gasket must be carefully scraped off and the gasket surfaces cleaned. If possible, spray the gasket first with a chemical gasket remover to help soften the gasket. Stubborn gasket material can also be soaked using a rust penetrant or solvent. However, depending on the gasket type and how hard the gasket has set up, the chemical may only soften the outer or exposed part of the gasket, so when scraping the gasket, only one layer of the gasket will tear away. While it is necessary to reapply the spray, using a chemical gasket remover is still the safest way to remove gaskets that are difficult to remove.

28 The use of a chemical gasket remover may cause paint to peel or bubble. To control the chemical, first spray it into a plastic container, then apply it with an acid brush.

CAUTION:

Never use gasket removal solutions or caustic chemicals on plastic or other composite components.

29 A scraper can be fashioned from a piece of copper tubing by flattening and sharpening one end. Copper is recommended because it is usually softer than the surfaces to be scraped, which reduces the chance of gouging the part. Some gaskets can be removed with a wire brush, but regardless of the method used, the mating surfaces must be left clean and smooth.

30 Single-edge razor blades mounted in a holder are popular, but the extremely sharp blades can flex and

possibly snag and gouge the gasket surface. When using a razor blade, make an initial check by using both sides of the blade. Usually, one side of the blade is duller and the best choice to use.

31 Gasket stain is not a raised surface, but instead a normal appearance on gasket surfaces left by the previous compressed gasket. Do not attempt to remove the stain marks as the operation may gouge and damage the surface.

32 If for some reason the gasket surface is gouged, then a gasket sealer thick enough to fill scratches will have to be used during reassembly of the components. For most applications, a non-drying (or semi-drying) gasket sealer should be used.

Cleaning parts

33 Cleaning parts is one of the more overlooked, tedious and difficult service jobs performed in the home garage. To help with gasket removal and other parts cleaning jobs, several types of chemical cleaners and solvents are available for shop use. Most are poisonous and extremely flammable. To prevent chemical exposure, vapor buildup, fire and injury, read and observe the entire product label before using any chemical. Always know what type of chemical is being used, and whether it is poisonous and/or flammable.

34 Do not use more than one type of cleaning solvent at a time. If mixing chemicals is required, measure the proper amounts according to the manufacturer.

35 Work in a well-ventilated area.

36 Wear chemical-resistant gloves that are appropriate for the chemical being used.

37 Wear safety glasses or goggles.

38 Wear a vapor respirator if the chemical manufacturer instructions call for it.

39 Wash hands and arms thoroughly after cleaning parts.

40 Thoroughly clean all oil, grease and cleaner residue from any part that must be heated.

41 Use a nylon brush when cleaning parts. Metal brushes may cause a spark.

42 When using a parts washer, only use the solvent recommended by the manufacturer as some pumps are only designed to work with water-based cleaners. Also make sure the parts washer is equipped with a fusible link that will lower the metal lid in case of fire.

43 Keep chemicals away from children and pets.

Hose removal tips

44 Hose removal precautions closely parallel gasket removal precautions. Avoid scratching or gouging the surface that the hose mates against or the connection may leak. This is especially true for radiator hoses. Because of various chemical reactions, the rubber in hoses can bond itself to the metal spigot that the hose fits over. To remove a hose, first loosen the hose clamps that secure it to the spigot. Then, with slip-joint pliers, grab the hose at the clamp and rotate it around the spigot. Work it back and

forth until it is completely free, then pull it off. Silicone or other lubricants will ease removal if they can be applied between the hose and the outside of the spigot. Apply the same lubricant to the inside of the hose and the outside of the spigot to simplify installation.

45   As a last resort (and if the hose is to be replaced with a new one anyway), the rubber can be slit with a knife and the hose peeled from the spigot. If this must be done, be careful that the metal connection is not damaged.

46   If a hose clamp is broken or damaged, do not reuse it. Wire-type clamps usually weaken with age, so it is a good idea to replace them with screw-type clamps whenever a hose is removed.

Tightening sequences and procedures

47   Most threaded fasteners should be tightened to a specific torque value (torque is the twisting force applied to a threaded component such as a nut or bolt). Overtightening the fastener can weaken it and cause it to break, while undertightening can cause it to eventually come loose. Bolts, screws and studs, depending on the material they are made of and their thread diameters, have specific torque values, many of which are noted in each Chapter's Specifications. Be sure to follow the torque recommendations closely. For fasteners not assigned a specific torque, a general torque value chart is listed in this Chapter's Specifications.

48   Fasteners laid out in a pattern, such as cylinder head bolts, alternator cover screws, gearcase cover screws, etc., must be loosened or tightened in sequence to avoid warping the component. This sequence will normally be shown in the appropriate Chapter. If a specific pattern is not given, the following procedures can be used to prevent warping.

49   Initially, the screws, bolts or nuts should be assembled finger-tight only. Next, they should be tightened one full turn each, in a criss-cross or diagonal pattern. After each one has been tightened one full turn, return to the first one and tighten them all one-half turn, following the same pattern. Finally, tighten each of them one-quarter turn at a time until each fastener has been tightened to the proper torque. To loosen and remove the fasteners, the procedure would be reversed.

Heating components

WARNING:

Wear protective gloves to prevent burns and injury when heating parts.

CAUTION:

Do not use a welding torch when heating parts. A welding torch applies excessive heat to a small area very quickly, which can damage parts.

50   A heat gun or propane torch is required to disassemble, assemble, remove and install many parts and components in this manual. Read the safety and operating information supplied by the manufacturer of the heat gun or propane torch while also noting the following:

51   The work area should be clean and dry. Remove all combustible components and materials from the work area. Wipe up all grease, oil and other fluids from parts. Check for leaking or damaged fuel system components. Repair or remove these parts before beginning work.

52   Never use a flame near the battery, fuel tank, fuel lines or other flammable materials.

53   When using a heat gun, remember that the temperature can be in excess of 1000 degrees F (540 degrees C).

54   Have a fire extinguisher near the job.

55   Always wear protective goggles and gloves when heating parts.

56   Before heating a part installed on the vehicle, check areas around the part and those hidden that could be damaged or possibly ignite. Do not heat surfaces that can be damaged by heat. Shield materials near the part or area to be heated, for example, cables and wiring harnesses.

57   Before heating a part, read the entire procedure to make sure the required tools are available. This allows quick work while the part is at its optimum temperature.

58   Before heating parts, consider the possible effects. To avoid damaging a part, monitor the temperature with heat sticks or an infrared thermometer, if possible. Another way, though not as accurate, is to place tiny drops of water on the part. When the water starts to sizzle, the part is usually hot enough. Keep the heat in motion to prevent overheating.

Removing Frozen Fasteners

59   If a fastener cannot be removed, several methods may be used to loosen it. First, liberally apply penetrating oil, and let it penetrate for 10-15 minutes. Rap the fastener several times with a small hammer. Do not hit it hard enough to cause damage. Reapply the penetrating oil if necessary.

60   For frozen screws, apply penetrating oil as described, and then insert a screwdriver in the slot and rap the top of the screwdriver with a hammer. This loosens the rust so the screw can be removed in the normal way. If the screw head is too damaged to use this method, grip the head with locking pliers and twist it out.

61   If heat is required, refer to Steps 50 through 58 for additional information.

Removing Broken Fasteners

62   If the head breaks off a screw or bolt, several methods are available for removing the remaining portion (using a screw extractor is described in Step 63). If a large portion of the remainder projects out, try gripping it with locking pliers. If the projecting portion is too small, file it to fit a wrench or cut a slot in it to fit a screwdriver. Other popular methods include drilling the fastener with left-hand drill bits, and if fastener size and conditions allow, weld a nut on top of the fastener, then turn the nut to remove the fastener. If necessary, take the part to a machine shop and have them remove the broken fastener.

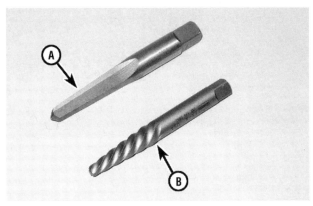

8.63a Taper type (A) and spiral type (B) screw extractors

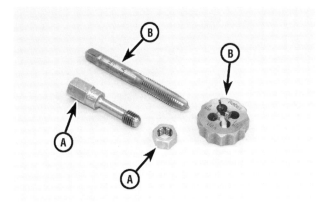

8.65a Thread chasers (A) and rethreading tap and die (B)

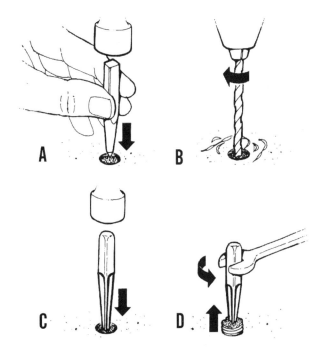

8.63b To use a taper type screw extractor, first center punch the exact center of the fastener (A) and then drill the correct size hole in the fastener (B). Tap the extractor into the hole until it is wedged in place (C) and turn it counterclockwise to remove the fastener (D). Spiral type screw extractors are used in a similar way, except you thread them counterclockwise into the hole. When the extractor grips the hole tightly, continue turning it to unscrew and remove the fastener

63 Screw extractors are popular because they are readily available, but they are made of very hard material and can break off inside the fastener. Always follow the manufacturer's instructions when selecting the drill and extractor sizes for the size fastener you are removing. Before using an extractor, it is necessary to drill a hole in the fastener. To help find and mark its center point, try to flatten the top of the broken fastener with a file or a suitable size bit installed in a hand grinder. Then locate the center point of the fastener as close as possible and mark it with a punch. Note that if the punch mark and hole is off-center, it will be more difficult to install and use the extractor successfully, as

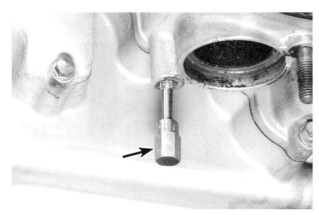

8.65b Thread chaser (arrow) being used to clean and repair a threaded hole in a cylinder head

the wall thickness will be thinner on one side. This is often the reason an extractor breaks off or slips when using it. It is also helpful to heat the area around a fastener before trying to turn and remove it **(see illustrations)**.

Repairing damaged threads

64 It is not uncommon to find damaged threads due to corrosion, seized fasteners and wear. Steps 65 through 70 describe tools and methods on repairing damaged threads.

Minor repair

65 If a fastener is difficult to start and has a nick or burr on the threads, use a thread chaser to repair and clean the threads. While rethreading taps and dies are more common, thread chasers are designed to clean and repair internal and external threads without removing material from the part, and are not designed to cut new threads. Depending on the work conditions and thread classification, rethreading taps and dies may remove material from existing threads and weaken them **(see illustrations)**.

Threaded insert

66 If an internal thread cannot be repaired by chasing it with a thread chaser, it is probably damaged and will

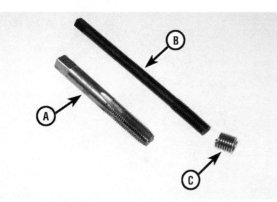

8.66a Typical Helicoil kit details (regular thread type)

A   *Screw thread insert (STI) tap*
B   *Installation tool*
C   *Insert*

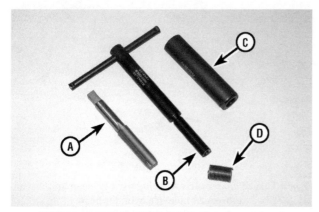

8.66b Typical Helicoil kit details (fine thread type)

A   *Screw thread insert (STI) tap*
B   *Installation tool*
C   *Prewinder tool (used for fine threads only)*
D   *Insert*

require a threaded insert to repair it. Steps 67 through 69 describe how to install a Helicoil **(see illustrations)**.

NOTE:

There are different Helicoil kits available, and some of the tools and kits will differ from those shown in this procedure. Read the instructions provided with the Helicoil kit while using the following information as a supplement.

67   Clean the damaged hole and then inspect the component for cracks and other damage. If the hole can be repaired, measure the fastener threads to determine the correct insert to use.
68   The following illustrations and captions describe how to install a regular thread type Helicoil, beginning with **illustration 8.68a**. Be sure to stay in order and read the caption accompanying each illustration.
69   When repairing a hole with fine threads, the Helicoil set will also include a prewinder tool along with the regular installation tool **(see illustration 8.66b)**. The prewinder tool compresses the insert for proper installation **(see illustration)**.

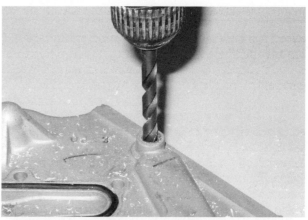

8.68a Refer to the manufacturer's instructions and select the correct size drill bit. Then drill the threaded hole to the correct depth. If possible, mount the assembly in a drill press to help ensure the drill bit is square with the hole. Failing to drill a hole square with the component is the biggest cause of failure when installing a threaded insert. When finished, clean the hole to remove chips and other debris

8.68b Tap the hole with the special STI (screw thread insert) tap included in the insert kit. Make sure and align the tap squarely with the hole. It must not be tilted. Depending on component material (steel or alloy) use the appropriate tapping fluid on the tap. After tapping the hole, thoroughly clean and dry the threads and hole with compressed air

8.68c Thread the insert fully onto the installation tool until you can hook the tang on the insert against the shoulder on the bottom of the tool (arrow). Before installing the insert, apply a medium strength threadlock onto the threads in the hole

8.68d With the installation tool mounted on a tap wrench, carefully align and slowly thread the insert into the threaded hole . . .

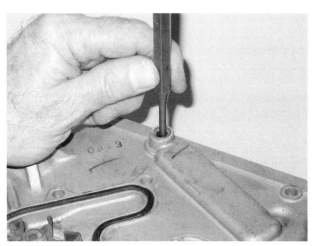

8.68g . . . and break it off with a punch or rod. Make sure to retrieve the tang so it doesn't remain in the hole or in the component you are repairing

8.68e . . . until the top thread on the insert is below the top of the hole (arrow) the amount specified on the instruction sheet included in the insert kit - usually 1/4 to 1/2 turn. Then reverse the installation tool and remove it from the insert

8.68h Thread the appropriate fastener into the insert to make sure it is positioned square with the hole

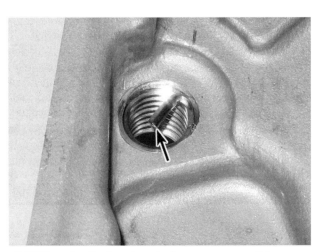

8.68f Examine the insert, and when you are sure it is properly installed, locate the tang (arrow) on the bottom of the insert . . .

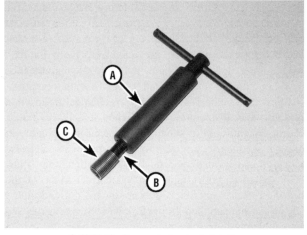

8.69 Helicoil prewinder tool details

A   Prewinder tool   C   Insert
B   Installation tool

70   Time-Sert thread inserts are another popular thread repair tool that works well when repairing a threaded hole where the threads must start at the top of a hole.

Stud Removal/Installation

71   A stud removal tool is available from most tool suppliers **(see illustration)**. This tool makes the removal and installation of studs easier. If one is not available and the threads on the stud are not damaged, thread two nuts onto the stud and tighten them against each other **(see illustration)**. Remove the stud by turning the lower nut.

72   Before removing the stud, measure its height above the surface. This dimension will be used when installing the new stud. Note that if the manufacturer lists a height measurement for a stud, it will be listed in the text.

73   Thread the stud removal tool onto the stud and tighten it, or thread two nuts onto the stud and tighten them together.

74   Remove the stud by turning the stud remover or the lower nut. If it is difficult to loosen the stud, it may have been installed with a high strength threadlock. If necessary, heat the area around the stud with a heat gun or hand-held torch, then loosen and remove it. After removing the stud, identify top and bottom threads as they may be different lengths, and the new stud must be installed with the correct side facing up.

75   Remove any threadlocking compound from the threaded hole. Clean the threads with an aerosol parts cleaner.

76   Install the stud removal tool onto the new stud, or thread two nuts onto the stud.

77   Apply threadlocking compounding compound to the threads on the end of the stud that will be installed in the component.

78   Using the same tools or methods, install the stud and position it at the height recorded in Step 72. Remove the tool or two nuts from the stud.

Bearings

General information

79   Bearings are precision parts and must be maintained with proper lubrication and the general maintenance of other components that can affect bearing operation. Bearings can be damaged through mechanical failure and through normal operating wear. When it is discovered a bearing is damaged, it should be replaced immediately to prevent secondary damage to other components. Because bearings can be damaged during installation, they must be installed carefully and with the correct tools. While bearing replacement procedures are included in individual Chapters where applicable, the following Steps can be used as a guideline for removing and installing bearings.

80   Read the appropriate Steps to determine what tools will be required. When using heat, make sure all of the

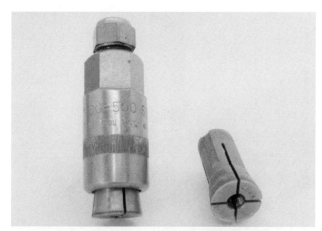

8.71a Stud removal tool with an additional collet

8.71b If the threads on a stud are in good condition, install and tighten two nuts (arrow) against each other, then turn the inner nut to remove the stud, and turn the outer nut when installing the stud

necessary tools are on hand so the procedure can be performed quickly (see Steps 99 through Step 110).

81   Unless otherwise specified, install bearings with the manufacturer's mark or number facing outward.

82   Before removing a bearing, check in the appropriate Chapter to see if there are any special instructions for bearing removal.

83   If a seal is installed on the outside of a bearing, remove the seal by referring to the procedure in the appropriate Chapter and to Steps 111 through 117.

84   Note and record the direction in which the numbers on the bearing face. This information will help to correctly align the new bearing with its bore. Also note if the bearing is installed at a certain depth and if there are any oil passages that must not be obstructed when installing the new bearing.

85   When a bearing is installed inside a bore, note which direction the bearing must be removed from. Bearings often seat against a shoulder and must be driven out the opposite way.

86   Bearing retainers are sometimes used to position and hold bearings in their bores. When a bearing retainer is used, it must be removed first, then the bearing. Before

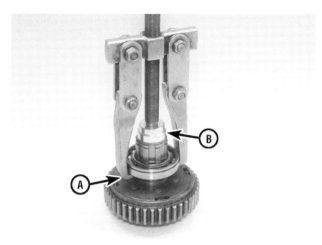

8.90a This 2-jaw puller has room to grab the bearing (A) -
note the spacer (B) used between the shaft and puller screw

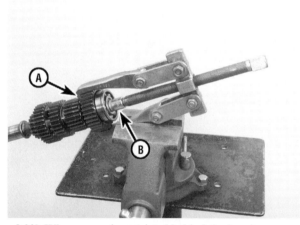

8.90b When access is restricted behind the bearing, mount
the puller jaws against the adjacent gear or component (A) -
note the spacer (B) used between the shaft and puller screw

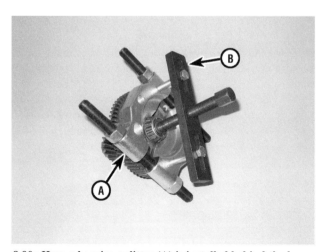

8.90c Here a bearing splitter (A) is installed behind the bearing and used with a bearing puller (B)

8.91 Set-up on how to use a bearing splitter (A), spacer (B)
and press to remove a bearing from a shaft - the spacer must
be sized so it can pass through the bearing without
any interference

removing a bearing retainer, note the fasteners used to secure them in place. These fasteners are usually secured with a threadlock and tightened securely. Heat the area around the screws to soften the threadlock, then loosen and remove them. When Phillips countersunk screws are used, first heat the area around the screws as described, then use a hand impact driver with the correct size Phillips bit to loosen them. These screws can be difficult to remove, and especially when the screw head is damaged.

87   Before removing a bearing from a shaft, make sure the shaft end is not damaged. Remove any burrs with a grinding stone or file.

88   Before installing a new bearing on a shaft, make sure the bearing surface on the shaft is clean and free of all burrs and raised surfaces.

89   Before installing a new bearing in a housing, make sure the housing is clean and the bearing bore is free of all burrs and raised surfaces. Any oil holes that align with the bearing bore in the housing must be clean.

Bearings installed on shafts

90   If using a 2- or 3-jaw puller, mount the puller so the jaws are positioned behind the bearing inner race or gear, depending on what the puller can grab against. When centering the puller screw against the shaft, place a spacer against the shaft to protect from damaging the shaft end, and especially if the shaft end is hollow. Also, if an oil jet or passage is centered in the end of the shaft, the spacer must be shaped so that it protects the oil jet or passage from damage. When space behind the bearing is limited, a bearing splitter and a puller that can thread into the splitter can be used (see illustrations).

91   When using a press to remove a bearing from a shaft, support the bearing with a bearing splitter on the press bed. Center the shaft so that it has room to pass through the press bed without contacting any of the blocks used to support the bearing. Also note that the moment the bearing is free from the shaft, the shaft will drop to the floor. Make sure to secure or hold the shaft to prevent it from falling. When using a press to remove bearing from a housing, support the housing with wooden blocks to prevent damage to the housing (see illustration).

8.92 When installing a bearing on a shaft, use a hollow driver that contacts only on the bearing's inner race - the driver must also be long enough to pass over the shaft without contacting it

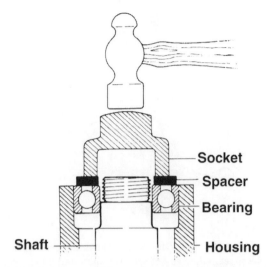

8.93 Set-up for installing a bearing over a shaft and into a housing at the same time

92   When installing a bearing on a shaft, apply pressure to the inner bearing race. Use a hollow driver (socket, pipe, etc.), making sure it is deep enough to avoid contacting the end of the shaft **(see illustration)**.

93   When installing a bearing over a shaft and into a housing at the same time, a tight fit will be required for both outer and inner bearing races. In this situation, install a spacer underneath the driver tool so pressure is applied evenly across both races **(see illustration)**. If the outer race is not supported, the balls will push against the outer bearing race and damage it.

Bearings installed in housings without blind holes

94   If a bearing can be driven out of a housing, first heat the housing to expand the bearing bore to help ease bearing removal. Then support the housing on wooden blocks near the bearing to prevent damage to the housing and gasket surfaces. If part of the outer race is accessible, place a driver so that it contacts this part of the bearing. If not, it will be necessary to remove the bearing by driving against its inner race. Use a hammer or press to drive the bearing out of the housing **(see illustration)**.

95   When installing a bearing into a housing, first support the housing on wooden blocks. If using a press, make sure the bearing in the housing is centered in the press bed and with the press ram. Then install and center the bearing into the bore with its correct side facing up. Sometimes a bearing will drop slightly in the bore and stop, or it will remain against the outer edge of the bore. Either way, it must be centered with the bore and remain centered as it is being installed. Heating the housing and freezing the bearing is a good way to install a bearing, as the temperature difference may allow the bearing to drop into and center itself in the bore (see Steps 105 through 110). Sometimes the bearing may drop all the way into the bore. If it does, make sure it bottoms completely. If force is required to install the bearing, place a driver against its outer race and drive or press it into the bore to its correct depth. Usually, bearings are installed until they bottom against a shoulder **(see illustrations)**.

8.94 Set-up for driving a bearing out of a housing

8.95a When using a bearing driver or socket to install a bearing in a housing, the tool must only contact the bearing's outer race (arrow)

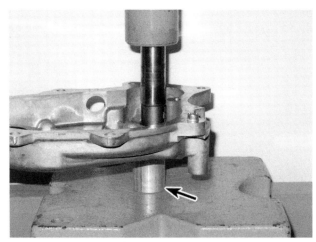

8.95b When installing a bearing in a housing, support the area underneath the bearing to prevent damage to the housing, especially when using a press, as the bearing, bearing bore and press ram must be centered - housings are often irregular in shape and difficult to support

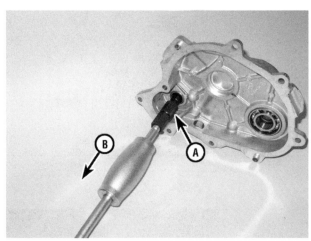

8.96 With the collet (A) locked against the backside of the bearing, operate the slide-hammer (B) to remove the bearing

8.103 Secure the bearing with a wire hook bent to hold it in the container of oil

Bearings installed in blind holes

96 When a bearing is installed in a blind hole, a blind bearing puller and the correct size collet are required. Collets are sized to match the inside diameter of bearings. Select the correct size collet and thread it fully onto the puller. Then insert the collet into the bearing and tighten it to expand and lock its shoulder against the backside of the bearing. While supporting the housing, hold the puller shaft and operate the slide-hammer to remove the bearing **(see illustration)**.

97 Sometimes it may be possible to heat the housing, and then tap it and have the bearing fall out of its bore. After heating the housing, turn it over and see if the bearing falls out. If not, it may be necessary to tap the housing with a plastic faced hammer, or tap the housing on a large wooden block.

98 Install bearings in blind holes as described in Step 95.

Interference fit

99 Removing and installing bearings can be made easier by applying heat to the housings and heat and cold to the bearings, depending on the application. This is especially true for bearings installed with an interference fit on a shaft or in a housing.

Bearings installed on shafts

> *CAUTION:*
>
> *Follow all safety precautions when heating a bearing. Do not heat the bearing above the specified temperature, and make sure all equipment used is suitable for this procedure.*

> *CAUTION:*
>
> *Do not heat the bearing with a torch. This can change the case hardening of the bearing and cause permanent damage.*

100 Remove the bearing from the shaft (see Steps 90 and 91).

101 When the shaft is ready for the bearing, secure the shaft in a vise with soft jaws and with the end of the shaft that the bearing is to be installed on facing up. Remove any burrs from the end of the shaft with a file. Then clean all oil and other residue from the bearing surface on the shaft.

102 Identify the bearing so that you install it with its correct side facing away from the shaft (toward the outside).

103 Support the bearing on a hook and lower it into a container of clean oil, making sure it does not contact the bottom or sides of the container **(see illustration)**. With the bearing in the oil, heat the oil to approximately 180-200 degrees F (82-93 degrees C). If the bearing is equipped with an integral seal, make sure the oil temperature does not exceed 200 degrees F (93 degrees C). Monitor the temperature with an infrared thermometer or a suitable thermometer placed in the oil. Do not allow the thermometer to contact the bottom or sides of the pan.

104 When the oil temperature is correct and while wearing clean gloves, lift the bearing out of the oil and quickly install it over the end of the shaft with the outside of the bearing facing toward the outside of the shaft (see illustration). The bearing should slide down the shaft and bottom in its correct position. As the bearing chills it will tighten on the shaft, so work quickly. Leave the shaft in the vise until the bearing is fully locked in position.

Bearings installed in a housing

105 Place the new bearing in a freezer for a minimum of two hours. Chilling a bearing slightly reduces its outside diameter while the heated bearing housing assembly is slightly larger due to heat expansion. This makes bearing installation easier.

106 The aluminum housings can be heated to help ease bearing removal and installation. Before heating a housing, clean it thoroughly to remove all oil and solvent residue. Then wash the housing with detergent and water and rinse with clear water. Repeat as necessary.

107 Remove any sensor/switch housings or other plastic parts, such as oil screens, to prevent the heat from damaging them.

108 Heat the housing to approximately 200 degrees F (93 degrees C) with a heat gun or on a hot plate. Monitor temperature with an infrared thermometer or place tiny drops of water on the housing as it is being heated; when they begin to sizzle and evaporate immediately, the temperature is approximately correct. Heat only one housing at a time.

109 When the housing is hot enough, tap it on a wooden block to see if the bearing falls. If the bearing did not fall out, tap it out with a driver or socket (see Step 94) or use a blind bearing puller (see Step 96) if the bearing is installed in a blind hole.

110 Reheat the housing, then install the bearing by hand, if possible. If necessary, tap the bearing into the housing (see Step 95).

Seals

111 Seals are used to contain oil, water, grease or combustion gasses in a housing or shaft (see illustration). Improper removal of a seal can damage the housing or shaft. Improper installation of the seal can damage the seal and its bore or shaft and cause a leak.

112 When there is no shaft running through the seal, prying is generally the easiest and most effective method of removing a seal from the housing. When necessary, place a rag under the pry tool to prevent damage to the housing. When positioning the pry tool, do not allow the edge of the tool to contact the seal bore as the tool will score the bore wall (see illustration).

113 To remove a seal that is contacting a shaft, use a No. 30 or No. 31 drill bit and drill a hole through the outer surface of the seal. Do not allow the drill bit to contact the shaft, bearing or housing shoulder located behind the seal. Thread a sheet metal screw part of the way into the hole. Then use

8.104 After removing the bearing from the oil, install it over the shaft with the correct side facing away from the shaft

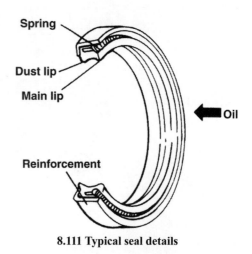

8.111 Typical seal details

8.112 To remove a seal that doesn't have a shaft running through it, pry it out of the housing with a tire iron or wide-blade screwdriver

8.113a After drilling a hole in the seal, thread a sheet metal screw into the seal and pry it out of the housing with a pair of pliers and a block of wood

8.113b The oil seal removed from the housing

8.114 Hook the tool against the inside of the oil seal and pry the seal out of the housing

8.117a Using a bearing driver to install a seal

8.117b Large seals can also be tapped into place with a soft-face hammer

a pair of 90 degree pliers and a block of wood and pry the seal out of its bore **(see illustrations)**. If the seal is tight or binding, drill another hole 180 degrees opposite from the first hole, then install a second screw and alternate between both screws to walk the seal out of the bore.

114 When a shaft passes through a seal but does not contact it, pry the seal out of the bore with a hooked type oil seal removal tool **(see illustration)**. If necessary, work around the seal to prevent it from binding.

115 Before installing a typical rubber seal, pack waterproof grease in the seal lips, unless instructed otherwise in the appropriate Step.

116 In most cases, install seals with the manufacturer's numbers or marks face out.

117 Install seals either by hand or with tools. First wrap the end of the shaft with thin plastic to prevent the splines on the end of the shaft from tearing the seal lip. Then carefully slide the seal over the plastic and center it into its bore. If you are installing a small seal, you may be able to install it by hand. Otherwise, install the seal with a socket or bearing driver placed on the outside of the seal **(see illustration)**. Drive the seal squarely into the housing until it is flush with its mounting bore or at a position described in the appropriate Chapter. Some large seals may require installation with a soft-face hammer **(see illustration)**. When selecting a hammer, choose one with a smooth face to avoid cutting or damaging the seal.

9   STORAGE

1   Vehicles that are to be stored for three months or more should be carefully prepared for storage. This is necessary to prevent damage to the engine, fuel system contamination, battery damage and a general deterioration of the vehicle. A properly stored vehicle is much easier to return to service.

2   If any repairs are needed, perform them now so the vehicle will be ready for you when taken out of storage. It is important that you can start and run the engine for a length of time to stabilize the fuel and fog the engine.

Preparation

3   The amount of preparation a vehicle should undergo before storage depends on the expected length of non-use, storage area conditions and personal preference.

4   Locate the clutch inlet and outlet duct openings (see Chapter 5) and cover them with plastic bags. If not, make sure you do not spray water where it can enter the ducts and contaminate the clutch belt and other components inside the clutch housing.

5   Plug the muffler and wash the vehicle thoroughly. If you use a power washer, use it carefully to prevent forcing water into areas and past seals that can cause deterioration and other damage. Make sure to remove all dirt, mud, sand and other debris from the vehicle.

6   After washing and drying the vehicle, remove the plastic bags from the clutch ducts and unplug the muffler.

7   Lubricate the throttle cable (see Chapter 2).

8   Inspect the air filter and replace it if necessary (see Chapter 2).

9   Make sure the cooling system contains the correct coolant mixture as coolant also contains important corrosion inhibitors. If necessary, drain and refill the cooling system with new coolant (see Chapter 2).

10   Fill the fuel tank. Then add Polaris Fuel Stabilizer (or equivalent) to the fuel tank. Add the specified amount as described on the container. Install the fuel cap.

11   Start the engine and run for 15-20 minutes to allow the treated fuel to pass through the fuel system. If the coolant was changed in Step 9, use this time to bleed the cooling system (see Chapter 2).

12   With the engine hot, change the engine oil and filter, regardless of the driving time since the last service (see Chapter 2).

13   Lubricate the driveshaft grease fitting(s) (see Chapter 2).

14   Check the front gearcase and transmission oil and change if necessary (see Chapter 2).

15   Add Polaris Carbon Clean to the fuel tank. Add the specified amount as described on the container. Install the fuel cap. Start the engine and run at idle speed for several minutes to allow the cleaner to reach the fuel injectors. Then turn the engine off.

16   Remove the spark plugs (see Chapter 2). Pour 2-3 tablespoons of engine oil into each cylinder. Install and tighten the spark plugs.

17   Apply a dielectric grease into each spark plug cap, but do not install them. Ground the spark plug caps with a grounding tool (see Section 6).

18   Operate the starter to turn the engine over several times to distribute the oil in each cylinder. Reinstall the spark plug caps.

19   Disconnect the cables from the battery terminals, negative cable first. In cold weather, remove the battery from the vehicle and store it inside. Check the battery voltage at least once a month, and recharge the battery if necessary to maintain it during the storage period. See Chapter 8.

20   Cover the exhaust and intake openings. If accessible, cover the clutch duct openings.

21   When storing in a coastal area (salt-air) or where there is high humidity, lightly coat exposed metal surfaces with oil. Do not coat rubber components with oil. Instead, use a protective substance designed for rubber products.

22   Inflate the front and rear tires to their recommended air pressure (see Chapter 2).

23   If it is safe to do so, support the vehicle on jackstands with the front and rear wheels off the ground.

Storage area

24   Cover the vehicle with a suitable cover, though do not use plastic as it can trap moisture and cause a buildup of condensation and corrosion.

25   Store the vehicle in a dry and covered area.

26   Consider the area's risk of fire, theft or vandalism. Check with your insurer regarding vehicle coverage while in storage.

Returning the Vehicle to Service

27   The amount of service required when returning a vehicle to service after storage depends on the length of non-use and storage conditions. In addition to performing the reverse of the above procedure, make sure the brakes, clutch, throttle and ignition switch work properly before operating the vehicle. Refer to the maintenance schedule in Chapter 2 and evaluate the service intervals to determine which areas require service.

28   Remove any covers or plugs used to block off the intake and exhaust systems and the clutch ducts (if covered).

29   Check the vehicle for insect and rodent nests.

30   If the vehicle was stored for longer than two months and the fuel was not treated with a fuel-stabilizer, drain the fuel tank and refill with fresh gasoline.

31   If the vehicle was stored for longer than four months, change the engine oil.

32   Check all of the fluid levels (see Chapter 2).

33   Inflate the tires to the proper air pressure (see Chapter 2).

34   Check the cooling system and the coolant level (see Chapter 2).

35   Perform the pre-ride inspection (see Chapter 2).

36   Test-ride the vehicle slowly at first while checking the brakes, lights and all controls for proper operation.

SPECIFICATIONS

Vehicle models, model number and engine model

Model	Model Number	Engine Model
2010 Ranger models		
XP 800	R10TH76AG, AH, AL, AR, AW, AY	EH076OLE
XP 800 EPS	R10TY76AZ	EH076OLE
HD 800	R10TY76AN	EH076OLE
Crew 800.	R10WH76AG, AH, AR, AV	EH076OLE
2011 Ranger models		
XP 800	R11TH76AA, AAC, AB, ABC, AC, ACC, AF, AFC, AG, AGC, AH, AHC, AK, AKC, AO, AOC, AR, ARC, AZ, AZC	1204172
XP 800 EPS	R11TH76AB, ABC, AG, AGC, AR, ARC, AV, AVC, AZ AZC	1204172
HD 800	R11TY76AN	1204172
Crew 800.	R11WH76AG, AR	1204172
Crew 800 EPS.	R11WY76AE, AH, AJ	1204172
2012 Ranger models		
XP 800	R12TH76AA, AAC, AG, AGC, AH, AHC, AI, AM, AMC, AR, ARC, AW, AWC	1204397
XP 800 EPS	R12TH7EAB, ABC, AG, AGC, AR, ARC, AZ, AZC	1204397
HD 800	R12TX7EAN	1204486
Crew 800.	R12WH76AB, AR	1204397
Crew 800 EPS.	R12WH7EAH, AV	1204397
2013 Ranger models		
4x4 800	R13TH76AG, AGC, AH, AK, AR, ARC, AZ, ASC	1204397
4x4 800 EPS	R13TH7EAG, AK, AKC, AZ, AZC	1204397
Crew 800.	R13WH76AG, AR	1204667
Crew 800 EPS.	R13WH7EAH, AI	1204667
2014 Ranger models		
4x4 800	R14TH76AA, AC, AR, AS	1204397
4x4 800 EPS	R14TH7EAK, AS	1204397
Crew 800.	R14WH76AA	1204667

General specifications

Year/model/category	Specifications
2010 Ranger models	
Cargo box capacity	1000 lbs. (454 kg)
Cargo box dimensions (L x W x H)	36 x 50 x 11 in. (91.4 x 127 x 27.9 cm)
Dry weight	
XP 800 and XP 800 EPS	1237 lbs. (561 kg)
HD 800	1262 lbs. (572 kg)
Crew 800	1510 lbs. (685 kg)
Gross vehicle weight	
XP 800 and XP 800 EPS	2887 lbs. (1310 kg)
HD 800	2912 lbs. (1321 kg)
Crew 800	3410 lbs. (1547 kg)
Ground clearance	
XP 800, XP 800 EPS and HD 800	12 in. (30.5 cm)
Crew 800	11.5 in. (29 cm)
Height	76 in. (193 cm)
Hitch tongue capacity	150 lbs. (68 kg)
Hitch towing capacity	2000 lbs. (907 kg)
Length	
XP 800, XP 800 EPS and HD 800	114 in. (289.6 cm)
Crew 800	145 in. (368.3 cm)
Maximum weight capacity	
XP 800, XP 800 EPS and HD 800	1500 lbs. (680 kg)
Crew 800	1750 lbs. (794 kg)
Turning radius	
XP 800 and XP 800 EPS	158 in. (401.3 cm)
HD 800	166 in. (422 cm)
Crew 800	255 in. (648 cm)
Width (cargo box)	60 in. (152.4 cm)
Width (tires)	58 in. (147.3 cm)
2011 and 2012 Ranger models	
Cargo box capacity	
XP 800 and XP 800 EPS	
49-state models	1000 lbs. (454 kg)
California models	600 lbs. (272 kg)
HD 800, Crew 800 and Crew 800 EPS	1000 lbs. (454 kg)
Cargo box dimensions (L X W X H)	36.5 x 54 x 11.5 in. (93 x 137 x 29 cm)
Dry weight	
XP 800	1237 lbs. (561 kg)
XP 800 EPS	1257 lbs. (570 kg)
HD 800	1262 lbs. (572 kg)
Crew 800	1495 lbs. (678 kg)
Crew 800 EPS	1515 lbs. (687 kg)
Gross vehicle weight	
HD 800	2912 lbs. (1321 kg)
All other models	Not specified
Ground clearance	
XP 800, XP 800 EPS and HD 800	12 in. (30.5 cm)
Crew 800 and Crew 800 EPS	11.5 in. (29 cm)
Height	76 in. (193 cm)
Hitch tongue capacity	150 lbs. (68 kg)
Hitch towing capacity	2000 lbs. (907 kg)

General Specifications (continued)

Year/model/category	Specifications
2011 and 2012 Ranger models (continued)	
Length	
XP 800, XP 800 EPS and HD 800.	114 in. (289.6 cm)
Crew 800 and Crew 800 EPS	145 in. (368.3 cm)
Maximum weight capacity	
XP 800 and XP 800 EPS	
49-state models	1500 lbs. (680 kg)
California models.	1100 lbs. (499 kg)
HD 800	1500 lbs. (680 kg)
Crew 800 and Crew 800 EPS	1750 lbs. (794 kg)
Turning radius	
XP 800, XP 800 EPS and HD 800.	158 in. (401.3 cm)
Crew 800 and Crew 800 EPS	255 in. (648 cm)
Width (cargo box).	60 in. (152.4 cm)
Width (tires)	58 in. (147.3 cm)
2013 and 2014 Ranger models	
Cargo box capacity	
4x4 800 and 4x4 800 EPS	
49-state models	1000 lbs. (454 kg)
California models.	600 lbs. (272 kg)
Crew 800 and Crew 800 EPS	1000 lbs. (454 kg)
Cargo box dimensions (L x W x H)	36.5 x 54 x 11.5 in. (93 x 137 x 29 cm)
Dry weight	
4x4 800	1237 lbs. (561 kg)
4x4 800 EPS	1257 lbs. (570 kg)
Crew 800.	1495 lbs. (678 kg)
Crew 800 EPS	1515 lbs. (687 kg)
Gross vehicle weight	Not specified
Ground clearance	11.5 in. (29 cm)
Height.	76 in. (193 cm)
Hitch tongue capacity.	150 lbs. (68 kg)
Hitch towing capacity.	2000 lbs. (907 kg)
Length	
4x4 800 and 4x4 800 EPS.	114 in. (289.6 cm)
Crew 800 and Crew 800 EPS	145 in. (368.3 cm)
Maximum weight capacity	
4x4 800 and 4x4 800 EPS	
49-state models	1500 lbs. (680 kg)
California models.	1100 lbs. (499 kg)
Crew 800 and Crew 800 EPS	1750 lbs. (794 kg)
Turning radius	
4x4 800 and 4x4 800 EPS.	158 in. (401.3 cm)
Crew 800 and Crew 800 EPS.	255 in. (648 cm)
Width (cargo box).	60 in. (152.4 cm)
Width (tires)	58 in. (147.3 cm)

Conversion formulas

Multiply:	By:	To get the equivalent of:
Length		
Inches	25.4	Millimeter
Inches	2.54	Centimeter
Miles	1.609	Kilometer
Feet	0.3048	Meter
Millimeter	0.03937	Inches
Centimeter	0.3937	Inches
Kilometer	0.6214	Mile
Meter	3.281	Feet
Fluid volume		
U.S. quarts	0.9463	Liters
U.S. gallons	3.785	Liters
U.S. ounces	29.573529	Milliliters
Liters	0.2641721	U.S. gallons
Liters	1.0566882	U.S. quarts
Liters	33.814023	U.S. ounces
Milliliters	0.033814	U.S. ounces
Milliliters	1.0	Cubic centimeters
Milliliters	0.001	Liters
Torque		
Foot-pounds	1.3558	Newton-meters
Foot-pounds	0.138255	Meters-kilograms
Inch-pounds	0.11299	Newton-meters
Newton-meters	0.7375622	Foot-pounds
Newton-meters	8.8507	Inch-pounds
Meters-kilograms	7.2330139	Foot-pounds
Volume		
Cubic inches	16.387064	Cubic centimeters
Cubic centimeters	0.0610237	Cubic inches
Temperature		
Fahrenheit	$(°F - 32) \times 0.556$	Centigrade
Centigrade	$(°C \times 1.8) + 32$	Fahrenheit
Weight		
Ounces	28.3495	Grams
Pounds	0.4535924	Kilograms
Grams	0.035274	Ounces
Kilograms	2.2046224	Pounds
Pressure		
Pounds per square inch	0.070307	Kilograms per square centimeter
Kilograms per square	14.223343	Pounds per square inch centimeter
Kilopascals	0.1450	Pounds per square inch
Pounds per square inch	6.895	Kilopascals
Speed		
Miles per hour	1.609344	Kilometers per hour
Kilometers per hour	0.6213712	Miles per hour

Technical abbreviations

ABDC	After bottom dead center
API	American Petroleum Institute
ATDC	After top dead center
AWD	All wheel drive
BBDC	Before bottom dead center
BDC	Bottom dead center
BTDC	Before top dead center
BARO	Barometric pressure sensor
C	Celsius (centigrade)
cc	Cubic centimeters
cid	Cubic inch displacement
CDI	Capacitor discharge ignition
CPS	Crankshaft position sensor
cu. in.	Cubic inches
DC	Direct current
ECU	Engine control unit
ECT	Engine coolant temperature
EFI	Electronic fuel injection
EPS	Electric power steering
EVAP	Evaporative emission
F	Fahrenheit
ft.	Feet
ft.-lb.	Foot-pounds
gal.	Gallons
H/A	High altitude
Hp	Horsepower
IAC	Idle air control
in.	Inches
in.-lb.	Inch-pounds
I.D.	Inside diameter
ISC	Idle speed control unit
kg	Kilograms
kgm	Kilogram meters
km	Kilometer
kPa	Kilopascals
L	Liter
LCD	Liquid-crystal display
LED	Light-emitting diode
m	Meter
MAG	Magneto
ml	Milliliter
mm	Millimeter
Nm	Newton-meters
O.D.	Outside diameter
OEM	Original equipment manufacturer
OSHA	Occupational Safety and Health Administration
oz.	Ounces
psi	Pounds per square inch
pt.	Pint
PVT	Polaris Variable Transmission
qt.	Quart
RPM	Revolutions per minute
RTV	Room temperature vulcanization
STI	Screw thread insert
T-BAP	Temperature and barometric air pressure sensor
T-MAP	Temp/Manifold absolute pressure sensor
TPS	Throttle position sensor
W	Watts

Standard Tap Drill Sizes

Thread size	Drill size	Thread size	Drill size
No. 0-80	3/64	12-13	27/64
No. 1-64	.53	1/2-20	29/64
No. 1-72	.53	9/16-12	31/64
No. 2-56	.51	9/16-18	33/64
No. 2-64	.50	5/8-11	17/32
No. 3-48	5/64	5/8-18	37/64
No. 3-56	.45	3/4-10	21/32
No. 4-40	.43	3/4-10	11/16
No. 4-48	.42	7/8-9	49/64
No. 5-40	.38	7/8-14	13/16
No. 5-44	.37	1-8	7/8
No. 6-32	.36	1-12	59/64
No. 6-40	.33	1 1/8-7	63/64
No. 8-32	.29	1 1/8-12	1 3/64
No. 8-36	.29	1 1/4-7	1 7/64
No. 10-24	.24	1 1/4-12	1 22/64
No. 10-32	.21	1 1/2-6	1 11/32
No. 12-24	.17	1 1/2-12	1 27/64
12-28	4.6 mm	1 3/4-5	1 9/16
1/4-20	.7	1 3/4-12	1 43/64
1/4-28	.3	2-4 1/2	1 25/32
5/16-18	F	2-12	1 59/64
5/16-24	I	2 1/4-4 1/2	2 1/32
3/8-16	O	2 1/2-4	2 1/4
3/8-24	Q	2 3/4-4	2 1/2
7/16-14	U	3-4	2 3/4
7/16-20	25/64		

Metric Tap Drill Sizes

Metric size	Drill equivalent	Decimal fraction	Nearest fraction
3 × 0.50	No. 39	0.0995	3/32
3 × 0.60	3/32	0.0937	3/32
4 × 0.70	No. 30	0.1285	1/8
4 × 0.75	1/8	0.125	1/8
5 × 0.80	No. 19	0.166	11/64
5 × 0.90	No. 20	0.161	5/32
6 × 1.00	No. 9	0.196	13/64
7 × 1.00	16/64	0.234	15/64
8 × 1.00	J	0.277	9/32
8 × 1.25	17/64	0.265	17/64
9 × 1.00	5/16	0.3125	5/16
9 × 1.25	5/16	0.3125	5/16
10 × 1.25	11/32	0.3437	11/32
10 × 1.50	R	0.339	11/32
11 × 1.50	3/8	0.375	3/8
12 × 1.50	13/32	0.406	13/32
12 × 1.75	13/32	0.406	13/32

Metric, Inch and Fractional Equivalents

mm	in.	Nearest fraction
1	0.0394	1/32
2	0.0787	3/32
3	0.1181	1/8
4	0.1575	5/32
5	0.1969	3/16
6	0.2362	1/4
7	0.2756	9/32
8	0.3150	5/16
9	0.3543	11/32
10	0.3937	13/32
11	0.4331	7/16
12	0.4724	15/32
13	0.5118	1/2
14	0.5512	9/16
15	0.5906	19/32
16	0.6299	5/8
17	0.6693	21/32
18	0.7087	23/32
19	0.7480	3/4
20	0.7874	25/32
21	0.8268	13/16
22	0.8661	7/8
23	0.9055	29/32
24	0.9449	15/16
25	0.9843	31/32
26	1.0236	1.1024
27	1.0630	1.1024
28	1.1024	1.1024
29	1.1024	1.1024
30	1.1024	1 3/16
31	1.2205	1 7/32
32	1.2205	1 1/4
33	1.2992	1 5/16
34	1.3386	1 11/32
35	1.3780	1 3/8
36	1.4173	1 13/32
37	1.4567	1 15/32
38	1.4961	1 1/2
39	1.5354	1 17/32
40	1.5748	1 9/16
41	1.6142	1 5/8
42	1.6535	1 21/32
43	1.6929	1 11/16
44	1.7323	1 23/32
45	1.7717	1 25/32
46	1.8110	1 13/16
47	1.8504	1 27/32
48	1.8898	1 7/8
49	1.9291	1 15/16
50	1.9685	1 31/32

Standard general fastener torque specifications

NOTE:

One foot-pound (ft.-lb.) of torque is equivalent to 12 inch-pounds (in.-lb.) of torque. Torque values below approximately 15 ft.-lbs. should be converted to in.-lbs. because torque wrenches are not accurate at these smaller values (ft.-lb. x 12 = in.-lb.).

Fastener size Screw/bolt/nut	Grade 2 ft.-lb. (N.m)	Grade 5 ft.-lb. (N.m)	Grade 8 ft.-lb. (N.m)
1/4-20	5 (7)	8 (11)	12 (16)
1/4-28	6 (8)	10 (14)	14 (19)
5/16-18	11 (15)	17 (23)	25 (35)
5/16-24	12 (16)	19 (26)	29 (40)
3/8-16	20 (27)	30 (40)	45 (62)
3/8-24	23 (32)	35 (48)	50 (69)
7/16-24	30 (40)	50 (69)	70 (97)
7/16-20	35 (48)	55 (76)	80 (110)
1/2-13	50 (69)	75 (104)	110 (152)
1/2-20	55 (76)	90 (124)	120 (166)

Metric General Fastener Torque Specifications

Fastener size Screw/bolt/nut	Grade 4.2 ft.-lb. (N.m)	Grade 4.8 ft.-lb. (N.m)	Grade 8.8/8.9 ft.-lb. (N.m)	Grade 10.9 ft.-lb. (N.m)	Grade 12.9 ft.-lb. (N.m)
M3	0.3 (0.5)	0.5 (0.7)	1.0 (1.3)	1.5 (2.0)	1.5 (2.0)
M4	0.8 (1.1)	1.0 (1.5)	2.0 (3.0)	3.0 (4.5)	4.0 (5.0)
M5	1.5 (2.5)	2.0 (3.0)	4.5 (6.0)	6.5 (9.0)	7.5 (10)
M6	3.0 (4.0)	4.0 (5.5)	7.5 (10)	11 (15)	13 (18)
M8	7.0 (9.5)	10 (13)	18 (25)	26 (35)	33 (45)
M10	14 (19)	18 (25)	37 (50)	55 (75)	63 (85)
M12	26 (35)	33 (45)	63 (85)	97 (130)	110 (150)
M14	37 (50)	55 (75)	103 (140)	151 (205)	177 (240)
M16	59 (80)	85 (115)	159 (215)	232 (315)	273 (370)
M18	81 (110)	118 (160)	225 (305)	321 (435)	376 (510)

CHAPTER ONE

TROUBLESHOOTING

CONTENTS

1   GENERAL INFORMATION

1   The troubleshooting procedures described in this chapter provide typical symptoms and logical methods for isolating the cause(s). There may be several ways to solve a problem, but only a systematic approach will be successful in avoiding wasted time and possibly unnecessary parts replacement. Gather as much information as possible to aid in diagnosis. Never assume anything and do not overlook the obvious. An engine needs the correct air/fuel mixture, compression and a spark at the correct time to run.

2   Learning to recognize symptoms makes troubleshooting easier. In most cases, expensive and complicated test equipment is not needed to determine whether repairs can be performed at home. On the other hand, be realistic and do not start procedures that are beyond your experience and equipment available. If the vehicle requires the attention of a professional, describe symptoms and conditions accurately and fully. The more information a technician has available, the easier it is to diagnose the problem.

3   Refer to *Safety First!* at the beginning of this manual before servicing the vehicle in this chapter.

2   STARTING THE ENGINE

1   Perform the daily pre-ride check (see Chapter 2, Section 1).

2   Apply the parking brake.

3   Shift the transmission into NEUTRAL.

4   Press the brake pedal and hold it in position when starting the engine.

NOTE:

Do not press or pump the throttle pedal when starting the engine.

5   Turn the ignition key to START and start the engine. Release the key after the engine starts.

NOTE:

Do not operate the starter motor for more than 5 seconds at a time. Wait approximately 10 seconds between starting attempts.

6   When the engine is running, vary the engine speed to help the engine warm up until it idles smoothly. Allow the engine to run at idle speed for several minutes before driving the vehicle.

CAUTION:

Do not race the engine during the warm-up period. Excessive wear and potential engine damage can occur when the engine is not up to operating temperature.

3   ENGINE DOES NOT START OR IS DIFFICULT TO START - IDENTIFYING THE PROBLEM

1   If the engine does not start, perform the following steps in the following sequence. If the engine fails to start after performing these checks, or starts but idles or runs roughly, refer to the troubleshooting reference guide in this Chapter (Section 10).

2   Turn the ignition switch On. If the CHECK ENGINE indicator on 2010 models or the CHECK ENGINE MIL on 2011 and later models remains On, refer to Chapter 7.

3   With the ignition switch On, check the fuel gauge on the instrument cluster. On 2010 and earlier models, if the fuel level is low, all of the fuel gauge segments will flash, the speedometer needle will blink and FUEL will be displayed on the LCD. On 2011 and later models, if the fuel level is low, all of the fuel gauge segments will flash. Refill the fuel tank and attempt to start the engine. If necessary, prime the fuel system as described in Chapter 7.

4   If the starter does not turn over, see Chapter 8, Section 5 on how to interpret low battery readings on the instrument cluster. If necessary, service the battery and recharge if necessary (see Chapter 8, Section 6). If the battery charge level is correct, check the battery for loose or corroded terminals. Then check the solenoid electrical connector for looseness and dirty or corroded connector terminals.

5   If the starter will not turn over and the problem was not found in Step 4, check the brake light switch for a loose or contaminated connector (see Chapter 8). Then disconnect the connector and clean the connector terminals and the terminals on the switch. With the connector disconnected, turn the ignition switch to On and press the brake pedal while checking for battery voltage at the brake light switch connector. If there is no battery voltage reading, check the wires for an open circuit (see Section 9).

6   If the starter will still not turn over, check the electrical connectors at the ECU for looseness and dirty or corroded connector terminals (see Chapter 7).

7   If the starter is turning over slowly, check the battery charge level and recharge if necessary (see Chapter 8). If the battery charge level is correct, check the battery for loose or corroded terminals.

NOTE:

If the starter is turning over correctly, the engine may not be receiving the correct amount of fuel. Continue with Step 8.

8   When the ignition switch is turned On, the ECU energizes the fuel pump, which will run for a few seconds to pressurize the fuel system for starting. During this initial start-up, you should be able to hear the pump run. If you cannot hear the fuel pump run immediately after turning the ignition switch On, the fuel pump is not working. Refer to Chapter 7 to test the fuel pump and check the fuel pressure.

9   If you can hear the fuel pump run and there is sufficient fuel in the fuel tank, remove both spark plugs immediately after attempting to start the engine (see Chapter 2). The

3.9a Fuel tank vent hose (2010 models)

3.9b Fuel tank vent hose (2011 and later models)

insulator on both plugs should be wet, indicating fuel is reaching the engine. If the plug tips are dry, fuel is not reaching the engine. To confirm, and with the engine turned Off, trace the fuel line from the fuel tank and disconnect it at the fuel rail (see Chapter 7, Section 8). Some fuel should seep out of the connection under pressure when it is disconnected. If not, check both ends of the fuel tank breather hose for clogging, then check the hose for proper routing **(see illustrations)**. Also make sure the breather hose nozzle on the fuel pump (2010 models) or on the fuel tank (2011 and later models) is not clogged. After checking/cleaning the breather hose, reattach the hose and attempt to start the engine. If the engine now starts, the breather hose was the problem. If not, disconnect the fuel pump electrical connector and check both terminal ends for corrosion and other damage. Reconnect the connector, and if the engine still will not start, test the fuel pump, inspect the fuel injectors and check the fuel pressure (see Chapter 7).

NOTE:

If there is fuel on the spark plugs and the engine will not start, the engine may not have adequate spark. Continue with Step 10.

4.1 A spark tester can be used in place of a spark plug to check spark - Motion Pro Ignition System Tester (part No. 08-0122) shown

4.6a Check spark with a new spark plug . . .

4.6b . . . or a spark tester

10   Make sure the spark plug cables are pushed fully inside the caps. Push the cap back onto the plug and slightly rotate to clean the electrical connection between the plug and the connector. If one or both spark plug caps feel loose and you cannot push them into place, the spark plug well may be filled with sand or other debris. Remove the spark plug caps and check for this condition, and clean the spark plug

wells if contaminated. When the plug caps are removed, also check them for water. If the plug caps are dry, in good condition and can be installed fully onto the spark plugs, and the engine does not start, continue with Step 11.

NOTE:
Cracked or damaged spark plug caps and cables can cause intermittent problems that are difficult to diagnose. If the engine occasionally misfires or cuts out, use a spray bottle to wet the spark plug cables and caps while the engine is running. Water that enters a damaged cap or cable causes an arc through the insulating material, resulting in an engine misfire.

11   Perform a spark test (see Section 4). If there is a strong spark at both spark plugs, perform Step 12.
12   If the fuel and ignition systems are working correctly, perform a cylinder compression test (see Section 5) and a cylinder leak-down test (see Section 6).

4   SPARK TEST

WARNING:
Do not perform this test if there is a fuel leak on the vehicle, or if you can smell fuel. The spark can ignite the fuel and catch the vehicle on fire.

1   Perform a spark test to determine if the ignition system is producing adequate spark. This test can be performed by removing the spark plug caps and then grounding new spark plugs against the engine. If available, a spark tester can also be used **(see illustration)**. Because the voltage required to jump the spark tester's gap is sufficiently larger than that of a normally gapped spark plug, the test results are more accurate than with a spark plug.
2   Perform this test when the engine is cold and then a second time when it is at normal operating temperature (if the engine will start).
3   On standard Ranger models, remove the seat base and seat back. On Crew models, remove the rear seat base and rear seat back. See Chapter 14.
4   Make sure the battery is fully charged (see Chapter 8).
5   Disconnect the spark plug caps and leave the original spark plugs in the cylinder head (see Chapter 2). Check for the presence of water in the plug caps.
6   Connect a separate new spark plug to each spark plug cap and ground them against the engine **(see illustration)**. If you have access to a spark tester, use it to replace one of the spark plugs and ground it the same way **(see illustration)**. Position the spark plugs/spark tester so the electrodes are visible.

WARNING:
Do not hold a spark plug or spark tester; a serious electrical shock may result.

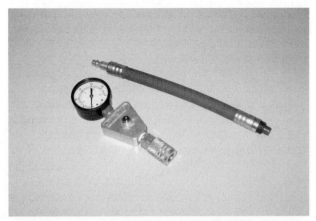

5.2 A compression gauge with a threaded end for the spark plug hole is preferable to the type which requires hand pressure to maintain a tight seal

5.6a Fuel pump electrical connector (2010 model)

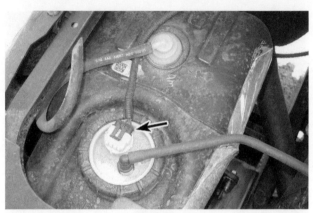

5.6b Fuel pump electrical connector (2011 and later models)

7   With the transmission in Neutral, turn the ignition switch On, apply the brake pedal and turn the key to turn the engine over. A fat blue spark should be evident between the spark plug and spark tester terminals.

8   If there is a spark at both spark plugs, the ignition system is functioning properly. At this point in your testing, it is necessary to remove and repeat the spark test with the original spark plugs to make sure they are not fouled and the cause of the problem (see Chapter 2).

9   If there was a good spark with both used spark plugs, check for a fault in the fuel system (see Chapter 7) or with engine compression (see Section 5).

10   If the spark was weak, check the ignition system (see Chapter 7).

11   If there was no spark at only one spark plug, check that spark plug's plug cap and wire for looseness or damage. Then test the ignition coil assembly (see Chapter 7).

12   If there was no spark at both spark plugs, check the ECM fuse (see Chapter 8). Then check for battery voltage at the ignition coil connector (see Section 9). If both are okay, check the ignition system (see Chapter 7).

5   CYLINDER COMPRESSION - CHECK

1   Among other things, poor engine performance, such as when the engine will start but not idle, may be caused by leaking valves, no valve clearance (worn camshaft lobes), a leaking head gasket, worn pistons, rings and/or cylinder walls and broken valve spring(s). A cylinder compression test checks the internal condition of the engine (piston rings, piston, head gasket, valves and cylinder).

2   Special tool: Use a screw-in type compression gauge with a flexible adapter **(see illustration)**. Before using the gauge, check that the rubber gasket on the end of the adapter is not cracked or damaged; this gasket seals the cylinder to ensure accurate compression readings.

3   On standard Ranger models, remove the seat base and seat back. On Crew models, remove the rear seat base and rear seat back. See Chapter 14.

4   Make sure the battery is fully charged to ensure proper engine cranking speed (see Chapter 8). If the starter does not turn the engine over fast enough, the compression reading will be incorrect.

5   Run the engine until it reaches normal operating temperature, then turn it off.

6   Disconnect the fuel pump electrical connector at the fuel pump. **(see illustrations)**.

7   Disconnect both spark plug caps at the spark plugs. Then remove one of the spark plugs (see Chapter 2).

8   Install a grounding tool in each of the spark plug caps and ground them against the cylinder head. This will help protect the engine control unit (ECU) from the excessive voltage created when the engine is turned over. To make a grounding tool for each spark plug cap, refer to Chapter 0, Section 6.

CAUTION:

While the spark plugs can be used to ground the ignition system, there is a risk of atomised fuel escaping from the combustion chambers and igniting when the spark plugs fire when the engine is turned over. The grounding tools are safer to use because they ground the ignition system without sparking.

5.9 A compression tester installed in the MAG side spark plug hole

6.6a While turning the drive clutch back and forth by hand . . .

6.6b . . . use a rod to help determine when the piston is at TDC

9   Lubricate the threads of the compression gauge adapter with a small amount of anti-seize compound and carefully thread the gauge into one of the spark plug holes (see illustration). Tighten the hose by hand to form a good seal.

10   Have an assistant press the throttle pedal fully to open the throttle, then operate the ignition switch to turn the engine over. Read the compression gauge until there is no further rise in pressure. The compression reading should

increase on each stroke. Compare the results to the value listed in this Chapter's Specifications.

11   If the compression built up quickly and evenly to the specified amount, you can assume the engine upper end is in good mechanical condition. Worn or sticking piston rings and worn cylinder will produce very little initial movement of the gauge needle, but compression tends to build up gradually as the engine spins over. Valve and valve seat leakage, or head gasket leakage, is indicated by low initial compression which does not tend to build up.

12   To isolate the problem to a valve or ring problem, perform a wet compression test. Pour about a teaspoon of engine oil into the spark plug hole to temporarily seal the piston rings, then repeat the compression test. If the compression increases significantly, the valves are good but the rings are defective. If the compression does not increase, the pressure is leaking past the valves or the head gasket. Leakage past the valves may be due to insufficient valve clearance (worn camshaft lobes), burned, warped or cracked valves or valve seats or valves that are hanging up in the guides.

13   If the compression readings are considerably higher than specified, the combustion chamber (piston crown and cylinder head surface) is probably coated with excessive carbon deposits. This will require removal of the cylinder head and pistons to decarbonize the combustion chamber (see Chapter 3).

14   Repeat for the other cylinder.

15   Installation is the reverse of removal.

16   Record the results for future reference.

6   CYLINDER LEAK-DOWN - TEST

1   A cylinder leak-down test can locate engine problems from leaking valves, a blown head gasket and broken, worn or stuck piston rings. This test is performed by positioning the piston at TDC on its compression stroke, then pressurizing the cylinder with compressed air supplied by an air compressor. The rate of air leaking from the combustion chamber is measured as a percentage. If the leakage rate is excessive, the leak-down test can also help locate the problem area before disassembling the top end.

2   Start and run the engine until it is warm. Turn it Off.

3   Remove the clutch outer cover (see Chapter 5).

4   Remove the air box (see Chapter 7).

5   Remove both spark plugs (see Chapter 2).

6   While the engine is not equipped with an accessible TDC timing mark, you can use a long, wooden rod to help indicate piston position in the cylinder and set it at TDC. Insert the rod through the spark plug hole and rest it on the piston. While holding the rod with one hand, have an assistant turn the drive clutch until you feel the rod rise to the top and then just start to move down, indicating the piston is approximately at TDC. While holding the rod, have your assistant slowly rock the drive clutch back and forth until you determine the point where the piston stops at the top of the bore and before it changes direction. This is TDC (see illustrations).

7   While you have just positioned the piston at TDC, it is unknown if the piston is at TDC on its compression stroke or on its exhaust stroke. However, this will be quickly determined once the cylinder is pressurized. Depending on the rate of leakage, it may be necessary to reposition the piston at TDC by turning the crankshaft 360 degrees.

WARNING:

Because the clutch belt is not under tension, and there is nothing to prevent the crankshaft from turning, pressurizing the cylinder will force the piston down and away from TDC, causing the crankshaft/drive clutch to spin rapidly. The most difficult step when perfoming the leak-down test will be how to safely lock the drive clutch to prevent the crankshaft from turning. Whatever method you choose, make sure the tool or object used to hold the drive clutch is secure and unable to release and fly outward, where under sufficient force it could injure you or anyone in the area, or damage the drive clutch or anything close by. If you do not feel you can safely lock the drive clutch in place, have a dealer service department perform the test.

8   Lock the drive clutch in a safe manner to prevent the crankshaft from spinning when the combustion chamber is pressurized.

9   Install a spark plug into the cylinder that is not being tested and tighten securely.

10   Thread the test adapter into the spark plug hole for the cylinder being tested. Connect the air compressor hose to the tester **(see illustration)**.

11   Using the leak-down tester, pressurize the cylinder following the manufacturer's instructions. With the cylinder pressurized, air will leak past the worn or defective parts. Read the leakage rate on the gauge. A leakage rate of 10 percent is considered normal. If the cylinder leakage rate is 15 per cent or higher, the leakage rate is excessive.

NOTE:

If the cylinder is showing 100 per cent leakage, it is likely the piston is not at TDC, its compression stroke, as either the piston moved when the cylinder was pressurized or the cylinder was positioned at TDC on its exhaust stroke. If the piston did not move, turn the crankshaft 360° and reposition the piston at TDC.

12   If the leakage rate is excessive, check the engine by listening for escaping air. If air is leaking out the muffler, an exhaust valve is leaking; air coming from the throttle body indicates a leaking intake valve. Remove the engine oil dipstick and listen for air coming from the crankcase, which indicates blow-by past the piston rings or a damaged cylinder. Remove the radiator cap. If the coolant is bubbling, air is traveling through the water jackets in the cylinder head and cylinder. This can be caused by a damaged head

6.10 The leak-down tester indicates the rate at which pressure leaks past the piston, rings, valves or head gasket in the combustion chamber

gasket, a warped cylinder head or cylinder block. In all cases, it will be necessary to remove and inspect the engine top end so the problem can be repaired (see Chapter 3).

13   Repeat for the other cylinder.

14   Installation is the reverse of removal.

15   Record the results for future reference.

7   ENGINE OIL PRESSURE - CHECK

1   Because the vehicle is not equipped with an oil pressure gauge or warning light, the oil pressure must be checked immediately when it is suspected there is a problem in the oil system. Low oil pressure can quickly cause severe engine damage.

2   To check the oil pressure, a suitable oil pressure gauge equipped with a 1/8 NPT threaded adapter will be needed.

3   The manufacturer bases the oil pressure readings on engines that are filled with the Polaris engine oil listed in the Chapter 2 Specifications. If a different oil is used, the oil pressure results observed in the test may vary.

4   Check the engine oil level and top off if necessary (see Chapter 2).

5   Warm the engine to normal operating temperature, then shut if off.

6   Thoroughly clean the area around the oil gallery plug installed in the upper crankcase near the oil filter **(see illustration)**. This threaded plug is in line with the main oil gallery. Remove the plug and thread the oil pressure gauge into the hole and tighten securely. Wipe up any oil that spilled from the hole.

WARNING:

Because the oil is hot and under pressure, the oil pressure gauge must be threaded carefully into the crankcase. If the hose blows off, severe burns will result if the oil contacts your skin.

7.6 To check the oil pressure, remove the oil gallery plug (arrow) from the upper crankcase, and thread an oil pressure gauge in its place

7   Start the engine and increase the engine speed to 6000 rpm. Read the oil pressure on the gauge and compare it to the values in this Chapter's Specifications. If the oil pressure reading is too low or too high, refer to Section 10 for a list of possible causes. If there is a problem, it must be found and corrected to prevent engine damage.

8   Installation is the reverse removal, noting the following:

   a) Apply sealant to the oil gallery plug and tighten securely.
   b) Check the engine oil level (see Chapter 2).
   c) After starting the engine, check the oil gallery plug for leaks.

8   ELECTRICAL SYSTEM FUNDAMENTALS

1   A thorough study of the many types of electrical systems used in today's vehicles is beyond the scope of this manual. However, a basic understanding of voltage, resistance and amperage is necessary to perform diagnostic tests.

Voltage

2   Voltage is the electrical potential or pressure in an electrical circuit and is expressed in volts. The more pressure (voltage) in a circuit, the more work can be performed.

3   Direct current (DC) voltage means the electricity flows in one direction. All circuits powered by a battery are DC circuits.

4   Alternating current (AC) means the electricity flows in one direction momentarily and then switches to the opposite direction. Alternator output is an example of AC voltage. This voltage must be changed or rectified to direct current to operate in a battery powered system.

Resistance

5   Resistance is the opposition to the flow of electricity within a circuit or component and is measured in ohms. Resistance causes a reduction in available current and voltage.

6   Resistance is measured in an inactive circuit with an ohmmeter. The ohmmeter sends a small amount of current into the circuit and measures how difficult it is to push the current through the circuit.

7   An ohmmeter, although useful, is not always a good indicator of a circuit's actual ability under operating conditions. This is due to the low voltage (6-9 volts) that the meter uses to test the circuit. The voltage in an ignition coil secondary winding can be several thousand volts. Such high voltage can cause the coil to malfunction, even though it tests acceptable during a resistance test.

8   Resistance generally increases with temperature. Perform all testing with the component or circuit at room temperature. Resistance tests performed at high temperatures may indicate false resistance readings and cause the unnecessary replacement of a component.

Amperage

9   Amperage is the unit of measure for the amount of current within a circuit. Current is the actual flow of electricity. The higher the current, the more work can be performed up to a given point. If the current flow exceeds the circuit or component capacity, the system will be damaged.

9   ELECTRICAL TESTING

1   This section describes electrical troubleshooting and the use of test equipment.

2   Never assume anything and do not overlook the obvious, such as a blown fuse or an electrical connector that is corroded, loose or has separated. Test the simplest and most obvious items first and try to make tests at easily accessible points on the vehicle. Make sure to troubleshoot systematically.

3   Refer to the color wiring diagrams in Chapter 8 to identify components and their connectors and to get a complete idea of what makes up that individual circuit. Use the wiring diagrams to determine how the circuit should work by tracing the current paths from the power source through the circuit components to ground. Also check any circuits that share the same fuse, ground or switch. If the other circuits work properly and the shared wiring is good, the cause must be in the wiring used only by the suspect circuit. If all related circuits are faulty at the same time, the probable cause is a poor ground connection or a blown fuse(s).

Preliminary Checks

4   Before starting any electrical troubleshooting, perform the checks in Steps 5 through 9.

5   Inspect the fuse for the suspected circuit, and replace it if blown (see Chapter 8).

6   Test the battery (see Chapter 8). Make sure it is fully charged and the battery leads are clean and securely attached to the battery terminals.

7   Electrical connectors and terminals are often the cause of electrical system problems (see illustration). Disconnect each electrical connector in the suspect circuit and make sure there are no bent terminals in the electrical connector or component. A bent terminal will not connect to its mate, causing an open circuit. Check the wires where they attach to the terminals for damage. When disconnecting a connector, never pull on the wires. Pull only on the connector housing.

8   Make sure each connector terminal is clean and free of corrosion (see illustration). Clean them, if necessary, and pack the connectors with dielectric grease. Make sure the terminals are pushed all the way into the connector. If not, carefully push them in with a narrow blade screwdriver or a terminal tool.

9   Push the connector halves together. Make sure the connectors are fully engaged and locked together.

Intermittent Problems

10   Problems that do not occur all the time can be difficult to isolate during testing. For example, when a problem only occurs when the vehicle is ridden over rough roads (vibration), when components become hot (heat related) or in wet conditions (water penetration).

11   Vibration is a common problem with loose or damaged electrical connectors. Perform a continuity test (see Steps 14 through 23). Then repeat the test while lightly pulling or wiggling the connectors. Do the same when checking the wiring harness and individual components, especially where the wires enter a housing or connector. A change in meter readings indicates a poor connection. Find and repair the problem or replace the part. Check for wires with cracked or broken insulation. An analog ohmmeter is useful when making this type of test as slight needle movements are visibly apparent, which indicate a loose connection.

12   Heat is a common problem with connectors or joints that have loose or poor connections. As these connections heat up, the connection or joint expands and separates, causing an open circuit. Other heat related problems occur when a component starts to fail as it heats up. If you suspect a heat related problem, troubleshoot to isolate the circuit. To check a connector, perform a continuity test as described in the appropriate Chapter or in Steps 14 through 23. Then repeat the test while carefully heating the connector with a heat gun. Do not overheat the connector as you can easily deform the connectors and damage the wiring. If the meter reading was normal (continuity) when the connector was cold, and then fluctuated or read infinity when heat was applied, the connection is bad. To check a component,

9.7 Check connectors and electrical components for bent pins and damaged sockets

9.8 After disconnecting a connector, check each half for dirt and corrosion and clean with electrical contact cleaner, if necessary

allow the engine to cool, and then start and run the engine. Note any operational differences when the engine is cold and hot. If the engine will not start, isolate and remove the suspect component. Test it at room temperature and again after heating it. A change in meter readings indicates a temperature problem.

13   When the problem occurs when riding in wet conditions or in areas with high humidity, start and run the engine in a dry area, if possible. Then, with the engine running, spray water onto the suspected component/circuit. Water-related problems often stop after the component heats up and dries.

Continuity checks

CAUTION:

To prevent damage to the ohmmeter, never connect it to a circuit that has power applied to it. Either disconnect the component connector or disconnect the battery negative lead before using an ohmmeter.

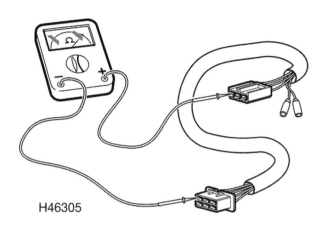

9.22 Testing for continuity in a wiring harness

14   Continuity is the uninterrupted flow of electricity through an electrical circuit. Continuity can be checked with a multimeter set either to its continuity function (a beep is emitted when continuity is found), or to the resistance (ohms / Ω) function, or with a dedicated continuity tester. Both instruments are powered by an internal battery, therefore the checks are made with the ignition Off. As a safety precaution, always disconnect the battery negative lead before making continuity checks, particularly if ignition system checks are being made (see Chapter 8).
15   Ohmmeters may be analog type (needle scale) or digital type (LCD or LED readout). Both types of ohmmeters have a switch that allows the user to select different ranges of resistance for accurate readings. The analog ohmmeter also has a set-adjust control which is used to zero or calibrate the meter (digital ohmmeters do not require calibration). Refer to the manufacturer's instructions to determine the correct scale setting.
16   If using a multimeter, select the continuity function if it has one, or the resistance (ohms) function. Touch the meter probes together and check that a beep is emitted or the meter reads zero, which indicates continuity. If there is no continuity there will be no beep or the meter will show infinite resistance. After using the meter, always switch it Off to conserve its battery.
17   A continuity tester can be used in the same way – its light should come on or it should beep to indicate continuity in the switch On position, but should be off or silent in the Off position.
18   Note that the polarity of the test probes doesn't matter for continuity checks, although care should be taken to follow specific test procedures if a diode or solid-state component is being checked.

Switch continuity checks

19   If a switch is at fault, trace its wiring to the wiring connectors. Separate the connectors and inspect them for security and condition. A build-up of dirt or corrosion

here will most likely be the cause of the problem – clean up using a dedicated electrical contact cleaner or sensor spray.
20   If using a multimeter, select the continuity function if it has one, or the resistance (ohms) function, and connect its probes to the terminals in the connector. Simple On/ Off type switches, such as brake light switches, only have two wires whereas combination switches, like the ignition switch, have many wires. Study the wiring diagram to ensure that you are connecting to the correct pair of wires. Continuity should be indicated with the switch On and no continuity with it Off.

Wiring continuity checks

21   Many electrical faults are caused by damaged wiring, often due to incorrect routing or chaffing on frame components. Loose, wet or corroded wire connectors can also be the cause of electrical problems.
22   A continuity check can be made on a single length of wire by disconnecting it at each end and connecting the meter or continuity tester probes to each end of the wire **(see illustration)**. Continuity should be indicated if the wire is good. If no continuity is shown, suspect a broken wire or a contaminated or damaged connector terminal.
23   To check for continuity to ground in any ground wire connect one probe of your meter or tester to the ground wire terminal in the connector and the other to the frame, engine, or battery ground terminal. Continuity should be indicated if the wire is good. If no continuity is shown, suspect a broken wire or corroded or loose ground.

Testing for a short with an ohmmeter

24   An analog ohmmeter or one with an audible continuity indicator works best for short testing. A self-powered test light may also be used.
25   Disconnect the negative battery cable.
26   Remove the blown fuse from the fuse panel (see Chapter 8).
27   Connect one test lead to the load side (battery side) of the fuse terminal in the fuse panel. Connect the other test lead to a good ground location. Make sure the ground is not insulated. If possible, use the battery ground connection.
28   Wiggle the wiring harness relating to the suspect circuit at small intervals. Watch the ohmmeter while progressing along the harness. If the ohmmeter needle moves or the ohmmeter beeps, there is a short-to-ground at that point in the harness.

Voltage checks

29   A voltage check can determine whether power is reaching a component. Use a multimeter set to the DC (direct current) voltage scale to check for power from the battery or regulator/ rectifier, or set to the AC (alternating current) voltage scale to check for power from the alternator. A test light can be used to check for DC voltage. The test light is

the cheaper component, but the meter has the advantage of being able to give a voltage reading.

30   Connect the meter or test light in parallel, i.e., across the load **(see illustration)**. Always check both sides of the connector because one side may be loose or corroded, thus preventing electrical flow through the connector.

31   Unless otherwise specified, make all voltage tests with the electrical connectors still connected. Insert the test leads into the backside of the connector and make sure the test lead touches the electrical terminal within the connector housing. If the test lead only touches the wire insulation, it will cause a false reading. Back probe pins can be used for these tests (see Step 51).

32   First identify the relevant wiring circuit by referring to the wiring diagram (see Chapter 8). If other electrical components share the same power supply (i.e., are fed from the same fuse), take note whether they are working correctly – this is useful information in deciding where to start checking the circuit.

33   When using a voltmeter, check first that the meter leads are plugged into the correct terminals on the meter (red to positive and black to negative). Set the meter to the appropriate volts function (DC or AC), where necessary, at a range suitable for the battery voltage – 0 to 20 VDC. Connect the meter red probe to the power supply wire and the black probe to a good ground on the vehicle's frame or directly to the battery negative terminal. Battery voltage, or the specified voltage, should be shown on the meter with the ignition switch, and if necessary any other relevant switch, On.

34   If using a test light, connect its positive probe to the power supply terminal and its negative probe to a good ground on the vehicle's frame. With the switch, and if necessary any other relevant switch, On, the test light should illuminate.

35   If no voltage is indicated, work back towards the power source continuing to check for voltage. When you reach a point where there is voltage, you know the problem lies between that point and your last check point.

Voltage drop test

36   The wires, cables, connectors and switches in the electrical circuit are designed to carry current with low resistance. This ensures current can flow through the circuit with a minimum loss of voltage. Voltage drop indicates where there is resistance in a circuit. A higher-than-normal amount of resistance in a circuit decreases the flow of current and causes the voltage to drop between the source and destination in the circuit.

37   Because resistance causes voltage to drop, a voltmeter is used to measure voltage drop when current is running through the circuit. If the circuit has no resistance, there is no voltage drop so the voltmeter indicates 0 volts. The greater the resistance in a circuit, the greater the voltage drop reading.

38   To perform a voltage drop test, connect the positive voltmeter test lead to the electrical source (where electricity

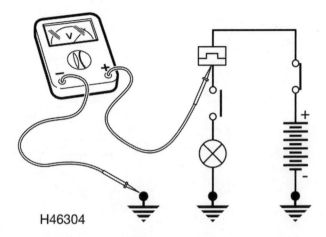

9.30 Connect the voltmeter in parallel (across the load) as shown

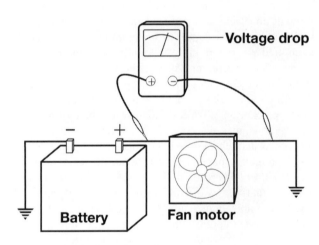

9.38 Measuring voltage drop in a circuit

is coming from) and negative test lead to the electrical load (where the electricity is going) **(see illustration)**. If necessary, activate the component(s) in the circuit. For example, if you're performing a voltage drop test on the brake light switch, apply the brake pedal when reading the voltmeter.

39   Read the voltage drop (difference in voltage between the source and destination) on the voltmeter. The voltmeter should indicate 0 volts. A voltage drop of 1 or more volts indicates that the circuit has excessive resistance. A voltage drop reading of 12 volts indicates an open in the circuit.

40   For example, consider a starting problem where the battery is fully charged but the starter turns over slowly. Voltage drop would be the difference in the voltage at the battery (source) and the voltage at the starter (destination) as the engine is being started (current is flowing through the battery cables). A corroded battery cable would cause a high voltage drop (high resistance) and slow engine cranking.

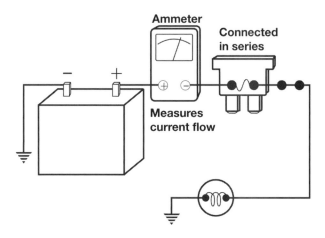

9.46 Setup when using an ammeter to measure current flow in a circuit

9.47 Ground connections (arrows) at the terminal block located near the battery

41   Common sources of voltage drop are loose or contaminated connectors and poor ground connections.

Testing for a short with a voltmeter

42   This test may be performed with a voltmeter or test light.
43   Remove the blown fuse from the fuse panel.
44   Connect the voltmeter across the fuse terminals in the fuse panel. Turn the ignition switch on and check for battery voltage.
45   With the voltmeter attached to the fuse terminals,

wiggle the wiring harness relating to the suspect circuit at approximately 6-inch (15.2 cm) intervals. Start next to the fuse panel and work systematically away from the panel. Note the voltmeter reading while progressing along the harness. If the voltmeter reading changes (test light blinks), there is a short-to-ground at that point in the harness.

Ammeter checks

46   Use an ammeter to measure the flow of current (amps) in a circuit **(see illustration)**. When connected in series in a circuit, the ammeter determines if current is flowing through the circuit and if that current flow is excessive because of a short in the circuit. Current flow is often referred to as current draw. Comparing actual current draw in the circuit or component to current draw specification (if specified by the manufacturer) provides useful diagnostic information.

Ground checks

47   Ground connections are made either directly to the engine or frame (such as the starter motor or ignition coil which only have a positive feed) or by a separate wire into the ground circuit of the wiring harness. Alternatively a short ground wire is sometimes run from the component directly to the vehicle's frame **(see illustration)**.
48   Corrosion is a common cause of a poor ground connection, as is a loose ground terminal fastener.
49   If total or multiple component failure is experienced, check the security of the main ground lead from the negative terminal of the battery, the ground lead bolted to the engine, and the main ground point(s) on the frame. If corroded, dismantle the connection and clean all surfaces back to bare metal. Reassemble and tighten the connection and prevent further corrosion from forming by smearing dielectric grease over the connection.
50   To check component ground, use an insulated jumper wire to temporarily bypass its ground connection – connect one end of the jumper wire to the ground terminal or metal body of the component and the other end to the vehicle's frame. If the circuit works with the jumper wire installed, the ground circuit is faulty.

How to back-probe connectors

51   Many voltage and resistance tests are performed with the component connectors connected and locked together. And because all of the wires entering the connectors are protected by seals, it is necessary to back-probe the connectors during testing. When back-probing a connector, you slip a small piece of metal in between the wire and insulator. See *Measuring tools* at the front of this manual for information on back-probe pins and how to use them.

Troubleshooting reference guide

CONTENTS

1   This Section provides an easy reference guide to the more common problems which may occur during the operation of your vehicle. These problems and their possible causes are grouped under headings denoting various components or operating conditions. They also refer you to the Chapter and/or Section which deals with the problem.

2   Remember that successful troubleshooting is not a mysterious art practiced only by professional mechanics. It is simply the result of the right knowledge combined with an intelligent, systematic approach to the problem. Always work by a process of elimination, starting with the simplest solution and working through to the most complex - and never overlook the obvious. Anyone can run the gas tank dry or leave the lights on overnight, so don't assume that you are exempt from such oversights.

3   Finally, always establish a clear idea of why a problem has occurred and take steps to ensure that it doesn't happen again. If the electrical system fails because of a poor connection, check the other connections in the system to make sure that they don't fail as well. If a particular fuse continues to blow, find out why - don't just replace one fuse after another. Remember, failure of a small componvent can often be indicative of potential failure or incorrect functioning of a more important component or system.

ENGINE DOESN'T START OR IS DIFFICULT TO START AND KEEP RUNNING

1   STARTER MOTOR DOESN'T TURN WHEN ATTEMPTING TO START ENGINE

1   Starting procedure incorrect (see Section 2).
2   Ignition switch OFF.
3   Fuse blown (Chapter 8).
4   Battery terminals connections loose or corroded (Chapter 8).
5   Battery voltage low. Check and recharge the battery (Chapter 8).
6   Battery damaged or faulty (Chapter 8).
7   Broken, loose or disconnected wiring in the starting circuit. Check all wiring connections and harnesses to make sure they are dry, tight and not corroded. Also check for broken or frayed wires that can cause a short to ground. See Chapter 8.
8   Ignition switch faulty (Chapter 8).
9   Starter motor faulty (Chapter 8).
10   Starter relay faulty (Chapter 8).
11   Rear brake light switch connector dirty or disconnected or switch faulty (Chapter 8).

2   STARTER MOTOR TURNS OVER SLOWLY

1   Battery voltage low. Check and recharge the battery (Chapter 8).
2   Battery ground cable loose or contaminated (Chapter 8).
3   Battery terminal connections loose or corroded (Chapter 8).
4   Starter motor faulty (Chapter 8).
5   Engine problem. Check whether the engine can be turned over by hand.

3   STARTER MOTOR TURNS BUT ENGINE DOES NOT TURN OVER

1   Starter drive faulty (Chapter 4).
2   Flywheel loose or flywheel gear damaged (Chapter 4).
3   Starter to starter drive damaged (Chapter 4).

4   NO FUEL FLOW

1   No fuel in tank.
2   Fuel tank breather hose plugged or damaged (Chapter 7).
3   Fuel pump faulty, or the internal fuel filter on the pump is blocked (Chapter 7).
4   Fuel hose clogged or damaged (Chapter 7).
5   Fuel rail or injector clogged. For both injectors to be clogged, foreign material entered the tank. The fuel filters installed on the fuel pump may be plugged or damaged. In some cases, if the vehicle has been unused for several months, the fuel turns into a varnish-like liquid which can cause an injector needle to stick to its seat. Drain the fuel tank and fuel system (Chapter 7).

5   ENGINE FLOODED

1   Starting technique incorrect (see Section 2). Under normal circumstances (i.e., if all of the fuel injection system components are good), the engine should start with the throttle closed.
2   Fuel injector needle worn or stuck open. A piece of dirt or other debris can cause the needle to seat improperly, causing excess fuel to be pumped to the throttle body. In this case, the injector should be cleaned and the needle and seat inspected (see Chapter 7). If the needle and seat are worn, the leaking will continue and the parts must be replaced. Long cranking times after the vehicle has been sitting overnight may indicate a fuel injector leaking into the engine (especially if there is a smoke cloud when the engine starts).

6   NO SPARK OR WEAK SPARK

1   Ignition switch Off.
2   Ignition switch shorted or damaged. This is usually caused by water, corrosion, damage or excessive wear.
3   Battery voltage low. Test and recharge battery as required (Chapter 8).
4   Spark plugs fouled, dirty, defective or worn out. Locate reason for fouled plug using spark plug condition chart and follow the plug maintenance procedures (see Chapter 2).

5   Spark plug cap not making good contact with either ignition coil or plug cap. Make sure the plug cap fits firmly over the plug end while twisting it back and forth. Sand and dirt can enter the spark plug well and prevent the plug cap from making full contact on the plug. Remove the spark plug cap and check for contamination (Chapter 2).

6   Rear brake light switch connector dirty or disconnected or switch faulty (Chapter 8).

7   Ignition coil defective. Test the coil (Chapter 7).

8   Fuel injection shutdown due to system fault (Chapter 7).

9   Crankshaft position sensor (CPS) defective (Chapter 7).

10   Camshaft phase sensor (2011 and later models) defective (Chapter 7).

11   Electronic control unit (ECU) defective (Chapter 7).

12   Wiring shorted or broken at the following components:

Ignition switch
Starter relay
ECU
Ignition coil
CKP sensor
Brake light switch
Camshaft phase sensor (2011 and later models)

13   Make sure that all wiring connections are clean, dry and tight. Look for chafed, burned and broken wires.

7   COMPRESSION LOW

1   Spark plugs loose. Remove the plugs and inspect the plug and cylinder head threads. Reinstall and tighten to the specified torque (Chapter 2).

2   Cylinder head not sufficiently tightened down. If a cylinder head is suspected of being loose, then there's a chance that the gasket or head is damaged if the problem has persisted for any length of time. This will require removal of the cylinder head and inspection. However, before removing the cylinder head, perform a leak-down test to see if there is any leakage past the head gasket (see Section 6). The head bolts should be tightened to the proper torque and in the correct sequence (Chapter 3).

3   Improper valve clearance. Because there is no valve adjustment on these models, this means the valve is not closing completely and compression pressure is leaking past the valve. Check the pushrods and valve lifters for damage (Chapter 3). Also check the camshaft for excessive lobe wear (Chapter 4).

4   Cylinder and/or piston worn. Excessive wear will cause compression pressure to leak past the rings. This is usually accompanied by worn rings as well. Top end overhaul is necessary (Chapter 3).

5   Piston rings worn, weak, broken, or sticking. Broken or sticking piston rings usually indicate a lubrication problem that causes excess carbon deposits to form on the pistons, rings in the piston ring grooves. Top end overhaul is required (Chapter 3).

6   Cylinder head gasket damaged. If the head is allowed to become loose, or if excessive carbon build-up on the piston crown and combustion chamber causes extremely high compression, the head gasket may leak. Retorquing the head is not always sufficient to restore the seal, so gasket replacement is necessary (Chapter 3).

7   Cylinder head warped. This is caused by overheating or improperly tightened head bolts. Machine shop resurfacing or head replacement is necessary (Chapter 3).

8   Valve spring broken or weak. Caused by component failure or wear; the spring(s) must be replaced (Chapter 3).

9   Valve not seating properly. This is caused by a bent valve (from over-revving), burned valve or seat, or an accumulation of carbon deposits on the seat (from fuel or lubrication problems). The valves must be cleaned and/or replaced and the seats serviced if possible (Chapter 3).

10   Rocker arm sticking or damaged. Remove the cylinder head cover to inspect the rocker arms while turning the engine over by hand (Chapter 3).

8   STALLS AFTER STARTING

1   Engine idle speed incorrect. On 2011 and later models, check the operation of the idle air control (IAC) mounted on the throttle body (Chapter 7).

2   Ignition timing incorrect due to ignition malfunction (Chapter 7).

3   Fuel injection system malfunction (Chapter 7).

4   Intake air leak. Check for loose intake boot and intake manifold clamps at the throttle body. Also check the boot and manifold for cracks and other damage (Chapter 7).

5   Fuel contaminated. The fuel can be contaminated with either dirt or water, or can change chemically if the vehicle has been unused for several months. Drain the tank and fuel system (Chapter 7).

9   ROUGH OR ERRATIC IDLE

1   Fuel system electrical connector contaminated or damaged (Chapter 7).

2   Air filter clogged or damaged. Replace the air filter element (Chapter 2).

3   Crankcase breather clogged (Chapter 3).

4   Throttle cable incorrectly adjusted (Chapter 2).

5   Intake air leak. Check for loose intake boot and intake manifold clamps at the throttle body. Also check the boot and manifold for cracks and other damage (Chapter 7).

6   Fuel rail or injector clogged. For both injectors to be clogged, foreign material entered the tank. The fuel filters installed on the fuel pump may be plugged or damaged. In some cases, if the vehicle has been unused for several months, the fuel turns into a varnish-like liquid which can cause an injector needle to stick to its seat. Drain the fuel tank and fuel system (Chapter 7).

7   Throttle body stop screw was turned from its original position and is now of adjustment with the ECU. This screw is mounted on the throttle body was pre-set at the factory. If the screw is turned, the throttle body will have to be replaced as the manufacturer does not provide adjustment

information or procedures (Chapter 7).

8   Spark plugs fouled, dirty, defective or worn out. Locate reason for fouled plug using spark plug condition chart and follow the plug maintenance procedures (see Chapter 2).

9   Throttle position sensor (TPS) damaged or out of adjustment (Chapter 7).

10   Ignition timing incorrect due to ignition malfunction (Chapter 8).

11   Engine compression low (see Section 5).

12   Valve tight or bent (Chapter 3).

13   Worn camshaft lobe(s) (Chapter 3).

14   Valve lifters worn or damaged (Chapter 3).

15   PVT belt dragging (Chapter 5).

16   Fuel contaminated. The fuel can be contaminated with either dirt or water, or can change chemically if the vehicle has been unused for several months. Drain the tank and fuel system (Chapter 7).

17   Engine idle speed incorrect. On 2011 and later models, check the operation of the idle air control (IAC) mounted on the throttle body (Chapter 7).

10   IDLE SPEED IS TOO LOW (BELOW 900 RPM WHEN ENGINE IS WARM)

1   Air filter clogged or damaged. Replace the air filter element (Chapter 2).

2   Throttle body stop screw was turned from its original position and is now of adjustment with the ECU. This screw is mounted on the throttle body was pre-set at the factory. If the screw is turned, the throttle body will have to be replaced as the manufacturer does not provide adjustment information or procedures (Chapter 7).

3   Fuel injector leaking (Chapter 7).

4   PVT belt dragging (Chapter 5).

11   IDLE SPEED TOO HIGH (ABOVE 1300 RPM WHEN ENGINE IS WARM)

1   Fuel system electrical connector contaminated or damaged (Chapter 7).

2   Throttle cable out of adjustment, dirty (sticking), incorrectly routed or damaged (Chapter 2).

3   Throttle body stop screw was turned from its original position and is now of adjustment with the ECU. This screw is mounted on the throttle body was pre-set at the factory. If the screw is turned, the throttle body will have to be replaced as the manufacturer does not provide adjustment information or procedures (Chapter 7).

POOR RUNNING AT LOW SPEEDS

12   SPARK WEAK

1   Battery voltage low. Check and recharge battery (Chapter 8).

2   Spark plugs fouled, dirty, defective or worn out. Locate

reason for fouled plug using spark plug condition chart and follow the plug maintenance procedures (Chapter 2).

3   Spark plug cap not making good contact with either ignition coil or plug cap. Make sure the plug cap fits firmly over the plug end while twisting it back and forth. Sand and dirt can enter the spark plug well and prevent the plug cap from making full contact on the plug. Remove the spark plug cap and check for contamination (Chapter 2).

4   Ignition coil defective. Test the coil (Chapter 7).

5   Electrical connector contaminated or damaged (Chapter 7).

13   FUEL/AIR MIXTURE INCORRECT

1   Fuel tank breather hose plugged or damaged (Chapter 7).

2   Fuel pump faulty, or the internal fuel filters on the pump are blocked (Chapter 7).

3   Fuel hose clogged or damaged (Chapter 7).

4   Fuel rail or injector clogged. For both injectors to be clogged, foreign material entered the tank. The fuel filters installed on the fuel pump may be plugged or damaged. In some cases, if the vehicle has been unused for several months, the fuel turns into a varnish-like liquid which can cause an injector needle to stick to its seat. Drain the fuel tank and fuel system (Chapter 7).

5   Intake air leak. Check for loose intake boot and intake manifold clamps at the throttle body. Also check the boot and manifold for cracks and other damage (Chapter 7).

6   Air filter clogged or damaged. Replace the air filter element (Chapter 2).

14   COMPRESSION LOW

1   Spark plugs loose. Remove the plugs and inspect the plug and cylinder head threads. Reinstall and tighten to the specified torque (Chapter 2).

2   Cylinder head not sufficiently tightened down. If a cylinder head is suspected of being loose, then there's a chance that the gasket or head is damaged if the problem has persisted for any length of time. This will require removal of the cylinder head and inspection. However, before removing the cylinder head, perform a leak-down test to see if there is any leakage past the head gasket (Section 6). The head bolts should be tightened to the proper torque and in the correct sequence (Chapter 3).

3   Improper valve clearance. Because there is no valve adjustment on these models, this means the valve is not closing completely and compression pressure is leaking past the valve. Check the pushrods and valve lifters for damage (Chapter 3). Also check the camshaft for excessive lobe wear (Chapter 4).

4   Cylinder and/or piston worn. Excessive wear will cause compression pressure to leak past the rings. This is usually accompanied by worn rings as well. Top end overhaul is necessary (Chapter 3).

5   Piston rings worn, weak, broken, or sticking. Broken

or sticking piston rings usually indicate a lubrication problem that causes excess carbon deposits to form on the pistons, rings in the piston ring grooves. Top end overhaul is required (Chapter 3).

6   Cylinder head gasket damaged. If the head is allowed to become loose, or if excessive carbon build-up on the piston crown and combustion chamber causes extremely high compression, the head gasket may leak. Retorquing the head is not always sufficient to restore the seal, so gasket replacement is necessary (Chapter 3).

7   Cylinder head warped. This is caused by overheating or improperly tightened head nuts and bolts. Machine shop resurfacing or head replacement is necessary (Chapter 3).

8   Valve spring broken or weak. Caused by component failure or wear; the spring(s) must be replaced (Chapter 3).

9   Valve not seating properly. This is caused by a bent valve (from over-revving), burned valve or seat or an accumulation of carbon deposits on the seat (from fuel or lubrication problems). The valves must be cleaned and/or replaced and the seats serviced if possible (Chapter 3).

10   Rocker arm sticking or damaged. Remove the cylinder head cover to inspect the rocker arms while turning the engine over by hand (Chapter 3).

15   POOR ACCELERATION

1   Timing not advancing. The crankshaft position sensor (CKP) or the engine control unit (ECU) may be defective (Chapter 7).

2   Air filter clogged or damaged. Replace the air filter element (Chapter 2).

3   Engine oil viscosity too high. Using a heavier oil than that recommended (Chapter 2) can damage the oil pump or lubrication system and cause drag on the engine.

4   Brakes dragging. Usually caused by debris which has entered the brake caliper piston seals, or from a warped disc or bent axle. Can also be caused by a plugged port in the master cylinder (see Chapters 11, 12, and 13).

5   Clutch and/or PVT belt problem (Chapter 5).

POOR RUNNING OR NO POWER AT HIGH SPEED

16   FIRING INCORRECT

1   Spark plug cap not making good contact with either ignition coil or plug cap. Make sure the plug cap fits firmly over the plug end while twisting it back and forth. Sand and dirt can enter the spark plug well and prevent the plug cap from making full contact on the plug. Remove the spark plug cap and check for contamination (Chapter 2).

2   Spark plugs fouled, dirty, defective or worn out. Locate reason for fouled plug using spark plug condition chart and follow the plug maintenance procedures (Chapter 2).

3   Incorrect spark plugs. Wrong type or heat range. Check and install correct plugs (Chapter 2).

4   Ignition coil defective. Test the coil (Chapter 7).

17   FUEL/AIR MIXTURE INCORRECT

1   Spark plugs fouled, dirty, defective or worn out. Locate reason for fouled plug using spark plug condition chart and follow the plug maintenance procedures (Chapter 2).

2   Fuel pump faulty, or the internal fuel filter on the pump is blocked (Chapter 7).

3   Fuel hose clogged or damaged (Chapter 7).

4   Fuel rail or injector clogged. For both injectors to be clogged, foreign material entered the tank. The fuel filters installed on the fuel pump may be plugged or damaged. In some cases, if the vehicle has been unused for several months, the fuel turns into a varnish-like liquid which can cause an injector needle to stick to its seat. Drain the fuel tank and fuel system (Chapter 7).

5   Intake air leak. Check for loose intake boot and intake manifold clamps at the throttle body. Also check the boot and manifold for cracks and other damage (Chapter 7).

6   Air filter clogged or damaged. Replace the air filter element (Chapter 2).

18   COMPRESSION LOW

1   Spark plugs loose. Remove the plugs and inspect the plug and cylinder head threads. Reinstall and tighten to the specified torque (Chapter 2).

2   Cylinder head not sufficiently tightened down. If a cylinder head is suspected of being loose, then there's a chance that the gasket or head is damaged if the problem has persisted for any length of time. This will require removal of the cylinder head and inspection. However, before removing the cylinder head, perform a leak-down test to see if there is any leakage past the head gasket (Section 6).The head bolts should be tightened to the proper torque and in the correct sequence (Chapter 3).

3   Improper valve clearance. This means the valve is not closing completely and compression pressure is leaking past the valve. Check the pushrods and valve lifters for damage (Chapter 3). Also check the camshaft for excessive lobe wear (Chapter 4).

4   Cylinder and/or piston worn. Excessive wear will cause compression pressure to leak past the rings. This is usually accompanied by worn rings as well. Top end overhaul is necessary (Chapter 3).

5   Piston rings worn, weak, broken, or sticking. Broken or sticking piston rings usually indicate a lubrication problem that causes excess carbon deposits to form on the pistons, rings in the piston ring grooves. Top end overhaul is required (Chapter 3).

6   Cylinder head gasket damaged. If the head is allowed to become loose, or if excessive carbon build-up on the piston crown and combustion chamber causes extremely high compression, the head gasket may leak. Retorquing the head is not always sufficient to restore the seal, so gasket replacement is necessary (Chapter 3).

7   Cylinder head warped. This is caused by overheating or improperly tightened head nuts and bolts. Machine shop resurfacing or head replacement is necessary (Chapter 3).

8 Valve spring broken or weak. Caused by component failure or wear; the spring(s) must be replaced (Chapter 3).
9 Valve not seating properly. This is caused by a bent valve (from over-revving), burned valve or seat or an accumulation of carbon deposits on the seat (from fuel or lubrication problems). The valves must be cleaned and/or replaced and the seats serviced if possible (Chapter 3).
10 Rocker arm sticking or damaged. Remove the cylinder head cover to inspect the rocker arms while turning the engine over by hand (Chapter 3).

19 KNOCKING OR PINGING

1 Carbon build-up in combustion chamber. Use of a fuel additive that will dissolve the adhesive bonding the carbon particles to the piston crown and chamber is the easiest way to remove the build-up. Make sure to follow the manufacturer's directions and change the engine oil and filter earlier than normal to remove the carbon deposits released from the combustion chamber. Otherwise, the cylinder head will have to be removed and decarbonized (Chapter 3).
2 Incorrect or poor quality fuel. Old or improper grades of fuel can cause detonation. This causes the piston to rattle, thus the knocking or pinging sound. Drain old fuel and always use the recommended fuel grade.
3 Spark plug heat range incorrect. Uncontrolled detonation indicates the plug heat range is too hot. The plug in effect becomes a glow plug, raising cylinder temperatures. Install the proper heat range plug (Chapter 2).
4 Improper air/fuel mixture. This will cause the cylinders to run hot, which leads to detonation. A blockage in the fuel system or an air leak can cause this imbalance (Chapter 7).

20 MISCELLANEOUS CAUSES

1 Throttle valve doesn't open fully. Check the throttle cable for damage. If the cable is okay, check and adjust the throttle cable freeplay (Chapter 2).
2 Clutch and/or PVT belt problem (Chapter 5).
3 Ignition timing advanced. The crankshaft position (CKP) or the engine control unit (ECU) may be defective (Chapter 7).
4 Engine oil viscosity too high. Using a heavier oil than the one recommended can damage the oil pump or lubrication system and cause drag on the engine. Drain the engine oil, change the oil filter, and refill with the correct oil (Chapter 2).

OVERHEATING

21 ENGINE OVERHEATS

1 Coolant level low. Check and add coolant (Chapter 2).
2 Radiator fins clogged with mud and other debris.

Carefully clean fins on radiator and check for damage (Chapter 9).
3 Air in cooling system. If the problem occurred right after changing the coolant, there could be air in the cooling system. Bleed the cooling system (Chapter 2).
4 Leak in cooling system. Check cooling system hoses and radiator for leaks and other damage. Check the coolant pipes and hoses mounted below the floor. Pressure test the cooling system to locate leaks (Chapter 9). Perform a leak-down test to determine if coolant is leaking from the cylinder head and cylinder water jackets into the engine (Section 6).
5 Thermostat stuck closed (Chapter 9).
6 Faulty pressure cap. Remove and pressure test the cap (Chapter 9).
7 Water pump damaged or impeller loose or damaged (Chapter 4).
8 Crankcase oil level low. Check and add oil (Chapter 2).
9 Fuel pump output low. Test fuel pump (Chapter 7).
10 Wrong type of oil. If you're not sure what type of oil is in the engine, drain it and fill with the correct type (Chapter 2).
11 Cooling fan not working. Check fan operation and repair as necessary (Chapter 9).
12 Air leak at throttle body intake joints. Check and tighten or replace as necessary (Chapter 7).
13 Worn oil pump or clogged oil passages. Replace pump or clean passages as necessary (Chapter 4).
14 Coolant passages clogged in radiator and/or engine. Have the entire system drained and flushed, then refill with fresh coolant and bleed the system (Chapter 2).
15 If the radiator was serviced, the diverter plate is missing from inside radiator. This prevents the coolant from flowing through the complete radiator.
16 Engine coolant temperature (ECT) sensor faulty. Test sensor and replace if necessary (Chapter 9).
17 Carbon build-up in combustion chamber. Use of a fuel additive that will dissolve the adhesive bonding the carbon particles to the piston crown and chamber is the easiest way to remove the build-up. Make sure to follow the manufacturer's directions and change the engine oil and filter earlier than normal to remove the carbon deposits released from the combustion chamber. Otherwise, the cylinder head will have to be removed and decarbonized (Chapter 3).

22 FIRING INCORRECT

1 Wrongly connected ignition coil wiring (Chapter 7).
2 Spark plugs fouled, dirty, defective or worn out. Locate reason for fouled plug using spark plug condition chart and follow the plug maintenance procedures (Chapter 2).
3 Incorrect spark plugs (Chapter 2).
4 Sheared flywheel key or loose flywheel (Chapter 4).
5 Faulty engine control unit (ECU) (Chapter 7).
6 Faulty ignition coil. Test the coil (Chapter 7).

23 FUEL/AIR MIXTURE INCORRECT

1   Fuel tank breather hose plugged or damaged (Chapter 7).
2   Fuel pump faulty, or the internal fuel filters on the pump are blocked (Chapter 7).
3   Air filter clogged or damaged. Replace the air filter element (Chapter 2).
4   Fuel rail or injector clogged. For both injectors to be clogged, foreign material entered the tank. The fuel filters installed on the fuel pump may be plugged or damaged. In some cases, if the vehicle has been unused for several months, the fuel turns into a varnish-like liquid which can cause an injector needle to stick to its seat. Drain the fuel tank and fuel system (Chapter 7).
5   Intake air leak. Check for loose intake boot and intake manifold clamps at the throttle body. Also check the boot and manifold for cracks and other damage (Chapter 7).

24 COMPRESSION TOO HIGH

1   Carbon build-up in combustion chamber. Use of a fuel additive that will dissolve the adhesive bonding the carbon particles to the piston crown and chamber is the easiest way to remove the build-up. Otherwise, the cylinder head will have to be removed and decarbonized (Chapter 3).
2   Improperly machined head surface or installation of incorrect gasket during engine assembly (Chapter 3).

25 ENGINE LOAD EXCESSIVE

1   PVT belt slipping. Can be caused by damaged, loose or worn PVT components. Refer to Chapter 5 for overhaul procedures.
2   Engine oil level too high. The addition of too much oil will cause pressurization of the crankcase and inefficient engine operation. Check Specifications and drain to proper level (Chapter 2).
3   Engine oil viscosity too high. Using a heavier oil than the one recommended in Chapter 2 can damage the oil pump or lubrication system as well as cause drag on the engine.
4   Brakes dragging. Usually caused by debris which has entered the brake caliper sealing boots, corroded calipers, a warped disc, contaminated master cylinder port or bent axle(s). Repair as necessary (Chapters 11, 12 and 13).

26 LUBRICATION INADEQUATE

1   Engine oil level too low. Friction caused by intermittent lack of lubrication or from oil that is overworked can cause overheating. The oil provides a definite cooling function in the engine. Check the oil level (Chapter 2).
2   Poor quality engine oil or incorrect viscosity or type. Oil is rated not only according to viscosity but also according to type. Some oils are not rated high enough for use in this engine. Check the Specifications section and

change to the correct oil (Chapter 2).
3   Oil pump failure (Chapter 4).
4   Camshaft or journals worn. Excessive wear causing drop in oil pressure (Section 7). Replace camshaft (Chapter 4). Abnormal wear could be caused by oil starvation at high rpm from low oil level or improper viscosity or type of oil (Chapter 2).
5   Crankshaft and/or bearings worn. Same problems as paragraph 4. Check and replace crankshaft assembly if necessary (Chapter 4).

EXCESSIVE EXHAUST SMOKE

27 WHITE SMOKE

1   It is normal to see white smoke or steam from the exhaust after first starting the engine in cold weather. This is actually condensation formed by the engine during combustion. As the engine warms to normal operating temperature, the water evaporates and exits the engine through the breather system. However, if the vehicle is driven for short trips or repeatedly started and stopped without allowing the engine to reach normal operating temperature, water will start to collect in the crankcase. As this water mixes with the oil in the crankcase, sludge is produced. Sludge can eventually cause engine damage as it circulates through the lubrication system and blocks off oil passages.
2   Piston oil ring worn. The ring may be broken or damaged, causing oil from the crankcase to be pulled past the piston into the combustion chamber. Replace the rings with new ones and check the cylinder bore for damage (Chapter 3).
3   Cylinders worn, cracked, or scored. Caused by overheating or oil starvation. If worn or scored, the cylinder block will have to be replaced and new pistons installed (Chapter 3).
4   Intake valve oil seals worn or damaged. Replace oil seals with new ones (Chapter 3).
5   Valve guides excessively worn. Valve guides are not replaceable. If the valve stem-to-guide clearance is excessive with new valves, replace the cylinder head (Chapter 3).
6   Engine oil level too high, which causes the oil to be forced past the rings. Drain oil to the proper level (Chapter 2).
7   Head gasket damaged. Causes oil to be pulled into the combustion chamber. Replace the head gasket and check the head for warpage (Chapter 3).
8   Abnormal crankcase pressurization, which forces oil past the rings. Check for a clogged breather hose and a damaged reed valve. The breather hose is installed between the cylinder head and air box. If the problem occurs in freezing weather, check for ice clogging the breather hose for. See Chapter 3.

28 BLACK SMOKE

1   Black smoke is an indication of a rich air/fuel mixture where an excessive amount of fuel is being burned in the combustion chamber.
2   Air cleaner clogged. Clean or replace the element (Chapter 2).
3   Leaking fuel injector. Remove the fuel injectors and check their O-rings for cracks and other damage. Check the fuel injectors for damage (Chapter 7).

29 BLUE SMOKE

Blue smoke indicates the engine is burning oil in the combustion chamber as it leaks past worn piston rings and/or worn intake valve stem seals. Excessive oil consumption is another indicator of an engine that is burning oil. Perform a compression test to isolate the problem (Section 5).

POLARIS VARIABLE TRANSMISSION (PVT) PROBLEMS

30 DRIVEBELT SLIPPING

1   Worn belt. Replace the belt (Chapter 5).
2   Oil or grease on belt. Clean belt and check for leaking engine and transmission seals (Chapters 4 and 6).
3   Water (not engine coolant) on belt. Check the clutch inner and outer covers for proper sealing (Chapter 5).

31 DRIVEBELT UPSIDE DOWN IN PULLEYS

1   Wrong drivebelt. Check part number on belt and replace with the correct belt if necessary.
2   Loose or broken engine or transmission mount. Check and tighten or replace as necessary (Chapters 4 and 6).

32 BURN MARKS OR THIN SPOTS ON DRIVEBELT

1   Excessive load on vehicle (weight on racks, heavy trailer, oversized accessory). Remove excessive load.
2   Brakes dragging. Usually caused by debris which has entered the brake caliper sealing boots, corroded calipers, warped disc, contaminated master cylinder reservoir port or bent axle(s). Repair as necessary (Chapters 11, 12 and 13).
3   Throttle is applied too slowly when starting out from a dead stop.
4   Applying throttle and continuously raising engine speed when the vehicle is not moving.

33 HARSH DRIVE CLUTCH ENGAGEMENT

1   Worn drivebelt. Replace the belt (Chapter 5).
2   Loose or broken engine or transmission mounts causing the drivebelt to run out of alignment. Check and tighten or replace as necessary (Chapters 4 and 6).
3   Clutch offset incorrect. Adjust offset by changing the number of shims behind the driven clutch (Chapter 5).

34 GRABBY OR ERRATIC ENGAGEMENT

1   Thin spots or overall wear on drivebelt. Inspect the belt and replace if necessary (Chapters 2 and 5). If there are thin spots, check possible causes described in Section 32 above.
2   Drive clutch bushings sticking. Inspect the bushings and replace if necessary (Chapter 5).

35 NOISY OPERATION

1   Worn belt or separated belt plies. Inspect the belt and replace it if necessary (Chapter 5).
2   Loose belt caused by loose or broken engine or transmission mounts causing the drivebelt to run out of alignment. Check and tighten or replace as necessary (Chapters 4 and 6).
3   Thin spots on belt. Replace the belt and check for causes of thin spots listed in Section 32 above.

36 MELTED PVT COVER

1   Air intake or outlet ducts clogged. Check the inlet and outlet for obstructions and clean as necessary (Chapters 2 and 5).
2   Belt slipping due to contamination and rubbing on cover. Clean away contamination. Check the cover for proper sealing against outside water. Check the engine and transmission for sources of any oil leaks (Chapters 4 and 6).
3   Transmission range (HIGH or LOW) incorrectly selected for driving conditions. Review driving conditions in owner's manual.
4   Rotating mechanical components hitting cover. Check for damage and repair as necessary (Chapter 5).

37 ENGINE RPM TOO LOW WHEN VEHICLE IS DRIVEN

1   First make sure engine is properly tuned and running correctly. If not, tune up engine (Chapter 2). If engine is properly tuned, consider the following.
2   Belt slipping. Inspect belt and replace as necessary (Chapter 5). Clean any grease from sheaves.
3   Drive clutch spring damaged or wrong spring installed. Remove and inspect spring and replace if required (Chapter 5).
4   Driven clutch spring broken or installed incorrectly. Inspect the spring and reinstall or replace it (Chapter 5).
5   Incorrect drive clutch shift weights (too heavy). Verify part number and install correct shift weights if necessary (Chapter 5).

38 ENGINE RPM TOO HIGH WHEN VEHICLE IS DRIVEN

1   Belt slipping. Inspect belt and replace as necessary (Chapter 5). Clean any grease from sheaves.
2   Incorrect drive clutch shift weights (too light). Verify part number and install correct shift weights if necessary (Chapter 5).
3   Incorrect drive clutch spring (spring rate too high). Verify part number and install correct spring if necessary (Chapter 5).
4   Binding drive clutch. Disassemble the clutch, clean away any dirt and inspect the buttons and shift weights. Reassemble the clutch without the spring and operate it through its full range by hand to check operation (Chapter 5).
5   Binding driven clutch. Disassemble the clutch, noting whether the location of the helix spring is correct. Clean away any dirt and inspect the sheave bushing and ramp buttons.

39 ENGINE RPM ERRATIC WHEN VEHICLE IS DRIVEN

1   Thin or burned spots on the drivebelt. Replace the belt and check for causes of thin spots listed in Section 32 above.
2   Binding drive clutch. Disassemble the clutch, clean away any dirt and inspect the shift weights. Clean and polish the hub of the stationary shaft, then reassemble the clutch without the spring and operate it through its full range by hand to check operation (Chapter 5).
3   Driven clutch damage. Disassemble the clutch and replace the ramp buttons. Inspect the movable sheave bushing for excessive clearance (Chapter 5).
4   Wear groove in sheave face. Replace the affected clutch (Chapter 5).

40 WATER ENTERING CLUTCH COVER

1   Check inner and outer clutch covers for looseness or damage (Chapter 5).
2   Water entering the clutch inlet when washing vehicle. Before washing the vehicle, cover the inlet with a plastic bag.
3   Water entering the clutch inlet duct when operating vehicle in deep water.

GEAR SHIFTING PROBLEMS

41 DOESN'T GO INTO GEAR

1   Insufficient or incorrect transmission oil. Check the oil and add or change it as necessary (Chapter 2).
2   Incorrect shift cable adjustment. Check and adjust as necessary (Chapter 6).
3   Wear or damage to external linkage or internal transmission components. To isolate the problem, disconnect the shift cable from the transmission (Chapter 6). Shift into gear by hand and operate the vehicle. If it now operates correctly, the problem is in the linkage. If not, the problem is internal.
4   Linkage problem. Recheck and verify proper adjustment. Check for worn linkage rod ends, bent linkage rods or damaged bellcranks. Replace damaged components and readjust as necessary (Chapter 6).
5   Internal problem. Take transmission to dealership for inspection. Replace worn or damaged components or install a new transmission unit (Chapter 6).
6   Engine idle speed incorrect. Refer to Sections 9, 10 and 11 above.
7   Select lever loose or damaged. Inspect select lever assembly and tighten loose fasteners or replace damaged parts (Chapter 6).
8   Loose or broken engine or transmission mounts causing the drivebelt to run out of alignment. Check and tighten or replace as necessary (Chapter 4 and 6).
9   After performing the services in this section, turn the ignition switch On and with the vehicle at rest, shift the transmission into each gear while watching the instrument cluster. Make sure the display on the instrument cluster indicates the correct transmission position when each gear change is made.

ABNORMAL ENGINE NOISE

42 KNOCKING OR PINGING

1   Carbon build-up in combustion chamber. Use of a fuel additive that will dissolve the adhesive bonding the carbon particles to the piston crown and chamber is the easiest way to remove the build-up. Otherwise, the cylinder head will have to be removed and decarbonized (Chapter 3).
2   Incorrect or poor quality fuel. Old or improper fuel can cause detonation. This causes the piston to rattle, thus the knocking or pinging sound. Drain the old fuel (Chapter 7) and always use the recommended grade fuel (Chapter 2).
3   Spark plug heat range incorrect. Uncontrolled detonation indicates that the plug heat range is too hot. The plug in effect becomes a glow plug, raising cylinder temperatures. Install the proper heat range plug (Chapter 2).
4   Improper air/fuel mixture. This will cause the cylinder to run hot and lead to detonation. See Section 23 above.

43 PISTON SLAP OR RATTLING

1   Cylinder-to-piston clearance excessive. Inspect and overhaul top end parts (Chapter 3).
2   Connecting rod bent. Caused by over-revving, trying to start a badly flooded engine or from ingesting a foreign object into the combustion chamber. Replace the damaged parts (Chapter 4).
3   Piston pin or piston pin bore worn or seized from wear

or lack of lubrication. Replace damaged parts (Chapter 3).
4   Piston ring(s) worn, broken or sticking. Overhaul the top end (Chapter 3).
5   Piston seizure damage. Usually from lack of lubrication or overheating. Replace the pistons and cylinder block, or have the cylinder bores replated, as necessary (Chapter 3).
6   Connecting rod upper or lower end clearance excessive (Chapter 4). Caused by excessive wear or lack of lubrication. Replace worn parts.

44   VALVE NOISE

1   Improper valve clearance. Check the pushrods and valve lifters for damage (Chapter 3). Also check the camshaft for excessive lobe wear (Chapter 4).
2   Valve spring broken or weak. Check and replace weak valve springs (Chapter 3).
3   Camshaft or cylinder head worn or damaged. Lack of lubrication at high rpm is usually the cause of damage. Insufficient oil or failure to change the oil at the recommended intervals are the chief causes (Chapters 3 and 4).

45   OTHER NOISE

1   Cylinder head gasket leaking. Check for oil leaks and perform a leak-down test (Section 6).
2   Exhaust pipe leaking at cylinder head connection. Caused by improper fit of pipe, damaged gasket or loose exhaust flange. All exhaust fasteners should be tightened evenly and carefully (Chapter 7). Failure to do this will lead to a leak.
3   Loose or broken engine or transmission mounts. Check and tighten or replace as necessary (Chapters 4 and 6).
4   Crankshaft runout excessive (Chapter 4). Caused by a bent crankshaft (from over-revving) or damage from an upper cylinder component failure.
5   Crankshaft bearings worn (Chapter 4).

ABNORMAL DRIVELINE NOISE

46   POLARIS VARIABLE TRANSMISSION (PVT) NOISE

See items in Section 35 above.

47   TRANSMISSION NOISE

1   Bearings worn. Also includes the possibility that the shafts are worn. Refer transmission inspection and overhaul to a dealership.
2   Gears worn or chipped. Refer transmission inspection and overhaul to a dealership.
3   Metal chips jammed in gear teeth. Probably pieces from a broken gear or shift mechanism that were picked

up by the gears. This will cause early bearing failure. Refer transmission inspection and overhaul to a dealership.
4   Transmission oil level too low (Chapter 2). Causes a howl from transmission. Also affects engine power and PVT operation.

48   FRONT GEARCASE NOISE

1   Bearings worn. Also includes the possibility that the pinion shaft, ring gear and output hub are worn. Refer front gearcase inspection and overhaul to a dealership.
2   Gears worn or chipped. Refer front gearcase inspection and overhaul to a dealership.
3   Metal chips jammed in gear teeth. This will cause early bearing failure. Refer front gearcase inspection and overhaul to a dealership.
4   Gearcase oil level too low (Chapter 2). Causes a howl from gearcase.

ABNORMAL CHASSIS NOISE

49   SUSPENSION NOISE

1   Shock absorber fasteners loose or missing (Chapters 11 and 12).
2   Shock spring(s) weak or broken. Makes a clicking or scraping sound. Check shock springs for any visual damage (Chapters 11 and 12).
3   Steering shaft bearings worn or damaged. Clicks when braking. Check and replace as necessary (Chapter 11).
4   Shock absorber fluid level incorrect. Indicates a leak caused by defective seal. Shock will be covered with oil. Replace or overhaul shock, depending on type (Chapters 11 and 12).
5   Internal shock damage, including bent damper shaft. Replace non-rebuildable shocks. If the shock is rebuildable, disassemble and inspect the parts; overhaul if possible or replace if necessary (Chapters 11 and 12).

50   DRIVEAXLE NOISE

1   Worn or damaged axle outer joint. Makes clicking noise in turns. Check for cut or damaged seals and repair as necessary (Chapters 11 and 12).
2   Worn or damaged axle inner joint. Makes knock or clunk when accelerating after coasting. Check for cut or damaged seals and repair as necessary (Chapters 11 and 12).

51   BRAKE NOISE

1   Brake pad adjust screw incorrectly positioned (Chapter 13).
2   Squeal caused by disc brake pad shim not installed or installed incorrectly (Chapter 13).
3   Squeal caused by dust on disc brake pads. Usually

found in combination with glazed pads. Clean using brake cleaning solvent (Chapter 13). If the pads are glazed, replace them.

4   Contamination of disc brake pads. Oil, brake fluid or dirt causing pads to chatter or squeal. Clean or replace pads and clean brake discs (Chapter 13).

5   Disc brake pads glazed. Caused by excessive heat from prolonged use or from contamination. Do not use sandpaper, emery cloth or carborundum cloth or any other abrasives to roughen pad surface as abrasives will stay in the pad material and damage the disc. A steel brush can be used, but pad replacement is suggested as a cure (Chapter 13).

6   Brake caliper loose or damaged (Chapter 13).

7   Disc warped. Can cause a chattering, clicking or intermittent squeal. Usually accompanied by a pulsating brake pedal and uneven braking. Measure disc runout and replace if necessary (Chapter 13).

8   Disc loose on hub. Check for loose and damaged disc studs (Chapter 13).

9   Loose or damaged wheel hub (Chapter 10).

10   Loose or damaged knuckle bearings (Chapter 10).

POOR HANDLING OR STABILITY

52   STEERING WHEEL HARD TO TURN

1   Flat or damaged tire(s). Inspect tires and replace if necessary (Chapter 11).

2   Wheel out of alignment. Caused by incorrect toe-in adjustment (Chapter 2) or bent tie-rod (Chapter 11).

3   Steering out of adjustment. Check toe adjustment and adjust if necessary (Chapter 2).

4   Tie-rods loose (Chapter 11).

5   Damaged front axles (Chapter 11).

6   Damaged steering assembly. Support vehicle with front wheels off the ground and check the steering assembly (Chapter 11).

7   If vehicle is equipped with electric power steering (EPS), refer to troubleshooting in Chapter 8.

8   Frame bent. Definitely suspect this if the machine has been rolled. May or may not be accompanied by cracking near the bend. Have frame inspected by a dealership.

9   Damaged frame. If vehicle was in a collision or roll-over, have frame and front end inspected by a dealership.

53   STEERING WHEEL SHAKES OR VIBRATES EXCESSIVELY

1   Tires worn or damaged. Remove and inspect tires (Chapter 10).

2   Knuckle bearings worn or damaged. Remove knuckles, inspect bearings and replace if necessary (Chapter 10).

3   Wheel rim(s) warped or damaged. Inspect wheels (Chapter 10).

4   Wheel hubs installed incorrectly (Chapter 10).

5   Wheel hubs damaged or wheel studs loose or damaged (Chapter 10).

6   Loose or missing fasteners in steering assembly (Chapter 11).

7   Steering bearing installed in pivot tube damaged (Chapter 11).

8   Steering shaft loose at either or both ends (Chapter 11).

9   On models with electric power steering (EPS), the power steering unit is loose. Check unit and replacing missing fasteners or tighten original fasteners (Chapter 11).

10   On models with EPS, power steering unit faulty (Chapter 11). Have unit inspected by a dealership.

11   Gearbox assembly damaged (Chapter 11). Have unit inspected by a dealership.

12   Engine mounts loose or damaged. Will cause excessive vibration with increased engine rpm (Chapter 4).

54   STEERING PULLS TO ONE SIDE

1   Uneven tire pressures (Chapter 2).

2   Frame bent. Definitely suspect this if the machine has been rolled. May or may not be accompanied by cracking near the bend. Have frame inspected by a dealership.

3   Wheel out of alignment. Caused by incorrect toe-in adjustment (Chapter 2) or bent tie-rod (Chapter 11).

4   Control arm bent or twisted. Caused by impact damage or age (metal fatigue). Replace the control arm (Chapters 11 and 12).

5   Damaged shock absorber (Chapters 11 and 12).

6   Damaged steering gearbox (Chapter 11).

7   Steering shaft bent. Caused by impact damage or by rolling the vehicle. Replace the steering shaft (Chapter 11).

55   FRONT OR REAR END TOO STIFF

1   Weak or damaged shock springs (Chapters 11 and 12).

2   Shock absorber damper rod bent or seized (Chapters 11 and 12).

3   Seized or damaged control arm pivot bolts (Chapters 11 and 12).

4   Aftermarket spring installed with too stiff spring rate. Change spring (Chapters 11 and 12).

56   FRONT OR REAR END TOO SOFT

1   Weak or damaged shock springs (Chapters 11 and 12).

2   Leaking damper rod oil seal where oil is visible on shaft and shock body. Replace non-rebuildable shocks. If the shock is rebuildable, disassemble and inspect the parts; overhaul if possible or replace if necessary (Chapters 11 and 12).

BRAKING PROBLEMS

57 SOFT OR SPONGY BRAKE PEDAL, DOESN'T HOLD

1   Air in brake line. Caused by inattention to master cylinder fluid level or by leakage from a loose or damaged brake hose/line. Locate problem and bleed brakes (Chapter 13).

2   Brake pads worn (Chapters 2 and 13).

3   Brake fluid leak. See paragraph 1.

4   Contaminated brake pads and brake discs. Caused by contamination with oil, grease, brake fluid, etc. Replace the brake pads. Clean brake discs thoroughly with brake cleaner (Chapter 13).

5   Brake fluid deteriorated. Fluid is old or contaminated. Drain system, replenish with new fluid and bleed the system (Chapter 13).

6   Master cylinder internal parts worn or damaged causing fluid to bypass. Replace master cylinder (Chapter 13).

7   Master cylinder bore scratched by foreign material or broken spring. Replace master cylinder (Chapter 13).

8   Master cylinder piston sticking in bore. Replace master cylinder (Chapter 13).

9   Worn or damaged brake caliper piston seals (Chapter 13).

10   Brake caliper piston sticking in bore. Remove and overhaul brake caliper and flush brake system (Chapter 13).

11   Brake caliper not sliding correctly on fixed shafts (Chapter 13).

12   Disc warped. Replace disc (Chapter 13).

58 BRAKE PEDAL PULSATES

1   Brake disc loose or warped. Replace brake disc (Chapter 13).

2   Axle bent. Replace axle (Chapters 11 and 12).

3   Wheel warped or otherwise damaged. Replace wheel. (Chapter 10).

4   Damaged knuckle bearing. Remove knuckle and replace bearing (Chapter 10).

5   Brake pedal assembly loose or damaged. Inspect the brake pedal and make any repairs as necessary (Chapter 13).

6   Front or rear hub damaged. Replace hub (Chapter 10).

59 BRAKES DRAG

1   Compensating port in master cylinder plugged with debris. Clean port with a thin piece of wire and flush the brake system (Chapter 13).

2   Brake pad adjust screw incorrectly positioned. Readjust screw (Chapter 13).

3   Master cylinder piston seized. Caused by wear or damage to piston or cylinder bore. Replace master cylinder (Chapter 13).

4   Brake pedal balky or stuck. Inspect the brake pedal

and make any repairs as necessary (Chapter 13).

5   Caliper piston seized in bore. Caused by wear or ingestion of dirt past deteriorated seal (Chapter 13).

6   Crushed brake hose (Chapter 13).

7   Brake pads improperly installed (Chapter 13).

60 BRAKES GRAB

1   Caliper bracket pad pins with steps or grooves along their surface. Replace the caliper bracket (Chapter 13).

2   Brake caliper not sliding correctly on pad pins. Remove caliper bracket and inspect pad pins (Chapter 13).

3   Warped brake disc. Replace brake disc (Chapter 13).

4   Loose brake disc mounting screws. Remove wheel and inspect the mounting screws (Chapter 13).

61 PARKING BRAKE DOES NOT HOLD

1   Parking brake cable out of adjustment (Chapter 2).

2   Worn parking brake pads (Chapter 13).

3   Parking brake disc severely worn or damaged (Chapter 13).

4   Parking brake lever loose or damaged (Chapter 13).

5   Parking brake lever ratchet mechanism stripped (Chapter 13).

6   Parking brake caliper assembly loose or damaged (Chapter 13).

62 PARKING BRAKE DOES NOT RELEASE

1   Parking brake cable out of adjustment (Chapter 2).

2   Parking brake cable frozen or seized (Chapter 13).

3   Parking brake caliper and brake pads contaminated or binding in place from rocks or other debris (Chapter 13).

4   Parking brake disc loose, warped or damaged (Chapter 13).

5   Parking brake lever seized or damaged (Chapter 13).

6   Seized transmission assembly (Chapter 6).

ELECTRICAL PROBLEMS

63 BATTERY DEAD OR WEAK

1   Battery faulty. Caused by sulfated plates which are shorted through sedimentation or low electrolyte level. Also, broken battery terminal making only occasional contact (Chapter 8).

2   Battery cables contaminated. Remove and clean cables. Apply dielectric grease to cable ends and reconnect (Chapter 8).

3   Battery cables loose and making poor contact (Chapter 8).

4   Load excessive. Caused by addition of high wattage lights or other electrical accessories. Perform current draw test (Chapter 8).

5   Ignition switch defective. Switch either grounds internally or fails to shut off system. Replace the switch (Chapter 8).
6   Regulator/rectifier defective (Chapter 8).
7   Stator coil open or shorted (Chapters 4 and 8).
8   Wiring faulty. Wiring grounded or connections loose in ignition, charging or lighting circuits (Chapter 8).

64 BATTERY OVERCHARGED

1   Test charging system to determine cause (Chapter 8).
2   Regulator/rectifier defective. Overcharging is noticed when battery gets excessively warm (Chapter 8).
3   Battery defective. Replace battery with a new one (Chapter 8).
4   Battery amperage too low, wrong type or size. Install manufacturer's specified amp-hour battery to handle charging load (Chapter 8).

SPECIFICATIONS

Engine compression and leak-down readings

Cylinder compression	165-185 psi (1138-1275 kPa)
Cylinder leak-down	15 per cent maximum

Oil pressure

Engine running at 6000 rpm	
Minimum	27 psi (186 kPa)
Standard	31 psi (214 kPa)
Maximum	
2012 and earlier models	35 psi (241 kPa)
2013 and later models	55 psi (379 kPa)

CHAPTER TWO

LUBRICATION, MAINTENANCE AND TUNE-UP

CONTENTS

1 INTRODUCTION TO TUNE-UP AND ROUTINE MAINTENANCE

1 This Chapter covers in detail the checks and procedures necessary for the tune-up and routine maintenance of your vehicle. Procedures that require more than minor disassembly or adjustment are covered in the appropriate Chapter. Section 1 includes the routine maintenance schedule, which is designed to keep the machine in proper running condition and prevent possible problems. The remaining Sections contain detailed procedures for carrying out the items listed on the maintenance schedule, as well as additional maintenance information designed to increase reliability. Maintenance information is also printed on decals, which are mounted in various locations on the vehicle. Where information on the decals differs from that presented in this Chapter, use the decal information.

2 Since routine maintenance plays such an important role in the safe and efficient operation of your vehicle, it is presented here as a comprehensive check list. For the driver who does all his own maintenance, these lists outline the procedures and checks that should be done on a routine basis.

3 Deciding where to start or plug into the routine maintenance schedule depends on several factors. If you have a vehicle whose warranty has recently expired, and if it has been maintained according to the warranty standards, you may want to pick up routine maintenance as it coincides with the next mileage or calendar interval. If you have owned the machine for some time but have never performed any maintenance on it, then you may want to start at the nearest interval and include some additional procedures to ensure that nothing important is overlooked. If you have just had a major engine overhaul, then you may want to start the maintenance routine from the beginning. If you have a used machine and have no knowledge of its history or maintenance record, you may desire to combine all the checks into one large service initially and then settle

into the maintenance schedule prescribed.

4   The Sections which actually outline the inspection and maintenance procedures are written as step-by-step comprehensive guides to the actual performance of the work. They explain in detail each of the routine inspections and maintenance procedures on the check list. References to additional information in applicable Chapters is also included and should not be overlooked.

5   Before beginning any actual maintenance or repair, the machine should be cleaned thoroughly, especially around the engine dipstick, front gearcase and transmission oil plugs, spark plugs, fuel injectors, etc. Cleaning will help ensure that dirt does not contaminate the engine and other components and will allow you to detect wear and damage that could otherwise easily go unnoticed.

2 Polaris Ranger 800 - Maintenance schedule

Daily (pre-ride)

☐ Check the fuel level and check the fuel system for leaks

☐ Check the engine oil level

☐ Check the engine coolant level and check for leaks - check throughout the day

☐ Check the pre-filter and clean or replace if necessary

☐ Check the air filter and replace if necessary - check throughout the day

☐ Check the brake operation and adjustment, including the parking brake; also check the brake fluid level and look for leakage; check that the brake pedal has some freeplay and to make sure pedal travel is not excessive

☐ Check the tires for damage, the presence of foreign objects and the correct air pressure

☐ Make sure the axle nut cotter pins are in place; if a cotter pin is missing, check the axle nut tightness and install a new cotter pin

☐ Check the wheel nuts for tightness; if necessary, tighten in a crossing pattern

☐ Check the throttle pedal for smooth operation and correct freeplay; make sure the throttle pedal returns when released

☐ Make sure the steering operates smoothly and there is no binding, excessive play or any abnormal noise; if necessary, support the vehicle with the front tires off the ground and check the steering

☐ Check the front and rear suspension for loose or damaged components

☐ Make sure the seat belts are securely attached to the vehicle and work properly; check the webbing for any tearing or heat related damage

☐ Check exposed fasteners for tightness; make sure all suspension cotter pins are in place

☐ Check the ignition switch and the proper operation of the headlights, taillights, brake lights and all instrument cluster lights

☐ Make sure any cargo is properly loaded and securely fastened

Weekly

☐ Check the air filter and replace if necessary

Every 10 hours, monthly or 100 miles (160 km), whichever comes first

☐ Check brake pad wear and replace if necessary

Every 20 hours, monthly or 200 miles (320 km), whichever comes first

☐ Check the battery box and the battery terminals

☐ Check the electrolyte level on conventional batteries

☐ Test the battery

Every 25 hours or one month, whichever comes first

☐ Check the parking brake system and adjustment and adjust if necessary

Initial 25 hours, one month or 250 miles (400 km), whichever comes first

☐ Change the engine oil and filter (also perform at this interval after rebuilding the engine)

Every 25 hours, monthly or 250 miles (400 km), whichever comes first

☐ Inspect the engine breather hose and replace if soft or damaged

☐ Check the front gearcase oil level and fill if necessary

☐ Check the transmission oil level and fill if necessary

**Every 50 hours, three months or
500 miles (800 km), whichever comes first**

☐ Lubricate the driveshaft

**Every 50 hours, six months or
500 miles (800 km), whichever comes first**

☐ Inspect and lubricate the shift cable; adjust
if necessary
☐ Lubricate the front and rear suspension
☐ Inspect the throttle pedal and lubricate the throttle
cable; check the throttle cable free play and a
djust if necessary
☐ Inspect the intake air duct assembly for loose or
missing hose clamps, air leaks and damage
☐ Inspect the clutch air duct for loose or missing hose
clamps, air leaks and damage; at the same time
inspect and service the clutch air duct filter
☐ Inspect the cooling system for leaks and damage;
pressure test the radiator cap and cooling system
☐ Inspect the drivebelt and replace if necessary

**Every 100 hours, six months or
1000 miles (1600 km), whichever comes first**

☐ Change the engine oil and filter
☐ Check the parking brake adjustment and
adjust if necessary

**Every 100 hours, 12 months or
1000 miles (1600 km), whichever comes first**

☐ Change the front gearcase oil
☐ Change the transmission oil
☐ Check the fuel system and system components for
leaks and other damage
☐ Inspect the spark plugs and replace if necessary
☐ Check and clean the PVT clutches; replace damaged
parts as required
☐ Inspect the radiator for leaks, loose or missing
fasteners and damage; clean the outside of the
radiator; measure the coolant specific gravity
☐ Inspect the coolant hoses for leaks, soft spots and
damage; replace if necessary
☐ Inspect the engine and transmission mounts; tighten
loose fasteners or replace the mounts if necessary

☐ Inspect the exhaust pipe and muffler for leakage,
loose and missing fasteners
☐ Check the wiring for chafing, wear and loose or
damaged routing guides; clean and pack connectors
subjected to dirt and moisture with dielectric grease
☐ Inspect the wheel bearings; replace if necessary

Every 100 hours

☐ Inspect the shocks for leaking oil seals and
other damage

**Every 200 hours, 24 months or
2000 miles (3200 km), whichever comes first**

☐ Change the brake fluid

**300 hours, 36 months or 3000 miles (4800 km),
whichever comes first**

☐ Clean the muffler

Every 500 hours

☐ Overhaul the shock absorbers to change the oil
and replace the oil seals (models with rebuildable
shock absorbers)

Every 2 years

☐ Replace the fuel line
☐ Flush the cooling system and change the coolant

Non-scheduled maintenance

☐ Check the axle boots for leakage and damage;
replace the boots if necessary
☐ Check the headlight aim and adjust if necessary
☐ Check the toe adjustment; adjust toe when necessary
or after replacing steering components

NOTE:
*Perform services more often if the vehicle
is operated in sand, water or under extreme
conditions.*

3.8a The dipstick is located on the PTO side of the engine

3.8b Pull the lever up . . .

3   FLUID LEVELS - CHECK

1   Check the fluid levels at the intervals listed in this Chapter's Specifications.
2   When removing the engine oil dipstick, caps and filler plugs to check fluid levels, check the O-rings and gaskets for damage or leakage, and replace if necessary.

Fuel level

3   Check the fuel level to make sure there is enough fuel for the planned ride. Check the fuel cap to make sure it is tight. Check the fuel hose and system components for leaks.

Engine oil

4   Check the engine oil level when the engine is cold, before the starting the engine. If the engine is hot, turn the engine off and wait several minutes for the oil to drain back into the crankcase to ensure an accurate reading. If the engine was just started, run it long enough for the oil to warm up sufficiently, and then turn the engine off and wait several minutes.
5   Park the vehicle on level ground, shift the transmission into gear and apply the parking brake.
6   On standard Ranger models, remove the seat base. On Crew models, remove the rear seat base. See Chapter 14.
7   Lift and remove the storage box located underneath the seat base (see Chapter 14).
8   Clean the top of the dipstick and the area around the dipstick. Then unlock and remove the dipstick **(see illustrations)**. Wipe the dipstick clean, then reinstall it fully so that the SAFE and ADD marks on the dipstick are facing up when the dipstick is installed through the dipstick tube. Do not lock the dipstick. Pull the dipstick back out and check the oil level by reading the level on the upper side of the dipstick. Reading the level on the lower side will the show the oil level as being higher than it really is. The oil level should be at or near the upper mark **(see illustration)**. If the oil level is near or below the lower mark, add a little

oil through the dipstick tube until it's near the upper mark.
9   When the oil level is correct, reinstall the dipstick and push its lever down to lock it in place **(see illustration 3.8b)**.
10   After starting and running the engine, check the oil level again after allowing the engine to cool and drain back into the crankcase.

Brake fluid

WARNING:

Brake fluid can harm your eyes and damage painted surfaces, so use extreme caution when handling and pouring it. Cover surrounding surfaces with a rag. Use brake fluid clearly marked DOT 4 and specified for disc brakes. Do not use silicone-based DOT 5 brake fluid, as it can cause brake component damage leading to brake system failure. Do not use brake fluid that has been standing open for some time, as it absorbs moisture from the air which can cause a dangerous loss of braking effectiveness.

WARNING:

If the reservoir is empty, or if the brake fluid level is so low that air has entered the brake system, the brake system must be bled (see Chapter 13). Simply adding brake fluid to the reservoir does not restore the brake system to its full effectiveness.

11   In order to ensure proper operation of the hydraulic brakes, the fluid level in the master cylinder reservoir must be properly maintained. The master cylinder is accessed through the front, left-side wheel well.
12   Park the vehicle on level ground, shift the transmission into gear and apply the parking brake.
13   Clean the master cylinder reservoir and the cap of all dirt and other debris. Clean the area above the cap to prevent debris from falling into the reservoir.

3.8c . . . to unlock the dipstick, then pull it out of the tube

3.14b Brake fluid level marks without the wheel panel

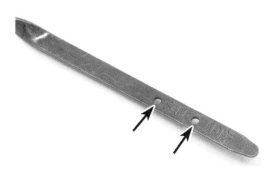

3.8d The oil level should be at or near the upper mark on the dipstick - if it isn't, add enough oil to bring it near the upper mark. Be sure to read the oil level on the UPPER side of the dipstick in relation to how it was removed from the engine

3.16 Inspect the O-ring (arrow) installed on the reservoir cap for cracks and other damage

14   The brake reservoir is marked with MAX and MIN level marks. Observe the brake fluid level through the translucent reservoir. The brake fluid level must be above the MIN level mark **(see illustrations)**.

15   If the level is low, turn the cap counterclockwise and remove it from the master cylinder. Add DOT 4 brake fluid up to the MAX level mark.

16   Before installing the cap, check the O-ring on the cap for any cracks, deterioration or other damage and replace if necessary **(see illustration)**.

NOTE:

When adding brake fluid to the reservoir, inspect the master cylinder reservoir diaphragm for tearing, cracks or other damage. A damaged diaphragm will allow moisture to enter the reservoir and contaminate the brake fluid.

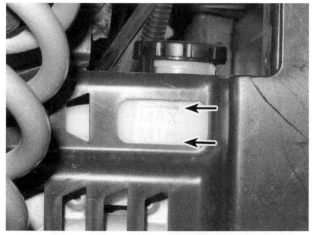

3.14a The brake fluid level is visible through the left side of the reservoir - it must be above the MIN mark (view through wheel panel)

17   Install the cap and turn it clockwise until the black tabs on the cap bottom against the stops on the reservoir.

Coolant check

18 Check the coolant level in the reservoir when the engine is a normal operating temperature.

19 Park the vehicle on level ground, shift the transmission into gear and apply the parking brake.

20 Raise the hood.

21 When the engine is hot, the coolant level must be between the MIN and MAX level marks on the reservoir **(see illustrations)**. If the reservoir is low, remove the reservoir cap and fill to the MAX mark with the correct antifreeze type and ratio listed in this Chapter's Specifications. Reinstall and tighten the reservoir cap. If you can't tighten the reservoir cap, it's probably cracked and should be replaced.

Front gearcase

22 Park the vehicle on level ground, shift the transmission into gear and apply the parking brake.

23 Clean the recess in the oil fill plug, which is located on the bottom, left side of the gearcase **(see illustration)**, and remove it with an Allen wrench. The oil should be level with the threads in the lower edge of the oil fill hole **(see illustration)**.

24 If the oil level is low, add the fluid listed in this Chapter's Specifications until it rises to the threads in the lower edge of the fill hole. Install the oil fill plug and its O-ring and tighten to the torque listed in this Chapter's Specifications.

Transmission

25 Park the vehicle on level ground, shift the transmission into gear and apply the parking brake.

NOTE:

On 2010 and 2011 models, the oil level check plug hole is also used as the oil fill hole. On 2012 and later models, a separate oil fill hole was added to the rear of the transmission housing.

26 Clean the oil level check plug located on the right side of the transmission and remove it and its O-ring. The oil should be level with the threads in the lower edge of the hole **(see illustrations)**.

27 If the oil level is low, add the oil listed in this Chapter's Specifications until it rises to the threads in the lower edge of the oil level check hole. On 2010 and 2011 models, add oil through the oil level check plug hole **(see illustration 3.26a)**. On 2012 and later models, add oil through the oil fill plug hole **(see illustration 3.26b)**. On all models, and especially because of the difficulty in accessing the oil level check plug hole on 2010 and 2011 models, it may be helpful to add oil with the use of a syringe and an attached hose **(see illustration)**. Install the plug(s) and gasket(s) and tighten to the torque listed in this Chapter's Specifications.

3.21a The coolant reservoir is mounted behind the radiator - the MAX and MIN markings (arrows) are visible on the reservoir

3.21b Remove the reservoir cap (arrow) to add coolant to the reservoir

3.23a Remove the front gearcase oil fill plug to check the oil level and add oil

3.23b The oil level should be level with the threads in the lower edge of the fill hole (arrow)

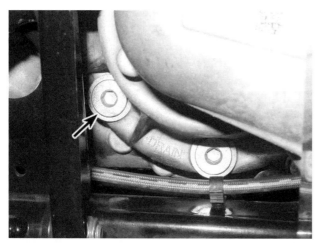

3.26a Remove the oil level check plug (arrow) to check the transmission oil level (2010 and 2011 models)

4.4a The pre-filter is mounted in the front air baffle box (arrow)

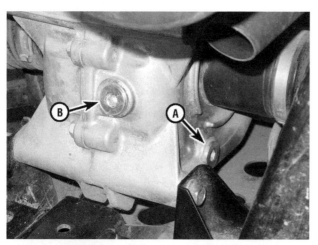

3.26b Oil plug details (2012 and later models)

A   Oil level check plug   B   Oil fill plug

4.4b Pinch the pre-filter with your hand . . .

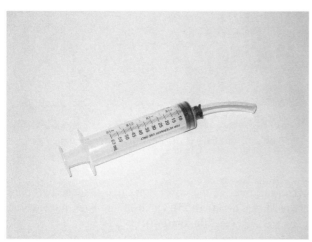

3.27 A syringe with an attached hose is a useful tool for adding oil to the transmission

4   FRONT AIR BAFFLE BOX PRE-FILTER - INSPECTION, CLEANING AND REPLACEMENT

1   A pre-filter is installed in the front air baffle box and connected to the air duct assembly that routes air into the air box. The pre-filter is an open mesh type filter that is installed dry. Inspect and service the pre-filter at the intervals specified in Section 1 or more often as required by weather and operating conditions.

2   Park the vehicle on level ground, shift the transmission into gear and apply the parking brake.

3   Open the hood.

4   Remove the pre-filter from the front air baffle box. If it is easier to do so, remove the front air baffle box first, then remove the pre-filter (see Chapter 7, Section 17) **(see illustrations)**.

4.4c . . . and pull it out of the front air baffle box

4.5 Inspect and clean the pre-filter before reinstalling it

5   Inspect the pre-filter for any clogging, tearing and other damage **(see illustration)**. Lightly pull on the filter to make sure none of the filter seams pull apart. If you can pull off some of the filter seams, discard the pre-filter and install a new one.

6   If there is no damage, clean the pre-filter in a high flash point solvent, then squeeze the solvent out of the filter and rewash the filter in soapy water, then rinse with clear water. Allow the filter to dry completely before reinstalling it. Do not oil the pre-filter. It is designed to operate dry.

7   Carefully install the pre-filter into the front air baffle box, making sure none of the sides are folded over.

8   Installation is otherwise the reverse of removal.

5   AIR FILTER - CHECK AND REPLACEMENT

1   Never run the engine without a properly serviced and installed air filter element. Likewise, running the engine with a contaminated, wet or damaged air filter element will allow dirt, sand and water to enter the engine. Frequent air filter inspection and replacement is a critical part of minimizing engine wear and maintaining engine performance. Inspect the air filter more often when riding in dusty, sandy and wet conditions.

NOTE:

If an aftermarket air filter is used, follow the manufacturer's instructions for servicing the filter element. Some aftermarket filters are designed to be cleaned, reoiled and reused. Always use the manufacturer's cleaning solvent and oil (if specified) to make sure the filter is properly serviced. When purchasing an aftermarket air filter, confirm that it is the correct filter for your vehicle.

2   Raise the cargo bed.

3   If necessary, clean the air box and cover before removing the cover.

4   Unhook the clips used to secure the air filter cover in

5.4a Release the clips (arrows) and remove the air filter cover. Here is the 2010 model cover . . .

5.4b . . . and here is the 2011 and later model cover

place and remove the cover. On 2010 models, two clips are used **(see illustration)**. On 2011 and later models, four clips are used **(see illustration)**.

5   Remove the air filter by sliding it out of the air box **(see illustration)**.

6   Plug the air box where it connects to the intake boot so

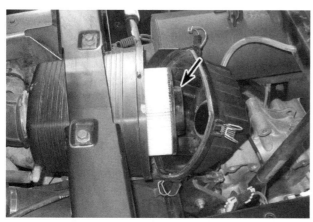

5.5 Slide the air filter out of the air box

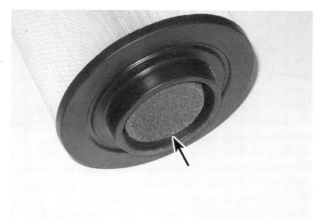

5.9 The foam pad fits into the closed end of the air filter (2011 and later models)

5.7 Inspect the air filter for any contamination, tearing and other damage - 2011 and later model air filter shown

5.12a Install the air box cover by aligning the raised shoulder on the air box cover with the mating slot in the air box (arrows) . . .

5.8 Apply grease to the inside of the filter shoulder (arrow) where it slides over the mating shoulder inside the air box

no debris can enter the intake boot, then clean the inside of the air box with a rag.

7   If the element has been soaked in water, oil or gasoline, or the element is saturated with dirt and sand, replace it with a new one (see illustration). Also inspect the inside of the air filter to make sure no debris passed through the paper element. Do not attempt to clean the paper type OEM filter and reuse it.

8   Before installing the air filter, apply a thick grease to the inside of the air filter shoulder (see illustration).

9   On 2011 and later models, before installing the air filter, make sure the foam pad is installed in the closed end of the air filter (see illustration).

10   Remove any cover or plug used to block off the intake boot that was installed in Step 6 and confirm the inside of the air box is clean and unobstructed. Then install the air filter over the shoulder inside the air box and push it firmly in place (see illustration 5.5). Make sure the air filter is fully seated and bottomed inside the air box.

11   Before installing the air box cover, check the O-ring in the cover groove for deterioration and other damage, and replace if necessary. If the O-ring was removed or replaced, lubricate it with grease before reinstalling it into the cover groove.

12   On 2010 models, refer to the illustrations to install and lock the air box cover (see illustrations).

13   On 2011 and later models, align the slot in the top

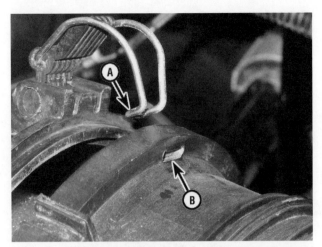

5.12b . . . then while holding the cover with one hand, pivot the clip handle to insert the clip (A) into the mating slot (B) . . .

5.12c . . . and push the clip handle down to lock the clip (arrow) in place. Repeat for the other clip

of the cover with the raised shoulder on the air box **(see illustrations)**, then engage and lock the four clips in place.

NOTE:

When securing the cover against the air box, make sure the clips lock the cover firmly in place - after locking the clips, make sure you can't turn the cover by hand. When our 2010 teardown vehicle arrived in the shop, we discovered the air filter cover was incorrectly installed. When we reinstalled the cover and locked it in place, it was too loose. Further investigation showed that an aftermarket air filter was used and it was too short for the air box. When operating this vehicle in rough terrain, the cover could have fallen off, allowing the filter to loosen or also fall off. This would allow sand, dirt and water to bypass the filter and enter the engine, causing rapid engine wear.

5.13a Air box cover and air box alignment position (arrow) . . .

6   BRAKE SYSTEM - GENERAL CHECK

1   Considering the environment and conditions these models operate in - mud, water, sand and competition - brake pad wear can occur rapidly, and it is critical that you inspect the brake system before each ride. A routine general check of the brakes will help to discover problems that can be remedied before driver and passenger safety is jeopardized. The complete brake system must be carefully inspected whenever the vehicle is involved in a crash or roll-over and when removed from storage.

2   Check the brake pedal for loose connections, excessive free play, and other damage. Replace any damaged parts with new ones (see Chapter 13).

3   Apply the brake pedal hard and hold it in position. If the pedal travel seems excessive or spongy, or if the pedal

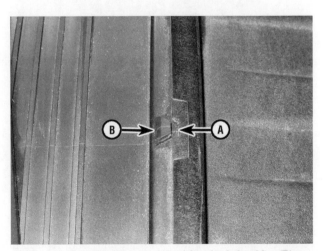

5.13b . . . align slot in cover (A) with raised shoulder (B) on air box and lock the four clips in place

6.5 Periodically check for brake fluid leaking from around the pushrod

7.4 Measure the brake pad lining thickness between the brake disc and the brake pad backing plate - measure each lining thickness separately

7.6 With the brake pads removed from the caliper, measure the brake pad thickness with a caliper

sinks to the floor, bleed the brake system (see Chapter 13).

4   Make sure the fluid level in the brake reservoir is correct (see Section 3). Because some of the brake hoses and brake lines are hidden and cannot be viewed quickly, it is important to monitor the fluid level in the reservoir. Any sudden fluid loss indicates a problem in the brake system.

5   Periodically inspect the front of the master cylinder where the pushrod is connected to the brake pedal **(see illustration)**. If brake fluid is leaking from around the pushrod, replace the master cylinder (see Chapter 13).

6   Inspect the brake hoses and brake lines for cracks, deterioration, leakage and other damage. Check each banjo bolt and flare nut for looseness.

7   Make sure all fasteners used in the brake system are tight.

8   Check the brake pads for wear and contamination (see Section 7).

9   Make sure the brake light operates when the brake lever is depressed.

10   Make sure the brake light is activated just before the brakes take effect.

11   The brake light switch is not adjustable. If it fails to operate properly, replace it (see Chapter 8).

7   BRAKE PADS - WEAR CHECK

1   Inspect and measure the front and rear brakes at the recommended intervals (see Section 1). Always replace pads as complete front or rear sets (both sides).

2   Remove the front or rear wheels (see Chapter 10).

3   Inspect the pads for oil or grease contamination, uneven wear and damage. Uneven wear may indicate that the caliper brackets are binding in the caliper. This will require cleaning of the brackets, lubrication of the sliding pins, and possible replacement of the rubber boots or other components. If there is brake fluid leaking from the caliper, remove the caliper and brake pads, then check for signs of leakage around the pistons. If the piston seals are leaking, the caliper must be overhauled to replace them.

4   With the pads installed in the caliper, measure the lining thickness on each brake pad with a caliper or ruler **(see illustration)**. Replace the brake pads when the lining thickness meets or is less than the limit listed in this Chapter's Specifications.

5   If it is difficult to determine the exact thickness of the remaining pad material by the above method, or if you are at all concerned about the condition of the pads, remove the caliper(s), then remove the pads from the calipers for further inspection (see Chapter 13).

6   Once the pads are removed from the calipers, clean them with brake cleaner and re-measure them with a caliper or ruler. You can measure the lining thickness as described in Step 4, or you can measure the complete thickness of the brake pad (lining and backing plate) and compare to the brake pad thickness dimensions listed in this Chapter's Specifications **(see illustration)**.

7   Installation is the reverse of removal.

8   PARKING BRAKE PADS AND DISC - INSPECTION AND WEAR CHECK

1   Inspect the parking brake pads and the parking brake disc at the intervals listed in Section 1.

Parking brake pads

2   Park the vehicle on level ground, shift the transmission into LOW gear and apply the parking brake. Block the rear wheels in case you release the parking brake in this procedure.
3   Raise the cargo bed.
4   Inspect the parking brake pads for any visual damage. The edges of the pads should be square with no indications of cracking or fluid contamination **(see illustration)**.

NOTE:
On 2010-2012 models, the outboard pad is thicker than the inboard pad. This is due to the difference in the thickness of the backing plates.

5   Check the pad wear. On 2010-2012 models, measure the thickness of each brake pad (includes both the backing plate and lining thickness). If the overall thickness of either pad is less than the thickness listed in this Chapter's Specifications, replace both parking pads as a set (see Chapter 13). On 2013 and later models, measure the pad lining thickness on each pad. Do not include the thickness of the backing plate. If the pad lining thickness of either pad is less than the thickness listed in this Chapter's Specifications, replace the parking brake caliper assembly **(see illustration)**.
6   If it is difficult to determine the exact thickness of the brake pads or lining, or if you are concerned about the condition of the pads, remove the caliper, then remove the pads from the caliper for further inspection (see Chapter 13).
7   Once the pads are removed from the caliper, clean them with brake cleaner and measure them as described in Step 5.
8   Installation is the reverse of removal.

Parking brake disc

9   Inspect the parking brake disc for wear and damage and measure its thickness as described in Chapter 13, Section 10.

9   PARKING BRAKE CABLE - CHECK AND ADJUSTMENT

1   To prevent the vehicle from being driven when the parking brake is applied, the parking brake switch signals the ECU when the parking brake lever is applied. The ECU uses this information and limits engine rpm to 1300 rpm. Because the clutch is unable to engage at this rpm, the vehicle cannot be driven. Otherwise, if you were to drive the

8.4 Parking brake pad details

A   Inboard brake pad   *B   Outboard brake pad*

8.5 Parking brake pad wear is determined by measuring the thickness of the complete brake pad (A) on 2010-2012 models, or just the lining thickness (B) on 2013 and later models. Measure each pad separately

vehicle with the parking brake applied, the parking brake pads and brake disc would overheat and suffer damage. For this safety feature to work, the parking brake cable must be properly adjusted. If you attempt to operate the vehicle when the parking brake cable adjustment is too loose, the parking brake indicator will automatically illuminate, reducing engine rpm and preventing clutch engagement. To maintain the correct parking brake cable tension, check the adjustment at the intervals specified in the maintenance schedule (see Section 1) or when necessary and adjust the cable if required.

Check and adjustment

2   Park the vehicle on a level surface. Jack up the vehicle so the rear rear wheels are off the ground and block the front wheels to prevent the vehicle from rolling off the jackstands (see Chapter 10). Shift the transmission into Neutral.

9.3 Before checking or adjusting the parking brake cable, make sure the cable is attached to the brake arm with the clevis pin (arrow) and clip

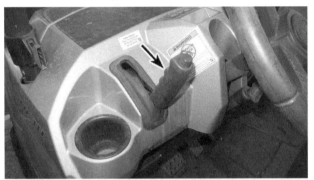

9.4a Press the button on top of the parking brake lever and pull the lever (arrow) until it clicks three times

9.4b The parking brake indicator (arrow) will light when the parking brake is applied - 2010 models

9.4c The word BRAKE appears on the instrument cluster when the parking brake is applied - 2011 and later models

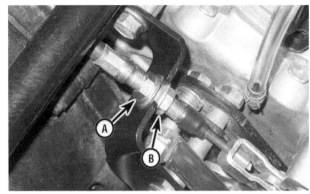

9.9 Parking brake cable adjustment details

A   Inner brake   B   Outer brake
     cable locknut   cable locknut

9.10 Reference mark (arrow) drawn across the outer locknut

3   Before checking the parking brake adjustment, make sure the brake cable is secured to the brake arm with the clevis pin and clip (see illustration).

4   Release the parking brake lever. Turn the ignition switch On, press the button on the top of the parking brake lever and pull the lever until you hear it click three times (see illustration). The parking brake indicator on the instrument cluster should illuminate (2010 models) or "BRAKE" should appear on the instrument cluster (2011 and later models) (see illustrations). Try to turn one of the rear wheels by hand. It should not turn.

5   Lower the vehicle so all four wheels are on the ground.

6   Pull the parking brake lever until you hear five additional clicks, so that a total of eight clicks of brake lever travel have been applied. Shift the transmission into Neutral and push the vehicle to see if it will move. It should not move.

7   If you were able to move the vehicle in Step 6, continue with Step 8 to adjust the parking brake cable.

8   Raise the vehicle so the rear wheels are off the ground and support it on jackstands.

9   Identify the inner and outer brake cable locknuts (see illustration).

10   Mark one edge on the outer locknut to use as a reference when turning the locknut (see illustration). Hold the inner locknut with a wrench, then loosen the outer locknut and back it out 1 1/2 turns (see illustration 9.9).

11 Hold the outer locknut with a wrench and turn the inner locknut clockwise while tightening it against the cable mounting bracket **(see illustration 9.9)**.

12 Recheck the parking brake cable adjustment (see Steps 4 through 6). Repeat until the adjustment is correct.

13 Release the parking brake lever and turn one of the rear wheels by hand to check for any brake drag. If there is any brake drag, the parking brake adjustment is incorrect. Repeat the adjustment as required.

14 If it is difficult to adjust the parking brake, check the brake disc and brake pad contact surfaces for mud and other contamination. Also check the parking brake assembly for any visible damage and loose or missing fasteners. Then check the brake cable to make sure it moves when the parking brake lever is applied and released, and that the linkage assembly at the parking brake caliper is not binding up.

15 After adjusting the parking brake, check its operation as follows. First make sure the main brake system is working properly - drive the vehicle and apply the brakes to stop it. If the main brake system is working correctly, drive the vehicle up a slight incline, then apply and hold the brake pedal to stop the vehicle, while making sure there is room behind the vehicle if it rolls backward. Shift the transmission into Neutral and pull the parking brake lever to apply the parking brake. Remove your foot from the brake pedal, while being ready to reapply it, and note whether the vehicle moves. If the vehicle moves, either the parking brake adjustment is incorrect or there is a problem with the parking brake assembly. This will require further inspection and adjustment. If the vehicle does not move, the parking brake is working correctly.

16 Do not operate the vehicle if the parking brake is not working correctly.

10 TIRES/WHEELS - GENERAL CHECK

1   Routine tire and wheel checks should be made before driving the vehicle. Worn tires can cause skidding, loss of traction and other handling problems that may cause loss of control of the vehicle. Also, problems may be found that could help prevent a flat or other problems when riding off-road.

2   Check for excessive wear, cuts, abrasions or punctures **(see illustration)**. Measure the tread depth at the center of the tire and replace worn tires with new ones when the tread depth is less than that listed in this Chapter's Specifications **(see illustration)**.

3   If a nail or other object is found in a tire, mark the location with a light crayon before removing it and patch the tire if it is safe to do so (see Chapter 10).

4   Check the valve stems for hardness, cracks and other damage, and replace if necessary (see Chapter 10). The rubber on valve stems hardens over time and are more prone to failure and damage than a newer, more flexible valve stem.

5   When the tires are cold, check and set the tire pressure to maintain good traction and handling and to prevent rim

10.2a Carefully check each tire for damage and other conditions that could cause handling problems or for a possible flat tire

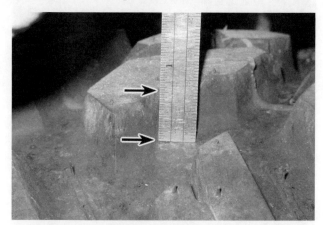

10.2b Measure tread depth (arrow) with a ruler to determine tire wear

10.5 Check tire pressure with a gauge that will read accurately at the low pressures used on these models

damage **(see illustration)**. See the tire pressure values listed in this Chapter's Specifications.

6   Check the wheels for cracks, dents and other damage **(see illustration)**. Rim damage may be sufficient to cause an air leak or affect wheel alignment. Improper wheel alignment can cause vibration and result in an unsafe driving condition.

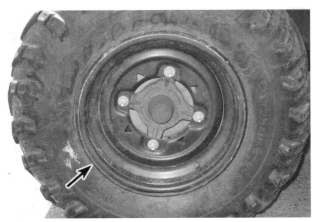

10.6 Check both sides of each rim for damage

11.1b . . . and at the throttle body (arrows) to make sure
both cable ends are fully seated (2010 model)

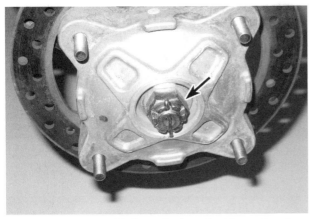

10.7 Make sure each hub nut is secured with a cotter pin
(front hub shown)

11.1c The throttle pedal (arrow) must operate smoothly and
under spring tension, and return fully when released

11 THROTTLE CABLE AND THROTTLE PEDAL - CHECK, LUBRICATION AND ADJUSTMENT

Throttle check

1   When inspecting the throttle cable, first make sure both ends of the cable are fully seated (see illustrations). Then operate the throttle pedal by hand to make sure it pivots easily from fully closed to fully open, and returns automatically from fully open to fully closed when released (see illustration).

2   If the throttle sticks, this is probably due to a dry or sticking throttle cable or a problem with the throttle pedal. Dirt and other debris entering the cable will also cause the cable to stick open. Before lubricating the throttle cable, inspect the cable sheath for cracks, splitting and other damage. Inspect the cable ends for fraying and other signs of damage. Check the cable operation by holding the sheath and then sliding the cable. Refer to Chapter 7 to replace the throttle cable and service the throttle pedal.

3   If the throttle pedal is working correctly and there are no problems with the throttle cable, check the throttle cable free play and adjust if necessary (see Steps 5 through 10).

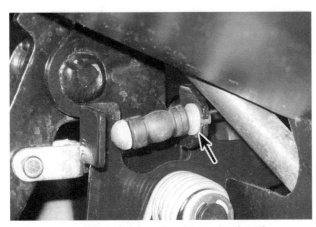

11.1a Check the throttle cable at the throttle
pedal (arrow) . . .

7   Whenever the wheels are removed, make sure the cotter pins are installed through the hub nuts with their ends bent to lock them in place (see illustration). If a cotter pin is missing, check the hub nut for tightness and install a new cotter pin (see Chapter 10).

8   Check that the wheel nuts are securely tightened on each wheel (see Chapter 10).

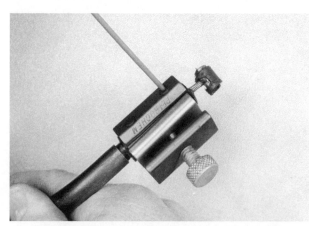

11.4 A cable lube tool mounted on the end of a cable

11.6a With the engine idling, measure throttle cable free play at the pedal (arrows) by pushing the pedal with your hand

Lubrication

4   To lubricate the throttle cable, first disconnect the cable at the throttle body and throttle pedal (see Chapter 7). At this point, the cable can be left in place as it is not necessary to remove it. Clamp a cable lube tool onto one end of the cable, and lubricate the cable with an aerosol cable lubricant **(see illustration)**. Forcing lubricant through the cable will also push dirt, sand and other debris that was trapped inside the cable out the opposite end. Continue until the lubricant exiting the cable is clear. Select a cable lubricant that is designed to be used in both hot and cold weather, and in wet and dry operating conditions. Reconnect both cable ends. Then adjust the throttle cable (see Steps 5 through 10).

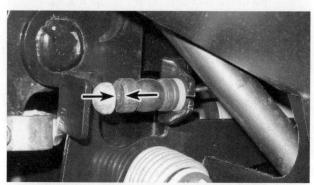

11.6b Measure throttle pedal free play between the throttle cable end and and its rubber cable stop (arrows) using a . . .

Throttle free play adjustment

5   Incorrect throttle free play can be caused by cable stretch, a damaged cable or the cable is out of adjustment. Excessive free play can cause a delay in throttle operation and prevent you from being able to open the throttle fully. If there is no cable freeplay, the engine idle speed may fluctuate and make it difficult for you to control throttle response, especially when accelerating.

6   Park the vehicle on level ground, shift the transmission into Neutral and apply the parking brake. Start the engine and allow it to warm up to normal operating temperature. With the engine running at idle speed, slowly push the throttle pedal and measure the amount of pedal freeplay at the pedal before the idle speed increases **(see illustration)**. Repeat this step several times to obtain an accurate measurement, then compare the freeplay to the value listed in this Chapter's Specifications. If the engine is not running, you can measure free play between the rubber boot and the flat part on the cable end **(see illustrations)**. With the pedal at rest, there should be clearance between the rubber cable stop and the flat part on the cable end. When you push the throttle pedal, the cable end will contact the rubber cable stop, taking up free play and moving the cable.

7   If the throttle free play adjustment is incorrect on

11.6c . . . metal scale . . .

11.6d . . . or different size drill bits (shank end)

11.8a The throttle cable adjuster is located inside a rubber cover (arrow) located near the throttle body

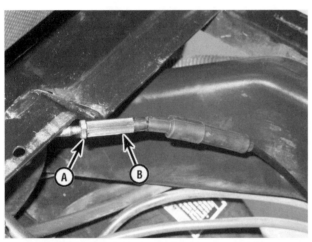

11.8b Throttle cable adjuster locknut (A) and adjuster (B) (2010 models)

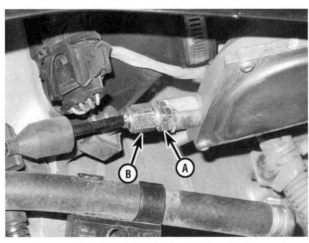

11.9 Throttle cable adjuster locknut (A) and adjuster (B) (2011 and later models)

standard Ranger models, remove the seat base. On Crew models, remove the rear seat base. See Chapter 14.

CAUTION:

On 2010 models, the throttle cable adjuster cover is a tight fit over the cable and adjuster. When sliding the cover off of the adjuster, do so carefully to prevent from kinking or otherwise damaging the throttle cable.

8   On 2010 models, locate the throttle cable and its adjuster **(see illustration)**. Then hold the cable and carefully pinch and slide the cover off the adjuster and down the cable.The cover is a very tight fit, so try not to tear it. Loosen the locknut and turn the adjuster until the specified amount of free play is obtained (see this Chapter's Specifications), then tighten the locknut **(see illustration)**. Check the adjustment again to make sure it did not change when the locknut was tightened.

9   On 2011 and later models, the throttle cable adjuster is located at the throttle body. Slide the boot away from the adjuster. Loosen the locknut on the throttle cable where is exits the throttle body. Turn the adjuster until the specified amount of free play is obtained (see this Chapter's Specifications), then tighten the locknut **(see illustration)**. Check the adjustment again to make sure it did not change when the locknut was tightened.

10   Start the engine and then press the throttle pedal several times. With the engine running at idle speed, recheck the throttle free play adjustment (see Step 6). Readjust the cable if necessary.

NOTE:

If the correct free play cannot be achieved, the throttle cable may be damaged or stretched to the point where it needs to be replaced (see Chapter 7).

11   Installation is the reverse of removal.

WARNING:

Turn the steering wheel all the way from side to side with the engine idling. The engine idle speed should not change. If it does, the cable may be adjusted or routed incorrectly or possibly damaged. Correct the condition before driving the vehicle.

12   STEERING SYSTEM - INSPECTION AND TOE ADJUSTMENT

Inspection

1   The steering system should be checked periodically for loose or missing parts, and worn or damaged parts that could cause excessive steering wheel play and other steering problems.

2   Park the vehicle on level ground and apply the parking brake.

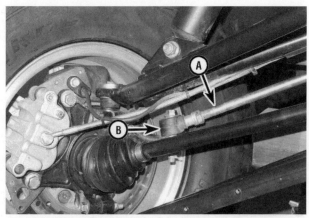

12.5 Move the tie-rod (A) in several directions while checking the tie-rod end (B) for play

12.9a Here a magnetic stand with a pointer is used to determine the centerline of the front hub . . .

3   Inspect all components of the steering system. Where used, check that the cotter pins are in place on the steering components. If you remove a cotter pin, replace it with a new one. Never reuse cotter pins as they may fail while the vehicle is under use. Repair or replace damaged steering components (see Chapter 11).

4   Make sure the front axle nuts are tight and secured in place with a cotter pin.

5   To check for play in a tie-rod ball joint, grasp the tie-rod and try to move it side-to-side and back and forth **(see illustration)**. If any play is detected, replace the tie-rod end (see Chapter 11). Repeat for the other tie-rod.

6   Turn the steering wheel from side to side and check for play before the wheels start to turn. If the play seems excessive, check the steering assembly (see Chapter 11).

7   Support the vehicle with the front wheel off the ground, then block the rear wheels to prevent the vehicle from rolling off the jackstands. Turn the steering wheel from side-to-side to check for any binding, catching or other problems, while making sure there is full side-to-side movement. Make sure all wiring harnesses, cables and hoses routed around the steering are properly routed and secured so they do not interfere with the steering.

12.9b . . . then used as a guide to identify the front center position of the tire, which is marked with a paint marker (arrow)

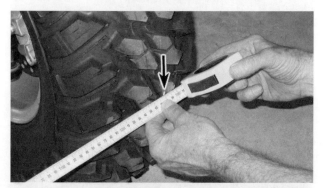

12.10 After marking each front tire, measure between the marks with a steel tape measure - this is the front measurement

Toe adjustment

8   Roll the vehicle forward onto a level surface and stop it with the front wheels pointing straight ahead.

9   Make a mark at the front and center of each tire, even with the centerline of the front hub **(see illustrations)**.

10   Measure the distance between the marks on both front tires with a steel tape measure **(see illustration)**.

11   Have an assistant push the vehicle forward or backward while you watch the marks on the tires. Stop when the tires have rotated exactly one-half turn, so the marks are at the back of the tires and even with the centerline of the front hub **(see illustration)**.

12   Measure the distance between the marks a second time to determine the rear measurement **(see illustration)**.

13   Subtract the front measurement from the rear measurement to get toe-out **(see illustration)**.

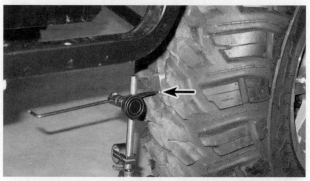

12.11 Use the magnetic stand to locate the paint mark placed on the centerline of one of the front tires after turning it one-half turn

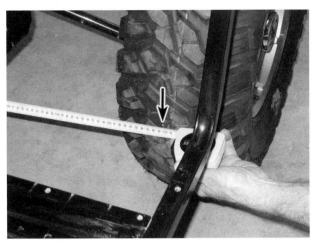

12.12 Measure between the marks once again to determine the rear measurement

13.4 Make sure all of the suspension arm pivot bolt nuts are tight - front upper suspension arm shown, rear suspension arms similar

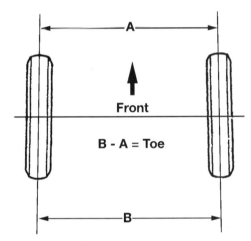

12.13 Toe-out measurement

14 If the toe-out measurement is different from the value listed in this Chapter's Specifications, hold each tie-rod end with a wrench and loosen the locknuts (see illustration). With a wrench placed on the tie-rod flats, turn each tie-rod an equal amount to change toe-out (see illustration). When toe-out is set correctly, tighten the locknuts to the torque listed in this Chapter's Specifications.

15 Drive the vehicle slowly on a flat, level surface to make sure the steering is correct.

13   SUSPENSION ARMS AND SHOCK ABSORBERS - CHECK

1 The suspension components must be maintained in top operating condition to ensure driver and passenger safety. Loose, worn or damaged suspension parts decrease the vehicle's stability and control.

2 Inspect each shock absorber for fluid leakage and tightness of the mounting nuts and bolts. If leakage is found, the shock should be rebuilt if possible, or replaced (see Chapters 11 and 12).

3 Have an assistant apply the brake while you push on the left front side of the vehicle to compress the shock absorber several times. See if the shock moves up-and-down smoothly without binding. If binding is felt, inspect the shocks as described in Chapters 11 and 12. Repeat for each shock absorber.

4 Check the tightness of all front and rear suspension arm pivot bolt nuts to be sure none have worked loose (see illustration).

5 If any of the fasteners checked in this section are loose, remove the nut and clean the exposed threads on the bolt. Then either install a new self-locking nut, or if reusing the original nut, apply a threadlock onto the bolt threads first. Hold the bolt and tighten the nut to the torque listed in the Chapter 11 Specifications or the Chapter 12 Specifications.

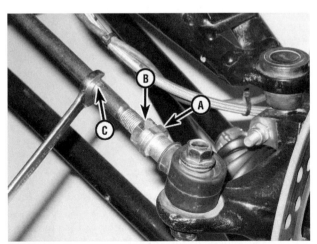

12.14 Hold the tie-rod end (A) and loosen the tie-rod locknut (B), then place an open end wrench on the flat (C) and turn both tie-rods an equal mount to adjust toe-out

14   SEAT BELTS AND OTHER SAFETY EQUIPMENT - INSPECTION

1   Make sure the seat belts and all safety equipment are properly installed, secured and work correctly. For information, refer to your owner's manual and Chapter 14.

15   FASTENERS INSPECTION

1   Since vibration tends to loosen fasteners, all nuts, bolts, screws, etc., should be periodically checked for proper tightness. Also make sure all cotter pins or other safety fasteners are correctly installed.
2   Pay particular attention to the following:

Spark plugs
All oil and fluid drain plugs
Oil filter
Brake pedal
Engine and transmssion mounts (see Section 32).
Steering fasteners
Front and rear hub nuts (see Section 10).
Wheel nuts (see Section 10).
Front and rear suspension fasteners
Skid plate screws

16   IGNITION SWITCH AND LIGHTING SYSTEM - INSPECTION

1   Turn the ignition switch on to check its operation and start the engine. Then check the lighting system for proper operation. Make sure the brake light comes on when the brake pedal is depressed. Also make sure the lights in the instrument cluster turn on and operate correctly.

17   BATTERY AND BATTERY BOX - CHECK

> *WARNING:*
> *Be extremely careful when handling or working around the battery. The electrolyte is very caustic and an explosive gas (hydrogen) is given off when the battery is charging.*

1   This section describes basic checks to make to the battery. See Chapter 8 if it is necessary to remove, test or charge the battery.
2   Note the external condition of the battery. Make sure the rubber protector is in place and covering the positive battery terminal. Check for any corroded or loose connections, cracks in the case or loose hold-down screws. Also check the entire length of each cable for cracks, and frayed conductors. On 2013 and earlier models, make sure the rubber hold-down strap is in place and doesn't show any signs of cracking or deterioration. On 2014 models,

17.4 The electrolyte level must be between the level lines (arrows)

17.6 Visually check sealed MF batteries for loose terminals and housing damage

make sure the battery hold down bracket is in place and its mounting screw is tight. If corrosion, which looks like white, fluffy deposits is evident around the battery terminals, remove and clean the battery and the battery terminals (see Chapter 8).
3   Check the battery box for any type of trail and road debris and clean if necessary.

Standard type batteries

4   The electrolyte level is visible through the translucent battery case - it should be between the MIN and MAX level lines **(see illustration)**.
5   If the electrolyte level is low, refer to Chapter 8 and remove the battery to top off the electrolyte and check specific gravity.

18.6 Locate the engine oil drain plug (arrow) through an opening in the skid plate

18.7 Unlock and remove the oil dipstick; oil is poured through the dipstick tube when refilling the engine

18.9a The oil filter is mounted on the PTO side of the engine

Maintenance free (MF) batteries

CAUTION:

Do not attempt to remove the strip at the top of the battery to check the electrolyte level or specific gravity. Removal will damage the strip, resulting in electrolyte leakage and battery damage.

6   If a sealed MF (maintenance free) battery has been installed, all that is required is to perform the basic checks described in Step 2 **(see illustration)**.

18   ENGINE OIL AND OIL FILTER - CHANGE

1   Consistent routine oil and filter changes are the single most important maintenance procedure you can perform on the Ranger engine. The oil not only lubricates the internal parts of the engine, it also acts as a coolant, a cleaner, a sealant, and protectant. Because of these demands, the oil takes a terrific amount of abuse and should be replaced often with new oil of the recommended grade and type. Saving a little money on the difference in cost between a good oil and a cheap oil won't pay off if it reduces the life and performance of the engine. The oil filter should be changed with every oil change.

2   Before changing the oil, warm up the engine so the oil will drain easily.

3   Park the vehicle on level ground, shift the transmission into gear and apply the parking brake.

4   On standard Ranger models, remove the seat base. On Crew models, remove the rear seat base. See Chapter 14.

WARNING:

The engine, exhaust system and oil are hot. Work carefully when removing the oil drain plug and oil filter to avoid contacting the oil or hot engine parts.

5   Clean the area around the dipstick, oil drain plug and oil filter.

6   Place a clean drain pan under the crankcase and remove the oil drain plug and crush washer **(see illustration)**. The drain plug is accessed through an opening in the skid plate.

7   With the oil draining, remove the oil dipstick to vent the crankcase and help speed up the flow of oil, and act as a reminder that there is no oil in the engine **(see illustration)**. Allow the oil to drain completely.

8   When the oil has stopped draining, install a new crush washer onto the oil drain plug. Then install the oil drain plug and washer and tighten to the torque listed in this Chapter's Specifications **(see illustration 18.6)**.

9   Place a rag or paper towels underneath the oil filter. Unscrew the oil filter using an oil filter socket **(see illustration)** and remove it from the engine. Some oil filters have a hex head mounted on the filter, which allows the filter to be loosened with a wrench. Hold the filter over

18.9b Use a ratchet, extension and oil filter socket . . .

18.9c . . . to remove the oil filter

the drain pan and pour out any remaining oil. Discard the oil filter **(see illustrations)**.

10   Clean the oil filter sealing surface on the crankcase. Do not allow any dirt or other debris to enter the engine.

11   Lubricate the O-ring on the new oil filter with clean engine oil, then screw the filter onto the engine by hand until the O-ring contacts the engine. From this point, tighten the filter an additional 1/2-turn to seat it.

12   Insert a funnel into the dipstick tube and fill the engine with the correct weight and quantity of oil specified in this Chapter's Specifications. Remove the funnel, then reinstall the dipstick and lock it in place **(see illustration 18.7)**.

13   Start the engine and let it run at idle speed for 1-2 minutes, then shut it off. Wait several minutes for the oil to drain back into the crankcase and check the oil level (see Section 3). If necessary, add more oil to raise the oil level to the upper mark on the dipstick. When the oil level is correct, reinstall the dipstick and lock it place. Check the oil drain plug and the oil filter for leaks.

14   The oil drained from the engine cannot be reused in its present state and should disposed of. Check with your local refuse disposal company, disposal facility or environmental agency to see whether they will accept the oil for recycling. Many automotive parts stores accept used oil for recycling and will sometimes provide a container that the oil can be drained and transported in. Don't pour used oil into drains or onto the ground. After the oil has cooled, it can be drained into a suitable container for transport to one of these disposal sites.

19   ENGINE BREATHER HOSE - INSPECTION

1   The engine is equipped with a crankcase breather system that consists of a breather hose, breather cover and reed valve. See Chapter 3 for a description of the system.

2   Inspect the breather hose, connected between the breather cover mounted on the valve cover and the air box, for soft spots and damage **(see illustrations)**. If the hose is in good condition, make sure both ends of the hose are clamped in place.

3   Check the breather cover **(see illustration)** for oil leaks, and if any leaks are found, remove and service the cover (see Chapter 3).

19.2a The breather hose is connected between the breather cover on the valve cover (arrow) . . .

19.2b . . . and the air box (arrow) - 2010 model

19.3 Check the breather cover (arrow) for oil leaks - 2011 and later models

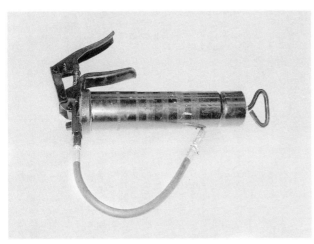

20.2 Use a grease gun with a flexible hose to force grease through grease nipples

20.4 The driveshaft grease nipple (arrow) is located on the yoke connected to the front output pinion shaft (standard Ranger shown)

21.4a Shift cable details (at select lever) - 2010 standard Ranger shown

A   Select lever
B   E-clip
C   Shift cable/boot
D   Cable locknut
E   Clip

20   DRIVESHAFT LUBRICATION

1   Lubricate the driveshaft at the specified intervals (see Section 1), after submerging the vehicle in water or before storing the vehicle for long periods of time.

2   A grease gun will be required to lubricate the driveshaft **(see illustration)**. When using a grease gun, force a little grease out of the hose nozzle to remove any dirt from the end of the gun. Wipe the nozzle clean with a rag before inserting it onto the grease nipple. When applying grease, first wipe off the grease nipple with a rag and push the nozzle firmly over it until you can feel it lock in place. Squeeze the trigger on the grease gun to force grease into the component. Apply enough grease to lubricate the component without damaging anything. If any grease oozes out of the joint, wipe off the excess with a rag. If grease escapes around the nozzle on the grease gun, the nipple is clogged or the nozzle is not completely seated on the grease fitting. Resecure the gun nozzle to the grease fitting and try again. Replace any grease nipple that is clogged or damaged.

3   Refer to the recommended lubricants listed in this Chapter's Specifications to obtain the correct type of grease required in this section.

4   Park the vehicle on a level ground. Locate the grease nipple at the rear part of the driveshaft **(see illustration)**. If necessary, shift the transmission into Neutral and roll the vehicle until the grease nipple is accessible. Then shift the transmission into gear and apply the parking brake. Lubricate the slip joint with grease (see Step 2). On Crew models, there is a second grease nipple located on the front driveshaft where it slides over the rear driveshaft.

21   SHIFT CABLE - INSPECTION AND LUBRICATION

1   Maintaining the shift cable in good condition and in proper adjustment is critical to vehicle operation. Failure to maintain and adjust the cable will result in poor shifting and possible transmission damage.

2   Park the vehicle on level ground and apply the parking brake.

3   Raise the dash to access the top part of the shift cable and the select lever (see Chapter 14).

4   Visually check that both ends of the shift cable are secured with a clip, and that the upper and lower cable locknuts are tight. Then check that the boot on each end of the cable is not torn, and that both ends of each boot fit tightly against the cable to prevent any debris from entering the cable. With the shift cable fully exposed, check it from end to end for any damage. Replace the shift cable if damaged (see Chapter 6) **(see illustrations)**.

5   To lubricate the shift cable, first disconnect the cable at the select lever and transmission (see Chapter 6). At this point, the cable can be left in place as it is not necessary to remove it. Clamp a cable lube tool onto one end of the cable, and lubricate the cable with an aerosol cable lubricant **(see illustration 11.4)**. Forcing lubricant through the cable

will also push dirt, sand and other debris that was trapped inside the cable out the opposite end. Continue until the lubricant exiting the cable is clear. Select a cable lubricant that is designed to be used in both hot and cold weather, and in wet and dry operating conditions. Reconnect both cable ends and adjust the shift cable (see Chapter 6).

6   Turn the ignition switch On. Move the select lever to check for full travel and correct gear engagement, while monitoring the shift position on the instrument cluster. If the transmission will not shift into each gear, or if it seems the transmission select lever is moving too far when shifting into a particular gear, check the shift cable adjustment (see Chapter 6).

7   Installation is otherwise the reverse of removal.

22   FRONT AND REAR SUSPENSION ARM LUBRICATION

1   While there are no grease nipples installed on the front rear rear suspension arms, it is a good idea to remove the suspension arms and clean and lubricate the pivot bolts and bushings at the intervals specified in this Chapter's Specifications **(see illustration)**. To do so, perform the removal and installation procedures in Chapters 11 and 12.

23   INTAKE AIR DUCT ASSEMBLY - INSPECTION

1   Inspect the intake air duct assembly, from the pre-filter to the throttle body for loose hose clamps or damaged duct housings. Refer to Chapter 7 for information on how to access the air baffle box and air duct assembly.

2   Refer to Section 4 in this Chapter for information on servicing the pre-filter.

24   CLUTCH AIR DUCT FILTER - CLEANING, INSPECTION AND REPLACEMENT

1   A filter is installed in the clutch air baffle box and connected to a duct assembly that routes air into the clutch housing. The filter is an open mesh type filter that is installed dry. Inspect and service the filter at the intervals specified in Section 1 or more often as required by weather and operating conditions.

2   Raise the cargo bed.

NOTE:

On all models, note the filter alignment when removing the filter from the clutch air baffle box. On some models, a notch is cut out of one side of the filter to allow it to align with the inside of the box.

3   On early 2010 models, remove the screws securing the clutch air baffle box cover in place, and remove the cover

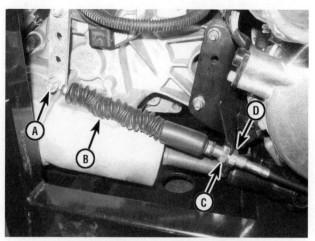

21.4b Shift cable details (at transmission) - 2010 standard Ranger shown

A   *Clip*   C   *Inside locknut*
B   *Shift cable/boot*   D   *Outside locknut*

22.1 Here is a good example of a suspension arm pivot bolt and the rust (arrow) that forms on the bolt from a lack of lubrication

while noting its O-ring. Then remove the filter from inside the clutch air baffle box.

4   On late 2010 and later models, remove the filter from the clutch air baffle box **(see illustrations)**.

5   Clean the filter in a high flash point solvent, then squeeze the solvent out of the filter and rewash the filter in soapy water, then rinse with clear water. Do not oil the filter. It is designed to operate dry.

6   After cleaning the filter, check it for clogging, tearing and other damage. Lightly pull on the filter to make sure none of the filter seams pull apart. If you can pull off some of the filter seams, discard the filter and install a new one.

7   Make sure all connecting points along the clutch air duct assembly are tight and in good condition. If it is necessary to service the clutch air duct assembly, see Chapter 5.

8   Installation is the reverse of removal. Make sure the filter is completely dry before reinstalling it.

2

24.4a Pinch the filter (arrow) with your fingers and remove it from the clutch air baffle box (late 2010 and later models)

24.4b Clutch air baffle box and filter. Note the notch cut in the top side of filter

25.3a Hose to thermostat

25.3b Hose to water pump

25.3c Sections of the coolant hoses (arrows) that pass underneath the floor should also be checked for leaks and damage

25 COOLING SYSTEM - INSPECTION

WARNING:
The engine must be cool before beginning this procedure.

NOTE:
Refer to Section 3 and check the coolant level before servicing the cooling system in this section.

1   The entire cooling system should be checked carefully at the recommended intervals. Look for evidence of leaks, check the condition of the coolant, check the radiator for clogged fins and damage and make sure the fan operates when required. Don't forget to check the skid plates for coolant, and if found, trace the coolant back to the source of the leak.

2   Remove body panels as necessary to access the cooling system components (see Chapter 14).

3   Examine each of the rubber coolant hoses along its entire length. Look for cracks, abrasions or other damage. Squeeze each hose at various points. They should feel firm, yet pliable, and return to their original shape when released. If they are dried or hard, replace them with new ones **(see illustrations)**.

4   On Crew models, check the aluminum water pipes for loose or missing fasteners, cracks and other damage. Check the hose clamp at each end of both pipes for looseness and tighten if necessary.

5   Check for coolant leakage at each cooling system joint. Tighten the hose clamps to prevent future leaks.

6   Check the coolant reservoir to make sure there is no coolant leakage from the reservoir or hoses. Also make sure the reservoir cap is not cracked and can be tightened firmly by hand.

7   Check underneath the water pump cover on the MAG

side of the engine for coolant leaking from the coolant weep hole located on the bottom of the stator housing **(see illustration)**. With the skid plate(s) mounted on the vehicle, you may first notice the coolant puddled underneath the water pump cover. When coolant is leaking from the weep hole, the water pump mechanical seal is damaged. If coolant is leaking from the weep hole, remove the stator housing to replace the water pump mechanical seal (see Chapter 4).

8   Check the radiator for evidence of leaks or other damage. Leaks in the radiator leave telltale scale deposits or coolant stains on the outside of the core below the leak. If leaks are noted, remove the radiator (see Chapter 9) and have it repaired by a radiator shop or replace it with a new one.

9   Check the radiator fins for mud, dirt, weeds and insects, which may impede the flow of water through the radiator. If the fins are dirty, force water or low pressure compressed air through the fins from the backside. If the fins are bent or distorted, straighten them carefully with a screwdriver.

10   Check the radiator for loose or missing mounting fasteners.

11   When the engine is cold, remove the radiator cap by turning it counterclockwise until it reaches a stop. If you hear a hissing sound (indicating there is still pressure in the system) wait until it stops. Now, press down on the cap with the palm of your hand and continue turning the cap counterclockwise until it can be removed. Check the condition of the coolant in the system. If it is rust colored or if accumulations of scale are visible, drain, flush and refill the system with new coolant. Check the cap and gaskets for cracks and other damage **(see illustration)**. Test the cap (see Chapter 9) or have the cap tested by a dealer service department. Replace the cap if necessary. Install the cap by turning it clockwise until it reaches the first stop, then push down on the cap and continue turning until it can turn no further.

12   Check the antifreeze content of the coolant with a coolant hydrometer **(see illustration)**. Sometimes coolant may look like it's in good condition, but might be too weak to offer adequate protection. If the hydrometer indicates a weak mixture, drain, flush and refill the cooling system (see Section 40).

13   Start the engine and let it reach normal operating temperature, then check for leaks again. As the coolant temperature increases, the fan should come on automatically and the temperature should begin to drop. If it doesn't, refer to Chapter 9 and check the cooling fan. Refer to Chapter 7 to check the engine coolant temperature (ECT) sensor. Also note that a low coolant level can prevent the fan from turning on, or possibly delay the fan from turning on at the proper time.

14   Pressure test the the cooling system (see Chapter 9). If you are not equipped to perform this test, have the test performed by a dealer service department or repair shop.

15   If the coolant level is consistently low, and no evidence of leaks can be found, perform a cylinder leakdown test to check for a damaged cylinder head gasket or a warped cylinder head (see Chapter 1).

25.7 Coolant weep hole location on bottom of stator housing

25.11 Replace the radiator cap if the gaskets on the underside of the cap are cracked or show signs of deterioration or other damage; at the same time, check the cap for any damage where it installed and mates against the radiator

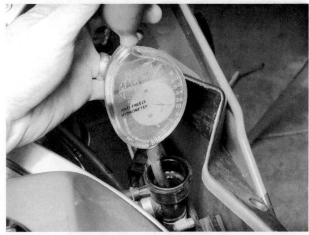

25.12 An antifreeze hydrometer is helpful in determining the condition of the coolant

26.2 Clutch cover drain plug (arrow)

27.3 Front gearcase oil drain plug (arrow)

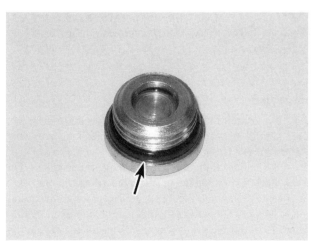

**27.4 Make sure the oil drain and and oil fill plug
O-rings (arrow) are in good condition
and properly installed**

26 DRIVEBELT - INSPECTION AND BELT DRYING

1   Inspect the drivebelt at the specified intervals (see Section 1). Refer to Chapter 5 for inspection and service procedures.

2   If water gets into the clutch housing, remove the clutch cover drain screw and allow any water trapped inside the clutch cover to drain **(see illustration)**. Then reinstall the drain screw. With the transmission in Neutral and the parking brake applied, start the engine. Rev the engine slightly above idle speed for 10-15 seconds to help blow dry the belt and clutch assemblies. If you choose to run the engine at a higher speed, do not operate at wide open throttle for more than 10 seconds. Then allow the engine to run at idle speed and shift the transmission into Low gear and attempt to drive off to make sure the belt doesn't slip.

3   If the belt slips, place the transmission back in Neutral and rev the engine some more. Once the belt stops slipping, drive the vehicle in Low gear to dry out any remaining water. If necessary, remove and service the drivebelt and the clutch assemblies (see Chapter 5).

4   Before putting the vehicle back in service, check the clutch air ducts for any loose hose clamps or connections, and make any repairs as necessary (see Section 24).

27 FRONT GEARCASE OIL - CHANGE

1   Drive the vehicle several miles to warm the oil in the front gearcase.

2   Park the vehicle on level ground, shift the transmission into gear and apply the parking brake.

3   Before removing the oil fill plug and the oil drain plug, clean both Allen recesses to avoid stripping the plugs when trying to loosen and tighten them. Then clean the area around both plugs to prevent dirt and sand from entering the gearcase.Place an oil drain pan underneath the front gearcase drain plug. Unscrew the oil fill plug **(see illustration 3.23a)** and the oil drain plug **(see illustration)** and allow the oil to drain into the pan.

4   Clean both plugs and replace the O-rings if necessary. Make sure an O-ring is installed on each plug **(see illustration)**.

5   Install and tighten the oil drain plug **(see illustration 27.3)** to the torque listed in this Chapter's Specifications.

6   Fill the front gearcase using the type and amount of oil specified in this Chapter's Specifications. The oil should come up to the threads in the lower edge of the fill hole **(see illustration 3.23b)**.

7   Install and tighten the oil fill plug **(see illustration 3.23a)** to the torque listed in this Chapter's Specifications.

8   Start the engine and drive the vehicle, then check for oil leaks.

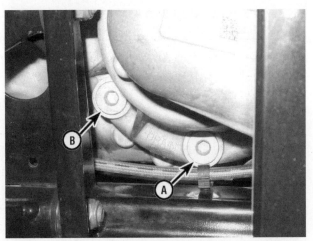

28.4a Transmission oil drain plug (A) - all models. Transmission oil level check plug (B) - 2010 and 2011 models

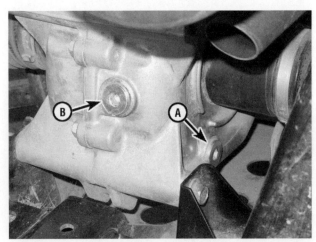

28.4b Transmission oil plug details (2012 and later models)

A   Oil level check plug   *B   Oil fill plug*

28   TRANSMISSION OIL - CHANGE

1   Drive the vehicle several miles to warm the oil in the transmission.

2   Park the vehicle on level ground, shift the transmission into gear and apply the parking brake.

3   Rinse off the transmission and the parts around it to prevent dirt and sand from entering the transmission. Make sure all of the oil plugs and the area around them are clean.

4   Place an oil drain pan underneath the oil drain plug located on the right side of the transmission. Unscrew the oil drain plug and the oil level check plug and allow the oil to drain into the pan **(see illustrations)**.

5   Clean the plugs and replace the O-rings if necessary. Make sure an O-ring is installed on each plug.

6   Install and tighten the oil drain plug **(see illustration 28.4a)** to the torque listed in this Chapter's Specifications.

NOTE:

On 2010 and 2011 models, the oil level check plug hole is also used as the oil fill hole. On 2012 and later models, a separate oil fill hole was added to the rear of the transmission housing.

7   Fill the transmission using the type and amount of oil specified in this Chapter's Specifications.On 2010 and 2011 models, add oil through the oil level check plug hole **(see illustration 28.4a)**. On 2012 and later models, remove the oil fill plug and add oil through the plug opening **(see illustration 28.4b)**. The oil should come up to the threads in the lower edge of the oil level check plug hole.

8   Install and tighten all of the transmission oil plugs to the torque listed in this Chapter's Specifications.

9   Use rags and paper towels to soak up the oil that pooled underneath the transmission housing when draining the oil. Cleaning the transmission and the area underneath it will allow you to spot an oil leak if one should occur from one of the plugs.

10   Start the engine and drive the vehicle, then check for oil leaks.

29   FUEL SYSTEM - INSPECTION AND FUEL FILTERS

WARNING:

Gasoline is extremely flammable, so take extra precautions when you work on any part of the fuel system. Don't smoke or allow open flames or bare light bulbs near the work area, and don't work in a garage where a natural gas-type appliance (such as a water heater or clothes dryer) is present. If you spill any fuel on your skin, wash it off immediately with soap and water. When you perform any kind of work on the fuel system, wear safety glasses and have a fire extinguisher suitable for class B type fires (flammable liquids) on hand.

Inspection

1   If you smell fuel while driving or after the vehicle has been sitting, inspect the fuel system immediately for leaks and damage.

2   On standard Ranger models, remove the seat base. On Crew models, remove the rear seat base. See Chapter 14.

3   Remove the fuel filler cap and inspect it for cracks and other damage. The gasket should have an unbroken sealing imprint. If the gasket is damaged, install a new one if available; otherwise, replace the fuel cap. After inspecting the fuel filler cap, reinstall it onto the fuel tank and tighten securely.

29.4a Make sure the fuel line is securely attached to the throttle body, fuel rail and fuel injectors and there are no leaks at the connectors or along the fuel line (see arrows). This is the fuel line assembly for 2010 models . . .

29.4b . . . and this is the fuel line assembly for 2011 and later models

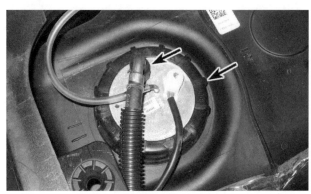

29.4c Also check the fuel line at the fuel pump (arrows) - 2010 model shown

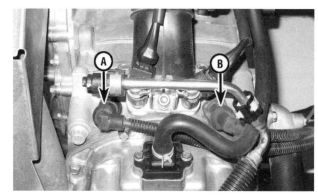

30.3a On 2010 models, identify either the MAG (A) or PTO (B) side spark plug cap

4   Check the fuel line, installed between the fuel tank and throttle body, for cracks, deterioration, leaks and other damage. Make sure the fitting at each end of the fuel line is in good condition (see illustrations). Note that the seals installed in the fittings are permanently attached to the fuel line. If a seal is leaking or damaged, it will be necessary to replace the fuel line.

5   Inspect the fuel injectors for any leakage or damage. If leakage is noted, the O-rings installed on the fuel injectors may be worn or damaged. Refer to Chapter 7 for information on the fuel injector O-rings.

6   Inspect the fuel tank for punctures, cracks and other damage. Make sure the metal clamps used to secure the fuel tank in place are securely attached.

7   Inspect the fuel pump vent hose to make sure it is clean and unobstructed. Then check the fuel pump where it is mounted into the fuel tank for leaks. See Chapter 7 to identify the parts on the different fuel pump assemblies.

8   If the joint between the fuel pump and the fuel tank is leaking, make sure the nut that secures the pump to the fuel tank is tight. If the leak continues, remove the fuel pump and inspect the fuel pump seal and the fuel tank for damage. Before removing the fuel pump, check with a dealership parts department to make sure a replacement seal is available. See Chapter 7.

9   Installation is the reverse of removal.

10   After installation, run the engine and check for fuel leaks.

Fuel filters

11   The fuel pump is equipped with two fuel filters and neither filter is replaceable. If fuel starvation is suspected, check the fuel pressure (see Chapter 7).

30 SPARK PLUGS - CHECK AND ADJUSTMENT

1   The spark plugs must be carefully removed to prevent dirt and sand from entering the combustion chamber. It is also important to know how to remove a plug that is seized, or is resistant to removal. Forcing a seized plug can destroy the threads in the cylinder head.

2   On standard Ranger models, remove the seat base and seat back. On Crew models, remove the rear seat base and rear seat back. See Chapter 14.

3   Note the spark plug cable routing from the engine to the ignition coil. On 2010 models, mark one of the spark plug caps to identify them so they can be correctly reconnected (see illustration). On 2011 and later models, the spark plug

cables are labeled either MAG or PTO - check each cable to make sure the label is attached, or mark one of the spark plug caps **(see illustration)**.

4   Twist the spark plug caps to break them free from the plugs and cylinder head, then lift and pull them off **(see illustration 30.3a)**.

5   Blow any dirt or sand that has accumulated around the spark plug **(see illustration)**.

6   Make sure your spark plug socket is the correct size before attempting to remove the plugs. The ceramic cover found on the top of a spark plug actually extends into the plug to prevent the spark from grounding through the plug's metal body and threads. The ceramic cover can be easily damaged from mishandling, such as when using an improper size socket. Fit the spark plug socket onto one of the spark plugs, then loosen and remove the plug by turning it counterclockwise **(see illustration)**. Repeat for the other plug.

7   If the plug is seized or drags excessively during removal, spray an aerosol penetrating lubricant around the base of the plug and allow it to set for 15 minutes. If the plug is completely seized, apply moderate pressure in both directions with the wrench. Only attempt to break the seal so lubricant can penetrate under the spark plug and into the threads. If this does not work, and the engine can still be started, install the spark plug caps. Then start the engine and allow it to completely warm up. The heat of the engine may be enough to expand the parts and allow the plug to be removed.

8   When a spark plug is loose, but drags excessively during removal, apply an aerosol penetrating lubricant around the spark plug threads. Turn the plug in (clockwise) to help distribute the lubricant onto the threads. Slowly remove the plug, working it in and out of the cylinder head while continuing to add lubricant. Do not reuse the spark plug.

9   After removing the spark plugs, inspect the threads in the cylinder head for damage. Clean and true the threads with a spark plug thread-chaser. Apply a thick grease onto the thread-chaser threads before using it to help trap some of the debris cut from the threads and preventing it from falling into the engine.

10   Inspect the electrodes for wear. Both the center and side electrodes should have square edges and the side electrode should be of uniform thickness. Look for excessive deposits and evidence of a cracked or chipped insulator around the center electrode. Check the threads, the washer and the ceramic insulator body for cracks and other damage **(see illustration)**.

11   Whether you are replacing the plugs at this time or intend to reuse the old plugs, compare each old spark plug with the chart at the front of this manual to determine the overall running condition of the engine. By correctly evaluating the condition of the plugs, engine problems can be diagnosed.

12   If the electrodes are not excessively worn, and if the deposits can be easily removed with a wire brush, the plug can be regapped and reused (if no cracks or chips are visible in the insulator). If in doubt concerning the condition of the plugs, replace both plugs as a set.

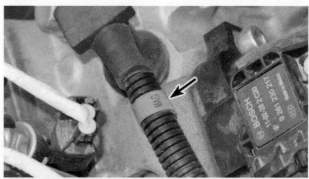

30.3b On 2011 and later models, the spark plug cables are identified either MAG or PTO - here is the MAG label

30.5 Here is a good example of why it's important to clean the area around the spark plugs before loosening and removing them. Just consider the engine wear and damage that would occur if some of the sand trapped in both spark plug wells fell into the engine

30.6 Loosen and remove the spark plugs with a 5/8 in. spark plug socket

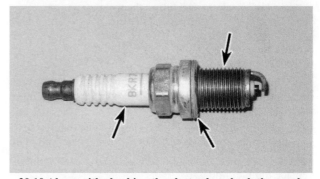

30.10 Along with checking the electrodes, check the spark plug for any visible damage, including the insulator body, washer and threads (arrows)

2

30.14a Spark plug manufacturers recommend using a wire type gauge when checking the gap - if the wire doesn't slide between the electrodes with a slight drag, adjustment is required

30.14b To change the gap, bend the side electrode only, as indicated by the arrows, and be very careful not to crack or chip the ceramic insulator surrounding the center electrode

13   Before installing a new plug, make sure it is the correct type and heat range (see this Chapter's Specifications). The reach (length) of a plug is also important. A shorter than normal plug causes hard starting, reduced engine performance and carbon buildup on the exposed cylinder head threads. These same conditions can occur if the correct length plug is used without a gasket. Trying to thread a spark plug into threads with carbon buildup may damage the threads in the cylinder head.

NOTE:

If the spark plugs you are using have an iridium center electrode, refer to the plug manufacturer's service recommendations as these plugs are serviced differently than conventional type spark plugs.

14   Check the gap between the electrodes, and even on new plugs as the gap is not preset. For best results, use a wire-type gauge rather than a flat gauge to check the gap **(see illustration)**. If there is a slight drag as the wire gauge passes through the gap, the setting is correct. If the gap must be adjusted, bend the side electrode only, and be very careful not to chip or crack the insulator nose **(see illustration)**. Make sure the washer is in place before installing the plug.

15   Due to the ultraseal shell used on the OEM recommended spark plug (see this Chapter's Specifications), it is not necessary to apply an anti-seize compound onto the plug threads. However, when using a different spark plug, refer to the manufacturer's instructions, and if it is necessary to do so, wipe a small amount of anti-seize compound onto the plug threads before installing the spark plug. Do not allow the compound to contact the electrodes.

16   Since the cylinder head is made of aluminum, which is soft and easily damaged, thread the plug into the head by hand. Slip a short length of hose over the end of the plug to use as a tool to thread it into place. The hose will grip the plug well enough to turn it, but will start to slip if the

plug begins to cross-thread in the hole - this will prevent damaged threads.

17   Once the plug is finger-tight, the job can be finished with a socket. If a torque wrench is available, tighten the spark plug to the torque listed in this Chapter's Specifications. If you do not have a torque wrench, tighten the plug finger-tight (until the washer bottoms on the cylinder head) then use a wrench to tighten it an additional 1/4 turn. Regardless of the method used, do not over-tighten it as you may crush the gasket and cause a compression leak, or damage the cylinder head threads.

18   Reconnect the spark plug caps by pushing them fully onto the plugs, while also making sure the the outer parts of the caps seal against the cylinder head.

19   Installation is the reverse or removal.

31   PVT CLUTCH - INSPECTION AND CLEANING

1   The Polaris Variable Transmission (PVT) should be inspected at the specified intervals (see Section 1). Check the clutch off-set alignment, pulley faces and clutch components for wear and damage and the clutch outer cover seal condition. If the clutch assemblies are dirty, remove the drivebelt and wipe them off with a dry rag. If the clutches have been contaminated with water, dirt or mud, remove, disassemble and clean them. Inspect and service the clutch housing, drivebelt and clutch assemblies as described in Chapter 5.

32   ENGINE AND TRANSMISSION MOUNTS - INSPECTION

1   The engine and transmission mounts should be inspected for loose or missing fasteners and damage at the specified intervals (see Section 1). Refer to the removal and installation procedures in Chapter 4 and Chapter 6 for specific information and tightening torques.

33.2 Make sure the screws that hold the exhaust manifold (arrow) to the cylinder head are tight

34.1 This alternator wire was pinched from improper routing

33 EXHAUST SYSTEM AND MUFFLER - CHECK AND CLEANING

1   On standard Ranger models, remove the seat base and the kickboard. On Crew models, remove the rear seat base and the rear kickboard. See Chapter 14.

2   Check the exhaust system for leaks and loose fasteners. The screws that secure the exhaust manifold or header pipe to the cylinder head are especially prone to loosening, which can reduce performance and possibly cause damage to the cylinder head **(see illustration)**. Check the exhaust manifold screws, and if loose, tighten them to the torque listed in the Chapter 7 Specifications. If necessary, remove the exhaust system to access the screws (see Chapter 7).

3   Check that all of the springs, exhaust pipe and muffler springs are properly installed.

4   Make sure all of the exhaust system heat shields are in place and their fasteners are tight (see Chapter 7).

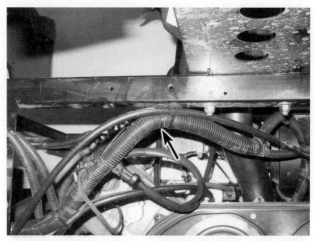

34.2 Here a flexible split loom conduit is used to guide and support wires routed from the front to the rear of the vehicle

34 WIRING HARNESS AND CONNECTORS - INSPECTION

1   The wiring harnesses are routed and secured in place with harness straps, tie mounts, tape and several different types of clamps. It is important these components are in good condition and correctly installed, as they hold the wiring harnesses in place to prevent flexing, and to prevent damage from moving parts, sharp edges and heat from the engine and exhaust system. Periodically inspect the wiring harness and connectors for missing harness guides and damage **(see illustration)**.

2   Some sections in the wiring harness must be flexible and able to move due to suspension and steering movement. These wires and harnesses are often enclosed in a flexible split loom conduit **(see illustration)**. Check these to make sure the plastic ties used to hold the conduit together are not missing.

3   Most connectors are disconnected by prying the locking tab on one connector away from the tab on its mating connector. After disconnecting the connectors, check the seal on one of the connector halves to make sure it is in place and not damaged **(see illustration)**.

34.3 One connector half is usually equipped with a seal (arrow) to keep water and other contaminants out of the connector joint

34.4 Visually inspect the connectors to make sure they are locked together (arrow)

34.5c Note the individual ground wires (arrow) attached to a single connector terminal and secured to the terminal block with a screw

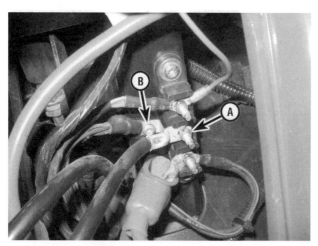

34.5a This is the engine ground cable (A) that is routed between the terminal block located under the hood and the engine. Also note the ground wire terminal connector and wires (B) attached to the same post on the terminal block

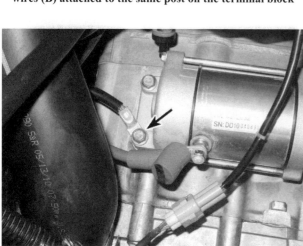

34.5b The engine ground cable (arrow) where it attaches to the starter - 2010 model shown. The ground attachment on 2011 and later models have two ground cables attached to a single connector terminal

4   Check the connector halves to make sure they are locked together (see illustration). Connectors that are subjected to direct mud and water spray should be packed with dielectric grease. Typical connectors to consider packing with grease would be those mounted at the front and rear of the vehicle, and those mounted near the wheels and suspension components.

5   The engine ground cable and a number of different ground wires are attached to the terminal block located underneath the hood (see illustrations). Because these terminals are subjected to water and other contaminants, periodically check them for corrosion and clean if necessary. When you do remove a nut from the terminal block to service a cable, note the condition of the ground strip, as its surface must be clean to ensure proper grounding. If necessary, use sandpaper to remove any rust or corrosion from the frame surface. When mounting additional ground terminals onto the terminal block, make sure the engine ground cable terminal is placed in position first, so that it seats directly against the ground strip.

6   To identify a particular connector or wire, refer to the appropriate wiring diagram in Chapter 8.

35   WHEEL BEARINGS - INSPECTION

1   Excessively worn or damaged wheel bearings will affect the steering and safe operation of the vehicle. Inspect the wheel bearings at the specified intervals (see Section 1) or whenever there is excessive play in the steering wheel, any wheel, or when there is any abnormal noise coming from a bearing.

2   Check that the wheel nuts are tight (see Chapter 10).

3   Park the vehicle on a level surface, then raise and support it on jackstands so the wheels to be checked clear the ground. Block the opposite set of wheels to prevent the vehicle from rolling off the stands.

4   Rotate the tire by hand. It should turn without any roughness, binding or grinding. Any problem here probably indicates a worn or damaged bearing.

5   Grasp one of the tires with both hands at the 12 o'clock and 6 o'clock positions and try to wiggle it back and forth. Then repeat by placing your hands at the 3 o'clock and 9 o'clock positions **(see illustration)**. Any movement may indicate a worn or damaged wheel bearing. Repeat the check for the other wheels and their bearings. If necessary, remove the knuckle, check the wheel bearing and replace if necessary (see Chapter 10).

36   BRAKE FLUID - CHANGE

1   The brake fluid should be replaced at the prescribed interval (see Section 1) or whenever you replace the master cylinder, replace or overhaul a brake caliper, replace a brake line, or when the fluid is dirty. Refer to the brake bleeding procedures in Chapter 13.

37   MUFFLER - CLEANING

WARNING:

When cleaning the muffler in this section, it will be necessary to start and run the engine. When doing so, never run the engine in an enclosed space such as a garage. Exhaust fumes contain carbon monoxide which is extremely poisonous; always do so in the open air or at least have the rear of the vehicle outside the workplace.

1   At the specified intervals (see Section 1), clean the muffler of carbon deposits.

2   With the engine cold, loosen and remove the cleanout plug from the bottom of the muffler **(see illustration)**. Note the washer installed on the plug and remove if it is stuck onto the muffler.

WARNING:

Have an assistant sit in the vehicle and operate the controls during the next steps as you'll need to be near the muffler. Don't stand directly behind or in front of the vehicle. Make sure the select lever is in Neutral or the vehicle will drive off when the engine is revved. Wear eye protection so you won't be injured by flying carbon chunks released from the muffler.

3   Shift the transmission into Neutral and apply the parking brake. Have your assistant start the engine and then rev it several times to expel carbon from the cleanout plug hole in the muffler. If carbon is blown out, put on a pair of welding gloves and cover the end of the muffler pipe with a rag **(see illustration)**. Have your assistant rev the engine several more times while you tap sharply on the

35.5 Grasp the tire at different positions and try to wiggle it back and forth to check for play in the wheel bearing

37.2 Unscrew the cleanout plug (arrow) threaded into the bottom of the muffler

37.3 Hold a rag against the muffler pipe and tap the muffler while an assistant revs the engine a few times to blow carbon out of the muffler

39.1 The fuel line (arrow) is attached between the fuel pump and fuel rail (2010 model shown)

39.2 When replacing the fuel hose, inspect the damper (arrow) at the same time and replace if necessary

muffler with a metal hammer or similar tool to loosen and remove carbon.

4   If you think there's still carbon in the muffler, back the vehicle up a slope so the rear end is about a foot higher than the front, then repeat Step 3.

5   If there's still carbon in the muffler, turn the vehicle around and drive it up the slope so the front is about a foot higher than the rear, then repeat Step 3.

6   Repeat Steps 4 and 5 until there are no longer any carbon particles expelled when the engine is revved.

7   Check the cleanout plug washer and replace if it is leaking or damaged. Then install the washer onto the plug and tighten the plug securely.

38 REBUILDABLE SHOCK ABSORBERS - OVERHAUL

1   If your vehicle is equipped with rebuildable shock absorbers, have a dealer service department or suspension specialist overhaul each unit and install new oil seals and refill with new oil at the intervals specified in Section 1.

39 FUEL LINE - REPLACEMENT

1   Replace the fuel line **(see illustration)** at the specified intervals, or sooner if leaking or damaged (see Chapter 7, Section 4).

2   On 2011 and later models, a damper **(see illustration)** is attached onto the opposite side of the fuel rail assembly. While there is no replacement interval for the damper, inspect it carefully when replacing the fuel hose. Replace the damper if it has started to deteriorate, feels soft, or if there are any signs of leakage or damage (see Chapter 7, Section 4).

40 COOLING SYSTEM - DRAINING, FLUSHING AND REFILLING/BLEEDING

WARNING:

Allow the engine to cool completely before performing this maintenance operation. Also, don't allow antifreeze to come in contact with your skin or painted surfaces of the vehicle. Rinse off spills immediately with plenty of water. Antifreeze is highly toxic if ingested. Never leave antifreeze lying around in an open container or in puddles on the floor; children and pets are attracted by its sweet smell and may drink it. Check with local authorities about disposing of used antifreeze. Many communities have collection centers which will see that antifreeze is disposed of safely. Antifreeze is also combustible, so don't store or use it near open flames.

WARNING:

Never remove the radiator cap with the engine warm. The coolant is scalding hot and under pressure. Opening the cap too soon will let it spray out forcefully and burn you. Let the engine cool, then remove the radiator cap and drain the cooling system.

1   At the intervals specified in Section 1, the cooling system should be drained, flushed and refilled to replenish the antifreeze mixture and prevent the formation of rust and corrosion. Failure to flush the cooling system and change the coolant at periodic intervals will eventually cause blockage in the cooling passages and result in engine overheating and engine damage. When replacing the coolant, all hoses and the radiator cap should be checked and replaced if necessary.

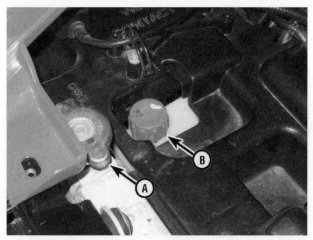

40.5 Radiator cap (A) and coolant reservoir cap (B)

40.6 Loosen the radiator drain screw to drain the cooling system

Draining

2   Park the vehicle on a level surface. Shift the transmission into Neutral and apply the parking brake. Once the engine is completely cool, continue with Step 3.

3   Open the hood.

4   It may be necessary to remove screws from the left side of the front cover so you can pull the cover away from the radiator cap. Reposition the front cover as necessary (see Chapter 14).

5   Remove the radiator cap by turning it counterclockwise until it reaches a stop **(see illustration)**. If you hear a hissing sound (indicating there is still pressure in the system) wait until it stops. Now, press down on the cap with the palm of your hand and continue turning the cap counterclockwise until it can be removed.

NOTE:

If the radiator is not equipped with a drain screw (Step 6), drain the cooling system as described in Step 7.

6   Place a clean pan beneath the drain screw, on the lower right side of the radiator **(see illustration)**. Loosen the screw and allow the coolant to drain into the pan.

7   If the radiator is not equipped with a drain screw, place a pan beneath the radiator hose, on the lower left side of the radiator. Open the clamp and disconnect the hose from the radiator and allow the coolant to drain into the pan **(see illustration)**.

8   Remove the two screws securing the coolant reservoir to the mounting bracket and lower the reservoir without disconnecting its hose. Remove the cap and drain the coolant into the drain pan. Flush the reservoir with clean water, then reinstall it and tighten its two mounting screws securely. Make sure the hose connected between the coolant reservoir and radiator is not kinked or pinched **(see illustrations)**.

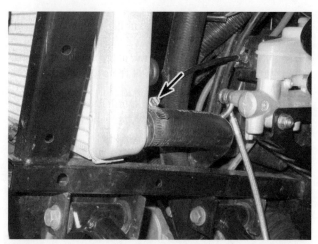

40.7 If the radiator is not equipped with a drain screw, loosen the hose clamp and disconnect the coolant hose at the bottom right side of the radiator (arrow) to drain the cooling system

40.8a Remove the two coolant reservoir mounting screws . . .

40.8b . . . then remove the coolant reservoir and its cap (arrow) and drain the coolant into a drain pan. Flush the coolant reservoir with clean water before reinstalling it

40.8c After reinstalling the coolant reservoir, make sure its hose (arrow) is not pinched or kinked - front cover removed to show hose routing (2010 model shown)

Flushing

9   Flush the system with clean water by inserting a garden hose into the radiator filler neck. Allow the water to run through the system until it is clear when it exits the radiator through the drain hole or hose fitting. If the radiator is extremely corroded, remove it (see Chapter 9) and have it cleaned at a radiator shop.

10   Tighten the radiator drain screw **(see illustration 40.6)** or reconnect the hose onto the radiator and secure it with the clamp **(see illustration 40.7)**.

Refilling/bleeding

40.11a The coolant bleed screw (arrow) on 2010 models is mounted on the thermostat cover

> *NOTE:*
>
> *When bleeding the cooling system, make sure to monitor the instrument cluster for any overheating, and especially if you are finding it difficult to bleed the system.*

11   Before refilling the cooling system, remove the coolant bleed screw and its washer. On 2010 models, the bleed screw is mounted on the outside of the thermostat housing **(see illustration)**. On 2011 and later models, the bleed screw is mounted on the top, left-hand side of the cylinder head **(see illustration)**. The passage hole inside the bleed screw must be clear. If not, clean it with a piece of wire or a drill bit **(see illustrations)**. Then reinstall the bleed screw with its crush washer and tighten hand-tight.

> *NOTE:*
>
> *If the bleed screw is plugged, air and coolant cannot escape and you will be unable to bleed the cooling system.*

12   Slowly fill the radiator with the proper coolant mixture (see this Chapter's Specifications). Pouring the coolant in slowly will reduce the amount of air entering the system

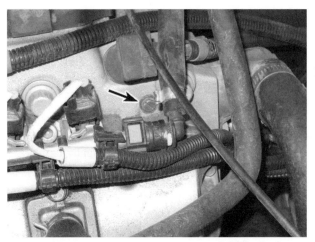

40.11b The coolant bleed screw (arrow) on 2011 and later models is mounted on the cylinder head

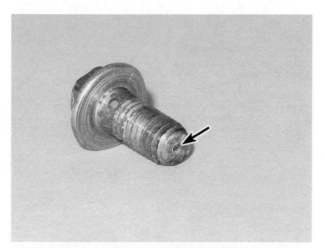

40.11c If the passage hole that runs through the bleed screw is blocked as shown here (arrow) . . .

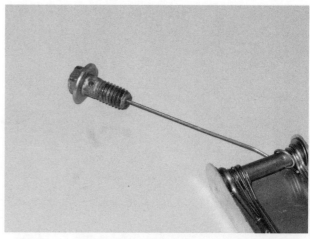

40.11d . . . clean the hole with a piece of wire or a drill bit

and help with bleeding. Fill until the coolant is at the bottom edge of the filler neck.

13 Fill the coolant reservoir with the proper coolant mixture **(see illustration 3.21a)**.

14 Start the engine and drive the vehicle onto an incline so the front part of the vehicle is elevated. If ramps are available, drive the vehicle onto the ramps, or raise the front of the vehicle with a jack and place a ramp under each front wheel **(see illustration)**, then lower the vehicle so the wheels are on the ramps. Shift the transmission into Neutral and apply the parking brake, then block the rear wheels.

> *WARNING:*
>
> *When using ramps to raise the front of the vehicle, make sure they are rated for the weight of the vehicle (see Specifications in the General Information chapter at the front of this manual).*

> *NOTE:*
>
> *Make sure the engine oil dipstick is installed and locked in place to prevent coolant from entering the dipstick tube and contaminating the engine oil when bleeding the cooling system.*

15 Make sure the coolant is at the bottom edge of the coolant neck, then start the engine and allow to idle for 5 to 10 minutes or until the thermostat opens and you can see coolant running through the radiator. The lower radiator coolant hose should also be hot. Then slightly loosen the coolant bleed screw to allow air in the coolant system to escape **(see illustrations 40.11a or 40.11b)**.

16 If there is air in the cooling system, the coolant will spit and bubble out of the bleed screw hole. You will also see coolant bubbling in the top of the radiator coolant neck **(see illustration)**. It may be helpful, while wearing thick gloves, to squeeze the upper radiator hose several times to expel any trapped air.

40.14 Automotive type ramps can be used to elevate the front of the vehicle when bleeding the cooling system

40.16 When the engine is running at idle speed and you can see coolant bubbling in the filler neck as shown here, air is trapped in the cooling system

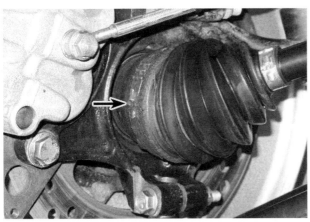

41.2 Two flexible boots are installed on each axle and must be in good condition and clamped tightly against the axle and CV-joint to prevent the loss of axle grease, while also preventing contamination of the grease and bearing assemblies. This boot is leaking and will require replacement and further inspection of the axle joint

17   When the coolant runs out in a steady stream, there is no air in the cooling system. Tighten the bleed screw to the torque listed in this Chapter's Specifications.
18   Install the radiator cap while the engine is still running, then drive the vehicle off the ramps (if used) and onto a level surface. Shut the engine off and let it cool down.
19   When the engine is cold, remove the radiator cap. Top off the coolant in the radiator until it is at the bottom edge of the coolant neck.
20   Check the coolant level in the reservoir and top it off if necessary.
21   Check the system for leaks.
22   Do not dispose of the old coolant by pouring it down the drain. Instead pour it into a plastic container, cap it tightly and take it to an authorized disposal site.

41 AXLE BOOTS - INSPECTION

1   The axle boots must be in good condition and secured tightly in place to keep dirt and moisture from contaminating the axle grease and causing CV-joint wear and damage.
2   Periodically check the boots on the front and rear axles for cracks, soft spots, tearing and other damage **(see illustration)**. Clean the axle and boots so they can be inspected. If a boot does not appear damaged, check for seepage where the boot is clamped to the axle and the CV-joint. Both mating areas must be dry. If there is any sign of grease and the boot is not damaged, one or both clamps may be loose or damaged. Check each boot and clamps for the same conditions.
3   If a boot is damaged or leaking, the axle must be removed from the vehicle and the boot removed from the axle so you can inspect the grease for contamination in Chapters 11 and 12. If the grease is contaminated with dirt and moisture, you will have to replace the CV-joint or the axle assembly. If the grease has a milky appearance, it has been contaminated by water. If the grease is not contaminated, it may be possible

to simply clean the parts, and reassemble with new grease, a new boot and clamps. However, this will require careful cleaning and inspection of the parts.

42 HEADLIGHT AIM

1   Check the headlight aim whenever it seems to be out of adjustment, or after a rollover or front end collision (see Chapter 8).

43 TOE ADJUSTMENT

1   Periodically check the toe adjustment to make sure it is not out of adjustment, which may indicate a damaged tie-rod or other steering component. Also check the toe whenever the vehicle doesn't track straight when the steering wheel is centered, or after replacing any steering components. See Section 12.

44 BREAK-IN

Engine

1   The performance and service life of a new or reconditioned engine depends greatly on a careful and sensible break-in for the first 25 hours of engine operation or approximately 14 gallons (53 liters) of fuel.
2   If possible, operate the vehicle on flat ground. Do not run in sand, mud or up hills. This will overload and possibly overheat the engine.
3   Avoid pulling any loads, and if it is necessary to do so, pull only light loads.
4   Vary the engine speed as much as possible while also avoiding hard acceleration for longer than 2-3 seconds at a time. After hard acceleration, lower the engine speed to reduce the build-up of heat in the engine.
5   Perform the pre-ride services in Section 1.
6   Install a new air filter (see Section 5).
7   Check the engine oil level.
8   Make sure the cooling system is full and bled of all air.
9   Start the engine and allow it to warm up. During this time, check for proper idle speed and leaks.
10   At the end of the the first 25 hours or one month, change the engine oil and filter (see Section 18).

PVT and drivebelt

11   After servicing the clutches and/or installing a new drivebelt, operate the vehicle at slower speeds while following the engine break-in information in Steps 2 through 4 for the first 10 hours of operation.

Brakes

12   After installing new OEM brake pads, bed in the pads as described in Chapter 13, Section 2.

SPECIFICATIONS

Spark plugs

Spark plugs
    Type . . . .   Champion RC7YC3
    Electrode gap . . . .   0.035 inch (0.90 mm)

Tire pressure

Tire pressure
    Standard Ranger models
        Front and rear . . . .   8-12 psi (55-83 kPa)
    Crew models
        Front . . . .   12 psi (83 kPa)
        Rear . . . .   16 psi (110 kPa)
Tire tread depth (minimum). . . . .   1/8 in. (3.2 mm)

Steering

Front wheel toe-out . . . .   1/8 to 1/4 inch (3.2-6.4 mm)

Miscellaneous

Brake pad lining minimum thickness
    (does not include backing plate thickness). . . . .   0.040 in. (1.0 mm)
Brake pad thickness (combined backing plate and lining thickness)
    Front and rear
        New . . . .   0.291-0.305 inch (7.39-7.75 mm)
        Minimum. . . . .   0.180 inch (4.6 mm)
Parking brake pad thickness (combined backing plate and lining thickness)
    2012 and earlier models
        Inboard pad
            New . . . .   0.304 inch (7.72 mm)
            Minimum . . . .   0.240 inch (6.1 mm)
        Outboard
            New . . . .   0.360 inch (9.14 mm)
            Minimum . . . .   0.310 inch (7.87 mm)
Parking brake lining thickness (does not include backing plate thickness)
    2013 and later models
        Minimum lining thickness.   0.040 inch (1.0 mm)
Throttle cable free play . . . .   1/16-1/8 inch (1.6-3.2 mm)

Recommended lubricants and fluids

Brake fluid . . . .   DOT 4 brake fluid
Coolant
    Type . . . .   Ethylene glycol-based antifreeze and water
    Mixture ratio. . . . .   60/40 (antifreeze/distilled water) or as required for freeze protection
                                        in operating area
    Capacity
        Standard Ranger models . . . .   3.25 qts. (3.1 l)
        Crew models . . . .   6.4 qts. (6.0 l)
Engine oil
    Type . . . .   Polaris PS-4 or similar 4-stroke engine oil
    Capacity . . . .   2 qt. (1.9L/1900 ml)
Front gearcase
    Type . . . .   Polaris Premium Demand Drive
    Capacity . . . .   9.0 oz. (266 ml)
Fuel requirement . . . .   87 octane minimum
Grease nipples . . . .   Polaris Premium U-joint Grease
Transmission
    Type . . . .   Polaris AGL Synthetic Gearcase Lubricant
    Capacity . . . .   33.8 oz. (1000 ml)

Torque specifications	Ft-lbs	In.-lb	Nm
Coolant bleed screw			
At thermostat housing	--	70	8
At cylinder head	--	60-80	7-9
Engine oil drain plug	14-18	--	19-24
Front gearcase			
Oil filler plug	8-10	--	11-14
Oil drain plug	8-10	--	11-14
Transmission			
Oil level check plug	10-14	--	14-19
Oil fill plug			
2012 and later models	10-14	--	14-19
Oil drain plug	10-14	--	14-19
Spark plugs	18	--	24
Tie-rod locknuts	12-14	--	16-19

2

MAINTENANCE LOG

Date	Miles	Type of Service

CHAPTER THREE

ENGINE TOP END

CONTENTS

1 GENERAL INFORMATION

1 The engine is a liquid-cooled, twin-cylinder, overhead valve type. The two valves per cylinder are operated by the camshaft via hydraulic lifters, pushrods and rocker arms. The camshaft, which is mounted in the crankcase, is gear-driven. The crankcase is divided vertically. Engine orientation is identified by its PTO (left) and MAG (right) sides.

2 The crankcase includes a wet sump, pressure-fed lubrication system, which uses a gear-driven rotor-type oil pump, a filter and a strainer screen. A balancer shaft,

mounted in the crankcase, reduces vibration. The crankshaft and connecting rods are a permanent assembly, which must be replaced as a unit if any problems are found.

3 This chapter provides service and overhaul procedures for the engine top end components including the cylinder head, valves, rocker arms, pushrods, valve lifters and pistons. These components can be serviced while the engine is in the frame. Most of the photographs in this chapter, however, show the engine being serviced on the bench. This is done for photographic clarity. Before starting any work, refer to the information to the General Information chapter at the front of this manual.

2   OPERATIONS POSSIBLE WITH THE ENGINE IN THE FRAME

1   The components and assemblies listed below can be removed without having to remove the engine from the frame:

NOTE:

Before servicing these components with the engine mounted in the frame, clean the engine, frame and other parts surrounding the engine to prevent sand and dirt from entering the engine. Because these vehicles operate in extreme off-road conditions, sand, dirt and other debris is always present, and can easily contaminate internal engine components if care is not taken before removing one or more engine covers.

a) *Valve cover*
b) *Rocker arms and pushrods*
c) *Cylinder head and valves*
d) *Cylinder, piston and rings*
e) *Water pump cover and impeller*
f) *Alternator cover*
g) *Flywheel, starter drive and stator coil*
h) *Stator housing*
i) *Starter motor*
j) *Cylinder block, pistons and rings*
k) *Camshaft*
l) *Water pump, oil pump and oil pump drive gear*
m) *Timing gears*

3   OPERATIONS REQUIRING ENGINE REMOVAL

1   It is necessary to remove the engine assembly from the frame to gain access to the following components:

a) *Balancer shaft*
b) *Crankshaft and connecting rods*
c) *Main bearings*
d) *Crankcase assembly*

4   MAJOR ENGINE REPAIR GENERAL NOTE

1   It is not always easy to determine when or if an engine should be completely overhauled, as a number of factors must be considered.

2   High mileage is not necessarily an indication that an overhaul is needed, while low mileage, on the other hand, does not preclude the need for an overhaul. Frequency of servicing is probably the single most important consideration. An engine that has regular and frequent oil and filter changes, as well as other required maintenance, will most likely give many miles of reliable service.

Conversely, a neglected engine, or one which has not been broken in properly, may require an overhaul very early in its life.

3   Exhaust smoke and excessive oil consumption are both indications that piston rings and/or valve guides are in need of attention. Make sure oil leaks are not responsible before deciding that the rings and guides are bad. Refer to Chapter 1 to perform a leak-down test and cylinder compression check. The results will help determine the nature and extent of the work required.

4   If the engine is making obvious knocking or rumbling noises, the connecting rod and/or main bearings are probably at fault.

5   Loss of power, rough running, excessive valve train noise and high fuel consumption rates may also point to the need for an overhaul, especially if they are all present at the same time. If a complete tune-up does not remedy the situation, major mechanical work is the only solution.

6   An engine overhaul generally involves restoring the internal parts to the specifications of a new engine. During an overhaul the piston rings are replaced and the cylinder walls are deglazed or honed. The crankshaft and connecting rod are permanently assembled, so if one of these components needs to be replaced both must be. Generally the valves are serviced as well, since they are usually in less than perfect condition at this point. While the engine is being overhauled, other components can be rebuilt also. The end result should be a like-new engine that will give as many trouble-free hours as the original.

7   Before beginning the engine overhaul, read through all of the related procedures to familiarize yourself with the scope and requirements of the job. Overhauling an engine is not all that difficult, but it is time consuming. Plan on the vehicle being tied up for a minimum of two weeks. Check on the availability of parts and make sure that any necessary special tools, equipment and supplies are obtained in advance.

8   Most work can be done with typical shop hand tools, although a number of precision measuring tools are required for inspecting parts to determine if they must be replaced. Often a dealer service department or repair shop will handle the inspection of parts and offer advice concerning reconditioning and replacement. As a general rule, time is the primary cost of an overhaul so it doesn't pay to install worn or substandard parts.

9   Several special tools are required and are described in the procedure.

10   The cylinders are identified as PTO (clutch side cylinder) and MAG (alternator side cylinder). When servicing the top end, label components that must be reinstalled in their original locations, so they can be easily identified.

11   As a final note, to ensure maximum life and minimum trouble from a rebuilt engine, everything must be clean, properly lubricated and assembled with care.

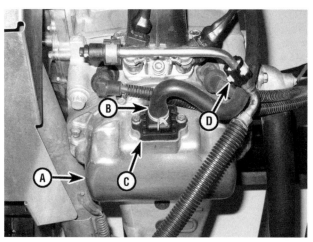

5.6a Valve cover details (2010 models)

A   *Valve cover*   C   *Breather cover*
B   *Breather hose*   D   *Fuel hose*

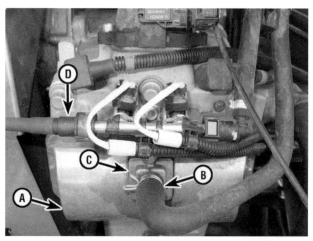

5.6b Valve cover details (2011 and later models)

A   *Valve cover*   D   *Fuel hose/fuel*
B   *Breather hose*   *rail assembly*
C   *Breather cover*

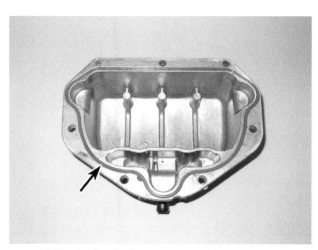

**5.9 The O-ring fits into a groove in the valve cover
(2010 model shown)**

5   VALVE COVER - REMOVAL, INSPECTION AND INSTALLATION

Removal

1 On standard Ranger models, remove the seat base, seat back, floor cover and kickboard (see Chapter 14).

2 On Crew models, remove the rear seat base, rear seat back and rear kickboard (see Chapter 14).

3 Before cleaning the engine, check the valve cover and breather cover for signs of oil leakage and damage. Note that the breather cover installed on the valve cover is a common source of oil leaks.

4 Clean the valve cover and the area around the valve cover to prevent dirt and other debris from entering the engine once the cover is removed. After cleaning the engine, park the vehicle on a level surface and apply the parking brake.

5 If the spark plugs will be removed, make sure to remove the plug caps from the plugs and clean the spark plug wells of all dirt, sand and other debris. See Chapter 2 or additional information.

6 Disconnect the breather hose from the breather cover **(see illustrations)**.

7 If it's necessary for access, disconnect the fuel hose (all models) and the fuel rail (2011 and later models) **(see illustration 5.6a or 5.6b)** and move it away from the valve cover (see Chapter 7).

8 Remove the valve cover mounting screws and the valve cover **(see illustration 5.6a or 5.6b)**. If the cover is stuck, tap its sides to break it loose. Don't pry between the valve cover and cylinder head as this could damage the parts and cause an oil leak.

9 If it was noted that oil was leaking from the valve cover (see Step 3), check the same area along the cover and O-ring for any damage. Then remove the O-ring and discard it **(see illustration)**.

Inspection

10 Clean the inside of the valve cover, though do not soak the cover in solvent with the breather cover and reed valve installed. If the inside of the cover will require scrubbing, first remove the breather cover and reed valve (see Section 6). Make sure the O-ring groove in the cover is clean. Then inspect the gasket surface for any scratches or scoring that could cause an oil leak.

11 Clean the valve cover screw threads and the mating threads in the cylinder head of all dirt and threadlock residue.

12 If necessary, service the breather cover and reed valve (see Section 6).

Installation

13 Make sure the valve cover and cylinder head cover surfaces are clean.

14 Lubricate a new O-ring with grease and fit it into the groove in the valve cover while making sure the index tab

5.16a Use a torque wrench . . .

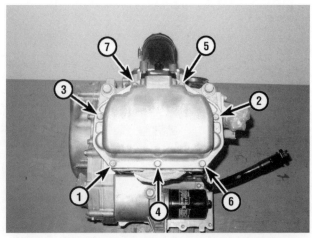

5.16b . . . and tighten the valve cover screws in numerical order and in two steps to the correct torque specification (2010 valve cover shown)

on the O-rings fits into the mating notch in the cover **(see illustration 5.9)**.

15   Spray the valve cover screw threads and the mating threads in the cylinder head with Loctite Primer N or an electrical contact cleaner and allow to dry. Then apply a medium strength threadlock onto the valve cover screw threads and place the screws on a clean paper towel until installation.

16   Install the valve cover onto the cylinder head, and align its screw holes with the threads in the cylinder head. After installing the cover, hold it in place with one hand when installing the screws to make sure the O-ring remains in its groove and does not become pinched between the valve cover and cylinder head. Because dowel pins are not used to align the valve cover with the cylinder head, install and start all of the cover screws before tightening them. If you start tightening them before all of the screws are installed, the final screws may not align correctly with the screw holes in the cover. When all of the screws are installed, tighten them finger-tight to hold the cover in place and center it on the cylinder head. Then tighten the valve cover screws in numerical order and in two steps to the torque listed in this Chapter's Specifications **(see illustrations)**.

17   The remainder of installation is the reverse of removal.

18   After starting and running the engine, check for oil leaks.

6   BREATHER COVER AND REED VALVE - REMOVAL, INSPECTION AND INSTALLATION

1   A breather cover and reed valve are mounted on the valve cover. A breather hose connects the breather cover to the air box **(see illustrations)**. When crankcase pressure rises to a certain level, the reed valve opens and vents the excessive pressure through the hose to the air box.

6.1a The breather hose is routed between the breather housing on the valve cover (2010 model shown) . . .

6.1b . . . and the air box

6.1c On 2011 and later models, note that the breather hose (A) is secured in place with a clamp (B)

6.7 Inspect the reed valve (arrow) for any cracks, warpage or other damage

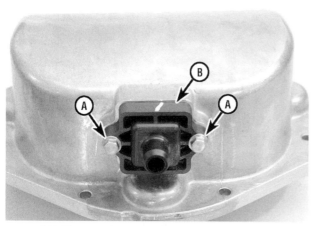

6.5a Remove the screws (A), breather cover (B) (2010 model shown) . . .

2   On standard Ranger, remove the seat base (see Chapter 14).

3   On Crew models, remove the rear seat base (see Chapter 14).

4   Disconnect the breather hose from the breather cover **(see illustration 5.6a or 5.6b)**.

5   Remove the screws, breather cover, gasket (2011 and later models) and reed valve **(see illustrations)**. Discard the gasket, if used.

6   Inspect the breather cover for any cracks or warpage and replace if necessary.

7   Inspect the reed valve for any visible damage and replace if necessary **(see illustration)**. The reed valve must lay flat against the reed block surface.

8   Install the components in the reverse order of removal, plus the following:

   a) *Apply a light coat of black RTV along the edges of the reed valve, and install the reed valve by aligning its index tab with the notch in the valve cover (see Step 5). Make sure not to allow any of the RTV to contact the reed valve.*

   b) *Install a new gasket (2011 and later models) and the breather cover and its mounting screws. Tighten the screws to the torque listed in this Chapter's Specifications.*

7   ROCKER ARMS AND PUSHRODS - REMOVAL, INSPECTION AND INSTALLATION

1   The rocker arms and pushrods can be removed with the engine in the frame.

Removal

2   Remove the valve cover (see Section 5).

3   If it's necessary for removal access, remove the exhaust

6.5b . . . and reed valve (A). Note how the index tab (B) on the reed valve fits into the notch in the valve cover. 2010 model shown, though the reed valve shown here is the same valve used on all model years

7.4 If reusing the parts, identify the rocker arm and pushrod sets so each can be installed in their original mounting position

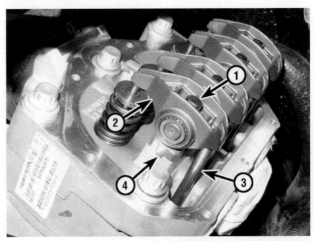

7.5 Rocker arm assembly details

1   *Rocker arm screw*
2   *Rocker arm*
3   *Pushrod*

4   *Rocker arm to cylinder head tab alignment*

system (see Chapter 7).

4   Label the rocker arms and pushrods so each can be reinstalled in its original location **(see illustration)**.

5   Remove a rocker arm screw and lift the rocker arm from the cylinder head. Then remove the pushrod **(see illustration)**.

6   Repeat for each rocker arm and pushrod.

Inspection

7   Use solvent to clean the rocker arms and their bearings. Then dry with compressed air. Inspect each rocker arm pad and pushrod cup for cracks, scoring and excessive wear. Compare these two wear points on all four rocker arms as each should have the same amount of wear and visual appearance **(see illustration)**.

8   Hold the rocker arm mounting block and pivot the rocker arm to make sure there is no binding or roughness with its bearings **(see illustration 7.7)**.

9   Clean a pushrod in solvent and then blow out the pushrod oil passage with compressed air while making sure air passes through the pushrod **(see illustration)**. If the oil passage cannot be cleared, replace the pushrod. If the oil passage is clear, slowly roll the pushrod on a flat surface and check for any runout. Replace any pushrod that is not straight. Check the pushrod ends for any scoring, cracks and other damage. Repeat for each pushrod.

Installation

10   Blow through each pushrod with compressed air.

11   Lubricate both pushrod ends with engine oil, and install each pushrod into its original position in the engine while centering each pushrod into the top of its valve lifter **(see illustration)**.

12   Lubricate the rocker arm bearing, rocker arm pad and pushrod cup with engine oil **(see illustration)**. Then

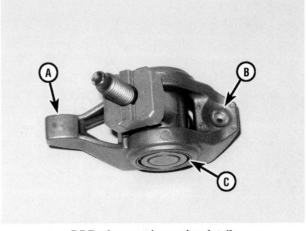

7.7 Rocker arm inspection details

A   *Rocker arm pad*
B   *Pushrod cup*

C   *Rocker arm bearing*

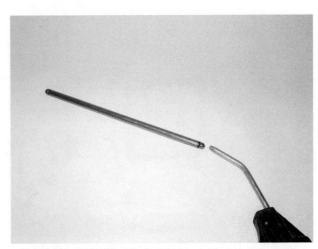

7.9 Clean the pushrod oil passages with compressed air

7.11 Lubricate both pushrod ends with engine oil, then install the pushrods by centering them into their valve lifters

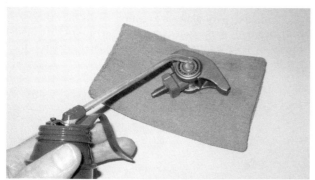

7.12 Lubricate both sides of the rocker arm bearing with engine oil

7.13a Install the rocker arm by inserting its shoulder into the cylinder head groove (A) and seating its cup over the pushrod (B)

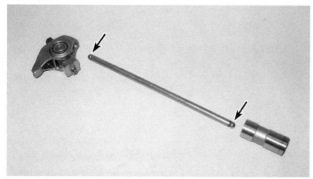

7.13b When tightening the rocker arm screw, make sure the pushrod ends remain centered against the rocker arm and valve lifter (arrows) - parts shown removed for clarity

7.14a Initially tighten the rocker arm screw until it feels like it has bottomed against the rocker arm . . .

7.14b . . . then tighten the screw to its final torque specification

lubricate the the valve stem end with engine oil. Repeat for rocker arm assembly.

13 Install the rocker arm in its original position by inserting its shoulder into the groove in the cylinder head and engaging it with the pushrod and valve stem (see illustration). Install the rocker arm screw and tighten finger-tight while making sure the pushrod remains centered against the rocker arm and the valve lifter (see illustration). Repeat to install the remaining rocker arms.

14 Before tightening the rocker arm screws, make a visual check to ensure each rocker arm is centered in its lifter and against the rocker arm cup. When the rocker arm is properly engaged with both the pushrod and valve stem, tighten its screw until you can feel the screw tighten to where it feels like it has bottomed against the rocker arm. Then tighten the screw to the torque listed in this Chapter's Specifications. Repeat for each remaining rocker arm (see illustrations).

15 Install the valve cover (see Section 5).

8.4 Disconnect the radiator hose (A) and the coolant temperature sensor connector (B) at the cylinder head (2010 model shown)

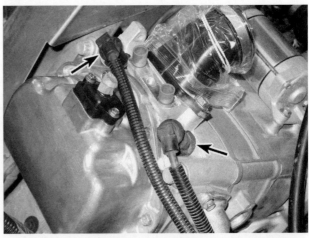

8.7 Note the spark plug wire routing across the cylinder head, then remove the spark plug caps (arrows) - 2010 model shown. Spark plug routing for 2011 and later models is the same as shown here

8   CYLINDER HEAD - REMOVAL AND INSTALLATION

1   The cylinder head can be removed with the engine in the frame.

Removal

2   Disconnect the negative battery cable at the battery (see Chapter 8).

3   Drain the coolant (see Chapter 2).

4   Open the clamp and disconnect the radiator hose from the thermostat cover at the cylinder head. Then disconnect the coolant temperature sensor electrical connector **(see illustration)**.

5   Remove the throttle body (see Chapter 7).

6   Remove the exhaust system (see Chapter 7).

7   Disconnect the spark plug caps at the spark plugs **(see illustration)**. If the cylinder head will be serviced, loosen, but do not remove, the spark plugs.

8   Remove the rocker arms and pushrods (see Section 7).

9   If you are servicing the cylinder head with the engine on the workbench and working alone, some means will be required to hold the engine steady when loosening and tightening the cylinder head mounting bolts. Note that this is more critical when tightening the bolts. One method is to mount a metal plate onto the engine, then lock the mounting plate in a vise **(see illustrations)**.

10   Using a crossing pattern, loosen each of the cylinder head mounting bolts 1/8 turn at a time until all of the bolts are loose **(see illustration)**. Then remove the bolts and washers. The washers are captive on the bolts and cannot be removed.

11   Tap the cylinder head with a rubber mallet to break it free from the head gasket and lift it off the cylinder block. Place the cylinder head on a wooden board to protect its gasket surface **(see illustration)**. Do not insert a

8.9a Here a metal plate has been mounted onto the front side of the engine . . .

8.9b . . . and then locked in a wheel vise mounted on a bike bench to hold the engine steady when loosening and tightening the cylinder head mounting bolts. A similar arrangement can be made by using a vise mounted on a secure workbench

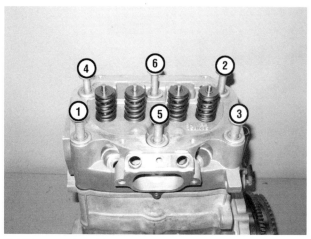

8.10 Loosen the cylinder head mounting bolts 1/8 a turn at a time in the numerical order shown here

8.11 Lift off the cylinder head

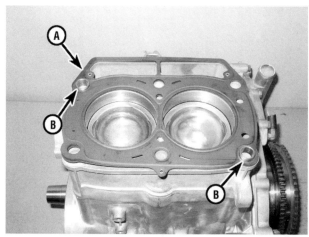

8.12 Remove and discard the cylinder head gasket (A). Because the dowel pins (B) are installed with what seems like a press fit, leave them in place unless they will be replaced

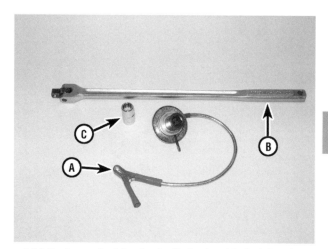

8.15 Tools required for final cylinder head bolt tightening

A   Torque angle meter (Lisle Tools 28100 shown)
B   1/2 inch breaker bar
C   14-mm socket (12-point)

screwdriver between the cylinder head and cylinder block to pry the cylinder head loose as this will damage the gasket surfaces.

CAUTION:

Be sure to note the information regarding the dowel pins in Step 12 to prevent from damaging them.

12   Remove and discard the cylinder head gasket as a new gasket must be installed. Note the two dowel pins installed in the cylinder block. Because these dowel pins are an extremely tight fit in the cylinder block, they are resistant to normal removal methods and should be left in place unless they will be replaced **(see illustration)**.

13   Clean all traces of old gasket material from the cylinder head and cylinder block gasket surfaces. Stuff clean rags or paper towels into the cylinder bores and pushrod tunnel to prevent gasket material from falling into the crankcase and cylinder bore if the pistons are not at TDC. After cleaning the cylinder head gasket surface, clean the coolant passages with compressed air.

14   To remove carbon from the combustion chambers, or if additional service is required, refer to Section 10.

Installation

15   Special tools: Because the cylinder head bolts are tightened to a specific torque angle, a torque angle meter, 1/2 in. breaker bar and a 14-mm socket (12-point) are required **(see illustration)**.

16   Make sure the cylinder head and cylinder block gasket surfaces are clean.

17   Clean the cylinder head bolt threads and their mating threads in the crankcase with Loctite Primer N. If the Loctite product is unavailable, clean the bolt threads with an electrical contact cleaner and allow to dry.

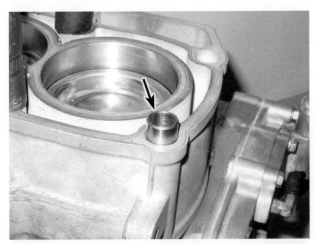

8.18a Center the dowel pin into the hole in the cylinder block

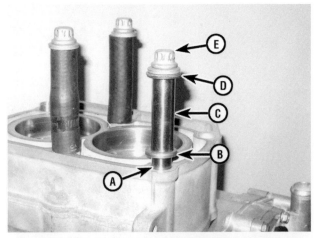

8.18b Mount a washer (B), hollow pipe (C) and a second washer (D) on top of the dowel pin (A). Then install a cylinder head bolt (E) through them and thread into the crankcase. When cutting the hollow pipe to length (C) to use as a spacer, make sure it is square on both ends

18 If the dowel pins were removed, **follow the accompanying illustrations, beginning with 8.18a**, to press them into the cylinder block. After installing a dowel pin, make sure it is completely bottomed in the cylinder block.

19 Install a new head gasket over the dowel pins, making sure all of the holes align **(see illustration 8.12)**. Never reuse the old gasket.

20 Carefully install the cylinder head over the dowel pins and seat it against the head gasket **(see illustration 8.11)**. The exhaust ports must face toward the front of the vehicle.

21 Apply clean engine oil to the cylinder head mounting bolt threads, under the bolt heads and to both sides of the washers **(see illustration)**. Then install the bolts through the cylinder head and thread them into the crankcase finger-tight only. Note that if new bolts are being installed, clean them in solvent to remove any anti-rust or protective coating and dry thoroughly. Then lubricate the bolts as described.

22 If the engine is mounted on a workbench, it will be necessary to secure it in place to prevent it from moving when tightening the cylinder head mounting bolts. You don't want the engine to move when tightening the bolts as a false torque reading may result. See Step 9 for additional information.

NOTE:

The cylinder head bolts are tightened in a unique sequence. Before tightening the bolts, read through Steps 23 through 28 to better understand the tightening procedure and how to use the tools described in Step 15.

23 Tighten the cylinder head bolts in two steps and in numerical order **(see illustration)** to the Step 1 torque listed in this Chapter's Specifications.

24 Following the numerical order shown in **illustration 8.10**, loosen each bolt by turning it five turns, taking

8.18c Tighten the cylinder head bolt to press the dowel pin (arrow) into the cylinder block until it bottoms. When pressing the dowel pin in place, make sure it enters the hole squarely

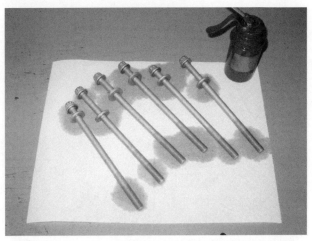

8.21 Lubricate the cylinder head mounting bolt threads, washers and underneath each bolt head with engine oil

3

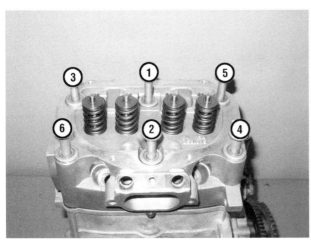

8.23 Tighten the cylinder head bolts in the numerical order shown here

8.26 Mark each bolt/crankcase with a marking pen to help gauge bolt movement

8.27 Tighten each bolt an additional 90 degrees (1/4 turn). Here a torque angle meter is used to accurately tighten the bolt to the proper angle

two or three steps to do so. When you're finished, the bolts may be completely loose, as we discovered on our teardown engine. This is the Step 2 torque sequence listed in this Chapter's Specifications.

25 Using three steps, tighten the cylinder head bolts in numerical order (see illustration 8.23) to the Step 3 torque listed in this Chapter's Specifications.

26 Make matching marks across each bolt/crankcase with a marker (see illustration). This will allow you to gauge the bolts' movement after tightening them.

27 Using a torque angle meter, turn each bolt clockwise in numerical order (see illustration 8.23) and in one continuous movement an additional 90 degrees (1/4 turn) (see illustration). This is the final torque setting and the Step 4 torque sequence listed in this Chapter's Specifications.

28 After tightening the bolts, compare the marks you made in Step 26 to make sure each bolt was turned to the proper angle.

29 The remainder of installation is the reverse of removal.

30 Fill and bleed the cooling system (see Chapter 2).

31 After running the engine and bleeding the cooling system, shut it off. Then check the coolant hose, valve cover and cylinder head for leaks.

9 VALVE/VALVE SEATS/VALVE GUIDES - SERVICING

1 Because of the complex nature of this job and the special tools and equipment required, servicing of the valves and the valve seats (commonly known as a valve job) is best left to a professional.

2 The home mechanic can, however, remove and disassemble the head, do the initial cleaning and inspection, then reassemble and deliver the head to a dealer service department or properly equipped motorcycle repair shop for the actual valve servicing (see Section 10).

3 The dealer service department will remove the valves and springs, recondition or replace the valves and valve seats, check and, if necessary, replace the valve springs, spring retainers and keepers, install new valve seals and reassemble the valve components. Note that replacement valve guides on this engine are not available. If any valve guide is severely worn or damaged, the cylinder head must be replaced.

4 After the valve job has been performed, the head will be in like-new condition. When the head is returned, be sure to clean it again very thoroughly before installation on the engine to remove any metal particles or abrasive grit that may still be present from the valve service operations. Use compressed air, if available, to blow out all the holes and passages.

10 CYLINDER HEAD AND VALVES - DISASSEMBLY, INSPECTION AND REASSEMBLY

1   Valve servicing and valve guide replacement should be done by a dealer service department or motorcycle repair shop (see Section 9). However, disassembly, cleaning and inspection of the cylinder head and valves can be done at home, with the right tools.

2   Before starting work, read this entire section. Obtain any special tools or supplies necessary to complete the job.

Disassembly

3   Special tool: To disassemble the valve components safely, a valve spring compressor is absolutely necessary. If you don't own a valve spring compressor, you may be able to rent one at a local tool rental yard, provided its pads are small enough to work on the size valves and spring seats used in the Polaris engine **(see illustration)**. The Polaris valve spring compressor (part No. PU-45257) is designed to remove the valves when the cylinder head has been removed from the engine, and to replace the intake valve seals when the cylinder head is installed on the engine **(see illustration)**. If you're unable to obtain a valve spring compressor, leave the following procedure to a dealer service department or motorcycle repair shop.

4   Remove the cylinder head (see Section 8).

5   Before removing the valves, clean the cylinder head and cylinder block gasket surfaces. If the gasket residue is hard to remove, place a solvent soaked rag across the cylinder head gasket surface to soften the deposits. Work slowly and do not nick or gouge the soft aluminum of the head.

6   Before removing the valves, check the combustion chambers for carbon. Because of the high operating temperatures found inside the combustion chamber, any carbon buildup will be difficult to remove. Start by chipping away large deposits with a dull screwdriver. Then switch and use a small wire brush mounted in a rotary hand grinder. Small brushes in various designs allow you to maneuver and hold them at different angles when working in the combustion chamber near the spark plug threads where the carbon is harder to access and remove, though don't expect these brushes to remove all of the carbon. While working through the different layers of carbon, switch between the tools and methods you are using. Work carefully to prevent from damaging the cylinder head and combustion chamber surfaces and the spark plug threads. Finally, use a piece of fine emery cloth to remove the small scratches left by the wire wheel or wire brush. If you want to check the valve seats for leakage before removing the valves, perform the solvent test in Step 48.

7   Before removing the valves, devise a method to label and store the valves with their related components in such a way that they can be installed in their original locations without getting mixed up **(see illustration)**. A good way to do this is to obtain a container which is divided into

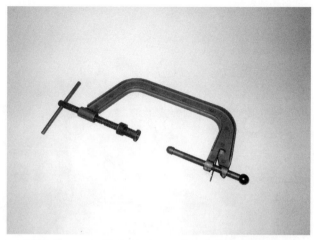

10.3a Common C-clamp type valve spring compressor

10.3b Polaris valve spring compressor (A) shown compressing spring to remove valve keepers (B)

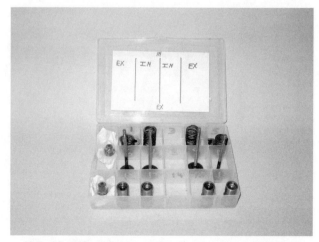

10.7a Identify and store each valve assembly in separate containers to prevent from mixing up the parts

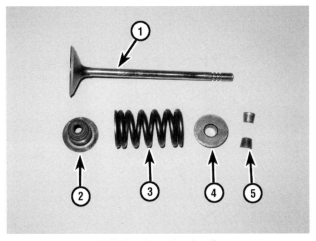

10.7b Intake valve details

1	Intake valve	4	Spring retainer
2	Oil seal	5	Valve keepers
3	Spring		

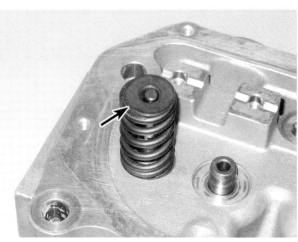

10.9a Remove the spring retainer . . .

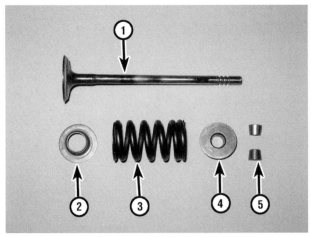

10.7c Exhaust valve details

1	Exhaust valve	4	Spring retainer
2	Spring seat	5	Valve keepers
3	Spring		

10.9b . . . then identify and remove the valve spring . . .

10.8 With the valve spring compressed, remove the valve keepers (arrow) from the end of the valve

compartments, and to label each compartment with the identity of the valve that will be stored in it. Plastic bags can also be used, though handle them carefully to prevent the loose parts from damaging the valve stem and seat **(see illustrations)**.

8   Mount the valve spring compressor across the valve, making sure it is correctly located onto each end of the valve assembly. Compress the valve spring until the valve keepers separate from the valve stem, making sure not to compress the spring any more than is absolutely necessary **(see illustration)**. Remove the valve keepers with a magnet or needlenose pliers, then slowly release the tool to relieve spring tension. Remove the valve spring compressor from the cylinder head.

9   Remove the spring retainer from the top of the spring **(see illustration)**. Place a paint mark on the top of the valve spring so that it can be reinstalled facing in its original position and remove it **(see illustration)**. Push on the valve

10.9c . . . and the valve

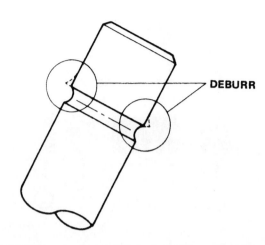

10.9d If the valve stem binds in the guide or there is noticeable roughness, deburr the area around the keeper groove

stem and slowly pull on the valve head **(see illustration)**
and remove the valve from the head. If the valve binds in
the guide or if you feel any roughness, push it back into the
head and deburr the area around the keeper grooves with a
very fine file or whetstone **(see illustration)**. However, if
the valve is still difficult to remove and its keeper groove
is free of any burrs, the valve stem is probably bent. And
because a bent valve will have damaged its valve guide,
both in operation and when removing it, it is necessary to
replace the cylinder head. Replacement valve guides are
not provided by the manufacturer.
10   After removing an intake valve, pull the valve stem
seal off the top of the intake valve guide with a pair of
pliers, making sure not to damage the top of the guide **(see
illustration)**. Discard the seal.
11   After removing an exhaust valve, remove the spring
seat **(see illustration)**. Note that the exhaust valves do not
use seals on the valve guides.
12   Clean the cylinder head with solvent and dry it
thoroughly. Compressed air will speed the drying process
and ensure that all holes and recessed areas are clean.
When the cylinder head is clean and dry, lubricate the valve
guides with engine oil to prevent rust.
13   Clean all of the valve springs, keepers, retainers and
spring seats with solvent and dry them thoroughly. Clean
one valve assembly at a time to keep the original parts
together.
14   Scrape off any deposits that may have formed on the
valve, then use a motorized wire brush to remove deposits
from the valve heads and stems. Again, make sure the
valves do not get mixed up.

Inspection

15   Inspect the head very carefully for damage. Inspect the
flat, machined rocker arm surfaces on the top of the head
for any cracks and other damage. Make sure the rocker arm

10.10 Remove the intake valve guide seal - note these seals
are a combination seal and spring seat assembly

10.11 Remove the exhaust valve spring seat - note the exhaust valves do not use seals

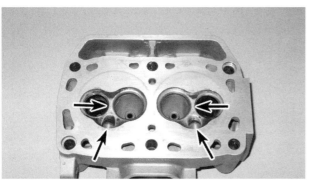

10.16 Check for cracks between the combustion chambers at the edge of the spark plug threads (arrows)

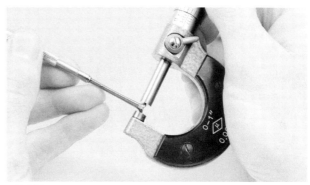

10.20 Measure the valve guide inside diameter with a small hole gauge, then measure the small hole gauge with a micrometer

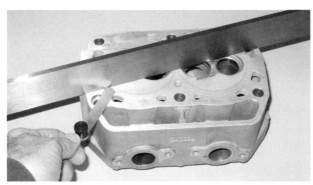

10.18 Check the cylinder head for warpage with a straight-edge and a feeler gauge

10.19a Inspect the valve seats and faces (arrows)

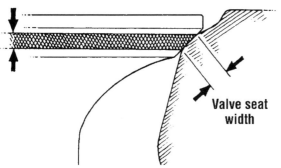

10.19b Measure the valve seat and face width

threaded holes are clean and there is no thread damage.

16 With the valves removed, inspect the areas between the valve seats and spark plugs for any cracks **(see illustration)**. If any cracks are found, a new cylinder head will be required.

17 Measure the installed height of the valve guides and compare to the valve guide protrusion value listed in this Chapter's Specifications to make sure the valve guides have not moved in the head. The valve guides are not replaceable.

18 Using a precision straightedge and a feeler gauge, check the head gasket mating surface for warpage **(see illustration)**. Lay the straightedge lengthwise, across the head and diagonally (corner-to-corner), intersecting the head bolt holes, and try to slip a feeler gauge under it, on either side of each combustion chamber. The gauge should be the same thickness as the cylinder head warp limit listed in this Chapter's Specifications. If the feeler gauge can be inserted between the head and the straightedge, the head is warped and must either be machined or, if warpage is excessive, replaced with a new one. Minor surface imperfections can be cleaned up by sanding on a surface plate in a figure-eight pattern with 400 or 600 grit wet or dry sandpaper. Be sure to rotate the head every few strokes to avoid removing material unevenly.

19 Examine the valve seats in each of the combustion chambers **(see illustration)**. If they are pitted, cracked or burned, the head will require valve service that's beyond the scope of the home mechanic. Measure the valve seat and face width with a machinist's scale or vernier caliper and compare it to the seat width listed this Chapter's Specifications. If it is not within the specified range, or if it varies around its circumference, valve service work is required **(see illustration)**.

20 Use solvent and a brush to clean the valve guides and remove any carbon and varnish buildup. Then measure the inside diameters of the guides (at both ends and the center of the guide and in two directions) with a small hole gauge and a micrometer **(see illustration)**. Insert the small hole gauge into the valve guide and expand it so there's a light drag when it's pulled out. Compare the results with the valve guide inside diameter value listed in this

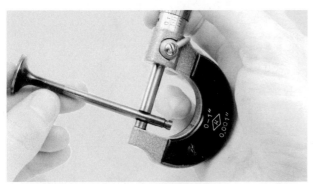

10.21 Measure the valve stem outside diameter with a micrometer

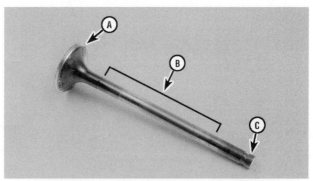

10.22 Inspect the valve face (A), stem (B) and keeper grooves (C) for signs of wear and damage

Chapter's Specifications. If the measurement on any guide is too large, it will be necessary to replace the cylinder head. Replacement valve guides are not available. If all of the guide measurements are within the recommended range, record the measurements for future reference. These measurements, along with the valve stem diameter measurements, will enable you to compute the valve stem-to-guide oil clearance listed in this Chapter's Specifications. This clearance will be one factor that will determine the extent of the valve service work required. For a final check of the guides, compare the guide measurements at the ends and at the center to determine if they are worn in a bell-mouth pattern (more wear at the ends). If they are, the cylinder head must be replaced.

21   Measure and then mark the section on the valve stems that actually operate inside the valve guides. Within this area, measure the valve stem outside diameter **(see illustration)** at the top, center and bottom of the valve stem. Then rotate the valve 90 degrees, and remeasure at the same three positions. By subtracting the valve stem outside diameter from the valve guide inside diameter (Step 20), the valve stem-to-guide oil clearance is obtained. If the clearance is greater than the value listed in this Chapter's Specifications and the valve stem outside diameters are within specification, the valve guides are excessively worn and the cylinder head will have to be replaced. You may notice more wear on the valve stems, and especially on the exhaust valves, where they operate at the bottom of the guides (combustion chamber/valve head side). The valve guides cannot be replaced separately.

22   Carefully inspect each valve face for cracks, pits and burned spots. Check the valve stem and the keeper groove area for cracks **(see illustration)**. Rotate the valve and check for any obvious indication that it is bent. Check the end of the stem for pitting and excessive wear. The presence of any of the above conditions indicates the need for valve servicing. Note the valve ends can be refaced with a valve grinding machine, provided the valve stem overall length remains within the range listed in this Chapter's Specifications. Refer this service to a dealer service department. Also refer to Steps 26 through 29 on how to check the valve seat contact surfaces.

23   Check the end of each valve spring for wear and

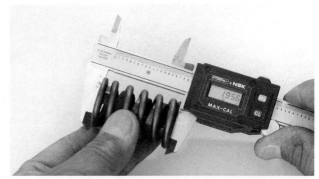

10.23a Measure the free length of the valve springs

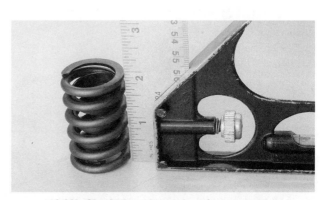

10.23b Check the valve springs for squareness

pitting. Measure the free length **(see illustration)** and compare it to this Chapter's Specifications. If any spring is shorter than specified it has sagged and must be replaced. Stand the spring upright on a flat surface and check it for squareness **(see illustration)**. If the bend in any spring appears visually excessive, it must be replaced.

24   Check the spring retainer and keepers for obvious wear and cracks. Any questionable parts should not be reused, as extensive damage will occur in the event of failure during engine operation.

25   If the inspection indicates that no service work is required, the valve components can be reinstalled in the head.

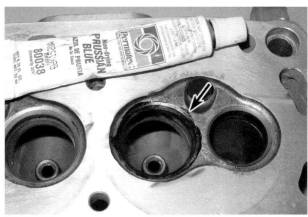

10.27 Here a thin layer of marking compound has been applied onto the valve seat in the cylinder head - also apply the compound onto the valve face

10.28 Tap the valve against the cylinder head (face-to-seat) several times - do not spin the valve when doing this

10.29 Compare the impression on valve seat and face, looking for any irregular or uneven wear and damage

Valve seat

26   One way to check the valve seats is to use a marking compound (non-drying Prussian Blue), available from auto parts and tool stores. This marking compound is used to locate high or irregular spots when checking or making close fits. Follow the manufacturer's directions.

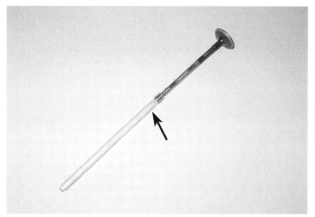

10.31a A length of hose (arrow) can be installed on the end of a valve and used to turn the valve during lapping - the wooden dowel installed in the hose helps to stiffen the hose and provide better hand control

NOTE:
Because of the close operating tolerances within the valve assembly, the valve stem and guide dimensions must be within tolerance; otherwise, the inspection results will be inaccurate.

27   Clean the valve and valve seat mating areas with contact cleaner **(see illustration 10.19a)**. When the parts are dry, spread a thin layer of marking compound evenly onto both valve seats **(see illustration)**.
28   Slowly insert the valve into its guide and tap the valve against its seat several times without spinning it **(see illustration)**.
29   Remove the valve and examine the impression left by the marking compound **(see illustration)**. If the impression (on the valve or in the cylinder head) is not even and continuous, and the valve seat width **(see illustration 10.19b)** is not within the specified tolerance listed in this Chapter's Specifications, replace the valve and reface the valve seat in the cylinder head. Refer this service to a dealer service department.

Valve lapping

30   If the valve seats were reground, consult with the dealership on whether the valves need to be lapped. Otherwise, before installing the valves in the head, they should be lapped to ensure a positive seal between the cylinder head and valve seats. This procedure requires coarse and fine valve lapping compound (available at auto parts stores) and a valve lapping tool.
31   If a lapping tool is not available, a piece of rubber or plastic hose can be slipped over the valve stem (after the valve has been installed in the guide) and used to turn the valve **(see illustration)**. When lapping a valve by holding it by its stem, it will be necessary to secure the cylinder head on the workbench to keep it steady and make sure

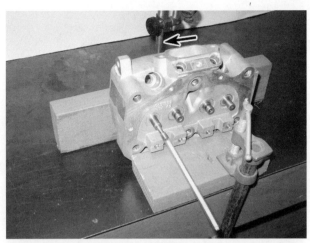

10.31b Wooden blocks and a clamp can be used to secure the cylinder head onto a workbench when turning the valve from its stem side. A magnetic stand (arrow) has been placed behind the rear wooden block to prevent the cylinder head from moving

10.32 Apply the lapping compound very sparingly, in small dabs, to the valve face only

the valve and cylinder head seats remain in contact. One way to do this is with wooden blocks and a clamp **(see illustration)**.

32 Lubricate the valve stem with engine oil. Then apply a small amount of coarse lapping compound to the valve face **(see illustration)** and slip the valve into the guide.

NOTE:

Make sure the valve is installed in the correct guide and be careful not to get any lapping compound on the valve stem or inside the guide.

33 Attach the lapping tool (or hose) to the valve and rotate the tool between the palms of your hands **(see illustration)**. Use a back-and-forth motion rather than a circular motion. Lift the valve off the seat and turn it at regular intervals to distribute the lapping compound properly. Continue the lapping procedure until the valve face and seat contact area is of uniform and specified width **(see illustration 10.19b)** and unbroken around the entire circumference of the valve face and seat **(see illustration)**. See this Chapter's Specifications for valve seat width values.

34 Carefully remove the valve from the guide and wipe off all traces of lapping compound. Use solvent to initially clean the valve and wipe the seat area thoroughly with a solvent soaked cloth.

35 Repeat the procedure with fine valve lapping compound, then repeat the entire procedure for the remaining valves.

36 When all of the valves have been lapped, clean the cylinder head and the valves in solvent, then with detergent and hot water. Rinse in cold water and dry with compressed air. Run a white cloth across each valve face and seat. If there is any color shown on the cloth, reclean the parts.

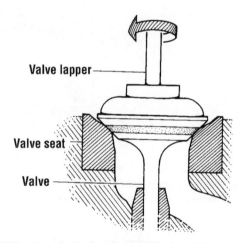

10.33a Operate the lapping tool back-and-forth to lap the valve

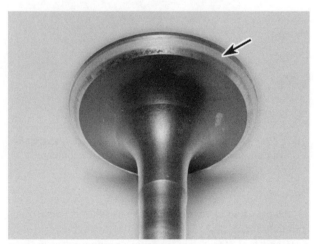

10.33b The valve face and seat should show a uniform unbroken ring (arrow), and when measured, be the specified width all the way round

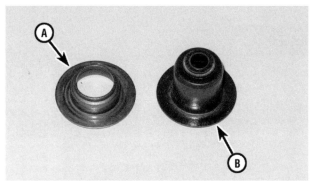

10.38 Exhaust valve spring seat (A) and intake valve seal (B)

10.42a With the intake valve installed in the cylinder head, install a new seal over the valve, then turn the seal while pushing it over the top of the valve and past the keeper grooves and down the valve stem

10.42b Use a socket and drive the seal base into the cutout in the cylinder head

10.42c Check that the seal is properly installed

10.43 Position the spring over the valve with the tightly wound coils (arrow) facing toward the cylinder head

Repeat until the parts are free of all lapping compound. Then lubricate the valve guides with engine oil to prevent rust.

CAUTION:
Any compound left on the valves or seats will cause excessive and rapid wear to these and other engine components.

37 Perform Steps 26 through 29 to check the valve seat contact areas.

Reassembly

38 Refer to **illustrations 10.7b and 10.7c** to identify the intake and exhaust valves. Note the difference in the spring seats used with the exhaust valves and the seals used with the intake valves **(see illustration)**.
39 Lubricate the valve guides and valve seats with engine oil.
40 When installing an exhaust valve, install the spring seat over the valve guide **(see illustration 10.11)**.

NOTE:
When installing an intake valve, the valve stem seal is installed after the valve is installed in the head.

41 Coat the valve stem on the valve with an assembly lube or a moly-based grease and install the valve by turning it into its guide **(see illustration 10.9c)**.
42 After installing an intake valve, lubricate the inside of a new valve stem seal with engine oil, then install it squarely over the valve stem and slide/turn it down until it contacts the top of the valve guide. Use your fingers and slide the seal firmly until the seal base contacts the cutout in the cylinder head. Then use a socket and drive the base of the seal into the cutout in the cylinder head until it bottoms. After installing the seal, do not remove the valve or the seal as the seal will be damaged **(see illustrations)**.
43 Lubricate a valve spring with engine oil and install it with its tightly wound coils facing down **(see illustration and illustration 10.9b)**.
44 Install and center the spring retainer on top of the spring **(see illustration 10.9a)**.

10.45 How the valve keepers must engage with the grooves in the valve stems

10.48a Check the valve seats for leakage by pouring solvent into each port . . .

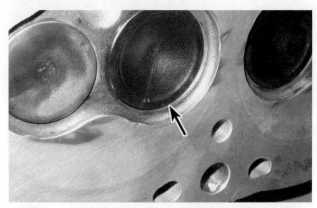

10.48b . . . and if fluid can be seen leaking into the combustion chamber (arrow), one or more valves are not seating correctly against their seat(s)

45   Apply a small amount of grease to the valve keepers to help hold them in place. Compress the spring with the spring compressor, making sure to depress it only as far as is absolutely necessary to slip the keepers in place **(see illustration 10.8)**. Make sure that the keeper ridges are securely locked in the retaining grooves in the valve stem **(see illustration)**. When both keepers are properly installed, release tension from the spring and remove the spring compressor.

46   Gently tap the spring retainer with a plastic-tipped hammer to set the keepers.

47   Repeat the procedure for the remaining valves. Remember to keep the parts for each valve together and separate from the other valves so they can be reinstalled in their original location.

48   After installing the valves, perform a solvent test to check the valve seats for leakage. Support the cylinder head with the intake port facing up and pour solvent into the port. Without turning the head over, check the combustion chamber for any sign of leakage. Pour the solvent out of the intake ports and wipe the combustion chamber dry with a rag. Then repeat for the exhaust valves. If the solvent leaked past any valve into the combustion chamber, the valve is not seating fully against its seat and additional work is required **(see illustrations)**.

11   CYLINDER BLOCK AND PISTONS - REMOVAL, INSPECTION AND INSTALLATION

1   The cylinder block and pistons can be removed with the engine in the frame.

Removal

2   Thoroughly clean the engine top end and the parts around it to prevent dirt from falling into the crankcase.

3   Remove the cylinder head (see Section 8).

11.5 Carefully lift and remove the cylinder block off the pistons

4   Lightly tap around the perimeter of the cylinder block with a soft-faced mallet to free it from its gasket.

5   Lift the cylinder block by rocking it forwards and backwards while sliding it off the pistons **(see illustration)**. Have an assistant reach in and hold the connecting rods to prevent the rods or pistons from falling and hitting against the crankcase. Stuff clean rags under the pistons

3

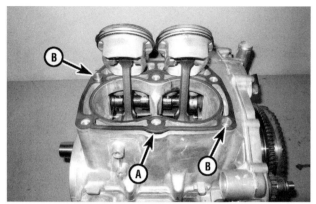

11.6 Remove the base gasket (A), but leave the dowel pins (B) in place unless they are going to be replaced

11.8 Mark each piston with its numbered cylinder position (A) and an arrow mark facing toward exhaust side of engine (B)

11.9 Wear eye protection when removing the circlips; they can pop out of the piston with sufficient force to cause an injury if they hit your eye

to support them and to prevent anything from falling into the crankcase.

6   Remove and discard the base gasket as a new one must be installed during assembly. Note the two dowel pins installed in the crankcase. Because these dowel pins are an extremely tight fit in the crankcase, they are resistant to

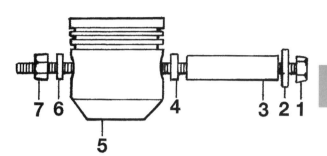

11.10 The piston pins should come out with hand pressure - if they don't, this removal tool can be fabricated from readily available parts

1   Bolt
2   Washer
3   Pipe (large enough for piston pin to fit inside)
4   Padding (large enough for piston pin to fit inside)
5   Piston
6   Washer (small enough to fit through piston pin bore)
7   Nut (small enough to fit through piston pin bore)

normal removal methods and should be left in place unless they will be replaced (see illustration).

7   Cover the crankcase opening with shop rags to prevent anything from falling into the crankcase.

8   Mark the top of each piston so it can be reinstalled in the correct cylinder, then mark the exhaust side of the piston so it be installed facing in its original direction (see illustration). While new pistons can be installed in either bore and facing in either direction, used pistons must be reinstalled in their original cylinders and with their original orientation.

9   Remove the circlip from the outboard side of the piston (see illustration).

CAUTION:

The piston pin operates with a sliding fit and can be removed by hand. However, problems such as varnish on the piston pin, a burred pin bore or circlip groove, or a damaged piston can make it difficult to remove the piston pin. Do not drive the pin out as the piston and connecting rod assembly may be damaged.

10   Push the piston pin out of the piston and lift the piston off the rod. If the pin is tight, insert a pair of external snap ring pliers into the pin, then open them to lock the pins against the inside of the pin and use them to work the pin out of the piston with a back-and-forth twisting motion. If the pin will not slide out, fabricate a piston removal tool from parts available from a hardware store (see illustration). Heat can also be applied to the top of the piston with a heat gun. When heating the piston, do not apply heat directly to the piston rings as it may cause the rings to lose tension.

11 Repeat for the other piston pin and piston.

12 Clean all traces of gasket from the crankcase mating surface while making sure not to allow any debris to fall into the crankcase. If a scraper is used, take care not to scratch or gouge the soft aluminum.

Inspection

Cylinder

13 The cylinder bores are Nikasil plated, which has a high resistance to wear. The cylinder bores cannot be bored oversize.

14 Soak the cylinder block surfaces in solvent, then carefully remove gasket material from the top and bottom mating surfaces with a scraper. Do not scratch or gouge the gasket surfaces or leakage may result.

15 Wash the cylinder block in solvent and dry with compressed air.

16 Measure the top of the cylinder for flatness **(see illustration)** and compare your measurements to the warpage limit listed in this Chapter's Specifications.

17 Inspect the cylinder walls thoroughly for grooves, scratches and score marks. Then check the dowel pin holes for cracks or other damage. If there is no visible damage, continue with Step 18.

18 Using a cylinder bore gauge or a telescoping gauge and micrometer, measure the cylinder diameter. Make three pairs of measurements (six in all), parallel and perpendicular to the crankshaft axis, 1/2 inch down at the top, in the middle and 1/2 inch up from the bottom of the cylinder **(see illustration)**. First, determine cylinder bore diameter. Take the largest measurement and compare it to the cylinder bore diameter listed in this Chapter's Specifications. Next, determine whether the cylinder is round. Compare the readings in one direction to the readings in the other direction, subtract the smaller readings from the larger readings and compare any differences to the allowable out-of-round listed in this Chapter's Specifications. Finally, determine whether the cylinder is tapered. Compare the largest reading to the smallest reading in each direction, subtract the two and compare the difference to the allowable taper listed in this Chapter's Specifications. If you do not have access to measuring equipment, have a dealer service department or motorcycle repair shop measure the cylinders.

19 If the bore diameter, taper or out-of-round is greater than specified (see Step 18), or if all of your measurements are within specification but one or both cylinder bores are badly scuffed, scored or there are signs that the plating is peeling, replace the cylinder block and pistons as a set, or have the cylinder block repaired.

NOTE:

When considering cylinder block repair, U.S. Chrome of Wisconsin is experienced in the repair of plated cylinder bores. You can contact them at www.usnicom.com.

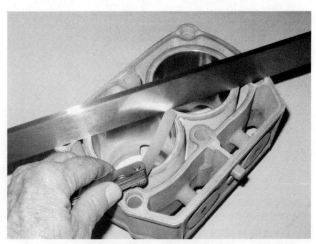

11.16 Use a straightedge and a feeler gauge to measure the top of the cylinder bore for flatness in a crossing pattern

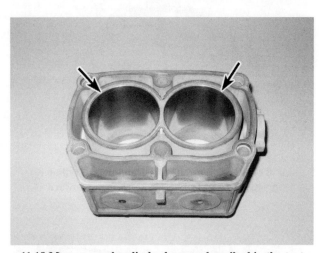

11.18 Measure each cylinder bore as described in the text

20 Determine piston-to-cylinder clearance as described in Step 34.

21 If all of the cylinder bore measurements are within specification, the bore surfaces are in good condition and the piston-to-cylinder clearance is within the allowable range, the cylinder block can be reused. If you are installing a new set of rings, you may want to have the cylinders honed to deglaze the surface. Because the manufacturer recommends the use of either a rigid hone or an arbor honing machine, refer this service to a dealership or motorcycle repair shop.

CAUTION:

A combination of soap and hot water is required to completely clean the cylinder walls. Solvent and kerosene cannot wash fine grit out of cylinder crevices. Any grit left in the cylinders will cause the piston rings and other engine parts to wear unnecessarily.

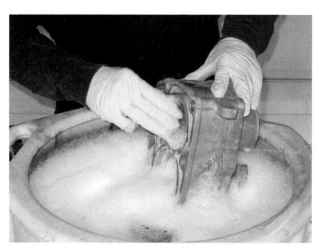

11.22 Thoroughly clean the cylinder bores in hot, soapy water to remove all grit and debris from the bore surfaces, then rinse with clear, cold water

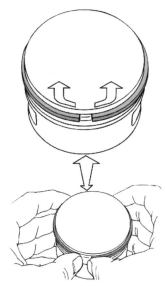

11.25a When removing a piston ring by hand, work carefully to prevent the ring from twisting and scratching the piston or the ring grooves

11.25b If possible, remove the piston rings with a ring removal and installation tool

22   After the cylinders have been measured and serviced, wash them thoroughly with warm soapy water to remove all traces of the abrasive grit produced during the honing operation **(see illustration)**. Also wash out any fine grit material from the coolant passages surrounding the cylinder bores. Be sure to run a brush through the bolt holes and flush them with running water. After washing the cylinder block, wipe each cylinder wall with a clean, white cloth. The cloth should not show any traces of grit or debris when it is removed from either cylinder. If the rag is the slightest bit dirty, the cylinders are not clean enough and must be washed again. When the cylinders are clean and dry, apply a coat of light, rust-preventative oil to all machined surfaces.

Pistons

23   Before removing the piston rings, hold the piston and turn the upper compression ring to make sure it floats and moves smoothly in its groove. If not, check for excessive carbon on both the ring and in the groove. A collapsed groove can also cause the ring to stick. Repeat for each ring.

24   Before inspecting the piston, the rings must be removed and the piston cleaned. When removing the piston rings, carefully note which way each ring fits and in which groove as they must be installed in their original positions if being reused.

25   Using your thumbs or a piston ring installation tool, carefully remove the rings from the pistons **(see illustrations)**. Because the rings will try to twist when removing them by hand, do not allow the ends of the rings to nick or gouge the piston.

26   Clean the piston thoroughly, making sure to note the identification marks made on the piston in case they are removed. Scrape all traces of carbon from the top of the piston. A hand-held wire brush or a piece of fine emery cloth can be used once most of the deposits have been scraped away. Do not, under any circumstances, use a wire brush mounted in a drill motor to remove deposits from the piston; the piston material is soft and will be eroded away by the wire brush.

27   Use a piston ring groove cleaning tool to remove any carbon deposits from the ring grooves. If a tool is not available, a piece cut off the old ring will do the job. When using a piston ring, make sure it is not thicker than the original ring. Be very careful to remove only the carbon deposits. Do not remove any metal and do not nick or gouge the sides of the ring grooves.

28   Once the deposits have been removed, clean the pistons with solvent and dry them thoroughly. Make sure the oil return holes below the oil ring grooves are clear.

29   If the identification marks previously made on the piston were removed, remark it to ensure it will be installed in its original bore and facing in its original direction **(see illustration 11.8)**.

30   Carefully inspect each piston for cracks around the skirt, at the pin bosses and at the ring lands. Normal piston

wear appears as even, vertical wear on the thrust surfaces of the piston and slight looseness of the top ring in its groove. If the skirt is scored or scuffed, the engine may have been suffering from overheating and/or abnormal combustion which caused excessively high operating temperatures. The oil pump should be checked thoroughly **(see illustration)**.

31 A hole in the piston crown, an extreme to be sure, is an indication that abnormal combustion (pre-ignition) was occurring. Burned areas at the edge of the piston crown are usually evidence of spark knock (detonation). If any of the above problems exist, the causes must be corrected or the damage will occur again.

32 Examine each ring groove for burrs, dented edges or other damage. Pay particular attention to the top compression ring groove as it usually wears more than the others. Because the oil rings are bathed in oil, these rings and grooves wear little compared to compression rings and their grooves. If there is evidence of oil ring groove wear or if the oil ring is tight and difficult to remove, the piston skirt may have collapsed due to excessive heat. Replace the piston.

33 Measure the piston ring-to-groove clearance by laying each piston ring in its groove and slipping a feeler gauge in beside it **(see illustration)**. Make sure you have the correct ring for the groove. Check the clearance at three or four locations around the groove. If the clearance is greater than specified in this Chapter's Specifications, replace the piston rings and remeasure the clearance using the new rings. If the clearance is still greater than that specified, the piston is worn and must be replaced with a new one.

34 Before checking the piston-to-cylinder clearance, first make sure the pistons and cylinders are correctly matched. Measure the piston across the skirt on the thrust faces at a 90-degree angle to the piston pin, at the distance from the bottom of the skirt listed in this Chapter's Specifications **(see illustration)**. If the piston diameter is within specifications, subtract the piston diameter from the bore diameter (Step 18) to obtain the clearance. If it is greater than specified in this Chapter's Specifications, the piston must be replaced (assuming the bore is within limits, otherwise a new cylinder block is also necessary).

35 Apply clean engine oil to the pin, insert it into the piston and check for freeplay by rocking the pin back-and-forth **(see illustration)**. If the pin is loose, new pistons and pins must be installed. For a more precise assessment of piston/piston pin wear, measure the diameter of the piston pin and compare your measurement to the piston pin diameter listed in this Chapter's Specifications. Replace the pin if it's excessively worn. Next, measure the inside diameter of the piston pin holes in the piston and compare to the values listed in this Chapter's Specifications. Replace the piston if the bore diameters are too large. If the piston bore diameters are within specification, subtract the diameter of the piston pin and compare your measurement to the piston pin clearance listed in this Chapter's Specifications. If the clearance exceeds the specified maximum, replace the piston and/or the piston pin (depending on whether the pin outside diameter or piston pin bore inside diameter is acceptable).

11.30 Check the piston pin bore and the piston skirt for wear and scoring

11.33 Measure the piston ring-to-groove clearance with a feeler gauge

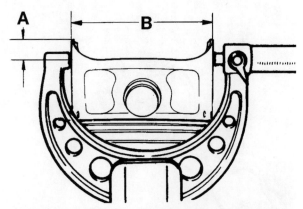

11.34 Measure the piston diameter with a micrometer

A   Specified distance from bottom of piston
B   Piston diameter

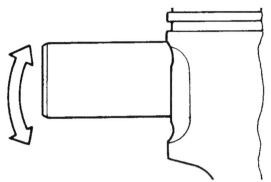

11.35 Check for excessive play between the piston pin and piston pin bore

11.41 Install the piston circlips with their open end toward the top of the piston

11.38 Lubricate both connecting rod big-end bearings with engine oil

11.39a Set-up for pressing the dowel pins into the crankcase

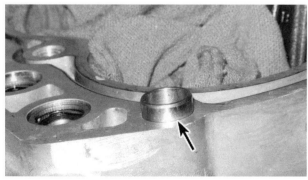

11.39b Visually check that both dowel pins are bottomed in the crankcase

Finally, measure the inside diameter of the small end of both connecting rods and compare to the dimension listed in the Chapter 4 Specifications. If the inside diameter is too large for any one connecting rod, replace the crankshaft. The connecting rods are not available separately.

Installation

36   Inspect and install the piston rings (see Section 12).
37   Check that the mating surfaces of the cylinder block and crankcase are clean and free from old gasket material. Then check the cylinder stud holes in the crankcase to make sure there is no debris in them and that the threads are clean and true.
38   Lubricate each connecting rod big-end with engine oil **(see illustration)**. Then rotate the crankshaft a few times and position the connecting rods at TDC.
39   If the dowel pins were removed, you can press new pins into the crankcase using the same technique as for the cylinder head dowel pins (see Section 8). Note that a longer pipe will be needed if you are using a cylinder head mounting bolt to press them in place **(see illustration)**. Make sure both dowel pins are fully bottomed in the crankcase **(see illustration)**.
40   If removed, install the valve lifters (see Section 13).
41   If you're installing the original pistons, identify each piston using the marks made on the pistons during their removal **(see illustration 11.8)**. New pistons can be installed in either bore and facing in either direction. After identifying the pistons, install a new circlip into the inboard side of each piston (do not reuse old circlips). Install the circlips so their open end toward the top of the piston **(see illustration)**. Make sure both circlips are correctly seated in their grooves.
42   Lubricate the connecting rod small-end bores, piston pins and the piston pin bores with engine oil.
43   Install the piston pin into the outboard side of the piston so the pin sits flush against the inboard edge of the piston boss. Repeat for the other piston and pin.
44   Install a new base gasket over the pistons and dowel pins **(see illustration 11.6)**. Make sure all of the holes align.

11.45 These piston holders were made by cutting 1 x 1 inch wooden blocks to length and connecting two halves together with a thin metal strap and screws

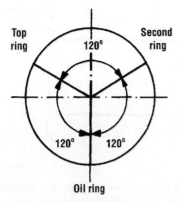

11.47 Stagger the piston ring end gaps like this

11.48 Raise the pistons to TDC and support each one on a piston holder. After lubricating the pistons and rings with engine oil, compress the piston rings with hose clamps (arrows)

11.50a Tap the cylinder down to compress the piston rings . . .

11.50b . . . and allow the hose clamps to slide down against the piston holders

45   Because the cylinder block and pistons are installed at the same time, it will be helpful to support each piston on a piston holder. Having the pistons supported by the holders is also helpful when installing the outer circlips in the pistons **(see illustration)**. After fabricating the holders, place them underneath the pistons.

46   Install the piston and push the pin through the connecting rod and into the other side of the piston. Install a new circlip into the outboard side of each piston (see Step 41).

47   Stagger the piston ring end gaps around the piston every 120-degrees **(see illustration)**.

48   With the pistons at TDC, support them on the piston holders. Then lubricate the pistons and rings with engine oil. Compress the piston rings on each piston with a hose clamp. When positioning the hose clamps, their screws must be facing toward the outside of the pistons. Do not overtighten the hose clamps, as you want them to move freely when contacted by the cylinder block as it slides over the rings and down the pistons **(see illustration)**.

49   Lubricate the cylinder bores with engine oil.

50   Align the cylinder block with the pistons, then carefully tap the cylinder block evenly to push each cylinder bore over the rings and pistons. Stop if any interference or roughness is felt. Push the cylinder block down until the pistons are fully compressed in the cylinder bores and the hose clamps are resting on the piston holders **(see illustrations)**.

51   Remove the hose clamps and piston holders, then use both hands to push the cylinder block down while seating it over the dowel pins and against the base gasket **(see illustration 11.5)**.

52   Cut two pieces of hose to length, and use them together with two washers and two cylinder head mounting bolts to hold the cylinder block in place **(see illustration)**. Then turn the engine over to make sure the pistons move inside the bores with no binding or roughness. If there is any interference, a piston ring may have broken during cylinder block installation. If necessary, remove the cylinder block

11.52 The hoses, washers and cylinder head mounting bolts shown here hold the cylinder block in place to prevent it from moving upward and snagging a ring when the engine is turned over to check for piston ring damage

12.3a Use the piston to square the ring in the cylinder . . .

12.3b . . . and measure the ring end gap with a feeler gauge

12.5 If the end gap is too small, clamp a file in a vise and file the ring ends (from the outside in only) to enlarge the gap slightly

and check for any damage.

53   Install the cylinder head (see Section 8).

54   Before starting the engine, remove and inspect the air filter and replace it if necessary (see Chapter 2). Then check the air box to make sure the passageway between the air filter and engine is clean. If there is dirt or sand in this area, it either passed through the air filter, the air filter was improperly sealed or the air box is not installed correctly or possibly damaged. It is critical to locate and repair any problems to prevent further debris from entering the engine and undoing the work you just performed.

12   PISTON RINGS

1   A three-ring type piston and ring assembly is used. The top and second rings are compression rings. The lower ring is an oil control ring assembly consisting of two ring rails and an expander. Lay out the pistons and the new ring sets so the rings will be matched with the same piston and cylinder during the end gap measurement procedure and engine assembly. If you haven't already done so, remove the piston rings from the pistons (see Section 11).

2   Before installing new piston rings, the ring end gaps must be checked.

NOTE:
When performing Step 3, it is critical to align the rings squarely with the bore when checking ring end gap; otherwise, a false reading will result.

3   Insert the top (No. 1) ring into the bottom of the first cylinder and square it up with the cylinder walls by pushing it in with the top of the piston. The ring should be about 1-2 inches (25-50 mm) above the bottom edge of the cylinder. To measure the end gap, slip a feeler gauge between the ends of the ring and compare the measurement to this Chapter's Specifications. Remove the ring and install it into the top of the cylinder and repeat the measurement. As before, the ring should be about 1-2 inches (25-50 mm) below the top edge of the cylinder **(see illustrations)**.

4   If the gap is larger or smaller than specified, double check to make sure that you have the correct rings before proceeding. If there is a difference between the two readings, check the cylinder for taper and out-of-round (see Section 11).

5   If the gap is too small, it must be enlarged or the ring ends may come in contact with each other during engine operation, which can cause the ring to break and/or score and severely damage the bore. The end gap can be increased by filing the ring ends very carefully with a smooth, double-cut flat file **(see illustration)**. When performing this operation, file only from the outside in and check your work often. Each time you file the ring, carefully deburr the ring ends to remove any sharp and raised edges before reinstalling the ring and checking its gap (see Step 3).

12.9a Install the oil ring expander first . . .

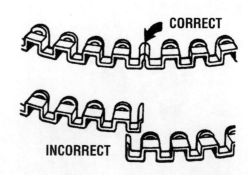

12.9b . . . while making sure the expander ends butt together

6   Excess end gap is not critical unless it exceeds the service limit. Again, double check to make sure you have the correct rings for your engine and the bore is not worn.

7   Repeat the procedure for each ring that will be installed in the first cylinder and for each ring in the remaining cylinder. Remember to keep the rings, pistons and cylinders matched up.

8   Once the ring end gaps have been checked/corrected, clean the rings in solvent, then with hot soapy water and rinse with clear water. When dry, they are ready to install onto the pistons, which should also be cleaned in the same manner.

9   The oil control ring (lowest on the piston) is installed first. It is composed of three separate components. Slip the expander into the groove, making sure the ends of the expander butt together **(see illustrations)**. Then install the lower side rail **(see illustration)**. Do not use a piston ring installation tool on the oil ring side rails as they are thin and may be damaged. Instead, place one end of the side rail into the groove between the spacer expander and the ring land. Hold it firmly in place and slide a finger around the piston while pushing the rail into the groove. Next, install the upper side rail in the same manner.

10   After the three oil ring components have been installed, check to make sure that both the upper and lower side rails can be turned smoothly in the ring groove.

11   The OEM compression rings can be identified by the following marks - the first (top) ring is marked with the letter "E," and the second ring is marked with the designation "M TOP" **(see illustration)**. These marks are located on one side of each ring, indicating the top side. On rings removed from the engine, these marks may be worn off or undecipherable. When purchasing a set of new OEM piston rings, you will note they are packaged and labeled for easy identification **(see illustration)**.

12   You can use the same technique or tool to install the compression rings as you used to remove them (see Section 11). However, to avoid breaking a ring or scratching the piston, it is helpful to use a piston ring installation tool **(see illustration 11.25b)**. Fit the second compression ring into the second groove on the piston with its identificaton mark facing up. Do not expand the ring any more than is necessary to slide it into place.

12.9c Installing an oil ring side rail - don't use a piston ring installation tool when installing the oil ring assembly

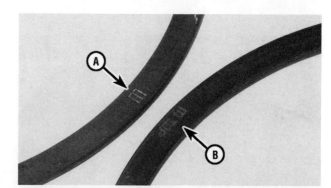

12.11a First (A) and second (B) compression ring identification marks. Make sure these marks face up when installing the rings on the pistons

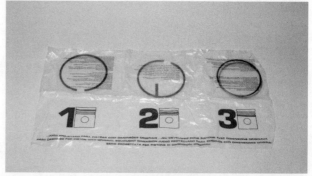

12.11b Replacement OEM piston rings are easily identified by their packaging

3

12.15 After installing the piston rings, make sure each ring moves freely in its groove

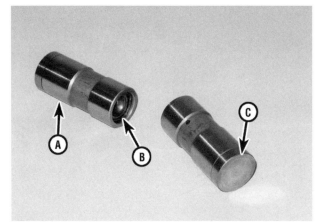

13.4 Lifter inspection details

A Body surface	C Bottom surface shape
B Clip	

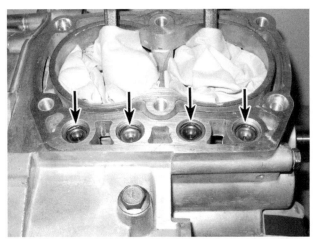

13.2a Identify each valve lifter after removing it from its bore inside the crankcase

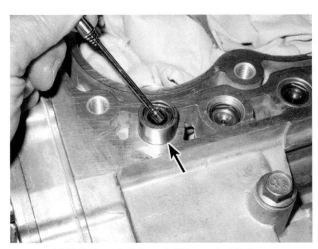

13.2b Lift and slide each lifter out of its bore

13   Finally, install the first (top) ring in the same manner. Make sure the ring's identification mark is facing up.

14   Repeat the procedure for the remaining piston and rings. Be very careful not to confuse the top and second rings.

15   Once the rings have been properly installed, check that they move freely **(see illustration)**. Before installing the cylinder block over the pistons, stagger the end gaps, including those of the oil ring side rails (see Section 11).

13   VALVE LIFTERS - REMOVAL, INSPECTION AND INSTALLATION

1   Remove the cylinder block (see Section 11).

NOTE:

If you cannot remove a valve lifter through the top of the crankcase, the bottom of the lifter has probably worn to a mushroom shape, or is damaged. Here, it is necessary to remove the camshaft first, then the lifter(s).

2   The valve lifters must be reinstalled in their original positions in the crankcase. Identify each lifter as it is removed so that it can be installed in its correct position **(see illustration)**. Use a magnet to remove each lifter **(see illustration)**.

3   Clean the lifers by dipping them in a container filled with clean engine oil. Then place on a clean towel.

4   Inspect each valve lifter for any scoring and other visual wear, while also making sure the clip in the top of the lifter is seated fully in its groove. Then check the bottom of each valve lifter as it should be slightly convex. If a lifter has a worn, flat bottom, it can only be used with the original camshaft and not a replacement camshaft. Replace all four lifters and the camshaft as a set if any lifter is worn or damaged. If the lifters could only be removed from the bottom side (after removing the camshaft), replace the lifters and camshaft as a set **(see illustration)**.

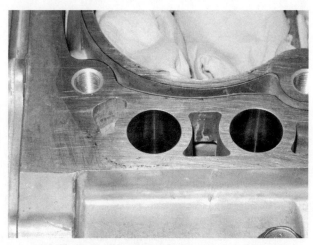

13.5 Check the lifter bores for grooves, scoring and other damage

13.6a Measure the lifter outside diameter . . .

5   Inspect the lifter bores inside the crankcase for any grooves, scoring and other damage **(see illustration)**. The bore surfaces must be smooth. If there is any noticeable damage, inspect the lifters for the same conditions.

6   Standard measurements can be made by measuring the valve lifter outside diameter and the valve lifter bore inside diameter (inside the engine crankcase) and comparing the results to this Chapter's Specifications **(see illustrations)**. If it is necessary to replace the valve lifters, refer to Step 4 for additional information. If the bore diameters are too large, it will be necessary to replace the crankcase assembly.

7   Lubricate both lifter ends with engine assembly lube **(see illustration)**. Then lubricate the sides of each lifter and the lifter bores inside the crankcase with engine oil.

8   If installing the original valve lifters, make sure to install them in their original positions. Install the lifters with their mating pushrod end facing up **(see illustration 13.2b)**.

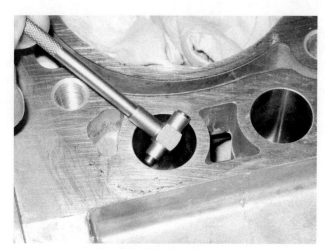

13.6b . . . and the lifter bore inside diameter

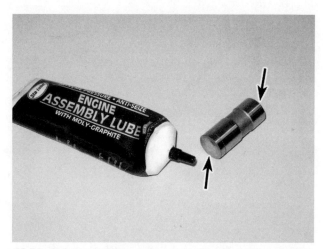

13.7 Lubricate the lifter ends (arrows) with engine assembly lube and the lifter body with engine oil

SPECIFICATIONS

General

Bore and stroke	3.1 x 3.0 in. (80 x 76.5 mm)
Compression ratio	9.78:1
Displacement	46.4 cu.-in. (760 cc)
Engine type	4-stroke, OHV, pushrod, twin cylinder
Lubrication system type	Pressurized wet sump

Cylinder head, valves and valve springs

Cylinder head standard height	3.478 inch (88.35 mm)
Cylinder head warpage limit	0.004 inch. (0.10 mm)
Valve guides	
Inside diameter	0.2364-0.2370 inch (6.005-6.020 mm)
Valve guide protrusion above head	0.803-0.811 inch (20.40-20.60 mm)
Valve seat width	
Intake	
Standard	0.039-0.055 inch (1.0-1.4 mm)
Limit	0.055 inch (1.4 mm)
Exhaust	
Standard	0.051-0.067 inch (1.30-1.70 mm)
Limit	0.071 inch (1.8 mm)
Valve springs	
Free length	1.735 inch (44.07 mm)
Installed height	
Intake	1.464 inch (37.19 mm)
Exhaust	1.474 inch (37.44 mm)
Valve stem outside diameter	
Intake	0.2352-0.2340 inch (5.974-5.944 mm)
Exhaust	0.2347-0.2355 inch (5.961-5.982 mm)
Valve stem overall length	
Intake	4.4952-4.5248 inch (114.180-114.930 mm)
Exhaust	4.5303-4.5603 inch (115.070-115.832 mm)
Valve stem-to-guide oil clearance	
Intake	0.0013-0.0033 inch (0.033-0.084 mm)
Exhaust	0.0018-0.0037 inch (0.046-0.094 mm)

Cylinder block

Bore diameter	3.1495 inches (80.00 mm)
Out-of-round limit	0.0003 inch (0.0076 mm)
Taper limit	0.00031 inch (0.008 mm)
Upper surface warpage limit	0.004 inch (0.10 mm)

Piston and pins

Piston	
Bore lining material	Nikasil
Diameter	3.1477-3.1483 inches (79.95-79.97 mm)
Measurement point	0.02 inches (5 mm) up from skirt, at 90-degrees to piston pin axis
Piston-to-cylinder clearance	0.0009-0.0021 inches (0.023-0.053 mm)
PIston pin fit in piston	Hand push at 68-degrees F (20-degrees C)
Piston pin outside diameter	0.70866-0.70846 inches (18.000-17.995 mm)
Piston pin bore in piston	0.7089-0.7091 inches (18.006-18.011 mm)
Piston pin clearance in piston	0.0002-0.0007 inches (0.0051-0.0178 mm)

Piston rings

Ring end gap installed

Top	0.0059-0.0138 inches (0.15-0.35 mm)
Second	0.0098-0.0197 inches (0.25-0.50 mm)
Oil ring side rail	0.010-0.030 inches (0.25-0.76 mm)

Ring-to-groove clearance

Top	0.0016-0.0032 inches (0.041-0.081 mm)
Second	0.002-0.005 inches (0.051-0.127 mm)
Oil ring side rail	Not specified

Valve lifters

Crankcase bore inside diameter	0.8432-0.8444 inches (21.417-21.448 mm)
Valve lifter outside diameter	0.8422-0.8427 inches (21.392-21.405 mm)

Torque specifications	Ft-lbs	In.-lb	Nm
Breather cover screws	--	15-25	2.0-3.0
Cylinder head bolts			
Step 1	13.5-16.5	--	18.3-22.4
Step 2	Loosen bolts/see text		
Step 3	31-39	--	42-53
Step 4	Turn bolts 90 degrees/see text		
Valve cover screws.............................	--	76-92	9-10
Rocker arm screws.............................	20-24	--	27-32

CHAPTER FOUR

ENGINE LOWER END

CONTENTS

1   GENERAL INFORMATION

1   This chapter provides service procedures for engine removal and service to the lower end components. These include the camshaft, flywheel, stator, timing gears, water and oil pump, crankshaft and crankcase.

2   ENGINE REMOVAL - METHODS AND PRECAUTIONS

1   If you've decided that the engine must be removed for overhaul or major repair work, several preliminary steps should be taken. Read all removal and installation procedures carefully prior to committing to this job.
2   Locating a suitable place to work is extremely important. Adequate work space, along with storage space for the vehicle, will be needed. If a shop or garage isn't available, at the very least a flat, level, clean work surface made of concrete or asphalt is required.
3   Clean the engine compartment and engine before beginning the removal procedure. This will make work much easier and help prevent sand, dirt and other debris from falling into some vital component.
4   After tightly wrapping water-vulnerable components, use a spray cleaner on everything, with particular concentration on the dirtiest areas where dirt and sand has collected. Oil leaks will not be difficult to spot as the dirt and sand will collect on these areas and have a moist appearance. If one section dries out, apply more cleaner. Depending on how dirty the engine is, let the cleaner soak in according to the directions, then hose off the grime and cleaner. Get the water down into every area that you can get at, then dry important components with compressed air (low pressure).
5   If you plan on removing an assembled engine, an engine hoist or A-frame will be helpful as the engine sits

low in the frame, is heavy and can be difficult to remove. Even when you have help, the use of an engine hoist is still a good idea. When using an engine hoist, make sure it can be maneuvered under and around the vehicle and is capable of lifting the assembly high enough out of the frame. Consider the ceiling height in the garage as this could restrict how high the engine hoist can be raised. Safety is of primary importance, considering the potential hazards involved in lifting the engine out of the vehicle. If necessary, remove the cab/frame to provide access to maneuver the engine hoist in place and remove the engine (see Chapter 14).

6   If you're a novice at engine removal, get at least one helper. One person cannot easily do all the things you need to do to raise the engine assembly out of the frame. Also helpful is to seek advice and assistance from someone who's experienced in engine removal.

7   Plan the operation ahead of time. Arrange for or obtain all of the tools and equipment you'll need prior to beginning the job. Some of the equipment necessary to perform engine removal and installation safely and with relative ease are a heavy duty floor jack, complete sets of wrenches and sockets as described in the front of this manual, wooden blocks, plenty of rags and cleaning solvent for mopping up spilled oil, coolant and gasoline. If the hoist must be rented, make sure that you arrange for it in advance and have everything disconnected and/or removed before bringing the hoist home. This will save you money and time.

8   Plan for the vehicle to be out of use for quite a while. A dealership can do the work that is beyond the scope of the home mechanic. Dealerships and machine shops often have a busy schedule, so before removing the engine, consult the shop for an estimate of how long it will take to rebuild or repair the components that may need work.

3   ENGINE - REMOVAL, INSPECTION AND INSTALLATION

Removal

1   Park the vehicle on a level surface. Because the engine is removed from the side, make sure you have adequate room on both sides of the vehicle.

2   Apply the parking brake. Make sure you have room to work around the back and sides of the vehicle, especially if you are going to use an engine hoist. Make sure there are no overhead lighting fixtures or other objects that could interfere with the engine hoist when lifting the engine out of the frame.

3   Review the information in Section 2.

4   Disconnect the negative battery cable from the battery (see Chapter 8). Place an insulator over the cable end so it cannot fall back across the battery and reconnect itself.

5   On standard Ranger models, remove the seat base, seat back, storage box, floor cover and kickboard (see Chapter 14).

6   On Crew models, remove the rear seat base, rear

seat back, rear lower floor and rear kickboard (see Chapter 14).

7   Remove any additional body components that will interfere with engine removal (see Chapter 14).

8   Clean the engine and the area around the engine where it is mounted in the frame.

9   Remove the skid plate(s) from underneath the frame (see Chapter 14). This will allow you to support the engine with a jack when it is necessary to do so in this procedure.

10   If the engine will be worked on, drain the engine oil (see Chapter 2).

11   Drain the engine coolant (see Chapter 2).

12   Before continuing, take several digital pictures of the engine compartment to show hose and cable routing.

13   Remove the exhaust system (see Chapter 7).

14   Remove the drive clutch, driven clutch and inner clutch housing (see Chapter 5).

15   Measure the clutch center distance as described in Chapter 6 and compare with the number listed in the Chapter 6 Specifications. If the distance measurement is incorrect, the adjustment was not set correctly, or the engine and/or transmission mounting fasteners are loose or were loose at one time and tightened without having the distance correctly adjusted. By recording the distance now, the number will serve as a guideline when it is time to install the engine in the frame and adjust the clutch center distance.

16   Several electrical connectors will be disconnected in this procedure. To protect the connectors from contamination after disconnecting them, enclose each connector half in a small plastic bag, then close and secure the bag with a rubber band (**see illustration**).

NOTE:
Because the fuel system is under pressure, some fuel will spray from the hose when it is disconnected. Protect yourself by wearing goggles and wrapping the hose with a rag. If you've never disconnected the quick-disconnect fuel hose connectors, refer to Chapter 7 for information on how to do this and for additional fuel hose information.

17   Disconnect the fuel hose at the fuel rail (**see illustrations**). Wipe up any spilled fuel, and store the fuel soaked rags in an approved storage container.

18   The fuel injector connectors are disconnected at their wiring harness connector ends and not at the injectors. Before disconnecting the fuel injector electrical connectors on 2010 models, use a marking pen to identify one of the connectors with its wiring harness connector - the connectors used on 2011 and later models are color coded. Then disconnect both connectors. Identifying one of the connectors on 2010 models will prevent any identification problems when reconnecting the connectors. Tie the wiring harnesses out of the way so they will not snag on anything and become damaged when removing the engine (**see illustrations**). See Chapter 7 for additional information on the fuel injector connectors.

3.16 To protect the exposed connector terminals and pins from sand and dirt after disconnecting them, cover each connector half in a plastic bag

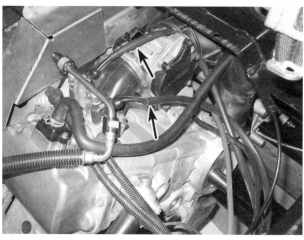

3.18a Before disconnecting the fuel injector wiring harness connectors, note their routing path from the fuel injectors to where they plug into the wiring harness (2010 model shown)

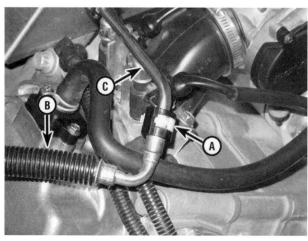

3.17a Fuel hose details (2010 models)

A	Fuel hose connector	C	Fuel rail
B	Fuel hose		

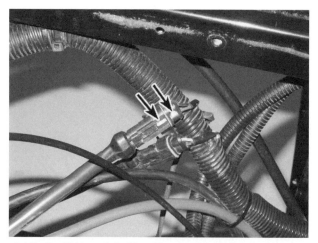

3.18b On 2010 models, identify one of the fuel injector connectors by marking both mating connector halves with a pen

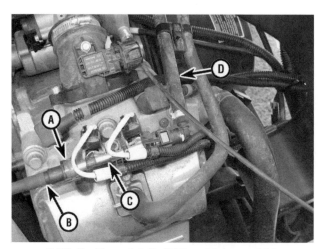

3.17b Fuel hose details (2011 and later models)

A	Fuel hose connector	C	Fuel rail
B	Fuel hose	D	Damper

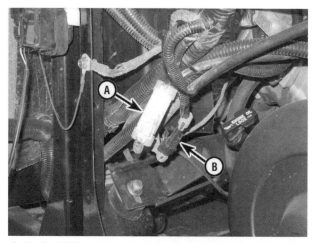

3.18c On 2011 and later models, the fuel injector connectors are color coded - gray/PTO side (A) and black/MAG side (B)

3.19 Disconnect the breather hose (arrow) at the engine

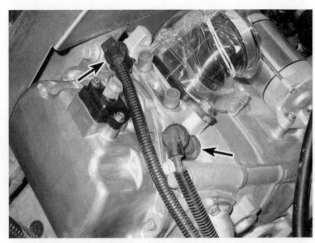

3.23a On 2010 models, identify one of the spark plug caps

3.22 With the connectors disconnected from the throttle body, set the throttle body aside without disconnecting the throttle cable

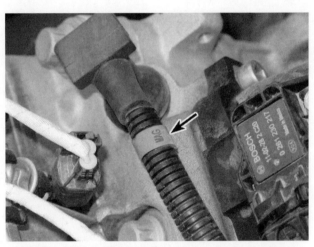

3.23b On 2011 and later models, the spark plug cables are labeled either MAG or PTO - here is the MAG label

19   Disconnect the breather hose at the valve cover **(see illustration)**.

20   To prevent damage to the fuel injectors when removing the engine, remove them from the cylinder head (see Chapter 7).

21   Remove the air box (see Chapter 7).

22   Remove the throttle body (see Chapter 7). If it is only necessary to relocate the throttle body during engine removal, leave the throttle cable connected and set the throttle body aside **(see illustration)**.

23   Note the spark plug cable routing from the engine to the ignition coil. On 2010 models, mark one of the spark plug caps to identify them so they can be correctly reconnected **(see illustration)**. On 2011 and later models, the spark plug cables are labeled either MAG or PTO - check each cable to make sure the label is attached, or mark one of the spark plug caps **(see illustration)**.

24   Disconnect the crankshaft position sensor and the stator wiring harness connectors **(see illustration)**. Both sensors are mounted on the MAG side of the engine.

3.24 Disconnect the crankshaft position sensor wiring harness connector (A) and the stator wiring harness connector (B)

4

3.25 The cam phase sensor is mounted above the oil filter

3.27 The engine coolant temperature (ECT) sensor is mounted on the PTO side of the cylinder head (2010 model shown)

3.26a Starter cable details

A   Starter cable (positive)   *B   Ground cable*

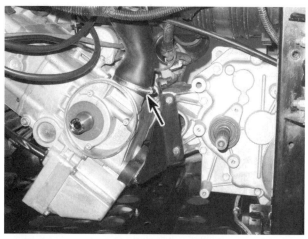

3.28 The rear clutch inlet hose (arrow) is mounted on the PTO side of the engine

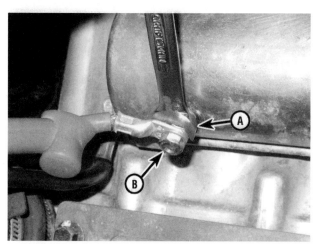

3.26b Hold the inner starter cable nut with a wrench (A) to prevent the insulator installed inside the starter housing from turning, then loosen and remove the outer nut (B)

25 On 2011 and later models, disconnect the cam phase sensor wiring harness connector **(see illustration)**.

26 Pull the rubber cap off the starter terminal. Then disconnect the starter cable by holding the inner nut with a wrench and removing the outer nut. Holding the inner nut prevents the terminal bolt from turning and damaging the insulator installed inside the starter. Then remove the lower starter motor mounting bolt and disconnect the ground cable. Reinstall the mounting bolt to prevent its loss. Note the starter and ground cable routing and remove them from the cable guide **(see illustrations)**.

27 Disconnect the engine coolant temperature (ECT) electrical connector **(see illustration)**.

28 Loosen the hose clamp and disconnect the rear clutch inlet hose at the engine **(see illustration)**.

3.29a Engine coolant hose (arrow) at the thermostat

3.30a Support the engine with a jack and wooden block . . .

3.29b Engine coolant hose (arrow) at the water pump

3.30b . . . making sure to first drill a hole in the
wooden block (arrow) for the engine drain bolt
to fit into (if necessary)

29   Disconnect the coolant hoses at the engine **(see illustrations)**.

30   Position a jack under the engine with a wooden block placed between the jack and lower crankcase. Make sure the jack is centered underneath the engine to prevent the engine from falling when the last mounting bolt is removed. If the engine oil drain bolt is a hex bolt and extends beyond the lower crankcase, drill a hole large enough in the wooden block for the bolt to fit into without any interference. Don't balance the engine on the drain bolt as the engine could easily tip and fall to either side **(see illustrations)**.

31   The engine is secured to frame with a front engine mount and a rear engine/transmission mount. Thick rubber dampers are used between the front engine mount and frame, and between the engine and the rear engine/transmission mount. When removing the engine, you may find washers installed on the rear engine/transmission mount dampers. Note the position of these so you can correctly reinstall them during engine installation. Raise the jack to remove tension from the engine without raising or binding the engine in the frame. Here you are using the jack to support the engine while removing pressure from the mounting fasteners, so they can be easily removed. Note that it may be necessary to reposition the jack as some of the fasteners are removed to remove weight or stress from the other fasteners to prevent them from binding. Remove the screws securing front engine mount to the engine **(see illustration)**. Remove the nuts

3.31a Front engine mount details

A   *Front engine mount. This mount will remain secured to the frame when you remove the engine from the frame*
B   *Rubber damper (one of two shown)*
C   *Rubber damper mounting nut (one of two shown)*

Note: *Hidden in this photograph are the two screws located in the center of the front engine mount that secure the mount to the engine. When removing the engine from the frame, you must remove these two screws*

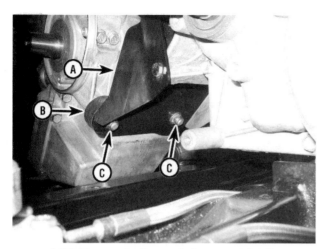

3.31b Rear engine/transmission mount details

A *Rear engine/transmission mount. This mount will remain attached onto the transmission when you remove the engine from the frame. However, if it is necessary to do so, you can remove the rear engine/transmission mount to provide additional clearance when removing the engine*

B *Rubber damper (one of two shown). These will remain on the engine during removal*

C *Rubber damper mounting nuts. Remove these to free the rear engine/transmission mount from the rubber dampers*

3.33 Remove the engine through the seat base opening (standard Ranger model shown)

securing the rear engine/transmission mount to the rubber dampers mounted on the engine **(see illustration)**.

32 Before attempting to remove the engine, make a final check for any remaining wiring harness connectors or hoses connected to the engine that could be damaged and interfere with engine removal.

WARNING:

Engine removal requires the aid of helpers or a hoist to safely remove the engine from the frame.

NOTE:

Keep in mind that if you are going to use a hoist, you must position it in such a way that you can roll it under the vehicle while centering its arm with the engine, and then be able to roll it out from under the vehicle with the engine hanging from the arm.

33 Roll the cylinder forward and remove it from the vehicle through the seat base opening **(see illustration)**. If the engine is difficult to remove, turn the engine with the valve cover facing toward the left side of the frame, then lift and remove the engine.

Inspection

34 With the engine removed from the frame, now is a good time to inspect parts that are not so easily accessible.

35 Touch up the frame with paint as required. Make sure all wiring harness connectors are protected inside plastic bags to prevent any damage from overspray.

36 Inspect and replace any damaged breather hoses.

37 Inspect the wiring harnesses for signs of damage that may have occurred when removing the engine. Repair damaged wires as required.

38 Inspect all of the coolant hoses and pipes that run between the radiator and engine for any leakage or damage. Tighten any loose hose clamps or replace any damaged part as required.

39 Inspect the brake hoses for leakage and damage. Make sure they are correctly routed and secured with any clips or plastic ties as required.

40 Inspect the engine mount fasteners for corrosion and thread damage. Clean each fastener in solvent and remove all threadlocking compound from the fastener threads where used. Replace damaged fasteners with original OEM fasteners.

Installation

41 Installation is the reverse of removal, noting the following:

CAUTION:

If the engine was disassembled and reassembled, the oil system must be primed before the engine is first started. Failure to do so may cause engine damage when the engine is first started.

a) *Make sure no wires, hoses or the throttle cable become trapped between the engine and other components when installing the engine assembly in the frame.*

b) *Before installing the engine in the frame, make sure the rear engine dampers are tightened fully against the engine. If washers were used on the rear engine/transmission mount dampers, make sure to reinstall them in their original positions as noted during removal.*

c) *Do not fully tighten the front or rear engine mounting fasteners until they have all been installed.*

d) *Tighten the front engine mount to engine screws to the torque listed in this Chapter's Specifications.*

e) *Tighten the rear engine/transmission mount damper nuts to the torque listed in this Chapter's Specifications.*

f) *Before installing the clutch assembly, check the clutch center distance and adjust if necessary (see Chapter 6).*

g) *When installing the clutch assembly, check the clutch offset and clutch alignment position and adjust if necessary (see Chapter 5).*

h) *Install a new gasket between the exhaust manifold and cylinder head. Replace any weak or damaged exhaust springs before starting the engine. See Chapter 7 for information on installing the exhaust system.*

i) *Make sure the throttle cable and all wires and hoses are correctly routed and connected, and secured by any clips or plastic ties as required.*

j) *If the engine oil was not drained, check the engine oil level and top off if necessary. If the engine oil was drained, install a new oil filter and refill the engine with oil. See Chapter 2.*

k) *If the engine was reassembled, the oil system must be primed before starting the engine for the first time. See Section 20 for information.*

l) *Refill and bleed the cooling system (see Chapter 2). Check the coolant hoses and pipes for leaks.*

m) *Start the engine and bleed the cooling system. Also check for oil, coolant and fuel leaks.*

n) *Turn the ignition switch on and with the vehicle at rest, shift the transmission into each gear while watching the instrument cluster. The display on the instrument cluster should indicate the correct transmission position when each gear change is made. If not, readjust the shift cable (see Chapter 6).*

o) *Slowly test ride the vehicle to ensure all systems are operating correctly.*

p) *If the engine top end was rebuilt, make sure to follow the break-in procedure (see Chapter 2).*

4   ENGINE MOUNTS - REMOVAL, INSPECTION AND INSTALLATION

1   The engine is secured in the frame with steel mounts and rubber dampers. The front dampers are installed between the front engine mount and frame. The rear dampers are installed between the rear engine/transmission mount and the engine. You may find washers installed on the rear engine/transmission mount dampers. Worn-out dampers can cause clutch problems if the engine shifts out of position.

4.4 The rear engine/transmission mount (arrow) can be removed without having to remove the engine or transmission from the frame

2   Rubber dampers degrade over time, and can be weakened prematurely by chemical contamination, such as engine and transmission oil and brake fluid. Damage can be detected by cracks and deterioration in the rubber material or separation of the rubber from its threaded stud. Operating the vehicle when the mounting fasteners are loose or missing can damage the dampers and steel mounts as the engine shifts in the frame. This will also damage the fasteners and possibly the threaded holes in the frame and engine. Periodically inspect the engine mounts and dampers for loose fasteners and damage, and especially when the engine seems to vibrate more than normal.

Removal

3   To access the front engine mount and rubber dampers, remove the engine from the frame (see Section 3). Remove the nuts securing the mount to the rubber dampers and lift off the mount. Then unscrew and remove the rubber dampers **(see illustration 3.31a)**.

4   The rear engine/transmission mount can be removed with the engine and transmission installed in the frame. Refer to Chapter 6, Section 5 and perform the procedures necessary to remove the rear engine/transmission mount and rubber dampers **(see illustration)**.

Inspection

5   Clean all of the parts, except for the rubber dampers, in solvent and dry with compressed air. Do not use solvent or any type of cleaning solution on the rubber dampers as these, along with oil, transmission and brake fluid, can weaken the rubber. Clean the rubber dampers with soapy water, then rinse with clear water and allow to dry.

6   Inspect the rubber dampers for cracks, softness or other damage **(see illustration)**. Then check the threaded studs on each damper for damage. If any one damper is damaged, replace all four dampers as a set to help reduce engine vibration. Don't attempt to repair a damaged damper or its threaded stud(s).

4.6 Inspect the rubber dampers and their studs for any damage. The threaded studs are embedded in the dampers and cannot be removed

4.7 Clean the metal mounts and inspect them for damage (rear engine/transmission mount shown)

5.5a Remove the alternator cover mounting screws and the alternator cover (arrow) . . .

7   Inspect the metal mounts for cracks, enlarged fastener holes and other damage **(see illustration)**. Do not attempt to repair a damaged mount, but instead, replace it to prevent any misalignment problems that could cause secondary damage to other parts and/or increase engine, clutch and transmission vibration.

8   Check all of the nuts and screws for thread damage. Replace damaged fasteners with OEM fasteners.

Installation

9   Installation is the reverse of removal, noting the following:

NOTE:

When a torque specification is not listed for a fastener, measure the fastener and use the general torque specification listed in the Specifications at the front of this manual.

a) *Remove all dirt and rust from surfaces where the rubber dampers and mounts rest against.*
b) *Tighten the rubber mounts securely by hand.*
c) *If washers were used on the rear engine/transmission mount rubber dampers, reinstall them in their original mounting positions.*
d) *Before installing the clutch assembly, check the clutch center distance and adjust if necessary (see Chapter 6).*
e) *If the engine was removed, tighten the front engine mount and the rear engine/transmission mount fasteners as described in Section 3 in this chapter.*
f) *If just the rear engine/transmission mount was removed, install and tighten its fasteners as described in Chapter 6.*

5   ALTERNATOR COVER - REMOVAL AND INSTALLATION

1   The alternator cover can be removed with the engine installed in the frame. Alternator cover removal is required when servicing the flywheel, starter drive, stator coil, stator housing and timing gears. If you are servicing the alternator cover and the parts located behind the cover as part of a complete engine overhaul, it will be easier to service these parts with the engine mounted on a workbench (see Section 3).

Removal

2   Clean the engine and the frame and body components around the alternator cover to prevent sand and dirt from entering the engine when performing the service in this section.
3   If it's necessary for removal access, remove the fuel tank (see Chapter 7).
4   Either disconnect the crankshaft position sensor wiring harness connector, or remove the sensor from the alternator cover (see Chapter 7).
5   Loosen and remove the alternator cover mounting screws, then remove the cover and locate the thrust washer installed on the starter drive **(see illustrations)**. If the thrust washer is not on the starter drive, look for it inside the cover.

5.5b . . . then locate and remove the thrust washer installed on the starter drive

5.7a Here is the upper dowel pin . . .

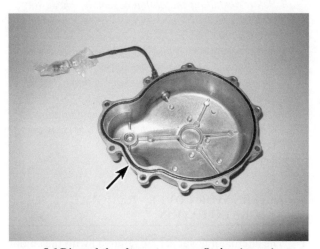

5.6 Discard the alternator cover O-ring (arrow)

5.7b . . . and the lower dowel pin

6   Remove and discard the O-ring from the groove in the alternator cover (see illustration). While the O-ring may still be serviceable, it is good practice to replace it now, considering how much time and work are required to remove the alternator cover.

7   Check for the two dowel pins, and remove them if loose (see illustrations).

8   If it is necessary to replace the alternator cover, remove the crankshaft position sensor if you haven't already done so (see Chapter 7).

Installation

9   The alternator cover screw threads were pre-coated with a dry film threadlock that releases evenly over the threads when the screws are installed and tightened. However, when loosening and removing the screws, the threadlock bond between the two thread sets is destroyed (see illustration). If you will reuse the original screws,

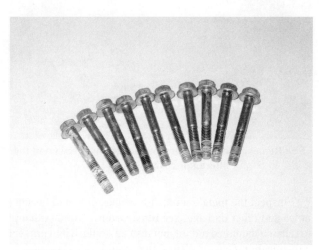

5.9 If reusing the alternator cover mounting screws, remove all of the threadlock remaining on the screw threads

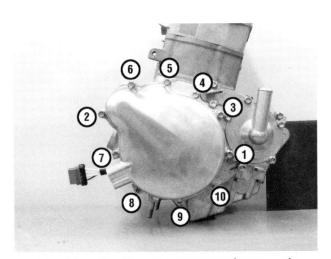

5.15 Tighten the alternator cover mounting screws in numerical order and in two or three steps

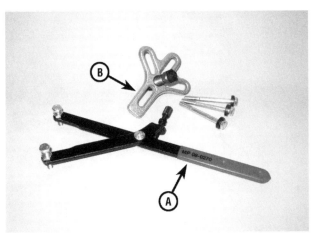

6.2a The Motion Pro Rotor & Sprocket Holder (part No. 08-0270) (A) and a universal type harmonic balancer puller (B) are used to hold and remove the flywheel in this section

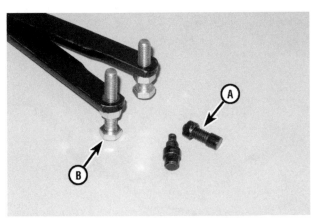

6.2b Before using the Motion Pro Rotor & Sprocket Holder, replace the original pins mounted on the holder (A) with bolts (B) long enough to reach and grab the slots in the flywheel. The actual bolt sizes we used are M8–1.25 x 35 mm and M8–1.25 x 45 mm. To hold the bolts in place, install a nut on each bolt and tighten against the holder

first run a thread chaser along the screws to remove any remaining threadlock from the thread grooves. A wire brush is also helpful. Then clean the screws with an aerosol electrical contact cleaner and allow to dry. Clean the screws now so they will be ready when installing the alternator cover.

10 Clean the screw holes in the stator housing with a thread chaser and/or a brush to remove all of the old threadlock that may be remaining in the thread grooves. Then clean the screw holes with electrical contact cleaner and allow to dry.

11 Clean the alternator cover and the mating surface on the stator housing of all oil and grease.

12 Lubricate the exposed starter drive shaft with dielectric grease. Then lubricate the thrust washer with the same grease and slide it onto the shaft (see illustration 5.5b).

13 If removed, install the two dowel pins (see illustration 5.7a and illustration 5.7b).

14 Lubricate a new O-ring with grease and install the O-ring into the alternator cover groove (see illustration 5.6).

15 Install the alternator cover, making sure it engages correctly onto the two dowel pins. Install new alternator cover mounting screws. If installing the original screws, make sure the threads are clean and dry (see Step 9). Then apply a medium strength threadlock onto the screw threads. When the screws are installed, tighten them finger-tight while making sure the cover is sitting squarely against the stator housing and the O-ring is not pinched between the gasket surfaces. Then tighten the screws in numerical order (see illustration) and in two or three steps to the torque listed in this Chapter's Specifications.

16 If removed, install the crankshaft position sensor (see Chapter 7).

17 The remainder of installation is the reverse of removal.

6 FLYWHEEL, STARTER DRIVE AND STATOR COIL - REMOVAL, INSPECTION AND INSTALLATION

1 This section covers removal and installation procedures for the flywheel, starter drive and stator coil. See Chapter 8 to test the stator coil (alternator test) and the charging system.

2 Special tools: A flywheel holder is required to hold the flywheel when loosening and tightening the flywheel nut. To remove the flywheel, the Polaris Flywheel Puller (part No. 2871043) or an equivalent aftermarket puller will be required. In this section readily available aftermarket tools are used (see illustrations).

Removal

3   Remove the alternator cover (see Section 5).

CAUTION:

When holding the flywheel with a holder like the one described in Step 2, make sure the pins or bolts on the holder do not contact the stator coil; otherwise, the windings on the stator coil could be permanently damaged. If you modify the Motion Pro tool as described in **illustration 6.2b***, you can adjust the length of the bolts and tighten them in place with the nuts.*

4   Hold the flywheel with a flywheel holder, then loosen and remove the flywheel nut and washer **(see illustration)**.

CAUTION:

To prevent from damaging the stator coil, use care when selecting and using a flywheel puller. When using a puller like the one described in Step 2 and shown in Step 5, do not thread the puller mounting screws so they extend past the inside of the flywheel, as the bolts could contact and damage the stator coil. Here you just need to make sure the mounting screws fully engage the threads inside the flywheel. If normal flywheel removal attempts fail, do not force the puller as excessive force could strip the flywheel threads, causing expensive damage. If necessary, take the engine to a dealer service department and have them remove the flywheel.

5   Before installing the flywheel puller, thread the flywheel nut (without the washer) back onto the end of the crankshaft and position it so that its outer edge is flush with the end of the crankshaft. This will leave a gap between the inside of the nut and the flywheel (check to make sure). Installing the nut serves two purposes. First, it prevents the flywheel from flying outward under force when it breaks free, thus preventing any damage to the stator. Second, the nut can be used as a thread chaser in case the pressure bolt mushrooms the threads on the end of the crankshaft. Install the flywheel puller by threading its three mounting screws into the threaded holes in the face of the flywheel, making sure the screws fully engage the threads in the flywheel. Turn the pressure bolt by hand to tension the puller, then check that the puller is positioned parallel with the flywheel. If not, readjust the puller screws as required. When the puller is properly installed, hold the flywheel with the holder and tighten the pressure bolt until the flywheel pops off the crankshaft taper. Remove the nut from the end of the flywheel, then remove the flywheel with the tool attached **(see illustration)**.

6   If the Woodruff key is loose, remove it from the crankshaft taper and place it in a small plastic bag or container to prevent its loss **(see illustration)**.

7   Remove the starter drive assembly, noting the thrust washer installed on each end **(see illustrations)**. The outer thrust washer may have been removed after the alternator cover was removed.

6.4 Use a flywheel holder (A) to hold the flywheel when loosening and removing the nut and washer (B)

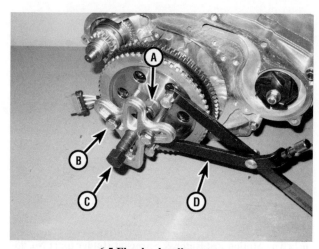

6.5 Flywheel puller setup

A   Flywheel nut
B   Flywheel puller mounting screws (x3)
C   Flywheel puller and pressure bolt
D   Flywheel holder

6.6 The Woodruff key (arrow) is installed in a keyway in the crankshaft

6.7a Remove the starter drive assembly (arrow) . . .

6.7b . . . while making sure to retreive both thrust washers

6.8 Wiring harness guide screws (A) and guide (B)

6.9 Stator coil assembly details

A   *Stator coil*
B   *Stator coil mounting screws*
C   *Wiring harness grommet*

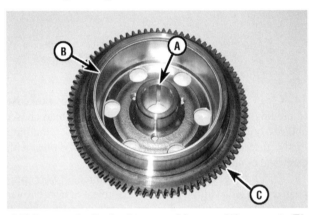

6.10 Inspect the flywheel taper and keyway (A), magnets (B) and starter drive gear teeth (C) for damage; make sure there are no screws or other metal parts stuck to the magnets

8   Remove the two screws and the wiring harness guide **(see illustration)**.

> *NOTE:*
>
> *With the two wiring harness guide screws removed, do not bump the stator cover as it is possible to break the gasket seal between the stator housing and crankcase. This will require removal of the stator cover in order to install a new gasket. If you do not plan on removing the stator housing, reinstall the two wiring harness guide mounting screws to hold the housing in place.*

9   Remove the stator coil mounting screws. Then free the wiring harness grommet from the notch in the stator housing, and remove the stator coil **(see illustration)**.

Inspection

10   Inspect the flywheel for cracks and other damage. Check the keyway in the flywheel to make sure the sides are straight and there is no sign of wear. Remove rust with sandpaper, then clean and dry the flywheel **(see illustration)**.

11   Check the gear teeth on the flywheel and the starter drive for excessive wear, cracks and other damage **(see illustration 6.10)**. These are mating gear teeth and should show the same wear patterns. Replace the flywheel and starter drive as a set if the gear teeth are damaged.

12   The flywheel is equipped with a 60-tooth ring gear and a gap with two consecutive teeth missing **(see illustration)**. This gap is the trigger that generates a signal in the crankshaft position sensor as the crankshaft rotates. Inspect and make sure there is no damage in this area.

13   Inspect the starter drive assembly for any visual wear or other damage while also referring to Step 11 to inspect the gear teeth. You should be able to slide the outer gear outward by hand to make sure it is not binding or damaged **(see illustration)**. The starter drive is not rebuildable.

Installation

6.12 The gap (arrow) left by the missing teeth on the ring gear is the signal trigger for the ignition system

NOTE:

If you previously installed the two wiring harness guide screws to hold the stator housing in place, remove them now.

14   Clean all of the exposed screw holes in the crankcase (including the stator coil screw holes) with a thread chaser and/or a brush to remove all of the old threadlock remaining in the thread grooves. Then flush the screw holes with electrical contact cleaner and allow to dry.

15   The wiring harness guide screw threads were pre-coated with a dry film threadlock that releases evenly over the threads when the screws are installed and tightened. However, when you loosen and remove the screws, the threadlock bond between the two thread sets is destroyed. If you will reuse the original screws, first run a thread chaser along the screws to remove any remaining threadlock from the thread grooves. A wire brush is also helpful. Then clean the screws with an aerosol electrical contact cleaner and allow to dry. Clean the screws now so they will be ready to use when installing the wiring harness guide.

16   Before installing the stator coil, check for an oil leak between the stator housing and crankcase. If necessary, remove the stator housing and install a new gasket (Section 8).

17   Align and install the stator coil over the crankshaft and seat it against the stator housing so that its wiring harness grommet is aligned with the notch in the stator housing. Then install the stator coil mounting screws and tighten to the torque listed in this Chapter's Specifications. Apply dielectric grease to the wiring harness grommet and push the grommet into the notch in the stator housing **(see illustration 6.9)**.

18   Install the wiring harness guide and two new screws. If installing the original screws, make sure the threads are clean and dry and apply a medium strength threadlock onto the screw threads (see Step 15). Tighten the screws in two or three steps to the torque listed in this Chapter's Specifications **(see illustration 6.8)**.

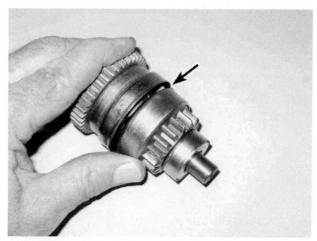

6.13 Slide the outer gear (arrow) outward by hand to make sure there is no binding or roughness

19   Lubricate the starter drive shafts and both thrust washers with dielectric grease, noting that the thrust washers are identical **(see illustration 6.7b)**. Then install a thrust washer onto the starter drive's inner and outer shafts, and install the starter drive assembly into its bore in the stator housing **(see illustration 6.7a)**. Turn the starter drive by hand to make sure there is no binding or roughness.

20   Install the Woodruff key into the keyway in the flywheel **(see illustration 6.6)**.

21   Spray the crankshaft and flywheel tapers with electrical contact cleaner to remove all oil and grease from these surfaces. Allow both surfaces to dry before installing the flywheel.

22   Check the inside of the flywheel to make sure there are no small screws or metal parts stuck to the magnets. Then install the flywheel by aligning its keyway with the Woodruff key. When the flywheel is seated on the

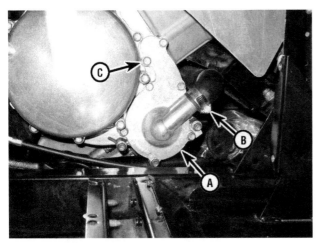

7.2 Water pump cover details

A   Water pump cover
B   Coolant hose and clamp
C   Water pump cover screws

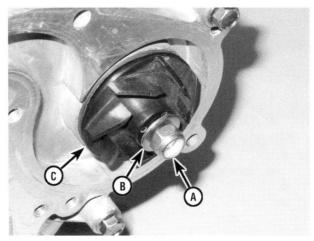

7.4a Remove the nut (A), washer (B) and impeller (C)

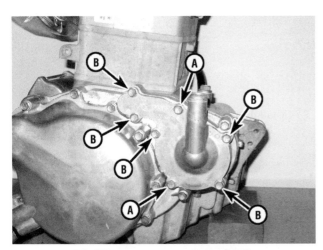

7.3a Water pump cover screw details

A   Long screws
B   Short screws

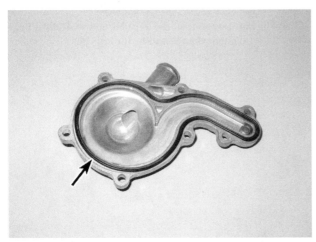

7.3b The O-ring fits in a groove in the water pump cover

crankshaft, use a flashlight and check that the Woodruff key aligns with the flywheel keyway and was not pushed out by the flywheel. Install the washer and the flywheel nut and tighten finger-tight. Hold the flywheel with the same tool used during removal and tighten the flywheel nut to the torque listed in this Chapter's Specifications.

23   Install the alternator cover (see Section 5).

7   WATER PUMP COVER AND IMPELLER - REMOVAL, INSPECTION AND INSTALLATION

1   The water pump cover, impeller and impeller seal can be serviced with the engine installed in the frame. The water pump mechanical seal is positioned behind the impeller and installed in the stator housing. To replace this seal, it is necessary to remove the stator housing (see Section 8). One way to check for a damaged water pump mechanical seal is to look for signs of coolant at the coolant weep hole located in the bottom of the stator housing (see Chapter 2, Section 25).

Removal

2   If the engine is mounted in the frame, drain the cooling system (see Chapter 2). Remove the fuel tank if it will provide additional access to the water pump cover (see Chapter 7). Then clean the coolant hose and the water pump cover to prevent sand and dirt from entering the engine. Loosen the hose clamp and disconnect the hose at the water pump cover **(see illustration)**.

3   Loosen and remove the water pump cover mounting screws, making sure to note the location of the two long screws **(see illustration)**. Tap the cover to free it and remove it with its O-ring **(see illustration)**. Discard the O-ring.

4   To remove the impeller, loosen and remove the nut and washer, then slide the impeller off its shaft **(see illustration)**.

7.4b If necessary, hold the flywheel with a holder to prevent the impeller from turning when loosening and tightening the nut (arrow)

If the engine has been removed from the frame, hold the flywheel with a holder to prevent the water pump shaft from turning when loosening the nut **(see illustration)**.

5   The impeller seal is now accessible **(see illustration)**. If necessary, remove this seal by sliding it off the shaft, first noting which side of the seal faces out.

Inspection

6   Clean the water pump cover and inspect it for cracks, warpage and other damage. Make sure the O-ring groove in the cover is clean.

7   Clean the impeller and inspect it for any heat related damage. Replace the impeller if necessary.

8   Inspect the impeller seal for any visible signs of wear and and replace if damaged. Note that this seal is only available with the purchase of a new water pump mechanical seal, as both are sold as a set. See Section 8 for additional information on both seals.

Installation

9   Clean the water/oil pump shaft. Install the impeller seal with its ceramic side seating against the water pump mechanical seal **(see illustration and illustration 7.5)**.

10   Align the flats on the impeller with the flats on the shaft **(see illustration)** and install the impeller over the shaft and seat it against its seal. Then install the washer and a new nut **(see illustration 7.4a)** and tighten to the torque listed in this Chapter's Specifications.

11   Install a new O-ring into the water pump cover groove **(see illustration 7.3b)**. Do not lubricate this O-ring as it should be installed dry.

12   Install the water pump cover and its mounting screws, making sure to install the two longer screws in their proper locations **(see illustration 7.3a)**. Tighten the screws in numerical order **(see illustration)** and in two steps to the torque listed in this Chapter's Specifications.

7.5 The impeller seal (arrow) is installed behind the impeller and seats against the water pump mechanical seal. Remove the seal by sliding it off the shaft

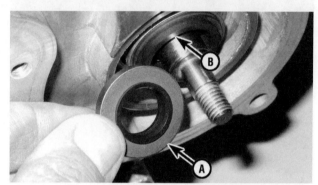

7.9 Install the impeller seal with its ceramic side (A) facing toward the water pump mechanical seal (B)

7.10 The flats (arrows) on the impeller and shaft must be aligned when installing the impeller

7.12 Tighten the water pump cover screws in numerical order and in two steps to the specified torque

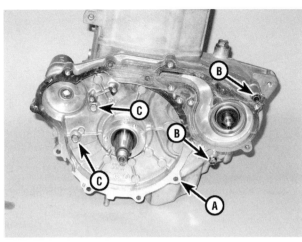

8.5a Stator housing details

A   Stator housing
B   Stator housing mounting screws
C   Wiring harness guide mounting screws

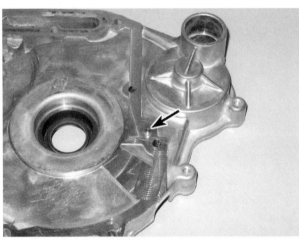

8.5b Note the alignment pin (arrow) installed in the stator housing

8.10 Drive the old crankshaft oil seal out of the stator housing with a seal driver or socket

13   The remainder of installation is the reverse of removal. If the engine is installed in the frame, fill and bleed the cooling system (see Chapter 2).

8   STATOR HOUSING - REMOVAL, SEAL REPLACEMENT AND INSTALLATION

1   The stator housing is installed on the MAG side of the engine between the alternator cover and the engine crankcase and can be replaced with the engine installed in the frame. Three seals are installed in the stator housing - right-side crankshaft oil seal, water pump mechanical seal and the inner water pump oil seal. Whenever the stator housing has been removed from the engine, replace these seals.

Removal

2   Remove the alternator cover (see Section 5).
3   Remove the flywheel, starter drive and stator coil (see Section 6).
4   Remove the water pump cover and impeller (see Section 7).
5   Remove the two stator housing mounting screws **(see illustration)**. If you reinstalled the two wiring harness guide screws after you removed the stator coil, remove them now. Tap the stator housing to break its seal and remove it from the engine. Don't pry between the housing and engine as this will damage the gasket surfaces. Locate the alignment pin pressed into the stator housing and remove if loose **(see illustration)**.

Seal replacement

6   The oil seals installed in the stator housing should be replaced whenever there are signs of oil or coolant leakage, or when the stator housing has been removed from the engine.
7   Before removing these oil seals, refer to the General Information chapter at the front of this manual for additional information on oil seal replacement.
8   Before removing an oil seal, note how it is installed in the stator housing and which side of the seal faces out.
9   To prevent from damaging the stator housing gasket surfaces, support the housing on wooden blocks or thick rubber pads when replacing the seals.

Crankshaft oil seal

10   Position the stator housing with its outside half facing up. Place a seal driver or socket against the seal and drive the seal out of its mounting bore **(see illustration)**.
11   Clean the seal bore and inspect it for any cracks, scoring or other damage.
12   Support the stator housing with its inside half facing up. The oil seal has a shoulder and must be installed from this side. Center the new seal into the bore with its shoulder facing up. Use a socket or driver that seats against the

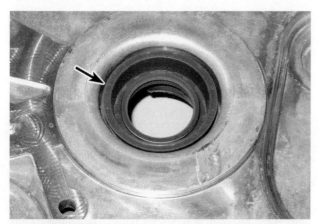

8.12a Center the new seal into the bore with its shoulder facing up toward the inside of the housing . . .

8.12b . . . then use a socket or bearing driver to drive the seal into its bore . . .

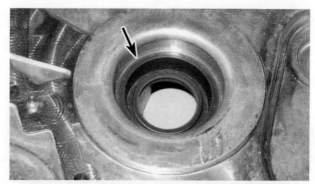

8.12c . . . until the seal's shoulder bottoms against the bore edge

8.14 Pry the inner oil seal out of its bore

8.15a Drive the water pump mechanical seal out of its bore from the inside out

8.15b The water pump mechanical seal removed from its bore - the blue debris pasted along the bore surface is sealer residue that peeled off the outside of the seal when it was removed

outer edge of the seal and drive it into the bore until its shoulder bottoms squarely against the edge of the bore **(see illustrations)**.

Water pump mechanical seal and inner oil seal

13   The water pump mechanical seal is installed on the outside of the housing, and the inner oil seal is installed on the inside of the housing.

14   Support the stator housing with its inside half facing up, and carefully pry the inner oil seal out of its bore with a large wide-blade screwdriver or similar tool. When removing the seal, place a rag placed between the pry tool and the housing to protect the housing gasket surface from damage **(see illustration)**.

15   With the stator housing still supported with its inside half facing up, use a socket and drive the water pump mechanical seal out of its bore **(see illustrations)**.

16   With both seals removed, inspect their bores for any surface roughness or other damage. If there is any sealer residue remaining on the water pump bore surface **(see illustration 8.15b)**, remove as much of the material as possible without scratching the seal bore.

8.17 The coolant weep hole in the seal bore must be clear before installing the water pump mechanical seal - push a Q-Tip through it to check

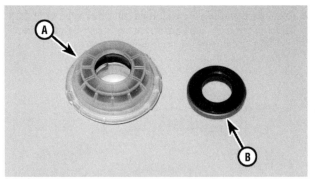

8.18a Purchase a new water pump mechanical seal (A), noting that the impeller seal (B) is included in the kit - set the impeller seal aside and install it later with the impeller

8.18b The water pump mechanical seal is installed in and protected by a stiff plastic cover. Using a pair of pliers, carefully bend the lip on the plastic cover outward in several places to free it from the seal

8.18c The seal and cover - discard the cover

8.18d Before installing the seal (A), locate a driver (B) that fits against the seal's shoulder, but does not contact the seal or its spring

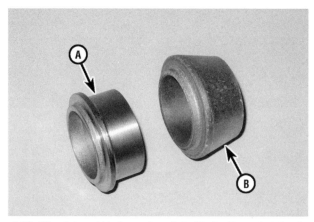

8.18e The driver (A) shown here is half of a discarded deadbolt assembly (used for a household door) with its shoulder machined on a lathe to fit the seal's shoulder - the other half of the deadbolt (B) is shown for comparison. The part No. for the Polaris Water Pump Mechanical Seal Installer is PA-44995

17 After cleaning the cover, make sure the coolant weep hole in the housing bore is clear and unobstructed (see illustration).

18 Follow the accompanying illustrations to install a new water pump mechanical seal (see illustrations 9.18a through 9.18h).

CAUTION:

In Step 18, if the inner oil seal is installed too deeply in its bore, it may block off the coolant weep hole (see illustration 8.18h).

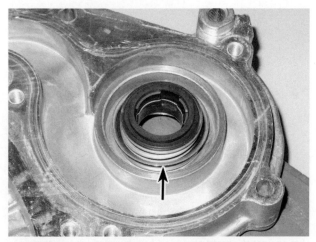

8.18f With the outside of the stator housing facing up, center the seal into its bore . . .

8.18h After installing the seal, turn the cover over and check that a portion of the coolant weep hole (arrow) is visible below the bottom of the seal

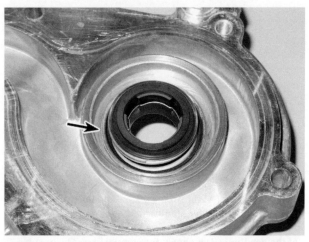

8.18g . . . and use the driver to drive the seal into its bore until its shoulder seats squarely against the stator housing

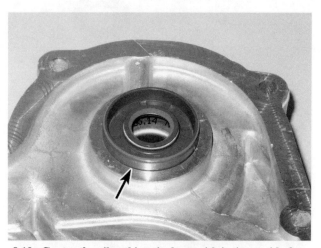

8.19a Center the oil seal into its bore with its inner side facing up . . .

19   Position the stator housing with its inner half facing up. Then center the inner oil seal into its bore with its open side facing up (away from the water pump mechanical seal installed in Step 18). Drive or press the seal into its bore until the edge of the seal is even with its bore's outer surface **(see illustrations)**.

Installation

20   Polaris recommends the use of two seal saver tools when installing the stator housing, one to protect the crankshaft seal and the other to protect the two water pump seals **(see illustration)**. The seal savers are thin plastic cylinders, open on one end and tapered on the other end. These tools are installed over the end of the crankshaft and water pump shafts with their tapered ends facing outward. When the stator cover is installed onto the engine, the

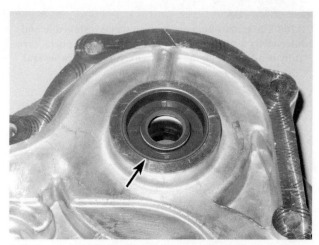

8.19b . . . and drive the seal into its bore until its edge is even with the bore surface

8.20 Polaris seal saver tools

A   *Crankshaft Seal Saver - part No. PA-45658*
B   *Water Pump Seal Saver - part No. PA-45401*

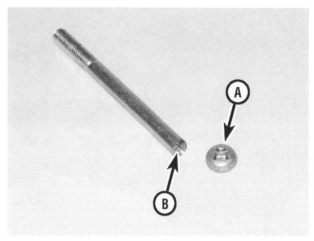

8.21c To make a guide pin, cut the head off of a suitable length screw (A), then cut a slot in the top of the screw (B) so that it can be turned with a screwdriver

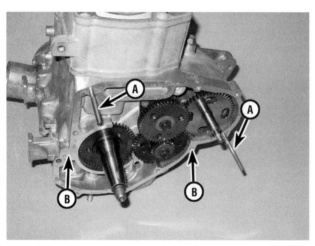

8.21a Thread two guide pins (A) into the crankcase, then apply a dab of sealant onto the two crankcase mating surface areas (B) . . .

8.21b . . . and install a new gasket over the guide pins and seat it against the crankcase. Leave the guide pins in place for now

scals installed in the cover pass over the seal savers, thus avoiding any contact with sharp edges on the shafts that could damage their lips. If you have access to the seal savers, use them as described in the procedure. If not, use care when installing the stator housing.

NOTE:

The crankshaft seal saver tool described in Step 20 was also used to form the lip on older style crankshaft seals with paper lips that were used in Polaris 800 engines installed in other models. After the crankshaft seal is installed in the stator housing, the tool is pushed through the back side of the seal, where its tapered end forms the seal's lip. The stator housing crankshaft seal used on Polaris Ranger 800 models does not use a paper lip.

21   Because there are no dowel pins that can be used to hold and align the gasket when installing the stator housing, thread two 6 mm guide pins into the crankcase. Apply a gasket sealant to the two seams formed by the upper and lower crankcase mating surfaces, then slide a new gasket over the guide pins and seat it against the crankcase. Leave the guide pins in place until removed in Step 25 **(see illustrations)**.

NOTE:

To fabricate a guide pin, use a hacksaw to cut the head off of a 6 mm screw that is long enough for the stator housing to pass over. Then cut a slot across the screw head so you can turn the screw with a screwdriver. Repeat to make a second screw (see illustration).

8.22 The water pump seal saver tool (arrow) installed on the water/oil pump shaft

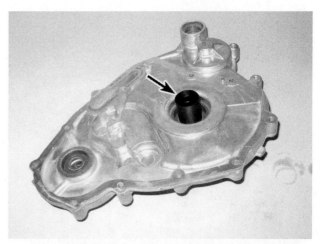

8.23 Using its tapered end first, push the crankshaft seal saver tool through the inside of the seal and leave it there until after the stator housing is installed

22   If available, install the water pump seal saver onto the water/oil pump shaft **(see illustration)**.

23   If available, and using its tapered end first, push the crankshaft seal saver tool through the inside of the seal and leave it there until after the stator housing is installed onto the engine **(see illustration)**.

24   Install the stator housing, while making sure the crankshaft seal saver tool (if used) passes over the crankshaft, and that the inner oil seal/water pump mechanical seal passes over the water pump seal saver tool (if used). When seating the housing, make sure the alignment pin in the housing seats into the hole in the crankcase **(see illustration 8.5b)**. If you are using the guide pins, the stator housing should align with and slide squarely against the gasket/crankcase **(see illustration)**. If you did not use the guide pins, check that the gasket aligns with the holes in the stator housing and crankcase.

25   If used, remove the two guide pins while holding the cover in place. Install and finger-tighten the two stator housing screws and the two wiring harness guide screws **(see illustration 8.5a)**. Note that you will remove the two wiring harness guide screws before you install the stator. With all four screws installed, tighten them in numerical order, and in two steps to the torque listed in this Chapter's Specifications **(see illustration)**. If used, remove the crankshaft and water pump seal saver tools **(see illustration 8.20)**.

26   The remainder of installation is the reverse of removal.

9   TIMING GEARS - TOOLS, REMOVAL, CAMSHAFT GEAR AND INSTALLATION

1   The timing gear assembly is installed on the MAG side of the engine behind the stator housing **(see illustration)**.

2   If any gear is worn or damaged, replace all three timing gears and the water/oil pump gear as a set.

8.24 Install the stator housing (arrow) over the guide pins and seat it against the gasket

8.25 Stator housing and wiring harness guide screw torque sequence

9.1 Timing gear assembly details and timing marks

A   *Crankshaft gear*
B   *Camshaft gear assembly*
C   *Balancer gear*
D   *Water/oil pump gear*
E   *Crankshaft gear and balancer gear timing marks*
F   *Camshaft gear and balancer gear timing marks*

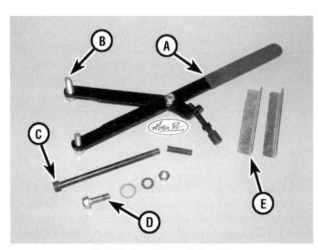

9.4 Timing gear tool details

A   *Motion Pro Rotor & Sprocket Holder (part No. 08-0270)*
B   *M8-1.25 x 35 mm and M8-1.25 x 45 mm bolts and nuts used to replace the original pins installed in the holder*
C   *M8-1.25 x 160 mm screw with the threads cut off. The screw shank is used as an alignment pin to hold and align the camshaft gear assembly during removal and installation*
D   *M8-1.25 x 25 mm bolt, flat washers and nut. These are used to hold the camshaft gear assembly together when assembling and aligning the gears*
E   *Aluminum plates used to soften the vise jaws when holding the camshaft gear assembly in a vise during its assembly*

Tools

3   The following Polaris factory tools, or equivalents, are needed when servicing the timing gears:

Cam spanner wrench: Polaris part number PU-45498. This tool is used to turn the engine when it is necessary to reposition the camshaft. This tool is only necessary if the rocker arms are installed on the engine and the camshaft

is under tension. If the rocker arms are removed from the engine, the camshaft can be turned by hand.

Cam gear alignment tool: Polaris part No. PU-45497-2. This tool is used to align the camshaft gear assembly (inner and outer camshaft gears) when removing and installing the gear.

Cam gear tooth alignment tool (three tapered pins): Polaris part No. PU-45497-1. These are used to align the camshaft gears after assembling them.

Gear holder: Polaris part No. PU-45838. This tool is used to hold the camshaft and balancer shaft gears when loosening and tightening their mounting bolts.

4   If you don't have access to the Polaris factory tools described in Step 3, the Motion Pro Rotor & Socket Holder (part No. 08-0270) and some metric fasteners can be used in their place **(see illustration)**. Before using the Motion Pro tool, it is necessary to remove the original pins from the tool and replace them with longer 8 mm bolts. The Motion Pro tool is used in this section to remove and install the timing gears and is referred to as a holder. Refer to Section 6 for additional information on the Motion Pro Rotor & Sprocket Holder and how to modify it.

5   To remove the balancer shaft and crankshaft gears in this section, the Polaris flywheel puller (part No. 2871043) or an equivalent aftermarket puller is required. This is the same tool used to remove the flywheel and described in Section 6. In this section, this tool is referred to as a flywheel puller.

Removal

6   Remove the alternator cover (see Section 5).
7   Remove the stator housing (see Section 8).
8   Remove the spark plugs (see Chapter 2).
9   Rotate the crankshaft clockwise, when viewed from the MAG side, until the timing marks on the crankshaft gear and balancer gear and the timing marks on the camshaft gear and the balancer gear align **(see illustration 9.1)**. Use a white marker and highlight each timing mark.

NOTE:

The camshaft gear is an assembly of two gears attached side-by-side and assembled so that the teeth on the outer gear are off-set by one-half of a tooth. The outer gear is also spring loaded. To install the camshaft gear, the teeth on the outer gear are first aligned with the teeth on the inner gear by inserting an alignment tool through both gears. After installing the camshaft gear assembly, the tool is removed and the springs force the outer gear to mesh against the balancer gear. Operating under tension, the outer gear helps to reduce backlash between the camshaft and balancer gears. Step 10 describes how to install an alignment pin in the gear so that when you remove the gear, it is not under tension and can be easily removed and not separate.

9.10a Hold the camshaft gear with the holder (A) and loosen the camshaft gear screw (B) - do not remove the screw at this time

9.10c After removing the camshaft gear screw and washer previously loosened, remove the camshaft gear assembly with the alignment pin (arrow)

9.10b Insert the alignment pin (arrow) through one of the 8-mm holes in the outer camshaft gear, then continue pushing it so that it enters the hole in the inner gear

9.11a Turn the camshaft until the timing marks on the crankshaft gear (A) and the balancer gear (B) are 180-degrees opposed, which positions the camshaft with its flat side facing toward the balancer gear (C)

10   The camshaft gear assembly is removed first. Insert the two bolts on the holder into the two 8 mm holes in the camshaft gear and prop the holder against a wooden block to hold it in place, then loosen, but do not remove, the camshaft gear screw **(see illustration)**. Remove the holder from the camshaft gear. Then install the alignment pin into one of the 8 mm holes and push it through both camshaft gears to hold the gears in alignment **(see illustration)**. Remove the camshaft gear screw and washer, then remove the camshaft gear assembly with the alignment pin **(see illustration)**.

11   If the rocker arms are installed on the engine, rotate the camshaft until the camshaft gear and balancer gear timing marks are 180-degrees opposed, which will align the flat part of the camshaft with the balancer gear **(see illustration)**. This alignment positions both pistons at bottom dead center, so there is no chance of piston-to-valve

9.11b Here the camshaft is being turned with the Polaris cam spanner wrench (arrow) . . .

4

9.11c . . . and with the camshaft gear installed on the camshaft, the camshaft is being turned with the holder (arrow). Here it is necessary to temporarily reinstall the camshaft gear so that it can be used to turn the camshaft

9.12c . . . or remove it with the same puller used to remove the flywheel

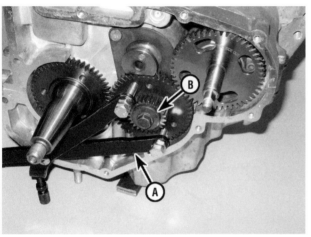

9.12a Hold the balancer gear with the holder (A) and remove the balancer gear screw and washer (B)

9.12d Remove and discard the Woodruff key

9.12b Try to remove the balancer gear by sliding it off its shaft. However, if the gear is tight, remove it with a knock puller (arrow) . . .

contact. To turn the camshaft while it is under tension, use the Polaris cam spanner wrench (see illustration) or temporarily reinstall the camshaft gear assembly onto the camshaft and turn the camshaft with the holder (see illustration).

NOTE:
Refer to Steps 15-19 to service and inspect the camshaft gear assembly.

12   Hold the balancer gear with the holder and remove its screw and washer (see illustration). Try to slide the balancer gear off its shaft by hand. If the gear is tight, either use a knock puller threaded into one of the gear's 6 mm bolt holes or use the flywheel puller used to remove the gear (see illustrations). Remove the Woodruff key from the balancer shaft and discard it (see illustration). A new one must be installed during installation.

9.13 Do not remove the crankshaft gear unless it is damaged, or if you are replacing the timing gear set, the crankshaft gear must be replaced as part of the set, along with the water/oil pump gear

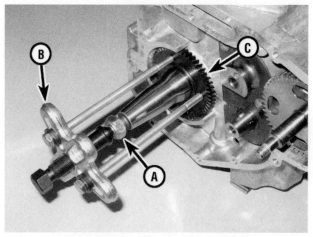

9.14 Crankshaft gear removal details

A   Flywheel nut
B   Flywheel puller
C   Crankshaft gear

13   Check each gear for broken or chipped teeth, including the crankshaft gear, which is still mounted on the crankshaft **(see illustration)**. If any gear is worn or damaged, replace all three timing gears and the water/oil pump gear as a set.

14   If replacing the crankshaft gear, first thread the flywheel nut onto the end of the crankshaft so the outer edge of the nut aligns with the end of the crankshaft. Note that installing the nut will allow you to use it to chase the crankshaft threads if the end of the crankshaft mushrooms when pressure is applied against it. Then mount the flywheel puller onto the crankshaft gear by threading the three puller screws fully into the gear. Make sure the puller is centered with the crankshaft, then turn the center screw on the puller and pull the gear off the crankshaft **(see illustration)**.

Camshaft gear

15   The tools described in Step 3 and Step 4 can be used to assemble and align the camshaft gear assembly.

WARNING:

Because the gear assembly is spring loaded and the springs may fly out when removing the outer gear, wear safety glasses or goggles to prevent eye injury.

16   Set the camshaft gear on the bench with the timing mark on the outer gear facing out **(see illustration)**. If you haven't done so, remove the alignment tool from the gears. Hold both gears with one hand to prevent them from flying apart, then with your other hand insert a small screwdriver between the gears and pry them apart to free the dogs on the outer gear from their contact with the springs. The outer gear is now free and can be removed **(see illustration)**.

17   Inspect the gear teeth and the dogs on the outer gear for any damage, then inspect the inner gear teeth for the same conditions **(see illustration 9.16b)**. Compare the length of the three springs, as they should all be the same.

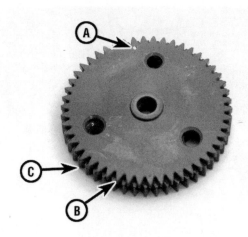

9.16a Camshaft gear details (assembled)

A   Timing mark
B   Outer gear
C   Inner gear

9.16b Camshaft gear details (disassembled)

A   Outer gear
B   Inner gear
C   Springs
D   Spring grooves
E   Dogs
F   Inner gear timing mark

9.18 For visual help when assembling the camshaft gear assembly, make a dot mark on the end of each spring groove as shown here (arrows) and use them to indicate the side of the groove where the dogs on the outer gear will be installed

9.19c Use a bolt, washers and nut to hold the gear assembly together. Do not tighten the nut as it will be necessary to turn the outer gear when aligning it

9.19a Begin assembly by marking the timing marks on the outer (A) and inner (B) gears with a white marker

9.19d Mount the inner camshaft gear (A) in a vise with soft jaws - do not clamp the outer gear (A) as you need to turn it when installing the alignment tool

9.19b Align the timing marks on both gears, then align the dogs on the outer gear with the gaps above the springs and install the outer gear into place against the inner gear - when assembled, the gear teeth will not align (this is normal)

Also inspect the springs for any cracked or stretched coils. Replace the gear assembly if any part is damaged. If just the springs require replacement, check with a dealership to see if a spring replacement kit is available. If not, the gear must be replaced as an assembly.

18   Install the springs into the grooves in the inner gear. Then make a mark above each spring groove and slide the springs away from the marks (see illustration). This positions the springs in their grooves while providing room for the dogs when installing the outer gear.

19   Follow the accompanying illustrations to assemble and align the camshaft gear assembly so that it is ready for installation into the engine (see illustrations 9.19a through 9.19f).

9.19e Mount the holder into two of the holes in the outer gear, and turn the outer gear (A) to align the teeth on both gears. When the gear teeth are in alignment, install the alignment pin (B) through both gears

Installation

> *WARNING:*
>
> *The crankshaft gear will be very hot when installing it onto the crankshaft. Welding gloves must be worn to protect your hands from serious burns.*

> *NOTE:*
>
> *When it is necessary to turn the crankshaft in this section, install the Woodruff key and flywheel onto the crankshaft, then turn the flywheel by hand*

20   If the crankshaft gear was removed, clean the end of the crankshaft with electrical contact cleaner and allow to dry as this surface must be free of all oil and grease when installing the gear. Then repeat to clean the new gear and allow it to dry. Place the gear on a hot plate or into a shop oven with the side marked "This Side Out" facing up. This side of the gear must be installed on the crankshaft so that it is facing out (away from the engine). Monitor the gear's temperature with an infrared thermometer and heat it to 250-degrees F (121-degrees C). When the gear is at the correct temperature, apply Loctite 242 to the gear's mating surface on the crankshaft. Then while wearing welding gloves, align the flat on the crankshaft gear with the shoulder on the crankshaft and quickly slide the gear onto the crankshaft until it bottoms **(see illustration)**.

21   If the rocker arms and pushrods are installed on the engine, perform Step 11 to turn the camshaft so that its flat faces toward the balancer shaft. If you do not have access to the Polaris cam spanner wrench described in Step 11, temporarily reinstall the camshaft gear assembly onto the camshaft, along with its bolt and washer and tighten finger-tight, then turn the camshaft with the holder until the flat on the camshaft is facing toward the balancer shaft **(see illustrations)**. If the camshaft is not under tension, you can

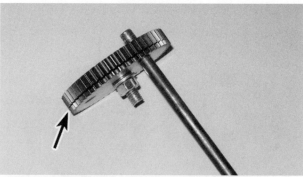

9.19f With the alignment pin installed, remove the nut, washers and bolt used to hold the gears together (arrow). Do not remove the alignment pin until after the gear assembly is installed on the engine. Set the gear assembly aside until you are ready to install it

9.20 Install the crankshaft gear onto the crankshaft with the side marked "This Side Out" (arrow) facing out

9.21a When the rocker arms and pushrods are installed in the engine, use the holder and camshaft gear assembly to turn the camshaft . . .

9.21b . . . until the flat on the camshaft (arrow) is facing toward the balancer shaft

9.22 Align the balancer gear (A) and crankshaft gear (B) timing marks

9.24b . . . and aligning the timing mark on the camshaft gear assembly with the timing mark on the balancer gear (arrows)

9.23 Hold the balancer gear with the holder (A) and tighten its screw (B) to the specified torque

9.24a Install the camshaft gear by inserting its pin (A) into the hole in the camshaft (B) . . .

turn it by hand to align it.

22 Install a new Woodruff key into the groove in the balancer shaft (see illustration 9.12d). Align the balancer gear keyway with the Woodruff key, and slide the gear part way onto the balancer shaft with its timing marks facing out. Then align the timing mark on the balancer gear with the timing mark on the crankshaft gear and push the balancer gear into place. The balancer gear must bottom on its shaft and mesh with the teeth on the crankshaft gear and the teeth on the water/oil pump gear (see illustration).

23 Install the balancer gear screw and its washer. Then hold the balancer gear with the holder, and tighten the balancer gear screw to the torque listed in this Chapter's Specifications (see illustration).

24 Install the camshaft gear by aligning its pin with the hole in the camshaft. If necessary, turn the balancer gear screw to help align the camshaft pin with the hole in the camshaft, and install the camshaft gear until it bottoms. Then check that the timing mark on the camshaft gear aligns with the timing mark on the balancer gear (see illustrations). When the camshaft gear is installed and the timing marks are aligned, hold the gear in place and remove the alignment pin.

NOTE:

If it is difficult to align the camshaft timing mark with the balancer gear timing mark, turn the camshaft as required. If the rocker arms are installed on the engine, you will not be able to turn the camshaft by hand. Instead, turn the camshaft as described in Step 11.

25 With all of the gears installed, check that the timing marks align (see illustration 9.1). If not, refer to the previous steps to remove and retime the gears. When the gears are properly timed, align the bevel washer with its concave side facing toward the engine, and place it on the camshaft gear's shoulder. Hold the washer in place and

9.25a Install the bevel washer onto the camshaft shoulder (arrow) with its concave side facing the engine. Install the screw and tighten finger-tight, then remove the alignment pin

9.25b Hold the camshaft gear with the holder (A) and tighten the camshaft gear screw (B) to the specified torque

install the screw finger-tight, then remove the alignment pin. Hold the camshaft gear with the holder and tighten the camshaft gear screw to the torque listed in this Chapter's Specifications **(see illustrations)**.

26 When the balancer shaft and crankshaft screws are tight, turn the crankshaft several times and then stop and make a final check that the timing marks are correct **(see illustration)**.

27 The remainder of installation is the reverse of removal.

9.26 Turn the engine over several times, then align the timing marks (arrows) to make sure they are correct

10 OIL PUMP - REMOVAL, INSPECTION, DISASSEMBLY, ASSEMBLY AND INSTALLATION

1 A single shaft installed inside the oil pump operates both the oil pump and water pump. The water pump/oil pump gear is pressed onto the shaft.

Removal

2 Remove the camshaft gear and balancer gear (see Section 9).

3 Rotate the water/oil pump gear until the oil pump mounting screws are visible through the holes in the gear. Then loosen and remove the screws and pull the pump from the crankcase, while at the same time using one hand to hold the back of the pump to prevent the rotors from falling out **(see illustrations)**.

Inspection

4 Mark the inner and outer rotors so they can be reinstalled with the same side facing out **(see illustration)**.

5 Insert a feeler gauge between the inner rotor tip and the outer rotor and measure the tip clearance **(see illustration)**.

10.3a Remove the oil pump mounting screws . . .

10.3b . . . and the oil pump - note that the rotors installed in the back of the pump can fall out if not held in place

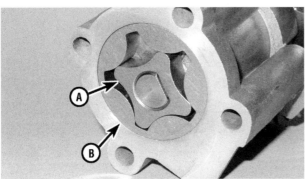

10.4 Mark the outside of the inner (A) and outer (B) rotors so they can be reinstalled facing in their original direction

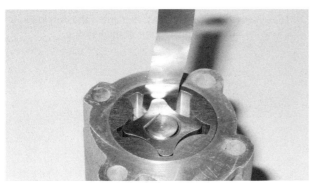

10.5 Measure the rotor tip clearance with a feeler gauge as shown

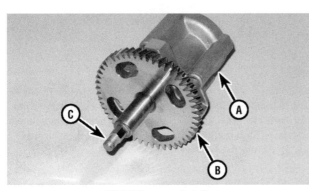

10.6 Oil pump details

A   Housing

B   Water pump/oil
    pump gear

C   Pump shaft

10.10 Inspect the pump rotors and the rotor bore for scoring and other damage

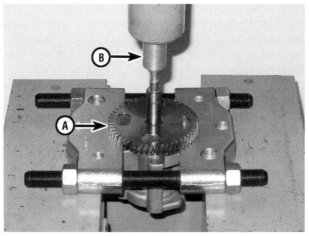

10.14 Support the gear (A) on a bearing splitter in a press, then place an aluminum drift (B) between the end of the shaft and the press to protect the shaft threads. Press the shaft out of the gear, making sure to catch the pump assembly to prevent it from falling to the floor

If the measurement exceeds the service limit listed in this Chapter's Specifications, replace the rotor assembly.

6   Rotate the pump shaft by hand to check the pump bearing **(see illustration)**. When turning the shaft, you shouldn't notice any noise or roughness coming from the bearing. If necessary, replace the bearing (see Steps 13 through 21).

7   Inspect the water pump/oil pump gear for missing or damaged gear teeth **(see illustration 10.6)**. If the gear is damaged, replace this gear and the timing gears as a set (see Section 9).

8   Remove the rotors, making sure they are marked for proper installation (see Step 4).

9   Clean all the components in solvent, making sure to remark the rotors so you can maintain their alignment.

10   Inspect the pump body and rotors for scoring and wear **(see illustration)**. If any damage, scoring, uneven or excessive wear is evident, replace the individual components or the complete pump assembly.

11   Inspect the pump shaft for bending, galling and other damage. Replace the shaft if necessary.

12   If oil pump service is required, continue with Step 13. If pump service is not required, remove any identification marks made on the original rotors. Lubricate the pump rotors with engine oil or assembly lube, then install the rotors facing in their original direction (see Step 4). Proceed to Step 22 to install the pump assembly.

Disassembly

13   Before disassembling the pump, check with a dealer parts department to make sure the replacement parts you need are available.

14   Support the water/oil pump gear in a press, and press the shaft from the gear **(see illustration)**. Be prepared to catch the pump assembly once the shaft releases from the gear.

15 Remove the snap ring from the groove in the housing. Then support the pump housing in a press with the bearing side of the housing facing down, and press the bearing and shaft assembly out of the housing **(see illustration)**.

16 Support the bearing in a press and press the shaft out of the bearing. Discard the bearing.

17 Discard the components that will be replaced and clean all of the reusable components in solvent.

Assembly

18 Support the new bearing in a press and press the shaft into the bearing until it bottoms. After removing the parts from the press, hold the bearing and turn the shaft by hand to make sure there is no binding or roughness. If the shaft turns roughly, the bearing was damaged when the shaft was installed.

19 Support the pump housing in a press with the snap ring groove side facing up. Position the bearing into its bore with the shaft's gear end facing up. Place a hollow driver against the bearing's outer race. The driver must not contact the shaft. Then press the bearing into its bore until it bottoms. Install a new snap ring into the groove in the pump housing. Make sure the snap ring is completely seated in the groove **(see illustration 10.15)**.

20 Support the pump housing in a press on two flat metal bars with the shaft's gear end facing up **(see illustration)**. The two metal bars provide clearance for the shaft, as it extends slightly past the bottom of the pump. Install the gear onto the shaft with the side marked "This Side Out" facing up and away from the pump housing. Then press the gear onto the shaft **(see illustration)**.

21 Remove any identification marks made on the original rotors. Lubricate the pump rotors with engine oil or assembly lube, then install the rotors into the pump facing in their original direction. Place the pump into a clean, plastic bag until installation.

Installation

22 The oil pump mounting screw threads were pre-coated with a dry film threadlock that releases evenly over the threads when the screws are installed and tightened. However, when loosening and removing the screws, the threadlock bond between the two thread sets is destroyed. If you will reuse the original screws, first run a thread chaser along the screws to remove any remaining threadlock from the thread grooves. A wire brush is also helpful. Then clean the screws with an aerosol electrical contact cleaner and allow to dry. Clean the screws now so they will be ready to use when installing the oil pump assembly.

23 Apply assembly lube or engine oil to the oil pump rotors **(see illustration)**. Then turn the pump shaft to distribute the lubricant.

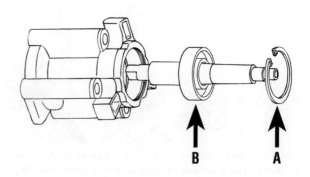

10.15 Remove the snap ring (A), then press the bearing and shaft assembly (B) out of the housing

10.20a Support the pump housing on two metal bars (A) to provide clearance for the pump shaft. Then place a hollow driver (B) over the shaft and rest it against the gear, and press the gear onto the shaft . . .

10.20b . . . with the side marked "THIS SIDE OUT" (arrow) facing away from the pump housing

10.23 Lubricate the oil pump rotors before installing the oil pump onto the engine

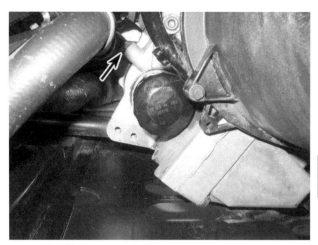

11.2 The oil pressure relief valve (arrow) is mounted in the upper crankcase, near the oil filter

10.25a When installing the oil pump, the pump and crankcase shoulders must align (arrows), then align the pump-to-crankcase screw holes

24   Clean the oil pump mounting screw threaded holes in the crankcase with electrical contact cleaner and allow to dry.

25   Install the oil pump into the crankcase and turn the gear until the holes in the gear align with the screw holes in the pump, and the shoulder on the pump aligns with the shoulder inside the crankcase (see illustration). Install new oil pump mounting screws. If reusing the original screws, apply Loctite 242 to the screw threads after cleaning the screws (see Step 22). Tighten the oil pump mounting screws in two steps and in numerical order to the torque listed in this Chapter's Specifications (see illustration).

26   Install the balancer gear and the camshaft gear (see Section 9).

11   OIL PRESSURE RELIEF VALVE - REMOVAL, INSPECTION AND INSTALLATION

1   The oil pressure relief valve can be serviced with the engine mounted in the frame.

2   Clean the area around the oil pressure relief valve bolt to prevent dirt and other debris from entering the oil passage when removing the bolt (see illustration).

NOTE:

The oil pressure relief valve is tapered on one end. When removing the valve, note which way the taper on one end of the valve is facing (it should be facing toward the engine). If the engine was recently rebuilt and is being serviced to troubleshoot a lubrication problem, the valve may have been installed upside down.

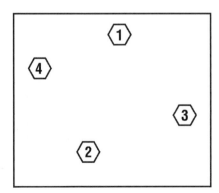

10.25b Tighten the oil pump mounting screws in numerical order and to the specified torque

3   Remove the bolt, washer, spring and the oil pressure relief valve **(see illustrations)**.

4   Clean the components in solvent. Do not scratch the oil pressure relief valve or the valve bore in the crankcase.

5   Inspect the spring for cracks and unevenly spaced spring coils. Do not attempt to stretch or repair the spring, as this will change the relief valve pressure setting, and possibly cause engine damage. Replace the spring if it appears stretched or damaged.

6   If the valve does not show any wear or damage, lubricate the valve and bore with new engine oil. Then install the valve into its bore with its tapered side facing down **(see illustration 11.3b)**. Install the spring, a new washer and the bolt **(see illustration 11.3a)**. Tighten the bolt to the torque listed in this Chapter's Specifications.

CAUTION:

Installing the oil pressure relief valve incorrectly (tapered end facing up) will affect the engine's oil pressure, and possibly cause severe engine damage. It will also affect the oil priming when first starting a reassembled engine.

12   CRANKCASE - DISASSEMBLY AND REASSEMBLY

1   To inspect and repair or replace the camshaft, balancer shaft, crankshaft, connecting rods, bearings, oil pickup and oil screen, the crankcase must be split into two parts.

Disassembly

2   Remove the engine unit from the frame (see Section 3).

3   Remove the starter motor (see Chapter 8).

4   Remove the valve cover (see Chapter 3).

5   Remove the rocker arms and pushrods (see Chapter 3).

6   Remove the cylinder head (see Chapter 3).

7   Remove the cylinder block and pistons (see Chapter 3).

8   Remove the valve lifters (see Chapter 3).

9   Remove the alternator cover (see Section 5).

10   Remove the flywheel, starter drive and stator (see Section 6).

11   Remove the water pump cover and impeller (see Section 7).

12   Remove the stator housing (see Section 8).

13   Remove the timing gears (see Section 9).

14   Remove the oil pump (see Section 10).

15   Remove the oil pressure relief valve (see Section 11).

16   Remove the Torx screws and the thrust plate **(see illustration)**.

17   Place the crankcase upside down on the workbench.

18   Two different length crankcase screws are used to secure the crankcase halves. Reverse the screw numerical order and loosen the crankcase screws in several stages and remove them **(see illustrations)**.

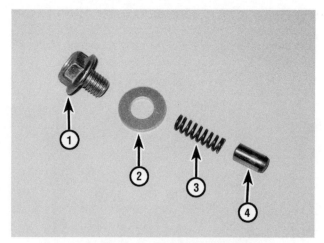

11.3a Oil pressure relief valve details

1   Bolt   4   Oil pressure
2   Washer   relief valve
3   Spring

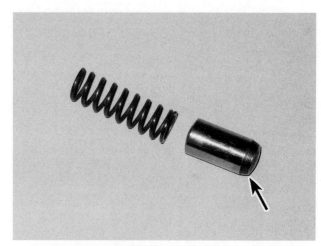

11.3b When removing the oil pressure valve, note that the tapered end should be facing down (arrow)

12.16 Remove the screws (A) and the thrust plate (B)

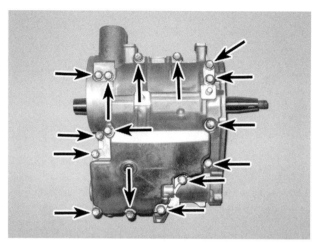

12.18a Crankcase mounting screw positions (arrows) in the lower crankcase

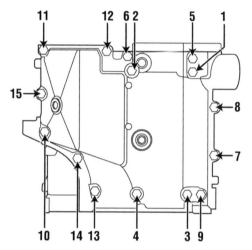

12.18b When loosening the screws, reverse the screw numerical order by starting with screw No. 15; when tightening the screws, follow the screw numerical order by starting with screw No. 1

12.19a Lift the lower crankcase half off the upper crankcase half - the crankshaft, balancer shaft and camshaft will remain in the upper crankcase half

12.19b Note the two dowel pin locations and remove them if loose

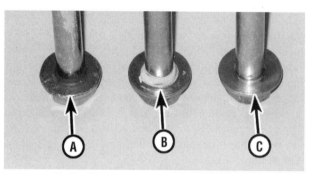

12.21a Crankcase screw and sealer details

A   New screw with pre-applied sealer
B   Used screw removed from engine showing remaining sealer
C   Used screw cleaned of all old sealer

19   Carefully lift the lower crankcase half from the upper half, using a soft-faced hammer to tap around the joint to initially separate the halves (see illustration). The lower crankcase half will come off leaving the crankshaft, balancer shaft and camshaft in the upper crankcase half. The oil pickup and baffle plate are installed in the lower crankcase half. Note that there will be one crankshaft main bearing insert and two balancer shaft bearing inserts installed in the lower crankcase half. Remove the two locating dowels from the crankcase if they are loose (they could be in either crankcase half), while noting their locations (see illustration).
20   Refer to Sections 14 through 19 for the removal and installation of the components housed within the crankcases.

Crankcase Assembly

21   The original crankcase mounting screws were installed with a pre-applied sealant under each screw flange, so that when the screws were tightened, the sealant would compress and provide an oil tight seal between the screw head and crankcase. When reassembling the crankcase halves, you have the option of installing new screws equipped with a pre-applied sealer, or you can reuse the original screws. When reusing the original screws, it is necessary to remove all of the original sealant from the screw flanges and clean the screws thoroughly (see illustration). Then right before

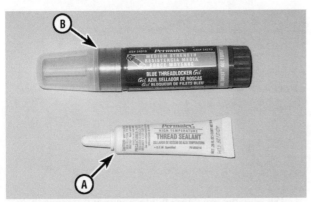

12.21b Permatex High Temperature Thread Sealant (A) - Permatex 242 Blue Threadlocker Gel (B)

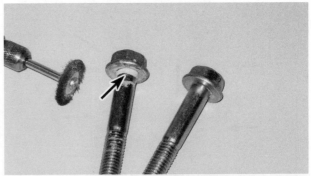

12.23 Remove stubborn bits of sealer from the screw flanges with a small wire wheel and grinder

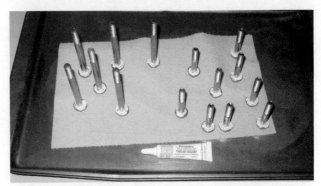

12.25 If reusing the crankcase screws, apply pipe sealant underneath each screw flange

12.26a Apply a suitable sealant to the upper crankcase mating surface . . .

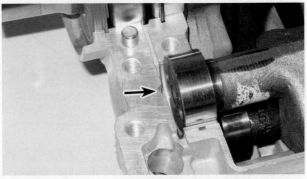

12.26b . . . making sure not to allow the sealant to enter or plug the camshaft relief hole (arrow) or contact the bearing inserts

you install the original screws, apply a ring of pipe sealant underneath each screw flange. The teardown engine shown in this section was assembled using Permatex High Temperature Thread Sealant (part No. 59214) on the screw flanges **(see illustration)**. Note that while this product is called a thread sealant, it is not a threadlocker. Also note that the Permatex High Temperature Thread Sealant used here was at one time sold under the name PST (Pipe Sealant With Teflon).

22 Clean and inspect the crankcase halves and all crankcase fasteners (see Section 13). Make sure to clean the threaded holes in the upper crankcase.

23 If you are reusing the original crankcase screws, remove the old sealant from the screw flanges, while also making sure the threads are clean **(see illustration)**. Then clean the screws with contact cleaner and allow to dry.

24 Ensure that all components and their bearings are in place in the upper and lower crankcase halves. Lubricate the connecting rod bearings with engine oil and turn the crankshaft by hand to help distribute the oil. Then soak a lint-free cloth with electrical contact cleaner and wipe it over the mating surfaces of both crankcase halves to remove all traces of oil. Allow the surfaces to dry before applying the sealer.

25 If reusing the original crankcase screws, apply a pipe sealant (see Step 21) underneath each screw flange and set them aside until installation **(see illustration)**.

26 Apply a thin layer of Polaris Crankcase Sealant (part No. 2871557), Hondabond 4, Yamabond 4, or an equivalent semi-drying gasket sealer to the mating surface of the upper crankcase half **(see illustration)**. Do not apply the sealant on or too close to any of the bearing inserts or surfaces. When applying sealant near the camshaft relief hole, do not apply the sealant directly against the hole where it can squeeze out and plug or enter the hole when the crankcase halves are assembled and tightened together **(see illustration)**. If you used a brush to apply the sealant, check the crankcase gasket surface and sealant for any bristles that may have broken off.

CAUTION:

Do not apply an excessive amount of sealant as it will ooze out when the case halves are assembled and may obstruct oil passages.

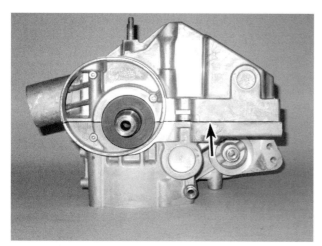

12.28a After installing the lower crankcase, make sure the gap (arrow) around the case halves is even

12.28b The crankshaft oil seal (arrow) must be fully seated in both case halves

27 Make sure the two dowel pins are installed in the upper crankcase half **(see illustration 12.19b)**.

28 Align and carefully install the lower crankcase half down onto the upper crankcase half, making sure the dowel pins locate correctly into the opposite crankcase half. Check that the lower crankcase half is correctly seated and the narrow gap between the case halves is even **(see illustration)**. Also check around the crankshaft seal to make sure it is fully seated against both case halves **(see illustration)**. If necessary, lightly tap the lower crankcase half to seat the dowel pins. While the crankcase halves should fit together without excessive force, it is normal to have to tap the crankcase in the area around the dowel pins to help them seat in both case halves.

NOTE:

The manufacturer specifies to apply a thread-locker onto the crankcase mounting screw

threads. Because most threadlocker fluids flow easily when applied, the fluid can run down the screw threads and along the case halves and contaminate the gasket sealer. When selecting a threadlocker, consider using a gel or stick type (see illustration 12.21b). A gel threadlocker will not run down the screw threads when the screws are installed in the case halves.

29 Apply a medium strength threadlock onto the crankcase screw threads. Do not apply an excessive amount as it can contaminate the gasket sealer if it runs onto the case half mating surfaces when installing and tightening the screws. If reusing the original crankcase screws, make sure a pipe sealant was applied underneath the screw flanges (see Step 21).

30 Install the crankcase screws and tighten finger-tight in numerical order. If a screw will not bottom against the lower crankcase, remove it and check its threaded hole for debris. Then tighten the screws in three steps, and in numerical order, to the torque listed in this Chapter's Specifications **(see illustration 12.18b)**.

31 When all of the crankcase screws have been tightened, rotate the crankshaft by hand to make sure there is no binding, roughness or tight spots. If there is a problem, stop and remove the crankcase screws and the lower crankcase. Remove the crankshaft and its bearings to make sure there is no lint or other debris caught between the crankshaft and its bearings, and between the bearings and their saddles in the crankcase. Also remove the dowel pins and check for debris in the bottom of either of their holes.

32 Apply a medium strength threadlock onto the thrust plate mounting screws, then install the plate and screws **(see illustration 12.16)** and tighten to the torque listed in this Chapter's Specifications.

33 If you removed the engine oil drain bolt, install a new gasket on the bolt, then install and tighten it to the torque listed in this Chapter's Specifications.

34 Install all other removed assemblies in the reverse order given in Steps 3 through 15.

35 After the engine is assembled, and before installing it into the frame, prime the oil system as described in Section 20.

13 CRANKCASE HALVES - CLEANING AND INSPECTION

1 After the crankcase halves have been disassembled and all of the internal components have been removed from them, the crankcase halves and fasteners must be thoroughly cleaned and inspected. When handling the crankcase halves on the workbench, place them on a rubber mat or on wooden blocks to protect the gasket surfaces from damage.

2 Apply solvent to the crankcase mating surfaces, and carefully remove all traces of sealant with a gasket scraper, making sure to work carefully to prevent from damaging

13.2 Remove all sealer residue from the gasket surfaces using gasket scrapers and brushes

13.3 When sealer sets up in screw holes it can be difficult to remove. Use a stiff cleaning brush to dislodge sealant in and around screw holes

the gasket and bearing surfaces **(see illustration)**. It may be helpful to soak the sealer with solvent to help soften it. Minor damage to the surfaces can be cleaned up with a fine sharpening stone and solvent.

3   When all of the sealer has been removed from the crankcase mating surfaces, clean the threaded holes in both crankcase halves of all oil, sealer and threadlock residue. These threads must be clean and dry to ensure proper tightening of the crankcase screws during assembly. Both a stiff brush and suitable size thread chasers are useful for cleaning threaded holes. Because gasket sealer will sometimes run and puddle into the bottom of threaded holes when the crankcase halves are assembled, check the bottom of each screw hole and remove any of this material **(see illustration)**.

4   Clean the threaded holes with compressed air, then check each hole, including the oil drain hole, for weak or damaged threads. Check by threading a suitable screw into each threaded hole, making sure the screw engages the threads fully and bottoms completely. If any damaged threads are found, repair them with a threaded insert (see the General Information chapter at the front of this manual).

5   When all of the crankcase mating surfaces and threaded holes are clean, clean the crankcase halves in solvent and dry with compressed air **(see illustration)**. Check that all oil passages and threaded holes are clear of sealant and other debris.

6   When the crankcase halves are clean, inspect them for fractures around all mounting and bearing bosses, stiffening ribs and threaded holes **(see illustration)**. If repair is required, refer inspection to a dealership or machine shop.

7   Clean and prepare the crankcase screws as described in Section 12.

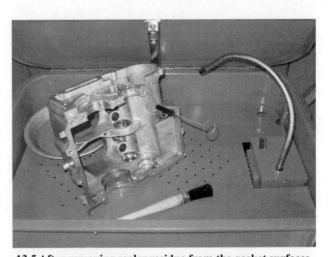

13.5 After removing sealer residue from the gasket surfaces, clean the case halves in solvent while making sure all oil passages and threaded holes are clear of debris

13.6 Inspect the crankcase halves carefully for any damage

14.1a The crankshaft oil seal

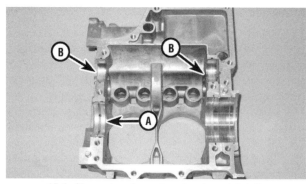
15.4a Upper crankcase bearing insert details

A   Crankshaft   *B   Balancer shaft*

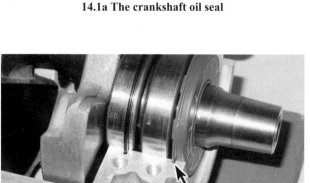
14.1b The crankshaft oil seal has a shoulder (arrow) that fits into grooves inside the upper and lower crankcase halves

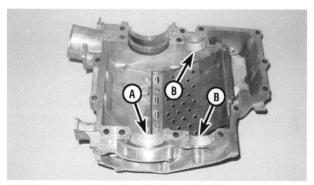
15.4b Lower crankcase bearing insert details

A   Crankshaft   *B   Balancer shaft*

15.2 Lift the crankshaft out of the upper crankcase

14   CRANKSHAFT OIL SEAL - REPLACEMENT

1   The crankshaft oil seal is installed on the PTO side of the engine (see illustration). Because this seal has a shoulder, it must be installed on the crankshaft before the crankshaft is installed in the engine. The shoulder then fits into grooves in the lower and upper case halves (see illustration). If this seal is damaged, it is necessary to remove the engine and split the engine cases to install a new OEM seal (see Section 15).

15   CRANKSHAFT - REMOVAL, INSPECTION, BEARING REPLACEMENT AND INSTALLATION

Removal

1   Separate the crankcase halves (see Section 12).
2   Lift the crankshaft out of the upper crankcase half, taking care not to dislodge the main bearing insert installed on the MAG side of the engine (see illustration).
3   Remove and discard the oil seal installed on the PTO side of the crankshaft (see illustration).
4   Remove the main bearing inserts from the upper and lower crankcase halves (see illustrations) by pushing at their center position toward the side, and lifting them out. Though the manufacturer recommends replacing the main bearing inserts any time the engine is disassembled, if the inserts will be reused, identify them as to upper or lower.

15.3 Slide the oil seal off the crankshaft and discard it

Inspection

5   The crankshaft and connecting rods cannot be serviced. If either the crankshaft or connecting rods are damaged, or if any specification is out of tolerance, the crankshaft and connecting rods must be replaced as an assembly. However, note that the crankshaft gear installed on the MAG side of the crankshaft can be replaced (see Step 17). Always replace the main bearing inserts when replacing the crankshaft.

6   Clean the crankshaft with clean solvent, while also using a small brush to scrub out the oil passages. If using a parts cleaning brush, make sure none of the bristles break or fall off and enter the oil passages inside the crankshaft. When cleaning the crankshaft, also clean the two ball bearings installed on the PTO side. Then dry the crankshaft with compressed air, making sure to blow through the oil passages. When the crankshaft is dry, lubricate both sides of the connecting rod (at the big end) with clean engine oil, and rotate the rods to distribute the oil. Then lubricate the two ball bearings.

7   Support the crankshaft and rotate each connecting rod by hand to check for any roughness, noise or damage. If a problem is detected, and the crankshaft has been cleaned and the connecting rod bearings were lubricated, replace the crankshaft.

8   Place the crankshaft on V-blocks and check the runout with a dial indicator. If the runout exceeds the limit listed in this Chapter's Specifications, replace the crankshaft.

9   Measure the connecting rod big end side clearance (the gap between the connecting rod big end and the crankshaft web) with a feeler gauge **(see illustration)**. If the clearance exceeds the specification listed in this Chapter's Specifications, replace the crankshaft.

10   Inspect the connecting rod small end inside diameter for any scoring or heat related damage. If there is no damage, measure the connecting rod small end inside diameter with a telescoping gauge **(see illustration)**. Then measure the gauge with a micrometer. If the small end is damaged, or if the inside diameter exceeds the specification listed in this Chapter's Specifications, replace the crankshaft. Repeat for the other connecting rod.

11   Support the crankshaft on V-blocks and place a dial indicator against the bottom of the connecting rod. Hold the small end of the connecting rod and move the rod back and forth and side-to-side to measure the connecting rod big end radial clearance **(see illustration)**. When measuring side-to-side movement, don't slide the connecting rod, but instead, twist the connecting rod at its small end. If the clearance in either check exceeds the specification listed in this Chapter's Specifications, replace the crankshaft.

12   Support the crankshaft on V-blocks and position the connecting rods at their top dead center position (parallel with the workbench). Place a dial indicator against the side of one of the connecting rod's small end **(see illustration)**. Without sliding the connecting rod at its big end, try to move it from side-to-side at its small end to measure the small end radial clearance. If the clearance exceeds the specification listed in this Chapter's Specifications, replace

15.9 Measure the connecting rod big end side clearance with a feeler gauge

15.10 Measure the connecting rod small end inside diameter

15.11 Set-up to check connecting rod big end radial clearance

15.12 Set-up to check connecting rod small end radial clearance

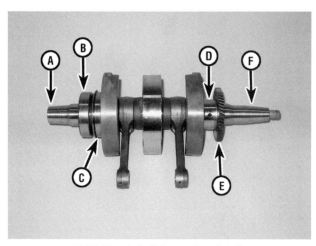

15.13 Crankshaft inspection details

A	Clutch taper	D	Main bearing journal
B	Outer bearing	E	Crankshaft gear
C	Inner bearing	F	Flywheel taper

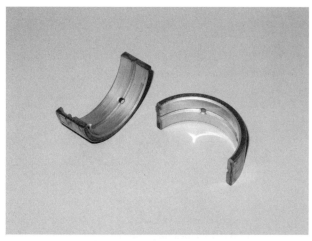

15.14 Crankshaft main bearing inserts

15.19 Crankshaft ball bearing details

A	Inner bearing	C	Outer bearing
B	Index ring		

the crankshaft. Repeat for the other connecting rod.

13 Inspect the crankshaft main bearing journal for scoring, pitting, heat discoloration or other defects **(see illustration)**. If there is any damage, the same type of damage will be present on the two main bearing inserts. If the journal is damaged, it will be necessary to install a new crankshaft. Note that undersize bearings are not available, thus preventing the option of regrinding the crankshaft.

14 While the manufacturer recommends replacing the main bearing inserts when reassembling the engine, it is still a good idea to inspect the original inserts before installing new inserts and rebuilding the engine. Inspect the main bearing inserts for peeling and other damage **(see illustration)**. Used bearings will normally show some light scoring and scratch marks. Heavier marks indicate a problem with dirt passing through the air filter or the engine has been operating with dirty oil. Deep score marks may indicate larger pieces of foreign debris are in the oil, which may have originated from a broken engine part (parts of a ring or gear). Bearing inserts that are black or blue and deeply scored or grooved indicate a lubricating problem. Inspect the oil pump for damage and replace it if necessary (Section 10). While the engine is apart, check for blocked and contaminated oil passages. Operating the engine with too little oil will also cause this type of damage.

15 Inspect the clutch and flywheel taper surfaces for pitting, scoring and other damage **(see illustration 15.13)**. Inspect the flywheel keyway for cracks and other damage. The sides of the keyway must be straight and with no signs of flaring or rounding. Replace the crankshaft if any damage is noted.

16 Check the threads on both ends of the crankshaft for contamination and damage. Use the correct size tap and die from a rethreading set to clean and/or repair any minor thread damage. Then check the threads by installing the original flywheel nut and clutch bolt. Make sure the threads are in good condition before installing the crankshaft into the engine.

17 Check the crankshaft gear for broken or chipped teeth. If the gear is damaged, replace the crankshaft gear, camshaft gear, balancer gear and the water/oil pump gear as a set (see Section 9).

18 Check the two crankshaft bearings by turning them individually by hand **(see illustration 15.13)**. There should be no roughness or binding. Working on one bearing at a time, try to push the bearing in and out to check for lateral play. Slight lateral play is normal. Then try to push the bearing up and down to check for radial play. Any radial play should be difficult to feel. If lateral play seems excessive, or if radial play is easily felt in any one bearing, replace both bearings as a set (see Steps 19 through 24).

Bearing replacement

19 The two ball bearings installed on the PTO side of the crankshaft can be replaced **(see illustration)**. Always replace both bearing as a set. Note that a spacer is installed between the two bearings.

20 Assemble a puller onto the end of the crankshaft as shown **(see illustration)**. Operate the puller to remove the outer bearing. Remove the spacer, then repeat to remove the inner bearing.

21 Inspect the bearing surface on the crankshaft for any burrs or scoring and remove with a fine-cut file.

22 Inspect the spacer installed between the bearings and replace if there is any noticeable thrust wear or heat damage.

23 Install the inner bearing with a driver that rests on the inner race of the bearing only - the index ring on the inner bearing must face out when the bearing is installed on the crankshaft **(see illustration 15.19)**. Install the spacer and seat it against the inner bearing. Then repeat to install the outer bearing **(see illustration)**.

24 Spin both bearings by hand to make sure they turn without any roughness or binding.

Installation

25 Make sure the upper crankcase is clean and ready for assembly (see Section 13).

26 Clean the bearing saddles (cut-outs) in the both crankcase halves with isopropyl alcohol and dry with compressed air or a lint-free cloth.

NOTE:

The manufacturer recommends installing new bearing inserts whenever reassembling the engine. If you choose to install the original inserts, they must be installed in their original locations as noted during removal.

27 Clean both sides of each bearing insert with isopropyl alcohol and dry with compressed air or use a lint-free cloth.

CAUTION:

No oil, dirt, lint or other material can be on the bearing saddle surfaces or bearing inserts when the bearing inserts are installed. If these parts are not clean, bearing seizure and engine damage may result.

28 Install the bearing inserts by pressing them into their locations in the upper and lower crankcase halves, making sure the anti-rotation tab on each bearing insert locks into the crankcase saddle notches correctly **(see illustration)**. Also make sure the oil hole in the upper bearing insert aligns with the oil hole in the crankcase. When the bearing inserts are correctly installed, reclean their outer surfaces with isopropyl alcohol and a lint-free cloth.

29 Clean the crankshaft main bearing journal with isopropyl alcohol and dry with a lint-free cloth **(see illustration 15.13)**.

30 Install a new oil seal onto the PTO side of the crankshaft with its flat side facing out. Bottom the oil seal against the bearing **(see illustration 15.3)**.

31 Lubricate the bearing inserts and the crankshaft main

15.20 Set-up for pulling the bearings off the crankshaft

A   Bearing splitter
B   Plug to protect crankshaft end and provide contact point for puller bolt
C   Puller

15.23 Install the bearings (one at a time) with a suitable driver

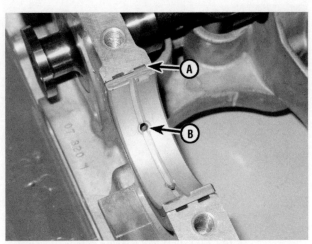

15.28 Press the bearing insert into its saddle and lock the anti-rotation tab into the notch (A). If there are any matching oil holes, make sure they align (B)

15.32 Make sure the index ring (A) and oil seal shoulder (B) fit into the saddle grooves

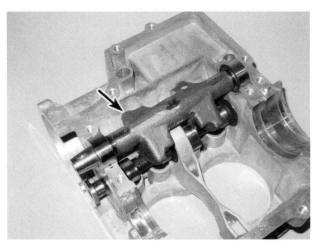

16.3 Remove the balancer shaft from the upper crankcase

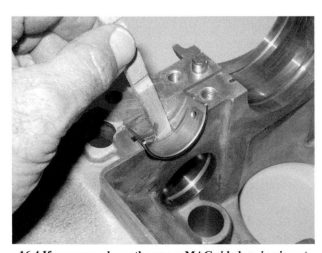

16.4 If necessary, lever the upper MAG side bearing insert out of its saddle with a wooden stick

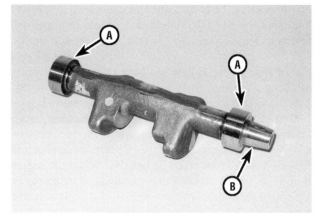

16.6 Balancer shaft details

A   Bearing journals   B   Taper and keyway

journal with engine assembly lube or clean engine oil.

32   Carefully align and install the crankshaft into the upper crankcase half. The index ring on the inner bearing must seat into the inner groove in the bearing saddle, and the shoulder on the oil seal must seat into the outer groove in the saddle **(see illustration)**.

33   Reassemble the crankcase halves (see Section 12).

16   BALANCER SHAFT - REMOVAL, INSPECTION AND INSTALLATION

1   The engine uses a rotating balancer shaft to dampen engine vibration. The balancer shaft weight is synchronized with the crankshaft, and is driven by a timing gear assembly located on the MAG side of the engine.

Removal

2   Separate the crankcase halves (see Section 12).

3   Lift the balancer shaft out of the upper crankcase half, taking care not to dislodge the bearing inserts **(see illustration)**.

4   Identify and remove the balancer shaft bearing inserts from the upper and lower crankcase halves **(see illustrations 15.4a and 15.4b)**. Most of the inserts can be removed by pushing at their center position toward one side, then lifting them out. The upper MAG side bearing may have to be levered out with a wooden stick **(see illustration)**. Identify each insert by its upper or lower and PTO or MAG positions.

Inspection

5   Clean the balancer shaft with clean solvent and dry with compressed air.

6   Inspect the balancer shaft journals for scoring, pitting, heat discoloration or other defects **(see illustration)**. If there is any damage, the same type of damage will be present on the bearing inserts. If the journals are damaged, it will be necessary to install a new balancer shaft and four new bearing inserts. Note that only one size bearing insert is available.

7 Inspect the balancer shaft bearing inserts for peeling and other damage **(see illustration)**. Used bearings will normally show some light scoring and scratch marks. Heavier marks indicate a problem with dirt passing through the air filter or the engine has been operating with dirty oil. Deep score marks may indicate larger pieces of foreign debris are in the oil, which may have originated from a broken engine part (parts of a ring or gear). Bearing inserts that are black or blue and deeply scored or grooved indicate a lubricating problem. Inspect the oil pump for damage and replace it if necessary (see Section 10). While the engine is apart, check for blocked and contaminated oil passages. Operating the engine with too little oil will also cause this type of damage.

8 Inspect the keyway on the MAG end of the balancer shaft for cracks and other damage **(see illustration 16.6)**. Each side of the keyway must be straight with no signs of flaring or rounding. Then fit the Woodruff key into the keyway to make sure the fit is snug.

9 Install the balancer shaft and the thrust plate and measure the balancer shaft end play with a dial indicator the same way you measure camshaft end play as described in Section 17. Compare the end play reading to the specification listed in this Chapter's Specifications. If the end play is excessive, inspect the thrust plate where the balancer shaft operates against it for any visual scoring or wear marks, and replace if necessary.

Installation

10 Clean the bearing saddles (cut-outs) in the both crankcase halves with isopropyl alcohol and dry with compressed air or a lint-free cloth.

11 Clean both sides of each bearing insert with isopropyl alcohol and dry with compressed air or use a lint-free cloth.

CAUTION:

No oil, dirt, lint or other material can be on the bearing saddle surfaces or bearing inserts when the bearing inserts are installed. If these parts are not clean, bearing seizure and engine damage may result.

12 Install the bearing inserts by pressing them into their locations in the upper and lower crankcase halves while making sure the anti-rotation tab on each bearing insert locks into the engine saddle notches correctly. Also make sure the oil holes in the bearing inserts align with the oil holes in the crankcase halves, if applicable. When the bearing inserts are correctly installed, reclean their outer surfaces with isopropyl alcohol and a lint-free cloth **(see illustration)**.

13 Clean the balancer shaft bearing journals with isopropyl alcohol and dry with a lint-free cloth **(see illustration 16.6)**.

14 Lubricate the bearing inserts and the balancer shaft main journals with engine assembly lube or clean engine oil.

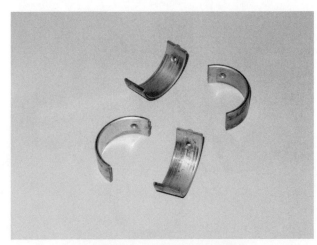

16.7 Balancer shaft bearing inserts

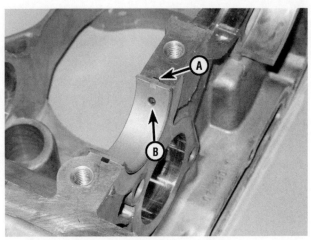

16.12 Press the bearing insert into its saddle and lock the anti-rotation tab into the notch (A). If there are any matching oil holes, make sure they align (B)

15 Carefully install the balancer shaft into the upper crankcase half. The tapered side on the balancer shaft must face toward the MAG side of the engine **(see illustration 16.3)**.

16 Reassemble the crankcase halves (see Section 12).

17 CAMSHAFT - REMOVAL, INSPECTION AND INSTALLATION

Removal

1 Separate the crankcase halves (see Section 12).

2 Remove the crankshaft (see Section 15).

3 Remove the balancer shaft (see Section 16).

4 Remove the camshaft by sliding it slowly out of the upper crankcase so the journals do not damage the camshaft journal bores in the crankcase **(see illustration)**.

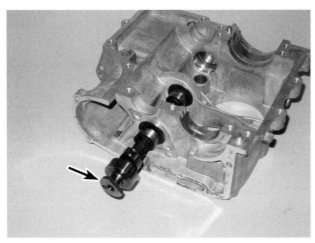

17.4 Slide the camshaft out of the upper crankcase

17.6c Measure the height of the camshaft lobes with a micrometer

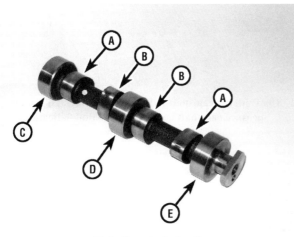

17.6a Camshaft details

A   Exhaust lobes   D   Center journal
B   Intake lobes   E   MAG side journal
C   PTO side journal

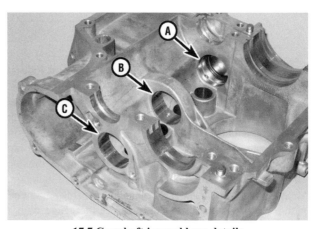

17.7 Camshaft journal bore details

A   PTO side   C   MAG side
B   Center

Inspection

NOTE:

If it is determined during inspection that the camshaft is worn or damaged and must be replaced, replace the valve lifters at the same time.

5   Clean the camshaft in solvent and dry thoroughly.

6   Check the camshaft lobes for heat discoloration (blue appearance), score marks, chipped areas, flat spots and pitting **(see illustrations)**. Measure the height of each lobe with a micrometer **(see illustration)** and compare the results to the individual specifications listed in this Chapter's Specifications. If damage is noted or wear is excessive, replace the camshaft.

7   Inspect the camshaft journal bore surfaces inside the upper crankcase and on the corresponding journals on the camshaft **(see illustration and illustration 17.6a)**. Check for signs of scoring (scratches or grooves in the journal surfaces) and pitting, both of which are usually caused by dirty or insufficient oil. If a journal bore surface is damaged, replace the crankcase halves as an assembly; if a camshaft journal is damaged, replace the camshaft.

17.6b Check the camshaft lobes for wear and visual damage; here's a good example of damage that will require camshaft replacement

17.8a Measure the outside diameter of each camshaft journal with a micrometer

17.8b Measure each camshaft journal bore inside diameter

8   Clean the camshaft journals and the camshaft journal bores in the upper crankcase, with a clean lint-free cloth. Identify the camshaft's MAG, center and PTO positions **(see illustration 17.6a)**. Then do the same for the journal bore inside diameters in the upper crankcase **(see illustration 17.7)**. Note that each of the measurement positions are a different size. Measure each camshaft journal outside diameter with a micrometer and record the dimension. Measure each camshaft journal bore inside diameter with a telescoping gauge, then measure the gauge with a micrometer and record the dimension **(see illustrations)**. Compare both sets of measurements to the values listed in this Chapter's Specifications. If any measurement is out of specification, replace the worn part.

9   To determine the oil clearance, subtract a camshaft journal outside diameter from its matching bore inside diameter recorded in Step 8, and compare the results to the value listed in this Chapter's Specifications. Repeat for each measurement position. If any one oil clearance measurement is out of specification, replace the camshaft and recheck the clearance. If the clearance is still excessive, replace the crankcase halves as an assembly.

10   Install the camshaft and thrust plate into the upper crankcase half. Tighten the thrust plate screws to the torque listed in this Chapter's Specifications. Mount the tip of a dial indicator against the camshaft. Slide the camshaft all the way into the case half, and zero the dial indicator **(see illustration)**. Slide the camshaft outward to measure end play, and compare to the value listed in this Chapter's Specifications. If the end play is excessive, inspect the thrust plate and the snap ring installed inside the case half for excessive wear and replace either or both if necessary **(see illustrations)**. When replacing the snap ring, position its end gap so that it doesn't block the oil hole in the crankcase **(see illustration)**. Then recheck the end play. If the end play is still excessive, replace the camshaft.

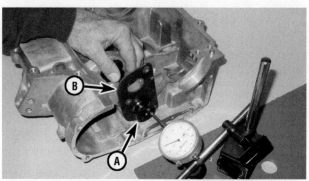

17.10a With the camshaft (A) and thrust plate (B) installed, measure camshaft end play with a dial indicator

17.10b Inspect the thrust plate . . .

17.10c . . . and snap ring for excessive wear

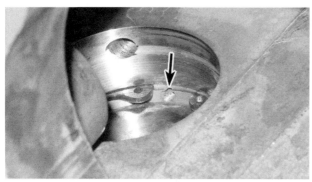

17.10d When replacing the snap ring, do not block the oil hole (arrow) in the crankcase

18.4d Note the threadlocker residue visible on the screw and case threads

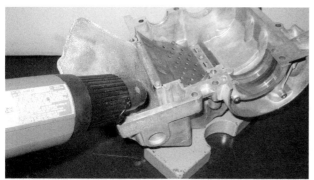

18.4a Heat the oil baffle screws to soften the threadlock - this must be done before attempting to loosen the screws

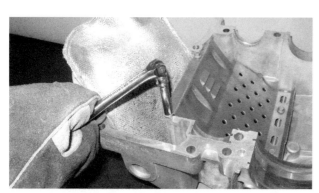

18.4b After heating the screws, loosen and remove them with a six-point socket . . .

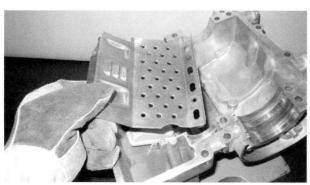

18.4c . . . and remove the oil baffle

Installation

11   Make sure the upper crankcase is clean and ready for assembly (see Section 13).

12   Apply assembly lube to the camshaft journals and to the camshaft journal bores in the upper crankcase.

13   Slide the camshaft into the upper crankcase half until the camshaft journals are completed seated in their bores. The side of the camshaft with the gear mounting flange must face toward the MAG side of the engine **(see illustration 17.4)**. When the camshaft is fully installed, rotate it by hand to make sure there is no roughness or binding.

14   Reassemble the crankcase halves (see Section 12).

18   OIL BAFFLE AND OIL PICKUP - REMOVAL, INSPECTION AND INSTALLATION

1   The oil baffle and oil pickup assemblies are mounted in the lower crankcase half. The oil pickup should be removed, cleaned and inspected whenever the engine is disassembled.

Removal

2   Separate the crankcase halves (see Section 12).

3   Clean the lower crankcase half (see Section 13).

CAUTION:

The oil baffle screws are secured in place with a threadlock. Before loosening these screws, heat them with a heat gun to soften the threadlock before trying to loosen them; otherwise, when you loosen the screws, it is possible to damage the screws and the screw threads in the lower crankcase half.

4   Heat the oil baffle screws with a heat gun to soften the threadlock **(see illustration)**. Using a six-point socket, loosen and remove the oil baffle screws and the baffle **(see illustrations)**. If one or more screws are difficult to loosen, stop and reheat them as required. The screws are small and the threadlock can form a strong bond on the screws and crankcase threads **(see illustration)**.

5   With the oil baffle removed, remove the screw, then pivot the oil pickup upward and slide it out of the oil passage and remove it **(see illustration)**. Remove and discard the O-ring installed on the oil pickup **(see illustration)**.

Inspection

6   Clean the oil pickup assembly in solvent and dry thoroughly with compressed air, if available. Inspect the oil pickup for any cracks or other damage, and replace if necessary **(see illustration)**.
7   Clean the oil baffle in solvent and dry thoroughly. Make sure all of the holes in the oil baffle are clear and that there are no cracks or other damage.
8   Clean and dry the oil pickup and oil baffle screws. Make sure and remove all threadlock material remaining on the screws and inside the threaded holes in the lower crankcase **(see illustration 18.4d)**. Replace damaged screws as required. Then carefully inspect the threaded holes for any chipped or otherwise damaged threads. If necessary, repair damaged crankcase threads with a threaded insert. Refer to the General Information chapter at the front of this manual.

Installation

9   Make sure the lower crankcase is clean and ready for assembly (see Section 13).
10   Lubricate a new O-ring **(see illustration 18.5b)** with grease and slide it onto the oil pickup, then carefully install the oil pickup into the engine to prevent from damaging the O-ring, and pivot it down so that it seats against the crankcase guide and the threaded hole **(see illustration 18.5a)**. Apply a threadlock onto the oil pickup screw threads, then install the screw and tighten to the torque listed in this Chapter's Specifications.
11   Position the oil baffle into the lower crankcase half. Apply a threadlock onto the oil baffle screw threads, then install the screws and tighten to the torque listed in this Chapter's Specifications.
12   After installing the oil baffle, temporarily install the balancer shaft inserts and the balancer shaft into the lower crankcase. Then turn the balancer shaft to make sure it doesn't contact the oil baffle **(see illustration)**. If it does, remove the oil baffle and inspect it for damage, then reinstall it, while making sure it is fully seated against the lower crankcase half.
13   Reassemble the crankcase halves (see Section 12).

19   ENGINE OIL DIPSTICK TUBE - REMOVAL AND INSTALLATION

1   The engine oil dipstick tube is mounted on the MAG side of the engine, near the oil filter.
2   If the engine is assembled and installed in the frame, clean the dipstick tube and the area around the dipstick tube and crankcase of all sand and dirt.
3   Remove the dipstick.

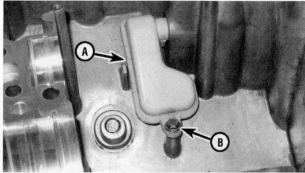

18.5a The oil pickup (A) is held in place with a fixed crankcase guide and a screw (B)

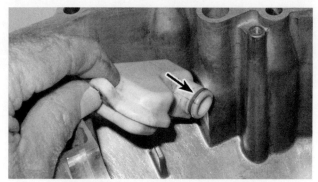

18.5b Remove and discard the O-ring

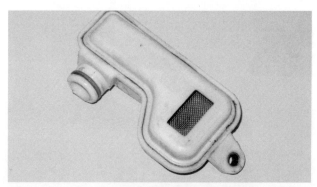

18.6 Inspect the oil pickup assembly carefully for any cracks or other damage

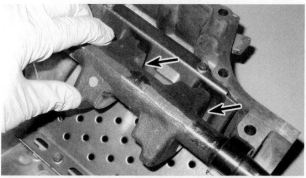

18.12 After installing the oil baffle, turn the balancer shaft to make sure it doesn't contact the baffle

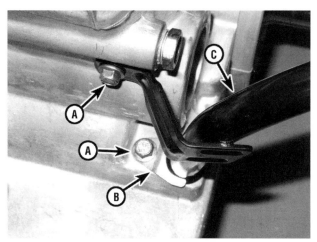

19.4 Engine oil dipstick tube details

A   *Screws*   C   *Dipstick tube*
B   *Clamp*

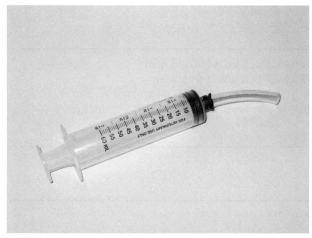

20.1 A large syringe, like the one shown here, and an attached hose, can be used to prime the engine

20.2 Fill the new oil filter 3/4 full (arrow) with new engine oil

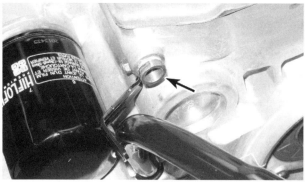

20.3 Primer plug position on crankcase

4   Remove the screws, clamp and withdraw the engine oil dipstick tube from the engine **(see illustration)**. Remove the O-ring from the dipstick tube and discard it.

5   Plug the dipstick tube opening in the crankcase to prevent objects and dirt from entering the engine.

6   Installation is the reverse of removal, noting the following:

a) *Lubricate a new O-ring with grease and install it onto the bottom of the engine oil dipstick tube.*

b) *Install the clamp so that the raised part of the clamp where it hooks around the dipstick tube is facing up. This position will apply pressure to the dipstick tube when the clamp screw is tightened.*

c) *If reusing the original screws, remove all thread-lock from the screw and cylinder threads. Then install the screws and tighten to the torque listed in this Chapter's Specifications.*

20   PRIMING THE OIL SYSTEM

CAUTION:
The engine oil system must be primed after reassembling the engine and before the engine is first started. Failure to prime the oil system may cause engine damage when the engine is first started.

1   Special tools: The Polaris oil system priming tool (part No. PU-45778) or a large syringe and hose will be required **(see illustration)**. Large syringes can usually be purchased at animal feed stores.

2   Fill a new oil filter 3/4 full with the recommended engine oil listed in the Chapter 2 Specifications. Allow the filter to set for approximately 10 minutes to allow the oil to soak into the filter element. Then install the oil filter onto the engine and fill the engine with the correct amount and type of engine oil (see Chapter 2) **(see illustration)**.

3   Loosen and remove the oil primer plug from the threaded plug in the upper crankcase half that is located near the oil filter **(see illustration)**. Thread a hollow adapter into the threaded plug, and connect the hose from

the syringe onto the hollow adapter. Remove the pump from the syringe and add approximately 3-5 ounces of engine oil into the syringe. Reinstall the pump and operate it to push the oil into the engine **(see illustration)**. Add all of the oil if possible, or stop when hard resistance is felt. Disconnect the hose and remove the hollow adapter. Clean the oil primer plug threads and the threaded plug threads of all sealer and oil. These threads must be clean and dry to prevent an oil leak. Then apply a sealer to oil primer plug threads. Install the oil primer plug and tighten to the torque listed in this Chapter's Specifications.

4   After reinstalling the engine into the frame and starting the engine, check the primer plug to make sure it is not leaking oil.

SPECIFICATIONS

Oil Pump

Rotor tip clearance (service limit)	0.006 in. (0.15 mm)

Crankshaft

Runout limit	0.0024 (0.061 mm)

Connecting rods

Big end radial clearance	0.0009-0.0021 inches (0.023-0.053 mm)
Big end side clearance	0.0059-0.0177 inches (0.15-0.45 mm)
Small end inside diameter	0.7096-0.7085 inches (18.024-18.000 mm)
Small end radial clearance	0.0006-0.0014 inches (0.015-0.036 mm)

Balancer shaft

End play	0.005 inch (0.127 mm)

Camshaft

End play	0.0069-0.0265 inches (0.1753-0.6731 mm)
Journal bore inside diameter	
MAG side	1.6556-1.6564 inches (42.052-42.073 mm)
Center	1.6366-1.6374 inches (41.569-41.589 mm)
PTO side	1.6166-1.6174 inches (41.062-41.082 mm)
Journal outside diameter	
MAG side	1.6536-1.6544 inches (42.001-42.022 mm)
Center	1.6336-1.6344 inches (41.493-41.514 mm)
PTO side	1.6136-1.6144 inches (40.985-41.006 mm)
Lobe height	
Intake	
2010 models	1.319 inches (33.512 mm)
2011 and later models	1.357 inches (34.477 mm)
Exhaust	
2010 models	1.319 inches (33.512 mm)
2011 and later models	1.342 inches (34.087 mm)
Oil clearance	0.002-0.004 inches (0.051-0.102 mm)

Torque specifications	Ft-lbs	In.-lb	Nm

NOTE

One foot-pound (ft-lb) of torque is equivalent to 12 inch-pounds (in-lbs) of torque. Torque values below approximately 15 ft-lbs are expressed in inch-pounds, because most foot-pound torque wrenches are not accurate at these smaller values.

	Ft-lbs	In.-lb	Nm
Alternator cover mounting screws	--	93-99	10-11
Balancer gear bolt	20-24	--	27-33
Camshaft gear bolt	20-24	--	27-33
Crankcase screws	20-24	--	27-33
Engine mount fastener			
Front engine mount to engine screws	25	--	34
Rear engine/transmission mount damper nuts	22	--	30
Engine oil dipstick tube screws	--	45-55	5-6
Engine oil drain bolt	14-18	--	19-25
Flywheel nut	58-72	--	79-98
Oil baffle screws	--	54-66	6-7
Oil pickup screw	--	54-66	6-7
Oil pressure relief valve bolt			
2010 models	20-24	--	27-33
2011 and later models	15-19	--	20-26
Oil primer plug	16-20	--	22-27
Oil pump mounting sccws	--	76-92	9-10
Stator coil mounting screws			
2012 and earlier models	--	93-99	10-11
2013 and later models	--	76-92	9-10
Stator housing screws			
2012 and earlier models	--	93-99	10-11
2013 and later models	--	84-108	9.5-12.2
Stator wiring harness guide screws	--		
2012 and earlier models	--	93-99	10-11
2013 and later models	--	84-108	9.5-12.2
Thrust plate screws	--	103-127	12-14
Water pump housing cover screws			
2012 and earlier models	--	93-99	10-11
2013 and later models	--	84-108	9.5-12.2
Water pump impeller nut	--	105-111	12-13

NOTES

CHAPTER FIVE

CLUTCH AND DRIVEBELT SYSTEM

CONTENTS

1   GENERAL INFORMATION

1   All of the vehicles covered in this manual use the Polaris Variable Transmission (PVT). This consists of a drive clutch, drivebelt and driven clutch, all mounted in a sealed housing on the PTO side of the engine and transmission **(see illustration)**. The PVT connects the engine to the transmission. The transmission on these models is a separate unit from the PVT. It allows the operator to select high, low, neutral and reverse range. Transmission service is covered in Chapter 6.

2   The PVT's drive and driven clutches control variable-diameter pulleys (sheaves). The drive clutch is mounted on the end of the engine crankshaft. The driven clutch is mounted on the transmission input shaft.

3   At low engine speeds, the drive clutch pulley has a small diameter and the driven clutch pulley has a large diameter. As engine speed increases, the drive pulley diameter gets larger and the driven pulley diameter gets smaller. This changes the effective gear ratio of the PVT.

4   The drive clutch changes its pulley diameter in response to changes in engine speed. At idle, the spring in the drive

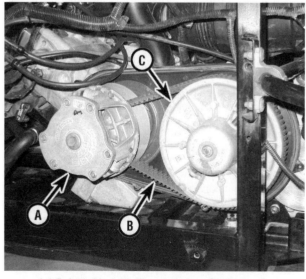

1.1 Polaris Variable Transmission (PVT) details

A   *Drive clutch*   C   *Driven clutch*
B   *Drive belt*

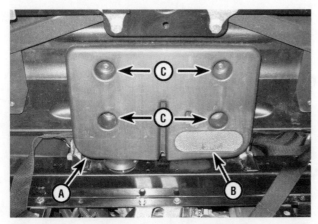

2.5a Clutch air baffle box details - late 2010 and later models

A   Clutch air baffle box
B   Filter
C   Mounting screws

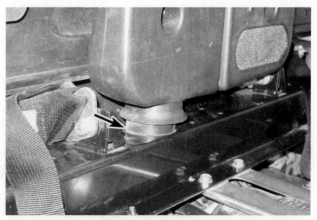

2.5b During service, note how the inlet air duct is connected to the clutch air baffle box - slip fit used on late 2010 and later models shown here. A clamp is used on early 2010 models

clutch forces the pulley halves apart, so the drivebelt is not gripped and no power is transferred to the driven clutch. As engine speed increases, the drive clutch spins faster. This causes the three shift weights (centrifugal levers) in the drive clutch to push the sliding pulley half toward the fixed pulley half. As a result, the drivebelt is gripped by the pulley and power is transferred to the driven clutch. As engine speed increases still more, the shift weights push the drive clutch's sliding pulley half closer to the fixed pulley half. This makes the pulley groove narrower, so the drivebelt rides higher in the pulley groove (closer to the outer edge of the pulley). This causes the driven pulley to be rotated more times for each rotation of the drive pulley (higher gearing).

5   Since the drivebelt doesn't change length, the driven clutch pulley must become smaller in diameter as the drive clutch pulley becomes larger. To make this happen, the driven clutch pulley changes diameter in response to the load placed on it by the drivebelt. At low engine speeds, the spring in the driven clutch pushes the pulley halves together, which causes the drivebelt to ride higher in the groove (closer to the outer edge of the pulley). This is the equivalent of a low gear in a conventional transmission. As engine speed increases, more power is applied to the drivebelt. The belt forces the driven pulley halves apart, causing the belt to ride lower in the pulley groove (closer to the center of the pulley). This is the equivalent of a higher gear in a conventional transmission. Two things control the rate at which the driven pulley halves are forced apart: the tension of the driven clutch spring and the angle of the helical cam that connects the centers of the two halves.

6   The PVT is air cooled. The cooling air is drawn into the housing by fins on the fixed half of the drive clutch pulley. The air enters a duct behind the driver and exits through another duct.

7   The system is designed so that at full throttle, engine rpm is maintained at a setting that produces peak power output. Springs, shift weights and driven clutch cams are specifically designed for each model. They must be replaced with the exact equivalents if new ones are needed.

In addition, the clutch components are balanced as a unit, so installing used parts from another clutch will probably cause vibration as well as reassembling the unit incorrectly (alignment marks were not made and followed).

8   Some models use the Engine Braking System (EBS). This consists of one-way clutches in the center of the drive and driven pulleys. When the throttle is released, compression braking from the engine is transferred through the pulleys to the drive train and wheels.

2   CLUTCH AIR DUCT ASSEMBLY

1   Inlet and outlet air ducts are used to provide air into and out of the clutch assembly. The inlet air duct is also equipped with a clutch air baffle box that contains a filter to prevent dirt and water from entering the clutch housing. Both ducts must be in good condition and sealed at all connecting points to provide air passage while preventing water and debris from entering the clutch cover assembly.

Inlet air duct and clutch air baffle box

2   On early 2010 models, the assembly consists of a clutch air baffle box, inlet air duct, nozzle and filter. The clutch air box halves separate to allow filter service (see Chapter 2). The inlet air duct is secured on both ends (engine and box fittings) with clamps.

3   On late 2010 and later models, the assembly consists of a clutch air baffle box, inlet air duct and filter. The clutch air baffle box is a sealed unit and does not separate. The inlet air duct is secured to the engine with a hose clamp, and the opposite end of the duct slides through the frame and into the bottom of the clutch air baffle box. A clamp is not used. The filter is serviced by removing it through the opening in the clutch air baffle box (see Chapter 2).

4   Raise the cargo bed.

5   To remove the clutch air baffle box, remove the screws securing the box to the frame (see illustrations). Loosen the hose clamp if used. Remove the box from the inlet duct

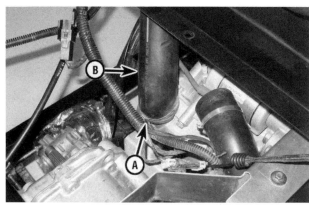

2.7a Loosen the hose clamp (A) and remove the inlet air duct (B) from the engine

2.7b Inlet air duct (arrow)

2.13 Cable and wiring harness routing around the clutch outlet air duct - 2010 standard model shown (other models may be different)

and remove it from the vehicle.

6   To remove just the inlet air duct, first remove the air box assembly (see Chapter 7).

7   On early 2010 models, loosen the clamp securing the inlet air duct to the clutch air baffle box. On all models, loosen the hose clamp securing the inlet air duct at the engine. Then release the inlet air duct from the engine and slide it off of or out of the clutch air baffle box and remove it (see illustrations).

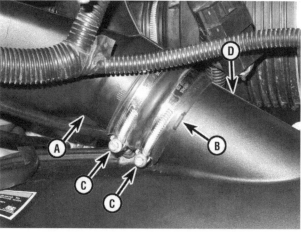

2.14a Outlet air duct mounting details

| A | Outlet air duct | C | Clamps |
| B | Rubber boot | D | Clutch outer cover |

2.14b Note how the rubber boot (arrow) fits onto the clutch outer cover so that it can be reinstalled correctly

8   Clean away any debris clogging the inlet air duct. Check the inlet duct for cracks, brittleness or deteriorated rubber and replace if necessary. Inspect the clutch air baffle box for cracks and other damage and replace if necessary.

9   If necessary, service the clutch air baffle box filter (see Chapter 2).

10   Installation is the reverse of removal.

Outlet air duct

11   The outlet air duct is connected onto the clutch outer cover with two hose clamps and a flexible rubber boot.

12   On Standard models, remove the seat base. On Crew models, remove the rear the seat base. To provide additional room and a better view of the cable and wiring harness routing, remove the storage box. See Chapter 14.

13   Before removing the outlet air duct, note the cable and wiring harness routing on both sides of the duct to help with proper alignment during installation (see illustration).

14   Loosen the rear clamp securing the outlet air duct rubber boot to the clutch outer cover (see illustrations).

15 Remove the mounting screw and the outlet air duct **(see illustration)**.

16 Clean away any debris clogging the outlet air duct. Check the outlet air duct for cracks and other damage and replace if necessary. Replace the rubber boot if torn or cracked.

17 Installation is the reverse of removal, noting the following:

a) *The rubber hose that connect the clutch outlet duct to the clutch outer cover is soft and folds under easily, which can cause a leak. After installing the clutch outlet duct, make sure the rubber hose fits squarely against the clutch outer cover.*

b) *After installing the outlet air duct hose onto the clutch outer cover, install and tighten the duct's mounting screw. This will position the duct correctly so the rubber hose fits onto the cover at the correct position.*

3 CLUTCH OUTER COVER - REMOVAL, INSPECTION AND INSTALLATION

1 The clutch outer and inner covers form a closed housing that protects the drivebelt and clutch assembly. The cover seal used between the clutch outer and inner covers, and the sealer applied to the inner cover are important because they keep water from leaking in and cooling air from leaking out. A wet or overheated drivebelt will slip on the pulleys.

2 Park the vehicle on a level surface and apply the parking brake.

3 On Standard models, remove the seat base. On Crew models, remove the rear seat base. Then remove the storage box. See Chapter 14.

4 Remove the clutch outlet air duct (see Section 2).

5 Remove the clutch outer cover screws and the cover **(see illustrations)**. If water drained out of the cover, try and determine how the water entered the cover assembly.

6 Clean the clutch outer cover and inspect it for cracks, warpage and heat damage.

7 Carefully check the cover seal while it is still installed in the inner cover **(see illustration)**. Check it for cracks, hardening and deterioration of the rubber. Also look for pinched spots caused by the outer cover being tightened while the seal was out of position. If you find any problems, remove and replace the seal. Install the seal by inserting it into the groove in the clutch inner cover with its shouldered side facing out **(see illustration)**.

8 Installation is the reverse of removal, noting the following:

a) *After installing the clutch outer cover, make sure the cover seal is properly seated around the entire perimeter of both the outer and inner covers. There must be no gaps. Then hold the cover in place and install the screws. Before tightening the screws, check the cover seal a final time.*

b) *Tighten the clutch outer cover screws to the torque listed in this Chapter's Specifications.*

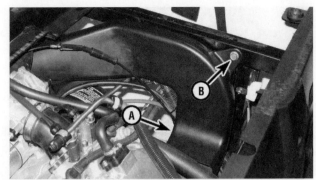

2.15 The outlet air duct (A) is secured to the frame with a mounting screw (B)

3.5a Remove the clutch outer cover (arrow) screws . . .

3.5b . . . and remove the cover

3.7a Make sure the cover seal (arrow) is fully seated in the clutch inner cover groove . . .

3.7b . . . with its shouldered side (arrow) facing out

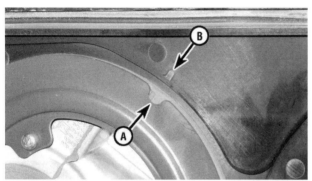

4.5 The notch in the retainer (A) must align with the index mark (B) on the clutch inner cover

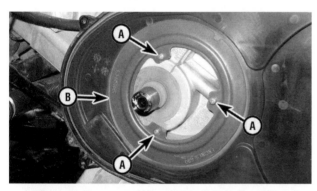

4.6 Remove the screws (A) securing the retainer (B) and clutch inner cover to the engine. If the retainer is loose, remove it from the cover; otherwise, remove the retainer with the cover, then remove it separately

4.7 Remove the screws (arrows) securing the clutch inner cover to the transmission screws - a combination steel and rubber washer set is installed on each screw

4.8 Remove the clutch inner cover from the engine and transmission

4.9 Lift the retainer off of the clutch inner cover

4   CLUTCH INNER COVER - REMOVAL, INSPECTION, SEAL REPLACEMENT AND INSTALLATION

Removal

1   Remove the clutch outer cover (see Section 3).
2   Remove the drivebelt (see Section 5).
3   Remove the drive clutch (Section 7).
4   Remove the driven clutch (see Section 9).
5   Before removing the clutch inner cover, note how the notch in the retainer aligns with the index mark on the cover **(see illustration)**. This alignment must be maintained during installation.
6   Remove the Phillips screws securing the retainer and clutch inner cover to the engine **(see illustration)**. If the screws are tight and difficult to turn, loosen them with a hand impact driver and a No. 2 Phillips bit.
7   Remove the screws and washers securing the clutch inner cover to the transmission **(see illustration)**.
8   Pull the clutch inner cover off the engine and transmission and remove it **(see illustration)**.
9   Remove the retainer if it remained on the clutch inner cover **(see illustration)**.

4.10 Inspect the clutch inner cover for cracks and warpage

**4.11 Inspect the clutch inner cover seal lip (arrow)
for damage**

Inspection

10   Clean the clutch inner cover and inspect it for cracks, warpage (heat damage) and other damage **(see illustration)**. Replace the cover if damaged, or if it does not seat squarely against the engine and transmission. These conditions make it difficult to keep water and dirt out of the clutch area, while at the same time allowing cooling air to escape and possibly causing the drivebelt to overheat.

11   Inspect the clutch inner cover seal for deterioration, cracks and other damage **(see illustration)**. If there is visual damage on the seal, or if it appears debris is passing past the seal and into the clutch housing, replace the seal (see Steps 14 through 16).

12   Clean the engine and transmission screws, making sure to remove any threadlock from the screw threads. Inspect the screws, making sure the threads are in good condition. The cross-slots in the engine screws must be sharp; otherwise, the screws cannot be properly tightened. Check the washers used on the transmission mounting screws, and replace if the rubber part has hardened, cracked or shows signs of deterioration **(see illustration)**. Note that the washers are permanently installed on the screws.

13   With the clutch inner cover removed, inspect the crankshaft and transmission oil seals for leaks and other damage and replace if necessary **(see illustration)**. Replace the crankshaft oil seal as described in Chapter 4, Section 14. Replace the transmission input shaft oil seal as described in *Service methods* in the General Information chapter at the front of this manual.

Seal replacement

14   Because silicone sealant is used to secure the clutch inner cover seal in place, the seal is difficult to break free **(see illustration 4.11)**. Work around the seal to find the point where it breaks loose, then carefully pull/pry it off the clutch inner cover. Do not use excessive force when

4.12 Clutch inner cover screw details

A   *Engine mounting screws*
B   *Transmission mounting screws*
C   *Washers (combination steel and rubber)*

4.13 Seal details

A   *Crankshaft oil seal*
B   *Transmission input shaft oil seal*

4.15a Install the clutch inner cover seal with the side marked "THIS SIDE TOWARD ENGINE" (arrow) facing the engine . . .

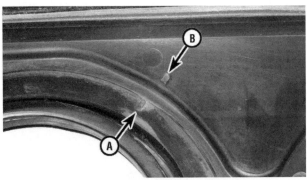

4.15b . . . while also aligning the index mark on the seal (A) with the index mark on the clutch inner cover (B)

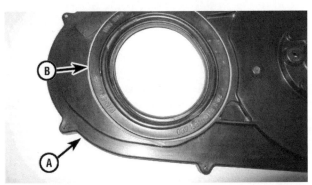

4.16 With the clutch inner cover inside surface facing up (A), install the seal (B), making sure it is properly aligned

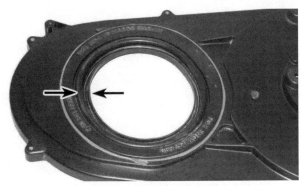

4.18a The groove formed in the clutch inner cover seal (arrows) . . .

4.18b . . . seats against the crankcase shoulder (arrow)

removing the seal or you will damage the clutch inner cover. After removing the cover seal, remove all traces of silicone sealant from the clutch inner cover. The cover must be clean and smooth to ensure the new cover seal can be correctly installed and sealed in place to prevent any leakage. When the cover is clean, inspect it for any damage.

15   Before installing the new seal onto the cover, note there are two alignments to make. First, install the seal with its side marked "THIS SIDE TOWARDS ENGINE" on the engine side of the cover (see illustration). Second, align the index mark on the new seal with the index mark on the cover (see illustration). If the seal is not correctly aligned, it will not properly seat against the engine, while also making it difficult to install the cover.

16   When you are ready to install the new seal, run a bead of silicone sealant around the seal mating surface on the clutch inner cover. Align the seal as described in Step 15 and push the cover seal into place (see illustration). Allow sufficient time for the silicone sealant to set up before installing the clutch outer cover on the engine.

Installation

NOTE:
If the parking brake caliper assembly has been removed from the transmission, install the caliper assembly before installing the clutch inner cover (see Chapter 13). It is easier to access the caliper assembly lower mounting screws without the clutch inner cover in place.

17   If the engine and/or transmission were removed and reinstalled into the frame, make sure the clutch center distance between the engine and transmission is properly adjusted before installing the clutch inner cover (see Chapter 6).

18   Check that the mating surfaces on the engine, transmission and clutch inner cover are clean and in good condition (see illustrations).

4.18c The shoulder (arrow) on the clutch inner cover . . .

4.18d . . . seats into the groove formed in the transmission input shaft oil seal (arrows)

19   Install the clutch inner cover by inserting the shoulder on the cover into the groove in the transmission input shaft oil seal **(see illustration)**, while also seating the cover seal against the crankcase shoulder **(see illustration)**. Hold the clutch inner cover in place and install the transmission mounting screws and washers finger-tight **(see illustration 4.7)**.

20   Apply a medium strength threadlock onto the engine mounting screw threads, and set the screws aside until installation **(see illustration 4.12)**.

21   Install the retainer by aligning the notch in the retainer with the index mark on the clutch inner cover **(see illustration 4.5)**, then install the engine mounting screws through the retainer and thread them into the engine **(see illustration 4.6)**.

22   Check that the clutch inner cover is seating flush against the engine and transmission, then tighten the engine mounting screws and the transmission mounting screws to the torque listed in this Chapter's Specifications.

23   The remainder of installation is the reverse of removal.

4.19a The shoulder (A) on the clutch inner cover fits into the groove (B) in the transmission input shaft oil seal

5   DRIVEBELT - REMOVAL, INSPECTION AND INSTALLATION

1   Early belt failure is abnormal. Determine the cause and correct the problem to prevent subsequent damage to the replacement belt. Always keep the clutch inner and outer covers installed on the vehicle and properly sealed and secured in place. When assembled together, the covers form a housing that helps cool the belt (with air provided and routed by the clutch air ducts) and keep water and debris off the belt.

2   Depending on model and model year, there have been several different drivebelts used. When purchasing a replacement drivebelt, make sure it is designed for your vehicle's model and model year. Aftermarket drivebelts are

4.19b Make sure the clutch inner cover seal seats flush against the crankcase shoulder and is not pinched or folded over

5.5 Refer to the manufacturer's marks, or draw an arrow on the belt indicating its direction of rotation - toward front of vehicle

5.6c . . . and remove it from the drive clutch

5

5.6a Push the drivebelt down hard to open the driven clutch sheaves . . .

5.6b . . . then lift and slide the belt off of the driven clutch . . .

also available. Because the drivebelt transmits power from the drive clutch to the driven clutch, belt width and length are critical to proper power transfer, so the correct size belt must be installed.

Removal

3   Park the vehicle on a level surface and set the parking brake.

4   Remove the clutch outer cover (see Section 3).

5   Check the manufacturer's marks on the drivebelt, noting how the belt is positioned on the pulleys so it can be reinstalled with the same orientation. If necessary, place an arrow on the belt in the direction of forward rotation **(see illustration)**.

6   On models without EBS (Engine Brake System), push the drivebelt down with your hand to open the driven clutch sheaves. The farther you can push the belt down, the farther the sheaves will open, and the more belt slack you will obtain. Then quickly lift and slide the belt off the driven clutch and remove it from the drive clutch **(see illustrations)**.

7   On models with EBS (Engine Brake System), remove the belt removal tool from the vehicle's tool kit (part No. 2877408). Insert the tool onto the driven clutch (above the exposed roller) and position it so that it is square with the movable (inner) sheave belt surface. Rotate the tool toward the driven clutch to open the sheaves. If the sheaves are not opening up, stop and make sure the tool is positioned correctly and facing squarely with the movable sheave. When there is sufficient slack in the belt, first slide the belt off the driven clutch, then the drive clutch.

Inspection

8   Inspect the drivebelt at the specified intervals (see Chapter 2, Section 1): when the belt is slipping, when you can smell rubber burning inside the clutch housing and

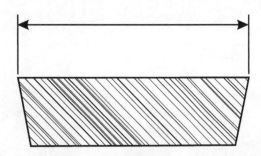

5.9 Inspect the drivebelt along its widest point for any irregular wear

5.11 When a problem with the drivebelt is experienced, visually inspect it to determine the cause

5.13a Install the drivebelt over the drive clutch and over the top of the driven clutch (arrow) . . .

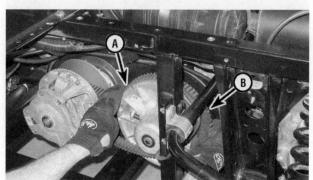

5.13b . . . then push down on the top of the belt halfway between the driven and driven clutch sheaves (A) to help open the driven clutch. At the same time, turn the driven clutch clockwise (B) to move the belt down onto the sheaves . . .

5.13c . . . while noting that if the belt becomes tight and difficult to move, check the belt's bottom run and straighten it by hand if it is twisting . . .

5.13d . . . then continue to pull and install the belt fully onto the driven sheave (arrow)

anytime the clutch outer cover is removed.

9   Note that the manufacturer does not list width specifications for the drivebelts used on these models. Instead, check for visible and irregular wear along the belt's widest point **(see illustration)**.

10   Inspect the drivebelt for oil and grease contamination. The belt should be dry. If the belt is contaminated, check the engine and transmission input shaft oil seals for leakage.

11   Inspect the belt for any visual damage **(see illustration)**. A burnt belt can be caused by a dragging brake. A frayed edge indicates belt misalignment that can be caused by incorrect clutch alignment or loose engine and/or transmission mounts. A belt worn in one section indicates excessive belt slippage. Belt disintegration is caused by severe belt wear or misalignment. Disintegration is also caused by the use of an incorrect belt. Sheared teeth are usually caused by violent drive clutch engagement, which indicates a damaged or improperly installed drive clutch.

Installation

12   If reinstalling a used belt, install the belt so it runs in the direction noted during removal (see Step 5).

13   On models without EBS, **follow the accompanying illustrations, beginning with 5.13a,** for the belt installation procedure.

14   On models with EBS, install the drivebelt over the drive

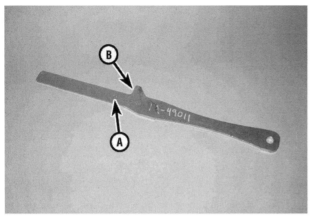

6.2 Polaris clutch alignment tool details

A *"TOP" mark - use the tool with this mark facing up*
B *Shoulder - rest the shoulder against the drive clutch when checking clutch alignment*

6.5a Clutch alignment details

A *Drive clutch fixed sheave*
B *Clutch hub bearing*

6.5b Lay the alignment tool across the driven clutch sheaves (arrows) . . .

clutch and over the top of the driven clutch **(see illustration 5.13a)**. Then install the belt removal tool (see Step 7) and rotate the tool toward the driven clutch to open the sheaves. Turn the driven clutch clockwise while pushing the belt onto the clutch sheaves until it is fully installed around the driven clutch. Remove the removal tool and turn the driven

6.5c . . . and slide it forward until its shoulder contacts the drive clutch (A). If the alignment is correct, the tool will rest against the clutch shaft bearing (B) and with the specified clearance between the edge of the tool and the drive clutch fixed sheave (C) . . .

clutch and belt by hand 5-7 times to seat the belt onto the driven clutch sheaves.

15 The remainder of installation is the reverse of removal.

16 If you installed a new drivebelt, following the break-in recommendations in Chapter 2.

6   CLUTCH OFF-SET ALIGNMENT - CHECK AND ADJUSTMENT

1   The driven clutch must be aligned with the drive clutch to allow the drivebelt to operate in proper alignment. To do this, washers are installed behind the driven clutch to position it inward or outward on the transmission input shaft. Perform this check after reinstalling the engine and/or transmission into the frame, and when the vehicle is experiencing clutch drag or other shifting problems.

Models without EBS

2   Special tool: The Polaris clutch alignment tool (part No. PA-49011) is required to check clutch alignment **(see illustration)**.

Check

3   Remove the drivebelt (see Section 5).
4   Make sure the drive clutch and driven clutch mounting bolts are tight (see Section 7 and 9).
5   **See illustration 6.2** to identify the adjustment tool. Lay the tool across the driven clutch sheaves with its "TOP" mark facing up, then slide the tool forward until its shoulder rests against the edge of the drive clutch. If the clutch alignment is correct, the tool will rest against the clutch hub bearing and there will be the specified clutch off-set alignment clearance between the tool and the fixed sheave on the drive clutch as listed in this Chapter's Specifications **(see illustrations)**.

6   If the measured clearance in Step 5 exceeds the specified amount, or if the tool hits the fixed sheave on the drive clutch before it contacts the clutch hub bearing, the adjustment is incorrect.

7   If the clutch adjustment is incorrect, first check for loose or missing engine and/or transmission mounting fasteners to make sure both units are properly secured in the frame (see Chapters 4 and 6). If the engine is loose, it will move the drive clutch. If the transmission is loose, it will move the driven clutch. If you find a problem here, perform the clutch center distance adjustment in Chapter 6. When the clutch center distance is correct and the engine and transmission mounting bolts are tight, recheck the clutch alignment (see Step 5).

8   If the engine and transmission mounts are correctly installed and tightened and the clutch adjustment is incorrect, perform Steps 9 through 16.

Adjustment

9   Remove the driven clutch (see Section 9).

10   Note the number and thickness of the washers installed on the transmission input shaft **(see illustration)**. Remove or add washers to position the driven clutch along the input shaft as required to adjust the clutch alignment position. Washers are available from a dealer parts department in two thicknesses: 0.030 in. (0.76 mm) and 0.060 in. (1.5 mm).

NOTE:

Increasing washer thickness will move the drive-belt toward the drive clutch movable sheave. Reducing washer thickness will move the drive-belt toward the drive clutch fixed sheave.

11   Reinstall the driven clutch, making sure to tighten its mounting bolt to the specified torque (see Section 9).

12   Repeat Step 5 to recheck clutch alignment.

NOTE:

If the measured clearance is still incorrect after installing different thickness washers, you may not be able to obtain the exact specified clearance, due to the thickness of the washers. In this case make sure there is measureable clearance between the tool and the fixed sheave. If the tool contacts the fixed sheave, indicating there is no clearance, premature belt wear and overheating will result.

13   Reinstall the drivebelt (see Section 5). Then check/measure the gap on both sides of the belt **(see illustration)**.

14   When the clutch alignment is correct, install the clutch outer cover (see Section 3). Roll the vehicle outside. While sitting in the driver's seat, apply the brake and start the engine. Continue to hold the brake and with the engine running at idle speed, shift the transmission into HIGH gear. When doing so, check for any sign of hard or difficult shifting and drive clutch drag.

6.5d . . . measure the clearance with a feeler gauge as shown here

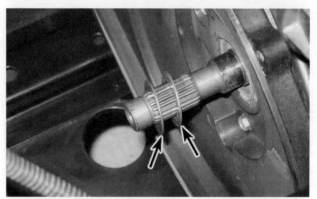

6.10 Clutch offset washers (arrows) installed on the transmission input shaft - the number and thickness can vary between different models

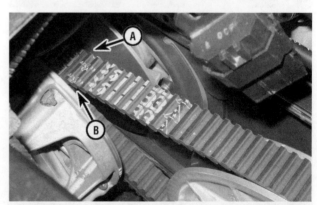

6.13 With the belt installed, the gap between the belt and the drive clutch fixed sheave (A) must be approximately 0.020 in. (0.51 mm); the gap between the belt and the drive clutch movable sheave (B) must be approximately 0.130 in. (3.3 mm)

15   If the shifting is still difficult, note whether the vehicle or the drive clutch is new. If so, allow the engine to run at idle speed for five minutes with the transmission in HIGH gear. This will allow time for the new drive clutch hub bearing to break in.

16   If the shifting is still difficult, but the vehicle and drive clutch are not new, check the drivebelt for damage (see Section 5). If the drivebelt is in good condition, repeat the clutch alignment procedure.

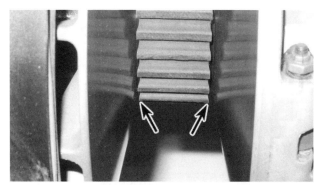

6.19a Belt is not touching either sheave (arrows) - clutch alignment is correct

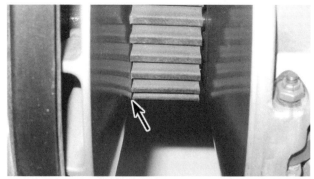

6.19b Belt is touching one sheave (arrow) - clutch alignment is incorrect

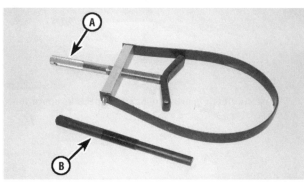

7.2 Drive clutch removal and installation tools

A   *Strap wrench type flywheel or sheave holder*
B   *Drive clutch puller*

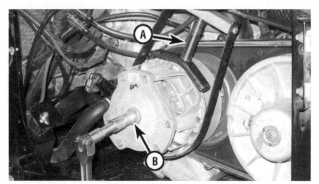

7.5a Hold the drive clutch with a holder (A) and loosen the drive clutch mounting bolt (B)

7.5b Drive clutch mounting bolt details

A   *Drive clutch mounting bolt*
B   *Lockwasher*
C   *Flat washer*
D   *Bushing*

Models with EBS

Check

17   Remove the clutch outer cover (see Section 3).

18   Turn the driven clutch by hand several times to seat the belt in the sheaves while making sure the belt is tight.

19   Visually inspect the drivebelt position in relation to the drive clutch sheaves. If the belt is not contacting either sheave, the clutch alignment is correct **(see illustration)**. If the side of the belt is contacting either sheave, the clutch alignment is incorrect and must be adjusted **(see illustration)**.

20   If the clutch alignment is incorrect, remove the drivebelt (see Section 5). Then perform Steps 9 through 16 to adjust the clutch alignment.

7   DRIVE CLUTCH - REMOVAL AND INSTALLATION

1   A machined taper fit aligns the drive clutch with the crankshaft. When the drive clutch mounting bolt is tightened, the fit between the clutch and crankshaft tightens significantly, thus stabilizing the drive clutch.

2   Special tools: When loosening and tightening the drive clutch mounting bolt, a holder is required to prevent the drive clutch from turning. Use the Polaris drive clutch holder (part No. 9314177) or a strap type flywheel or sheave holder. A puller is required to remove the drive clutch from the crankshaft. Use the RV Service Tools (www.rvservicetools.com) clutch puller (part No. 200101), the Polaris drive clutch puller (part No. 2870506) or an equivalent **(see illustration)**.

3   Remove the clutch outer cover (see Section 3).

4   Remove the drivebelt (see Section 5).

5   Hold the drive clutch with a strap wrench or drive clutch holder, then loosen the drive clutch mounting bolt **(see illustration)**. Slide the bolt out of the drive clutch along with its lockwasher, flat washer and bushing **(see illustration)**. Leave the strap wrench or holder mounted on the drive clutch.

7.6a Thread the puller (arrow) into the drive clutch by hand until it bottoms . . .

7.6b . . . then hold the drive clutch and turn the puller to break the drive clutch free of the crankshaft

6   Thread the drive clutch puller into the drive clutch by hand until it bottoms. Hold the drive clutch with the holder and turn the clutch puller to break the drive clutch from the crankshaft taper **(see illustrations)**. You will hear a pop and feel the drive clutch move outward when it breaks free. Depending on the tools used, either remove them first, then the drive clutch, or remove the drive clutch with the tools attached and separate them later. Work carefully to prevent damage to the crankshaft and drive clutch tapered surfaces.

7   With the clutch free, check the clutch bearing operation by turning it by hand **(see illustration)**. On models without EBS, the bearing should turn in both directions with only slight drag. Replace the bearing if it binds or turns roughly in either direction. On models with EBS, the bearing should only rotate clockwise as viewed from the cover plate side, and lock when turned counterclockwise. Replace the bearing if it turns in both directions. See Section 8 if it is necessary to replace the clutch bearing.

8   Installation is the reverse of removal, plus the following:

a) *Clean the crankshaft taper and the taper inside the drive clutch with contact cleaner and allow to dry. Both surfaces must be clean and free of grease and oil.*

b) *Install the drive clutch onto the crankshaft until it stops, then install the mounting bolt with the lockwasher, flat washer and bushing (see Step 5). Thread the mounting bolt into the crankshaft by hand.*

c) *Hold the drive clutch with the same tool used during removal and tighten the drive clutch mounting bolt to the torque listed in this Chapter's Specifications.*

d) *If you installed a new drive clutch bearing, or installed a new drive clutch, follow the break-in recommendations in Chapter 2.*

8   DRIVE CLUTCH - DISASSEMBLY, INSPECTION AND REASSEMBLY

1   Before servicing the drive clutch, identify the major components **(see illustration)**.

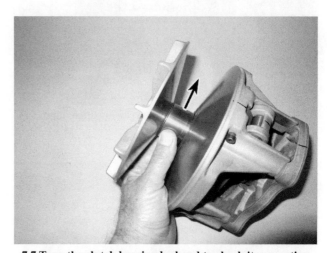

7.7 Turn the clutch bearing by hand to check its operation

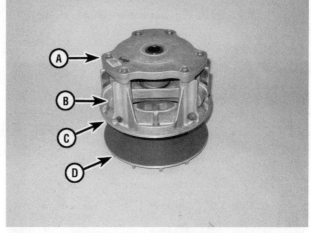

8.1 Drive clutch details

A	Cover plate	C	Sliding sheave
B	Spider	D	Fixed sheave

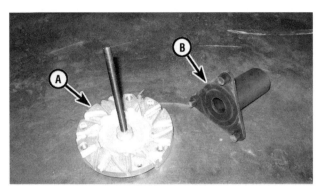

8.2 Drive clutch overhaul tools

A   *Clutch holding fixture*
B   *Spider removal tool*

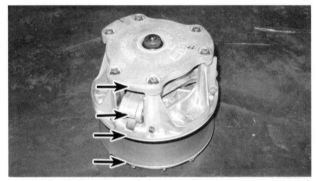

8.5 Mark the major clutch components (arrows) so they can be aligned during assembly to maintain clutch balance

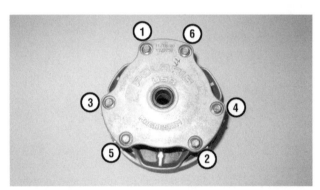

8.6a Loosen the cover plate screws in a criss-cross pattern until all spring tension is released from the cover, then remove the screws . . .

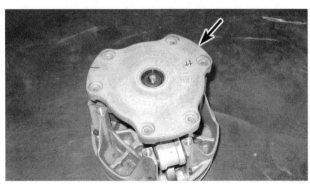

8.6b . . . the cover plate . . .

8.6c . . . and spring

2   Special tools: Because the spider is threaded onto the stationary sheave and tightened to a high torque, special tools are required when disassembling and reassembling the drive clutch. To hold the stationary sheave when loosening and tightening the spider, use the Polaris clutch holding fixture (part No. 2871358). To loosen and tighten the spider, use the RV Service Tools (www.rvservicetools.com) spider removal tool (part No. 200110) or the Polaris spider removal tool (part No. 2870341) **(see illustration)**. In addition, a torque wrench capable of tightening the spider to its high torque value is required.

Disassembly

3   Secure the clutch holding fixture onto a workbench or in a large, heavy-duty vise that is properly secured to the floor or on a workbench **(see illustration 8.2)**.
4   Install the drive clutch over the shaft on the clutch holding fixture and engage the fins on the outside of the fixed sleeve with the notches in the fixture. Thread the nut onto the clutch holding fixture to hold the drive clutch in place. Now check that the clutch cannot be turned by hand on the holding fixture.
5   Use a permanent marker and make alignment marks across the cover plate, spider, sliding sheave and fixed sheave so these parts can be aligned during assembly to maintain clutch balance **(see illustration)**.

WARNING:
The cover plate is under spring pressure. Remove the cover plate screws as described in Step 6 to prevent the cover from binding or flying off the clutch.

6   Loosen the cover plate screws in numerical order and in small increments until spring tension against the cover plate is released. When there is no spring tension cover against the cover plate, remove the screws, cover plate and spring **(see illustrations)**.

NOTE:
If you're just removing the spring, the remaining disassembly steps can be skipped. Begin reassembly at Step 40.

8.7 Limiter spacer (arrow) used on models without EBS

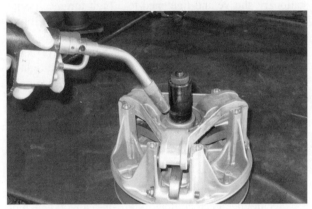

8.8a Heat the spider threads with a torch . . .

8.8b . . . then loosen the spider by turning the spider re-moval tool counterclockwise . . .

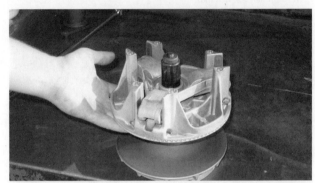

8.8c . . . and lift the spider and the sliding sheave off the fixed sheave

8.9a The spacer (A), clutch bearing (B) and shims (not visible here) assembled length determines the drivebelt to sheave clearance - installing the parts in their correct order help maintain clutch balance

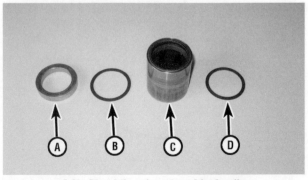

8.9b Clutch bearing assembly details

A	Spacer	C	Clutch bearing
B	Shim	D	Shim

7   On models without EBS (Engine Brake System), remove the limiter spacer from the top of the spider (**see illustration**).

8   Before attempting to loosen the spider, make sure the drive clutch is securely fastened in the clutch holding fixture. Because the spider is tightened to a high torque value, it is helpful to heat the spider with a torch where it threads onto the fixed sheave. Then install the spider removal tool over the top of the spider and engage the posts on the tool firmly against the arms on the spider. Turn the tool counterclockwise to loosen the spider. When the spider is loose, turn and remove it and the sliding sheave from the fixed sheave (**see illustrations**). Then lift and remove the spider from the sliding sheave, while checking to see if any of the buttons mounted on the spider fell off. If so, retrieve them so they are not lost.

9   The assembled length of the spacer, clutch bearing and shims installed on the fixed sheave determines the drivebelt to sheave clearance, while installing the parts in their correct order helps maintain clutch balance (**see illustration**). It is critical to identify these parts during their removal so that you when you assemble the clutch assembly, all of the parts are installed in their original order and facing in their original direction. Also note that the number of shims used on the clutch you are servicing may differ from the number of shims shown in the teardown illustrations (**see illustration**).

8.10a First remove the spacer, noting that the side with the chamfer (arrow) faces toward the bearing . . .

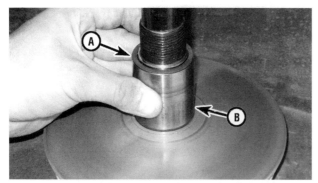

8.10b . . . then remove the upper shim(s) (A) and clutch bearing (B) . . .

8.10c . . . noting that if a one-way clutch bearing is used, the end with the needle bearing (arrow) faces toward the fixed sheave . . .

8.10d . . . and finally remove the lower shim(s) (arrow)

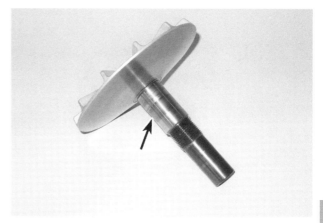

8.15 Fixed sheave assembly with arrow pointing to the clutch bearing operating surface - this surface is critical to clutch operation. Measure the clutch bearing operating position outside diameter with a micrometer and compare to the service limit listed in this Chapter's Specifications

10   Remove the spacer, noting that the side of the spacer facing the bearing has a chamfer. The side of the spacer facing away from the bearing is flat. With the spacer removed, remove the outer shim(s). Slide the clutch bearing off the shaft, noting that if a one-way clutch bearing is used, the bearing must be installed facing in its original position. Then remove the lower shim(s). Note the number of shims used and their thicknesses. The same number of shims with the same thicknesses must be reinstalled (see illustrations).

Inspection

11   The cover plate, spider, sliding sheave and fixed sheave are not available separately. If any of these parts are damaged, the drive clutch must be replaced as an assembly.

12   Clean all parts in solvent, and dry with compressed air. Take care not to remove the alignment marks made in Step 5. If necessary, remark the parts.

13   Check the cover plate, spider, sliding sheave and fixed sheave for cracks or damage. Inspect the belt surface on each sheave for a buildup of rubber or corrosion, and if found, carefully remove with a fine steel wool pad, then clean with a lint-free cloth. The sheave surfaces must be clean and smooth. If you used steel wool to clean the sheaves, reclean the sheaves in solvent once again to remove all residue, and dry thoroughly.

14   Inspect the threads on the fixed sheave and spider for damage. Make sure these threads are clean and dry (free of all oil and debris). Then thread the spider onto the fixed sleeve by hand, making sure there is no binding or roughness when engaging the threads on the two parts.

15   Inspect the clutch bearing operating surface on the fixed sheave shaft for any scoring, cracks and other damage (see illustration). If the surface appears okay, measure its outside diameter with a micrometer and compare to the

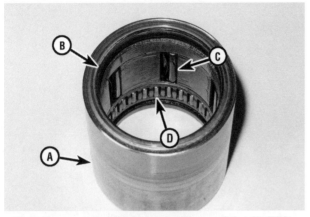

8.16 One-way clutch bearing details - models with EBS

A   Outer bearing surface
B   Seal (installed in each end of bearing)
C   One-way clutch rollers
D   Needle bearing rollers

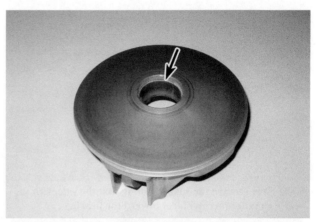

8.19 Bushing wear is determined by its appearance - replace a bushing when more brass than Teflon is visible on its surface (sliding sheave bushing shown)

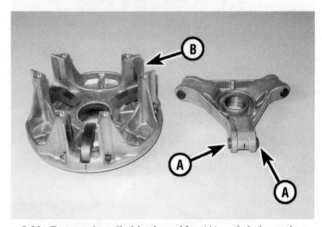

8.20a Buttons installed in the spider (A) and their mating contact surfaces on the sliding sheave towers (B)

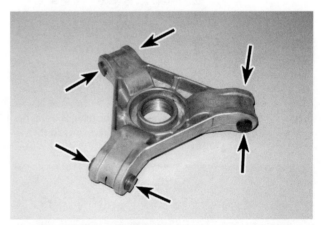

8.20b Identify and remove the buttons from the spider

service limit listed in this Chapter's Specifications. If the surface is damaged or the outside diameter is too small, replace the drive clutch assembly.

16 Inspect the clutch bearing assembly for wear and damage. On models with EBS, inspect the rollers in the one-way clutch for bluing and other signs of damage. Check the needle bearing unit assembly for missing needles and any needles with flat spots, cracks and other damage. Minor scuffing on the outside of the bearing is normal, but any surface roughness that can be felt requires bearing replacement. **(see illustration)**. Except for the one-way clutch rollers, the same inspection procedures described here apply to the standard type clutch bearing used on models without EBS.

17 Measure the thickness of the bearing shims **(see illustration 8.9b)** and compare to the thickness values listed in this Chapter's Specifications. Replace any shim that is too thin.

18 Inspect the spring for cracks or distortion. Make sure the spring coils parallel one another. Then measure the spring free length with a vernier caliper and compare to the values listed in this Chapter's Specifications. If the spring is too short, replace it with a spring with the same color and wire diameter as the original spring. When ordering a replacement spring, have a dealer parts department confirm that it is the correct spring.

19 Inspect the bushing in the sliding sheave and the bushing in the cover plate for severe wear **(see illustration)**. Each brass bushing is Teflon coated. A bushing is considered worn and must be replaced when more brass than Teflon is showing on the bushing surface. Do not remove a bushing unless it must be replaced.

NOTE:

A number of special tools are needed to re-place the clutch bushings. If a bushing must be replaced, take the clutch to a dealer ser-vice department for this service.

Button clearance and replacement

20 Buttons installed in the spider contact the towers in the sliding sheave during clutch operation **(see illustration)**. Identify the button positions, then slip them out of the spider and inspect them for cracks, uneven wear or other damage **(see illustration)**. Then inspect the sliding sheave

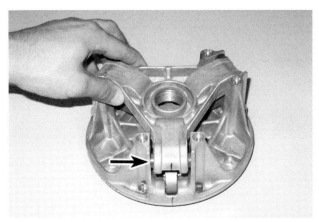

8.21 Check for worn buttons by measuring between each button and its mating surface on the slider tower

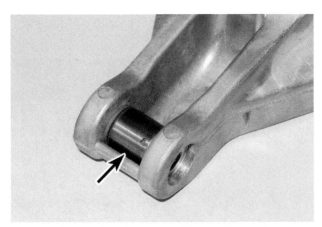

8.22 Inspect the rollers for galling, binding and any visual damage

8.24a Spider supported on a socket while using a pin punch to remove the roller pin

where the buttons operate for any scoring or other damage. All of the button and sliding sheave contact surfaces must be smooth.

21   Reinstall the buttons into the spider in their original positions **(see illustration 8.20b)**. The rubber side on each button must be installed inside of the spider. With

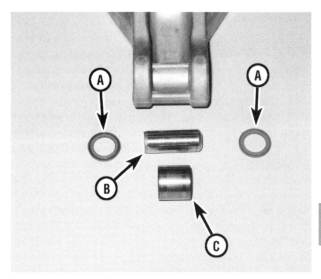

8.24b Roller and roller pin details

A	Thrust washers	C	Roller
B	Roller pin		

the buttons installed in the spider, align the spider and sliding sheave index marks (see Step 5) and install the spider between the towers on the sheave, compressing the buttons while making sure all of the buttons remain in place. Measure the clearance between each button and tower with a feeler gauge **(see illustration)**. Compare the actual clearance with the value listed in this Chapter's Specifications. If the clearance is excessive. Replace all of the buttons as a set.

Rollers, roller pins and thrust washers

22   The spider is equipped with three sets of rollers, roller pins and thrust washers, where each roller is installed over a roller pin. The roller pins are a press fit in the spider, and a thrust washer is installed on the outside of each roller and roller pin. Inspect the roller assemblies for binding and other damage. Draw a metal rod across each roller or roll them with a finger **(see illustration)**. If any resistance, galling or flat spots are noticed, replace all three roller assemblies.

23   Remove the buttons if they were not previously removed (see Step 20).

24   Support the spider with a socket, then use a pin punch and drive the roller pin out of the spider. Then remove the roller and both thrust washers from the spider **(see illustrations)**.

25   If reusing the parts, make sure the roller is a slip fit on the roller pin. The parts must be free of all rust, corrosion and burrs that could cause binding.

26   Reverse these steps to install the roller pins, roller and thrust washer sets. After reassembly, make sure each roller turns freely on its roller pin.

Shift weights

27 Visually inspect the shift weights for any sign of wear and damage **(see illustration)**. The machined contact surface on each weight must be smooth and consistent in appearance with the other weights. If there is any noticeable wear, dents or other damage to an individual weight, replace all three weights as a set. Then pivot the shift weights to check for any binding or roughness. If necessary, remove the the shift weights to replace them and/or service their pivot bolts. If a weight is damaged, check its mating roller assembly for a stuck or damaged roller (see Step 22).

28 Remove the nut, pull the pivot bolt and remove the shift weight from the sheave. Discard the nut **(see illustration)**.

29 With the parts removed, inspect the pivot bolt and the bore inside the shift weight for signs of fretting, which can be identified by the presence of a fine red iron oxide dust on the mating parts **(see illustration)**. Note that this dust is not rust, and is very abrasive and will cause severe pitting and wear to the contact surfaces if not removed. If there is pitting on the pivot bolts or inside the shift weight bores, replace the shift weights and pivot bolts as a complete set. Do not intermix new and worn parts.

30 If replacing the weights, refer to the manufacturer's part number in the OEM parts catalog for your vehicle's exact model and model year. Because the weights installed in your clutch were selected because of how they control clutch shift patterns and engagement RPM, always install the same weights, unless you are familiar with clutch adjustment and how the weights affect clutch operation. After receiving the new weights, compare the numbers on the new weights with the numbers on the old weights. If these number sets do not match, the weights removed from your clutch may have been replaced by a different owner.

31 Installation is the reverse of these steps. Install the pivot bolts from the direction shown in **illustration 8.28**. This correctly places the nuts on the trailing side of the clutch. Hold the pivot bolt, then install a new nut and tighten securely.

32 Repeat for each shift weight assembly.

Assembly

33 Make sure all parts are clean and free of oil. Do not lubricate the Teflon bushings, as they are self-lubricating.

34 Install the lower shim over the fixed sheave shaft **(see illustration 8.10d)**. Then install the clutch bearing. If installing a one-way bearing, install it with the needle bearing end facing toward the fixed sheave **(see illustration 8.10c)**. Install the upper shim and seat it on top of the bearing **(see illustration 8.10b)**.

35 Install the spacer with its chamfer side facing down toward the clutch bearing and seat it against the upper shim **(see illustration 8.10a)**.

36 If removed, install the buttons into the spider (Step 21). Align the alignment mark on the spider with the alignment mark on the sliding sheave (Step 5), then compress the buttons and install the spider into the sheave.

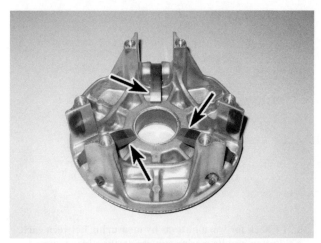

8.27 Inspect the shift weights (arrow) for severe wear, damage and any binding or roughness

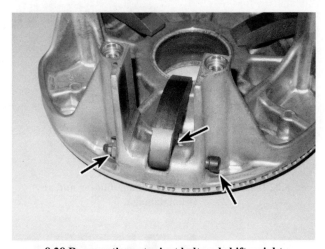

8.28 Remove the nut, pivot bolt and shift weight

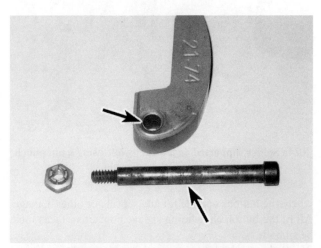

8.29 When fretting is apparent (fine red dust) as shown here (arrows), the debris must be removed or pitting and severe wear will damage the pivot bolt and shift weight contact surfaces

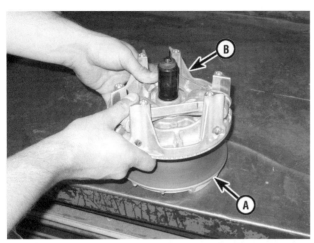

8.37 Here the fixed sheave (A) is engaged securely onto the clutch holding fixture while the spider (B) is threaded onto the fixed sheave threads

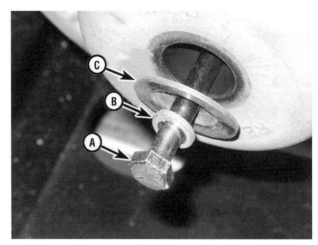

9.3b . . . then remove the bolt (A), lockwasher (B) and cupped washer (C)

8.38 Use the spider removal tool (A) and a torque wrench (B) and tighten the spider to the torque listed in this Chapter's Specifications

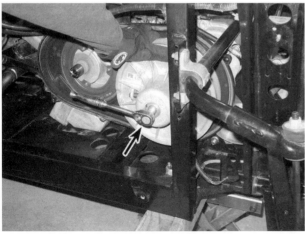

9.3a Hold the driven clutch to prevent it from turning and loosen its mounting bolt (arrow) . . .

37   Secure the fixed sheave onto the clutch holding fixture and thread the spider onto the fixed sheave until it stops **(see illustration)**.

38   Install the spider removal tool over the top of the spider and engage the posts on the tool against the arms on the spider. With a torque wrench mounted on the spider removal tool, tighten the spider to the torque listed in this Chapter's Specifications **(see illustration)**. After torquing the spider, remove the tools but leave the fixed sheave locked onto the clutch holding fixture.

39   On models without EPS, install the limiter spacer over the fixed sheave shaft and seat it against the top of the spider **(see illustration 8.7)**.

40   Install the spring into the spring seat in the spider **(see illustration 8.6c)**.

41   Install the cover plate by aligning its alignment mark with the alignment mark on the spider. At this point, all of the alignment marks made in Step 5 must be aligned **(see illustration 8.5)**.

42   Install the cover plate screws into the threaded holes in the sliding sheave. Tighten the screws in a crossing pattern **(see illustration 8.6a)** and in several steps to the torque listed in this Chapter's Specifications.

43   Remove the drive clutch from the clutch holding fixture.

9   DRIVEN CLUTCH - REMOVAL AND INSTALLATION

1   Remove the clutch outer cover (see Section 3).

2   Remove the drivebelt (see Section 5).

3   Hold the driven clutch with your hand or with a strap wrench, and loosen the mounting bolt **(see illustration)**. Then remove the mounting bolt with the lockwasher and cupped washer **(see illustration)**.

4   Slide the driven clutch off the transmission input shaft **(see illustration)**. Then note the number and thickness of the washers installed on the input shaft and place them where they won't be lost **(see illustration)**. These washers are used to adjust the clutch off-set alignment (see Section 6).

5   Installation is the reverse of removal, noting the following:

   a) *Install the same number and thickness of washers on the transmission input shaft.*
   b) *Clean the transmission input shaft splines and the splines inside the driven clutch of all grease. Then lightly lubricate the splines with new grease.*
   c) *Align the splines inside the driven clutch with those on the transmission input shaft, and slide the driven clutch onto the input shaft.*
   d) *Install the lockwasher and cupped washer onto the mounting bolt. Position the cupped washer on the mounting bolt with its cupped shoulder facing into the driven clutch (see Step 3).*
   e) *Hold the driven clutch to prevent it from turning and tighten the driven clutch mounting bolt to the torque listed in this Chapter's Specifications.*
   f) *If you installed a new driven clutch, follow the break-in recommendations in Chapter 2.*

10   DRIVEN CLUTCH - DISASSEMBLY, INSPECTION AND REASSEMBLY

Models without EBS

WARNING:

The driven clutch is under considerable spring pressure. Do not attempt to disassemble the driven clutch without a clutch compression tool. Personal injury could result. If this tool is unavailable, have the service performed by a dealership. Wear eye protection when removing and installing the snap ring.

1   Special tool: Because the driven clutch is under considerable spring pressure, disassembly and reassembly will require a clutch compression tool when removing and installing the snap ring installed in the clutch shaft. Use the RV Service Tools (www.rvservicetools.com) Polaris Clutch Compression Tool (part No. 900101), the Polaris Clutch Compression Tool (part No. PU-50518) or an equivalent tool.

Disassembly

2   Locate the "X" mark on the outside of the fixed and sliding sheaves **(see illustration)**. If these marks align with each other, you can use them as a reference when reassembling the clutch. If the "X" marks do not align, scribe alignment marks across the fixed and sliding sheaves **(see illustration)**. The sheaves must be aligned during assembly to maintain clutch balance.

9.4a Remove the driven clutch . . .

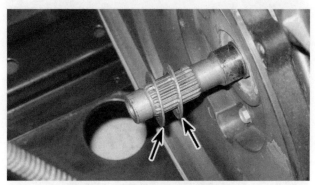

9.4b . . . and the washers (arrows)

10.2a Fixed sheave "X" alignment mark - check to see if the "X" mark on each sheave aligns . . .

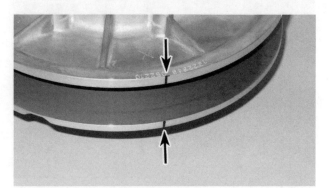

10.2b . . . if not, draw an alignment mark (arrows) across the fixed and sliding sheaves to help align them during clutch assembly

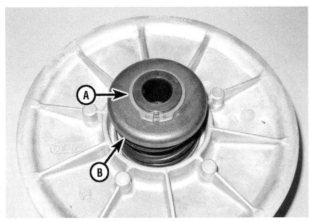

10.3a Driven clutch snap ring (A) and outer spring retainer (B)

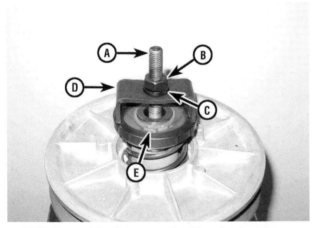

10.3b Support the driven clutch with a clutch compression tool. The tool used in this sequence consists of a large threaded rod (A), nut (B), washer (C) and support plate (D). Note how the support plate seats completely around the outer spring retainer. Center the tool onto the clutch so the snap ring end gap (E) is accessible

10.4a Center the support plate against the outer spring retainer, and turn the nut to compress the spring and move the retainer down the clutch shaft. When there is a small gap between the outer spring retainer and snap ring (arrow), indicating there is no tension against the snap ring, remove the snap ring from the groove in the shaft with a pair of snap ring pliers

10.4b When the snap ring is free, remove the pliers and allow the snap ring (arrow) to rest against the end of the shaft . . .

10.4c . . . then reverse the clutch compression tool and slowly release all tension from the outer spring retainer (arrow)

10.5a Remove the snap ring (A), outer spring retainer (B) . . .

3   Mount the driven clutch onto the clutch compression tool so that the exposed snap ring is facing up, while following the tool manufacturer's instructions **(see illustrations)**.

4   If you're using a tool like the one shown in **illustration 10.3b** to compress the spring and remove the snap ring from the clutch shaft, **follow the accompanying photos, beginning with illustration 10.4a**. If you're using a different type of spring compression tool, follow the instructions that came with the tool.

5   Remove the snap ring, outer spring retainer, spring and the lower spring retainer **(see illustrations)**.

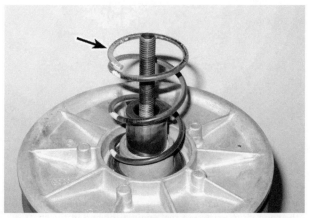

10.5b . . . spring (arrow) . . .

10.5c . . . and the inner spring retainer

6   Turn and lift the sliding sheave to remove it from the fixed sheave **(see illustration)**.

7   Remove the fixed sheave from the clutch compression tool **(see illustration)**.

Inspection

8   The sliding sheave and fixed sheave are not available separately. If any one of these parts is damaged, the driven clutch must be replaced as an assembly.

9   Clean all parts in solvent. Dry them with compressed air. Take care not to remove the alignment marks made during removal. If necessary, remark the parts.

10   Check the sliding and fixed sheaves for cracks or damage **(see illustration)**.

11   Check the sliding sheave and fixed sheave for cracks or damage. Inspect the belt surface on each sheave for a buildup of rubber or corrosion, and if found, carefully remove with a fine steel wool pad, then clean with a lint-free cloth. The sheave surfaces must be clean and smooth. If you used steel wool to clean the sheaves, reclean the sheaves in solvent once again to remove all residue, and dry thoroughly.

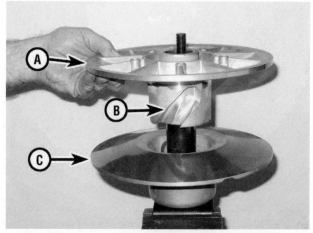

10.6 Turn and lift the sliding sheave (A) to disconnect its cam (B) from the rollers mounted inside the fixed sheave (C)

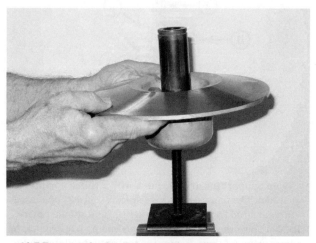

10.7 Remove the fixed sheave if it is still mounted on the clutch compression tool

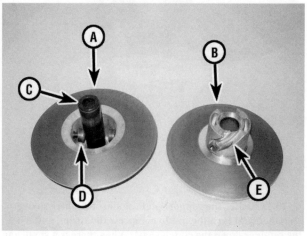

10.10 Clutch sheave details

A Fixed sheave	D Rollers
B Sliding sheave	(one indicated)
C Clutch shaft	E Cam slot (one shown)

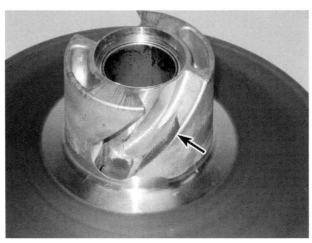

10.12 The cam groove and surface (arrow) must be smooth to allow the sliding sheave to move in and out along the fixed sheave rollers during clutch operation

10.14b Inner bushing

10.13 Check the rollers by turning them by hand to make sure they turn freely and without any binding or roughness. Inspect each roller for burrs, cracks and other surface damage

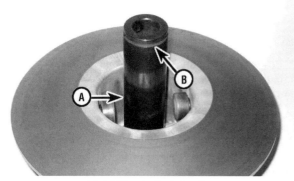

10.15 Clutch shaft details

A   Shaft   B   Snap ring groove

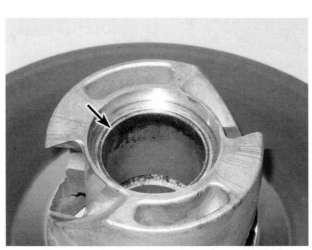

10.14a Outer bushing

12   Inspect the cam on the sliding sheave for signs of wear or damage (see illustration). If there is any noticeable wear or damage, check the rollers (Step 13) for the same conditions.

13   Inspect the rollers on the fixed sheave for wear of damage (see illustration). If these rollers are damaged, replace the driven clutch assembly as the rollers are not available separately.

14   Visually inspect the bushings installed inside the sliding sheave for excessive and uneven surface wear (see illustrations). These bushings are Teflon coated, and as the coating wears, the actual bushing surface becomes visible, which is indicated as a visual contrast between the remaining Teflon and the bushing. It is common to see some bushing wear on a used clutch. A bushing is considered excessively worn when more of the bushing surface than Teflon is showing. Note that replacement bushings are not available. If the bushings are excessively worn or damaged, it is necessary to replace the driven clutch as an assembly.

15   Inspect the clutch shaft for any burrs, roughness and other conditions. The shaft must be smooth to prevent premature and rapid clutch bushing wear (Step 14). Check the snap ring groove for damage (see illustration).

16   Inspect the splines inside the fixed sheave for twisting, galling and metal transfer **(see illustration)**. If any damage is noted, check the mating splines on transmission input shaft splines for the same conditions. When both spline sets are clean, slide the fixed sheave onto the transmission input shaft and slide it back and forth to check it for any roughness or binding.

17   Check the snap ring for twisting, cracks and other signs of weakness or damage. Inspect the outer and inner spring seats for cracks that could cause failure when the clutch is assembled and the spring is under tension. Inspect the spring for cracks or distortion. Make sure the spring coils parallel to one another. When replacing the spring, note the color-code on the spring and have it matched by a dealer parts department **(see illustration)**.

18   Inspect the driven clutch mounting bolt, lockwasher and cupped washer for damage **(see illustration)**. Check the bolt for straightness and the threads for any damage. Check the cupped washer for any cracks or other damage. Make sure all of the parts are clean and dry before installing them.

Assembly

19   Before assembling the drive clutch assembly, make sure the splines inside the fixed sheave **(see illustration 10.16)** are clean and dry. Also make sure the clutch shaft is dry (no oil or grease) and do not lubricate the bushings installed inside the movable sheave.

20   Install the fixed sheave onto the clutch compression tool following the manufacturer's instructions **(see illustration 10.7)**.

21   Install the sliding sheave over the fixed sheave by aligning the cam grooves with the rollers **(see illustration 10.6)**. Turn and lower the sliding sheave into place. Then check that the index marks used in Step 2 align. If not, remove the sliding sheave and turn it 180 degrees, and reinstall it. The index marks should now align.

22   Install the inner spring retainer into the sliding sheave with its cupped side facing up **(see illustration 10.5c)**. Then install the spring and seat it into the inner spring retainer **(see illustration 10.5b)**. Install the outer spring retainer with its cupped side facing down and seat it on top of the spring, then place the snap ring on top of the outer spring retainer with its flat side facing up **(see illustration 10.5a)**.

23   Use the clutch compression tool as before, and compress the outer spring retainer until the snap ring groove on the shaft is exposed. Install the snap ring into the shaft groove, making sure it is fully seated **(see illustration 10.4a)**. After releasing the snap ring pliers and before removing tension from the spring, check the snap ring to make sure it is a tight fit in the groove. You should only be able to turn the snap ring with the pliers after slightly opening them. If you can move the snap ring by hand, or if it just feels loose, it has weakened and must be replaced.

24   Once the snap ring is fully seated, slowly release the spring compression tool and allow the outer spring retainer to seat against the snap ring. Remove the driven clutch assembly from the tool.

10.16 Clean the splines (arrow) of all old grease and inspect them for damage

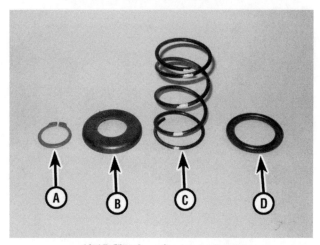

10.17 Clutch spring components

A   Snap ring   C   Spring
B   Outer spring retainer D   Inner spring retainer

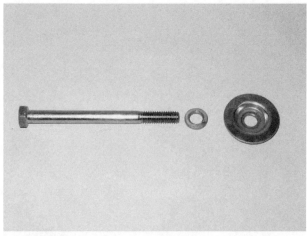

10.18 Driven clutch mounting bolt, lockwasher and cupped washer

10.26 Scribe an alignment mark across all of the parts to help realign them during assembly

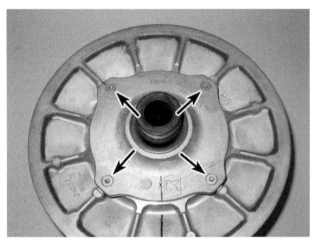

10.27a Remove the screws (arrows) . . .

10.27b . . . and the cam

10.29 With the clutch held in the clutch compression tool and with pressure applied against the spider (no pressure against snap ring), remove the snap ring (arrow) from the groove in the shaft

5

Models with EBS

WARNING:
The driven clutch is under considerable spring pressure. Do not attempt to disassemble the driven clutch without a clutch compression tool. Personal injury could result. If this tool is unavailable, have the service performed by a dealership. Wear eye protection when removing and installing the snap ring.

25 Special tool: Because the driven clutch is under considerable spring pressure, disassembly and reassembly will require a clutch compression tool. Use the RV Service Tools (rvservicetools.com) Polaris Clutch Compression Tool (part No. 900101), the Polaris Clutch Compression Tool (part No. PU-50518) or an equivalent tool.

Disassembly

26 Use a permanent marking pen and make alignment marks across the shaft, cam and the fixed and sliding sheaves so these parts can be aligned during assembly to maintain clutch balance **(see illustration)**.
27 Loosen and remove the screws securing the cam assembly to the sliding sheave, then lift the cam off **(see illustrations)**. Note that the cam is under tension and will twist slightly when the last screw is removed.
28 Mount the clutch assembly into the clutch compression tool with the sliding sheave side facing up, following the manufacturer's instructions. The RV Service Tools clutch compression tool (part No. 900101) is used in this procedure.
29 Close the handle on the clutch compression tool and compress the spider assembly into the sliding sheave cavity. Lock the tool handle with the chain provided on the tool. With the tool handle locked in place, check that all pressure has been relieved from the snap ring. If not, recheck the tool setup to make sure it is being properly used. When there is no pressure against the snap ring, remove it with a pair of snap ring pliers **(see illustration)**. Then push

10.30a Remove the spider assembly (A) and spring (B) . . .

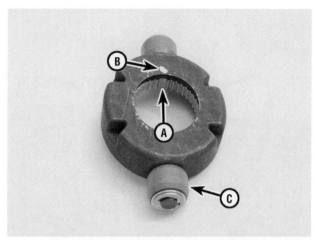

10.31a Locate the master spline (A) on the inner spider and the mark on the outer spider (B) - repaint the mark if necessary to help with reassembly. Note how the master spline and mark align with the rollers (C)

10.30b . . . and the thrust washer (if used)

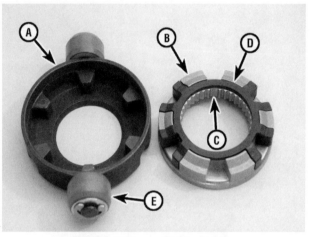

10.31b Spider assembly details

A   Outer spider
B   Inner spider
C   Master spline
D   Damper

E   Clutch roller
     assembly (E-clip,
     washer and roller)

10.34a Remove the roller pin spring pins with a punch (arrow) . . .

the tool handle and unlock it from the chain restraint, and slowly release tension from the spider assembly. Remove the clutch assembly from the tool.

30   Remove the spider assembly, spring and thrust washer (if used) from the clutch shaft **(see illustrations)**.

31   Before disassembling the spider, note how the master spline on the inner spider aligns with a mark on the outer spider. Make a new mark on the outer spider if the original mark is faint or illegible **(see illustration)**. Then remove the inner spider and damper from the outer spider **(see illustration)**.

32   Remove the E-clip, washer and clutch roller from each arm on the spider **(see illustration 10.31b)**.

33   Remove the driven clutch from the compression tool.

34   Use a punch and drive the spring pin from each roller pin in the sliding sheave. Then slide each roller pin and roller assembly out of their groove in the fixed sheave **(see illustrations)**.

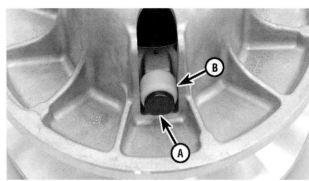

10.34b ... and remove the roller pins (A) and rollers (B)

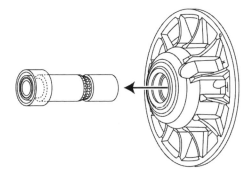

10.37 Support the fixed sheave and press the shaft and bearing out in the direction shown here

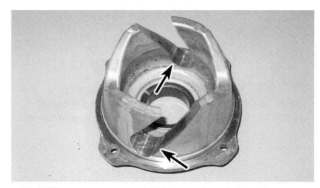

10.43 The cam ramps must be smooth and show the same amount of wear

10.44 Visually inspect the bushing (arrow) in the end of the cam for cracks, uneven wear and other damage. Then slide the shaft into the bushing - the fit should be snug

35   Lift the fixed sheave off the sliding sheave.

36   If it is necessary to remove the bearing and shaft from the fixed sheave, support the fixed sheave assembly in a hydraulic press with the shaft facing down.

37   Center the shaft under the press ram, and press the shaft and bearing assembly from the fixed sheave **(see illustration)**. Make sure to catch these parts once they are free of the fixed sheave.

Inspection

38   The shaft, sliding sheave and fixed sheave are not available separately. If any one of these parts is damaged, the driven clutch must be replaced as an assembly.

39   Hold the shaft and spin the bearing by hand. If the bearing turns roughly or there is any catching or noise, replace it. Remove the snap ring from the groove in the shaft. Note how the bearing is facing on the shaft so you can install the new bearing facing the same way. Support the bearing in a press and press the shaft out of the bearing. Discard the bearing. Clean the shaft, then check for and remove any burrs from the end of the shaft and the snap ring groove. Support the shaft and press the new bearing onto the shaft, making sure it faces in the direction of the original bearing. Use a bearing driver placed against the bearing's inner race when pressing it onto the shaft. Then install a new snap ring into the shaft groove, making sure it seats in the groove completely.

40   Clean all parts in solvent, taking care not to remove the alignment marks made during disassembly. If necessary, remark the parts (see Step 26).

41   Check the sliding sheave and fixed sheave for cracks or damage. Inspect the belt surface on each sheave for a buildup of rubber or corrosion, and if found, carefully remove with a fine steel wool pad, then clean with a lint-free cloth. The sheave surfaces must be clean and smooth. If you used steel wool to clean the sheaves, reclean the sheaves in solvent once again to remove all residue, and dry thoroughly.

42   Inspect the sliding sheave rollers and the spider rollers for wear and damage and replace in sets of two, if necessary.

43   Inspect the ramps on the cam for scoring, gouging or other signs of excessive wear or damage **(see illustration)**. Smooth the ramp area with No. 400 wet or dry sandpaper. Replace the cam if any ramp is damaged, or if there is clearly uneven wear when comparing both ramps.

44   Inspect the bushing pressed into the outside of the cam **(see illustration)**. If the bushing is damaged, or if the shaft is a loose fit in the bushing, replace the cam.

45   Inspect the teeth inside the outer spider for cracks, wear and other damage. Inspect the mating teeth and slots on the inner spider for the same conditions. Inspect the clutch roller arms on the outer spider for scoring and excessive wear. If there is any visible damage, inspect the bore inside each roller for the same conditions. Inspect the damper for signs of wear and damage. Replace any part as required **(see illustration 10.31b)**.

Assembly

46   Clean the bearing bore in the fixed sheave. Then align and press the bearing into the bore until it bottoms. Place a bearing driver against the bearing's outer race when pressing it into the bore. After pressing the bearing into place, turn the shaft to make sure there is no roughness or binding.

47   Align the marks made during disassembly **(see illustration 10.26)** and fit the sliding sheave into the fixed sheave.

48   Invert the sheave assembly so the fixed sheave faces up.

49   Install a roller onto each roller pin. Then insert a roller/pin assembly through the fixed sheave and into the boss in the sliding sheave. Make sure the flat side of the roller pin faces down. Repeat for the roller/pin assembly on the other side **(see illustration 10.34b)**.

50   Invert the sheave assembly so the fixed sheave faces down.

51   Drive a new spring pin through the boss in the sliding sheave and into the roller pin until it sits flush with the sheave boss. Check that the roller pin is secured in place. Repeat for the other side.

52   Install the thrust washer (if used) over the shaft **(see illustration 10.30b)**. Then install the spring over the shaft **(see illustration)**.

53   Set the clutch assembly into the clutch compression tool with the sliding sheave facing up.

54   Assemble the spider by installing a roller and washer onto one spider arm and securing them in place with a new E-clip **(see illustration 10.31b)**. Then repeat for the other roller. Align and install the damper onto into the inner spider **(see illustration 10.31b)**. Then install the inner spider into the outer spider while making sure the master spline on the inner spider aligns with the index mark on the outer spider **(see illustration 10.31a)**.

55   Install the spider onto the shaft by aligning the master spline on the inner spider with the marked spline on the shaft **(see illustration)**.

56   Use the clutch compression tool and compress the spider into place until the snap ring groove on the shaft is exposed. Then lock the tool handle with the chain. If the spider is difficult to install, stop and check the master spline alignment (see Step 55). Install the snap ring into the shaft groove, then release the chain and slowly release the tool handle **(see illustration 10.29)**. Make sure the marks on the spider and shaft align, and the snap ring is fully seated in the shaft groove **(see illustration)**. Remove the clutch assembly from the tool.

57   Install the cam over the shaft and onto the sliding sheave **(see illustration 10.27b)**, while engaging it with the rollers and aligning the index marks made during disassembly **(see illustration 10.26)**. If it is difficult to install the cam, the sheaves may not be aligned. To align them, position the clutch on the workbench with the cam side facing down. Grasp the sliding sheave with your hands and press it downward to free the cam, then reinstall the cam.

10.52 Install the spring over the shaft

10.55 Install the spider assembly by aligning the master spline on the inner spider (A) with the marked spline on the shaft (B)

10.56 After installing the snap ring (A), make sure the index marks on the spider and shaft align (B)

10.58 Tighten the cam screws in a crossing pattern to their final torque

58 Hold the driven clutch and turn the cam to align its screw holes with the threaded holes in the sliding sheave. Install and tighten the cam screws in a crossing pattern until they bottom, then tighten to the torque listed in this Chapter's Specifications **(see illustration)**.

5

SPECIFICATIONS

Clutch adjustment specifications

Clutch off-set alignment clearance
    Models without EPS............................ 0.020 in. (0.51 mm)
    Models with EPS .... --

Drive clutch specifications

Button clearance
    2010 models................................. 0.000-0.001 in. (0.000-0.025 mm)
    2011 and later models........................ 0.000-0.005 in. (0.000-0.127 mm)
Fixed sheave outside diameter (clutch bearing operating surface)
    New .... 1.3745-1.3750 in. (34.91-34.93 mm)
    Service limit .... 1.3730 in. (34.87 mm)
Clutch bearing shim thickness
    New .... 0.030 in. (0.76 mm)
    Service limit .... 0.025 in. (0.64 mm)

Drive clutch spring specifications

Spring part number	Color	Wire diameter	Free length
7043594	Black	0.177 in. (4.50 mm)	2.68-2.93 in. (68.07-74.42 mm)

Torque specifications	Ft-lbs	In.-lb	Nm

NOTE

One foot-pound (ft-lb) of torque is equivalent to 12 inch-pounds (in-lbs) of torque. Torque values below approximately 15 ft-lbs are expressed in inch-pounds, because most foot-pound torque wrenches are not accurate at these smaller values.

	Ft-lbs	In.-lb	Nm
Clutch outer cover screws	--	45-50	5.1-5.6
Clutch inner cover mounting screws			
At engine side................................	--	50	5.6
At transmission side	12	--	16
Drive clutch cover plate screws.....................	--	90	10.2
Driven clutch cam screws			
Models with EBS	--	42-52	4.7-5.9
Drive clutch mounting bolt	47	--	64
Driven clutch mounting bolt	17	--	23
Spider	200	--	271

CHAPTER SIX

TRANSMISSION

CONTENTS

1   GENERAL INFORMATION

1   The vehicles covered in this manual use a combination gear-drive/final gearcase assembly in addition to the belt-drive transmission (Polaris Variable Transmission, or PVT) covered in Chapter Five. In this chapter, the assembly will be referred to as the transmission. On all models, the driver can select High and Low forward gears as well as Neutral and Reverse. When the vehicle is parked, apply the parking brake.

2   This chapter covers the shift cable, select lever and transmission assembly. The transmission can be removed without having to remove the engine from the frame.

2   SHIFT CABLE - ADJUSTMENT AND REPLACEMENT

1   This section services the shift cable connected between the select lever in the driver's compartment and the transmission. The shift cable must be kept in proper adjustment or the transmission will not shift correctly.

Adjustment

2   Shift cable adjustment is performed with the two shift cable locknuts located at the transmission. The shift cable can go out of adjustment from cable stretch and possibly

from worn parts in the select lever assembly. When experiencing shifting or transmission problems, check the shift cable adjustment before checking the transmission.

3   Special tool: When adjusting the shift cable, two 3/4 in. open end wrenches are required to hold and turn the cable locknuts located at the transmission. However, because of space limitations around the cable locknuts, and the shoulder on the cable holder, it can be difficult to turn or hold the wrenches without having them slip and round off the flats on the nuts. To obtain a firmer grip, make a flare-nut wrench by using a hand grinder and cutoff wheel to cut a section from a 3/4 in. box end wrench that is wide enough to allow the wrench to slip over the shift cable. The larger contact area provided by the wrench will allow you to turn and hold the locknut with a firmer grip **(see illustrations)**.

CAUTION:

To prevent transmission damage, do not shift the transmission while the vehicle is moving. Always bring the vehicle to a complete stop, then select a different gear.

4   Park the vehicle on level ground and apply the parking brake.

5   Loosen the outside locknut and turn it 1 1/2 turns counterclockwise to create a gap between the locknut and the cable holder. Then hold the outside locknut to prevent it from turning, and turn the inside locknut clockwise and tighten it securely against the cable holder **(see illustration)**.

6   Turn the ignition switch ON, and with the vehicle at rest, shift the transmission into each gear while watching the instrument cluster. The display on the instrument cluster should indicate the correct transmission position when each gear change is made.

7   Start the engine and shift the transmission through all of the gears while the vehicle is at rest. If it appears that gear selection in each gear is equal, shift and drive the vehicle in LOW, then come to a stop and shift into HIGH and drive the vehicle. Then repeat for NEUTRAL and REVERSE. Note how the transmission operates in each gear position. If there is any ratcheting noise when driving the vehicle in LOW, HIGH or REVERSE, the shift cable is not adjusted correctly. If the vehicle creeps when the transmission is in NEUTRAL, the shift cable is not adjusted correctly. Repeat the adjustment until the transmission shifts properly.

NOTE:

If there is still a ratcheting noise when driving in gear, and the shift cable is properly adjusted, check for a problem inside the transmission (see Section 6).

8   If you are unable to properly adjust the shift cable and cannot find a problem at one of the cable attachment points, the cable may have stretched to the point where it must be replaced (see Steps 9 through 18).

2.3a A hand grinder equipped with a cutoff wheel was used to cut a section from this 3/4 in. box end wrench. The amount removed from the wrench must be wide enough to allow the wrench to slip over the shift cable

2.3b Slip the wrench over the cable . . .

2.3c . . . and engage the locknut

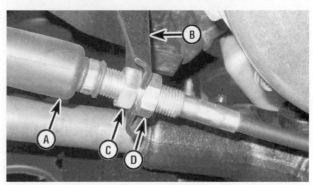

2.5 Shift cable details

A *Shift cable*	C *Inside locknut*
B *Cable holder*	D *Outside locknut*

2.10 Select lever details

A   Select lever
B   Shift cable
C   Cable locknut (upper end)

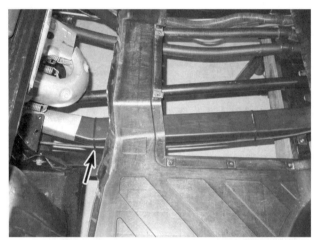

2.12 Note the shift cable routing and the plastic ties and guides that secure the cable (arrow) in place (2010 Ranger shown)

2.13a Shift cable attachment point details (upper end)

A   Clip   C   Shift cable end
B   Washer   D   Select lever

2.13b After removing the shift cable from the select lever, remove the bushing (arrow)

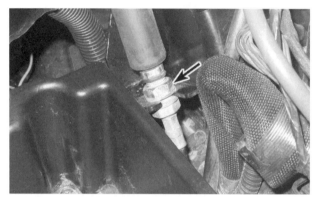

2.14 Loosen the locknut (arrow) that secures the front part of the cable to the mounting bracket

Replacement

CAUTION:

If the shift cable will be disconnected at one or both ends, but the cable will not be removed, do not bend or damage the loose cable end(s) when servicing other components on the vehicle.

9   Park the vehicle on level ground and apply the parking brake.

10   Raise the dash and slide it up the cab/frame assembly to access the select lever (see Chapter 14). It should not be necessary to remove the cab/frame assembly to access the select lever and the upper cable end **(see illustration)**.

11   Trace the shift cable from the select lever at the front of the vehicle to the transmission. Then remove the seat(s) and body panels, according to your model, as necessary to access the shift cable from end to end (see Chapter 14).

12   Note the shift cable routing from the select lever to the transmission and any guides that the cable passes through **(see illustration)**. Cut any plastic ties that are not designed to be reused.

13   Remove the clip and washer and slide the shift cable end off the select lever **(see illustration)**. Then remove the bushing **(see illustration)**.

14   Loosen the locknut securing the shift cable to the select lever mounting bracket **(see illustration)**.

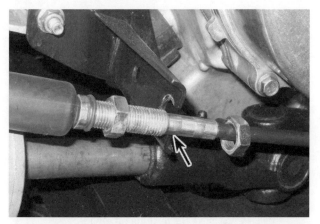

2.15 At the transmission, loosen the two cable locknuts and remove the shift cable (arrow) from the cable holder

15   Loosen the two shift cable locknuts at the transmission to release the cable from the cable holder **(see illustration)**.

16   Remove the clip and washer and slide the shift cable end off the transmission shift lever. Then remove the bushing **(see illustrations)**.

17   With the shift cable disconnected at both ends, remove it from the vehicle while noting its routing path.

18   Installation is the reverse of removal steps, plus the following:

    a) *Inspect the clips, washers and bushings installed on each end of the shift cable, and replace if weak or damaged.*

    b) *After installing and routing the cable, make sure it is not twisted.*

    c) *Replace the cable clips if weak or damaged, and install new plastic ties where they were previously used. After installing the clips make sure they are locked in place. Check that the shift cable is routed and secured in place and that it does not interfere with any steering or suspension component.*

    d) *Adjust the shift cable (see Steps 2 through 8). Then make sure the shift cable locknuts are tight.*

3   SELECT LEVER ASSEMBLY - REMOVAL AND INSTALLATION

Removal

1   Park the vehicle on level ground and apply the parking brake.

2   Raise the dash to access the select lever assembly (see Chapter 14). It shouldn't be necessary to remove the cab/frame assembly to access the select lever.

3   Disconnect the shift cable at the select lever (see Section 2).

4   Remove the E-clip and washer and slide the select lever off the pivot shaft **(see illustration)**. Note the two bushings installed inside the select lever and remove them **(see illustration)**.

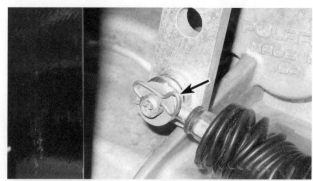

2.16a At the shift lever, remove the clip (arrow) . . .

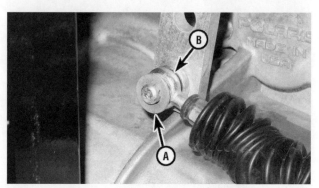

2.16b . . . washer (A), shift cable end (B) . . .

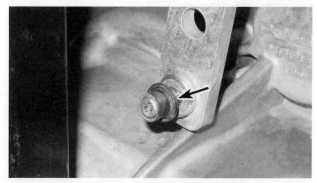

2.16c . . . and bushing (arrow)

3.4a Remove the E-clip (A) and select lever (B) from the pivot shaft

3.4b Remove the bushings (arrows) from inside the select lever bore

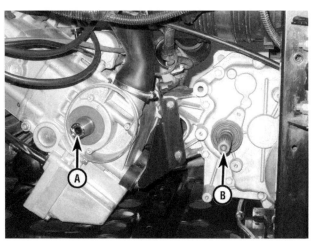

4.1 Clutch center distance is the distance between the center of the crankshaft (A) and the center of the transmission input shaft (B)

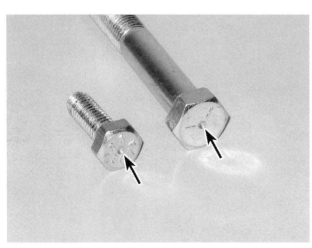

4.2 After drilling a dimple mark in each bolt head (arrows), the bolts can be used as centering points when measuring the clutch center distance between the crankshaft and the transmission input shaft

Installation

5   Installation is the reverse of removal, plus the following:

   a) Clean the select lever bore and its pivot shaft of all sand and dirt. Replace the pivot bushings installed inside the select lever if severely worn or damaged. Always replace these bushings in sets of two.

   b) Turn the ignition switch ON and with the vehicle at rest, shift the transmission into each gear while watching the instrument cluster. Make sure the display on the instrument cluster indicates the correct transmission position when each gear change is made. If not, check the shift cable adjustment (see Section 2).

4   CLUTCH CENTER DISTANCE ADJUSTMENT

1   Clutch center distance is the center-to-center distance between the crankshaft and the transmission input shaft, measured on the left side of the vehicle **(see illustration)**. This distance is critical to clutch and transmission operation. Clutch center distance must be checked after installing the engine or transmission into the frame, and adjusted if necessary. If the measured distance is incorrect, it is necessary to loosen the engine and/or transmission mounting fasteners and slide the engine and/or transmission forward or rearward in the frame. Clutch center distance should also be checked when you notice the clutch is dragging, or when the vehicle is experiencing shifting problems while running at idle speed.

NOTE:

This adjustment only centers the two clutch assemblies with each other at a specified distance. Clutch off-set alignment is a different adjustment procedure, and covered in Chapter 5.

2   Special tool: The recommended method used to check the clutch center distance is to install the 10 in. Polaris Center Distance Tool (part No. 2871710) over the crankshaft and the transmission input shaft at the same time. If the tool will not fit across the ends of both shafts, the clutch center distance is incorrect. If you don't have access to the factory tool, you can purchase two bolts and have a machine shop use a center drill to drill a dimple in the center of each bolt head. You then install the bolts into the ends of the shafts, and use a metal scale to measure between the dimple marks to determine the clutch center distance. You will need a 5/16 – 18 x 1 bolt and 7/16 – 20 x 3 bolt **(see illustration)**.

3   If installed, remove the drive and driven clutch units (see Chapter 5). It is not necessary to remove the clutch inner cover when measuring the clutch center distance, unless adjustment is required.

4   If using the factory tool described in Step 2, try to align it with the crankshaft and transmission input shaft

ends, following the manufacturer's instructions. If the tool fits, the clutch center distance is correct and no adjustment is required - reinstall the clutch units (see Chapter 5). If not, continue at Step 6.

5   If using the bolts described in Step 2, thread the 5/16 in. bolt into the transmission input shaft and tighten finger-tight. Then thread the 7/16 in. bolt into the end of the crankshaft and turn it so that its bolt head is even with the 5/16 in. bolt head **(see illustrations)**. This alignment will allow you to measure squarely across both bolts to obtain a more accurate measurement. Now use a metal scale and measure the distance between the dimple marks **(see illustration)**, and compare to the measurement listed in this Chapter's Specifications. If the reading is correct, no adjustment is required - reinstall the clutch units (see Chapter 5). If the reading is incorrect, continue with Step 6.

6   If the clutch center distance is incorrect, remove the clutch inner cover if installed on the engine/transmission (see Chapter 5). Then loosen the engine (see Chapter 4) or transmission (see Section 5) mounting fasteners, depending on which unit was recently installed into the frame, and move it forward or rearward in the frame until the clutch center distance measurement is correct. Tighten the fasteners and remeasure. If the correct distance measurement cannot be achieved by moving just the engine or transmission, loosen the mounting fasteners for the other unit and reposition it as required.

7   When the clutch center distance is correct, remove the modified bolts (if used).

8   Install the clutch inner cover, drive clutch and driven clutch assemblies (see Chapter 5). Do not install the drivebelt.

9   Check the clutch off-set alignment (see Chapter 5).

10   When the clutch off-set alignment is correct, install the drivebelt and the clutch outer cover (see Chapter 5).

5   TRANSMISSION - REMOVAL, INSPECTION AND INSTALLATION

Removal

1   Wash the transmission and rear axles to prevent dirt and other debris from entering the transmission when the axles are removed.

2   Park the vehicle on a level surface and apply the parking brake.

3   On Standard Ranger models, remove the seat back and seat base. On Crew models, remove the rear seat back and rear seat base. Then remove the storage container. See Chapter 14.

4   Remove the skid plate from underneath the frame (see Chapter 14).

5   While the transmission can be removed with the cargo box mounted on the vehicle, it is easier to work around and maneuver the transmission with the cargo box removed (see Chapter 14).

6   If the transmission will be serviced, drain the

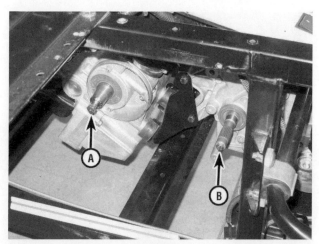

4.5a The modified bolts installed into the crankshaft (A) and transmission input shaft (B)

4.5b Because the exposed part of the crankshaft is shorter than the transmisson input shaft, turn the 7/16 in. bolt installed in the crankshaft (arrow) until it is even with the 5/16 bolt

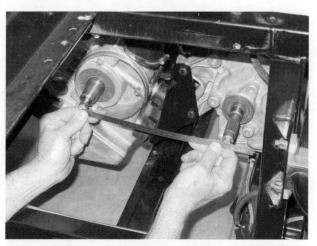

4.5c With the two bolts installed, measure the center-to-center distance between the crankshaft and transmission input shaft and compare to the specification listed in this Chapter's Specifications

5.8 On 2010 models, the brake switch wiring connector is positioned below the clutch outer cover - disconnect the connector and set the wiring harness aside

5.16 The gear position switch is mounted on the right side of the transmission. Disconnect its connector (arrow) and set the wiring harness aside

6

5.13 Vehicle speed sensor - 2011 and later models

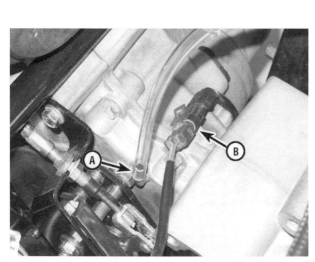

5.15 Disconnect the transmission vent hose (A) and the rear differential solenoid electrical connector (B) routed over the transmission

transmission oil (see Chapter 2).

7   Remove the rear wheels (see Chapter 10). Then block the front wheels to prevent the vehicle from rolling off the jackstands or other support.

WARNING:

Recheck the vehicle to make sure the jackstands are securely supporting the vehicle rear end and the front wheels are blocked to prevent them from rolling.

8   On 2010 models, disconnect the brake switch wiring harness connector at the brake light switch mounted below the clutch outer cover **(see illustration)**.

9   Remove the clutch outer cover, drivebelt, drive clutch, driven clutch and the clutch inner cover (see Chapter 5).

10   Measure the clutch center distance as described in Section 4 in this Chapter. Compare your measurement with the specified measurement listed in this Chapter's Specifications. Both measurements should be the same; otherwise, the adjustment was not correctly set, or the engine and/or transmission mounting fasteners are loose.

11   Remove the air box (see Chapter 7).

12   Remove the muffler (see Chapter 7).

13   On 2011 and later models, disconnect the wiring harness connector at the vehicle speed sensor mounted on the right side of the transmission **(see illustration)**.

14   Disconnect the rear axles from the transmission (see Chapter 11 and Chapter 12).

15   Disconnect the vent hose at the transmission and the rear differential solenoid electrical connector **(see illustration)**.

16   Disconnect the gear position switch electrical connector at the switch **(see illustration)**.

17   Disconnect the shift cable at the transmission (see Section 2). Reposition the cable so that it doesn't interfere with transmission removal.

18   Remove the parking brake caliper from the left side of

5.19 Support the engine with a jack and wooden block. If necessary, drill a hole in the wood block for the engine oil drain plug to fit into

5.20b Remove the two nuts (arrows) . . .

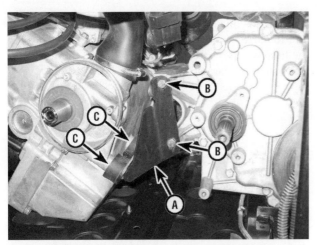

5.20a Rear engine/transmission mount details

A   *Rear engine/transmission mount*
B   *Mounting bolts*
C   *Rubber dampers*

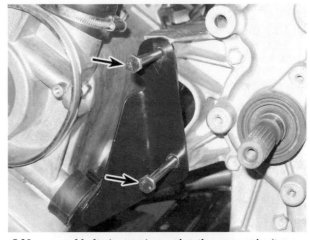

5.20c . . . and bolts (arrows) securing the rear engine/transmission mount to the transmission

the transmission (see Chapter 13).

19   Position a jack under the engine with a wooden block placed between the jack and engine. Make sure the jack is centered underneath the engine to prevent the engine from falling when the last mounting bolt is removed. If the engine oil drain plug extends past the crankcase, drill a hole large enough in the wooden block for the bolt to fit into. Don't balance the engine on the drain bolt. Raise the jack and apply light tension to the engine **(see illustration)**.

20   The transmission is secured to the engine with a rear engine/transmission mount, and directly to the frame with mounting bolts. Dampers are used between the engine and the rear engine/transmission mount **(see illustration)**. **Follow the accompanying photos, beginning with illustration 5.20b**, to remove the engine/transmission mount.

21   Remove the two nuts and bolts that secure the transmission to its mounting brackets welded onto the

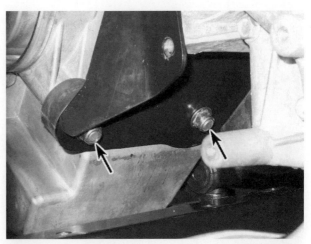

5.20d Remove the two nuts securing the two engine dampers to the engine/transmission mount and pull the mount away from the dampers . . .

5.20e . . . then loosen and remove the two engine dampers from the engine..

5.21b . . . and the front bolt (arrow). Because this bolt is difficult to access . . .

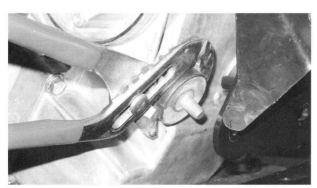

5.20f . . . using pliers if necessary to turn them . . .

5.21c . . . use a 9/16 in. universal joint (arrow) and extension . . .

5.20g . . . and remove the rear engine/transmission mount (arrow) from the left side of the vehicle

5.21d . . . to hold the bolt (arrow) when loosening its nut

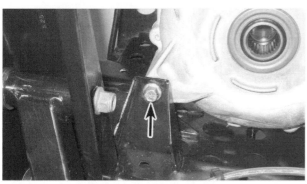

5.21a Here is the rear transmission-to-frame bolt (arrow) . . .

frame **(see illustrations)**. Because it is difficult to hold the front bolt straight on, hold it with a 9/16 in. universal joint when loosening its nut **(see illustrations)**.

22 If the rear axles are still attached to the knuckles, secure each rear axle to its lower control arm to prevent them from interfering with transmission removal.

23 Remove the rear stabilizer bar assembly from the frame (see Chapter 12).

24 Raise the exhaust pipe and tie it to the frame to provide clearance when removing the transmission.

25 If the cargo box is installed on the vehicle, secure it in its raised position so it can't fall. Then remove the clip and pin securing the damper to the frame and tie the

5.26 Note the brake hose routing at the rear of the vehicle to prevent from damaging them when removing the transmission (2010 Ranger shown)

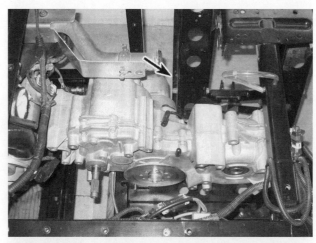

5.27a Before the transmission can be removed from the vehicle, move it towards the left side of the vehicle to clear the vertical frame brace (arrow)

5.27b After removing the transmission, place it on a movable jack, if available

5.28a Transmission - left side

damper so that it is out of the way. However, if additional room is needed, remove the damper from the vehicle (see Chapter 14, Section 19).

26 Check to make sure everything necessary has been disconnected or removed from the transmission. Then note the position of the brake hoses routed around the transmission **(see illustration)**. These can be damaged if the transmission falls against them.

WARNING:

Because the transmission is a long and heavy unit, assistance will be required to safely remove it from the frame. To prevent personal injury, do not attempt to remove the transmission by yourself.

NOTE:

If available, position a moveable jack at the rear of the vehicle to support the transmission on immediately after removing it from the vehicle.

27 With an assistant, lift the transmission and move it towards the left-side of the frame to that it will not contact the vertical frame brace during its removal **(see illustration)**. Then lift and slide the transmission rearward. If the cargo box is installed on the frame, close it so that it doesn't interfere with transmission removal. Then lift and remove the transmission from the rear of the vehicle **(see illustration)**.

Inspection

28 Inspect the transmission for any visible damage or oil leaks **(see illustrations)**. If service is necessary, refer service to a dealer service department.

29 Inspect the shift lever to make sure its mounting nut is tight and the lever is not slipping on its shaft. If necessary,

5.28b Transmission - right side

5.33a Position the transmission into the frame . . .

5.30 Check the front and rear transmission mounts welded onto the frame for cracks and other damage - rear transmission mount shown here

5.33b . . . while aligning the splines and installing the front output shaft into the driveshaft (arrow). Wipe off any excess grease

5.32a Clean and lubricate the front output shaft splines (arrow) . . .

5.32b . . . and the driveshaft splines with grease. Inspect the O-ring (arrow) located inside the driveshaft joint and replace if damaged

remove the nut and shift lever and inspect the mating splines for damage. If the splines are okay, reinstall the shift lever by aligning the key on the shaft with the spline on the shift lever. Install the shift lever nut and tighten to the torque listed in this Chapter's Specifications.

30   Clean the transmission mounts on the frame and inspect them for any cracks or other damage (see illustration).

31   Clean and dry all of the transmission fasteners and inspect them for damage. Roll the long mounting bolts on a flat surface to check for bending. If a fastener is bent, or there is any thread or other visible damage, replace it with a new OEM fastener.

Installation

32   Clean the front output shaft splines and the mating splines inside the driveshaft. Replace the O-ring installed in the driveshaft joint if damaged. Then lubricate the splines with Polaris Premium All Season Grease or an equivalent grease (see illustrations).

33   With an assistant, install the transmission from the rear side of the vehicle (see illustration 5.27b) while aligning/ engaging the front output shaft splines with the driveshaft splines (see illustrations). Make sure to position the transmission so it is positioned between the front and rear transmission mounts welded on the frame.

34   Install the engine/transmission mount between the

engine and transmission (see illustration 5.20g). Then thread the two rubber dampers onto the engine and tighten securely (see illustration 5.20e). Install the engine/transmission mounting bracket over the two rubber dampers and secure in place with the two nuts (see illustration 5.20d).

35   Install the front and rear transmission through bolts through the transmission and frame mounts from the right side (see illustration 5.21a and illustration 5.21b). Install the nuts and tighten finger-tight. When installing the front bolt, make sure it bottoms against the transmission and doesn't pinch the brake hose. These are 3/8 inch bolts.

36   Install the front mounting bolts through the engine/transmission mount from the right side (see illustration 5.20c). Install the nuts and tighten finger-tight. These are 5/16 inch bolts.

37   Adjust the clutch center distance (see Section 4).

38   Tighten the 5/16 inch bolts to the torque listed in this Chapter's Specifications. Then tighten the 3/8 inch bolts to the torque listed in this Chapter's Specifications. When these four bolts are tight, tighten the rubber damper nuts securely. Recheck the clutch center distance (see Step 37).

39   Install the clutch inner cover, drive clutch and driven clutch assemblies (see Chapter 5). Do not install the drivebelt.

40   After installing the drive and driven clutch units, check the clutch offset and clutch alignment position and adjust if necessary (see Chapter 5).

41   When the clutch off-set alignment is correct, install the drivebelt and the clutch outer cover (see Chapter 5).

42   If the transmission oil was previously drained, refill the transmission with the correct type and quantity oil (see Chapter 2).

43   The remainder of installation is the reverse of removal, noting the following:

   a) *Check the brake hoses to make sure they are properly secured in place and were not damaged when removing and installing the transmission.*
   b) *Make sure both ends of the transmission vent hose are open before reconnecting it onto the transmission.*
   c) *Reconnect and adjust the shift cable (see Section 2).*
   d) *Test drive the vehicle to make sure the transmission shifts properly.*

6   TRANSMISSION - OVERHAUL

1   Overhaul of the transmission requires several special tools. If the transmission housing or gears require attention, take the complete unit to a Polaris service department for service. If you previously drained the transmission oil to inspect it, pour it in a clean plastic container and take it with you so the service department can examine it for metal debris.

SPECIFICATIONS

Service specifications

Clutch center distance	10.05 in. (255 mm)

Torque specifications	Ft-lbs	Nm
Shift lever nut.	12-18	16-24
Transmission mounting bolts		
5/16 inch bolts	20	27
3/8 inch bolts	37	50

CHAPTER SEVEN

ENGINE MANAGEMENT SYSTEM

CONTENTS

1 GENERAL INFORMATION, SERVICE INFORMATION AND PRECAUTIONS

General information

Fuel system

1 The fuel injection system consists of the fuel tank assembly, incorporating the fuel pump and fuel pressure regulator, the fuel hose to the fuel rail on the throttle body, and the fuel injectors located in the intake manifold.

2 Fuel is supplied under pressure to the injectors by the pump, mounted inside the fuel tank. Excess fuel is returned to the tank by the pressure regulator.

3 The injectors are valves that open for precisely controlled lengths of time, allowing pressurized fuel to spray into the throttle body. The injectors open once for each time the pistons come to top dead center, injecting half of the amount of fuel needed for one four-stroke cycle into the intake port. In both systems, the fuel is pulled into the cylinder when the intake valve opens.

4 The entire fuel injection system is controlled by the engine control unit (ECU) which monitors data sent from the various system sensors and adjusts fuel delivery to the engine accordingly. If a problem develops in the injection system, the malfunction indicator light (MIL) illuminates on the instrument cluster. Trouble codes, which can be easily accessed on the instrument cluster, indicate where in the system the problem lies.

5 The fuel pump and pressure regulator are supplied only as a complete unit. If diagnosis shows a fault with any of the tank assembly components, the fuel pump must be replaced as an assembly. On some models, it may be necessary to replace the fuel tank with the fuel pump installed as a unit.

Ignition system

6   The electronic ignition system is combined with the fuel injection system, both being controlled by the ECU (engine control unit). The ignition consists of a rotor (flywheel), crankshaft position sensor (CKP sensor), engine control unit (ECU), ignition coil and camshaft phase sensor (2011 and later models).

7   The flywheel is equipped with a 58-tooth ring gear with two consecutive teeth missing. The missing teeth are the triggers that generate a signal in the CKP sensor as the crankshaft rotates. The CKP sensor sends that signal to the ECU, which in conjunction with the information received from the other ignition and fuel system sensors, calculates the ignition timing and supplies the ignition coil with the power necessary to produce a spark at the spark plugs. There is no method or procedure for checking or adjusting the ignition timing.

8   The ignition coil is a separate unit with two secondary wires and plug caps that connect to the spark plugs.

EFI system components

9   The EFI system components used on the Ranger 800 models are as follows:

   a) *Fuel tank, fuel pump, pressure regulator and fuel level sender, internal filters (assembly)*
   b) *Fuel injectors (one for each cylinder)*
   c) *Fuel rail*
   d) *Throttle body*
   e) *Throttle position sensor (TPS)*
   f) *Engine coolant sensor (ECT)*
   g) *Crankshaft position sensor (CPS)*
   h) *Camshaft phase sensor (2011 and later models)*
   i) *Idle air control (IAC) (2011 and later models)*
   j) *Intake air temperature /barometric air pressure sensor (T-BAP) (2010 models)*
   k) *Temperature/manifold absolute pressure sensor (T-MAP) (2011 and later models)*
   l) *Engine control unit (ECU)*
   m) *Ignition coil and secondary wires and caps*
   n) *Spark plugs*

Service information

10   To prevent damaging components in the fuel injection system, certain information and precautions must be observed.

11   Do not start the engine when the battery cables are not properly secured to the battery. When making tests, secure the cables in place with the screws, instead of just laying or wedging them against the battery terminals. Vibration from the engine running may cause the cables to disconnect.

12   Never disconnect the battery when the engine is running.

13   When working on the electrical system, always know whether the ignition switch is turned on or off. Never disconnect or reconnect the electrical connector at the ECU or any other electrical component when the ignition switch is turned on. This could produce a voltage spike and damage the ECU.

14   Because of the harsh environment these vehicles operate in, always clean the connector halves before disconnecting them. The mating contact terminals inside the connectors are small, and any dirt contamination can cause performance problems after the connectors have been reconnected and when attempting to start the engine or during engine operation.

15   Do not use compressed air or water to clean the vehicle when any of the fuel or electrical system connectors are disconnected and exposed. Enclose the connectors in plastic bags to protect them from dirt and water contamination.

16   Before welding on the vehicle, disconnect the electrical connector at the ECU.

Precautions

> *WARNING:*
> *Gasoline is extremely flammable, so take extra precautions when you work on any part of the fuel system. Don't smoke or allow open flames or bare light bulbs near the work area, and don't work in a garage where a gas-type appliance (such as a water heater or clothes dryer) is present. Since gasoline is carcinogenic, wear gasoline-resistant gloves when there's a possibility of being exposed to fuel, and if you spill any fuel on your skin, rinse it off immediately with soap and water. Mop up any spills immediately and do not store fuel-soaked rags where they could ignite. The fuel system is under constant pressure, so, if any fuel lines are to be disconnected, the fuel pressure in the system must be relieved first. When you perform any kind of work on the fuel system, wear safety glasses and have a Class B type fire extinguisher on hand.*

17   Read *Safety first!* in the General Information chapter at the front of this manual carefully before starting work.

18   Always perform service procedures in a well-ventilated area to prevent a build-up of fumes.

19   Never work in a building containing a gas appliance with a pilot light, or any other form of naked flame. Ensure that there are no naked light bulbs or any sources of flame or sparks nearby.

20   Do not smoke (or allow anyone else to smoke) while in the vicinity of gasoline or of components containing it. Remember the possible presence of vapor from these sources and move well clear before smoking.

21   Check all electrical equipment belonging to the house, garage or workshop where work is being undertaken. Remember that certain electrical appliances such as drills, grinders, etc., create sparks in the normal course of operation and must not be used near gasoline or any component containing it. Again, remember the possible presence of fumes before using electrical equipment.

22   Safety glasses or goggles must be worn when relieving fuel pressure and when disconnecting any fuel hose.

23   Always mop up any spilled fuel and safely dispose of the rag used.

2.3a On 2010 models, the quick connect plug (A) is mounted on one end of the fuel rail and the fuel hose (B) is connected onto the opposite end. You can disconnect either connector to relieve the fuel pressure

2.3b On 2011 and later models, the damper (A) is mounted on one end of the fuel rail and the fuel hose (B) is connected onto the opposite end. You can disconnect either connector to relieve the fuel pressure

2.3c The fuel hose (arrow) can also be disconnected at the fuel pump to relieve fuel pressure (2010 model fuel tank shown)

24 Any stored fuel that is drained off during servicing work must be kept in sealed containers that are suitable for holding gasoline, and clearly marked as such; the containers themselves should be kept in a safe place. Note that this last point applies equally to the fuel tank if it is removed from the machine; also remember to keep its filler cap closed at all times.

25 Owners of machines used in the U.S., particularly California, should note that their machines must comply at all times with Federal or State legislation governing the permissible levels of noise and of pollutants such as unburned hydrocarbons, carbon monoxide etc., that can be emitted by those machines. All vehicles offered for sale must comply with legislation in force at the date of manufacture and must not subsequently be altered in any way which will affect their emission of noise or of pollutants.

26 After working on the fuel system, turn the ignition switch on and off several times to pressurize the fuel system, then check for fuel leaks. If there is a fuel leak, do not start the engine until the problem has been repaired or the damaged part replaced.

2 FUEL SYSTEM PRESSURE RELIEF

WARNING:
Fuel injection systems operate under high pressure, which remains high even with the engine off. Be sure to relieve the fuel system pressure before disconnecting any fuel lines. Gasoline is extremely flammable and is always present when working on the fuel system. Refer to the precautions given in Section 1 before starting work.

WARNING:
Safety glasses or goggles must be worn when relieving fuel pressure by disconnecting any fuel hose, quick connector plug (2010 models) or damper (2011 and later models) from the fuel system.

1 Disconnect the negative battery cable before disconnecting any fuel hose to relive fuel pressure (see Chapter 8).

2 There is no specific procedure or test valve for relieving residual fuel pressure before working on the fuel system, only that you have shop rags handy to catch any spilled fuel. Observe the precautions in the Warnings above.

3 You can depressuize the fuel system by either removing the quick connect plug (2010 models) or the damper (2011 and later models) mounted on one end of the fuel rail, or disconnecting one of the fuel hose connectors **(see illustrations)**. Before disconnecting a plug, damper or hose, place a clean rag over the part to prevent fuel from spraying outward. See Section 4 for steps on how to disconnect and reconnect the connectors.

3   FUEL INJECTION SYSTEM - PRIMING

1   The fuel injection system must be primed to expel air from the lines whenever the system has been disassembled, or when there is no fuel in the system, including the fuel hoses.

2   Turn the ignition switch to ON, wait three seconds, and turn it to OFF. You should be able to hear the fuel pump run, then switch off as fuel pressure builds up.

3   Repeat Step 2 five more times.

4   Crank the engine. If the engine starts, the fuel system is primed. If the engine doesn't start within five seconds, turn the ignition switch to OFF.

5   If the engine didn't start, repeat Steps 2 through 4 two more times.

6   If the engine still doesn't start, refer to Chapter 1 to troubleshoot the starting problem.

4   QUICK-CONNECT FUEL HOSE CONNECTORS - DISCONNECTING AND RECONNECTING

WARNING:

Gasoline is extremely flammable and is always present when working on the fuel system. Refer to the precautions given in Section 1 before starting work.

1   Models are equipped with a single fuel hose connected between the fuel rail and fuel pump. The hose is equipped with quick-connect connectors on both ends.

2   Refer to Section 2 for information on relieving the fuel system pressure.

3   If necessary, clean the connectors on each end of the fuel hose to prevent dirt from contaminating the fuel hose, fuel rail and fuel pump.

4   **Follow the accompanying illustrations** when disconnecting the quick-connect connectors. Be sure to stay in order and read the caption under each illustration. Wrap the connector with a rag when disconnecting it to catch fuel that will spray from the hose while under pressure.

5   Reconnecting the hoses is the reverse of these steps, while noting the following:

   a) *Make sure the fuel hose connectors and pipe ends are clean.*

   b) *Slide the fuel hose/connector onto the pipe until you feel it snap in place. Then push the clip through the connector and over the pipe until it locks the connector in place. Pull the connector to make sure it is locked in place and doesn't slide off the pipe.*

   c) *Turn the ignition switch on to pressurize the system, then check the connectors and fuel hose(s) for leaks.*

   d) *If the engine is difficult to start, prime the fuel system (see Section 3).*

4.4a Squeeze the clip tabs (arrows) with your fingers . . .

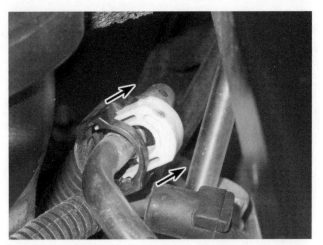

4.4b . . . and push the clip away from the fuel hose and pipe . . .

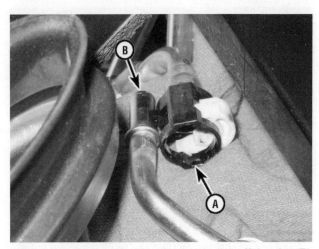

4.4c . . . then pull the fuel hose/connector (A) off the pipe (B)

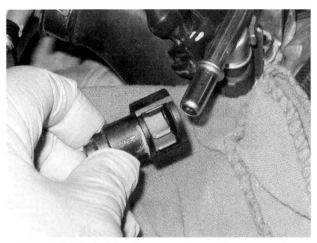

5.5a On 2010 models, disconnect the quick connect plug from the end of the fuel rail

5.5b On 2011 and later models, disconnect the damper (arrow) from the end of the fuel rail

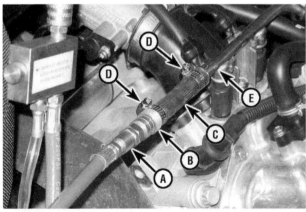

5.5c Aftermarket fuel pressure gauge end of line connection details at fuel rail

A	Fuel pressure gauge hose	C	Connecting hose
		D	Hose clamps
B	Adapter	E	Fuel rail

5   FUEL PRESSURE CHECK

WARNING:

Refer to the precautions given in Section 1 before starting work.

1   Special tools: To check the fuel pressure, a suitable gauge, gauge hose and adapters will be needed. Polaris provides service tools: fuel pressure gauge kit (part No. PU-43506-A) and fuel pressure gauge adapter (part No. PV-48656) for this purpose. The hose fittings on this tool match those used on the fuel hose. Aftermarket fuel pressure gauge kits are also available and can be used, provided you can attach them securely to the fuel rail.

2   Park the vehicle on level ground and apply the parking brake. Because the engine will be running when making this check, make sure there is adequate ventilation if the vehicle is parked in an enclosed building.

3   The fuel pump is located inside the fuel tank. When the ignition is switched ON, you should hear the pump run for a few seconds until the system is up to pressure. If you didn't hear the pump run, first check the EFI fuse (2010) or fuel pump fuse (2011 and later models). Then check the EFI relay (2010 models) or fuel pump relay (2011 and later models). See Chapter 8. If they are good, check the wiring and terminals at the fuel pump for physical damage or loose or corroded connections and repair as necessary. If the problem still hasn't been found, perform voltage and continuity tests at the fuel pump as described in Section 6.

4   If you're using the Polaris fuel pressure gauge kit, disconnect the fuel hose at the fuel pump to depressurize the fuel system (see Section 2). Connect the fuel pressure gauge adapter between the fuel hose and the fuel pump. Then connect the fuel pressure gauge to the test valve on the fuel pressure gauge adapter. Take the bleed-off hose connected to the fuel pressure gauge and place it in a fuel storage can.

WARNING:

Step 5 describes how to attach a fuel pressure gauge that doesn't have a factory fitting to the fuel rail. However, if you cannot securely attach the hose leading from the gauge to the fuel rail, do not perform the fuel pressure test. Because the hose is under high pressure, if it slips off the fuel rail, fuel will spray out and flood the vehicle, causing an extreme fire hazard.

5   If you're using an aftermarket fuel pressure gauge kit and it doesn't include a fitting that can attach directly to the fuel pump, it will be necessary to measure fuel pressure at the fuel rail, so make sure you read the manufacturer's instructions on how to assemble and attach the gauge. Remove the quick connect plug (2010 models) **(see illustration)** or the damper (2011 and later models) **(see illustration)** from the end of the fuel rail and depressurize the fuel system (see Section 4). Install the connecting hose from the fuel pressure gauge in its place, and tighten its hose

clamps securely so the hose cannot slip off the fuel rail. The aftermarket gauge shown here uses an adapter to connect the fuel pressure gauge hose to a separate connecting hose clamped onto the fuel rail (see illustration). If the gauge assembly is equipped with a bleed-off hose, place the end of the hose into a fuel storage can.

6   Turn the ignition switch ON, start the engine and allow to run at idle. Check the pressure reading on the gauge (see illustration), and compare to the value listed in this Chapter's Specifications.

7   Turn the ignition switch OFF. If using the Polaris fuel pressure gauge, or an aftermarket tool equipped with a pressure release button, press the button to relieve fuel pressure (see illustration). If the tool is not equipped with a pressure release button, hold a rag over the gauge when you disconnect it, as this will release fuel pressure from the system. Then disconnect the gauge and adapters, using a rag to catch any residual fuel. Depending on the tester used, reconnect the fuel hose to the pump, or reinstall the quick connect plug (see illustration 5.5a) or damper (see illustration 5.5b) onto the end of the fuel rail.

8   If the fuel pressure is out of specification (too low or too high), replace the fuel pump (see Section 6). Normally, you would first check for a plugged fuel filter or a faulty fuel pressure regulator, but both of these are permanently installed on the fuel pump, and cannot be serviced or replaced separately.

NOTE:

If you're working on an unfamiliar model, and the fuel pressure reading is higher than specified, don't assume the fuel pump is faulty without first making sure the pump you are testing is the correct pump for the vehicle's model year. A previous owner may have replaced the stock fuel pump with a higher capacity fuel pump to solve a fuel system problem.

9   After reconnecting the fuel hose, quick connect plug or damper, turn the ignition switch ON to allow the fuel system to pressurize the system, then check for fuel leaks. Turn the ignition switch OFF.

6   FUEL PUMP - CHECK AND REPLACEMENT

WARNING:

Refer to the precautions given in Section 1 before starting work.

1   The OEM electric fuel pump is installed inside the fuel tank and is a combined unit incorporating the fuel pump regulator, fuel sending unit and two non-serviceable filters. None of these parts are available separately from the manufacturer. If any one of these parts is damaged or fails to properly operate, the fuel pump must be replaced as an assembly. However, note that aftermarket fuel pumps are available, and when installing an aftermarket fuel pump,

5.5d The fuel pressure gauge assembled and attached to the fuel rail

5.6 Correct fuel pressure reading for a 2010 Ranger with the engine running at idle speed. Note that the fuel pressure reading for your model year can differ, depending on model year - refer to the Chapter Specifications for the actual fuel pressure reading

5.7 Depress the button on the gauge to depressurize the fuel system

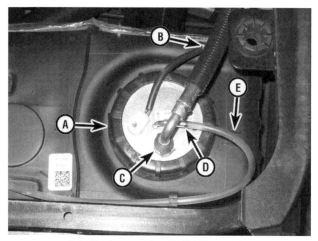

6.6a Fuel pump details (2010 models)

A	Fuel pump and nut	D	Vent hose
B	Electrical connector	E	Vent hose
C	Fuel hose		alignment marks

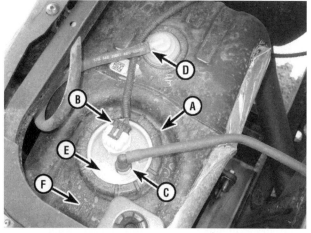

6.6b Fuel pump details (2011 and later models)

A	Fuel pump and nut	E	Fuel pump
B	Electrical connector		arrow mark
C	Fuel hose	F	Fuel tank
D	Vent hose		alignment marks

follow the manufacturer's instructions. This section covers the OEM fuel pump assembly.

2   When the ignition switch is turned ON, the ECU energizes the fuel pump, which will run for a few seconds to pressurize the fuel system for starting. During this initial start-up, you should be able to hear the pump run.

3   To prevent flooding, the ECU will turn the fuel pump off if the ignition key is not turned immediately to the start position, if the engine stops running when the ignition key is in the ON position, and when the engine will not start. If one of the these conditions occurs, the Check Engine Light will illuminate. However, the Check Engine Light will turn off if the engine can be turned over (four revolutions) and the ECU determines the fuel system is working correctly. The fuel pump will remain on when the engine is running.

Check

4   If you cannot hear the fuel pump run immediately after turning the ignition switch ON, perform the following voltage and resistance tests.

5   On standard Ranger models, remove the seat base. On Crew models, remove the rear seat base. See Chapter 14.

6   Disconnect the fuel pump electrical connector. On 2010 models, a short wiring harness is used at the pump **(see illustration)**. On 2011 and later models, the electrical connector plugs directly into the pump **(see illustration)**.

7   On 2010 models, connect a voltmeter across terminals A (red wire or red/black wire) and C (brown wire) on the harness side connector. On 2011 and later models, connect a voltmeter across terminals 3 (red/blue wire) and 4 (brown wire) on the harness side connector. Turn the ignition switch ON, read the voltmeter and compare to the fuel pump voltage test value listed in this Chapter's Specifications.

8   If the voltage is below 7 volts, make sure the battery is fully charged. If necessary, test the battery (see Chapter 8) and service it if necessary to make sure the correct amount of voltage is available at the connector. If the battery is fully charged and the voltage is still below 7 volts, the problem may be in the ECU relay, fuse, ignition switch or wiring harness and/or connector. Refer to Chapter 8 to inspect, test or replace these parts.

9   If the voltage reading at the two harness side connector terminals was correct, connect an ohmmeter between the corresponding two terminals identified in Step 7 in the pump side harness connector. The ohmmeter should indicate continuity. If the ohmmeter reading is infinity, replace the fuel pump.

Replacement

10   When replacing the fuel pump, refer to the manufacturer's instructions included with the replacement fuel pump, while using the following information to supplement the instructions.

11   Special tool: The fuel pump is secured to the fuel tank with a large nut that is tightened to a high torque. The Polaris fuel pump nut wrench (part No. PU-50326) is required to loosen and tighten nut. This tool is machined with notches on its inner ring that grip the raised shoulders on the nut. The tool is also equipped with a 1/2 inch square hole that allows it to be turned with a breaker bar and torque wrench.

NOTE:

If you are removing the fuel pump, but not to replace it, note that the gasket used between the fuel pump and fuel tank is not available separately. When removing the fuel pump, work carefully to prevent damage to the gasket.

12   The fuel pump can be replaced with the fuel tank mounted in the frame. However, before removing the fuel pump, make sure the fuel cap is secured tightly and then

use a hose and spray the tank with water to prevent any dirt and sand from entering the tank when removing the pump.

13 On standard Ranger models, remove the seat base. On Crew models, remove the rear seat base. See Chapter 14.

14 Disconnect the negative battery cable at the battery (see Chapter 8).

15 Remove the fuel cap from the fuel tank and use a siphon to remove as much fuel from the fuel tank as possible. Store the fuel in a safety approved gasoline storage can.

16 The fuel pump is accessed at the top of the fuel tank.

17 Depressurize the fuel system by disconnecting the fuel hose at the fuel pump (see Section 2) **(see illustration 6.6a or 6.6b)**.

18 Disconnect the electrical connector at the fuel pump **(see illustration 6.6a or 6.6b)**.

19 Place the fuel pump nut wrench over the nut on the fuel pump, then mount a breaker bar onto the tool and turn the nut to loosen and remove it. It is helpful to press on the fuel pump flange when loosening the nut. Remove the nut when it is free of the pump.

20 Lift the fuel pump and tilt it as required to prevent damage to the float and filter assemblies mounted at the bottom of the pump.

21 Inspect the bottom of the fuel tank for any sand, mud and other debris. If necessary, remove the fuel tank and clean it (see Section 8).

22 Cover the opening in the fuel tank until the pump is reinstalled.

23 If installing a new fuel pump, carefully remove it from its original packaging. A new nut, gasket and cleaning wipes should be included with the pump.

24 Use the cleaning wipes to clean the threads on the new fuel pump nut and those on the fuel tank.

25 Slip the new gasket carefully over the bottom of the fuel pump and seat it against the pump shoulder.

26 On 2010 models, carefully install the fuel pump into the fuel tank by aligning the vent hose fitting on the pump between the two alignment marks on the top of the fuel tank **(see illustration 6.6a)**.

27 On 2011 and later models, carefully install the fuel pump into the fuel tank by aligning the arrow mark on the top of the pump between the two alignment marks on the top of the fuel tank **(see illustration 6.6b)**.

28 Apply downward pressure against the fuel pump and carefully thread the new nut onto the fuel tank. Tighten the nut hand-tight while checking to make sure the alignment marks made in Step 26 or Step 27 are still aligned.

29 Position the fuel pump wrench onto the nut, and using a torque wrench, tighten the nut. On 2010 models, tighten the nut to the torque listed in the manufacturer's instructions that came with the replacement fuel pump. On 2011 and later models, tighten the nut to the torque listed in this Chapter's Specifications. After tightening the nut, check the alignment marks one more time to make sure they are properly aligned.

CAUTION:

If the fuel pump is not properly aligned with the fuel tank, the float mounted on the side of the pump may contact the inside of the fuel tank, which will prevent the fuel level gauge from registering the correct level of fuel in the tank.

30 The remainder of installation is the reverse of removal, noting the following:

a) *Check the fuel pump by turning the ignition switch on and off several times to pressurize the system and check for leaks. Then start the engine and allow it to run for several minutes to help purge air from the system.*

b) *If the engine is difficult to start, prime the fuel system (see Section 3).*

c) *After driving the vehicle a short distance, stop and check the fuel pump for leaks.*

7   FUEL LEVEL SENDER - TESTING

1 The fuel level sender measures the level of fuel in the fuel tank and signals this information to the instrument cluster where the level is displayed on the fuel gauge. If the fuel gauge does not work, or if the reading on the fuel gauge seems to differ from the amount of fuel inside the fuel tank, test the fuel level sender. The fuel level sender is an integral part of the fuel pump. If the fuel level sender is faulty, it will be necessary to replace the fuel pump as an assembly.

2 Before testing the fuel level sender, check the wiring circuit between the fuel pump and the instrument cluster for an open or short circuit. Also check the connectors at both ends for contamination, corrosion and damaged terminals. Spray the terminals with electrical contact cleaner, allow to dry, then reconnect them. Turn the ignition switch ON and recheck the fuel gauge reading. If the reading is still incorrect or questionable, continue with Step 3.

NOTE:

The resistance tests can also be performed with the fuel tank removed from the vehicle and empty of fuel. To do so, tilt the fuel tank to position the float in raised and lowered positions when performing the tests.

NOTE:

When removing the fuel pump in Step 3, note the alignment of the pump where it is installed in the tank. If the problem started after the fuel pump was installed into the fuel tank, the pump may be incorrectly aligned, causing the float to be out of position and contacting the side of the fuel tank.

3 Remove the fuel pump (see Section 6). Before testing

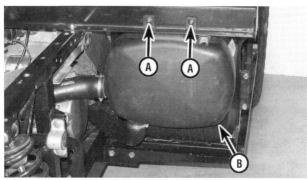

8.10 Remove the two screws (A) securing the rear engine air baffle (B) to the frame. The two hoses can remain attached to the baffle

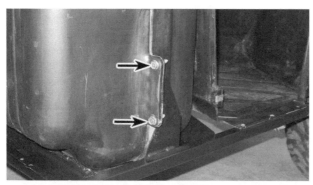

8.11a Outer fuel tank mounting screws

8.11b Inner fuel tank mounting screws (one screw shown)

8.11c Slide the fuel tank past the rear engine air baffle (arrow) when removing it

the fuel level sender, check for a loose or damaged float, or a bent float rod.

4   To check the operation of the fuel level sender, an ohmmeter is required. Connect the test leads to the brown and purple/white terminals on the fuel pump side connector. Measure the resistance of the fuel level sender with the float raised (tank full) and lowered (tank empty), and compare to the values listed in this Chapter's Specifications.

5   If the tests show the fuel level sender is faulty, replace the fuel pump with a new one.

6   If the tests show the fuel level sender to be good, repeat the checks in Step 2.

7   Installation is the reverse of removal.

8   FUEL TANK - REMOVAL AND INSTALLATION

WARNING:

Refer to the precautions given in Section 1 before starting work.

1   Park the vehicle on level ground and apply the parking brake.

2   On standard Ranger models, remove the seat base. On Crew models, remove the rear seat base. See Chapter 14.

3   On standard Ranger models, remove right rocker panel. On Crew models, remove the right rear rocker panel. See Chapter 14.

4   Disconnect the negative battery cable (see Chapter 8).

5   Before removing the fuel tank, note how any cables, hoses and wiring harnesses are routed around and over the fuel tank.

6   Depressurize the fuel system by disconnecting the fuel hose at the fuel pump (see Section 2).

7   Use a siphon and remove as much fuel from the fuel tank as possible. Store the fuel in a clean fuel storage can so it can be poured back into the fuel tank after reinstalling it.

8   On 2010 models, disconnect the electrical connector at the fuel pump **(see illustration 6.6a)**.

9   On 2011 and later models, disconnect the electrical connector at the fuel pump, and the vent hose from the nozzle on the fuel tank **(see illustration 6.6b)**.

10   Remove two screws securing the rear engine air baffle to the frame **(see illustration)**. You can leave the hoses connected to the baffle and slide the fuel tank past it during removal.

11   Remove the screws securing the fuel tank to the frame **(see illustrations)**. Then slide the fuel tank past the rear engine air baffle and remove it **(see illustration)**.

12   Installation is the reverse of removal, noting the following:

   a) *Refill the fuel tank with gasoline.*
   b) *Turn the ignition switch ON and OFF several times to pressurize the system and check for leaks.*
   c) *If the engine won't start, prime the fuel system (see Section 3).*

9   FUEL INJECTION SYSTEM TROUBLESHOOTING

1   All models covered by this manual are equipped with on-board diagnostics. When the ECU recognizes a malfunction in the engine management system, it illuminates the CHECK ENGINE indicator on 2010 models, or the CHECK ENGINE MIL (Malfunction Indicator Light) on 2011 and later models. The ECU will continue to display the indicator until the problem is fixed and the trouble code is cleared from the ECU's memory. You can access any trouble code without the use of a scan tool.

Scan tools

2   Scan tools are available that can be used when troubleshooting the Polaris Ranger engine management system. These tools simplify the procedure for extracting trouble codes from your vehicle's engine management system. While you can extract trouble codes without special tools on the models covered in this manual, a scan tool allows you to read ECU data, perform diagnostic procedures, adjust the throttle position sensor (TPS), and perform other functions, depending on the model and its requirements for its engine management system. The MS5950 Scan Tool (www.griffin-tools.com) is one such tool that can be purchased by a do-it-yourselfer that comes with one activation token to activate the scan tool software for a particular manufacturer **(see illustration)**, which in this case would be for Polaris. For independent shops, scan tools are available that are programmed with software required to cover a larger number of different powersport manufacturers - the MS5950 Scan Tool (www.griffin-tools.com) is one such tool.

3   Before using a scan tool, refer to the manufacturer's instructions. Before plugging a scan tool into the diagnostic connector, make sure there's no corrosion on the pins and that no pins are bent or damaged. Also make sure the wires going into the connector are tight and there are no loose or open wires. Repeat this check on the cable included with the scan tool.

4   The diagnostic connector is mounted under the hood **(see illustration)**. If necessary, refer to the appropriate wiring diagram at the end of this chapter to identify the diagnostic connector and its wire colors. Remove the dummy plug from the connector before hooking up the scan tool and its cable to the diagnostic connector.

2010 models

5   When the CHECK ENGINE indicator is illuminated on the instrument cluster, retrieve trouble codes as described in Steps 6 through 11 **(see illustration)**.

6   To display any stored trouble codes, first shift the transmission into NEUTRAL and apply the parking brake. Then turn the ignition switch from OFF to ON three times within five seconds and leave it ON. The word WAIT will appear on the instrument cluster as the ECU searches for

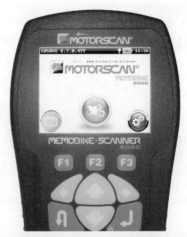

9.2 Scan tools like the MS6050 Motorcycle, Scooter & ATV Diagnostic Scan Tool is a powerful diagnostic aid - programmed with comprehensive diagnostic information, and with updates available from the distributor

9.4 The diagnostic connector is located underneath the hood - 2010 standard Ranger model shown

9.5 CHECK ENGINE indicator (arrow) - 2010 models

9.6 The word WAIT displayed on the instrument cluster indicates the ECU is searching for any trouble codes stored in memory

9.7 The word END displayed on the instrument cluster indicates there are no codes stored in memory or all of the codes have been displayed

any trouble codes **(see illustration)**. If any trouble codes are stored in memory, the code number will appear as flashes on the instrument cluster. A code 21, for example, will show as two flashes, then a pause, then one flash. If more than one code is stored, all of the codes will be displayed from the lowest number to the highest. The pause between codes is longer than the pause between the two digits of a code number.

7   When the word END is displayed on the instrument cluster, either there are no codes stored in memory or all of the codes have been displayed **(see illustration)**.

8   Write down any displayed codes. Check the affected circuits by referring to the wiring diagrams (see Chapter 8,

Section 40). If the wiring and connections are good, refer to the different Sections in this chapter to check individual components.

9   Poor wiring connections are by far the most common cause of fuel injection system problems. Before replacing a component in the fuel injection system, check the wiring and connections carefully.

10   Once the problem is solved, make sure the ignition switch is turned OFF, then disconnect the battery negative cable for 20 seconds to clear the stored codes from the ECU and turn out the check engine light.

11   Note the codes and identify the faults from the following table:

Trouble code	SAE code	Faulty component - symptoms
21	P0355	Loss of synchronization
22	P0122	Throttle position sensor circuit - short or open ground circuit
22	P0123	Throttle position sensor circuit - open ground circuit or short circuit to battery
22	P1120	Throttle position sensor circuit - available voltage too low
23	P0601	Defective ECU
23	P1601	Defective ECU
25	P0914	Incorrect gear switch signal voltage
26	P0500	Vehicle speed sensor failure
27	P1121	Throttle position sensor circuit - set error
41	P0112	Intake air temperature sensor circuit - short circuit to ground
41	P0113	Intake air temperature circuit - short or open circuit to battery
42	P0117	Engine coolant temperature circuit - short circuit to ground
42	P0118	Engine coolant temperature circuit - short or open circuit to battery

Trouble code	SAE code	Faulty component - symptoms (continued)
45	P0107	Barometric pressure sensor circuit - low voltage
46	P0108	Barometric pressure sensor circuit - high voltage
51	P0261	Injector circuit No. 1 - short circuit to ground
51	P0262	Injector circuit No. 1 - short circuit to battery
51	P1260	Injector circuit No. 1 - open driver circuit
52	P0264	Injector circuit No. 2 - short circuit to ground
52	P0265	Injector circuit No. 2 - short circuit to battery
52	P1263	Injector circuit No. 2 - open driver circuit
53	P1691	Rear differential lock control circuit - open circuit
53	P1692	Rear gearcase lock control circuit - short circuit
53	P1693	Rear gearcase lock control circuit - short to ground
54	P0655	Engine coolant temperature lamp circuit - open circuit
54	P1657	Engine coolant temperature lamp circuit - short circuit to ground
54	P1658	Engine coolant temperature lamp circuit - short circuit to battery
55	P1652	Malfunction indicator lamp circuit - short circuit to ground
55	P1653	Malfunction indicator lamp circuit - Short circuit to battery
56	P1231	Fuel pump relay circuit - open circuit
56	P1232	Fuel pump relay circuit - short circuit to ground
56	P1233	Fuel pump relay circuit - short circuit to battery
61	--	End of trouble code sequence

2011 and later models

12   When the CHECK ENGINE MIL is illuminated on the instrument cluster, retrieve trouble codes as described in Steps 13 through 18 **(see illustration)**.

13   Turn the ignition switch ON. If the CHECK ENGINE MIL **(see illustration 9.12)** is illuminated, toggle the MODE button on the instrument cluster until CK ENG appears on the instrument cluster LCD **(see illustration)**. Release the MODE button.

14   Press and hold the MODE button to enter the diagnostic code menu, and three different groups of numbers will appear on the LCD **(see illustration)**. These numbers are used together to determine the trouble code:

* **The single digit number on the left side of the screen represents the number of trouble codes (possible total of nine) occuring in the system. For example, number 1 is shown here, indicating there are two trouble codes identified by the ECU. If the number 0 was shown, it would indicate that only one trouble code has been identified**

9.12 Instrument cluster details - 2011 and later models

A CHECK ENGINE MIL	B MODE button
	C LCD screen

9.13 Check engine display as it appears on the instrument cluster LCD

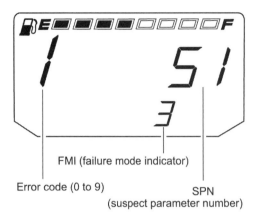

FMI (failure mode indicator)

Error code (0 to 9)

SPN
(suspect parameter number)

9.14 Diagnostic code details

* The number on the upper, right side of the screen is the suspect parameter number (SPN). For example, the number 51 is shown here, indicating a failure in the throttle position circuit

* The number on the lower, right side of the screen is the failure mode indicator (FMI). For example, the number 3 is shown here, indicating excessive voltage is present in the throttle position sensor circuit

NOTE:
Use the SPN and FMI numbers to identify the component and its operating condition listed in the accompanying table to determine the possible cause of the problem.

15   If the single digit number indicates there is more than one trouble code present, press the MODE button one time to advance to the next trouble code. Repeat until all of the trouble codes have been recorded on paper.

16   Poor wiring connections are by far the most common cause of fuel injection system problems. Before replacing a component in the fuel injection system, check the wiring and connections carefully.

17   Once the problem is solved, clear the trouble codes. To do this, press and hold the MODE button, then turn the ignition switch OFF.

18   Note the codes and identify the faults from the following table:

SPN	FMI	Digital Wrench P-code	Faulty component - symptoms
51	3	P0123	Throttle position sensor - excessive voltage
51	4	P0122	Throttle position sensor - low voltage
84	2	P0503	Vehicle speed sensor - no or intermittent signal
84	19	C1069	Vehicle speed sensor - signal error
102	3	P0108	Manifold absolute pressure sensor circuit - high voltage
102	4	P0107	Manifold absolute pressure sensor circuit - low voltage
105	3	P0113	Intake air temperature sensor circuit - high voltage
105	4	P0112	Intake air temperature sensor circuit - low voltage
110	3	P0118	Engine coolant temperature sensor circuit - high voltage
110	4	P0117	Engine coolant temperature sensor circuit - low voltage
110	16	P0217	Engine coolant temperature sensor circuit - engine temperature too high

SPN	FMI	Digital Wrench P-code	Faulty component - symptoms (continued)
110	0	P1217	Engine coolant temperature sensor circuit - engine shutdown from overheating
168	3	P0563 or C1063	System voltage - high voltage
168	4	P0562 or C1064	System voltage - low voltage
190	0	C1059	Electric power steering circuit - engine speed too high
190	19	C1066	Electric power steering circuit - engine speed input error
523	4	P0916	Transmission switch signal - low voltage
628	12	C1073	ECU memory - failure
630	13	C1074	Calibration - error
636	2	P0335	Crankshaft position sensor circuit - circuit malfunction
637	8	P0340	Camshaft phase sensor circuit - circuit malfunction
651	5	P0261	Injector No. 1 circuit - open or grounded circuit
651	3	P0262	Injector No. 1 circuit - short to B+
651	4	P1262	Injector No. 1 circuit - improper ground
652	5	P0264	Injector No. 2 circuit - open or grounded circuit
652	3	P0265	Injector No. 2 circuit - short to B+
652	4	P1265	Injector No. 2 circuit - improper ground
746	5	P1691	Transmission (rear differential) - open or grounded circuit
746	3	P1692	Transmission (rear differential) output circuit - short to B+
746	4	P1693	Transmission (rear differential) - improper ground
1071	5	P1481	Fan relay circuit - open or grounded circuit
1071	3	P1482	Fan relay circuit - short to B+
1071	4	P1483	Fan relay circuit - improper ground
1268	3	P1353	Ignition coil No. 1 circuit - short to B+
1269	3	P1354	Ignition coil No. 2 circuit - short to B+
1347	5	P0230	Fuel pump primary circuit - grounded circuit
1347	3	P0232	Fuel pump secondary circuit - short to B+
1347	4	P0231	Fuel pump secondary circuit - grounded circuit
3597	3	P16A2	ECU output supply voltage 1 - high voltage
3597	4	P16A1	ECU output supply voltage 1 - low voltage
3598	3	P16A9	ECU output supply voltage 2 - high voltage

SPN	FMI	Digital Wrench P-code	Faulty component - symptoms (continued)
3598	4	P16A8	ECU output supply voltage 2 - low voltage
520207	5	P1836	All wheel drive control circuit - open or grounded circuit
520207	3	P1835	All wheel drive control circuit - short to B+
520207	4	P1834	All wheel drive control circuit - improper ground
520221	6	C1050	Steering over current shut down - current too high or grounded circuit
520222	6	C1051	Steering current error - current too high or grounded circuit
520223	31	C1052	Steering torque partial failure
520224	31	C1053	Steering torque full failure
520225	16	C1054	Electric power steering inverter temperature - over 230 degrees F (110 degrees C)
520225	0	C1055	Electric power steering inverter temperature - over 248 degrees F (120 degrees C)
520226	2	U0100	EPS CAN receive error - no RX message for two seconds
520227	2	U1100	EPS CAN receive error - no TX message for two seconds
520228	11	C1065	Position encoder error
520229	12	C1070	Electric power steering software error
520230	31	U0131	Electric power steering circuit offline
520231(1)	31	C1071	EPS power save condition - ignition key ON, engine off for more than 5 minutes
520267(2)	5	P1505	Idle air control valve (Pin 1) - open or grounded circuit
520267(2)	3	P1509	Idle air control valve (Pin 1) - short to B+
520267(2)	4	P1508	Idle air control valve (Pin 1) - grounded circuit
520231	31	C1071	Electric power steering circuit in power save timeout
520268	5	P1515	Idle air control valve (Pin 3) - open or grounded circuit
520268	3	P1519	Idle air control valve (Pin 3) - short to B+
520268	4	P1518	Idle air control valve (Pin 3) - improper ground
520269	5	P1525	Idle air control valve (Pin 4) - open or grounded circuit
520269	3	P1529	Idle air control valve (Pin 4) - short to B+
520269	4	P1528	Idle air control valve (Pin 4) - improper ground
520270	5	P1535	Idle air control valve (Pin 6) - open or grounded circuit
520270	3	P1539	Idle air control valve (Pin 6) - short to B+

(1) 2013 and later models.
(2) 2011 models
(3) 2012 and later models.

SPN	FMI	Digital Wrench P-code	Faulty component - symptoms (continued)
520270	4	P1538	Idle air control valve (Pin 6) - improper ground
520271(3)	5	P1505	Idle air control valve (Pin 1) - open or grounded circuit
520271(3)	3	P1509	Idle air control valve (Pin 1) - short to B+
520271(3)	4	P1508	Idle air control valve (Pin 1) - improper ground

(1) 2013 and later models.
(2) 2011 models
(3) 2012 and later models.

10   FUEL INJECTION SENSORS

1   If a fault is indicated on any of the system components, first check the wiring and connectors between the appropriate component and the engine control unit (ECU) - see Section 11. A continuity test of all wires will locate a break or short in any circuit. Inspect the terminals inside the wiring connectors and ensure they are not loose or corroded. Spray the inside of the connectors with an electrical contact cleaner and allow to dry before reconnecting them. Where appropriate, remove the sensor and check the sensor head and clean it if it is dirty – an accumulation of dirt could affect the signal it transmits. See Chapter 8, Section 3 for additional information.

NOTE:

Dirty and contaminated wiring harness connectors are by far the most common cause of fuel injection problems. Check the wiring and connectors carefully.

2   It is possible to perform some checks on system components using a multimeter and comparing the results with the values listed in this Chapter's Specifications. When testing components, keep in mind that different meters may give slightly different results to those specified even though the component being tested is not faulty – before discarding a component, have your test confirmed by a dealer service department if possible. See Chapter 8, Section 2 for additional information.

3   If after a thorough check of the fuel and electrical systems the source of a fault has not been identified, it is possible that the ECU is faulty. Polaris provides no test specifications for the ECU. In order to determine conclusively that the unit is defective, it should be substituted with a known good one. If the problem is then rectified, the original unit is faulty. However, to prevent from purchasing a new ECU and finding out that the original ECU is good and not the problem, have this check performed by a dealer service department. See Section 11 for additional information.

10.5 Location of the crankshaft position sensor (arrow) on the alternator cover

4   When servicing the sensors in this section, first park the vehicle on level ground and apply the parking brake.

Crankshaft position sensor (CPS) - check and replacement

5   The CPS is externally mounted on the bottom, left side of the alternator cover **(see illustration)**.

Check

6   If a trouble code indicates a problem with the CPS or the CPS circuit, perform the following checks.

7   Make sure the ignition switch is turned OFF. Locate the CPS on the MAG side of the engine **(see illustration 10.5)** and trace its wiring harness to its three-pin connector and disconnect it **(see illustration)**. Using a multimeter set to the ohms scale, measure the resistance between the yellow and white terminals on the sensor side of the connector **(see illustrations)**. If it's within the range listed in this Chapter's Specifications, the sensor is good. Go to Step 8. If the sensor is faulty, replace it (see Steps 10 through 16).

10.7a Crankshaft position sensor electrical connector (arrow)

10.16 Lightly lubricate the CPS O-ring (arrow) with engine oil

7

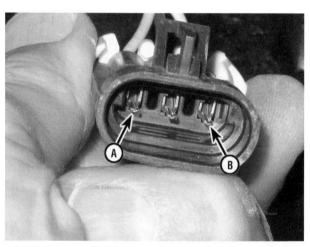

10.7b Measure the resistance between the yellow (A) and white (B) connector terminals . . .

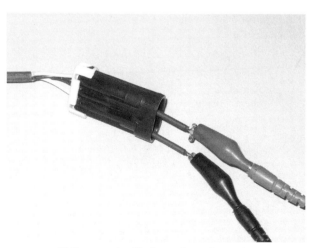

10.7c . . . using T-pins and an ohmmeter

8 Follow the main wiring harness from the CPS connector to the ECU and check the corresponding CPS wires, connector and mating terminals at the ECU. Disconnect the connector at the ECU (see Section 11). Test the wiring harness by checking the continuity in each of the CPS wires for breaks and loose or contaminated terminals. If the wiring harness and the CPS terminals at the ECU are in good condition, go to Step 9.

9 Make sure the screw used to secure the CPS in the alternator cover is tight. If so, remove the CPS (see Steps 10 through 16) and check its sensor end for any corrosion or damage. If possible, use a mirror and flashlight and look through the CPS hole in the alternator cover to check for any damage on the flywheel ring gear. If the problem hasn't been found, and the CPS trouble code is still set, remove the alternator cover and check the flywheel for a sheared Woodruff key or a damaged ring gear (see Chapter 4).

Replacement

10 Raise the cargo bed.

11 If it's necessary for removal access, remove the fuel tank (see Section 8).

12 Clean the alternator cover and the area around the CPS to prevent sand and dirt from falling into the engine.

13 Make sure the ignition switch is turned OFF. Locate the CPS **(see illustration 10.5)** on the MAG side of the engine and trace its wiring harness to its three-pin connector and disconnect it **(see illustration 10.7a)**.

14 Remove the Allen screw, then twist and remove the CPS from the alternator cover **(see illustration 10.5)**.

15 Before installing the new CPS, clean the mounting hole in the alternator cover.

16 Installation is the reverse of removal. Lubricate a new O-ring with engine oil and slide it onto the CPS **(see illustration)**. Tighten the mounting screw to the torque listed in this Chapter's Specifications.

10.17a Throttle position sensor (arrow) - 2010 models

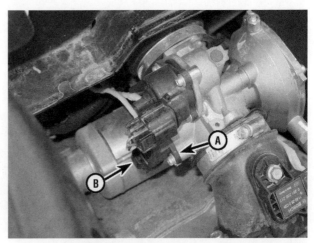

10.17b Throttle position sensor (A) and electrical connector (B) - 2011 and later models

Throttle position sensor (TPS) - check and replacement

17   The TPS is mounted on the throttle body assembly **(see illustrations)**. The TPS is adjustable and precisely set at the factory. Special tools are required to check, service and adjust the TPS.

18   If a trouble code related to the TPS is set, disconnect the TPS electrical connector **(see illustration or illustration 10.17b)**. Then disconnect the wiring harness connector at the ECU (see Section 11). Follow the main wiring harness from the TPS connector to the ECU and check the corresponding TPS wires, connectors and mating terminals at the ECU. Test the wiring harness by checking the continuity in each of the TPS wires for breaks and loose or contaminated terminals. If the wiring harness and the TPS terminals at the ECU are in good condition, refer testing and replacement to a dealer service department.

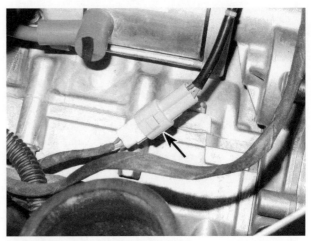

10.18 TPS electrical connector (arrow) - 2010 models

Engine coolant temperature (ECT) sensor - check and replacement

19   The ECT sensor is located on the PTO side of the engine and threaded into the cylinder head **(see illustration)**. If an ECT sensor fault is indicated by the fuel injection system diagnostic system, or if the cooling fan does not operate when the engine is hot, check the sensor.

Check

20   Perform Step 25 to access the ECT sensor and its electrical connector.

21   A quick test can be performed by disconnecting the electrical connector at the ECT sensor **(see illustration 10.19)**. Start the engine and allow it to run at idle speed. Within a few seconds, the fan should turn on. On 2011 and later models, the CHECK ENGINE MIL should turn on (see Section 9). These actions indicate the wiring harness, connectors and all other

10.19 Engine coolant temperature sensor (arrow)

10.29 Engine coolant temperature sensor and washer (arrow)

10.32a T-BAP sensor location (arrow) on the intake boot - 2010 models

10.32b T-MAP sensor (arrow) location on the intake manifold - 2011 and later models

components related to ECT sensor operation are working correctly.

22   With the engine at room temperature, disconnect the electrical connector at the ECT sensor **(see illustration 10.19)**. Set a multimeter to the ohms scale and connect the test leads between the sensor terminals and compare the reading to the appropriate ambient temperature value listed in this Chapter's Specifications.

23   Start and warm the engine to normal operating temperature. If the sensor is working correctly, the resistance should drop substantially as the engine warms up. Specific temperature and resistance readings are listed in this Chapter's Specifications.

24   If the ECT sensor doesn't perform as described, replace it.

Replacement

25   On standard Ranger models, remove the seat base. On Crew models, remove the rear seat base. See Chapter 14.

26   Let the engine cool, then drain the coolant below the level of the sensor (see Chapter 2).

27   Disconnect the electrical connector at the ECT sensor, then loosen and remove the sensor from the cylinder head **(see illustration 10.19)**.

28   Remove all thread sealant residue from the threads in the cylinder head.

29   Note the washer that comes installed on the new ECT sensor **(see illustration)**, then apply thread sealant onto the sensor threads. Install the sensor and tighten to the torque listed in this Chapter's Specifications. Reconnect the sensor electrical connector.

30   Fill and bleed the cooling system (see Chapter 2).

31   The remainder of installation is the reverse of removal.

Temperature and barometric air pressure sensor (T-BAP) (2010 models) and Temp/Manifold absolute pressure sensor (T-MAP) (2011 and later models) - check and replacement

32   The T-BAP sensor (2010 models) is a combined sensor for intake air temperature and barometric pressure and is mounted on the intake boot **(see illustration)**. The T-MAP sensor (2011 and later models) is a combined sensor for intake air temperature and manifold absolute pressure and is mounted on the intake manifold **(see illustration)**. Refer to the appropriate wiring diagram in Chapter 8 to identify the sensor wiring harness colors.

Check

33   Testing the sensor requires the Polaris Digital Wrench Diagnostic Software or an aftermarket scan tool. If a trouble code related to the T-BAP or T-MAP is set, disconnect the electrical connector at the sensor **(see illustration 10.32a or illustration 10.32b)**. Then disconnect the wiring harness connector at the ECU (see Section 11). Follow the main

7

wiring harness from the sensor connector to the ECU and check the corresponding T-BAP or T-MAP wires, connectors and mating terminals at the ECU. Test the wiring harness by checking the continuity in each of the T-BAP or T-MAP wires for breaks and loose or contaminated terminals. If the wiring harness and the terminals at the ECU are in good condition, refer testing to a dealer service department.

Replacement

2010 models

34   Raise the cargo bed.

35   Remove the air box (see Section 16).

36   Loosen the hose clamp and slide the intake boot off of the throttle body with the T-BAP mounted on the intake boot **(see illustration)**.

37   Disconnect the electrical connector at the sensor. Remove the sensor mounting screw, then turn the sensor back and forth to work it loose and remove it from the intake boot, noting the O-ring installed on the sensor **(see illustrations)**.

38   Clean the sensor bore in the intake boot. Then apply a light coat of engine oil to the sensor O-ring to ease installation and install the sensor **(see illustration 10.32a)**. Install the mounting screw and tighten to the torque listed in this Chapter's Specifications.

39   The remainder of installation is the reverse of removal. Check the intake boot alignment with the air box as described in Section 16.

2011 and later models

40   Disconnect the electrical connector at the sensor. Remove the sensor mounting screw, then turn the sensor back and forth to work it loose and remove it from the intake manifold, noting the O-ring installed on the sensor **(see illustration 10.32b)**.

41   Clean the sensor bore in the intake manifold. Then apply a light coat of engine oil to the sensor O-ring to ease installation and install the sensor **(see illustration 10.32b)**. Install the mounting screw and tighten to the torque listed in this Chapter's Specifications.

42   The remainder of installation is the reverse of removal.

Idle air control (IAC) (2011 and later models) - check and replacement

43   The idle air control (IAC) is mounted on the top, right side of the throttle body **(see illustration)**.

Check

44   Disconnect the electrical connector at the IAC **(see illustration 10.43)**.

45   Connect an ohmmeter between the specified terminals on the IAC **(see illustration)** and compare to the corresponding values listed in this Chapter's Specifications. If any reading is not as specified, replace the IAC. Refer to the wiring diagrams at the end of this manual to verify the IAC wire colors and terminal numbers.

10.36 Loosen the hose clamp and remove the intake boot (A) with the T-BAP (B) still attached

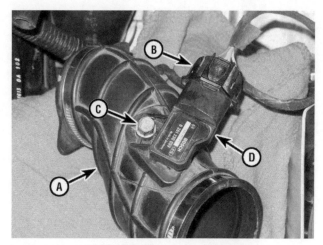

10.37a T-BAP mounting details

A	Intake boot	C	Mounting screw
B	Electrical connector	D	T-BAP sensor

10.37b The sensor is equipped with an O-ring

10.43 Idle air control sensor (A) and electrical connector (B) - 2011 and later models

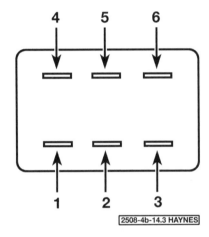

10.45 Idle air control (IAC) terminal numbers

10.49 The cam phase sensor is mounted above the oil filter

Replacement

46   On standard Ranger models, remove the seat base. On Crew models, remove the rear seat base. See Chapter 14.

47   Disconnect the electrical connector at the IAC, then remove the mounting screws and the IAC from the throttle body **(see illustration 10.43)**. Note the O-ring installed on the IAC.

48   Installation is the reverse of removal. Lubricate the O-ring with engine oil, then install the IAC. Install and tighten the IAC mounting screws to the torque listed in this Chapter's Specifications.

Cam phase sensor (2011 and later models) - check and replacement

49   The cam phase sensor is mounted on the crankcase, directly above the oil filter and below the cylinder block **(see illustration)**. It can be identified by its three-wire electrical connector.

Check

50   If a trouble code related to the cam phase sensor is set, turn the engine OFF. Then disconnect the electrical connector at the sensor. Set a digital multimeter to the volts scale and connect the test leads between the harness side connector red/dark blue (+) and brown (-) wire terminals. Battery voltage should be present when the ignition switch is turned to ON. If battery voltage is not present, check the red/dark blue and brown wires for an open circuit or loose or damaged terminals. If battery voltage is present, disconnect the wiring harness connector at the ECU (see Section 11). Follow the main wiring harness from the sensor connector to the ECU and check the corresponding cam phase sensor wires, connectors and mating terminals at the ECU. Test the wiring harness by checking the continuity in each of the cam phase sensor wires for breaks and loose or contaminated terminals. If the wiring harness and the terminals at the ECU are in good condition and you are unable to determine the problem, refer further testing to a dealer service department.

Replacement

51   On standard Ranger models, remove the seat base. On Crew models, remove the rear seat base. See Chapter 14. Lift and remove the storage container installed underneath the seat base, if used.

52   Disconnect the electrical connector at the cam phase sensor **(see illustration 10.49)**. Then remove the screw and remove the sensor from the crankcase. Note the O-ring installed on the sensor.

53   Clean the sensor bore in the crankcase.

54   Installation is the reverse of these removal steps. Apply a light coat of engine oil to the O-ring to ease installation. Tighten the screw to the torque listed in this Chapter's Specifications.

11.3a Engine control unit (2010 standard Ranger model shown)

11.3b Engine control unit (2011 Crew model shown)

11   ENGINE CONTROL UNIT (ECU) - GENERAL INFORMATION AND REPLACEMENT

General information

1   Test specifications for the engine control unit (ECU) are not available. Determining whether the ECU is faulty requires eliminating other possible causes through troubleshooting. If the testing procedures described in this Chapter and Chapter 8 indicate that all ignition and fuel injection system components are functioning correctly, yet a problem exists, take the vehicle to a dealer service department for testing. No procedures are available for checking the ECU. Oftentimes, dealers will install a known good ECU to see if the original unit is faulty. If you attempt to swap ECU units when troubleshooting, make sure the replacement ECU is from the same model and has the same part number.

2   The ECU is a permanently sealed unit. Attempting to open or tamper with the ECU in any way will void the warranty. Likewise, there are no adjustments that can be performed to the ECU, either internally or externally.

3   On standard Ranger models, the ECU is mounted on the kickboard on the driver's side **(see illustration)**. On Crew models, the ECU is mounted on the rear kickboard, on the left passenger's side **(see illustration)**.

Replacement

NOTE:

The manufacturer states that the ECU should not be replaced without factory authorization. Always contact a dealer service department before ordering and installing a replacement ECU. If you do replace an ECU, note that the unit is expensive, so be sure it is faulty before purchasing a new one. Most dealerships do not accept the return of electrical components (see Chapter 8, Section 2).

11.6 Carefully use compressed air (low pressure setting) to clean the ECU connector before disconnecting it

4   On standard Ranger models, remove the seat base. On Crew models, remove the rear seat base. See Chapter 14.

5   Turn the ignition switch OFF.

6   Carefully use compressed air (set on low pressure) to remove any dirt and sand from the ECU connector **(see illustration)**. This will help prevent sand and other debris from entering the connector terminals when disconnecting and separating the connectors.

7   Disconnect the electrical connector at the ECU. Then remove the screws and the ECU. If the ECU will not be immediately reinstalled, cover the harness connector with a clean plastic bag to prevent the connector terminals from being contaminated with sand and dirt **(see illustration 11.3a or illustration 11.3b)**.

8   Installation is the reverse of removal. Tighten the ECU mounting screws to the torque listed in this Chapter's Specifications.

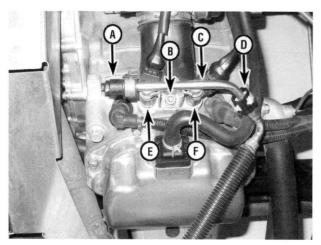

12.1a Fuel injectors and fuel rail details (2010 model)

A Quick connect plug
B Fuel rail
   mounting screw
C Fuel Rail
D Fuel hose and fitting

E Fuel injector -
   MAG side
F Fuel injector -
   PTO side

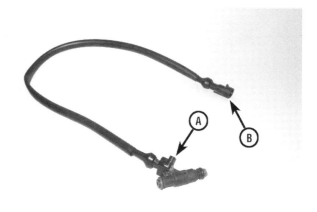

12.2 A section of the wiring harness is permanently bonded onto each fuel injector (A) - when servicing a fuel injector, disconnect it at its wiring harness connector (B). 2010 model fuel injector shown. The fuel injectors used on 2011 and later models are similar

7

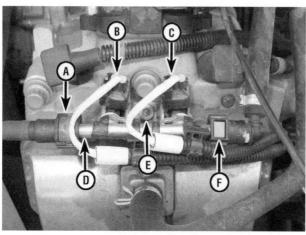

**12.1b Fuel injectors and fuel rail details
(2011 and later models)**

A Fuel hose and fitting
B Fuel injector -
   MAG side
C Fuel injector -
   PTO side

D Fuel rail
E Fuel rail
   mounting screw
F Quick connect plug
   and damper hose

12   FUEL INJECTORS AND FUEL RAIL - CHECK, REMOVAL AND INSTALLATION

WARNING:

Refer to the precautions given in Section 1 before starting work.

WARNING:

Wait until the engine is completely cool before beginning this procedure.

1   Note the hose and wiring harness routing around the fuel injectors and fuel rail when servicing these components in this section **(see illustrations)**.

2   When servicing the fuel injectors in this section, note that the wiring harness connector installed at the injector is permanently bonded in place. Do not attempt to disconnect the wiring harness at the injector, as you will damage the injector and wiring harness. Instead, disconnect the injector harness connector at the main wiring harness **(see illustration)**.

Check

CAUTION:

When testing and handling the fuel injectors, do not apply voltage directly to an injector. Also, do not apply a ground directly to an injector when the ignition switch is turned ON. Either condition will damage the injector.

3   Refer to Steps 9 through Step 19 on how to access, disconnect and remove the fuel injectors.

4   The following checks can be made with the fuel injectors installed on the throttle body.

5   Start the engine and allow to idle. Place a long screwdriver or a mechanic's stethoscope against an injector. You should hear/feel a steady clicking as the engine runs, indicating the fuel injectors are opening and closing. If an injector is quiet, either the injector is damaged, or there is a problem with its wiring harness and/or connector. Repeat for the other injector.

6   Turn the engine off. Disconnect the fuel injector wiring harness connector from the main wiring harness (see Steps 2 and 13). Use a multimeter set to the ohms R x 1 scale and measure the resistance between the injector terminals and

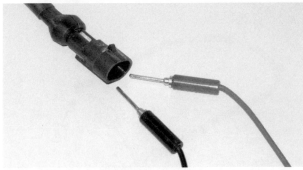

12.6 Measure fuel injector resistance between the two wire terminals

12.11 Remove the fuel injector wiring harness clip (arrow) from the fuel rail

compare the result with the specification in this Chapter's Specifications **(see illustration)**. If the result is good, check that there is no continuity between each terminal and ground. If the results are not as specified, the injector is probably faulty. If necessary, refer further testing to a dealership service department.

7   If the fuel injector resistance is correct, but you did not hear or feel the injector when the engine was running, inspect the fuel injector wiring harness for an open circuit.

8   Look and feel around the fuel injector where it enters the throttle body and fuel rail. Check for any fuel leaks.

Removal

9   On standard Ranger models, remove the seat base. On Crew models, remove the rear seat base. Then remove the storage box located underneath the seat base. See Chapter 14.

10   Clean the area around the fuel injectors to prevent sand and dirt from falling into the cylinder head.

11   On 2011 and later models, remove the clip that secures the fuel injector wiring harnesses to the fuel rail **(see illustration)**.

12   Relieve the fuel system pressure (see Section 2). Then disconnect the fuel hose at the fuel rail **(see illustration 12.1a or illustration 12.1b)**.

NOTE:

Before disconnecting the fuel injector wiring harness connectors, see Step 2 for additional information.

13   On 2010 models, when looking at the wiring harness side fuel injector connectors, the wires in the MAG side connector are red/black and black, and in the PTO connector, the wires are red/black and white. However, the connectors attached to the fuel injectors themselves are not color coded, and either can be connected into the MAG or PTO wiring harness side connectors. To identify these connectors, mark one connector set, either MAG or PTO, with a marking pen **(see illustration)**. On 2011 and later models, the wiring harness and fuel injector connector sets are color coded. The MAG side injector connectors are black and the PTO side injector connectors are gray **(see illustration)**. After you have identified the fuel injector

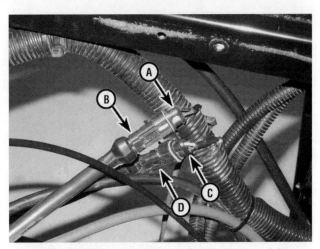

12.13a Fuel injector connector details (2010 models)

A   *Wiring harness side connector - MAG side*
B   *Fuel injector side connector - MAG side*
C   *Wiring harness side connector - PTO side*
D   *Fuel injector side connector - PTO side*
     (Note the alignment marks drawn across the MAG side connector halves)

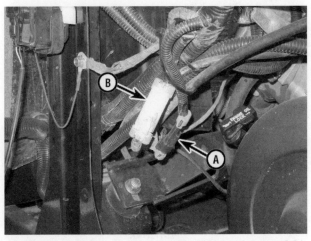

12.13b Fuel injector connector details (2011 and later models)

A   *Black connectors - MAG side*
B   *Gray connectors - PTO side*

12.14 Disconnect the engine breather hose (arrow) and move it away from the fuel injectors (2010 models)

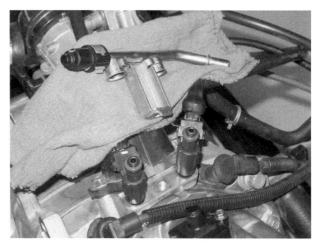

12.16b The fuel rail removed with both fuel injectors remaining in the cylinder head (2010 model shown)

12.15 Remove the fuel rail mounting screw (A) with an L-shaped Allen wrench - if necessary, use a piece of pipe (B) as an extension (2010 model shown)

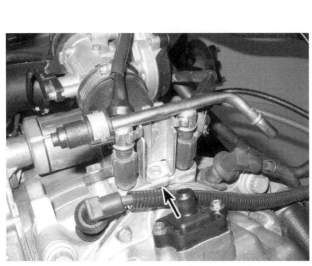

12.16a Fuel rail (arrow) and fuel injector mounting position in the cylinder head (2010 model shown)

wiring harness connectors, disconnect them at the wiring harness.

14   On 2010 models, disconnect the engine breather hose from the valve cover (see illustration).

NOTE:

The fuel rail Allen screw is tight and can only be accessed from one side. Before loosening the Allen screw in Step 15, clean the recess in the top of the screw to make sure your Allen wrench engages the screw fully. If the Allen wrench slips under heavy pressure, it could damage the hex shoulders in the top of the screw, making it difficult to loosen and re-move the screw.

15   Use an L-shaped Allen wrench to loosen and remove the Allen screw securing the fuel rail to the cylinder head. Because of the lack of working space with the engine installed in the frame, it may be helpful to slide a piece of pipe over the end of the Allen wrench to increase leverage when loosening the screw (see illustration).

16   Before removing the fuel rail/fuel injector assembly, reroute the wiring harness connected to each fuel injector so they are not damaged during removal. Then lift the fuel rail and remove it (see illustration). Note that one or both fuel injectors will remain in the cylinder head and/or inside the fuel rail (see illustration).

CAUTION:

An O-ring is installed on both ends of the fuel injectors, and because they are designed to prevent fuel leakage, the fuel injectors can be difficult to remove, and especially from the cylinder head. When removing a fuel injec-tor, hold the injector by its body, and not its wiring harness or connector. If you damage the connector, it will be necessary to replace the fuel injector and its wiring harness as an assembly.

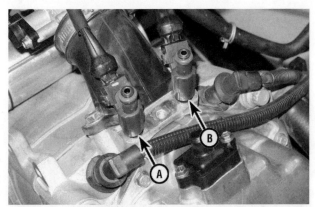

12.17a To remove each fuel injector from the cylinder head or fuel rail, simultaneously twist and pull it out of its mounting position. Identify the mag (A) and PTO (B) fuel injectors, and remove them from the cylinder head . . .

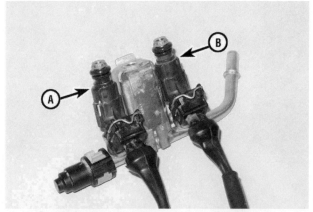

12.17b . . . or the fuel rail (2010 model shown)

12.18 Small tapered plugs (arrows) work well for blocking the fuel injector openings in the cylinder head

12.19 Fuel injector details (2010 model shown)

A   *Upper O-ring (blue)*
B   *Lower O-ring (black)*
C   *Wiring harness connector (do not disconnect)*

17   Remove the fuel injectors from either the cylinder head or fuel rail **(see illustrations)**.

18   Cover the fuel injector openings to prevent sand, dirt and other debris from falling into the cylinder head **(see illustration)**.

19   If you intend to reuse the same fuel injectors, note that the O-rings installed on the injectors are not available separately from the manufacturer **(see illustration)**. If one or more O-rings require replacement, it will be necessary to purchase new fuel injectors, or possibly source new fuel injector O-rings from an aftermarket supplier.

20   Inspect the injector nozzles for blockage and carbon buildup. Modern fuels contain detergents which should, along with the filters installed on the fuel pump, injector design and high fuel pressure, keep the injectors clean and free of gum or varnish. While the manufacturer does not recommend cleaning the fuel injectors, if either injector is suspected of being blocked, try and flush it thoroughly with injector cleaner. Injectors can become blocked or clogged due to dirty or poor-quality fuel, clogged or damaged fuel pump filters, or running the engine for short operating intervals (engine does not come up to operating temperature). When fuel quality is suspect, use a fuel injection cleaner or additive.

21   Inspect the injectors for any cracks and other damage. If the O-rings are cracked or damaged in any way, it will be necessary to replace the fuel injectors, or try and find replacement O-rings from an aftermarket supplier that are designed on work on the Polaris injectors **(see illustration 12.19)**. Do not attempt to disconnect the wiring harness connector from an injector, as it is permanently sealed in place with epoxy; see Step 2 for additional information.

22   Inspect the fuel rail for cracks and other damage. Make sure the bore through the fuel rail and the two fuel injector cups is clean and free of any debris. If the upper injector O-rings are torn or damaged, check for any rubber residue sticking to the inside of both cups **(see illustration)**. If any rubber residue is found, remove it carefully to keep from

scratching the cup surface and causing a fuel leak. Make sure the quick connect plug on the end of the fuel rail is not leaking or damaged.On 2011 and later models, check the damper hose mounted on the end of the quick connect plug for damage and a loose hose clamp.

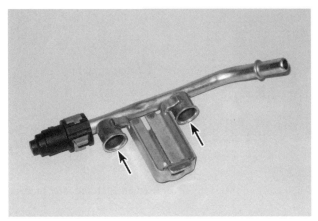

12.22 Inspect the fuel rail for cracks and other damage. Make sure the cups (arrows) where the injectors are installed are clean and free of any torn O-ring residue

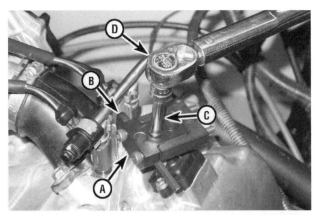

12.26 Because the Allen screw cannot be accessed from its top side, the Motion Pro adjustable torque wrench adapter (A) - part No. 08-0380, an L-shaped Allen wrench (B), ratchet extension (C) and torque wrench (D) are used here to tighten the Allen screw. If you don't have access to a torque adapter, tighten the screw securely, making sure not to overtighten it and damage the threads in the cylinder head

Installation

23   Lightly lubricate the injector O-rings with engine oil to help seat them in place when installing the injectors into the cylinder head and when installing the fuel rail.

24   Because the fuel injectors can be difficult to install, it is easier to install each injector one at a time into the cylinder head, instead of attempting to install both at the same time when they are installed in the fuel rail. Before installing the fuel injectors, first identify the MAG and PTO side fuel injectors, then install them in their correct positions and with their connectors facing toward the back of the engine **(see illustration 12.1a or illustration 12.1b).**

25   With both fuel injectors installed in the cylinder head, install the fuel rail, making sure it is fully seated over the O-rings.

26   Install and tighten the fuel rail mounting screw to the torque listed in this Chapter's Specifications **(see illustration).**

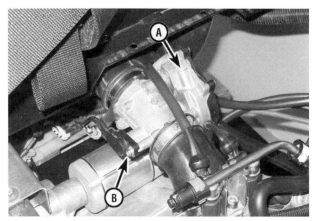

13.1a When servicing the throttle body, do not turn the throttle body stop screw (A) or loosen the TPS mounting screw (B) - 2010 model

27   The remainder of installation is the reverse of removal, noting the following:

 a) *Turn the ignition switch ON to activate the fuel pump for a few seconds, then turn the ignition switch OFF when the fuel pump stops running. When the fuel pump runs, fuel pressure rises in the fuel system. Repeat this sequence two or three times. Then turn the ignition switch OFF and check for fuel leaks around the fuel injectors, fuel rail, fuel hose and the quick connect plug.*

 b) *When you are sure there are no fuel leaks from the fuel injectors, fuel rail or fuel hoses, start the engine and allow to run at idle speed. Then check to make sure you hear the fuel injectors opening and closing (see Step 5).*

13   THROTTLE BODY - REMOVAL, INSPECTION AND INSTALLATION

WARNING:
Refer to the precautions given in Section 1 before starting work.

NOTE:
Unless otherwise noted, the illustrations in this section show the service being performed on a 2010 model. Service procedures for 2011 and later models are similar.

1   When servicing the throttle body in this section, it is important to observe the following. Do not turn the throttle body stop screw. Because this screw sets the throttle valve position and calibrates the throttle body air flow, its position is pre-set at the factory and sealed in place. If the sealer is removed and the screw is turned, the throttle body will have to be replaced. Likewise, the throttle position sensor (TPS) angle position on the throttle body has been pre-set at the factory. If the TPS mounting screw is loosened, the TPS must be recalibrated and its position adjusted by a dealer service department **(see illustrations).**

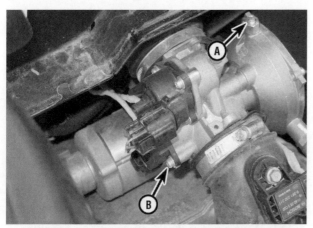

13.1b When servicing the throttle body, do not turn the throttle body stop screw (A) or loosen the TPS mounting screw (B) - 2011 and later models

13.7a Remove the screws holding the throttle cable cover (arrow) to the throttle body. This is the cover used on 2010 models . . .

13.7b . . . and this is the cover used on 2011 and later models

13.7c Turn the throttle wheel by hand to provide slack in the throttle cable (arrow) . . .

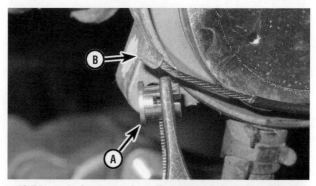

13.7d . . . and remove the collar (A) and throttle cable (B) from the throttle wheel (2010 model shown)

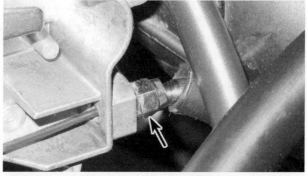

13.7e Loosen the cable nut (arrow) and remove the throttle cable from the throttle body (2010 model shown)

Removal

2   On standard Ranger models, remove the seat base. On Crew models, remove the rear seat base. See Chapter 14.

3   Raise the cargo bed, if necessary, to access the intake boot installed between the air box and throttle body.

4   Make sure all engine openings are closed or blocked off, then use compressed air to remove loose sand and dirt from the throttle body, intake boot and intake manifold.

5   Disconnect the TPS electrical connector (see Section 10). See Step 1 for additional information on the TPS.

6   On 2011 and later models, disconnect the IAC electrical connector (see Section 10).

7   Remove the throttle cable cover and disconnect the throttle cable at the throttle body **(see illustrations)**. After removing the cable, set it aside so that it cannot become kinked or damaged. Note the O-ring installed in the throttle cable cover. On 2011 and later models, the throttle cable adjuster is mounted facing toward the front side of the throttle body assembly.

13.8 Before removing the throttle body, note where the tab on the intake boot aligns with the throttle body (2010 model shown). On 2011 and later models, the intake boot tab is on the left side

13.9 Loosen the clamps (arrows) securing the throttle body to the intake boot and intake manifold. Note that alignment on your model may differ from the alignment shown here (2010 Ranger model shown)

13.13 The intake boot (A), intake manifold (B) and both clamps must be in good condition to prevent sand and dirt from entering the throttle body and engine

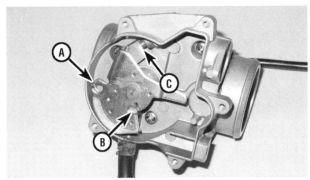

13.14 Move the throttle wheel (A) by hand to check for any binding or roughness; mvake sure the return spring is hooked onto the throttle wheel (B) and is not loose or damaged. When the throttle wheel is at rest, the throttle stop must rest against the stop screw (C) - 2010 model shown

8   Before removing the throttle body in Step 9, locate the large tab on the intake boot and where it aligns with the throttle body (see illustration). If the air box is removed, this alignment must be maintained with the throttle body.

9   Loosen the throttle body clamps and carefully remove the throttle body, first from the intake boot, then the intake manifold (see illustration). When removing the throttle body, handle it carefully to prevent from damaging the TPS wiring harness. Stuff a clean rag into the intake manifold and intake boot to prevent sand and dirt from falling inside.

10   After removing the throttle body, inspect it and the intake boot for any sand and dirt that may have passed through the air filter. If any debris is found, inspect the air box, air filter and intake boot for any damage, and correct the problem before putting the vehicle back into service.

Inspection

11   Other than basic cleaning and inspection, there is not much you can do or are required to do to the throttle body. To prevent from causing any calibration or operating problems with the throttle body or TBS, read the information in Step 1 before continuing with Step 12.

CAUTION:

When handling and inspecting the throttle body, do not damage the throttle valve or throttle valve bore as this may cause the engine to idle roughly, and require replacement of the throttle body.

12   Inspect the throttle body for cracks or other damage that could cause an air leak and operating problems.

13   Inspect the intake boot and intake manifold where they seal against the throttle body for cracks and other damage (see illustration). Check the condition of the clamps for the intake boot and intake manifold and replace if you noticed a problem when loosening them, of if they are damaged. If the intake manifold was removed, clean it and its mating surface on the cylinder head, and tighten its mounting screws to the torque listed in this Chapter's Specifications.

14   Check that the throttle wheel moves smoothly and freely, taking into account spring pressure. When turning the throttle wheel by hand, maintain pressure on the wheel so the throttle valve does not slam shut against the stop screw. Also, do not push against the throttle valve by hand to check its movement, as the spring pressure is too great and will give you a false impression of its movement. Then inspect the spring for any cracks and other damage, while making sure it is hooked tightly against the throttle wheel. The return spring and the area enclosed by the throttle cable cover must be clean (see illustration).

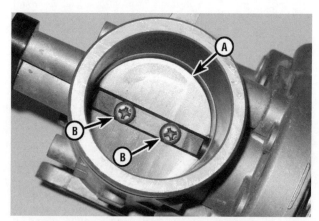

13.15 Check the throttle valve (A) and bore for carbon, and both mounting screws (B) for looseness

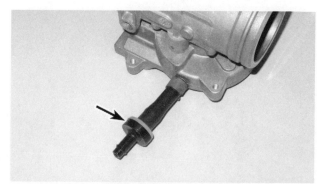

13.16 The check valve (arrow) used on 2010 models must be in good condition and installed onto the throttle body so that it faces in the direction shown here

15 Make sure the throttle valve is clean (no carbon) and its mounting screws are tight **(see illustration)**.

16 On 2010 models, inspect the check valve and hose mounted on the bottom of the throttle body for any damage, while making sure the end of the hose is open. If the check valve is removed, reinstall it facing in its original position **(see illustration)**.

17 Check the O-ring installed in the cover for cracks and deterioration and replace if necessary **(see illustration)**. Before installing the O-ring, make sure the groove in the cover is clean so that the O-ring will set flush when installed.

13.17 A small O-ring (arrow) fits into the cover groove and helps seal the area behind the cover (2010 model shown)

Installation

18 Remove the rags from the intake boot and intake manifold. Then check to make sure there is no debris in the boot or manifold.

19 On 2010 models, if the intake boot was removed, make sure it doesn't pinch the fuel injector wiring harness **(see illustration)**.

20 Install the throttle body into the intake manifold and intake boot. On 2010 models, align the tab on the throttle body with the notch in the intake manifold and push the throttle body all the way in **(see illustration)**. Then position the intake boot over the throttle body. If the air box was removed, make sure the tab on the air box is in the same alignment with the throttle body **(see illustration 13.8)**. Tighten the intake manifold and intake boot clamps securely **(see illustration 13.9)**.

21 The remainder of installation is the reverse of removal, plus the following:

a) *Before reconnecting the throttle cable, inspect the cable end for fraying and other damage. Also check the outer sheath for bending, creases or other damage. If any damage is found, replace the cable (see Section 18).*

b) *Adjust the throttle free play (see Chapter 2).*

22 While sitting in the driver's seat, start the engine. Turn the steering wheel from side to side, making sure the engine idles properly and does not speed up.

13.19 When installing the intake boot on 2010 models, lift the fuel injector wiring harness to make sure the boot seats fully against the throttle body

13.20 On 2010 models, the throttle body tab (arrow) must align with the notch in intake manifold

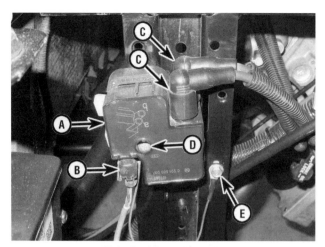

15.1a Ignition coil details

A   Ignition coil assembly
B   Primary electrical connector
C   Secondary coil wires (2010 model shown)
D   Mounting screw
E   Ignition coil ground wire and screw (2010 model shown)

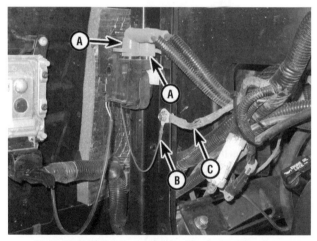

15.1b 2011 and later model ignition coil differences

A   Secondary coil wires
B   Ignition coil ground wire and screw
C   Wiring harness ground wire

14   IGNITION SYSTEM CHECK

1   If the CHECK ENGINE indicator (2010 models) or the CHECK ENGINE MIL (2011 and later models) on the instrument cluster stays on, refer to Section 9 to retrieve the trouble codes and troubleshoot the fuel injection system. Otherwise, if you feel there is a problem on the ignition side of the fuel injection system and a code has not been set, perform Steps 2 through 12 to isolate the problem. If necessary, refer to Chapter 1 for additional troubleshooting information and procedures.

2   Carefully check all of the ignition system wiring and connectors for corrosion, loose and damaged pins or other problems. Refer to the wiring diagrams at the end of this manual.

3   Check the fuses, relays and circuit breakers (see Chapter 8).

4   Check and charge the battery. When the battery is fully charged, perform a load test to make sure the battery is in good condition and is not the problem. Refer to Chapter 8 for information on battery charging and testing. Note that when battery voltage is below 7 volts, the ECU cannot signal and operate the fuel system.

5   Check for worn or fouled spark plugs (see Chapter 2).

6   Perform a spark test (see Chapter 1). If there is a strong spark at each spark plug, the ignition system is working correctly. If there is no spark at one or both spark plugs, or the spark is weak, continue with Step 7.

7   Check for loose or damaged spark plug caps. Measure the secondary wire resistance to check the secondary wires and spark plug caps (see Section 15).

8   Test the ignition coil (see Section 15).

9   Test the ignition switch (see Chapter 8).

10   Test the crankshaft position sensor (see Section 10).

11   On 2011 and later models, test the camshaft phase sensor (see Section 10).

12   If the problem has not been found, have a dealer service department substitute the engine control unit (ECU) and retest. See Section 11 for information on the ECU and its replacement.

15   IGNITION COIL - REMOVAL, TESTING AND INSTALLATION

1   The ignition coil is mounted below the seat base on standard Ranger models and below the rear seat base on Crew models. Because a plastic insulator is used between the ignition coil and frame, a separate ground wire is installed between the ignition coil and its mounting screw and frame **(see illustrations)**.

Removal

2   Make sure the ignition switch is turned OFF.

3   On standard Ranger models, remove the seat base. On Crew models, remove the rear seat base. See Chapter 14.

4   Disconnect the primary electrical connector at the ignition coil **(see illustration 15.1a or illustration 15.1b)**.

NOTE:

Make sure to identify the secondary wires as described in Step 5. If you switch the wires at the ignition coil or spark plugs, an engine misfire will result. Note that on all models, the secondary wires are different lengths. On 2011 and later models, the secondary wires are marked either PTO or MAG.

5   Identify the secondary wires before disconnecting them at either the spark plugs or ignition coil. To remove the ignition coil without disconnecting the spark plug caps, disconnect the secondary wires from the ignition coil **(see illustration 15.1a or illustration 15.1b)**. To remove the

15.6a The plastic insulator shown here (arrow) fits between the ignition coil and the frame

15.7 The ignition coil mounting screw threads into a nut clip (arrow) installed in the frame

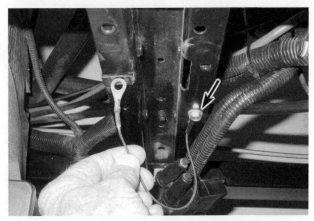

15.6b The ignition coil ground wire will free itself after removing the mounting screw and ignition coil

15.8 Inspect each coil (arrows) for cracks and other damage

ignition coil with the secondary wires attached, disconnect the spark plug caps at the spark plugs.

6   Remove the screw and the ignition coil assembly, while noting the plastic insulator and the ground wire attached to the ignition coil mounting screw **(see illustrations)**. The ground wire will slip out from between the plastic insulator and ignition coil when the coil is removed from the frame.

7   Note the nut clip installed in the frame **(see illustration)**.

Testing

8   Inspect the coil for cracks and other damage **(see illustration)**. If either coil is obviously damaged, replace the ignition coils as an assembly. If the coil assembly is undamaged, continue with the next Step.

NOTE:

If any of the ignition coil or secondary coil wire terminals look dirty or corroded, perform the following tests and record the results before cleaning the terminals. Then clean the terminals and repeat the tests. If the second

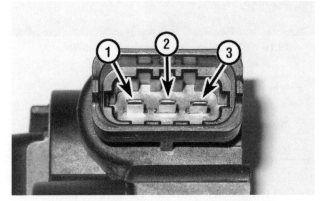

15.9 Ignition coil primary terminal identification

test results are different and within specification, this may have been the problem.

9   Use a multimeter set to the ohms R X 1 scale and measure the primary coil resistance across terminals 1 and 2, then across terminals 2 and 3 **(see illustration)**. Compare the results with the specifications listed in this Chapter's Specifications.

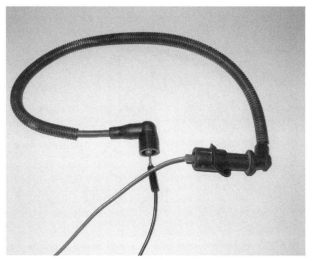

15.10a Measuring the secondary wire resistance

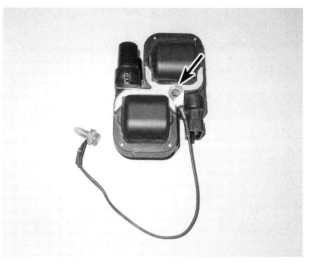

15.14 Place the ground wire against the ignition coil (arrow) before installing the plastic damper

7

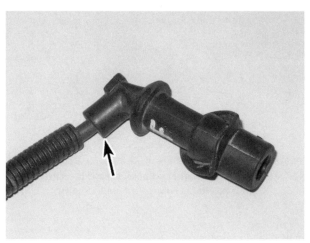

15.10b Make sure the spark plug cap is tightened fully on the secondary wire

10   Set the ohmmeter to the K-ohms scale and measure the secondary wire resistance between the spark plug terminal and the end plug terminal **(see illustration)**. Compare the result with the specifications listed in this Chapter's Specifications. If the results are erratic, check for a loose spark plug cap, then repeat the test **(see illustration)**.

11   If either test is out of specification, have the test results confirmed by a dealer service department before replacing any parts.

12   Clean the ground wire ends and the frame contact point to make sure the ignition coil will be properly grounded when reinstalled **(see illustration 15.6b)**.

Installation

13   Make sure the nut clip is installed in the frame **(see illustration 15.7)**.

14   Install the ground wire and seat it against the ignition coil **(see illustration)**, then align and install the plastic damper against the ignition coil **(see illustration 15.6a)**. Hold the parts in place and install the mounting screw through the ignition coil, ground wire and plastic damper. Install the ignition coil and tighten the screw to the torque listed in this Chapter's Specifications.

15   Reconnect the secondary wires while referring to your identification marks made during removal (see Step 5).

16   The remainder of installation is the reverse of removal.

16   AIR BOX - REMOVAL AND INSTALLATION

1   The air box is located at the rear of the engine and underneath the cargo box. A boot and two hoses are connected to the air box - intake boot, rear engine baffle box hose, and engine breather hose. Because of the environment these vehicles operate in, maintaining the air filter, air box, intake boot and hoses is key to engine operation and longevity. Inspect and service the air filter as described in Chapter 2.

Removal and installation

2   Park the vehicle on level ground and apply the parking brake.

3   Raise the cargo box (see Chapter 14).

16.4a Air box details (2010 models)

A   Air box
B   Mounting screws
C   Engine breather hose
D   Intake boot
E   Plugged hose nozzle
F   Engine rear baffle
     box hose
G   Air filter cover

16.4b Air box details (2011 and later models)

A   Air box
B   Mounting screws
C   Engine breather hose
D   Intake boot
E   Plugged hose nozzle
     (not visible here)
F   Engine rear baffle hose
G   Air filter cover

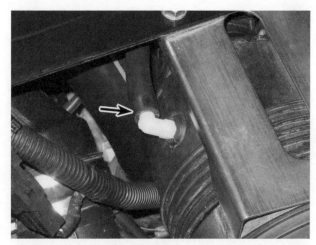

16.6 The engine breather hose (arrow) is a slip fit on the air box hose fitting (2010 model shown)

16.7 The engine rear baffle box hose (arrow) is secured to the air box with a clamp (2010 model shown)

16.8 The intake boot (arrow) is secured to the air box with a clamp (2010 model shown)

4   Before servicing the air box, check the air box, air filter cover, boot and hoses carefully for any loose fittings or damage **(see illustrations)**.

5   Make sure all engine openings are closed or blocked off, then use compressed air to remove loose sand and dirt from the air box, throttle body, intake boot and intake manifold.

6   Disconnect the the engine breather hose at the air box **(see illustration)**.

7   Loosen the clamp securing the engine rear baffle box hose to the air box **(see illustration)**.

8   Loosen the clamp securing the intake boot to the air box **(see illustration)**.

9   Remove the screws securing the air box to the frame, then carefully release the boot and hoses previously loosened and remove the air box assembly. Cover the throttle body boot and engine rear baffle box hose to prevent sand and

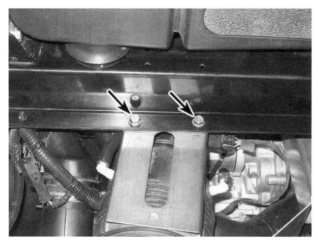

16.9a Remove the air box mounting screws (arrows) . . .

16.13a Here the air box is fully installed, but there is still a gap (arrows) between the air box and the intake boot . . .

16.9b . . . and the air box (2010 model shown)

16.13b . . . to close the gap (arrows), it was necessary to loosen the hose clamp at the throttle body and turn the intake boot

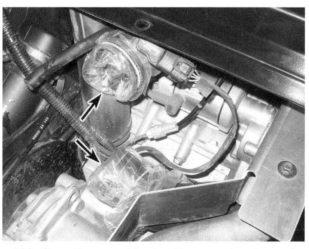

16.9c Cover the exposed boot and hose openings (arrows)

dirt from entering (see illustrations).

10   Remove the air filter and clean the air box of all sand and dirt. Also clean the shoulder inside the air box where the air filter is clamped onto it of all old grease. Remove and service the air filter, if necessary (see Chapter 2).

11   Inspect the clamps used to secure the boot and hoses and replace any that are weak or damaged. If necessary, remove and clean the clamps so the screws turn easily.

12   Before installing the air box, remove any rags or plastic bags used to block off the boot and hoses.

13   Make sure the intake boot and hoses are fully installed and seated against the shoulders on the air box (see illustrations). Use your finger and feel around the boot and clamp to make sure each are fully installed and not pinched. Then position the hose clamps and tighten securely.

14   Replace any hose clamp(s) that will not tighten correctly.

15   The remainder of installation is the reverse of removal.

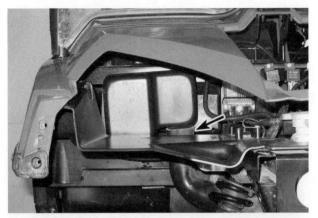

17.6a Loosen the hose clamp at the connecting hose (arrow) . . .

17.6b . . . and remove the front air baffle box (arrow)

17.9 Rear air baffle box details

A   Rear air baffle box
B   Air box hose
C   Air duct rear connecting hose
D   Mounting screws

17.14a A hose clamp secures the air duct (A) to the front air baffle boxv connecting hose (B)

17   AIR BAFFLE BOX AND INTAKE AIR DUCT - REMOVAL AND INSTALLATION

1   Air entering the engine through the air filter first passes through a filtered front air baffle box located at the front of the vehicle. Air then passes through a long plastic air duct, through the rear air baffle box, and into the air box. All of the components in this system must be in good condition and sealed at all connecting points to prevent water from entering the air box and contaminating the air filter.

Front air baffle box

2   The front air baffle box is located under the hood and behind the right front headlight.
3   Park the vehicle on level ground and apply the parking brake.
4   Raise the hood.
5   Remove the front cover to easier access the front air baffle box (see Chapter 14).
6   Loosen the hose clamp and remove the front air baffle box from the hose connected to the air duct **(see illustrations)**.
7   To service the pre-filter mounted in the front air baffle

box, refer to Chapter 2.
8   Installation is the reverse of removal.

Rear air baffle box

9   The rear air baffle box is connected between the air duct's rear connecting hose and and the air box **(see illustration)**. This box is not equipped with a filter.
10   Open the cargo box (see Chapter 14).
11   Disconnect the two hoses at the rear air baffle box. Then remove the screws and the box (see illustration 17.9).
12   Check the box for any contamination and flush with water if necessary. Allow the box to dry before reinstalling it back onto the vehicle.
13   Installation is the reverse of removal.

Air duct(s)

14   One or more air ducts are used to connect the front air baffle box to the air box at the throttle valve **(see illustration)**. The air duct is routed lengthwise across the

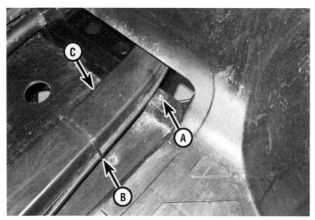

17.14b Torx screws (A) and plastic ties (B) secure the air duct (C) to the frame

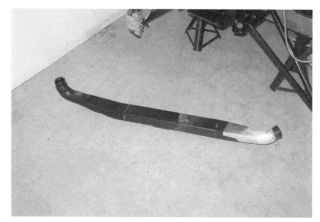

17.16b Air duct removed from a standard Ranger model

17.15 Here the front gearcase was removed to allow removal of the air duct (2010 model)

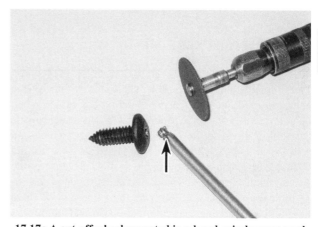

17.17a A cut-off wheel mounted in a hand grinder was used to cut a circular groove (arrow) below the screwdriver tip to make a ball end Torx screwdriver

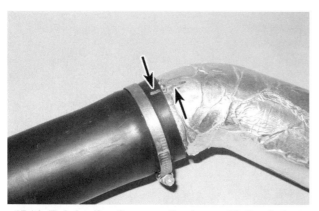

17.16a To help align the connecting hoses with the air duct during installation, scribe alignment marks across the parts (arrows) before separating them

top of the lower main frame tubes and secured in place with Torx screws and plastic ties **(see illustration)**. Because of the increased wheelbase on Crew models, three air ducts are used - one long air duct and a short air duct on each end. The air duct can be left in place when performing the majority of the service procedures described in this manual. On occasion, however, it may be necessary to disconnect the hoses at the air duct and move it aside to provide access to other components.

15   Remove the seat base, floor cover and any other body components, according to your model, as necessary to access the air duct (see Chapter 14). On some models, it may be necessary to remove the front gearcase before the air duct can be removed from the vehicle (see Chapter 11) **(see illustration)**.

16   Before removing the air duct, scribe alignment marks across the air duct and both connecting hoses to help align the parts during assembly **(see illustrations)**.

17   If an air duct screw is mounted underneath the floor and its access is restricted, try to use a T-25 ball end Torx screwdriver. Because the head of the screwdriver has a groove machined above the tip, the screwdriver can be used at an angle, instead of straight on. If you cannot locate the correct size ball end Torx screwdriver, you can easily modify a regular T-25 Torx screwdriver as described in **illustrations 17.7a through 17.7c**.

18   Periodically check for loose or missing hose clamps at the air duct. Plastic ties are also used to secure the air duct, and replace any that are loose or have broken.

19   Installation is the reverse of removal.

17.17b Here the ball end Torx screwdriver is inserted underneath the floor at an angle . . .

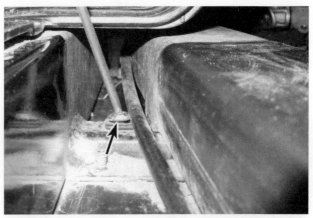

17.17c . . . and used to access the air duct screw (arrow)

18   THROTTLE CABLE - REMOVAL AND INSTALLATION

1   Problems with the throttle cable are primarily due to water, mud and other debris entering the cable. When operating the vehicle in freezing weather, water inside the cable can cause the inner cable to freeze, which can result in a stuck or broken cable. Mud can pack around the cable ends and cause the cable to stick. Because of the environment these vehicles operate in, it is a good idea to periodically remove and lubricate the cable with a cable lube tool and a cable lubricant. Note also that lubing the cable flushes contaminants out of the cable. Refer to the information in Chapter 2 on how to inspect and lubricate the throttle cable.

18.4 Plastic tie (arrow) used to secure throttle cable in place. Note where and how the throttle cable is routed and held in place before removing it

NOTE:

The following information should be used as a general guide when removing and installing the throttle cable. Note that the clamps and routing on your vehicle may differ from the way they are shown in this Section, due to model and manufacturing changes, or changes made by a previous owner. If necessary, refer this procedure to a dealer service department or independent repair shop.

2   Park the vehicle on level ground and apply the parking brake.
3   Remove the left wheel panel (see Chapter 14).
4   During the procedure, note the throttle cable routing from the throttle pedal to the throttle body. Also note any guides and plastic-ties the cable passes through **(see illustration)**. If possible, take pictures of the cable routing for your actual model to help with rerouting and installation.
5   Disconnect the throttle cable at the throttle body (see Section 13).
6   Disconnect the throttle cable end and remove the brake and throttle pedal mounting bracket with both pedals

18.8 Remove the two throttle cable mounting bracket screws (arrows)

attached (see Chapter 14).
7   On standard Ranger models, remove the floor. On Crew models, remove the front floor. See Chapter 14.
8   Working inside the driver's compartment, remove the two screws securing the throttle cable mounting bracket to the frame plate **(see illustration)**.

18.9a Pull the throttle cable mounting bracket (arrow) forward . . .

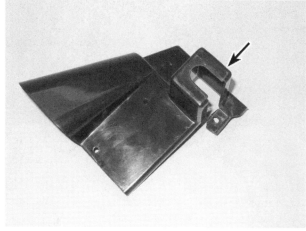

18.13 Check the plastic cover for any damage, and especially at the top, where any damage could allow the throttle cable mounting bracket to slip or move as the vehicle is being driven

18.9b . . . to free it from the plastic housing

bracket is installed over **(see illustration)**. Check the cover for any cracks or other damage that could allow the throttle cable mounting bracket to move, and possibly cause the throttle cable to stick open while the vehicle is being driven. Replace the cover if any damage is found.

14 Installation is the reverse of removal, noting the following:

a) *Replace any damaged cable guides or plastic ties.*
b) *Refer to your notes when routing and installing the new throttle cable. Work carefully so you don't kink or bend the cable.*
c) *Tighten the throttle cable mounting bracket screws securely.*
d) *Before adjusting the throttle free play, check the throttle cable routing again to make sure it is properly routed through all cable guides and plastic ties.*
e) *Adjust the throttle free play (see Chapter 2).*

WARNING:
Turn the steering wheel all the way from side to side with the engine idling. Idle speed should not change. If it does, the cable may be adjusted or routed incorrectly. Correct this condition before driving the vehicle.

19 THROTTLE PEDAL - REMOVAL AND INSTALLATION

Removal

1 Park the vehicle on level ground and apply the parking brake.

2 Working at the throttle body, loosen the locknut and the throttle cable adjuster to obtain slack in the throttle cable (see Section 13). Then working in the driver's compartment, push the throttle cable rearward to unlock

9 Pull the throttle cable mounting bracket forward (with the cable attached) and remove it from the plastic housing that supports it **(see illustrations)**. Once the throttle cable is free, don't remove the mounting bracket from the cable. New OEM cables come with the mounting bracket attached.

10 With the throttle cable free at both ends, check the cable routing again, and note how the cable passes through any cable guides and plastic ties. Open and/or remove any cable guides that the cable cannot pass through. If required, cut any plastic ties, noting their original position and tightness against the cable.

11 Carefully remove the throttle cable from the frame. If necessary, remove any additional body components to provide complete access to the throttle cable (see Chapter 14).

12 Compare the new and old cables. See a dealer parts department if there are any differences in the two cables.

13 Check the plastic cover that the throttle cable mounting

19.2a Hold the throttle cable around its end piece, and push it rearward . . .

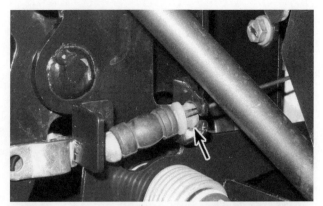

19.2b . . . to unlock and release it from the throttle pedal

and release it from the throttle pedal **(see illustrations)**. Make sure not to bend or kink the throttle cable when releasing it from the throttle pedal.

3   Note the return spring position against the throttle pedal **(see illustration)**. Grab the return spring with a pair of locking pliers, then pull the spring over the nut and release its hooked end from the throttle pedal **(see illustration)**.

4   Remove the E-clip and slide the throttle pedal off of its pivot shaft **(see illustration 19.3a)**. Note the nylon pedal bushings and remove them also.

5   Inspect the nylon pedal bushings for excessive wear and damage. Replace these bushings in sets of two.

6   Inspect the pedal bore and its pivot shaft for excessive wear. Also check the pivot shaft for cracks, bending and other damage. The E-clip groove on the end of the pivot shaft must have sharp edges and be in good condition to prevent the E-clip from releasing. The bore and pivot shaft surfaces must be smooth.

Installation

7   Installation is the reverse of these steps, plus the following:

   a) *Install the two bushings and throttle pedal onto the pivot shaft. Install a new E-clip into the shaft groove, making sure it is fully seated. Then move the throttle pedal from side-to-side to make sure the E-clip does not pop out of its groove. Pivot the throttle pedal to make sure there is no binding or roughness.*

   b) *Install the throttle cable by pushing its end piece into the throttle pedal to lock it in place. Make sure the end piece is bottomed against the throttle pedal and there is no gap between the two parts (see Step 2).*

   c) *Adjust the throttle assembly and check the throttle pedal operation (see Chapter 2).*

WARNING:

After adjusting the throttle assembly, turn the steering wheel all the way from side to side with the engine idling. Idle speed should not change. If it does, the cable may be adjusted or routed incorrectly. Also make sure the

19.3a Throttle pedal details

A   *Throttle pedal*
B   *Return spring position - hooked against pedal*
C   *Return spring position - resting against nut on inside*
D   *E-clip*
E   *Throttle cable*

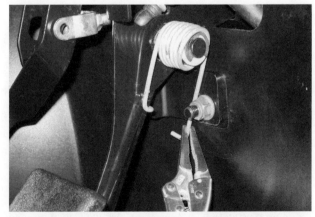

19.3b Lift the return spring over the nut, then disconnect the hooked spring end from the throttle pedal

throttle pedal pivots smoothly in all positions and there is no binding or roughness. Correct these conditions before driving the vehicle as they could lead to a loss of control.

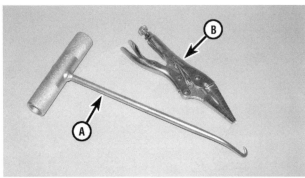

20.3a A spring hook tool (A) and a pair of locking pliers (B) are helpful when disconnecting and reconnecting the springs

20.3b The muffler is secured in place with two very strong springs (arrows)

20.3c To lengthen a spring before attempting to remove it, use locking pliers to wedge thin metal shims between the spring coils (arrows) . . .

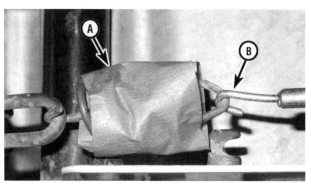

20.3d . . . then wrap the spring with tape to hold the metal shims in place when the spring is pulled. Then pull one end of the spring with a spring removal tool (B) . . .

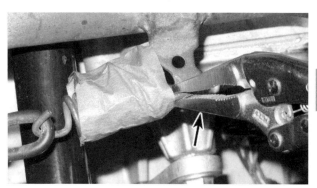

20.3e . . . or a pair of locking pliers (arrow) and disconnect it from the muffler

20   EXHAUST SYSTEM - REMOVAL AND INSTALLATION

WARNING:

If the engine has been running, the exhaust system will be very hot. Allow the system to cool before carrying out any work.

Removal

1   Park the vehicle on a level surface and apply the parking brake.

2   On standard Ranger models, remove the seat base and the kickboard. On Crew models, remove the rear seat base and the rear kickboard (see Chapter 14).

WARNING:

Wear eye protection and thick gloves when removing the exhaust system springs to help protect yourself should the tool you are using to remove the springs slips off the springs while they are under tension.

NOTE:

The muffler can be removed without having to disturb any of the other exhaust components or their fasteners.

3   Remove the springs that secure the muffler in place. Because these springs are strong and difficult to remove, see the accompanying illustrations for tools and methods **(see illustrations 20.3a through 20.3e)**.

NOTE:

The two muffler springs are different from the five springs used to secure the manifold joint pipe to the exhaust manifold and exhaust pipe. Store the two spring sets in different containers.

20.4a Slide the muffler rearward to release its pins from the grommets (arrow) and remove it from the vehicle

20.4b Exhaust pipe-to-muffler gasket

4   With both springs removed, slide the muffler rearward to disconnect it from the exhaust pipe and the frame mounted grommets **(see illustration)**. With the muffler removed, note the gasket installed on the exhaust pipe **(see illustration)**. If you will be reusing this gasket, you can leave it installed on the exhaust pipe.

NOTE:

Steps 5 through 9 describe removal of the remaining exhaust system components.

5   Remove the screws securing the front right heat shield to the frame and remove it from the vehicle **(see illustration)**.
6   Remove the screws securing the front heat shield to the exhaust manifold mounting bracket **(see illustration)**.

NOTE:

The information in Step 3 also applies to the manifold joint springs removed in Step 7.

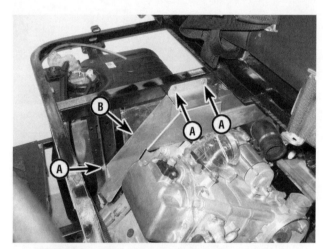

20.5 Remove the screws (A) and the heat shield (B)

7   Wedge a wooden block between the manifold joint pipe and frame to hold the joint pipe in place, then remove the springs and the joint pipe **(see illustration)**. Note the gaskets installed on the exhaust manifold and manifold joint pipe **(see illustrations)**. If you will be reusing these gaskets, you can leave them installed in place. The heat shield installed on the joint pipe can also be left in place, unless replacement is necessary.
8   Remove the nut, washer and bolt securing the exhaust pipe to the frame and remove the exhaust pipe with the heat shield attached **(see illustration)**. After removing the exhaust pipe, note and remove the damper assembly installed between the exhaust pipe and frame **(see illustration)**.
9   Remove the screws securing the exhaust manifold to the cylinder head **(see illustration)**. Release the manifold from its gasket and remove it.

20.6 Remove the screws (A) and the heat shield (B)

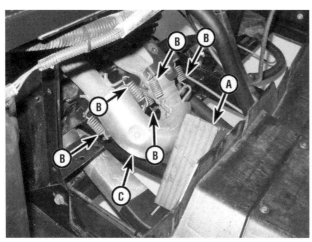

20.7a To prevent the manifold joint pipe from moving outward when removing the last spring, wedge a wooden block between the manifold joint pipe and frame (A). Then remove the five springs (B) and the manifold joint pipe (C)

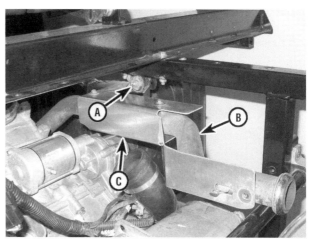

20.8a Remove the nut, washer and bolt (A) securing the exhaust pipe (B) to the frame and remove the exhaust pipe with the heat shield (C) attached

20.7b Exhaust manifold-to-manifold joint pipe gasket

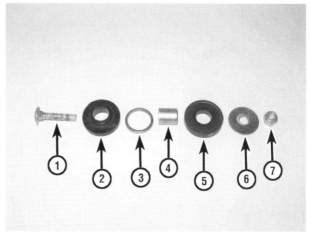

20.8b Exhaust pipe damper details

1	Bolt	5	Rubber washer
2	Vibration damper	6	Flat washer
3	Washer	7	Nut
4	Collar		

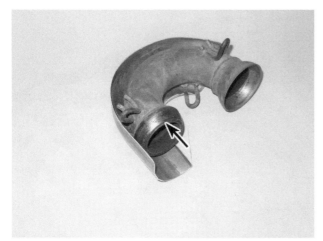

20.7c Manifold joint pipe-to-exhaust pipe gasket

20.9 Remove the screws (A) and the exhaust manifold (B)

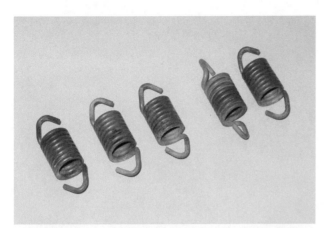

20.12 Inspect the springs for stretched coils and bent, worn or damaged hooks - manifold joint pipe springs shown

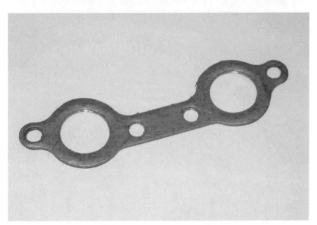

20.13 Install a new exhaust gasket

20.14a Position the vibration damper (A) with its shoulder facing up. Install the washer (B) over the damper shoulder and install the collar (C) through the damper . . .

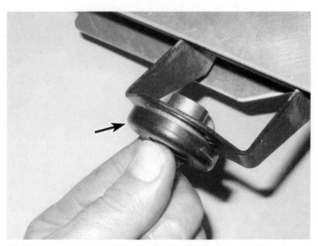

20.14b . . . then install the collar through the outside exhaust pipe mounting bracket (arrow) . . .

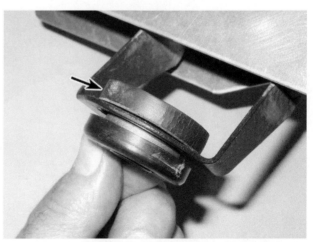

20.14c . . . and install the rubber washer (arrow) over the collar to hold the damper assembly in place

10 Carefully scrape the gasket from the cylinder head and exhaust manifold surfaces.

11 Replace any leaking or damaged seals used to seal the different exhaust pipe components when they are joined together.

12 Compare the two muffler springs with each other, then the five manifold joint springs with each other **(see illustration)**. The springs in each separate group should be the same approximate length. Then check the hooks on each spring for cracks or obvious wear marks indicating a hook is worn or damaged. When a spring is relaxed, there should not be a gap between any two coils. Replace any weak or damaged springs.

Installation

13 Install a new exhaust gasket, making sure to properly align it with the cylinder head exhaust ports **(see illustration)**. Then install the exhaust manifold **(see illustration 20.9)** and tighten its mounting screws to the torque listed in this Chapter's Specifications.

14 Before installing the exhaust pipe, assemble and install the damper assembly onto the exhaust pipe mounting bracket **(see illustrations)**.

15   Install the exhaust pipe assembly and secure to the frame with the bolt, flat washer and nut **(see illustration 20.8a)**. Install the bolt through the outside of the frame and index its shoulder with the square hole in the frame. Install the nut and tighten finger-tight at this time.

16   The remainder of installation is the reverse of removal, noting the following:

   a) *If a gasket was removed and it's in good condition, install it with its tapered side facing in its original direction (see Step 4 and Step 7).*

   b) *After installing the manifold joint pipe and muffler and securing them in place with their springs, tighten the exhaust pipe nut installed in Step 15 (see Step 8).*

   c) *Install the heat shields and tighten the fasteners securely. If you didn't remove the heat shield mounted on the exhaust pipe, check the mounting screws for looseness and tighten if necessary.*

   d) *Start the engine and allow to idle. Then check for any exhaust leaks.*

SPECIFICATIONS

Component test data

Crankshaft position sensor (CPS) resistance	504-616 ohms (at 68 degrees F/20 degrees C)
Engine coolant temperature sensor resistance	
At 68 degrees F (20 degrees C)	2.35-2.65 k-ohms
At 86 degrees F (30 degrees C)	1.6-1.8 k-ohms
At 104 degrees F (40 degrees C)	1.1-1.3 k-ohms
At 122 degrees F (50 degrees C)	784-884 ohms
At 140 degrees F (60 degrees C)	560-632 ohms
At 158 degrees F (70 degrees C)	409-461 ohms
At 176 degrees F (80 degrees C)	304-342 ohms
At 194 degrees F (90 degrees C)	228-258 ohms
At 212 degrees F (100 degrees C)	175-197 ohms
Fuel injector resistance	
2010 models	13.8-15.2 ohms
2011 and later models.	11.4-12.6 ohms
Fuel level sender resistance	
Empty	
2010 models	5 ohms
2011 and later models	85.5 -94.5 ohms
Full	
2010 models	90 ohms
2011 and later models	5-7 ohms
Fuel pressure	
2010 models	36-42 psi (2.5-2.9 Bar)
2011 through 2012 models	43-47 psi (3.0-3.2 Bar)
2013 and later models.	56-60 psi (3.9-4.1 Bar)
Fuel pump voltage test.	7-14 volts
Idle air control (IAC) resistance	
2011 and later models	
Between terminals 1 and 2	28.8-31.2 ohms
Between terminals 2 and 3	28.8-31.2 ohms
Between terminals 1 and 3	57.6-62.4 ohms
Between terminals 4 and 5	28.8-31.2 ohms
Between terminals 5 and 6	28.8-31.2 ohms
Between terminals 4 and 6	57.6-62.4 ohms

Ignition coil

Primary coil resistance.	0.4 ohms
Secondary wire resistance	
2010 models	5.0 k-ohms
2011 and later models.	6.6-7.4 k-ohms

7

Torque specifications	Ft-lbs	In.-lb	Nm

NOTE

One foot-pound (ft-lb) of torque is equivalent to 12 inch-pounds (in-lbs) of torque. Torque values below approximately 15 ft-lbs are expressed in inch-pounds, because most foot-pound torque wrenches are not accurate at these smaller values.

	Ft-lbs	In.-lb	Nm
Cam phase sensor mounting screw			
2011 and later models	--	45-55	5.1-6.2
Crankshaft position sensor (CPS) mounting screw	--	25	2.8
Electronic control unit (ECU) mounting screws	--	10	1.1
Engine coolant temperature (ECT) sensor	17	--	23
Exhaust manifold screws	16-20	--	22-27
Fuel pump nut			
2011 and later models	65-75	--	88-102
Fuel rail mounting screw	16-20	--	22-27
Idle air control (IAC) mounting screws			
2011 and later models	--	17.7	2.0
Intake manifold screws	16-20	--	22-27
Ignition coil mounting screw	--	75	8.5
Temperature and barometric air pressure sensor (T-BAP)			
mounting screw (2010 models)	--	29	3.3
Temp/Manifold absolute pressure sensor (T-MAP)			
mounting screw (2011 and later models)	--	22.5-27.5	2.5-3.1

CHAPTER EIGHT

ELECTRICAL SYSTEM

CONTENTS

1   GENERAL INFORMATION

1   All of the machines covered by this manual are equipped with a 12-volt electrical system. The components include a three-phase permanent magnet alternator and a regulator/rectifier unit. The regulator/rectifier unit maintains the charging system output within the specified range to prevent overcharging and converts the AC (alternating current) output of the alternator to DC (direct current) to power the lights and other components and to charge the battery.

2   An electric starter is mounted on the engine case. The starting system includes the starter, the battery, the starter relay and the various wires and switches.

2 ELECTRICAL COMPONENT REPLACEMENT

1   Most dealerships and parts suppliers will not accept the return of any electrical part. If you cannot determine the exact cause of any electrical system malfunction, have a dealership retest that specific system to verify your test results. If you purchase a new electrical component(s), install it, and then find that the system still does not work properly, you will probably not be able to return the unit for a refund.

2   Consider any test result carefully before replacing a component that tests only slightly out of specification, especially resistance. A number of variables can affect test results dramatically. These include the testing meter's internal circuitry, ambient temperatures and conditions under which the vehicle has been operated. All instructions and specifications have been checked for accuracy; however, successful test results depend largely upon individual accuracy when performing the test.

3 ELECTRICAL CONNECTORS

1   Corrosion-causing moisture can enter electrical connectors and cause poor electrical connections leading to component failure. Troubleshooting an electrical circuit with one or more corroded electrical connectors can be time-consuming and frustrating. Before reconnecting electrical connectors, pack them with a dielectric grease compound. Do not use a substitute that may interfere with the current flow within the electrical connector. Do not use silicone sealant, as doing so will make it nearly impossible to disconnect the connectors later on.

4 BATTERY - PRECAUTIONS, GENERAL INFORMATION, REMOVAL, INSTALLATION, MAINTENANCE AND STORAGE

1   All models were originally equipped with conventional fillable batteries. Sealed maintenance-free batteries are a popular upgrade and can be found in use when working on an unfamiliar model. Refer to this Chapter's Specifications for battery specifications.

Precautions

WARNING:
Protect your eyes, skin and clothing, even when working on a sealed battery; electrolyte is corrosive and can cause severe burns and permanent injury. The battery case may be cracked and leaking electrolyte. If electrolyte gets into your eyes, flush your eyes thoroughly with clean, running water and get immediate medical attention. Always wear safety goggles when servicing the battery.

WARNING:
While batteries are being charged, highly explosive hydrogen gas forms in each cell. Some of this gas escapes through a vent opening and may form an explosive atmosphere in and around the battery. This condition can persist for several hours. Sparks, an open flame or a lighted cigarette can ignite the gas, causing an internal battery explosion and possible serious injury.

2   To prevent accidental shorts that could blow a fuse when working on the electrical system, always disconnect the negative battery cable from the battery.
3   Do not disconnect live circuits at the battery. A spark usually occurs when a live circuit is broken.
4   Do not smoke or permit any open flame near any battery being charged or which has been recently charged.
5   Take care when connecting or disconnecting a battery charger. Be sure the power switch is turned off before making or breaking connections. Poor connections are a common cause of electrical arcs, which cause explosions.
6   Keep children and pets away from the charging equipment and battery.

General information

7   When servicing the battery, certain precautions should be observed to prevent from damaging the engine control unit (ECU).
8   When making tests when the cables must be connected to the battery, do not start the engine if the cables are not properly secured. Secure the cables to the battery with the proper bolts, instead of just laying or wedging them against the battery terminals. Vibration from a running engine may cause the cables to disconnect.
9   Never disconnect the battery cables when the engine is running.
10 When charging the battery when it is installed in the vehicle, disconnect the battery cables first. Never charge the battery with the cables connected. If possible, charge the battery after first removing it from the vehicle.
11 Never charge the battery with the ignition switch turned ON.

Removal and installation

NOTE:
When installing a new battery, be sure to turn in the old battery at that time. The lead plates and the plastic case can be recycled. Most dealerships accept old batteries in trade when purchasing a new one. Never place an old battery in household trash; it is illegal, in most states, to place any acid or lead (heavy metal) contents in landfills.

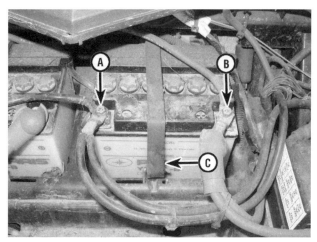

4.16a Conventional battery (2010 through 2013 models)

A *Negative terminal*   C *Mounting strap*
B *Positive terminal*

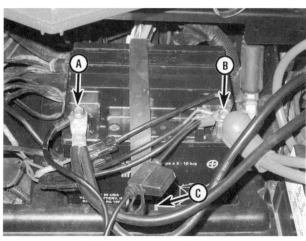

4.16b Maintenance free battery

A *Negative terminal*   C *Mounting strap*
B *Positive terminal*

4.16c Dual battery setup

4.16d To keep track of accessory terminals that were connected to the battery, secure them to the appropriate battery terminal with a plastic tie

12   Park the vehicle on a level surface and apply the parking brake.

13   Turn the ignition switch OFF.

14   On 2010 through 2013 models, open the hood.

15   On 2014 models, remove the seat base (see Chapter 14).

16   Before disconnecting the the battery leads, note how the battery is installed in the box and how the leads are routed **(see illustrations)**. Remove the negative terminal bolt first and disconnect the negative lead from the battery. Then remove the positive terminal bolt and disconnect the positive lead. If several electrical accessory terminals were connected to the battery terminals, tie them together with a plastic tie until installation **(see illustration)**.

NOTE:

If only the negative battery cable is being disconnected, insulate it so it cannot accidentally reconnect the battery circuit.

17   On 2010 through 2013 models, disconnect the rubber strap, and lift the battery out of the battery box. On 2014 models, remove the screw securing the battery strap to the battery box, then disconnect the strap from the battery box and remove it from around the battery. Lift the battery out of the battery box and remove it.

18   Clean and service the battery as described in Steps 23 through 32, depending on battery type.

19   Coat the battery leads with dielectric grease.

20   When installing the battery, connect the positive cable first, then the negative cable.

21   When connecting accessory wiring connectors to the battery, you may find that the original terminal bolt is too short and a longer bolt is necessary. When selecting a longer bolt, make sure it is not too long. After positioning the cables and tightening the bolt, tug on the cables to

8

4.21 The arcing marks visible on the positive battery cable and an aftermarket headlight cable shown here resulted from a terminal bolt that was too long. This allowed the cables to move as the vehicle was being driven

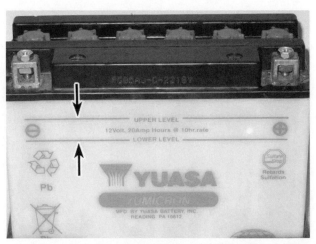

4.24 Electrolyte should between the UPPER and LOWER level marks

make sure they are not loose (see illustration). In addition, always place the battery cable against the battery post, then place the accessory cables on top.

CAUTION:

Be sure the battery cables are connected to their proper terminals. Connecting the battery backward reverses the polarity and damages components in the electrical system. When installing a replacement battery, make sure the negative and positive terminals on the battery are in the same positions.

22   On 2010 through 2013 models, when the battery is in place, stretch the rubber strap across the battery and hook both ends into their slots in the battery box. Then close the hood. On 2014 models, hook the battery strap into the battery box, then install and tighten the mounting screw to secure the strap over the battery. Install the seat base.

Maintenance

Conventional battery

23   A conventional lead/acid type battery is stock on all models. Maintenance requires regular checks of the electrolyte level and cleaning the battery and battery cables. To properly service the battery, remove it as described in Steps 12 through 17.

24   The electrolyte level is visible through the translucent battery case - it should be between the UPPER and LOWER level marks (see illustration).

25   If the electrolyte level is low, clean the top of the battery case to prevent sand and dirt from entering and contaminating the cells. Then unscrew and remove the cell caps and fill each cell to the upper level mark with distilled water (see illustrations). Do not use tap water (except in an emergency), and do not overfill. It may help to use a clean plastic squeeze bottle with a small spout or a syringe

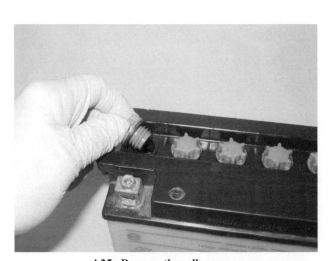

4.25a Remove the cell caps . . .

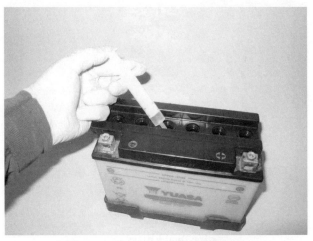

4.25b . . . and top-up with distilled water

4.26 The vent tube on this battery is disconnected (arrows). Corrosive gas released from this battery can damage wiring harnesses routed near the battery and corrode metal parts

4.32 After a maintenance-free battery has been serviced, never remove the sealing bar (arrow) at the top of the battery to check or add electrolyte

to add the water. Install the battery cell caps, tightening them securely.

26 Check the battery vent tube to make sure it is connected to the battery and is not pinched or obstructed **(see illustration)**.

27 Check the battery terminals and leads for tightness and corrosion. If corrosion is evident, unscrew the terminal bolts and disconnect the leads from the battery (negative lead first). Clean the terminals and lead ends with a wire brush or emery paper. When reconnecting the leads, connect the negative terminal last, and apply a thin coat of petroleum jelly or battery terminal grease to the connections to slow further corrosion.

28 The battery case should be kept clean to prevent current leakage, which can discharge the battery over a period of time (especially when it sits unused). Make sure the cell caps are tight, then wash the outside of the case with a solution of baking soda and water. Rinse the battery thoroughly, then dry it.

29 Look for cracks in the case and replace the battery if any are found. If acid has been spilled in the battery box or on the frame, neutralize it with a baking soda and water solution, dry it thoroughly, then touch up any damaged paint. Also check the electrical components and wiring near the battery for damage.

30 If the vehicle sits unused for long periods of time, service the battery as described in Steps 33 through 36.

31 To determine battery condition, refer to Section 5.

Maintenance-free battery

32 The maintenance-free battery is sealed and the battery electrolyte level cannot be serviced. Never attempt to remove the sealing bar from the top of the battery **(see illustration)**. Because the battery is permanently sealed, it does not require periodic electrolyte inspection or refilling. However, the battery should be serviced at regular intervals as described in Steps 27 through 31.

Storage

33 When the vehicle is driven infrequently or put in storage for an extended amount of time, the battery must be periodically charged to ensure it will be capable of working correctly when returned to service.

34 Remove the battery (see Steps 12 through 17).

35 Clean and inspect the battery and the battery cables. See Steps 23 through 32, depending on battery type.

36 Charge the battery (see Section 6). Store the battery in a cool dry place. Continue to charge the battery once a month when stored in temperatures below 60 degrees F (16 degrees C) and every two weeks when stored in temperatures above 60 degrees F (16 degrees C).

5   BATTERY - SPECIFIC GRAVITY CHECK, VOLTAGE TEST AND LOAD TEST

WARNING:
Refer to the precautions given in Section 4 before starting work.

1 Refer to the battery specifications in this Chapter's Specifications when testing the battery.

2 2010 models are equipped with a low battery/over voltage indicator light on the instrument cluster. When this light illuminates, it indicates the battery state of charge is too low or too high. To determine which condition is present, it is necessary to measure the voltage directly across the battery with a voltmeter when the engine is running. On 2011 and later models, a readout on the LCD display informs of battery voltage problems. When battery voltage drops below 11 volts, Lo is displayed along with the current battery voltage. When battery voltage drops

below 8.5 volts, the LCD display icons and backlighting turn off. When battery voltage is over 15 volts, OV is displayed along with the current battery voltage. When battery voltage increases above 16.5 volts, the LCD display icons and backlighting turns off.

3   When driving the vehicle at low speed for extended periods of time, excessive idling and/or when the cooling fan is running and possibly there are other electrical accessories turned on, the warning indicator may indicate the engine rpm is too low to keep the battery fully charged. If this happens, drive the vehicle at a higher rpm. If the light does not turn off on 2010 models, or if the warning indicator does not turn off on 2011 and later models, test the battery.

Specific gravity check (conventional batteries)

4   This test uses a hydrometer to test the specific gravity of the electrolyte to determine a conventional battery's state of charge. Specific gravity is the weight of the electrolyte compared to the weight of pure water. The test results do not indicate if a battery has enough current to operate the starter motor or other electrical systems. When selecting a hydrometer, try and use a temperature corrected hydrometer with numbered graduations from 1.100 to 1.300. However, if the hydrometer requires a large amount of electrolyte to raise the float during the measurement, it may be necessary to use a smaller hydrometer that uses color-coded bands or floating balls. You can then convert the reading based on temperature (see Step 12 to obtain an accurate reading.

5   Clean and dry the top of the battery as described in Section 4.

6   Remove the cell caps from the top of the battery. Examine the fluid level in each cell. If a cell is low, add distilled water to correct the level. Then charge the battery for 15-20 minutes to ensure the water and electrolyte are mixed thoroughly. Because the cells are diluted with water, do not test a battery with a hydrometer immediately after adding water to the cells. A lower specific gravity reading will result.

7   Squeeze the rubber ball and insert the tip of the hydrometer into one of the cells. Slowly release the ball to suck electrolyte into the tube. Draw enough electrolyte to float the weighted float inside the hydrometer. When using a temperature-compensated hydrometer, release the electrolyte and repeat this process several times to make sure the thermometer has adjusted to the electrolyte temperature before taking the reading.

8   Hold the hydrometer vertically at eye-level and note the number in line with the surface of the electrolyte. This is the specific gravity for this cell. Make sure the float is not dragging against the inside of the hydrometer. If a temperature-compensated hydrometer is being used, note the temperature on the thermometer.

9   Slowly squeeze the bulb to return the electrolyte to the cell from which it came.

10   Record the specific gravity reading and repeat these steps for each battery cell.

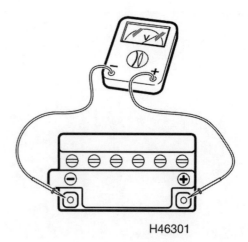

H46301

5.16 Checking battery voltage (static test) with a digital voltmeter

11   The specific gravity of the electrolyte in each battery cell is an excellent indication of their condition. A fully charged cell reads 1.265-1.280. To determine the state of charge for the battery you are testing, refer to the state of charge readings listed in this Chapter's Specifications.

12   Because the specific gravity of electrolyte changes with temperature, hydrometers are temperature calibrated at 77 degrees F (25 degrees C). At colder temperatures, electrolyte thickens and its specific gravity raises (gaining gravity). At higher temperatures, electrolyte thins and its specific gravity lowers (loses gravity). If a temperature-compensated hydrometer is not used, add 0.001 to the specific gravity reading for every 3 degrees above 77 degrees F (25 degrees C). For every 3 degrees below this reading, subtract 0.001. Compare the reading to battery state of charge readings listed in this Chapter's Specifications. If necessary, charge the battery.

Voltage test (all battery types)

Static

13   This is the easiest test to perform when checking and maintaining the battery, and is often referred to as an open circuit voltage test. A low voltage reading indicates that the battery should be charged and tested. Use a digital voltmeter to test the battery while it is mounted on the vehicle.

14   Turn the ignition switch OFF.

15   Refer to Section 4 to access the battery.

   Note: To prevent false test readings, do not test the battery if the battery terminals are corroded. Remove and clean the battery and terminals as described in this section, then install and test the battery.

16   Check the battery condition by measuring the voltage at the battery terminals. Connect the voltmeter positive probe to the battery positive terminal and the negative probe to the battery negative terminal **(see illustration)**. Record

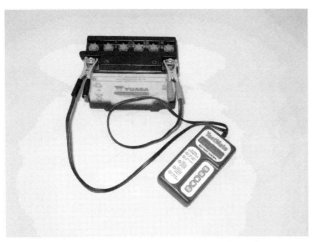

5.25a Digital battery load tester connected to a battery

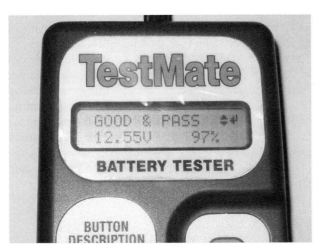

5.25b Battery test reading - good

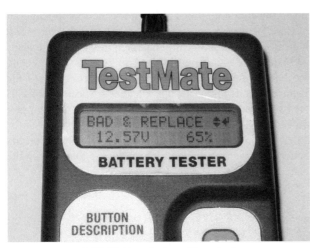

5.25c Battery test reading - bad

the voltage reading and compare to the voltage reading specifications listed in this Chapter's Specifications. If the voltage reading is 75 percent or lower, recharge the battery (see Section 6) and then perform a load test (see Steps 21 through 25).

Starting

17 This procedure tests the battery's capacity when starting the vehicle. This is a good test to perform when the battery has been charged, but doesn't seem to be holding a charge as it should.

NOTE:

To prevent false test readings, do not test the battery if the battery terminals are corroded. Remove and clean the battery and terminals as described in this section, then install and test the battery.

18 Refer to Section 4 to access the battery.
19 Connect a digital voltmeter between the battery positive (+) and negative (–) leads **(see illustration 5.16)**. To prevent a short, make sure the voltmeter leads attach firmly to the battery terminals.
20 Start the vehicle while reading the voltmeter. If the voltage drops below 9.5 volts, recharge the battery (see Section 6) and then repeat the test. If the voltage still drops below 9.5 volts, replace the battery.

Load Test (all battery types)

Low load test

21 Refer to Section 4 to access the battery.
22 Connect a digital voltmeter between the battery positive (+) and negative (–) leads **(see illustration 5.16)**.
23 Turn the ignition switch ON while making sure the headlights are ON.
24 The voltmeter should read a minimum of approximately 11.5 volts. Turn the ignition switch OFF and disconnect the voltmeter. If the voltage reading is lower, charge the battery (see Section 6) and retest.

High load test

25 This test requires a battery load tester **(see illustrations)**. This load test checks the battery's performance with a current draw or load applied and is the best indication of battery condition. When using a load tester, follow the manufacturer's instructions. If necessary, remove the battery and take it to a dealership for testing. Before going to the service department, check to see if the parts department has a load tester, and if so, they may test your battery without charging you any labor time.

6   BATTERY - CHARGING AND NEW BATTERY INITIALIZATION

WARNING:

Refer to the precautions given in Section 4 before starting work.

WARNING:

During the charging process, highly explosive hydrogen gas is released from the battery. Charge the battery only in a well-ventilated area away from any open flames including pilot lights on home gas appliances. Do not allow any smoking in the area. Never check the charge of the battery by connecting screwdriver blades or other metal objects between the terminals; the resulting spark can ignite the hydrogen gas.

6.1 A typical smart battery charger

1   For home use, it is suggested to use a smart battery charger because they automatically switch to a float or maintenance mode to prevent overcharging when a battery is fully charged **(see illustration)**. However, while a smart battery charger can be connected to maintenance free batteries for long periods of time, note that that when a smart battery charger is connected to a conventional battery for extended periods, it is still necessary to check the battery water levels and top off when the levels drop. Likewise, care must be observed when using a trickle or taper charger, because if left connected to the battery for too long a time, they can overcharge a battery and damage it. Before using any battery charger, refer to the manufacturer's instructions.

2   Remove the battery from the vehicle (Section 4).

3   Measure the battery voltage (see Section 5) and compare to the value listed in this Chapter's Specifications to determine the battery's state of charge.

NOTE:

If the voltage reading is very low, internal resistance in the battery may prevent it from recovering when following normal charging attempts. When a battery's state of charge is 11.5 volts or less, it is necessary to increase the charging voltage of the battery by applying a low current rate to allow the battery to recover. This will require an adjustable battery charger with a separate amp and volt meter. However, some smart battery chargers are programmed to diagnose and recover deep-discharged batteries. These chargers can also charge and maintain batteries during all normal battery service without overcharging or overheating the battery. Refer to the charger manufacturer's instructions and specifications for making this test.

4   Clean the battery terminals and battery case (see Section 4).

5   Connect the positive (+) charger lead to the positive battery terminal and the negative (–) charger lead to the negative battery terminal.

6   Turn the battery charger on and charge the battery following the manufacturer's instructions. Smart battery chargers are usually equipped with LED displays that display the battery status/charger operation. If using an adjustable battery charger, charge the battery at a slow charge rate of 1/10 its given capacity. To determine the current output in amps, divide the battery amp hour capacity by 10. For example, a 30Ah battery should be charged at 3.0 amps (30Ah divided by 10 equals 3 amps). If using a trickle or taper battery charger, make sure the charge rate does not exceed the specified charge rate for the battery, and do not allow the charger to remain on the battery for periods longer than recommended by the manufacturer. When the battery is charging, periodically check the battery case for overheating. If the battery feels hot, disconnect the battery charger and allow the battery to cool down 6 to 12 hours before continuing charging.

NOTE:

When using an adjustable battery charger, follow the manufacturer's instructions. Do not use a larger output battery charger or increase the charge rate on an adjustable battery charger to reduce charging time. Doing so can cause permanent battery damage.

7   After the battery has charged for the specific amount of time, or if you are using a smart battery charger and it indicates the battery is fully charged, disconnect the leads and allow the battery to set for 1 to 2 hours. Then check the battery with a digital voltmeter and compare to the voltage specifications in this Chapter's Specifications. If the battery is not 100 per cent charged, repeat the charging procedure. If the voltage reading is less than 12.6 volts, either the battery was not charged long enough or the battery is defective. In this case, perform a load test on the battery (see Section 5).

NOTE:

The battery should only self-discharge approximately one percent of its given capacity each day. If a battery not in use, without any loads connected, loses its charge within one week after charging, the battery is defective.

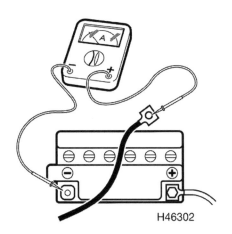

7.16 Ammeter connected in series with a battery

New battery initialization

8   Before installing and using a new battery, it must be fully charged. Otherwise, the battery will never be able to hold more than an 80 percent charge. Charging a new battery after it has been used will not bring its charge to 100 per cent. When purchasing a new battery from a dealership or parts store, verify its charge status. If necessary, have them perform the initial or booster charge before accepting the battery, or charge the battery with your own equipment, following the battery manufacturer's instructions.

7   CHARGING SYSTEM TEST

1   The charging system supplies power to operate the engine and electrical system components and keeps the battery charged. The charging system consists of the battery, alternator and a regulator/rectifier. Refer to the appropriate wiring diagram to identify the alternator and regulator/rectifier terminals (see Section 40).

2   Alternating current generated by the alternator is rectified to direct current. The regulator/rectifier maintains constant voltage to the battery and additional electrical loads, such as lights or ignition, despite variations in engine speed and load.

3   Whenever there is a problem with the charging system, follow the steps in order to help isolate the problem. If a test indicates that a component is working properly, reconnect the electrical connections (if disconnected) and proceed to the next step. Systematically work through the tests until the problem is found. Repair or replace the defective parts as required.

4   Check and charge the battery (see Section 6). When the battery is fully charged, perform a load test to make sure the battery is in good condition and is not the problem (see Section 5).

5   Perform the current draw test (see Steps 13 through 18).

6   Perform the charging voltage test (see Steps 19 through 23).

7   Perform the break even test (see Steps 24 through 33).

8   Perform the stator coil resistance and ground check (see Section 8).

9   Perform the stator coil AC voltage test (see Section 8).

10   If the problem has not been found, locate the red wire at one of the regulator/rectifier wiring harness connectors (see Section 9). Disconnect the connector and check for battery voltage at the red wire on the wiring harness side connector. If there is no voltage, check the wiring harness for an open circuit. Also make sure the terminal(s) inside the connector is making contact with the red wire. On some models, a fusible link is installed in the red wire. Refer to the appropriate wiring diagram to see if the fusible link is used on your model (see Section 40). If there is an open circuit, check the fusible link for damage and replace if necessary.

11   If the battery is in good condition and the problem has not been found, the regulator/rectifier may be faulty (see Section 9).

12   Once a repair has been made or a part replaced, repeat the charging voltage test to confirm the charging system is working correctly (see Steps 19 through 23).

Current draw test

13   A short circuit will increase current draw and drain the battery. Adding electrical accessories can also drain the battery. Perform this test to check for shorts and to check the current draw of accessories added to the electrical system.

CAUTION:

Always connect an ammeter in series, never in parallel with the battery; otherwise, it will be damaged. Do not turn the ignition ON or operate the starter motor when the ammeter is connected - a sudden surge in current will blow the meter's fuse.

NOTE:

Perform this test before and after adding electrical accessories to determine baseline readings that can be referred to if charging system problems occur at a later time.

14   Turn the ignition switch OFF.

15   Disconnect the negative battery cable at the battery (see Section 4).

16   Set a digital multimeter to the ampere scale and connect its negative lead to the battery negative terminal, and the positive lead to the disconnected negative battery lead **(see illustration)**. Always set the meter to a high ampere range initially and then bring it down to the mA (milliamperes) range; if there is a high current flow in the circuit it may blow the meter's fuse. Do not turn the ignition switch ON once this connection is made.

7.22 Charging voltage reading with the engine running in NEUTRAL at 3000-4000 rpm

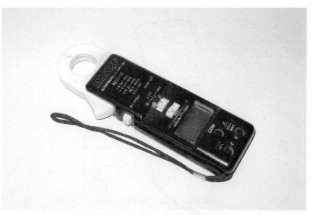

7.25 Inductive ammeter used to measure DC amperage during the break even test

17   Read the current draw in mA and compare to the value listed in this Chapter's Specifications. If the current draw is excessive, there is a short circuit in the system, or aftermarket electrical accessories have been added that exceed the maximum allowable limit. Other possible causes include a damaged battery, faulty regulator/rectifier or loose, dirty or damaged electrical connectors.

18   To locate the problem that is causing the excessive current draw, refer to the appropriate wiring diagram (see Section 40). Then identify and disconnect different electrical connectors (or remove fuses) one by one while monitoring the ammeter (reconnect the connector before disconnecting the next one). When the current draw rate returns to an acceptable level, the faulty circuit is indicated. Test the circuit further to find the problem. If you have added electrical accessories to the system, don't forget to disconnect them also, as they may be the problem.

NOTE:

When installing electrical accessories, do not wire them onto the battery or into a live circuit where they will stay on all the time as this will drain the battery. Refer to the accessory manufacturer's instructions.

Charging voltage test

19   Start and run the engine until it reaches normal operating temperature. Then park the vehicle on a level surface. Shift the transmission into NEUTRAL and apply the parking brake. Turn the engine OFF.

20   To obtain accurate test results, the battery must be fully charged (see Section 5).

21   Connect a digital voltmeter to the battery terminals (positive-to-positive and negative-to-negative). To prevent a short, make sure the voltmeter leads attach firmly to the battery terminals **(see illustration 5.16)**.

22   Start the engine and allow it to idle. Gradually increase engine speed between 3000 and 4000 rpm while reading the voltage indicated on the voltmeter **(see illustration)**. Compare the result with the charging voltage listed in this

Chapter's Specifications.

23   If the charging voltage reading is incorrect, perform Steps 13 through 18 to check for excessive current draw in the system. If the current draw is within specifications, but the charging voltage is too low, check for an open or short circuit in the charging system wiring harness, an open or short in the alternator, high resistance in the regulator/rectifier and/or positive battery cable or connector at the terminal block, or a damaged regulator/rectifier. If the charging voltage is too high, check for a poor regulator/rectifier ground, a damaged regulator/rectifier, or a damaged battery.

NOTE:

If the battery is often discharged, but the charging voltage tested normal during Step 4, the battery may be damaged. Perform a load test on the battery (see Section 5).

NOTE:

Clues to a faulty regulator/rectifier are constantly blowing bulbs, bulb brightness varying considerably with engine speed, and battery overheating.

Break even test

24   The break even test allows you to determine whether or not the charging system is producing electrical current at the correct engine rpm to begin charging the battery.

25   An inductive ammeter that can measure DC amperage is required for this test **(see illustration)**.

CAUTION:

When making this test, do not disconnect the negative battery cable and connect an ammeter in series with the battery and start the engine. The current surge will blow the meter's fuse or damage the meter.

26   The battery must be fully charged when performing this test (see Section 5).

27   Switch the inductive ammeter to its DC amperage

8.2 Cut the plastic tie (A) and disconnect the stator coil four-pin wiring harness connector (B)

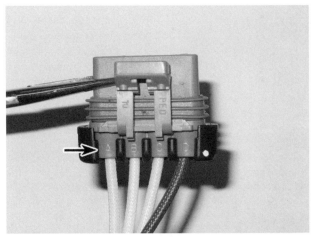

8.3 Identify the alternator connector terminals by referring to the letters on the connector (arrow)

8.4a Check for continuity between each yellow wire - there should be continuity

scale and clamp it around or onto the negative battery cable, following the manufacturer's instructions.

28   Turn the ignition switch to ON and turn the lights ON, but do not start the engine. The ammeter should show a negative amperage reading (battery is discharging).

29   Turn the lights and all electrical loads OFF.

30   Make sure the transmission is in NEUTRAL and the parking brake is applied. Start the engine and allow to run at idle speed. The ammeter should still show a negative amperage reading.

31   While reading the ammeter, slowly increase the engine speed and note the RPM when the ammeter starts to display a positive reading (battery is charging). When the amperage reading on the ammeter changes from a negative to positive reading, this is considered the charging system break even point. With the lights and all electrical loads turned OFF, the break even point should occur when the engine is running at approximately 1500 RPM or lower.

32   Now turn the lights ON and apply the brake pedal so the brake lights stay ON. Repeat the test and with the lights turned ON, the break even point should occur when the engine is running at approximately 2000 rpm or lower.

33   If the break even rpm reading is incorrect, visually check the stator wires for any damage. Also check the stator connector for contamination, loose pins and damage. If the wires appear to be in good condition, perform the stator coil AC voltage test (see Section 8).

8   ALTERNATOR - CHECK, REMOVAL AND INSTALLATION

Check

1   Raise the cargo box.

2   Locate the three yellow wires and the one brown wire leading out of the left side of the engine to the stator coil four-pin connector and disconnect it **(see illustration)**.

> *NOTE:*
> *If any of the stator coil tests in this section result with incorrect readings, and before condemning the stator coil as the problem, make sure the problem is not due to contaminated or damaged wiring, or loose terminals between the connector and stator.*

Stator coil resistance and ground check

3   Note the letters A, B, C and D on the stator coil side wiring harness connector. Use the letters A, B and C to identify the individual stator coil wires **(see illustration)**. The brown wire (D) is the ground wire.

4   Use a multimeter set to the ohms scale and measure resistance between the following sets of wires on the stator coil side wiring harness connector - A to B, A to C and B to C - and compare the results with the stator coil resistance listed in this Chapter's Specifications **(see illustration)**.

Then check for continuity between each yellow terminal and the brown terminal (ground); there should be no continuity **(see illustration)**.

5   If the individual stator coil resistance tests are within specification, and there is no continuity (infinity) between any of the stator wire terminals and the brown wire (ground), the stator coil assembly is in good condition. If not, the stator coil assembly is faulty and must be replaced. Before replacing the stator coil, have the tests confirmed by a dealer service department.

Stator coil AC voltage test

6   This check measures the AC voltage output of the stator coil with the engine running at different speeds. Three separate tests will be made at three different pairs of wires.

7   Set a digital multimeter to the AC ampere scale. See Step 3 to identify the stator coil wire terminals in the connector **(see illustration 8.3)**. Start the test by connecting the test leads between the A and B wire terminals on the stator coil side wiring harness connector. Start the engine and read the AC voltage with the engine running at 1300, 3000 and 5000 rpm and compare each reading to the stator coil AC voltage values listed in this Chapter's Specifications. Then repeat the test for the A to C and B to C connector wire terminals. If one pair of wires gives the wrong reading, the stator coil may be defective. Before replacing the stator coil, have the tests confirmed by a dealer service department.

Removal and installation

8   Refer to Chapter 4 to remove and install the stator coil assembly.

9   REGULATOR/RECTIFIER - CHECK, REMOVAL AND INSTALLATION

Check

1   The regulator/rectifier is tested by a process of elimination (when all other possible causes of charging system failure have been checked and eliminated, the regulator/rectifier is defective). Since it's easy to miss a problem it's worthwhile to have the charging system tested by a dealer service department, or if possible, substitute a known good regulator/rectifier (with the same part number) before buying a new one.

2   The regulator/rectifier is designed to turn itself off when it become too hot. When troubleshooting the regulator/rectifier, first check for mud and any other obstructions that may be blocking air from reaching it.

Removal and installation

3   Turn the ignition switch OFF.

4   Remove the grill (see Chapter 14).

5   The regulator/rectifier is mounted on a bracket in front of the radiator **(see illustration)**. Disconnect the regulator/

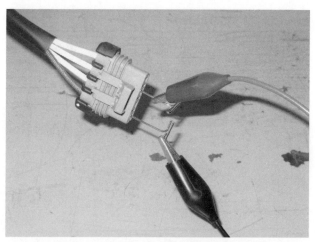

8.4b Check for continuity between each yellow wire and the brown wire - there should be no continuity

9.5a Regulator/rectifier mounting position in front of the radiator

9.5b Regulator/rectifier wiring harness connectors (2010 model shown). On 2011 and later models, the wiring harness plugs into the regulator/rectifier

9.5c The regulator/rectifier mounting bracket is secured to the frame with screws (arrows)

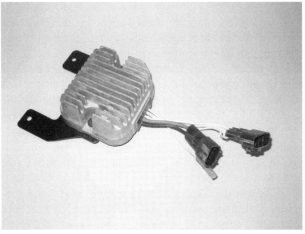

9.6 Regulator/rectifier used on 2010 models with integral wiring harness and connectors

rectifier wiring harness connectors. On 2010 models, the connectors plug into a set of wires and connectors leading out of the regulator/rectifier (see illustration). On 2011 and later models, the wiring harness connectors plug directly into the regulator/rectifier. After disconnecting the connectors, remove the mounting screws and remove the regulator/rectifier and its mounting bracket (see illustration).

6 Inspect the regulator/rectifier wiring harness and connectors for any damage (see illustration). Repair any damage before reinstalling the regulator/rectifier.

7 Installation is the reverse of removal. Make sure all wiring harnesses are properly routed and the connectors are connected and secured tightly.

10   STARTING SYSTEM TEST

1 When the ignition is turned on and the ignition switch is operated, current is transmitted from the battery to the starter relay. When the relay is activated, it activates the starter solenoid that mechanically engages the starter with the engine.

2 A starting system problem may be electrical or mechanical. Refer to the troubleshooting reference guide (Chapter 1) for general troubleshooting procedures to help isolate starting problems. To troubleshoot the starting system, continue with Step 3. Refer to the appropriate wiring diagram (see Section 40) to identify the wiring called out in the following steps.

3 Check and charge the battery (Section 6). When the battery is fully charged, perform a load test (Section 5) to make sure the battery is in good condition and is not the problem.

4 On 2010 models, disconnect the 2-pin connector at the starter relay. Set a digital multimeter to the voltage scale and connect the red lead (+) to the white/red wiring harness

connector terminal and the black lead (-) to the brown/yellow wiring harness connector terminal. Apply the brake pedal and turn the ignition switch to its START position. The voltmeter should read battery voltage. If there is no voltage, turn the ignition switch to its ON position and apply the rear brake pedal. Then check for battery voltage at the 20 amp main fuse. If there is no voltage, check for a blown fuse. If the fuse is good, check the orange wire at the 20 amp main fuse for an open circuit. Then check for battery voltage at the ignition switch. If there is battery voltage at the ignition switch but not at the relay, test the ignition switch (Section 26).

5 On 2011 and later models, disconnect the 2-pin connector at the starter relay. Set a digital multimeter to the voltage scale and connect the red lead (+) to the dark green/white wiring harness connector terminal and the black lead (-) to the orange wiring harness connector terminal. Apply the brake pedal and turn the ignition switch to its START position. The voltmeter should read battery voltage. If there is no voltage, turn the ignition switch to its ON position and apply the rear brake pedal. Then check for voltage on both sides of the 20 amp ECM fuse and ignition switch. If the voltage readings are correct, remove and test the ignition switch (Section 26).

6 Remove and test the starter relay (Section 13). Depending on the test results, reinstall the original or new starter relay.

NOTE:
Steps 7 through 9 are voltage drop tests.

7 Connect the black voltmeter lead to the battery positive terminal at the battery. Connect the red voltmeter lead to the battery-to-solenoid cable at the solenoid end. Apply the brake pedal and turn the ignition switch to its START position. The voltmeter should read 0.1 volts or less. If the reading is 0.1 volts or less, continue with Step 8. If the

reading exceeds 0.1 volts, remove, clean and inspect the battery-to-solenoid cable. Make sure both cable ends and their mating terminals at the battery and solenoid are clean. Replace the cable if damaged.

8   Connect the black voltmeter lead to the battery-to-solenoid cable at the solenoid end. Connect the red voltmeter lead to the solenoid-to-starter cable at the solenoid end. Apply the brake pedal and turn the ignition switch to its START position. The voltmeter should read 0.1 volts or less. If the reading is 0.1 volts or less, continue with Step 9. If the reading exceeds 0.1 volts, replace the solenoid.

9   Connect the black voltmeter lead to the solenoid-to-starter cable at the solenoid end. Connect the red voltmeter lead to the same cable at the starter end. Apply the brake pedal and turn the ignition switch to its START position. The voltmeter should read 0.1 volts or less. If the reading is 0.1 volts or less, continue with Step 10. If the reading exceeds 0.1 volts, remove, clean and inspect the solenoid-to-starter cable. Make sure both cable ends and their mating terminals at the solenoid and starter are clean. Replace the cable if damaged.

10   If the problem has not been found and the starter still will not turn, remove and bench test the starter (see Section 11 and 12).

11   STARTER - REMOVAL AND INSTALLATION

NOTE:

Replacement parts for the starter are not shown on current manufacturer parts fiche pages. When removing and installing the starter in this section, work carefully to prevent from tearing the boot installed over the starter terminal and the two O-rings installed on the starter shoulder where the starter is installed into the engine. If you need a part for the starter, contact a dealer parts department.

Removal and installation

1   Park the vehicle on a level surface and apply the parking brake.
2   Disconnect the negative battery cable at the battery (see Section 4).
3   Raise the cargo box (see Chapter 14).
4   Remove the air box (see Chapter 7).
5   The starter motor is mounted behind the engine **(see illustration)**.
6   Carefully pull the rubber cover off the starter motor terminal and slide it up the cable. To disconnect the starter cable, hold the inner nut with a wrench, then loosen and remove the outer nut, lockwasher and cable. Holding the inner nut prevents the terminal bolt from turning, which could damage the positive brush holder and insulator installed inside the starter **(see illustrations)**.

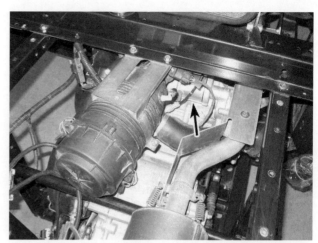

11.5 Starter mounting position (arrow) with engine installed in the frame

11.6a The rubber cover (arrow) fits tightly over the starter cable and positive terminal bolt to keep them clean and dry - during installation, reposition the cover carefully to prevent from tearing it

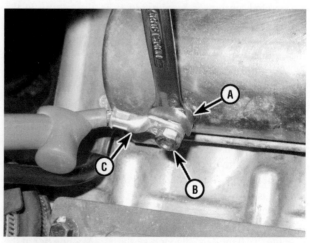

11.6b Hold the inner nut (A) to prevent the terminal bolt from turning, then loosen and remove the outer nut (B) and disconnect the positive battery cable (C)

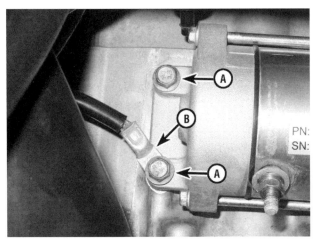

11.7 Remove the starter mounting screws (A) and disconnect the ground cable (B) - 2010 model

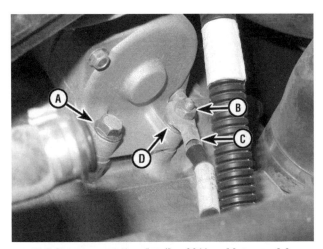

11.8 Starter mounting details - 2011 and later models

A   *Screw (on 2012 and later models, a metal bracket is mounted on this screw)*
B   *Nut*
C   *Ground cable*
D   *Stud*

7   On 2010 models, remove the screws and the ground cable **(see illustration)**.

8   On 2011 and later models, remove the nut and ground cable from the stud. Then loosen and remove the stud and the mounting screw. On 2012 and later models, remove the metal bracket after removing the upper mounting screw **(see illustration)**.

9   Slide the starter out from the crankcase and remove it from the engine. If necessary, tap the starter with a plastic mallet to free it from the crankcase.

10   Inspect the two O-rings installed on the end of the starter for deterioration, flat spots and other damage. If the O-rings are damaged, it will be necessary to match O-rings from a different source as replacement O-rings are not

available from the manufacturer.

11   Installation is the reverse of removal, noting the following:

a) *Clean the free ends on both cables of all dirt and corrosion.*
b) *Lubricate the starter O-rings with grease.*
c) *On 2010 models, note that the lower screw is used as a pilot screw to align the starter with the starter drive unit. Thus, it is important to tighten the lower screw first, then the upper screw. Before installing the lower screw, make sure to install the starter ground cable on it. Tighten both screws to the torque listed in 7 this Chapter's Specifications.*
d) *On 2011 and later models, install the screw in the upper hole, then install the stud. Tighten the screw first, then the stud, to the torque listed in this Chapter's Specifications. Then install the cable onto the stud and tighten the nut securely. On 2012 and later models, install the metal bracket and secure it with the upper mounting screw.*
e) *When tightening the starter cable nut, hold the inner nut on the starter terminal with a wrench and tighten the outer nut securely (see Step 6).*
f) *Install the rubber cover over the starter terminal so that it fits tightly against the terminal insulator washer (see Step 6).*

12   STARTER - DISASSEMBLY, INSPECTION AND REASSEMBLY

1   This section describes how to disassemble, inspect and reassemble the starter. While the manufacturer does not offer replacement parts for the starter, aftermarket rebuild kits may be available. The information in this section has been provided to help with starter inspection and troubleshooting.

NOTE:

Replacement parts for the starter are not shown on current manufacturer parts fiche pages. When servicing the starter in this section, work carefully to prevent from damaging any parts. If you need a part for the starter, contact a dealer parts department.

Disassembly

2   Remove the starter (see Section 11).

3   As you disassemble the starter, lay each part out in the order of removal. This is an easy way to maintain the correct alignment of all parts and help with assembly.

4   Carefully remove the O-rings from the end of the starter.

5   Find the alignment marks across the armature housing and both end covers. If necessary, paint the marks to

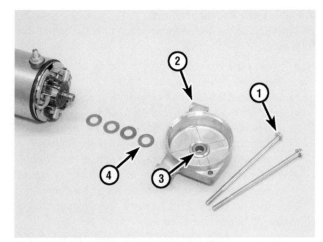

12.6 Rear end cover details

1	Starter assembly screws	3	Bushing
2	Rear end cover	4	Shims

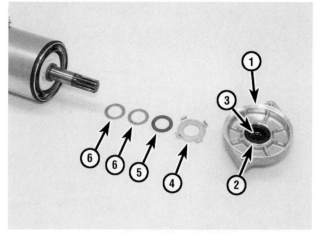

12.7 Front end cover details

1	Front end cover	4	Toothed washer
2	Oil seal	5	Insulated washer
3	Needle bearing	6	Shims

identify them or scribe new marks.

NOTE:

When disassembling the starter, note that shims and washers are installed on both armature shafts. Also note that the number of shims shown in the illustrations in this section can vary from the number of shims used on the starter you are servicing. When reassembling the starter, the shims and washers must be reinstalled in their correct order and number. Failing to install the correct number of shims and washers may increase armature end play, which may cause the starter to draw excessive current. Record the thickness and alignment of each shim and washer removed during disassembly.

6   Remove the starter assembly screws, rear end cover and shims **(see illustration)**.

NOTE:

If you're disassembling the starter to just check the condition of the brushes, you only need to remove the rear end cover. The brushes can be quickly inspected and the cover reinstalled if further disassembly is not required. When doing so, make sure to locate and reinstall the shims onto the armature in the order they were removed.

7   Remove the front end cover, toothed washer, insulated washer and shims **(see illustration)**.
8   Hold the housing and remove the armature **(see illustration)**.
9   After removing both end covers, carefully remove the two large O-rings from the housing.
10   Before removing the brush holder, set a multimeter to the ohms scale and perform the tests described in Steps 11 through 14. The positive brushes have insulated sleeves

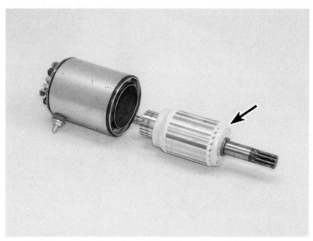

12.8 Remove the armature (arrow) from the housing

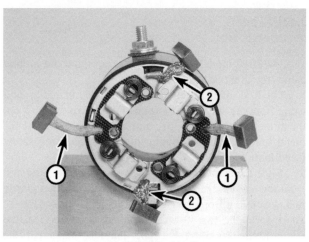

12.10 Brush details

1	Positive brushes	2	Negative brushes

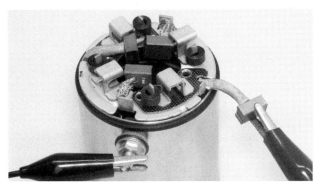

12.11 Checking the terminal bolt and positive brushes for continuity - there should be continuity

12.12 Checking for continuity between the terminal bolt and starter housing - there should be no continuity

12.13 Checking for continuity between the positive (A) and negative brushes (B) - there should be no continuity

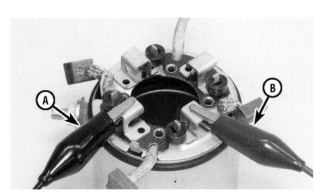

12.14 Check for continuity between the positive (A) and negative brush holders (B) - there should be no continuity

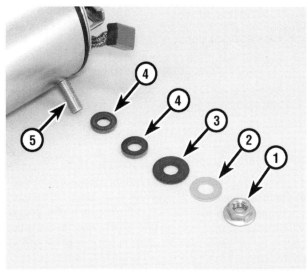

12.15 Terminal bolt details (outer)

1	Inner nut	4	Small insulators
2	Steel washer	5	Terminal bolt
3	Large insulator		

installed over their wire leads. The negative brush wires leads do not. Before making the tests, slide the brushes out of the brush holder **(see illustration)**.

11   Check for continuity between the terminal bolt and each positive brush **(see illustration)**. There should be continuity. If there is no continuity at both brushes, check for corrosion where the terminal bolt contacts the positive brush holder. If there is no continuity at only one brush, check for damage where the brush is fixed onto the brush holder.

12   Check for continuity between the terminal bolt and starter housing **(see illustration)**. There should be no continuity. If there is continuity, check for damaged, missing or improperly installed insulators on the terminal bolt. Note the alignment of the installed insulators and their condition when removing them.

13   Check for continuity between the positive and negative brushes **(see illustration)**. There should be no continuity. If there is continuity, check the positive brush wires for damaged insulation sleeves. The insulation sleeves must be installed through the brush holder plate so the positive brush wires do not short out.

14   Check for continuity between the positive and negative brush holders on the brush plate **(see illustration)**. There should be no continuity. If there is continuity, the brush holder plate is shorted.

15   Remove the inner nut, steel washer, large insulator and the two small insulators from the terminal bolt. Remove the O-ring if it is accessible, or remove it after removing the terminal bolt **(see illustration)**.

16   Straighten the positive brush wires and remove

the brush plate with the negative brushes attached **(see illustration)**. Do not damage the insulation sleeves on the positive brush wires.

17 Remove the positive brush holder and insulator ring from inside the housing **(see illustration)**.

18 Remove the O-ring and disassemble the terminal bolt, insulator and positive brush holder assembly **(see illustration)**.

Inspection

19 The manufacturer does not provide replacement parts to overhaul the starter. If severely worn or damaged parts are found, it will be necessary to purchase a new starter, rebuild the starter with usable parts from a discarded starter, or use parts from an aftermarket starter rebuild kit (if available).

20 The internal parts in a used starter are contaminated with carbon and copper dust released from the brushes and commutator. Before assembling the starter, the parts must be carefully cleaned to prevent from damaging them. Clean all parts (except the armature, insulated washers, brush plate and brushes and starter housing) in solvent. Use a rag lightly damped with solvent to wipe off the armature, insulated washers, brush plate and brushes and the starter housing (inside and outside). Use a fine grade sandpaper to clean the brushes. Do not use emery cloth as its fibers may insulate the brushes. Use only crocus cloth to clean the commutator. Do not use emery cloth or sandpaper. Any abrasive material left on or embedded in the commutator may cause excessive brush wear. Do not leave any debris on or between the commutator bars.

> *NOTE:*
>
> *A dirty or rough commutator will result in poor brush contact and cause rapid brush wear. In addition, carbon dust resulting from brush wear accumulates between commutator segments and partially shorts out starter current.*

21 Inspect the bushing in the front cover for wear or damage.

22 Inspect the seal and needle bearing in the front cover for damage **(see illustration 12.7)**.

23 Check the lockwasher, shims and insulated washers for damage.

24 Inspect each brush for cracks and other damage. Inspect the insulation sleeves on the positive brushes for tearing and other damage **(see illustration)**. Check each brush where it is fixed to its holder for looseness or damage. Measure the length of each brush and compare to the service limit in this Chapter's Specifications. If the brushes are too short, consult with a dealer parts department to see if replacement brushes are available.

25 Inspect the brush springs for damage. The springs can be considered serviceable if they snap the brushes firmly

12.16 Spread the positive brushes to release them from the brush plate and remove the brush plate with the negative brushes attached

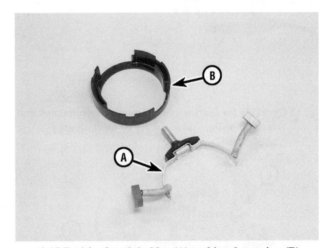

12.17 Positive brush holder (A) and insulator ring (B) removed from the housing and separated

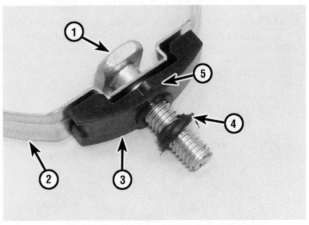

12.18 Terminal bolt details (inner)

1	*Terminal bolt*	*4*	*O-ring*
2	*Positive brush holder*	*5*	*Index tab on*
3	*Insulator*		*insulator*

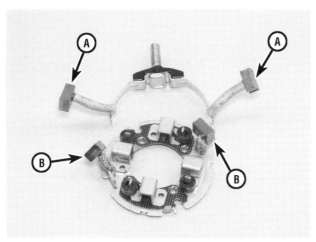

12.24 Inspect the positive (A) and negative (B) brush sets

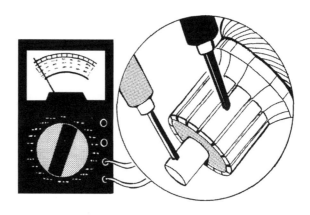

12.29 Checking for an improper ground between the armature shaft and commutator

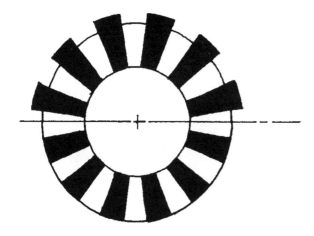

12.27 Inspect the commutator for excessive wear

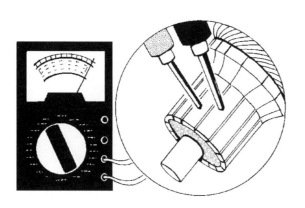

12.28 Checking for continuity between the commutator bars

8

in position against the commutator when assembling the starter.

NOTE:

Worn brushes and weak springs can cause poor brush contact, resulting in starting problems.

26 Inspect both armature shafts for scoring and other damage. If the needle bearing and/or bushing installed in the end covers are damaged, one or both shaft ends may be damaged. Then inspect the armature windings for any visual damage. To check the armature for a short circuit, have it tested on a growler by a dealership or automotive electrical repair shop.

27 Inspect the commutator bars for visual damage, then clean the commutator surface (see Step 20). The mica must be below the surface of the copper bars. On a worn commutator the mica and copper bars may be worn to the same level **(see illustration)**. If the mica level is too high or if its shape is too narrow or V-shaped, undercut the mica with a hacksaw blade. Inspect the commutator copper bars for discoloration. If a pair of bars are discolored, grounded armature coils are indicated.

28 Use a multimeter set to the ohms scale and check for continuity across all adjacent pairs of commutator bars **(see illustration)**. There should be continuity across all pairs of bars. If an open circuit exists between a pair of bars, the armature is damaged.

29 Use an ohmmeter and check for continuity between the armature shaft and each commutator bar **(see illustration)**. There should be no continuity.

12.30 Checking for an improper ground between the armature coil core and the commutator bars

12.33 Insulator ring, positive brush holder and terminal bolt installed inside housing

30 Check for continuity between the armature coil core and each commutator bar **(see illustration)**. There should be no continuity. If there is continuity, replace the armature.

31 Inspect the starter housing for cracks or other damage. Then inspect for loose, chipped or damaged magnets.

Assembly

32 Install the terminal bolt through the positive brush holder, then install the insulator over the bolt **(see illustration 12.18)**. The O-ring will be installed in Step 35. Note that the insulator has an index tab on one side **(see illustration 12.18)**. When installing the terminal bolt assembly, the index tab on the insulator must face up and toward the brush plate.

33 Install the positive brush holder into the insulator ring with the index tab on the insulator facing up. Then install the assembly into the housing **(see illustration)**.

34 Install the brush plate by aligning the tab on the plate with the notch in the housing **(see illustration)**. At the same time position the two positive brush wires into the notches in the plate **(see illustration 12.10)**. Make sure the wires are not pinched between the plate and housing.

12.34 Align the tab on the brush plate with the notch in the housing

NOTE:

In Step 35, make sure to reinstall all parts in the order described to insulate the terminal bolt and positive brushes from the housing.

35 Slide the O-ring onto the terminal bolt until it fits squarely in the hole in the starter housing. Then install the two small insulators, large insulator, steel washer and inner nut **(see illustration 12.15)**.

36 Perform the continuity checks in Steps 11 through 14 to check the positive brushes and terminal bolt for proper installation.

37 To keep spring pressure off the brushes when installing the armature, insert a strip of stiff plastic

12.37a Place a plastic strip (arrows) between each spring and spring holder to hold the brushes back when installing the armature

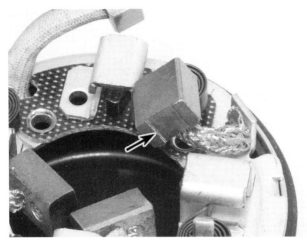

12.37b Install each brush into its holder with its grooved side (arrow) facing toward the spring

12.38 After installing the armature and removing the plastic strips, check that the springs are pushing the brushes squarely against the commutator

between each spring and brush holder **(see illustration)**. Then install the brushes into their holder. Note that one side of each brush is machined with a groove **(see illustration)**. The groove side faces toward the spring and not the commutator.

NOTE:

In Step 38, a strong magnetic force will pull the armature against the coils inside the starter housing. When installing the arma-ture, hold it tightly to avoid damaging the coils or brushes.

38   Install the armature into the starter housing until the commutator is aligned with the brush holders. Then remove the plastic strips to release the brush springs and allow them to push the brushes squarely against the

commutator **(see illustration)**. Also make sure the brush wires are properly routed.

39   Install the shims (rear cover side) onto the armature shaft **(see illustration 12.6)**.

40   Install the O-ring onto the commutator side of the starter housing, making sure it seats squarely in the groove and is not twisted.

41   Apply a thin coat of grease onto the armature shaft.

42   Install the rear cover over the armature shaft and seat it against the O-ring/housing. Align the index mark on the rear cover with the mark on the housing (see Step 5).

43   Lubricate the needle bearing in the front end cover with grease, then lightly lubricate the seal lip with grease **(see illustration 12.7)**. Wipe off all excess grease from the front end cover so it doesn't contaminate the brushes.

44   Install the metal shims onto the armature shaft, noting that the number of shims found on the starter you are working on may vary from the number of shims shown here. Then install the insulated washer and seat it against the shims **(see illustration 12.7)**.

45   Install the O-ring onto the front side of the starter housing, making sure it seats squarely in the groove and is not twisted.

46   Install the toothed washer into the front end cover **(see illustration 12.7)**. The teeth on the washer must face toward the front end cover. Then install the front end cover by aligning the index mark on the cover with the mark on the housing (see Step 5). Install the starter assembly screws and tighten to the torque listed in this Chapter's Specifications.

NOTE:

If one or both screws will not pass through the starter, the covers and/or the brush plate are installed incorrectly.

47   Lubricate the O-rings with grease and install them into the front cover grooves.

48   Hold the starter and turn the armature shaft by hand. The armature should turn with some resistance, but should not bind or lock up. If the armature does not turn properly, disassemble the starter and check the shim, insulated washer and lockwasher alignment.

CAUTION:

Because of the large amount of current that will flow from the battery to the starter, use a large diameter cable when making the test in Step 49. To avoid damaging the starter, do not leave the battery connected for more than a few seconds.

49   Before installing the starter onto the engine, test starter operation by using an auxiliary battery and battery cables to apply battery voltage directly to the starter. When selecting a battery for this test, make sure it is fully charged and capable of turning the starter. Clamp the negative battery cable end to

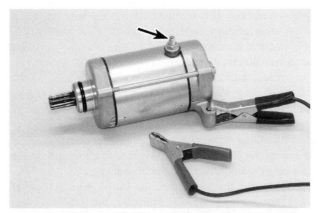

12.49 Test the starter with a fully charged 12-volt battery and jumper cables - connect the negative cable to the starter housing and the positive cable to the terminal bolt (arrow)

13.4 Starter relay mounting position underneath the dash (arrow)

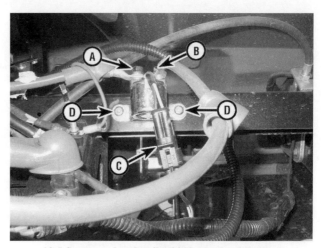

13.5 Starter relay details (2010 standard Ranger model shown)

A	Battery cable	C	Wiring harness connector
B	Starter cable	D	Mounting screws

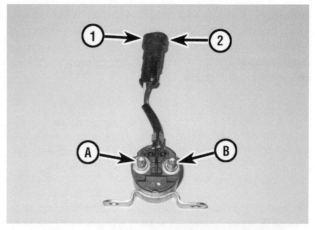

13.8 The two wiring harness connector terminals are identified by the numbers 1 and 2 found on the connector. The relay terminals are identified by letters A (battery terminal) and B (starter terminal)

the starter housing and then briefly touch the positive cable end to the terminal bolt on the starter **(see illustration)**. The starter should turn when battery voltage is applied directly to the terminal bolt. If the starter did not turn, disassemble and inspect the starter as described in this section.

50   Install the starter (see Section 11).

13   STARTER RELAY - REMOVAL, INSTALLATION AND TESTING

1   The starter relay connects the battery to the starter and is designed to temporarily carry the high electrical load to the starter when the ignition switch is turned to the START position. The brake pedal must be applied when starting the engine.

Removal and installation

2   Turn the ignition switch OFF.
3   Disconnect the negative battery cable (see Section 4).
4   The starter relay is mounted underneath the dash, on the left-hand side of the frame **(see illustration)**. If necessary, remove the left-hand headlight assembly and/or remove some of the dash fasteners, according to your model, to access the starter relay.
5   Slide the rubber boots away from the two cable ends at the starter relay. Then remove the two nuts and disconnect the starter motor and battery leads at the starter relay, noting where each cable is originally installed. With the two cables disconnected, disconnect the starter relay wiring harness connector. Then remove the two screws and the starter relay **(see illustration)**.
6   Installation is the reverse of these steps. Clean the battery and starter cable leads before connecting them to the relay. Tighten both cable nuts securely.

Testing

7   Remove the starter relay (see Steps 2 through 5).
8   Identify the starter relay terminals before testing **(see illustration)**.

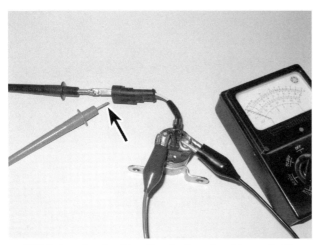

13.9 Set-up for checking the starter relay. Momentarily touch the negative battery terminal (arrow) to the wiring harness connector's No. 1 terminal

9   Set a multimeter to the ohms scale, and connect its two leads across the relay's starter and battery terminals. Then connect the positive terminal of a 12 volt battery to the wiring harness connector No. 2 terminal. While reading the ohmmeter, momentarily touch the negative battery terminal to the wiring harness connector No. 1 terminal. The relay should click and there should be continuity or a small ohms reading. Compare the reading to the specified resistance listed in this Chapter's Specifications **(see illustration)**.

10   If the test result is correct, the relay is in good condition. If the relay failed the test, have a dealer service department confirm the test results before replacing the relay.

14   LIGHTING SYSTEM - CHECK

1   The battery provides power for operation of the headlights, taillight and brake light. If none of the lights operate, always check battery voltage before proceeding. Low battery voltage indicates either a faulty battery or a defective charging system. Refer to Section 5 for battery checks and Section 7 for charging system tests. When checking the lighting system, note the following:

   a)   *Refer to the appropriate wiring diagram to identify the protection devices (fuses, relays and circuit breakers) used in the lighting circuit (see Section 40).*
   b)   *When all of the lights fail to operate, check for a blown light fuse (see Section 37).*
   c)   *When it is necessary to make voltage and resistance tests in the lighting circuit, refer to Chapter 1, Section 9 for information on electrical troubleshooting tips and procedures.*
   d)   *When one headlight fails to work, check the bulb and bulb wiring harness connectors first. Then try installing the bulb from the opposite working*

headlight unit. If this solves the problem, replace the defective bulb. If not, check for voltage and ground at the bulb's wiring harness connector.
   e)   *When checking headlight bulbs and the headlight circuit on 2011 and later models, make sure to select either HIGH or LOW beam at the headlight switch, depending on which circuit you are testing.*
   f)   *When one LED taillight fails to work, install the working LED taillight in its place. If this solves the problem, replace the defective LED taillight as an assembly. If not, turn the ignition switch ON and check for voltage at the LED wiring harness side connector - check both the taillight and brake light circuits. Then use an ohmmeter and check that the ground wire is properly grounded. If voltage is present during the tests and the ground is good, replace the LED taillight. If there is no voltage reading, the problem lies in the wiring or one of the switches is damaged.*
   g)   *When testing indicates there's no voltage at a connector, the problem lies in the wiring or one of the switches in the circuit. Test the switch as described in this Chapter.*

15   HEADLIGHT BULB - ADJUSTMENT AND REPLACEMENT

1   Single element headlight bulbs are used on 2010 and earlier models. Models from 2011 and later use dual element bulbs that allow the driver to select HIGH and LOW beam headlight positions.

2   Always use the correct size bulb specified in this Chapter's Specifications. Using the wrong size bulb produces a dim light or may cause the bulb to burn out prematurely.

3   When riding in mud and other harsh conditions, make sure to keep the headlight and taillight lenses clean to provide optimum lighting, and to help drivers in other vehicles see you.

NOTE:

When handling quartz-halogen type headlight bulbs, do not touch the bulb glass because skin acids and grease will shorten the bulb's service life. If the bulb is accidentally touched, clean it carefully with a rag soaked in isopropyl alcohol and allowed to dry before installation. Always use a new paper towel or dry cloth when handling bulbs to increase bulb life.

Adjustment

4   Each headlight housing is equipped with two horizontal pins that fit into slots in the front cover. A thick O-ring is twisted and installed on the outside of each pin to hold the headlight housing in place. A single headlight adjust screw

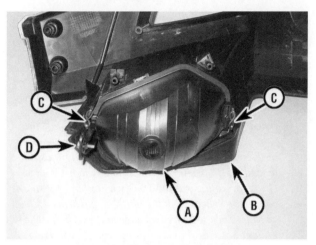

15.4 Headlight housing details

A   Headlight housing   D   Headlight adjust
B   Front cover   screw
C   O-rings

15.10a The headlight adjust screw is located on the outside of the headlight housing. The mark on the dash (arrow) approximates the adjust screw position inside the wheel-well

15.10b Headlight adjust screw (arrow) with the headlight housing removed for clarity

is installed on the outside of the headlight housing, and is used to adjust the headlight beam while also securing the housing in place **(see illustration)**.

5   The headlight can only be adjusted vertically.

6   Park the vehicle on a level surface so the headlights are approximately 25 feet (7.6 meters) from a wall.

7   Measure the height from the floor or ground to the center of the headlight. Mark the wall at this height.

8   Start the engine. On 2010 models, turn the headlight on. On 2011 and later models, turn the headlight on to HIGH beam. On all models, a driver must be sitting in the front seat when checking and adjusting the headlight.

9   The brightest section of the beam should be 8 in. (20 cm) below the centerline mark on the wall made in Step 7. Check the adjustment for both bulbs.

10   If adjustment is necessary, working inside the wheel-well, loosen the headlight adjust screw **(see illustrations)**. Then pivot the headlight housing by hand to raise or lower the beam to the desired height. Tighten the screw and recheck the adjustment.

11   Repeat for the other headlight.

Replacement

WARNING:
If the headlight just burned out or it was just turned off, it will be hot. Do not touch the bulb until it cools off.

12   On 2010 models, turn the bulb 90 degrees counterclockwise, then remove it from the housing **(see illustration)**. Disconnect the wiring harness connector from the bulb.

13   On 2011 and later models, turn the bulb counterclockwise 90 degrees and remove it from the headlight housing.

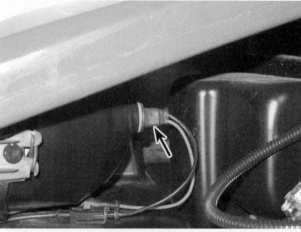

**15.12 Turn the bulb counterclockwise to remove it from the headlight housing
(2010 model with an aftermarket bulb holder shown)**

15.13a Turn the bulb counterclockwise 90 degrees and slip it out of the headlight housing . . .

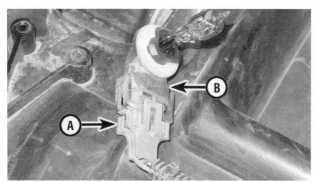

15.13b . . . then disconnect the wiring harness connector (A) and remove the bulb (B)

16.3 O-ring (arrow) used to secure headlight housing - note how it is twisted and installed in place

17.2a Remove the LED light assembly mounting screws (arrows) and the light from the cargo bed . . .

Then disconnect the wiring harness connector from the bulb **(see illustrations)**.

14   Installation is the reverse of these steps, noting the following:

a) *Make sure the wiring harness connector terminals are clean.*

b) *Install the bulb/holder by aligning the tabs on the bulb/holder with the notches in the housing. Then turn the bulb/holder 90 degrees clockwise and lock it in place.*

c) *Start the engine and turn the headlights ON. Make sure both the left and right headlights work correctly. If the vehicle is equipped with both HIGH and LOW headlight beams, check the light operation in both positions and on both sides. Do not drive the vehicle until both headlights work properly.*

16   HEADLIGHT HOUSING - REMOVAL AND INSTALLATION

1   Remove the headlight bulb for the housing to be removed (see Section 15).

2   Remove the front cover to access the headlight housings (see Chapter 14).

3   Remove the headlight adjust screw. Note how the O-rings are twisted and installed in place, then stretch and remove the O-ring from each side of the headlight housing **(see illustration)**. Pull the headlight housing to release it from the mounting brackets on the front cover **(see illustration 15.4)**.

4   Inspect the O-rings for any cracks and replace if weak or damaged.

5   Installation is the reverse of these steps, plus the following:

a) *To tension the O-rings, twist them into a figure-eight pattern when installing them.*

b) *Adjust the headlights (see Section 15).*

17   TAILLIGHT - REPLACEMENT

1   All models are equipped with an LED taillight on each side of the cargo bed. There are no individual bulbs to replace. If one or both taillight assemblies do not work, refer to Section 14.

2   Remove the two screws securing the LED light assembly to the cargo bed and pull it outward until the wiring harness connector is accessible. Disconnect the connector and remove the LED light assembly **(see illustrations)**.

3   Installation is the reverse of removal, noting the following:

a) *Pack the wiring harness connector with dielectric grease before reconnecting it.*

b) *Turn the ignition switch ON and check the tail/ brake light operation.*

8

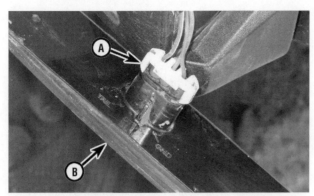

17.2b . . . then disconnect the wiring harness connector (A) and remove the LED light assembly (B)

18.3b . . . then lift and remove the instrument panel from the dash

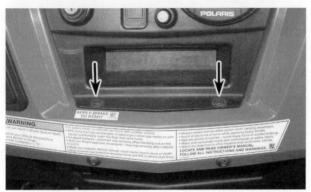

18.3a Remove the two push pins (arrows) . . .

18   INSTRUMENT PANEL - REMOVAL AND INSTALLATION

1   The instrument panel is installed in the dashboard and can be removed to access the switches and the instrument cluster.

2   Disconnect the negative battery cable at the battery (see Section 4).

3   Remove the two push pins securing the instrument panel to the dashboard and remove the instrument panel **(see illustrations)**.

4   Installation is the reverse of removal, noting the following:

a) *Install the instrument panel by inserting its two hooks into the two notches in the dash. Then install and lock the push pins.*

b) *After reconnecting the negative battery cable, turn the ignition switch ON and check all of the switch functions to make sure each switch operates correctly.*

19   INSTRUMENT CLUSTER - REMOVAL AND INSTALLATION

1   A single instrument cluster is used on all models. A rubber grommet installed on the outside of the instrument cluster is used to align and hold the instrument cluster in the dash **(see illustrations)**.

19.1a Instrument cluster (arrow) used on 2010 models

19.1b Instrument cluster (arrow) used on 2011 and later models

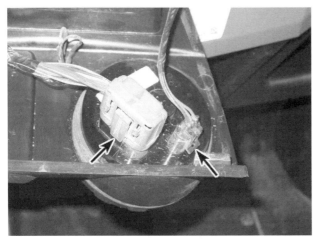

19.3 On 2010 models, disconnect the two wiring harness connectors (arrows) from the backside of the instrument cluster. On 2011 and later models, one wiring harness connector is used

19.5 Align the index tab on the rubber grommet with the notch in the instrument panel (arrows)

19.4a Remove the instrument cluster (A) by pushing it out of the instrument panel, while leaving its rubber grommet (B) in place

Removal and installation

2   Remove the instrument panel (see Section 18).

3   Disconnect the wiring harness connector(s) and remove the instrument cluster **(see illustration)**.

4   Use your hand and push the instrument cluster out of the instrument panel, while leaving its rubber grommet in place, if possible **(see illustration)**. When removing the instrument cluster, note how the shoulder on the instrument cluster aligns with the notch in the rubber grommet **(see illustration)**.

5   If the rubber grommet came off with the instrument cluster, or if you are replacing it, install it by inserting its index tab into the notch in the instrument panel **(see illustration)**. Then seat the rubber grommet fully against the instrument panel. Do not lubricate the rubber grommet when installing it.

6   Installation is otherwise the reverse of removal, noting the following:

   a) Once the rubber grommet is properly aligned and installed in the instrument panel (Step 5), spray the outside of the instrument cluster with soapy water. Then align the shoulder on the instrument cluster with the notch in the rubber grommet, and push the instrument cluster into place until it bottoms against the grommet (Step 4).

   b) Make sure the wiring harness connector terminals are clean, and if necessary, spray the terminals with an electrical contact cleaner and allow to dry. Then reconnect the connector(s) and lock in place.

   c) Turn the ignition switch ON and make sure the instrument cluster works properly.

8

19.4b Note the instrument cluster and rubber grommet alignment (arrows) - the shoulder and notch alignment must be maintained during installation

20 INSTRUMENT CLUSTER - TESTING

Testing

NOTE:

If test results in this section indicate the instrument cluster is damaged, note the information in Section 2 before replacing the instrument cluster.

2010 models

1   When it is necessary to do so during testing, disconnect the 16-pin wiring harness connector at the instrument cluster (see Section 19).

2   When testing the instrument cluster in this section, check for voltage at the 16-pin wiring harness connector when instructed to do so in a specific test **(see illustration)**. To match the connector pin numbers and wire colors, refer to the appropriate wiring diagram (see Section 40).

3   Check the terminal pins in the instrument cluster for damage and corrosion **(see illustration)**.

No display on instrument cluster

4   If there is no display on the instrument cluster when the ignition switch is turned to its ON position, turn the ignition switch OFF and wait ten seconds. Then turn the ignition switch to the ON position once again. If there is still no display, continue with Step 5.

5   Turn the ignition switch to the ON position. Using a multimeter set to the volt scale, place the positive probe against the No. 1 pin and the negative probe against the No. 8 pin **(see illustration 20.2)**. Note the voltmeter reading. Now place the positive probe against the No. 2 pin and the negative probe against the No. 8 pin. Battery voltage should be recorded in each test. If battery voltage is not indicated in one or both tests, start at the wiring harness connector and check the wires for an open circuit.

Odometer does not work

6   If the odometer reading does not change when the vehicle is being driven, but the speedometer arm is moving to indicate vehicle speed, the odometer function in the instrument cluster is damaged, and it is necessary to replace the instrument cluster. However, if the speedometer arm doesn't move when the vehicle is being driven, have a dealer service department check the wheel speed sensor operation. Special tools are required to accurately check the wheel speed sensor.

Odometer changes but speedometer needle does not move

7   The speedometer unit is damaged. Replace the instrument cluster and retest.

Fuel gauge does not work

8   Perform this test when the instrument cluster and speedometer work correctly, but the fuel gauge does not.

9   Check the No. 12 terminal (violet/white wire) at the wiring harness connector **(see illustration 20.2)** and the mating pin at the instrument cluster **(see illustration 20.3)**

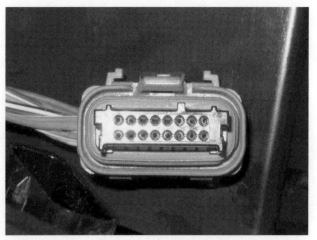

20.2 Instrument cluster wiring harness connector 16-pin number/wire color details

1	Red (12 volt constant)	10	Orange/red (parking
2	Red/white		brake indicator)
	(12 volt switch)	11	Black/white
3	Grey/orange		(malfunction indicator)
	(mode button)	12	Violet/white
4	Not used		(fuel gauge)
5	Not used	13	Brown
6	Not used		(ground terminal)
7	Yellow/red	14	White (gear
	(rpm input)		indicator)
8	Brown/red	15	Not used
	(ground terminal)	16	Brown/white (AWD
9	Blue/white (engine		control terminal)
	overheat switch)		

20.3 Check the terminal pins in the instrument cluster (arrow) when troubleshooting an electrical problem

for corrosion and damage. Then check the violet/white fuel gauge wire for an open circuit. Make any repairs to the connector, instrument cluster and/or wiring harness as required. Then reconnect the wiring harness connector and recheck the fuel gauge operation.

10   If the fuel gauge still doesn't work, check the fuel level sender operation (see Chapter 7).

11   If the tests show the fuel level sender is faulty, replace

20.15 AWD coil wiring harness connector (arrow)

the fuel pump (see Chapter 7).

12 If the tests show the fuel level sender is good, replace the instrument cluster (see Section 19).

AWD drive is not functional and the AWD icon is or is not displayed

13 The AWD icon should be displayed on the instrument cluster when the AWD switch is turned ON. If AWD is not functional, perform the following to isolate the problem.

14 Perform Steps 4 through 7 to check the speedometer operation. When you have confirmed the speedometer is working correctly, continue with Step 15.

15 Turn the ignition switch to the ON position, shift the transmission into gear, and turn the AWD switch ON. At the front gearcase, locate the AWD hub coil wiring harness connector **(see illustration)**. Do not unplug the connector. Instead, it is necessary to back-probe the connector when checking for voltage (see Chapter 1, Section 9). Use a multimeter set to the volt scale and place the positive probe against the brown/white terminal and the negative probe against the gearcase (ground). The voltmeter should read battery voltage.

16 If the voltmeter did not read battery voltage, check the AWD coil along with its wiring harness connector and wiring harness (see Section 33).

17 If the voltmeter read battery voltage, leave the AWD switch in its ON position and turn the ignition switch OFF. Disconnect the instrument cluster 16-pin wiring harness connector (see Section 19). Turn the ignition switch to the ON position. Using a voltmeter, place the positive probe against the brown/white terminal and the negative probe to the front gearcase (ground). The voltmeter should read battery voltage.

18 If the voltmeter did not read battery voltage, check the brown/white wire for an open circuit.

19 If the voltmeter read battery voltage, turn the ignition switch to its OFF position and reconnect the instrument cluster 16-pin wiring harness connector.

20 Turn the ignition switch to its ON position and shift the transmission into LOW or HIGH gear with the AWD switch turned ON.

21 If the AWD icon did not turn ON, replace the instrument cluster and retest.

22 If the AWD icon turned ON, but the vehicle will not operate in AWD, the clutch assembly in the front gearcase may be damaged. Refer further testing to a dealer service department.

No AWD safety limiter

23 Problems with the AWD safety limiter (mounted in the front gearcase unit) can prevent the AWD icon from turning ON and prevent the AWD function from operating. Perform the following steps to isolate the problem to either an electrical or mechanical problem with the AWD safety limiter. See Section 33 for additional information.

24 Perform Steps 4 through 7 to check the speedometer operation. When you have confirmed the speedometer is working correctly, continue with Step 25.

25 Shift the transmission into NEUTRAL and start the engine. Toggle the mode button on the instrument cluster until the engine RPM is displayed. Increase the engine speed and hold it in a fixed position until the RPM reading on the digital display stabilizes. Does it seem the rpm reading is accurate?

26 If the rpm reading seems accurate, go to Step 30 to continue troubleshooting.

27 If the rpm reading does not seem accurate, turn the ignition switch OFF. Disconnect the instrument cluster 16-pin wiring harness connector (see Section 19). Restart the engine and allow to run at idle speed. Set a digital multimeter to the AC amperage scale and place the positive probe against the yellow/red terminal and the negative probe to the brown/red terminal in the wiring harness side connector. The voltmeter should read more than 3 volts AC.

28 If the AC voltage is correct, replace the instrument cluster and retest.

29 If the AC voltage is incorrect, test the charging system (see Section 7).

30 Shift the transmission into NEUTRAL. Apply the parking brake and support the vehicle with both front wheels off the ground (see Chapter 10). Also block the rear wheels to prevent the vehicle from rolling off the jackstands.

31 Turn the AWD switch OFF. Then start the engine and increase the engine speed above 3100 rpm and turn the AWD switch ON. The front gearcase unit should not engage the front wheels. Lower the engine RPM and turn the engine OFF.

32 If the front drive did not engage, there is no problem with the safety limiter assembly in the front gearcase.

33 If the front drive engaged, note whether the AWD icon on the instrument cluster turned ON.

34 If the AWD icon did not turn on, the problem is in the AWD coil assembly in the front geacase. Refer further testing to a dealer service department.

8

35 Disconnect the AWD coil wiring harness connector **(see illustration 20.15)**. Use a multimeter set to the ohms scale and check for continuity between the brown/white terminal in the gearcase side connector and the front gearcase (ground) - there should be no continuity.

36 If there is continuity, there is a short circuit in the AWD coil brown/white wire. Repair the wiring harness and retest.

37 If there is no continuity, the instrument cluster is damaged. Replace the cluster and retest.

2011 and later models

38 Specific troubleshooting procedures are not provided for the 2011 and later model instrument cluster. When a problem is experienced with the instrument, refer to Chapter 1, Section 9 for electrical troubleshooting information and to the appropriate wiring diagram (see Section 40) to identify the power and ground terminal numbers and wire colors.

21 SWITCH CONTINUITY TESTING - GENERAL INFORMATION

1 Test switches for continuity with an ohmmeter or a self-powered test light as described in the individual sections in this Chapter. Disconnect the switch connector and check continuity at the terminals on the switch side of the connector. Operate a switch in each of its operating positions and compare the results with the information listed in the text. See Chapter 1, Section 9 for information on electrical troubleshooting.

2 When testing switches, note the following:

   a) *Before testing a switch, check the appropriate circuit protection device to make sure it is not blown or open (see Section 37).*

   b) *If you are testing a switch, and it has not been disconnected from the circuit, disconnect the negative battery cable at the battery (see Section 4).*

   c) *Before disconnecting two connectors, check them for any locking tabs or arms that must be pushed or opened. If two connectors are difficult to separate, do not force them as damage may occur. Also, after time, the connectors become brittle and the small locking arms and tabs are easily damaged.*

   d) *When separating two connectors, pull on the connector housings and not the wires.*

   e) *After locating a defective circuit, check the connectors to make sure they are clean and properly connected. Check all wires going into a connector housing to make sure each wire is properly positioned and the wire ends are not loose. Before replacing a switch, make sure the problem is not with its connectors and/or wiring harness.*

   f) *When replacing a switch, make sure the wiring harness is properly routed and secured in place.*

   g) *When reconnecting electrical connector halves, push them together until they click or snap into place.*

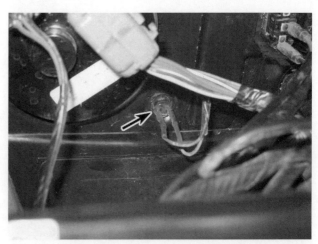

22.3 Mode switch (arrow) position behind instrument panel

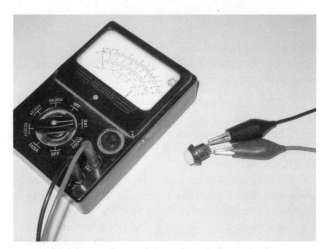

22.4 Set-up for testing mode switch continuity

22 MODE SWITCH (2010) - TEST AND REPLACEMENT

1 The mode switch is mounted on the instrument panel and is used to toggle back and forth through the diagnostic functions on the instrument cluster.

Test and replacement

2 Remove the instrument panel (see Section 18).

3 Push the mode switch and its wiring harness out of the dashboard from the inside out **(see illustration)**. Then disconnect the two wiring harness connectors and remove the switch.

4 Use a multimeter set to the ohms scale and connect the leads across the two switch terminals **(see illustration)**. There should be continuity with the button pressed, and no continuity with the button released. Replace the switch if it failed either part of this test.

5 Installation is the reverse of removal. Check the mode switch operation.

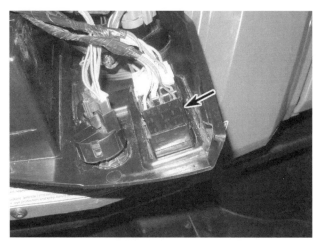

23.2 Disconnect the wiring harness connector (arrow) at the headlight switch

23.11 Compress the clip on each side of the switch (arrows) and push the switch out of the instrument panel

23.3 Set-up for testing the ignition switch with an ohmmeter

23 HEADLIGHT SWITCH - TEST AND REPLACEMENT

Test

NOTE:

The illustrations used in this section show the headlight switch used on 2010 models. Procedures required to service the headlight switch used on 2011 and later models are similar.

1   Remove the instrument panel (see Section 18).
2   Disconnect the wiring harness connector at the headlight switch **(see illustration)**.
3   Test the switch with an ohmmeter or a continuity test light by checking for continuity between the terminals on the switch, and with the switch in different operating positions (see Steps 4 through 9, depending on model year) **(see illustration)**. Refer to the numbers on the side of the headlight switch and to the appropriate wiring diagram (see Section 40) to identify the headlight switch terminal

numbers. Replace the headlight switch if it fails any part of the test.

2010 models

4   Flip the switch to its ON position. There should be continuity between terminals 2 (yellow) and 3 (dark green).
5   Flip the switch to its OFF position and repeat the test in Step 4 There should be no continuity between these same two terminals.
6   With the switch in either the ON or OFF position, check continuity between terminals 6 and 7. This is the switch back-light circuit. Then check for continuity between terminals 3 and 8. This is the ON indicator. There should be continuity in both tests.

2011 and later models

7   Turn the switch OFF. There should be continuity between terminals 1 (blank - no wire) and 2 (white).
8   Turn the switch to LOW. There should be continuity between terminals 2 (white) and 3 (dark green) and between terminals 4 (white) and 5 (red/yellow).
9   Turn the switch to HIGH. There should be continuity between terminals 2 (white) and 3 (dark green) and between terminals 5 (red/yellow) and 6 (yellow).

Replacement

10   Perform Step 1 and Step 2 to access the switch and disconnect its electrical connector.
11   Working inside the dashboard, compress the clips holding the headlight switch in place, and push the switch forward to remove it **(see illustration)**.
12   When installing the switch, make sure it is right-side up, then push it into the instrument panel until it locks in place. Reconnect the wiring harness connector, then start the engine and test the switch in each of its operating positions.

24 ALL WHEEL DRIVE (AWD) SWITCH - TEST AND REPLACEMENT

1   This switch is also referred to as the AWD/TURF switch or the 2WD/AWD switch.

Test

NOTE:

The illustrations used in this section show the AWD switch used on 2010 models. Procedures required to service the AWD switch used on 2011 and later models are similar.

2   The AWD switch is accessed in the same way as for the headlight switch (see Section 23) **(see illustration)**.

3   Test the switch with an ohmmeter or a continuity test light by checking for continuity between the terminals on the switch, and with the switch in different operating positions (see Steps 4 through 10, depending on model year) **(see illustration)**. Refer to the appropriate wiring diagram (see Section 40) to identify the AWD switch terminal numbers. Replace the AWD switch if it fails any part of the test.

2010 models

4   Push the switch to AWD. There should be continuity between terminals 2 (orange/white) and 3 (gray).

5   Push the switch to 2WD. There should be no continuity between any two terminals.

6   Push the switch to TURF. There should be continuity between terminals 4 (white/dark green) and 5 (brown).

2011 and later models

7   Flip the switch to AWD. There should be continuity between terminals 2 (brown) and 3 (gray) and between terminals 5 (brown) and 6 (blank).

8   Flip the switch to 2WD. There should be no continuity between any two terminals.

9   Flip the switch to TURF. There should be continuity between terminals 1 (brown) and 2 (brown) and between terminals 4 (white/dark green) and 5 (brown).

10   With the switch in either the ON or OFF position, there should be continuity between terminals 7 (red/dark green) and 8 (brown). This is the switch back-light circuit.

Replacement

11   Replace the switch as described in Section 23.

25 BRAKE LIGHT SWITCH - TEST AND REPLACEMENT

1   All models use a non-adjustable hydraulic brake light switch. On 2010 models, the switch is mounted on the frame, near the clutch outer cover. On 2011 and later

24.2 AWD switch and connector (arrow) position on instrument panel

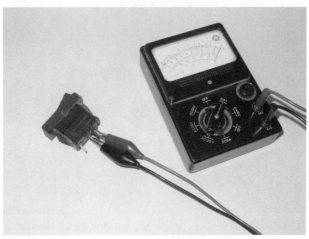

24.3 Bench set-up for testing the AWD switch with an ohmmeter. Switch can also be tested while installed in the instrument panel

models, the switch is mounted on the master cylinder. When the brake pedal is applied, unequal pressure on the normally open switch causes it to close, and voltage is applied to the rear brake lights. Because the rear brake pedal must be applied when starting the engine, the brake light switch is also wired to the starter relay. A faulty brake light switch will prevent the starter relay from operating.

Test

2   If the rear brake lights do not work, first make sure the LED taillights are in good condition and there is voltage at both connectors (see Section 17). Then check the circuit protection device for a blown fuse or an open circuit (see Section 37). If everything is okay, perform the following continuity tests on the brake light switch.

3   On 2011 and later models, remove the left wheel panel (see Chapter 14).

25.4a Brake light switch (2010 model)

25.10 Loosen and remove the brake light switch (arrow) -
2010 models

25.4b Brake light switch (2011 and later models)

25.5 Brake light switch test setup (2010 model shown)

4   Disconnect the wiring harness connector(s) at the brake light switch **(see illustrations)**.

5   With the brake pedal released, use a multimeter set to the ohms scale and check for continuity across the two switch terminals **(see illustration)** - there should be no continuity. If there is continuity, the switch is faulty and must be replaced.

6   Apply the brake pedal and repeat the test - there should be continuity (0 ohms). If the ohmmeter shows a reading greater than 0.5 ohms, clean the switch contacts and repeat the test. If the reading is still greater than 0.5 ohms, replace the switch.

Replacement

7   Perform Step 3 (2011 and later models) and Step 4.

8   Clean the brake light switch and the area around the switch to prevent dirt and debris from entering the brake system when the switch is removed.

9   Wrap a plastic cloth below the rear brake light switch assembly to prevent brake fluid from contacting other parts when the switch is removed.

NOTE:

Make sure there is no pressure applied to the brake pedal when removing the brake light switch.

10   On 2010 models, loosen and remove the brake light switch from the hose joint **(see illustration)**.

11   On 2011 and later models, loosen and remove the brake light switch from the hose joint on the master cylinder **(see illustration 25.4b)**.

12   Install the new brake light switch and tighten securely. Reconnect the electrical connector(s) at the switch.

13   Bleed the brake system (see Chapter 13).

14   Installation is the reverse of these steps. Start the engine, making sure the starter turns over and the rear brake lights turn ON when you apply the brake pedal.

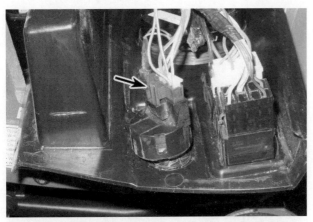

26.2 Ignition switch wiring harness connector (arrow)

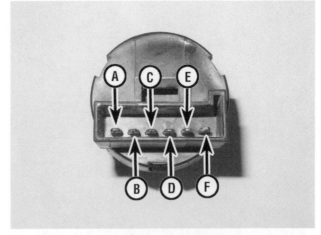

26.3 Test the ignition switch with an ohmmeter or continuity test light at the switch terminals

26   IGNITION SWITCH - TEST AND REPLACEMENT

Test

1   Remove the instrument panel (see Section 18).

2   Disconnect the wiring harness connector from the ignition switch **(see illustration)**.

3   Insert the ignition key into the switch. Test the switch with an ohmmeter or a continuity test light by checking for continuity between the specified terminals on the switch, and with the switch in different operating positions (see Steps 4 through 6) **(see illustration)**. Replace the ignition switch if it fails any part of the test.

4   Turn the switch OFF. There should be continuity between terminals E and F.

5   Turn the switch ON. There should be continuity between terminals C and D and between terminals A and F.

6   Turn the switch to START. There should continuity between terminals A and B and between terminals C and D.

Replacement

7   Perform Steps 1 and 2.

8   Remove the nut, plastic washer and remove the ignition switch from inside the instrument panel **(see illustration)**.

9   When installing the switch, align the tab on the switch with the slot in the instrument panel **(see illustration)**. Then install the washer and nut and tighten the nut securely. Reconnect the wiring harness connector, then turn the ignition switch ON and check the switch in each of its operating positions.

27   GEAR POSITION SWITCH - TEST AND REPLACEMENT

Test

1   Park the vehicle on a level surface. Because it is necessary to shift the transmission into each gear when testing the gear position switch, you may have to rock the vehicle back and forth to make sure the proper gear is engaged. After selecting a gear, apply the parking brake to

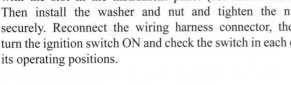

26.8 The ignition switch is secured to the instrument panel with a large plastic nut (arrow) and washer

26.9 Install the ignition switch by aligning its tab with the slot in the instrument panel (arrow)

27.2 Gear position switch details (2010 model shown)

A   Gear position switch
B   E-clip
C   Wiring harness connector

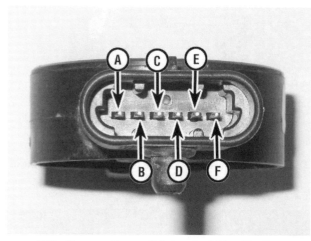

27.3a Gear position switch terminal identification

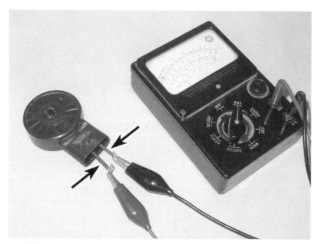

27.3b To prevent the test leads from shorting across the switch terminals when connecting them, make and use a pair of insulated T-pins (arrows) - switch removed for clarity

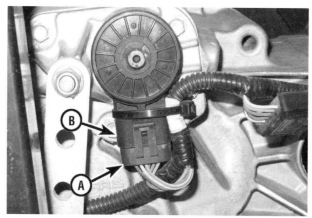

27.9 Refer to wire colors and the letters on the wiring harness connector (A) when testing the gear position switch (B) for continuity in each gear position

prevent the vehicle from rolling.
2   Disconnect the gear position switch wiring harness connector located at the switch on the right side of the transmission (see illustration).

2010 models

3   Test the switch while it is mounted on the transmission. Use a multimeter set to the ohms scale and connect the test leads across the specified connector terminals on the switch as described in Steps 4 through 7 (see illustration). If it is difficult to access the terminals on the bottom of the switch, use a pair of insulated T-pins between the switch terminals and your meter's test leads (see illustration). Using T-pins and heat shrink, you can easily make a set of insulated test pins as described in *Measuring tools* at the front of this manual.
4   Shift the transmission into HIGH gear. There should be continuity across terminals A and C.
5   Shift the transmission into LOW gear. There should be continuity across terminals B and C.
6   Shift the transmission into NEUTRAL. There should be continuity across terminals C and D.
7   Shift the transmission into REVERSE. There should be continuity across terminals C and E.
8   If any one test result is incorrect, the switch is faulty and must be replaced.

2011 models

9   Test the switch while it is mounted on the transmission. Use a multimeter set to the ohms scale and connect the test leads across the specified connector terminals on the switch as described in Steps 10 through 13 (see illustration). If it is difficult to access the terminals on the bottom of the switch, use a pair of insulated T-pins between the switch terminals and your meter's test leads (see Step 3).
10   Shift the transmission into HIGH gear. There should be continuity across terminals C (violet/white) and A (dark blue).

11   Shift the transmission into LOW gear. There should be continuity across terminals C (violet/white) and B (yellow).
12   Shift the transmission into NEUTRAL. There should be continuity across terminals C (violet/white) and D (dark green).
13   Shift the transmission into REVERSE. There should be continuity across terminals C (violet/white) and E (red).

NOTE:

Disregard the F terminal (orange wire) in the gear position switch and connector. The F terminal is designated for a transmission PARK position, which is not used on these models.

14   If any one test result is incorrect, the switch is faulty and must be replaced.

2012 and later models

15   Use a multimeter set to the ohms scale and connect the test leads across the two switch connector terminals (labeled A and B on the switch). Leave the ohmmeter leads connected to these two terminals when making the following switch tests.
16   It is necessary to shift the transmission and test the switch in each gear position. First, shift the transmission into HIGH gear and measure the switch resistance. Compare the reading to the value listed in this Chapter's Specifications.
17   Repeat Step 16 to measure the resistance of the switch in each remaining gear position - LOW, NEUTRAL and REVERSE. Compare each individual resistance reading with the values listed in this Chapter's Specifications.

NOTE:

Disregard the gear position switch PARK terminal identified on the wiring diagram (see Section 40). The PARK position is not used on these models.

18   If any one test result is incorrect, the switch is faulty and must be replaced.

Replacement

19   Disconnect the gear position switch wiring harness connector (see Step 2).
20   Remove any cable guides securing the gear position switch wiring harness in place.
21   Remove the E-clip and slide the gear position switch off the transmission shaft **(see illustration 27.2)**.
22   Before installing the switch, lightly lubricate the transmission shaft with grease.
23   There are two alignments to make when installing the switch. First align the flat on the switch with the flat on the shaft. Second, align the pin on the backside of the switch with the cutout in the transmission housing **(see illustrations)**.
24   Install the E-clip into the groove in the shaft and reconnect the wiring harness connector **(see illustration 27.2)**.

27.23a Install the switch by aligning the two flats (arrows) . . .

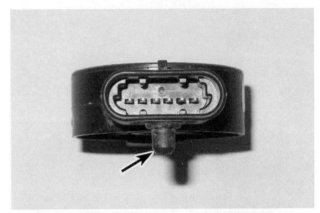

27.23b . . . while inserting the pin (arrow) on the backside of the switch . . .

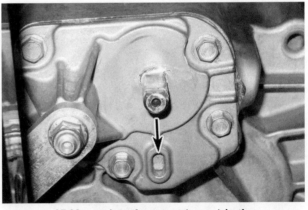

27.23c . . . into the cutout (arrow) in the transmission housing

28   RESISTOR MODULE (2010 AND 2011 MODELS) - TEST AND REPLACEMENT

1   The resistor module is connected to the gear position switch mounted on the transmission. Depending on the transmission gear selection, the instrument cluster on 2010 models, or the ECM on 2011 models interprets the resistance from the resistor module so the correct gear

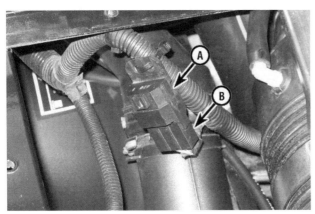

28.3a Resistor module (A) and its wiring harness connector (B) - 2010 model shown

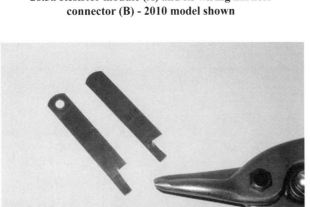

28.3b Cut a section out of two feeler gauges (0.013 in. gauges used here) that are wide enough . . .

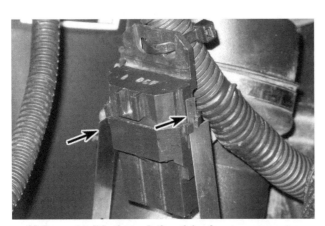

28.3c . . . to slide through the wiring harness connector guides and compress the locks on the resistor module . . .

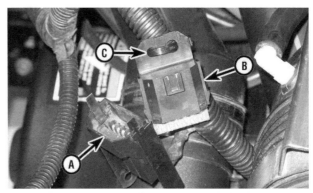

28.3d . . . so you can disconnect the wiring harness connector (A) from the resistor module (B). Then cut the plastic-tie (C) that secures the resistor module to the wiring harness and remove it

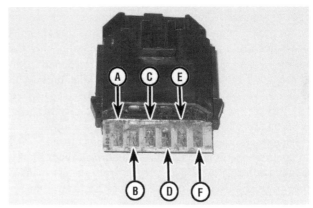

28.4 Resistor module terminal identificaiton

position is displayed on the instrument cluster. If the correct gear position is not displayed on the instrument cluster, test the resistor module to determine if it is the cause of the problem.

2   This test measures the resistance of the different circuits in the resistor module. On 2010 models, the test is made directly at the module terminals. On 2011 models, the test is made at the gear position switch wiring harness connector. The resistance readings for both the 2010 and 2011 resistor modules are the same.

2010 models

3   Disconnect the wiring harness connector at the resistor module **(see illustration)**. Because of how the wiring harness connector locks onto the resistor module, it can be difficult to disconnect the connector from the module. To easily disconnect the wiring harness connector using two modified feeler gauges, follow the accompanying illustrations **(see illustrations 28.3b through 28.3d)**.

4   Use a multimeter set to the ohms scale and connect one test lead across the A terminal on the resistor module - leave this test lead in place when making the following tests. Take the other ohmmeter lead and touch the C (REVERSE), D (NEUTRAL), E (LOW) and F (HIGH) terminals one at a time, and compare each resistance reading to the resistance readings listed in this Chapter's Specifications **(see illustration)**.

NOTE:

Disregard the B (PARK) terminal position on the resistor module.

5   If any one resistance reading is incorrect, the resistor module is faulty and must be replaced.

6   Before installing the resistor module, clean the connector with electrical contact cleaner and allow to dry **(see illustration)**. Then push the resistor module into the connector until it locks in place.

7   Installation is otherwise the reverse of removal.

8   Turn the ignition switch ON and shift the transmission into each gear to make sure the correct gear selection is displayed on the instrument cluster.

2011 models

9   Disconnect the gear position switch wiring harness connector. The resistor module is wired directly to the connector through a sub-wiring harness **(see illustration)**.

10   Using a T-pin, back-probe the white wire at the resistor module. Then with a multimeter set to the ohms scale, connect one test lead across the T-pin - leave this T-pin and test lead in place when making the following tests. Take the other ohmmeter lead, and using a second T-pin, separately back-probe the dark blue (HIGH), yellow (LOW), dark green (NEUTRAL), red (REVERSE) and orange (PARK) terminals in the gear position switch wiring harness connector. Compare each resistance reading to the resistance readings listed in this Chapter's Specifications. Refer to *Measuring tools* in the General Information chapter at the front of this manual for information on T-pins and how to use them to back-probe wires and connectors when making electrical tests **(see illustration)**.

11   If any one resistance reading is incorrect, the resistor module is faulty and must be replaced.

12   If the resistor module is faulty, purchase a new sub-wiring harness with the resistor module attached. Inspect the old and new parts to make sure they are identical, and if not, have a dealer parts department explain the differences before you install the new part. Then remove the old sub-wiring harness and replace it with the new one, making sure to route it following its original path. Make sure all of the connectors are clean before reconnecting them.

13   Installation is otherwise the reverse of removal.

14   Perform Step 8.

29 PARKING BRAKE SWITCH - TEST AND REPLACEMENT

1   The parking brake switch is mounted on the parking brake lever mounting bracket and is accessed from inside the dash. The switch is equipped with a movable arm that rests against the parking brake lever, and depending on the position of the parking brake lever, the arm moves to open and close the switch. When the parking brake lever is applied, the switch closes, signaling the ECU to reduce engine rpm to 1300. At this low rpm, the clutch cannot engage and the vehicle cannot be driven, preventing the parking brake pads and

28.6 Clean the resistor module wiring harness connector before installing the module

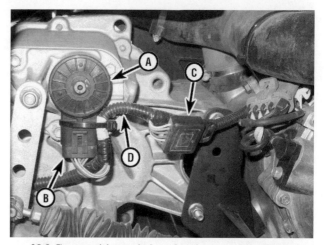

28.9 Gear position switch and resistor module details

A   *Gear position switch*
B   *Wiring harness connector*
C   *Resistor module*
D   *Sub-wiring harness between wiring harness connector and resistor module*

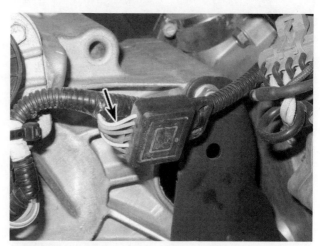

28.10 Back-probe the white resistor module wire (arrow) with a T-pin. The white wire is the resistor module output signal wire to the ECM. Then back-probe each individual wire as described in Step 10

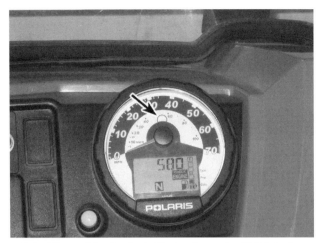

29.1a The parking brake indicator (arrow) will light when theparking brake is applied - 2010 models

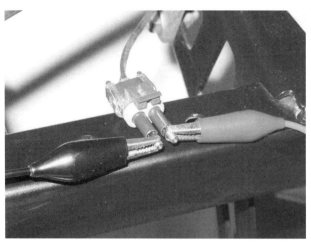

29.4 Ohmmeter test leads connected to the parking brake switch connector terminals

29.1b The word BRAKE appears on the instrument cluster when theparking brake is applied - 2011 and later models

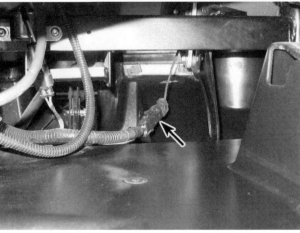

29.3 Parking brake switch wiring harness connector (arrow)

brake disc from overheating. A display on the instrument cluster will indicate when the parking brake is applied **(see illustrations)**.

Test

2   Remove the front cover (see Chapter 14).
3   Working through the left-side headlight area, disconnect the parking brake switch wiring harness connector **(see illustration)**.
4   Test the switch while it is mounted on the parking brake lever. Use a multimeter set to the ohms scale and connect the test leads across the two terminals **(see illustration)** on the switch side connector. There should be continuity with the parking brake lever applied, and no continuity when the lever is released. If the readings are incorrect, clean the connector terminals with electrical contact cleaner, allow to dry, then repeat the test. If the results are the same, the switch is faulty and must be replaced.

Replacement

NOTE:

The parking brake switch is difficult to access with the dash mounted on the vehicle. The following steps show how to remove the switch by working through the headlight opening inside the dash. If you're unable to remove the switch this way, it will be necessary to release the dash and slide it up the cab/frame assembly to access the switch from the top side (see Chapter 14).

5   Park the vehicle on a level surface and shift the transmission into LOW gear. Because it will be necessary to release the parking brake, block the front and rear wheels to prevent the vehicle from rolling.

29.8a The parking brake switch is located behind this frame member (arrow) - dash installed on vehicle

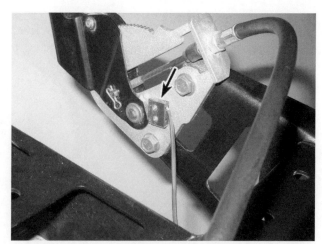

29.8b Here is the parking brake switch (arrow) mounting position on the parking brake lever - dash removed from vehicle

6   Perform Step 2 and Step 3 to disconnect the parking brake switch wiring harness connector.

7   Release the parking brake lever. This will remove tension from the arm on the switch.

8   Remove the two screws securing the parking brake switch to the parking brake lever, and remove the switch **(see illustrations)**.

9   Installation is the reverse of removal. Turn the ignition switch ON, and check the switch operation by applying and releasing the parking brake. When the parking brake is fully applied, the brake display on the instrument cluster should be turned ON **(see illustration 29.1a or illustration 29.1b)**.

30   12 VOLT ACCESSORY OUTLET - REPLACEMENT AND TEST

1   All models are equipped with two 12 volt accessory outlets mounted in the dash panel **(see illustration)**. On Crew models, two additional 12 volt accessory outlets are mounted in the rear mid floor and positioned in front of the rear passenger seat.

2   Disconnect the negative battery cable (see Section 4).

3   On 2010 through 2013 models, if removing one of the front 12 volt accessory outlets, remove the battery to access the outlet so you can push it out of the dash panel (see Section 4).

4   If removing a rear 12 volt accessory outlet on Crew models, remove the front storage box (see Chapter 14).

5   Push the outlet out of the dash panel from the inside out. When removing a rear outlet on Crew models, push it out of the rear mid floor. When the outlet is accessible, disconnect the negative and positive leads from its backside and remove it **(see illustrations)**.

6   Install the outlet by aligning the shoulder on the side of the outlet with the notch in the dash panel or rear mid floor **(see illustration)**.

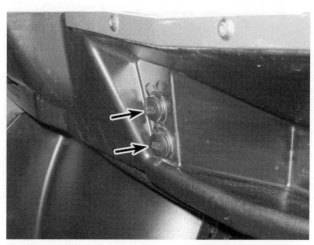

30.1 12 volt accessory outlets mounted in dash panel

30.5a Push the outlet out . . .

30.5b . . . then disconnect the negative (A) and positive (B) terminals and remove the outlet

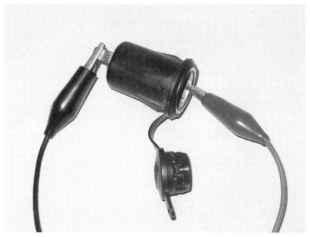

30.9b Testing the negative terminal end-to-end - there should be continuity

30.6 Install the outlet by inserting its shoulder into the notch (arrow) in the dash panel or rear mid floor

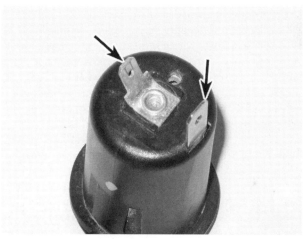

30.9c Check for continuity across positive and negative terminals (arrows) - there should be no continuity

7   Installation is otherwise the reverse of removal. Plug an accessory power plug into the outlet to make sure it powers the accessory device correctly.

Test

8   Perform Steps 2 through 5 to remove the 12 volt accessory outlet.

9   Test the outlet with an ohmmeter or a continuity test light by checking for continuity on both sides of the positive terminal, and then on both sides of the negative terminal. There should be continuity during each test, indicating the terminals are not corroded or broken. Then test for continuity between the positive and negative terminals. There should be no continuity. Replace the outlet if it failed any one test **(see illustrations)**.

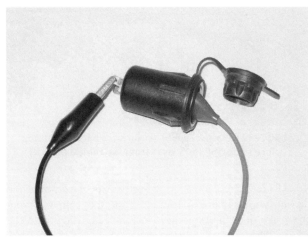

30.9a Testing the positive terminal end-to-end - there should be continuity

31 WHEEL SPEED SENSOR (2010 MODELS) - CHECK AND REPLACEMENT

Check

1   If the speedometer needle on the instrument cluster fails to register the correct vehicle speed, check the wheel speed sensor operation. If you don't have access to the special tools, have a dealer service department check the wheel speed sensor.

2   Special Tools:The Polaris static timing light harness (part No. 2871745) and the hall sensor probe harness (part No. 2460761) are required for this test. Three jumpers wires can be used in place of the hall sensor probe harness. Make sure the 9 volt battery used to power the static timing light harness is fully charged.

3   Park the vehicle on a level surface and apply the parking brake. Raise the vehicle front end and secure both sides with jackstands. During the test, it is necessary to rotate the right front wheel.

4   Trace the wheel speed sensor wiring harness from the sensor to its connector, then disconnect the connector from the wiring harness. Identify the A, B and C terminals on the vehicle speed sensor wiring harness connector. Look for the A, B and C marks on the connector and how the connector is labeled on the wiring diagram (see Section 40).

5   If using the hall sensor probe harness, connect it between the wheel speed sensor wiring harness connector and the static timing light harness.

6   If using jumper wires, connect the first jumper wire between the wheel speed sensor wiring harness connector A terminal and the BROWN wire on the static timing light harness. Connect the second jumper wire between the B connector terminal and the WHITE wire. Connect the third jumper wire between the C connector terminal and the BLACK wire.

7   Turn the right front wheel by hand. If the light on the static timing light harness flashes, the vehicle speed sensor is in good condition. If necessary, have the test confirmed by a dealer service department.

Replacement

8   Park the vehicle on a level surface and apply the parking brake. If the right front wheel will be left on the vehicle, turn the steering wheel to the right side so the wheel speed sensor is accessible.

NOTE:
If you're only removing the wheel speed sensor to service the brake caliper, it is not necessary to cut the plastic ties that secure the sensor to the brake hose.

9   Remove the speed sensor mounting screw, then remove the speed sensor from the caliper. Remove the cover and plate from the speed sensor to prevent their loss. Do not cut the plastic ties securing the speed sensor wiring harness to the brake hose, unless necessary **(see illustrations)**.

31.9a Remove the mounting screw (A) and the wheel speed sensor (B) from the front right caliper . . .

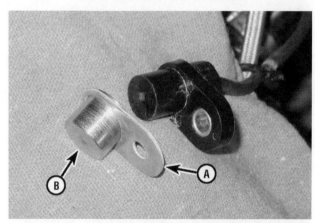

31.9b . . . then remove the plate (A) and cover (B) from the wheel speed sensor

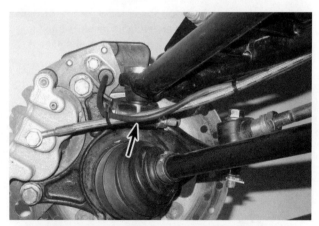

31.10 Note the wheel speed sensor wire harness routing before removing the sensor from the vehicle (arrow)

10 If you're replacing the wheel speed sensor, note the sensor wiring harness routing from the caliper, along the brake hose, and to where its connector plugs into the wiring harness **(see illustration)**. Then cut the plastic-ties, disconnect the connector and remove the wheel speed sensor and its wiring harness.

11 Installation is the reverse of removal. Support the

32.5 Vehicle speed sensor A, B and C terminals

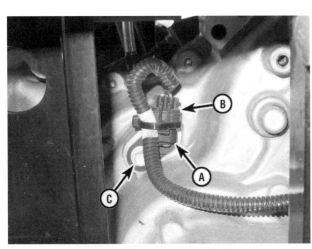

32.7 Vehicle speed sensor details

A Vehicle speed sensor
B Wiring harness connector
C Mounting screw

32.8 Vehicle speed sensor and O-ring (arrow)

vehicle on jackstands with the front wheels off the ground (see Step 3). Turn the steering wheel to make sure there is adequate slack in the wheel speed sensor wiring harness at the caliper. If the wiring harness pulls or binds when the steering wheel is turned, reposition it along its routing path to obtain the necessary amount of slack.

32 VEHICLE SPEED SENSOR (2011 AND LATER MODELS) - CHECK AND REPLACEMENT

Check

1   If the display on the instrument cluster fails to display the correct speedometer reading, check the vehicle speed sensor operation. If you don't have access to the special tools, have a dealer service department check the vehicle speed sensor.

2   Special Tools: The Polaris static timing light harness (part No. 2871745) and the hall sensor probe harness (part No. 2460761) are required for this test. Three jumpers wires can be used in place of the hall sensor probe harness. Make sure the 9 volt battery used to power the static timing light harness is fully charged.

3   Remove the vehicle speed sensor from the transmission (see Step 7).

4   If using the hall sensor probe harness, connect it between the vehicle speed sensor wiring harness connector and the static timing light harness.

5   If using jumper wires, identify the A, B and C terminals on the vehicle speed sensor (see illustration). Connect the first jumper wire between the vehicle speed sensor wiring harness connector A terminal and the BROWN wire on the static timing light harness. Connect the second jumper wire between the B connector terminal and the WHITE wire. Connect the third jumper wire between the C connector terminal and the BLACK wire.

6   Pass a screwdriver back and forth in front of the sensor tip. If the light on the static timing light harness flashes, the vehicle speed sensor is in good condition. If necessary, have the test confirmed by a dealer service department.

Replacement

7   Clean the area around the speed sensor to prevent dirt from entering the transmission. Then disconnect the wiring harness connector at the speed sensor. Remove the screw and slide the vehicle speed sensor out of the transmission (see illustration).

8   If installing the original vehicle speed sensor, replace the O-ring if leaking or damaged (see illustration). Lubricate the O-ring with gear oil and install the sensor by twisting it into the transmission to prevent from tearing its O-ring. Align the mounting hole on the sensor with the transmission, then install and tighten the mounting screw securely. Reconnect the wiring harness connector.

33.1a AWD indicator (2010 model)

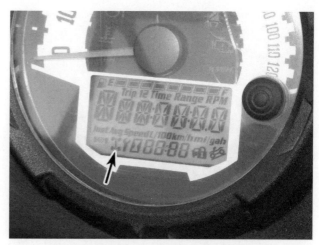

33.1b AWD indicator (2011 and later models)

33 ALL WHEEL DRIVE (AWD) COIL - TESTING AND REPLACEMENT

1   All of the vehicles in this manual are equipped with all wheel drive (AWD). When the AWD switch is turned ON, the AWD function is active and the AWD icon is displayed on the instrument cluster **(see illustrations)**. When the AWD drive switch is turned ON, the front gearcase engages and the front wheels become drive wheels if the rear wheels lose traction. Once the rear wheels regain traction, the front gearcase disengages. This is accomplished through the AWD coil installed in the front gearcase.

2   If AWD will not engage, make the following resistance and voltage tests to help isolate the problem as either electrical or mechanical.

3   Park the vehicle on a level surface and apply the parking brake.

4   At the front gearcase, trace its wiring harness and disconnect the AWD coil wiring harness connector **(see illustration)**.

5   Using a multimeter set to the ohms scale, measure the resistance between the grey and brown/white terminals on the coil side of the connector **(see illustration)**. Compare the reading with the value listed in this Chapter's Specifications. If the reading is incorrect, the AWD coil must be replaced.

6   If the reading in Step 5 is correct, shift the transmission into either LOW or HIGH gear. Turn the ignition and AWD switches ON. Using a voltmeter, check for battery voltage between the grey and brown/white terminals on the wiring harness side connector. If the voltage is less than battery voltage, check the wiring harness connector for poor contact and corroded terminals. If the connector is good, check the grey and brown/white wires for a short or open circuit.

7   If the AWD drive resistance and voltage tests are correct, and the AWD switch (see Section 24) is good, the front gearcase will have to be disassembled to inspect the AWD coil assembly for excessive wear and/or damage. Remove the front gearcase (see Chapter 11) and take the unit to a dealer service department for disassembly and inspection.

33.4 Disconnect the AWD coil wiring harness connector (arrow)

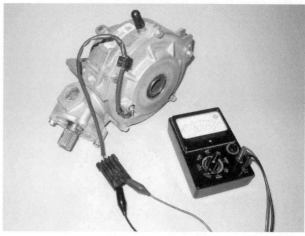

33.5 Testing the AWD coil resistance with an ohmmeter (front gearcase removed for clarity)

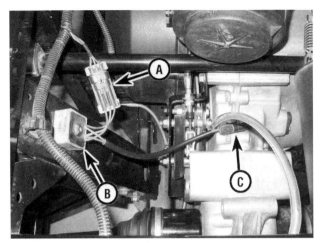

34.4 Rear differential solenoid relay details

A   Solenoid relay-to-main wiring harness connector
B   Rear differential solenoid relay
C   Solenoid relay-to-rear differential solenoid wiring
      harness connector

34.8 Rear differential solenoid (arrow)

34   REAR DIFFERENTIAL SOLENOID - TESTING, REMOVAL AND INSTALLATION

1   All models are equipped with a TURF mode that is controlled by a rear differential solenoid mounted on the right side of the transmission, a clutch gear and yoke installed in the transmission, and a separate rear differential solenoid relay. When the TURF mode on the AWD switch is selected, the ECU grounds the rear gearcase relay. This energizes the relay, and the relay supplies power to the solenoid. When powered, the solenoid unlocks the rear gearcase to reduce steering effort for greater maneuverability and to minimize damage to sensitive terrain. AWD and 2WD modes are also available. All three modes (AWD, 2WD and TURF) are controlled by the AWD switch.

Testing

2   If the transmission does not respond to the different traction modes, first test the AWD switch (see Section 24). If the switch is okay, continue with Step 3.
3   Raise the cargo bed.
4   Disconnect the electrical connectors at the rear differential solenoid relay and check both harness connectors for loose terminals, corrosion and damage **(see illustration)**.
5   Turn the ignition switch ON, and using a multimeter set to the volts scale, make sure the main wiring harness side connector is receiving voltage when the AWD switch is in the TURF mode. Refer to the test information in Section 24 and to the appropriate wiring diagram in Section 40 to identify the relay connectors and wiring colors.

CAUTION:

In Step 6, do not apply battery voltage to the solenoid for more than one second; otherwise, the solenoid may be damaged.

6   If there is voltage at the connector, remove the solenoid (see Steps 7 and 8). Using a fully charged 12 volt battery, momentarily apply battery voltage directly to the solenoid wiring harness connector terminals. When voltage is applied, the plunger on the end of the solenoid should move. If the plunger failed to operate as described, replace the solenoid.

Removal and installation

7   Raise the cargo box.
8   Disconnect the rear differential solenoid wiring harness connector **(see illustration 34.4)**. Then use a wrench and loosen and remove the solenoid from the transmission **(see illustration)**.
9   Check the plunger tip on the end of the solenoid. The tip should be round. If the tip is flat or appears damaged, discard the solenoid.
10   Replace the solenoid O-ring if leaking or damaged.
11   Installation is the reverse of removal. Lubricate the solenoid O-ring with gear oil. Tighten the rear differential solenoid to the torque listed in this Chapter's Specifications.

35   ELECTRIC POWER STEERING (EPS) - GENERAL INFORMATION AND TROUBLESHOOTING

General information

1   Electric power steering (EPS) is available on some models. This system uses an electric power steering unit installed between the upper and lower steering shafts (see Chapter 11, Section 5). The lower steering shaft is then connected directly to the steering gearbox. Other

8

components include a system fuse, one or two relays, diagnostic connector and related wiring to the instrument cluster and engine control unit (ECU).

2   The system uses input torque at the steering column and output torque at the front wheels as the basis for determining the correct amount of steering assistance to be applied by the electric power steering unit. Power is supplied by the vehicle's 12 volt battery.

3   The EPS system constantly monitors battery voltage, engine speed and the vehicle speed at the front wheels. If the EPS fuse blows, the battery voltage is too low or high, or a component in the EPS system fails, the EPS fault indicator (2010 models) or the power steering malfunction indicator on the instrument cluster (2011 and later models) will illuminate. When the indicator is turned on, power steering is shut down and the vehicle resorts to mechanical steering.

4   It is important to note that to conserve battery power, the EPS system will shut down when the ignition key is left in the ON position for five minutes when the engine is not running. When this happens, the EPS fault indicator (2010 models) or power steering malfunction indicator (2011 and later models) will illuminate. To restart power steering, it is necessary to turn the ignition switch OFF, then turn it ON and restart the engine.

5   If the power steering unit does not work, first make sure the battery is fully charged and the 30A EPS fuse is good. If both are OK and the power steering still does not work, before troubleshooting the EPS system, take the vehicle to a dealer service department and have them reflash the power steering unit. A reflash may solve the problem and prevent unnecessary troubleshooting and the replacement of parts that are still in good condition. If reflashing the system does not correct the problem, troubleshoot the system as described in Steps 6 through 31, depending on model.

Troubleshooting

6   When the power steering shuts down, note whether the EPS fault indicator (2010 models) or the power steering malfunction indicator (2011 and later models) is illuminated **(see illustrations)**. Then refer to the appropriate section to troubleshoot the system.

7   When troubleshooting, refer to the correct wiring diagram to identify the wire color codes, connectors, fuse, fusible link, and relay(s) used in the EPS system (see Section 40).

8   If it is thought the EPS relay is bad, remove and replace it with a known good relay. You can either install a new relay, or quickly use one of the other relays from the fuse box. If the system now works, the relay was the problem. If not, troubleshoot the system as described. Refer to Section 37 for additional information on fuses, relays and fusible links.

Indicator OFF (power steering not functional)

2010 models

9   Turn the ignition wwitch ON and measure battery voltage, then turn the ignition switch OFF. The voltage

35.6a EPS fault indicator (2010 models)

**35.6b Power steering malfunction indicator
(2011 and later models)**

reading should be greater than 12 volts when the ignition switch is turned ON. If the voltage reading is less than 12 volts, test the battery to determine its condition. See Section 5.

10   If the battery voltage is good, turn the ignition switch ON and note if the EPS fault indicator illuminated for one second **(see illustration 35.6a)**.

11   If the EPS fault indicator did illuminate for one second, take the vehicle to a dealer service department and have them check the system with their diagnostic tester.

12   If the EPS fault indicator did not illuminate, remove the EPS fault relay from its socket (see Section 37). Use a multimeter set to the ohms scale and check for continuity between relay terminals 87a and 30 (the numbers are marked on the relay). If there is no continuity, replace the relay.

13   If the EPS fault indicator did not illuminate, make the following test at the EPS fault relay wiring harness socket

(relay was disconnected in Step 12). Switch an ohmmeter to the volts scale and connect its test leads across the relay's wiring harness socket red/white and white/black terminals. Turn the ignition switch ON while reading the voltmeter. There should be no voltage for one second after the ignition switch is turned ON, then the voltmeter should read battery voltage. Turn the voltmeter off. If the readings were incorrect, check each wire between the EPS fault relay socket and the power steering unit 8-pin connector for an open circuit. Also check for any loose, corroded or damaged socket terminals.

14   If the voltage test in Step 13 was correct, test the EPS fault indicator (see Section 36).

2011 and later models

15   Perform Step 9 to measure battery voltage.

16   If the battery voltage is correct, check for a blown EPS fuse and replace if necessary (Section 37).

17   If battery voltage is correct and the EPS fuse is good, disconnect the 2-pin wiring harness connector at the power steering unit. Turn the ignition switch ON, and using a multimeter set on the volts scale, check for battery voltage across the wiring harness side connector orange and brown terminals.

18   If battery voltage is not present, replace the EPS relay (see Section 37). If the EPS relay is good, check the orange wire between the EPS relay socket and the power steering unit 2-pin connector for an open circuit. If okay, check the red wire between the EPS relay socket and the 30A EPS fuse for an open circuit. If the orange and red wires are okay, check the brown wire (ground) at the EPS relay socket for an open circuit.

19   If battery voltage at the 2-pin EPS wiring harness connector is present, disconnect the 8-pin wiring harness connector at the power steering unit. Turn the ignition switch ON and using a multimeter set to the volts scale, check for battery voltage at the orange terminal (No. 3) on the wiring harness side connector. If voltage is not present, check the wiring harness from the connector to the ignition switch for an open circuit. If the wiring is good, check the ignition switch wiring harness for an open or short circuit (see Section 26).

20   If the problem has not been found after performing Steps 15 through 19, turn the ignition switch ON while observing the instrument cluster, then start the engine. The EPS malfunction indicator should illuminate when the ignition switch is turned to the ON position and turn OFF when the engine starts and runs.

21   If the EPS malfunction indicator performed as described in Step 20, take the vehicle to a dealer service department and have them check the EPS system with their diagnostic tester.

Indicator ON (power steering not functional)

2010 models

22   Perform Step 9 to measure battery voltage.

23   If battery voltage is good, check for a blown 30A EPS

fuse (see Section 37).

24   If the fuse is blown, install a new fuse and check the system operation again. If the fuse blows again, check the B+ wire between the terminal block and the EPS relay red (#30) wire at the relay connector for a short circuit.

25   If the fuse is good, disconnect the 2-pin wiring harness connector at the power steering unit. Turn the ignition switch ON, and using a multimeter set on the voltage scale, check for battery voltage across the red (+) and black (-) terminals on the wiring harness side connector.

26   If battery voltage was not present in Step 25, reconnect the 2-pin wiring harness connector at the power steering unit. Locate the EPS relay underneath the dash but do not disconnect it (see Section 37). Turn the ignition switch ON. When doing so, the EPS relay should click. Turn the ignition switch OFF. If the relay did not click, remove the EPS relay from its connector. Use a multimeter set to the volts scale and connect the test leads across the relay connector red/white (#85) and brown (#86) terminals. Turn the ignition switch ON and read the voltmeter. The voltmeter should read battery voltage with the ignition switch ON. If not, check the red/white and the brown wires for an open circuit. If there is voltage, check for voltage between connector red (#30) terminal and ground. There should be battery voltage when the ignition switch is turned ON and OFF. If not, check the red wire between the connector and the 30 amp power steering fuse for an open circuit. If the tests are correct, replace the relay.

27   If battery voltage was present in Step 25 disconnect the 8-pin wiring harness connector at the power steering unit and check for voltage between the red/white (No. 3) terminal on the wiring harness side connector and ground. If there is no voltage present, check for a blown 20A chassis fuse (see Section 37). If the fuse is good, check the red/white wire in the 8-pin connector for an open or short circuit. If the red/white wire is good, check the ignition switch (see Section 26). If voltage is present, take the vehicle to a dealer service department and have them check the EPS system with their diagnostic tester.

2011 and later models

28   Perform Steps 15 through 19 to make sure the battery is fully charged and there is voltage present at the power steering unit 2-pin and 8-pin wiring harness side connectors. If the battery is in good condition and there is voltage at both connectors, take the vehicle to a dealer service department and have them check the EPS system with their diagnostic tester.

Indicator ON (power steering functional)

2010 models

29   Disconnect the EPS fault lamp relay from its wiring harness socket (see Section 37).

30   Perform the voltage test in Step 13. If voltage is present as described (battery voltage present one second after turning the ignition switch ON), continue with Step 31. If voltage was not present, take the vehicle to a dealer

service department and have them check the EPS system with their diagnostic tester.

31   Remove the EPS fault relay from its socket underneath the dash (see Section 37). Turn the relay over and note the terminal numbers on the relay housing. Switch a multimeter to its ohms scale and measure the resistance across the No. 85 and No. 86 relay terminals and compare to the value listed in this Chapter's Specifications. Then check for continuity across the No. 30 and No. 87A terminals. Continuity should be present. If either test result was incorrect, replace the relay.

32   If you replaced the relay and the problem still occurs, take the vehicle to a dealer service department and have them check the EPS system with their diagnostic tester.

36   ELECTRONIC POWER STEERING (EPS) FAULT INDICATOR (2010 MODELS WITH EPS) - TEST AND REPLACEMENT

Test

1   The EPS fault indicator is mounted in the instrument panel and should illuminate for one second when the ignition switch is turned ON and then turn OFF (see illustration 35.6a).

2   If the indicator did not illuminate for one second, turn the the ignition switch OFF. Working inside the dashboard, disconnect the wiring harness connector at the EPS fault indicator. Use a multimeter set to the ohms scale and measure the resistance across pin 7 (white wire) and pin 8 (brown wire) on the EPS fault indicator. Resistance should be less than the resistance reading listed in this Chapter's Specifications. If not, replace the indicator.

3   The EPS fault indicator can also be checked by applying voltage directly across pin 7 (+) and pin 8 (-). The indicator should illuminate when voltage is applied. If not, replace the indicator.

4   If the indicator tested correctly, check its white and brown wires for a short or open circuit.

Replacement

5   Remove the instrument panel (see Chapter 14).

6   Disconnect the wiring harness connector at the EPS fault indicator **(see illustration 35.6a)**.

7   Compress the clips holding the EPS fault indicator in place in the dash, and push it forward to remove it.

8   Installation is the reverse of removal. Turn the ignition switch ON and check the EPS fault indicator operation.

37   CIRCUIT PROTECTION AND RELAYS

1   The electrical system is protected by a circuit breaker, fusible links, fuses and relays. To determine the circuit protection used on your model, refer to the appropriate

37.2 Circuit breaker location (2010 model shown)

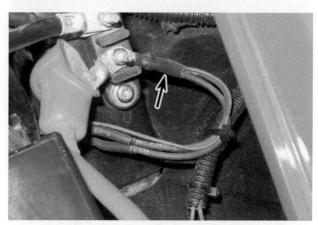

37.6 Typical fusible links (arrow) attached to the terminal block

wiring diagram in Section 40. Circuit breaker and fuse ratings are listed in this Chapter's Specifications.

Circuit breaker

2   The circuit breaker is installed in the wiring harness leading into the fuse box **(see illustration)**.

3   If the circuit breaker trips repeatedly, check the wiring for a short.

4   Never, under any circumstances, use a higher rated circuit breaker or bridge the breaker terminals as damage to the electrical system, or even a fire, could result.

5   Occasionally a circuit breaker will trip for no obvious reason. Corrosion on the circuit breaker terminals may occur and cause poor contact. If that happens, remove the corrosion with a wire brush or emery paper, then spray the terminals with electrical contact cleaner.

Fusible links

6   A fusible link is a length of thin wire in a thicker wire **(see illustration)**. It is designed to melt if overheated, cutting off current flow in the circuit to prevent damage to the wiring.

7   Fusible links are mounted between the solenoid

37.10a Fuse box location near the battery with cover installed and label identifying fuses and relays

37.10b Fuses and relays

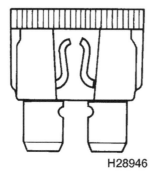

H28946

37.11 A blown fuse can be identified by a break in its element

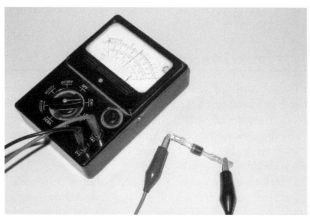

38.2 Set-up for testing the 6 amp diode (2011 model shown)

(positive battery cable side) and different electrical devices, depending on model. See the appropriate wiring diagram in Section 40 to identify the fusible links used on your model and what circuits they protect.

8   If the insulation of a fusible link is swollen or discolored, disconnect the negative battery cable at the battery. Then check the fusible link for continuity with an ohmmeter or test light.

9   Replacement fusible links are sized for specific amperage ratings. If you replace a fusible link, be sure to install the correct size as determined by a dealer parts department. Never, under any circumstances, use a higher rated fusible link.

Fuses

10   The circuit fuses are mounted in the fuse box, located underneath the hood (see illustrations). A label on the fuse box cover identifies the fuses and relays installed in the fuse box. Fuse ratings are also listed in this Chapter's Specifications. To identify a fuse not located in the fuse box, refer to the wiring diagram for your model (see Section 40).

11   The fuses can be removed and checked visually. If you can't pull the fuse out with your fingertips, use a pair of needle-nose pliers. A blown fuse is easily identified by a break in the element (see illustration). A spare fuse of each rating is installed in the fuse box and can be identified by the label on the fuse box cover. When a spare fuse is used, always replace it with a new one so that a spare of each rating is carried on the vehicle at all times.

NOTE:
On 2010 models with electric power steering (EPS), a 120 ohm resistor is mounted in the fuse box. This resistor is required for use with the OEM diagnostic tester when it is plugged into the diagnostic connector during trouble-shooting.

12   On 2010 models with EPS, the fuse is referred to as the steering fuse. On 2011 and later models, the fuse is referred to as the EPS fuse. On all model years, the fuse is mounted in the fuse box.

13   On 2012 and later models, the EPS fuse is located in separate fuse holder. Start at the power steering unit and trace the wiring harness until you locate the fuse holder.

WARNING:
Never substitute any metal object for a fuse. Never use a higher amperage fuse than specified. An overload could cause a fire and the complete loss of the vehicle.

14   If a fuse blows, be sure to check the wiring circuit very carefully for evidence of a short-circuit. Look for bare wires and chafed, melted or burned insulation. If the fuse is replaced before the cause is located, the new fuse will blow immediately.

15   Occasionally a fuse will blow for no obvious reason. Corrosion of the fuse ends and fuse box terminals may occur and cause poor fuse contact. If a fuse blows and the cause cannot be determined, check for and remove corrosion with a wire brush, then spray the fuse ends and terminals with electrical contact cleaner.

Relays

16   Several electrical accessories in the vehicle, such as the fuel injection system and fan, use relays to transmit the electrical signal to the component. Relays use a low-current circuit (the control circuit) to open and close a high-current circuit (the power circuit). If the relay is defective, that component will not operate properly.

17   Relays installed in the fuse box are identified on the fuse box label **(see illustration 37.10a)**. To identify relays not located in the fuse box, refer to the wiring diagram for your model (see Section 40).

18   The relays are easily unplugged or plugged into the relay terminal strip **(see illustration 37.10b)** or in a separate relay socket. Because only 4-terminal and 5-terminal relays are used, there is no danger of installing a relay in the wrong position. The 4-terminal relays are identical, and the 5-terminal relays are identical.

19   On 2010 models, the EPS relay and the EPS fault relay are located underneath the dash and accessed from inside the driver's compartment. Start at the power steering unit and trace the wiring harness until you locate the relay sockets.

20   On 2011 models, the EPS relay is located in the fuse box.

21   On 2012 and later models, the EPS relay is located in a separate socket. Start at the power steering unit and trace the wiring harness until you locate the EPS relay socket.

22   A questionable relay can be quickly checked by exchanging it with a known good relay. To do this, first identify the relay as a 4-terminal or 5-terminal type. Unplug the relay and plug in the new relay.

38   DIODES (2011 AND LATER MODELS) - GENERAL INFORMATION AND TESTING

1   On 2011 and later models, a 6 amp diode is installed in the ignition switch circuit. On 2011 models, the diode is located underneath the fuse box. On 2012 and later models, the diode is plugged into the wiring harness. See the appropriate wiring diagram in Section 40 on how the diode is connected in the wiring harness.

2   To test a diode, disconnect and remove the diode. Set a multimeter to the ohms R x 1 scale. Connect the test leads across the two diode leads and check for continuity **(see illustration)**. Then reverse the test leads and check for continuity in the opposite direction. If the diode is in good condition, there should be continuity or a small resistance reading in one direction and no continuity when the test leads are reversed. If not, replace the diode.

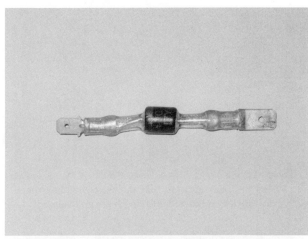

38.3 The 6 amp diode used on 2011 models - note the different size terminal ends

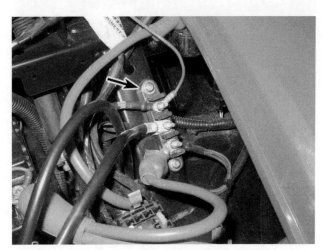

39.1 Typical insulated block with attached wires and cables (2010 model shown)

3   When installing the 6 amp diode on 2011 models, note that terminals on each end of the diode are a different size **(see illustration)**. When installing the diode, make sure to match the correct terminals with the matching connectors.

39   TERMINAL BLOCK

1   An insulated terminal block is installed under the hood and used to connect different circuits together. The block is equipped with several integral studs that allow individual wires and cables equipped with ring type blade connectors to be secured in place with nylon locknuts **(see illustration)**.

2   Before disconnecting a wire or cable from the terminal block, disconnect the negative battery cable at the battery (see Section 4). Then identify the wires on the terminal

you will be removing them from as you want to make sure they are returned to their original position. If necessary, refer to the wiring diagram for your model to identify the circuits and how they are grouped on the terminal block (see Section 40).

3   Periodically check the wire and cable ends mounted onto the terminal block for corrosion, and if necessary, remove and clean them with a wire brush.

40 COLOR WIRING DIAGRAMS

1   Color wiring diagrams are included at the end of this manual for all models. When selecting a wiring diagram, look for the title that matches the vehicle you are working on. Models covered in this manual are listed in the Specifications at the front of this manual. For the most part, complete wiring diagrams are shown. When necessary, wiring diagrams identifying separate circuits are used. When selecting a wiring diagram, always check to see if a separate circuit diagram is used.

2   When working on an unfamiliar vehicle, check for any electrical accessories that may have been added by a previous owner, as any additional wiring required for these accessories is not shown on the diagrams.

3   While the wiring diagrams are in color, the following list indicates the wire coding for the Polaris models covered in this manual, listing both the wire colors and their letter code:

Beige or tan - BG

Black - BK

Brown - BN

Clear- CL

Dark blue - DB

Dark green - DG

Gray - GY

Light blue - BU

Light green - GN

Orange - OG

Pink - PK

Red -RD

Violet or purple - VT

White - WH

Yellow - YE

8

SPECIFICATIONS

Battery specifications

Type and capacity
    Stock (conventional battery)...................... Yuasa YB30L-B, 12V, 30Ah
    Battery upgrade (maintenance-free batteries)......... Yuasa GYZ32HL, YIX30L, YIX30L-BS
Open circuit voltage (static test)
    Yuasa YB30L-B (conventional battery type) .... 12.7 volts or higher
    Maintenance-free battery type .... 12.8 volts or higher
Charging time
    Conventional battery.......................... 3 to 5 hours @ 3.0A or when specific gravity reading is 1.270 or higher
    Maintenance-free battery .... See separate Table in this Section

Battery state of charge - conventional batteries

State of charge		Specific gravity	5-ball hydrometer	Digital voltmeter*
100%	....	1.265-1.280	4 or 5 balls floating	12.70
75%	....	1.210	3 balls floating	12.50 volts
50%	....	1.160	2 balls floating	12.20 volts
25%	....	1.120	1 ball floating	12.0 volts
0-25%	....	1.100 or less	0 balls floating	Less than 11.90 volts

*100 percent charge for Yuasa batteries with Sulfate Stop is 12.80 volts. For other conventional batteries, 12.65 volts is usually considered fully charged. Always refer to the battery manufacturer's specifications for specific state of charge information

Battery state of charge - maintenance-free batteries

State of charge		Digital voltmeter
State of charge	....	Digital voltmeter
100%	....	12.8-13.0 volts
75-100%	....	12.5-12.8 volts
50-75%	....	12.0-12.5 volts
25-50%	....	11.5-12.0 volts
0-25%	....	11.5 volts or less

Maintenance-free battery charging times

State of charge/battery type		Voltage reading	Approximate charging time
100%			
30Ah	....	12.8 or higher	Not required*
75-100%			
30Ah	....	12.6-12.8	3-6 hours
50-75%			
30Ah	....	12.3-12.6	5-11 hours
25-50%			
30Ah	....	12.0-12.3	13 hours minimum
0-25%			
30Ah	....	12.0 or less	20 hours minium

*Consider the battery fully charged if it maintains this voltage reading after it has been removed from the charger for 1 to 2 hours.

Charging system

Alternator maximum output	500 watts @3000 rpm
Break even test rpm	See text
Current draw	10 mA (maximum)
Charging voltage	13.0-14.6 volts @ 3000-4000 rpm
Stator coil resistance	
2012 and earlier models	0.16-0.22 ohms
2013 and later models	0.19-0.25 ohms
Stator coil AC voltage	
2010 through 2012 models	
1300 rpm	13.5-22.5 volts AC
3000 rpm	31-53 volts AC
5000 rpm	48-80 volts AC
2013 and later models	
1300 rpm	16.5-27.5 volts AC
3000 rpm	37-61 volts AC
5000 rpm	60-100 volts AC

Starter

Brush length service limit	0.312 inch (8 mm)

Starter relay

Starter relay resistance	0-0.5 ohms

Bulb specifications

Headlights	
2010 models	50W x 2
2011 and later models	60/55W x 2
Taillight/brake light assembly	
Type	LED
Capacity	
Brake light	3.1W
Taillight	0.3W

Gear position switch test specifications - 2012 and later models

Transmission gear position	Resistance reading
Reverse	300 ohms
Neutral	160 ohms
Low	75 ohms
High	24 ohms

Resistor module test specifications - 2010 and 2011 models

Transmission gear position	Resistance reading
Reverse	75 ohms
Neutral	160 ohms
Low	300 ohms
High	620 ohms

All wheel drive (AWD) test specification

All wheel drive (AWD) resistance	21.6-26.4 ohms

EPS fault relay - 2010 models

EPS relay resistance	111-135 ohms

SPECIFICATIONS (continued)

EPS fault indicator - 2010 models

EPS fault indicator resistance . . . .   150 ohms

Circuit breaker rating

2010 models . . . .   15 amp
2011 and later models . . . .   20 amp

Fuses

2010 models
    Accessory . . . .   15 amp
    ECU . . . .   15 amp
    EFI . . . .   15 amp
    Lights . . . .   15 amp
    Main chassis . . . .   20 amp
    EPS* . . . .   30 amp
2011 and later models
    Accessory . . . .   20 amp
    Drive . . . .   20 amp
    ECU . . . .   20 amp
    EPS* . . . .   30 amp
    Fuel pump . . . .   10 amp
    Lights . . . .   20 amp
*Models equipped with electric power steering (EPS)

Circuits protected by relays

2010 models . . . .   Brake light, EFI, EPS, fan and rear diff
2011 and later models . . . .   Chassis, ECM, EPS, fan, fuel pump and rear diff

Torque specifications	Ft-lbs	In.-lb	Nm

NOTE

One foot-pound (ft-lb) of torque is equivalent to 12 inch-pounds (in-lbs) of torque. Torque values below approximately 15 ft-lbs are expressed in inch-pounds, because most foot-pound torque wrenches are not accurate at these smaller values.

	Ft-lbs	In.-lb	Nm
Rear differential solenoid	23-27	--	31-37
Starter assembly screws	--	35-52	4.0-5.9
Starter mounting fasteners			
2010 models	9	--	12
2011 and later models	7	--	9.5

CHAPTER NINE

COOLING SYSTEM

CONTENTS

9

1 GENERAL INFORMATION

1   The models covered by this manual are liquid-cooled. The liquid-cooling system uses a water/antifreeze mixture to carry away excess heat produced during engine operation. The water pump impeller is mounted on the MAG side of the engine and is driven by the oil pump shaft. The rotating impeller pumps coolant through a channel formed by the water pump cover and stator housing, where it flows through the water jackets surrounding the cylinder block and cylinder head. When the thermostat is open, coolant passes through the thermostat and travels up into the radiator (which is mounted at the front of the vehicle, to take advantage of maximum air flow), where it is cooled by the passing air, then flows through another hose back to the water pump, where the cycle is repeated. On standard Ranger models, long flexible hoses connect the radiator to the engine. On Crew models, long aluminum pipes with a flexible hose on each end connect the radiator to the engine.

2   An electric fan, mounted behind the radiator and automatically controlled by the engine coolant temperature (ECT) sensor mounted in the cylinder head, provides a flow of cooling air through the radiator when the coolant temperature exceeds a specified limit.

3   The ECT sensor senses the temperature of the coolant and signals the information to the ECU. At a specified temperature, the ECU closes the fan relay circuit, which turns the fan on. When the coolant temperature reaches a dangerous level, the ECU turns on a warning indicator on the instrument cluster to warn the driver the engine is overheating. On 2010 models, the word HOT appears on the check engine warning indicator. On 2011 and later models, when the engine begins to overheat, the engine temperature indicator will flash. When the engine overheating condition becomes severe, the indicator will stop flashing and remain ON.

4   Refer to Chapter 7 to service and test the ECT sensor.

5   The fan circuit is protected by a 15-amp (2010 models) or a 20-amp (2011 and later models) circuit breaker.

6   The entire system is sealed and pressurized. The pressure is controlled by a valve which is part of the radiator cap. By pressurizing the coolant, the boiling point is raised, which prevents premature boiling of the coolant. An overflow hose, connected between the radiator and reservoir tank, directs coolant to the tank when the radiator cap valve is opened by excessive pressure. The coolant is automatically siphoned back to the radiator as the engine cools.

7   Many cooling system inspection and service

procedures are considered part of routine maintenance and are included in Chapter 2.

WARNING:

Do not allow antifreeze to come in contact with your skin or painted surfaces of the vehicle. Rinse off spills immediately with plenty of water. Antifreeze is highly toxic if ingested. Never leave antifreeze lying around in an open container or in puddles on the floor; children and pets are attracted by its sweet smell and may drink it. Check with local authorities about disposing of used antifreeze. Many communities have collection centers which will see that antifreeze is disposed of safely.

WARNING:

Do not remove the radiator cap when the engine and radiator are hot. Scalding hot coolant and steam may be blown out under pressure, which could cause serious injury. To open the radiator cap, remove the rear screw from the right side panel on the inside of the fairing (if equipped). When the engine has cooled, lift up the panel and place a thick rag, like a towel, over the radiator cap; slowly rotate the cap counterclockwise to the first stop. This procedure allows any residual pressure to escape. When the steam has stopped escaping, press down on the cap while turning counterclockwise and remove it. Likewise, do not remove or disconnect any cooling system component that is under pressure when the engine hot.

2   PRESSURE TEST

WARNING:

The engine must be completely cool before beginning this procedure.

1   Special tool: A cooling system tester is required to test the radiator cap and to pressurize the cooling system when checking for leaks. The tester is a small hand-pump with fittings that allow it to be installed on the radiator in place of the radiator cap. Adapters are usually provided that allow the radiator cap to be mounted on the tester so it can be tested separately. If you do not have access to a tester, refer the tests to a dealer service department or to an independent repair shop.

2   If problems such as overheating and loss of coolant occur, check the entire cooling system (see Chapter 2). If no visible damage is found, pressure test the cooling system and the radiator cap. Both tests require the use of a cooling system tester (Step 1).

3   Open the hood. Locate the radiator cap and remove any

2.4 To remove the radiator cap, turn it counterclockwise to the first stop, let any residual pressure escape, then resume turning the cap counterclockwise until it's free and lift it off; do not remove the radiator cap when the engine is hot

2.5 Maintain the coolant level at the radiator filler neck (arrow)

debris packed around the cap or on top of the radiator to prevent it from falling into the radiator and contaminating the coolant.

4   With the engine cold, remove the radiator cap **(see illustration)**.

5   Add coolant to the radiator to bring the level up to the filler neck **(see illustration)**.

6   Check the rubber washers on the inside of the radiator cap and replace the cap if the washers show signs of deterioration, cracking or other damage.

CAUTION:

Applying excessive pressure to the cooling system may damage some of the components. Only apply the pressure specified in the test procedure.

7   Lubricate the rubber washer on the inside of the radiator cap with coolant and install it on a cooling system

2.7 Testing the radiator cap with a cooling system pressure tester

3.3 Radiator cap (silver) and coolant reservoir cap (red)

3.4 On some models, a coolant drain tap (arrow) is located on the bottom, right side of the radiator

pressure tester **(see illustration)**. Operate the pump and apply the amount of pressure specified in this Chapter's Specifications. Replace the cap if it cannot hold the specified amount of pressure.

8   Before testing the cooling system, inspect the radiator filler neck seat for dents, distortion or contaminants. Wipe the sealing surface with a clean cloth. Then mount the pressure tester onto the radiator filler neck and pressure test the cooling system to the pressure reading specified in this Chapter's Specifications. If the cooling system cannot hold this pressure for a minimum of five minutes, check for a leak within the cooling system. Usually, if there are any leaks present, coolant will be expelled through the opening once the system is pressurized. When checking for a possible slow leak, pump the tester up to the specified pressure and leave it on the system for a period of time until the leak can be found.

9   If the cooling system failed the pressure test, inspect the cooling system for any visible damage (see Chapter 2). If a leak is not found, inspect the radiator filler neck and cap mounting flange for damage.

NOTE:

It may be helpful to remove the skid plate(s) while the vehicle is parked over a clean shop floor, then pressure test the cooling system. This way, you can spot coolant leaks from the hoses or other parts in the cooling system, and see where coolant has dripped onto the floor.

10   If the test pressure drops rapidly, but there are no visible coolant leaks, coolant may be leaking into the combustion chamber. To check, perform a cylinder leak-down test (see Chapter 1). If air can be heard escaping through the radiator filler neck during the test, or if you can see the coolant bubbling in the radiator, coolant is leaking between the cylinder head and cylinder. Another indicator of this problem is when the coolant level falls in the reservoir and radiator and there are no external signs of a coolant leak.

11   Remove the tester and install the radiator cap.

12   Installation is otherwise the reverse of removal.

3   RADIATOR - REMOVAL AND INSTALLATION

WARNING:

The engine must be completely cool before beginning this procedure.

1   Remove the hood and front cover (see Chapter 14).

2   Remove the wheel panels (see Chapter 14).

3   Clean the radiator cap and the area around it to prevent any sand or dirt from falling into the radiator. Then remove the radiator cap **(see illustration)**.

4   If the radiator is equipped with a drain tap, place a clean container underneath it that is large enough to hold all of the antifreeze, especially when draining the cooling system on a Crew model. Open the drain tap and drain the cooling system **(see illustration)**. If the radiator is not equipped

3.5a After disconnecting its hose at the radiator, remove the coolant reservoir mounting screws (arrows) . . .

3.5b . . . and remove the reservoir from its mounting bracket

3.6 Trace the wiring harness from the fan motor to its connector and disconnect it (2010 standard Ranger model shown)

3.7a Remove the left side fan/motor shroud mounting screws (arrows) . . .

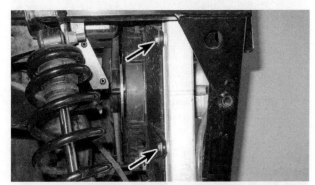

3.7b . . . and the right side screws (arrows). Then pull the fan/motor shroud away from the radiator

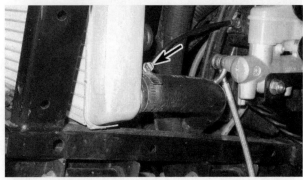

3.8 Loosen the hose clamp and disconnect the lower radiator hose (arrow) at the radiator. If the radiator is not equipped with a drain tap, allow the coolant to drain into the pan

with a drain tap, you will drain the cooling system when disconnecting the lower radiator hose in Step 8.

5   Disconnect the coolant reservoir hose at the radiator, then unscrew and remove the coolant reservoir from its mounting bracket **(see illustrations)**.

6   Disconnect the fan motor electrical connector **(see illustration)**.

7   Remove the screws securing the fan motor/shroud to the radiator and maneuver the assembly away from the radiator **(see illustrations)**.

8   On all models, place a clean container underneath the lower radiator hose. If the radiator is not equipped with a drain tap, make sure the container is large enough to catch all of the coolant that will drain out, and especially on Crew models. Then loosen the hose clamp and disconnect the lower hose at the radiator **(see illustration)**.

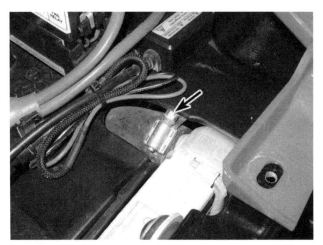

3.9 Loosen the hose clamp and disconnect the upper radiator hose (arrow) at the radiator

3.12b These two grommets (arrows) support the bottom of the radiator

3.11 After removing its fasteners, lift the dash liner (arrow) far enough to so the radiator can slide past it during its removal

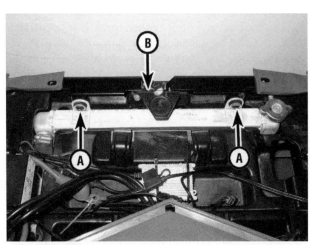

3.12a The radiator mounting screws (A) are located behind the radiator. On 2010 and 2011 models, the hood latch spring seat (B) must be removed before removing the radiator

9   Loosen the hose clamp and disconnect the upper hose at the radiator **(see illustration)**.

10   On 2010 and 2011 models, remove the hood latch spring seat (see Chapter 14).

11   Visually check to see if the dash liner is installed over the radiator. If so, remove the battery on 2010 through 2014 models (see Chapter 8) and the air baffle box (see Chapter 7). Then partially remove the dash and slide it up the cab/frame assembly as described in Chapter 14. With the dash out of the way, remove the screws securing the dash liner **(see illustration)** in place and lift/maneuver the liner as required to obtain enough clearance to lift and slide the radiator beside it. When lifting the dash liner, check all of the wiring harnesses and connectors mounted on and routed across the liner and reposition as necessary to avoid damaging them.

12   Remove the two radiator mounting screws **(see illustration)**. Then carefully lift the radiator to release it from its two mounting grommets **(see illustration)** and guide the radiator out of the vehicle. Note that any coolant remaining in the radiator will drain out as the radiator is tilted during removal.

13   Clean the exterior of the radiator with a garden hose on low pressure while preventing any dirt from entering the radiator. Spray the front and back sides to remove all debris. Carefully use a whisk broom or stiff paint brush to remove any stubborn dirt.

14   Check both sides of the radiator for bent or flattened cooling fins and carefully straighten them with a small screwdriver. If a large area of the cooling surface is damaged, replace the radiator.

15   Check the seams and other soldered connections for corrosion (green or white residue). If corrosion is evident, there could be a leak in that spot. Refer any necessary repair to a radiator repair shop.

16   Fill the radiator with water and check the flow rate out of the radiator. If the flow rate is slow, or if corrosion or

9

other buildup is seen, take the radiator to a radiator repair shop to have it flushed and inspected.

17 Replace the grommets mounted on the top of the radiator and on the lower radiator mounting bracket if weak, deteriorated or damaged.

18 Inspect the radiator hoses for cracks, tears and other damage and replace if necessary. Also replace weak or damaged hose clamps.

19 Before reinstalling the radiator, remove the fan/shroud assembly and inspect the blades for cracks and other damage. Also check the shroud for any buildup of dirt and other debris, and clean thoroughly to prevent overheating.

20 Installation is the reverse of removal, noting the following:

  a) *If removed, install the fan/shroud into position in the frame before installing the radiator.*
  b) *Tighten the radiator mounting screws securely, but don't overtighten them and distort the grommets.*
  c) *Fill the cooling system and bleed it of air (see Chapter 2).*
  d) *Check for coolant leaks.*

4   COOLING FAN - CHECK AND REPLACEMENT

Check

1 If the engine is overheating and the fan is running, turn the engine off and check for broken or missing fan blades. Then check for dirt and other debris built up inside the fan shroud that could be reducing air flow through the radiator when the fan is running.

2 If the engine is overheating and the fan isn't coming on, first make sure the cooling system is full of coolant, the coolant reservoir is full and all air has been purged from the system (see Chapter 2). One or both conditions, if present, can delay or prevent fan operation. After checking the coolant and confirming the level is correct, and there is no air in the system, continue with Step 3. For 2011 and later models, coolant temperatures for when the fan should turn ON and OFF are listed in this Chapter's Specifications.

3 Park the vehicle on a level surface and apply the parking brake.

4 To test the fan motor, first disconnect its wiring harness connector **(see illustration 3.6)**. Using a 12-volt battery and two jumper wires, connect the battery positive terminal to the orange/black wire terminal on the fan side of the wiring harness connector, and the battery negative terminal to the brown wire terminal. Once connected the fan should operate. If it does not, check the connector and the wiring for any damage. Also make sure the connector pins are clean and free of all corrosion. If the connector and wiring are in good condition, then the fan motor is faulty. If the fan motor operated during the test, continue with Step 5.

5 Disconnect the engine coolant temperature (ECT) sensor wiring harness connector at the sensor **(see illustration)**.

4.5 Engine coolant temperature (ECT) sensor and wiring harness connector (arrow) at the cylinder head

6 Turn the ignition switch ON. The fan should run.

7 If the fan did not run, check the fan relay (see Chapter 8). If the relay is good, check the fan motor wiring harness for an open or short circuit. Also check the fan ground connection.

8 If the fan ran with the ECT sensor wiring harness connector disconnected, but does not run when the engine is hot, test the ECT sensor (see Chapter 7).

Replacement

9 Remove the radiator (see Section 3).

10 Remove the fan and shroud assembly from the vehicle.

11 Installation is the reverse of removal.

5   THERMOSTAT - REMOVAL, INSPECTION, TESTING AND INSTALLATION

1 The thermostat is located in the cylinder head on the PTO side of the engine. The thermostat is a temperature sensitive valve used to control the flow of coolant into the radiator. When the engine is cold, the thermostat is closed to retain coolant in the water jackets that surround the cylinder block and cylinder head. This helps the engine to warm up quickly. When the engine reaches a specified temperature, the thermostat opens and coolant flows between the engine and radiator, where it is cooled.

2 If the thermostat is functioning correctly, the engine should warm up quickly, within a few minutes (unless the ambient temperature is cold). A stuck thermostat causes the engine to warm up slowly (when it is stuck open) or causes overheating (when it is stuck partially or fully closed). Check by starting the engine (when cold) and allow it to warm to normal operating temperature. During this time, carefully touch the top radiator hose. If the hose becomes hot quickly, the thermostat is probably stuck open. This

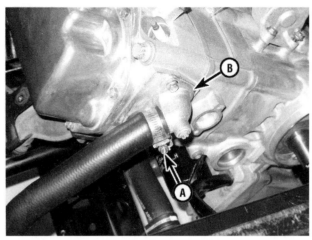

5.5 Coolant hose (A) and thermostat housing (B) located on the PTO side of the engine (2010 Ranger model shown)

5.7 A seal fits around the outside of the thermostat - wide seal edge (arrow) faces out

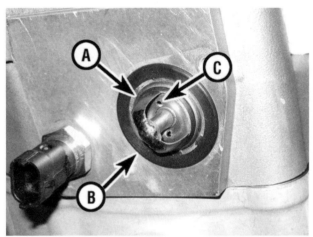

5.6a Thermostat installation details

A   Thermostat   C   Air bleed hole (1 of 2)
B   Seal

5.6b Thermostat assembly details

A   Thermostat housing (2010 models)
B   Screws
C   Bleed screw (2010 models)
D   Washer (2010 models)
E   Seal
F   Thermostat

condition will cause the engine to run colder for a longer period. If the hose gradually warms and then becomes hot, the thermostat is probably operating correctly. However, if the upper hose and radiator do not feel hot after the engine has run long enough to warm to normal operating temperature, the thermostat is probably stuck closed and is blocking coolant flow through the radiator. This condition will cause the engine to overheat.

WARNING:
The engine must be completely cool before beginning this procedure.

Removal

3   Remove seat base, storage box and other components required on your model to access the thermostat (see Chapter 14).
4   Drain the cooling system (see Chapter 2).
5   Place a rag underneath the thermostat to catch any residual coolant spilled from the hose and thermostat housing. Then loosen the hose clamp and disconnect the hose **(see illustration)**. Hold the hose over a clean pan to catch the coolant.
6   Remove the screws and the housing **(see illustration 5.5)**, then remove the thermostat and its seal from the cylinder head **(see illustrations)**.
7   Remove the seal (arrow) from the lip around the thermostat and replace it if cracked or deteriorated, or if coolant was leaking from the cover **(see illustration)**.

Inspection

8   Rinse the thermostat in clear water and inspect it for damage. Make sure the spring has not sagged or broken.
9   Visually check the thermostat for corrosion, cracks and other damage. If the thermostat valve was open when it was removed, the thermostat is defective and must be replaced.

Testing

10   Support the thermostat and a thermometer in a pan of cold water **(see illustration)**. The thermometer must be rated higher than the test temperatures specified in this Chapter's Specifications. The thermostat and thermometer must not touch the sides or bottom of the pan or a false reading will result. An infrared thermometer can also be used to measure water temperature. Gradually heat the water in the container with a hot plate or stove while monitoring the temperature and watching the valve on the top of the thermostat. Note the temperature when the thermostat valve just starts to open and compare it to the value listed in this Chapter's Specifications. Continue to monitor the thermostat and note the temperature when the valve is fully open, and compare it to the value listed in this Chapter's Specifications **(see illustration)**.

5.10a Heat the thermostat in a pan of water and note the temperatures when it starts to open and when it is fully open

NOTE:

On 2010 models, a valve lift specification is listed in this Chapter's Specifications that indicates what the valve lift should be when the thermostat is fully open. However, it is difficult to accurately measure valve lift because the valve will start to close almost immediately after the thermostat is removed from the water. Instead, use the thermostat's fully open temperature to determine when the valve is fully open. If you do try to measure valve lift, it may be necessary to repeat the step several times until an accurate measurement can be made.

11   After heating the thermostat and then removing it from the water and placing it on the workbench, the valve should start to close, and then close fully in a short time. If you have an infrared thermometer, measure the valve's closing temperature and compare to the value listed in this Chapter's Specifications.

12   Repeat the test several times, noting that the test results should be consistent. Replace the thermostat if the valve failed to perform at the specified temperatures. Replace the thermostat if the valve did not open fully at the specified temperature. Replace the thermostat if the valve remains open at room temperature.

13   Always replace the thermostat with one of the same temperature rating. If a temperature rating is stamped on the thermostat, this is the temperature when the thermostat valve should start to open. If there is no temperature rating on the thermostat, confirm the part number on the new thermostat to make sure it is correct.

CAUTION:

Installing an incorrectly rated thermostat can cause engine overheating problems (valve opens too late). However, low engine temperatures can also cause problems by reducing fuel economy and possible lubrication problems from the condensation of water in the crankcase (valve opens too early).

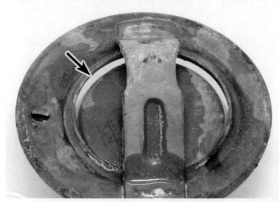

5.10b Arrow indicates how a thermostat valve looks when open

Installation

14   The outer seal edge is tapered. Slip the seal onto the outside edge of the thermostat with the wide edge side facing out **(see illustration 5.6b)**. Check that the seal is seated completely around the thermostat and is not folded under. If reusing the original seal, check it for cracks, deterioration and other damage, and replace if necessary.

15   Install the thermostat into the cylinder head, spring end first, and position it so that one of its air bleed holes is at the top **(see illustration 5.6a)**.

16   Install the housing over the thermostat, then install the screws and tighten to the torque listed in this Chapter's Specifications. Slide the coolant hose over the housing, and depending on the type of clamp used, either release the clamp or tighten it to secure the hose in place **(see illustration 5.5)**.

17   Refill and bleed the cooling system (see Chapter 2). Check the cover and hose for leaks.

6   WATER PUMP

1   The water pump and oil pump share a common shaft. Refer to Chapter 4 to service the water pump impeller and the water pump seals.

SPECIFICATIONS

General

Coolant type...................................	See Chapter 1
Mixture ratio	See Chapter 1
Fan operation	
Off	
2010 models	--
2011 and later models	194 degrees F (90 degrees C)
On	
2010 models	--
2011 and later models	205 degrees F (96 degrees C)
Radiator cap pressure relief pressure..................	13 psi (90 kPa)
Radiator (cooling system) pressure test................	10 psi (69 kPa) for five minutes
Thermostat operation	
Opens.....................................	180 degrees F (82 degrees C)
Closes	
2010 models	171 degrees F (77 degrees C)
2011 and later models	175 degrees F (79 degrees C)
Fully open	
2010 models	203 degrees F (95 degrees C)
2011 and later models	202 degrees F (94 degrees C)
Valve lift	
2010 models	0.24 in. (6 mm)
2011 and later models	--

Torque specifications	In.-lb	Nm
Thermostat housing mounting screws	76-92	9-10.4

9

NOTES

CHAPTER TEN

WHEELS, TIRES AND HUBS

CONTENTS

10

1   GENERAL INFORMATION

1   Models were originally equipped with aluminum (cast) wheels or steel wheels.
2   The front and rear knuckles are each equipped with a single wheel bearing.

2   WHEELS - REMOVAL AND INSTALLATION

1   Flange nuts are used on aluminum wheels and lug nuts are used on steel wheels. Torque procedures and specifications are different for each wheel type.

Removal

2   Park the vehicle on level ground and apply the parking brake.
3   Clean the wheels thoroughly to remove mud and dirt that may interfere with service or mask defects.
4   If the front or rear wheel sets will be removed at the same time, identify their normal operating direction

2.4 When directional arrows are molded into the tire, they should face forward

by marking each tire with a piece of chalk, or locate the directional marks on the tires, if used, so the wheels can be reinstalled on the correct side of the vehicle **(see illustration)**.

2.5 Loosen the nuts in a crossing pattern (cast wheel shown)

2.14a Use a torque wrench and tighten the lug nuts in a crossing pattern to the initial torque specified in this Chapter's Specifications . . .

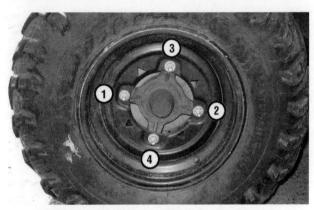

2.12 Tighten the steel wheel flange nuts (arrows) in a crossing pattern

2.14b . . . then use a breaker bar and socket and tighten each lug nut . . .

5   Loosen the wheel flange nuts or lug nuts in a crossing pattern before raising the vehicle **(see illustration)**. The weight of the vehicle will help prevent the wheels from turning.

6   Park the vehicle on a level surface, then raise and support it on jackstands. Block the wheels on the opposite side of the vehicle from the wheel being removed, to prevent the vehicle from rolling off the stands. On aluminum wheels, remove the flange nuts and wheel. On steel wheels, remove lug nuts, washers and wheel.

7   Check the tires and wheels as described in Chapter 2.

Installation

8   Make sure the threads on the lug nuts or flange nuts and the threads on the hub studs are clean and dry.

9   Make sure the hub and wheel mating surfaces are clean and dry. Do not use any lubricant on the threads.

10   Install the wheel over the studs so that it is facing in its original direction, with the valve stem facing outward, and the directional arrow, if used, facing forward. Then install the washers and flange nuts or lug nuts and tighten finger-tight, while making sure the wheel is seating squarely against the hub.

11   Lower the vehicle so the wheel is resting on the ground

2.14c . . . an additional 90 degrees (1/4 turn)

so the weight of the vehicle will prevent the wheels from turning when tightening the flange nuts and lug nuts.

12   On models with steel wheels **(see illustration)**, tighten the flange nuts in a crossing pattern to the torque listed in this Chapter's Specifications.

13   On 2010 models with aluminum wheels, tighten the lug nuts in a crossing pattern to the torque listed in this Chapter's Specifications **(see illustration 2.5)**.

14   On 2011 and later models with aluminum wheels, refer to **illustrations 2.14a through 2.14c** on how to tighten the lug nuts in two steps.

3.6a Break the upper tire bead with a bead breaker . . .

3.6b . . . then turn the wheel over and break the other bead

3.7 Insert two tire irons between the rim and tire and at the point where the rim protectors are placed

3   TIRES

1   All models are equipped with tubeless, low pressure tires designed specifically for off-road use. Rapid tire wear will occur if the vehicle is ridden on paved surfaces. This section describes how to remove a tire from the rim and install a plug patch and permanent cold patch.

Tires - changing

2   A bead breaker tool is required to change the tires. Follow the manufacturer's directions while using the

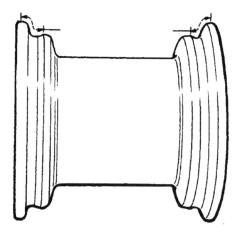

3.9 The rim sealing surfaces must be straight and smooth in order to seal properly

following procedure as a guide.

3   Remove the tire from the vehicle (see Section 2).

4   If necessary, clean the tire and wheel.

5   Remove the valve stem cap and core and deflate the tire. Do not reinstall the core at this time.

6   Position the wheel into the bead breaker tool. Lubricate the tire bead and rim flanges with water. Then lower the leverage bar so both blades are below the rim lip. Throughout the procedure, make sure the blades stay in contact against the tire and do not contact the the top of the rim. If necessary, adjust the bead breaker so that the blades contact the tire and not the rim. Press the leverage bar down to break the tire bead away from the rim **(see illustrations)**. Work around the rim, using the bead breaker and hand pressure to break the upper tire bead free. Relubricate the tire as required.

CAUTION:

Failure to use rim protectors could allow the tire irons to damage the bead seating area on the rim and cause an air leak.

7   Place rim protectors or other padding on the rim flange where the tire irons will be inserted. Then relubricate the upper tire bead and rim flange. Insert the tire irons between the rim and tire **(see illustration)**. Pry the bead over the rim. If removal is difficult, move the tire irons closer together and work small sections at a time to prevent from tearing the tire bead.

8   When the upper sidewall is free, lift the lower sidewall and pry it over the rim to remove the tire.

9   Clean and inspect the rim sealing surfaces **(see illustration)**. If necessary, use a fine grade steel wool to clean these areas.

10   If you're replacing the valve stem, first remove the old valve stem. If necessary, cut the outside of the stem, making sure not to contact the rim, and push it out through the inside. Clean the valve stem hole of all dirt and rubber

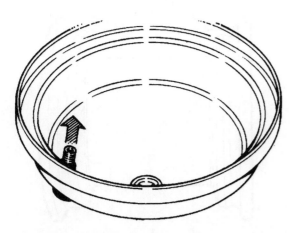

3.10 Install the valve stem by pulling it from the inside of the rim until it seats in place

3.15 Place the tire on the rim with the directional arrow facing forward, then work the first bead over the rim flange

residue. Lubricate the new valve stem with water or a tire lubricant. Do not use oil. Insert the new valve stem through the rim hole from the inside. Then mount a tire valve installation tool onto the valve stem, and pull the valve stem outward until it snaps into place **(see illustration)**. Remove the tool from the valve stem. Check the valve stem for any torn rubber or other damage that could cause an air leak.

11   Inspect the tire bead for cleanliness and the inside of the tire for any foreign objects.

12   Place the rim on the work surface with the valve stem facing up.

13   Check the tire sidewall for the direction arrow and orient the tire with the outside of the wheel so the arrow will point forward when the tire is mounted **(see illustration 2.4)**.

WARNING:

The sidewall arrow on the tire must be oriented properly when the tire is mounted. If the tire is installed backward (arrow pointing to the rear), the tire ply may fail during operation.

14   Wet the lower tire bead and rim surface with water.

15   Place the tire onto the rim with the sidewall directional marking pointing forward, and hand-fit as much of the lower bead over the rim flange as possible **(see illustration)**. Then use the rim protectors and tire irons to finish installing the lower bead.

16   Push the tire down and lubricate the upper bead and rim surface with water. Then use tire irons to start the second bead over the rim flange and continue until the bead is completely installed **(see illustrations)**.

17   Install the valve stem core, if removed.

18   Apply water to both rim beads, then inflate the tire to the bead seating pressure, indicated on the sidewall.

WARNING:

Do not inflate the tire past the specified bead seating pressure. Tire explosion and severe personal injury is possible.

3.16a Use tire irons to start the second bead over the rim flange . . .

3.16b . . . and continue until the upper bead is completely installed over the rim flange - if necessary, hold the bead in place with your knee while you work the last section of it over the rim flange

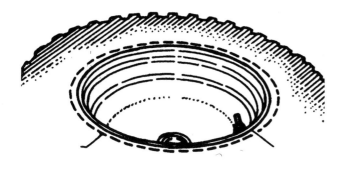

3.19 After seating the beads on the rim, make sure the rim lines are parallel with the rim flanges

NOTE:

If the tire beads will not seat because of air leakage, a tight strap placed around the perimeter of the tread will aid in driving the beads into place.

19   After inflation, check the rim lines on both sides of the tire to ensure the beads are seated. If the beads are seated correctly, the rim lines will be parallel with the rim flanges on both sides of the tire **(see illustration)**. If the beads are not seated correctly, deflate the tire and break the bead so additional lubricant can be applied to the tire bead. Reinflate the tire and check the bead alignment.

20   Adjust the tire pressure to the operating pressure listed in the Chapter 2 Specifications. Then apply water to the beads and valve stem to check for leaks.

21   Install the wheel on the vehicle (see Section 2).

WARNING:

After installing the wheel, ride at slow to moderate speeds to make sure the tire is properly seated on the rim while stopping occasionally to check the tire and wheel. A loss of air pressure can cause loss of control.

Tire Repair

22   A tire can be plugged while mounted on the vehicle. A more permanent repair can be made by removing the tire from the rim and installing a cold patch inside the tire. Follow the patch manufacturer's instructions when using a rubber plug or cold patch repair kit. If instructions are not available, use the following procedures.

Rubber plug repair

23   These steps describe tire repair using a universal rubber plug repair kit available at most automotive parts stores.

24   Check the tire for the object(s) that punctured the tire.

25   Mark the puncture location with chalk, then remove the object while noting its puncture path through the tire.

26   Lubricate the spiral probe on the insert tool with cement and insert it through the puncture hole. Move the probe up and down three times to clean and lubricate the hole, then remove it.

27   Center a rubber tire plug through the hole in the spiral probe and lubricate it with cement.

28   Push the spiral probe through the puncture hole until the plug is slightly above the tire. Twist the spiral probe and remove it from the tire, leaving the plug in the puncture hole.

29   Use a razor blade and trim the plug 1/4 inch (6 mm) from the tire.

30   Allow the cement to dry. Refer to the plug manufacturer's recommendations on drying time.

31   Inflate the tire and apply a small amount of cement around the plug. The cement will bubble if there is a leak.

32   If there is a leak, perform the cold patch repair in this section.

33   If the tire holds air, inflate the tire to the pressure listed in the Chapter 2 Specifications.

Cold patch repair

34   These steps describe how to install a flat rubber patch inside the tire. This type of repair works best after a rubber plug has been installed in the puncture.

35   Remove the tire from the rim (see Steps 4 through 8).

36   If a plug was not installed in the tire, check the tire for the object(s) that punctured the tire and mark the location with chalk. Then remove the object(s).

37   If a plug was previously used, use a razor blade and trim its exposed end until it is flush with the inside of the tire.

38   Working inside the tire, roughen the area around the puncture that is larger than the patch you will be using. If the repair kit does not provide a tool to roughen the area, use coarse sandpaper, a wire brush or any object that will lightly scrape and roughen the surface.

39   Clean all rubber dust and dirt away from the roughened area.

40   Apply a small amount of cement to the roughened area and allow to dry until it becomes tacky. Do not touch the area with fingers.

41   Remove the backing from the patch, making sure not to touch its exposed surface.

42   Center the patch over the puncture, then press the patch into place. Do not attempt to raise or slide the patch once it contacts the cement.

43   Burnish the patch with a roller, checking that the edges are tightly sealed. If a roller is not available, use a smooth hard object (sockets work well) to burnish the patch.

44   Install the tire on the rim (see Steps 12 through 20).

10

4.3 Bend back the cotter pin and pull it out of the front axle, then discard it

4   FRONT HUB - REMOVAL, INSPECTION, STUD REPLACEMENT AND INSTALLATION

Removal

1   Park the vehicle on level ground and and apply the parking brake.

2   Remove the front wheel for the side being worked on (see Section 2). Make sure the frame is supported with jackstands and the rear wheels are blocked to prevent the vehicle from rolling off the stands.

3   Remove the cotter pin and discard it **(see illustration)**.

4   Have an assistant apply the brake while you loosen the front axle nut. If an assistant is not available, or if the front axle still turns with the brake applied, see Step 6 on how to loosen the axle nut.

5   Remove the front brake caliper (see Chapter 13). It is not necessary to disconnect the brake hose from the caliper unless it will be removed from the vehicle. If the caliper will remain on the vehicle, support it with a stiff piece of wire so it doesn't hang by its brake hose.

6   If the axle nut is difficult to loosen, use an impact wrench and impact socket. If an impact wrench is unavailable, hold the hub in place with a long metal bar placed over two of the hub studs and then lock it in place in place with two nuts. The metal bar must be long enough to contact the ground so that it can lock the hub in place. Then loosen the axle nut with a breaker bar and socket **(see illustration)**.

7   With the axle nut loose, remove it and the two cone washers, noting how they are installed on the axle **(see illustration)**.

8   Hold the axle with one hand to prevent it from falling against its bearing, and slide the front hub off the axle and remove it **(see illustration)**. If the hub is seized onto the axle splines, remove it with a puller secured across the hub studs or hub shoulders **(see illustration)**. Do not strike the hub or brake disc.

4.6 A long metal bar, secured to the front hub and resting against the ground, can be used to lock the front hub when loosening the axle nut (arrow)

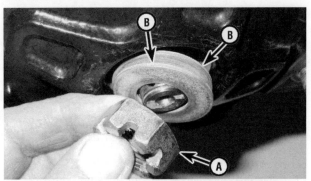

4.7 Remove the axle nut (A) and the two cone washers (B), noting the direction the washers are installed on the axle

4.8a Remove the front hub and brake disc assembly (arrow)

4.8b If the hub is stuck, use a two-jaw puller or a slide hammer with an attached coupling mounted across the hub studs to pull the hub off the axle splines

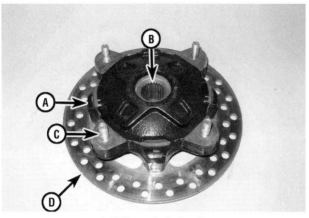

4.10 Front hub details

A	Front hub	C	Studs
B	Splines	D	Brake disc

4.14b Splines on the stud (A) bite into the hub hole (B) - always inspect the holes for cracks and other damage. Remove rust and corrosion from the stud holes with a stiff brush

4.11 Inspect each stud for thread damage and a loose fit in the hub

4.15 Square the stud with the hole so that its splines bite evenly into the stud hole - then drive the stud into the hole until it bottoms

11   Inspect the wheel studs for thread damage and looseness in the hub **(see illustration 4.10)**. If the studs are damaged, replace them (see Steps 12 through 16). If one or more studs are loose, the stud bores in the hub may be damaged, requiring replacement of the hub. Loose studs are usually discovered when loosening and tightening the wheel nuts.

Stud replacement

12   The studs must be in good condition and pressed securely in the hub to properly secure the wheels. Remove damaged studs and inspect the hub carefully before installing new studs.

13   Remove the brake disc from the hub (see Chapter 13).

14   If the stud will be reused, thread a nut onto its end to protect its threads. Then use a hammer and drive against the stud until the nut bottoms. Remove the nut, then carefully use a punch to complete stud removal. Repeat for each stud **(see illustrations)**.

15   Install the stud into the hub hole with the threaded side of the stud facing out. Center the splines on the stud with the hole and drive the stud into the hub with a hammer until it bottoms **(see illustration)**.

16   Install the brake disc (see Chapter 13).

4.14a Remove the studs by driving them out with a hammer - if the stud will be reused, protect its threads with a nut

Inspection

9   Clean and dry the hub. Then clean the brake disc with brake cleaner and allow to dry.

10   Check the hub for any cracks and other damage. Check the splines carefully for twisting, cracks and other damage. Check for cracks and damage around the stud holes **(see illustration)**.

Installation

17   Clean the wheel bearing, axle splines and axle threads of all dirt and grease **(see illustration)**. Then lubricate the axle splines with anti-seize **(see illustration)**. Do not lubricate the axle threads or axle nut threads. These threads must be clean and dry when the axle nut is tightened.

18   Clean the brake disc with brake cleaner and allow to dry.

19   Slide the front hub onto the axle so that its shoulder passes through the bearing and bottoms **(see illustration 4.8a)**.

20   Install both cone washers with their convex sides facing out **(see illustration 4.7)**.

21   Install the front axle nut and tighten to the torque listed in this Chapter's Specifications. If necessary, tighten the axle nut an additional amount to align its cotter pin slots with the hole in the axle. Don't loosen the nut to align the slots. Install a new cotter pin and bend it to secure the nut **(see illustration 4.3)**. If it is necessary to lock the front hub in place when tightening the axle nut, mount a long bar onto the hub as described in Step 6 **(see illustration)**.

22   Install the front brake caliper (see Chapter 13).

23   Install the front wheel (see Section 2).

5   FRONT STEERING KNUCKLE AND WHEEL BEARING - REMOVAL, INSPECTION, BEARING REPLACEMENT AND INSTALLATION

1   The front steering knuckles work like a hinge that pivots on balljoints and support the front wheels. A tie-rod is also attached to each knuckle, which controls knuckle movement to steer the vehicle. A wheel bearing is pressed into each steering knuckle and is secured in place with a high-strength retaining compound and a snap ring.

Removal

2   Park the vehicle on level ground and apply the parking brake.

3   Support the vehicle with jackstands so the front wheels are off the ground. Block the rear wheels so the vehicle cannot roll off the stands.

4   Before removing the front wheel, inspect the wheel bearing (see Chapter 2). If the bearing appears excessively worn or damaged, replace it after removing the steering knuckle (see Steps 13 through 22).

5   Remove the front wheel (see Section 2).

NOTE:

Before removing the components, note how the brake hose is routed from the master cylinder to the brake caliper.

6   Remove the front hub (see Section 4).

7   Remove the cotter pin at the tie-rod, then hold the bolt and remove the nut and both washers. Remove the bolt and

4.17a Front axle and wheel bearing details

A   *Wheel bearing*   C   *Axle threads*
B   *Axle splines*

4.17b Lubricate the axle splines with anti-seize

4.21 Using a long metal bar to hold the hub/axle when tightening the axle nut

5.7 Tie-rod mounting details

A   Bolt
B   Tie-rod
C   Washers
D   Nut
E   Cotter pin

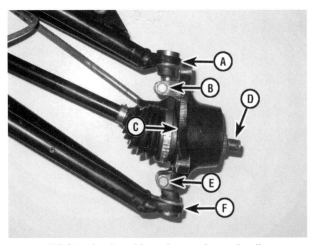

5.8 Steering knuckle and control arm details

A   Upper control arm
B   Upper control arm pinch bolt (nut hidden)
C   Steering knuckle
D   Front axle
E   Lower control arm pinch bolt (nut hidden)
F   Lower control arm

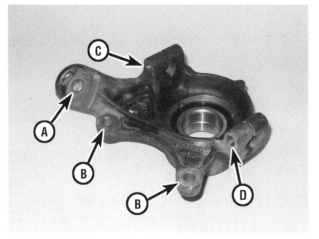

**5.10 Front steering knuckle component attachment points -
inspect these areas carefully for damage**

A   Steering tie-rod balljoint
B   Brake caliper
C   Upper control arm balljoint
D   Lower control arm balljoint

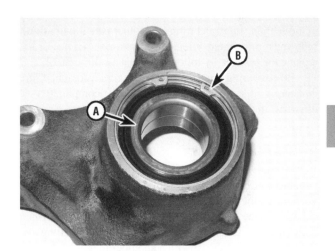

**5.11a The front wheel bearing (A) is pressed into the steering
knuckle and secured in place with a retaining compound and
a snap ring (B)**

move the tie-rod away from the steering knuckle. Discard the cotter pin **(see illustration)**.

8   Remove the nuts and pinch bolts securing the upper and lower control arm balljoints to the steering knuckle. Then tap on the upper arm to free it from the steering knuckle. When the upper arm is free, secure it away from the steering knuckle. Repeat to free the lower arm, then carefully remove the steering knuckle from the front axle and remove it **(see illustration)**.

Inspection

9   Before cleaning the knuckle, cover the bearing with plastic to prevent dirt and sand from entering the bearing.

If the knuckle is caked with dirt, first scrape it with a wire brush, then clean it with a solvent soaked rag. Do not submerge the knuckle in solvent, or spray it with an aerosol cleaner, as either method will contaminate the bearing.
10 Inspect all of the steering component attachment points on the knuckle for cracks and other damage **(see illustration)**. Inspect the knuckle body for corrosion and damage.
11 Even if the front wheel bearing did not show any wear when performing Step 4, inspect it carefully while the knuckle is removed from the vehicle **(see illustration)**. There should be no rust, corrosion, cracks or any other visible damage on the bearing. Also check for any moisture contamination between the middle of the bearing where the inner races separate. Then turn the inner bearing races by

5.11b Move each inner bearing race by hand to check for excessive play

5.13a The bearing driver used to install the wheel bearing must be fabricated with a shoulder (A) that only contacts the bearing's outer race - because the bearing's inner race (B) sets higher than the outer race, a flat bearing driver will contact the inner race and damage the bearing

hand to check for any roughness or binding. The bearing should turn smoothly. Hold the bearing inner races and try to move them sideways from each other **(see illustration)**. Sideways movement should be minimal. If necessary, replace the bearing by following Steps 13 through 22.

12   If the bearing does not need to be replaced, make sure the snap ring seats in the knuckle groove completely **(see illustration 5.11a)**.

Bearing Replacement

13   Special tools: The wheel bearing installed in each knuckle can be difficult to replace without certain tools. To remove the bearing, a heat source, punch and a large collar or piece of pipe that can support the knuckle when removing the bearing are required. When installing the bearing, a bearing driver with a shoulder that only contacts the bearing's outer race is required **(see illustrations)**. Other tools include a large pair of internal snap ring pliers and a press to install the bearing. Loctite 603 retaining compound is required when installing the bearing. If you're not equipped to replace the bearing, refer replacement to a dealer service department or machine shop.

14   Remove the snap ring from the groove in the knuckle **(see illustration)**.

5.13b Note how the bearing driver is only contacting the bearing's outer race (arrow)

CAUTION:

Do not attempt to pry the snap ring out of its groove as the pressure exerted by the pry tool could damage the snap ring groove and require knuckle replacement. Use the correct tool when removing and installing the snap ring.

WARNING:

The knuckle will be hot after heating it. Welding gloves must be worn to prevent burns and severe injury.

5.14 Remove the snap ring with a large pair of internal snap ring pliers

5.15 A MAPP torch is being used to heat the steering knuckle to soften the retaining compound (and also expand the bearing bore) before attempting to remove the bearing

5.16a Locate the three notches inside the knuckle . . .

5.16b . . . then alternately use a punch to drive the bearing squarely out of the knuckle bore - note the large round collar (arrow) that the knuckle is placed on so the bearing can pass through as it is driven out of the knuckle

5.16c Here the bearing has started to move down the bore . . .

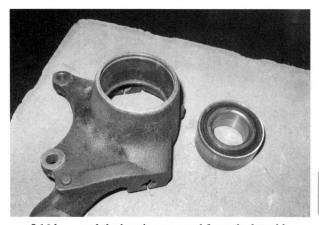

5.16d . . . and the bearing removed from the knuckle

15 A high-strength retaining compound was applied to the outer bearing race when the bearing was originally installed into the knuckle. Because the compound must be softened before the bearing can be removed, heat the outside of the knuckle around the bearing bore with a torch **(see illustration)**. Heating the knuckle will also expand the bearing bore and help ease bearing removal.

CAUTION:

When driving the bearing out in Step 16, work carefully to prevent the punch from sipping outward and gouging the bore surface. Note that as you drive the bearing downward, this will increasingly become a problem as more of the bore surface is exposed.

16 Locate the three notches in the back of the steering knuckle. While alternating between these notches, use a punch and hammer and drive the bearing squarely out of the knuckle. Work carefully to prevent the bearing from binding, as this could damage the bore inside the knuckle. Note that before the end of the bearing exits the bearing bore, you must place the knuckle on a large collar or piece of pipe that has an internal diameter large enough for the bearing to pass through **(see illustrations)**.

5.17 The dried retaining compound shown here (arrow) must be removed to allow the new bearing to bottom against the knuckle shoulder when it is installed

5.19 Apply a high-strength retaining compound (Loctite 603 shown here) around the bearing outer race (arrow) and inside the knuckle bore

17 Clean the knuckle bearing bore of all oil, dirt, corrosion and retaining compound **(see illustration)**. The bore surface must be clean and dry when installing the new bearing. Also make sure the snap ring groove in the knuckle is clean and there are no cracks or damage.

18 Before installing the new bearing, clean the knuckle bore and the bearing outer race with electrical contact cleaner and allow to dry. Do not allow any of the cleaner to enter the bearing.

19 Apply a thin film of a high-strength retaining compound around the bearing outer race and inside the knuckle bore **(see illustration)**.

20 Support and center the knuckle in a press with the bearing bore facing up. Center the bearing into the bore and place a driver against the bearing so that it only contacts the bearing outer race. Press the bearing into the bore until it bottoms. Make sure the bearing enters the bearing bore squarely. If the bearing is tilted, stop and remove it, then repeat the procedure **(see illustrations)**.

21 Check for any retaining compound that was forced out of the bore when the bearing was installed, and remove it with a rag. Likely places are at the top of the bearing and inside the snap ring groove.

22 Install the snap ring into the knuckle groove, making sure it seats in the groove completely **(see illustration 5.11a)**.

Installation

NOTE:

If both steering knuckles were removed, make sure to install them on their correct side.

23 Clean the splines on the front axle. Then install the front axle through the steering knuckle and hold the assembly in place.

24 Slip the upper or lower control arm balljoint shaft into the steering knuckle. Then align the notch in the

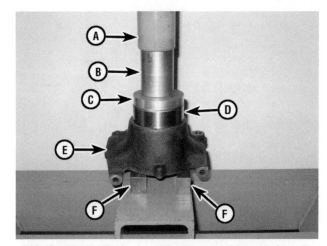

5.20a Set-up details for installing the wheel bearing into the knuckle

A	Press ram	F	Metal support bars
B	Pipe extension		used to level the
C	Bearing driver		knuckle in the press
D	Bearing		bed
E	Knuckle		

5.20b The new bearing installed and bottomed in the knuckle bore

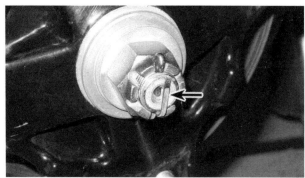

6.3a Bend back the cotter pin and pull it out of the axle, then discard it

6.3b Remove the axle nut (A) and the two cone washers (B), noting how they are installed on the axle

6.5a Remove the rear hub and brake disc assembly (arrow)

6.5b If the hub is stuck, use a two-jaw puller or a slide hammer with an attached coupling mounted across the hub studs to pull the hub off the axle splines

balljoint shaft with the hole in the knuckle and install the pinch bolt and a new Nyloc nut and thread into place by hand until it stops. If you are reusing the original nuts, clean the nut and pinch bolt threads, then apply a threadlock onto the pinch bolt threads and install the nuts. If the pinch bolt is difficult to install, the balljoint shaft is not fully installed in the steering knuckle. The bolt should slip into place as it passes by the notch machined in the shaft. Do not drive the bolt into place as this will damage the balljoint shaft. Repeat for the other control arm **(see illustration 5.8)**.

25   With the upper and lower balljoints installed onto the steering knuckle, hold the pinch bolts and tighten the nuts to the torque listed in this Chapter's Specifications.

26   Grab the steering knuckle and pivot it from side to side to make sure there is no binding or roughness.

27   Wipe off the tie-rod boot and clean its bore in the knuckle of all dirt and corrosion. Install the tie-rod and secure it to the steering knuckle with the bolt, two washers and nut. On all models, the tie-rod end is installed on top of the steering knuckle. The washers fit on each side of the steering knuckle **(see illustration 5.7)**. Hold the bolt and tighten the nut to the torque listed in this Chapter's Specifications. Install a new cotter pin through the hole in the bolt and bend the ends over to lock it in place.

28   Install the front hub (see Section 4).

29   Install the front wheel (see Section 2).

6   REAR HUB - REMOVAL, INSPECTION, STUD REPLACEMENT AND INSTALLATION

Removal

1   Park the vehicle on level ground and apply the parking brake.

2   Remove the rear wheel (see Section 2). Make sure the frame is supported with jackstands and the front wheels are blocked to prevent the vehicle from rolling off the stands.

3   Remove the cotter pin and discard it **(see illustration)**. Then loosen and remove the axle nut and both cone washers, noting how they are installed on the axle **(see illustration)**.

4   Remove the rear brake caliper (see Chapter 13). It is not necessary to disconnect the brake hose from the caliper unless it will be removed from the vehicle. If the caliper will remain on the vehicle, support it with a stiff piece of wire so it doesn't hang by its brake hose.

5   Hold the axle with one hand to prevent it from falling against its bearing, and slide the rear hub off the axle and remove it **(see illustration)**. If the hub will not slide off the axle splines, remove it with a puller **(see illustration)**. Do not strike the hub or brake disc.

Inspection

6   Clean and dry the hub. Then clean the brake disc with brake cleaner and allow to dry.

10

7   Check the hub for any cracks and other damage. Check the splines carefully for twisting, cracks and other damage. Check for cracks and damage around the stud holes (see illustration).

8   Inspect the wheel studs for thread damage and looseness in the hub (see illustration 6.7). If the studs are damaged, replace them (see Step 9). If one or more studs are loose, the stud bores in the hub may be damaged, requiring replacement of the hub.

Stud replacement

9   Stud replacement is similar to the procedures required when replacing the studs in the front hub (see Section 4).

Installation

10   Clean the wheel bearing, axle splines and axle threads of all dirt and grease (see illustration). Then lubricate the axle splines with anti-seize (see illustration). Do not lubricate the axle threads or axle nut threads. These threads must be clean and dry when the axle nut is tightened.

11   Clean the brake disc with brake cleaner and allow to dry.

12   Slide the rear hub onto the axle so that its shoulder passes through the bearing and bottoms (see illustration 6.5a).

13   Install both cone washers with their convex side facing out (see illustration 6.3b).

14   Install the rear axle nut and tighten to the torque listed in this Chapter's Specifications. If necessary, tighten the axle nut an additional amount to align the cotter pin slots with the hole in the axle. Don't loosen the nut to align the slots. Install a new cotter pin and bend it to secure the nut (see illustration 6.3a).

15   Install the rear brake caliper (see Chapter 13).

16   Install the rear wheel (see Section 2).

7   REAR KNUCKLE AND WHEEL BEARING - REMOVAL, INSPECTION, BEARING REPLACEMENT AND INSTALLATION

1   The rear knuckles work like a hinge to support the rear axles and rear wheels. The rear upper and lower control arms are attached to the knuckles with pivot bolts and collars, and operate on bushings installed in the knuckles. Each knuckle is equipped with a wheel bearing.

Removal

2   Park the vehicle on level ground and apply the parking brake.

3   Support the vehicle with jackstands so the rear wheel is off the ground. Block the front wheels so the vehicle cannot roll off the stands.

4   Before removing the rear wheel, inspect the wheel bearing (see Chapter 2). If the bearing appears excessively worn or damaged, replace it after removing the knuckle (see Step 19).

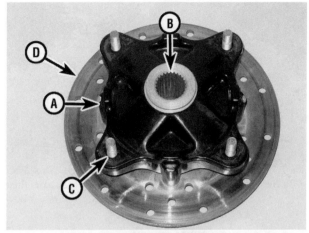

6.7 Rear hub details

A	Rear hub	C	Studs
B	Splines	D	Brake disc

6.10a Rear axle and wheel bearing details

A	Wheel bearing	C	Axle threads
B	Axle splines		

6.10b Lubricate the axle splines with anti-seize

5   Remove the rear wheel (see Section 2).

NOTE:

Before removing the rear knuckle, note how the brake hose is routed from the brake caliper and along the control arms.

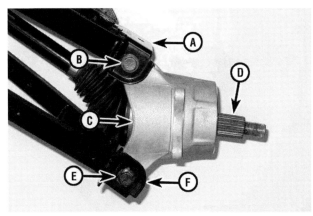

7.8 Rear knuckle and control arm details

A   *Upper control arm*
B   *Upper control arm pivot bolt and nut*
C   *Rear knuckle*
D   *Rear axle*
E   *Lower control arm pivot bolt and nut*
F   *Lower control arm*

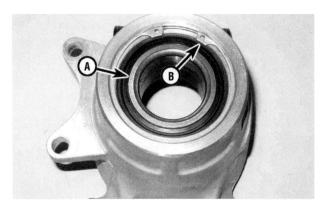

7.12 The rear wheel bearing (A) is pressed into the knuckle and secured in place with a liquid retaining compound and a snap ring (B)

7.14a Pry two of the bushings out of the knuckle, then remove the collars and the opposite two bushings

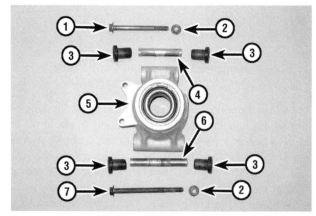

7.14b Rear knuckle details

1	*Pivot bolt (short)*	*5*	*Rear knuckle*
2	*Nuts*	*6*	*Collar (long)*
3	*Bushings*	*7*	*Pivot bolt (long)*
4	*Collar (short)*		

6   Remove the rear hub (see Section 6).
7   Place a small jack or wooden blocks underneath the lower control arm to hold the rear knuckle in place.
8   Remove the upper and lower control arm pivot bolt nuts. Then remove the pivot bolts and the rear knuckle **(see illustration)**.

Inspection

9   Perform Step 14 through Step 18 to service the bushings and collars installed inside the knuckle.
10   Before cleaning the knuckle, cover the bearing with plastic to prevent dirt and sand from entering the bearing. If the knuckle is caked with dirt, first scrape it with a wire brush, then clean it with a solvent soaked rag. Do not submerge the knuckle in solvent, or spray it with an aerosol cleaner, as either method will contaminate the bearing.
11   Inspect the knuckle for cracks and other damage **(see illustration 7.14b)**.
12   Even if the rear wheel bearing did not show any wear when performing Step 4, inspect it carefully while the knuckle is removed from the vehicle **(see illustration)**. There should be no rust, corrosion, cracks or any other visible damage. Also check for any moisture contamination between the middle of the bearing where the inner races separate. Then turn the inner bearing races by hand to check for any roughness or binding. The bearing should turn smoothly. Hold the bearing inner races and try to move them sideways from each other **(see illustration 5.11b)**. Sideways movement should be minimal. If necessary, replace the bearing (see Step 19).
13   If the bearing does not need to be replaced, make sure the snap ring seats in the knuckle groove completely **(see illustration 7.12)**.

Collar and bushing inspection and replacement

14   Remove the bushings from one side of the knuckle, then remove the collars and the other two bushings **(see illustrations)**.
15   Clean all of the parts in solvent and dry with compressed air, if available.

10

16   Inspect the bushing inner and outer surfaces for cracks, distortion and other damage **(see illustration)**.

17   Inspect the collars and pivot bolts for rust and corrosion and remove any debris with a wire wheel. Slide each pivot bolt through its collar to make sure it turns easily and there is no binding or roughness **(see illustration)**. If one or both bolts are difficult to install, check them for bending and replace if necessary. Do not attempt to straighten them.

18   Install the bushings and collars into their correct positions in the knuckle **(see illustration 7.14b)**.

Bearing replacement

19   The rear wheel bearings are replaced the same way as the front wheel bearings. See Section 5.

Installation

NOTE:

If both steering knuckles were removed, make sure to install them on their correct side.

20   Clean the splines on the rear axle. Then install the axle through the knuckle and hold the assembly in place.

21   Reconnect the lower and upper control arms onto the steering knuckle, and install the pivot bolts from the rear side **(see illustration 7.8)**, then install a new Nyloc nut on each pivot bolt. If you are reusing the original nuts, clean the nut and pivot bolt threads, then apply a threadlock onto the pivot bolt threads and install the nuts. Hold the pivot bolts and tighten the nuts to the torque listed in this Chapter's Specifications.

22   The remainder of installation is the reverse of removal.

7.16 Make sure the bushing surfaces are clean and show no signs of damage

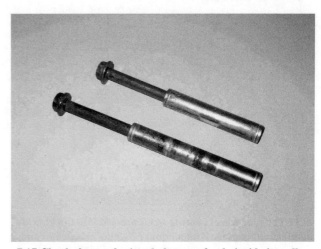

7.17 Check that each pivot bolt turns freely inside its collar

SPECIFICATIONS

Wheels and Tires

Tires	Make/model/tire size
2010 models	
XP 800 models	
Front	Carlisle/PXT/26x9 R12; Titan/AT489/25x10 R12
Rear	Carlisle/PXT/26x11R 12; Titan/AT489/25x11 R12
HD 800 and Crew models	
Front	Carlisle/PXT/26x9 R12
Rear	Carlisle/PXT/26x11 R12
2011 and 2012 models	
XP 800 models	
Front	Carlisle/AT489/25x10 R12; Carlisle/PXT/26x9 R12
Rear	Carlisle/AT489/25x11 R12; Carlisle/PXT/26x11 R12
HD 800 and Crew models	
Front	Carlisle/PXT/26x9 R12
Rear	Carlisle/PXT/26x11 R12
2013 and later models	
Standard Ranger models	
Front	Carlisle/AT489/25x10 R12; Carlisle/PXT/26x9 R12
Rear	Carlisle/AT489/25x11 R12; Carlisle/PXT/26x11 R12
Crew Models	
Front	Carlisle/PXT/26x9 R12
Rear	Carlisle/PXT/26x11 R12
Tire Pressure	See Chapter Two
Tire tread depth	See Chapter Two
Wheel size/type*	
Front	12x6/steel or cast aluminum
Rear	12x8/steel or cast aluminum

HD 800 models were only equipped with cast aluminum wheels.

Torque specifications	Ft-lbs	Nm
Balljoint pinch bolt nuts* (at steering knuckle)		
2010 models	17	23
2011 and later models	23	31
Front axle nuts	80	108
Rear axle nuts	110	150
Rear control arm pivot bolt nuts* (at rear knuckle)	30	41
Tie-rod nuts	40	54
Wheel nuts		
Aluminum (cast) wheels		
2010 models	90	122
2011 and later models		
First step (initial torque)	30	41
Second step	Turn 90 degrees (1/4 turn)	--
Steel wheels	35	47

Replace all Nyloc nuts with new ones.

10

NOTES

CHAPTER ELEVEN

FRONT SUSPENSION, STEERING AND FRONT GEARCASE

CONTENTS

11

1   GENERAL INFORMATION

Front suspension

1   The front suspension on these models is fully independent. The steering knuckles are connected to upper and lower control arms by balljoints. The control arms are secured to the frame with pivot bolts. The shock absorbers are bolted to brackets on the frame and the lower ends are bolted to the upper control arms. Each control arm is equipped with a balljoint that mounts in the steering knuckle. Depending on model, different types of shock absorbers have been used. The standard oil damper type shock absorbers can be adjusted for spring preload only and cannot be rebuilt. The Walker Evans shock absorbers installed on some models offer both spring preload and compression adjustments and can be rebuilt.

Steering system

2   The steering system consists of a steering wheel and upper and lower steering shafts that are connected to a steering gearbox assembly. On some models, electric power steering (EPS) is available. The tie-rods mounted on the steering gearbox have a rod end that mounts on their respective steering knuckle. When the steering wheel turns, it rotates the steering shaft, which connected to the steering gearbox, pushes or pulls the tie-rods to turn the steering knuckles or struts, and with them the front wheels.

3   The front axles are mounted between the steering knuckles and wheel hubs and a front gearcase unit. On standard Ranger models, the front gearcase is connected to the transmission by a single piece driveshaft. Crew models are equipped with two driveshafts.

Fasteners

4   Fasteners used to assemble front suspension and steering system components are critical to the safe operation of the vehicle. During installation, replace all Nyloc nuts with new ones. Likewise, replace all screws that have a dry-film type locking compound applied to their threads. These fasteners are designed for one-time use and may loosen when used a second time. However, if you are unable to obtain the correct fastener, clean the threads on the original fastener and apply a threadlock onto its threads before installing it. See *Fasteners* at the front of this manual for additional information on self-locking fasteners.

NOTE:

After working on the front suspension and steering systems, test ride the vehicle slowly at first to make sure that each system is working correctly before putting the vehicle into hard or severe service.

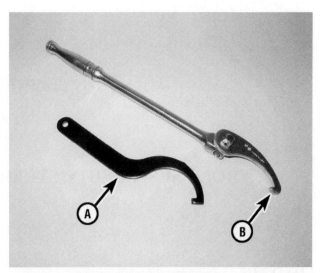

2.6a Stock (A) and aftermarket (B) spanner wrenches used for adjusting spring preload

2   FRONT SHOCK ABSORBERS - ADJUSTMENT, REMOVAL, INSPECTION, SPRING REPLACEMENT AND INSTALLATION

WARNING:

Do not attempt to disassemble the shock absorbers. The oil damper shocks (no reservoir) are not designed to be rebuilt. The gas-oil damper shocks (with reservoir) are nitrogen charged and under high pressure. While these shocks are designed to be rebuilt, service should be referred to a dealer service department or suspension specialist. Severe personal injury can occur from mishandling these shocks when trying to disassemble them.

1   Three types of shock absorbers have been used on the models covered in this manual - oil damper (no reservoir), Nivomat (self-leveling) and gas-oil damper (with reservoir). If your vehicle is equipped with aftermarket shock absorbers, refer to the manufacturer's instructions for adjustment and service.

Adjustment

WARNING:

If you stiffened the shock preload in order to carry a heavy load, make sure to decrease the preload after removing the load fom the vehicle. Without the additional weight, the stiffer preload may reduce your vehicle's handling and stability.

Oil damper shock absorbers

2   These are considered standard shock absorbers and are not equipped with a reservoir mounted on the shock body. These shocks can only be adjusted for spring preload.

3   While the proper spring preload setting helps establish your vehicle's ride height, the manufacturer does not list stock spring preload settings for these shock absorbers. When determining a spring preload setting, note that when carrying heavy loads or pulling a trailer, it may be necessary to increase the spring preload for a stiffer ride to help maintain adequate ground clearance during operation. When the load is removed, it may be necessary to return the shock to a softer preload setting. When operating your vehicle, record the loads used and the most optimum spring preload settings in a notebook. You can then use this information as a guide when determining spring preload settings for different loads and conditions.

4   On most models, both the front and rear shock absorbers are equipped with preload adjusters. On some models, only the front shock absorbers have preload adjusters - the rear shock absorbers are Nivomat type shock absorbers (see Step 7).

5   Depending on the shock absorber being adjusted, jack up the vehicle and support it securely on jackstands. The shock absorbers must be fully extended when adjusting spring preload.

6   Preload is the amount the spring is compressed from its free length. Use a spanner wrench to turn the adjusting cam located below the spring. Turning the adjusting cam counterclockwise decreases spring preload, while turning the adjusting cam clockwise increases it **(see illustrations)**.

2.6b To turn the adjusting cam, insert the pin on the spanner wrench into one of the notches in the top of the cam

2.7 Nivomat self-leveling shock absorber

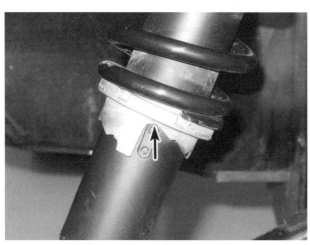

2.6c Softest spring preload position . . .

2.6d . . . stiffest spring preload position

Nivomat shock absorbers

7   Some models are equipped with Nivomat self-leveling shock absorbers on the rear end **(see illustration)**. Shock adjustment takes place mechanically when the vehicle starts moving, as a pump mechanism inside the shock absorber builds pressure to level the vehicle. The benefit of Nivomat shock absorbers is how they prevent the vehicle from squatting when heavy loads are placed in the cargo bed. These shock absorbers are not equipped with any type of external adjuster, though they operate in conjunction with a coil spring and internal damping.

Gas-oil damper shock reservoirs

8   The factory installed Walker Evans gas-oil damper shock absorbers are equipped with a reservoir. Each shock is equipped with compression damping adjuster and a spring preload adjuster.

Compression damping

9   Compression damping controls the shock absorber rate, after hitting a bump. This setting has no effect on the rebound rate of the shock.

10   The compression adjuster is a large three-fingered knob mounted on top of the shock reservoir. To set the adjuster to its standard setting, turn the adjuster counterclockwise until it stops (fully open position). Then turn the adjuster clockwise while counting the number of clicks listed in this Chapter's Specifications. To increase the compression damping, turn the adjuster clockwise. To decrease the compression damping, turn the adjuster counterclockwise.

NOTE:

Make sure the compression adjuster is located in one of the detent positions and not in between any two settings.

11

Spring preload

11   Preload is the amount the spring is compressed from its free length. Preload is set with the threaded adjuster at the top of the shock absorber. By tightening the adjuster, spring preload is increased. By loosening the adjuster, spring preload is decreased.

12   Jack up the vehicle and support it securely on jackstands. The shock absorbers to be adjusted must be fully extended when adjusting spring preload.

NOTE:

Before adjusting spring preload, clean the threads on the shock body to prevent thread damage.

13   To determine if the spring preload is set at the factory setting, measure the length of the compressed spring between the top of the spring and the bottom of the spring and compare the setting with the factory preload setting listed in this Chapter's Specifications **(see illustration)**. If adjustment is necessary, turn the adjuster with a spanner wrench to set the spring preload to the factory preload setting, or set it to the desired spring preload setting for the cargo load you are carrying.

14   Always set both front shock absorbers to the same preload setting. Always set both rear shock absorbers to the same preload setting.

Shock mounting adjustment position (all models)

15   To increase or reduce suspension stiffness, the frame has two upper shock mounting positions for each wheel - the inside position is softer and the outside position is stiffer **(see illustration)**. Refer to Steps 16, 17, 19 and 49 for information on how to remove, reposition and tighten the upper shock mounts when making this adjustment. See Chapter 12, Section 2 for information on how to change the rear shock absorber mounting position.

Removal

16   Support the vehicle with the front wheels off the ground and apply the parking brake. Block the rear wheels to prevent the vehicle from rolling off the jackstands.

17   Place a jack underneath the lower control arm to prevent the front wheel/suspension assembly from dropping when the shock absorber mounting bolts are removed. By using a jack instead of wooden blocks, you can adjust it to reduce tension on the bolts when removing and installing them.

18   Remove the nut and bolt from the lower end of the shock absorber and allow the lower control arm to settle against the jack **(see illustration)**.

NOTE:

Before removing the upper shock absorber mount from the frame in Step 19, note which adjustment hole (inner or outer) the shock is mounted in (see Step 15).

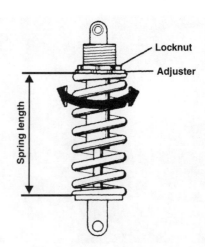

2.13 Measure spring preload between the top and bottom of the spring; to adjust the spring preload, turn the adjuster as required to obtain the desired preload setting - note that a locknut is not used on these shock absorbers

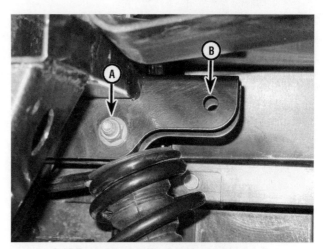

2.15 Front shock adjustment position details

A   *Inside position - softer*
B   *Outside position - stiffer*

2.18 Remove the nut and bolt at the bottom of the shock

2.19 Remove the nut and bolt at the top of the shock absorber and remove the shock assembly

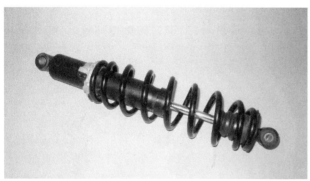

2.20a Standard type oil damper shock absorber used on Ranger models

2.20b Check for oil leaking around the damper rod where it enters the shock

2.20c Here oil is leaking past a damaged oil seal on a gas-oil damper shock - this shock can be rebuilt to replace the oil seal and change the shock fluid

2.22a Remove the collar (A) and both bushings (B) from each shock eye (standard oil damper shock shown)

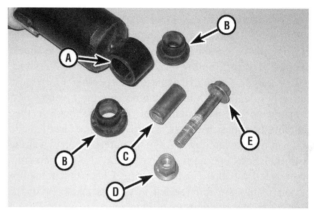

2.22b Shock bushing details (standard oil damper shock shown)

A	Shock eye	D	Nut
B	Bushings	E	Mounting bolt
C	Collar		

19   Remove the nut and bolt from the upper end of the shock absorber and remove it from the frame **(see illustration)**.

Inspection

> *NOTE:*
>
> *This section inspects and services the standard oil damper and Walker Evans shock absorbers. Refer all Nivomat shock service to a dealer service department.*

20   Before cleaning the shock absorber, inspect the damper rod for signs of pitting and oil leakage **(see illustrations)**. On gas-oil damper shocks, also inspect the reservoir for oil leakage. If leaking, oil damper shocks will have to be replaced as they cannot be rebuilt. Gas-oil damper shocks can be rebuilt to replace a leaking oil seal and to change the shock fluid. Refer this service to a dealer service department or suspension specialist.

21   Inspect the shock body for severe dents that can affect shock operation. On gas-oil damper shocks, also inspect the reservoir for dents and other damage.

22   On standard oil damper shock absorbers, push out the collar and remove both bushings from the shock eye **(see illustrations)**.

11

23   On Walker Evans gas-oil damper shocks, remove the collar and O-ring from each shock eye. Do not remove the spherical bearing unless it will be replaced **(see illustration)**.

24   Remove dirt, rust and corrosion from the pivot bolts and collars with a wire wheel **(see illustration)**. Then inspect the collar and bolt contact surfaces for cracks, wear, grooves and other damage.

25   On Walker Evans gas-oil damper shocks, wipe off the spherical bearing with a clean rag. Then inspect the bearing by holding it with two fingers and pivoting it laterally. If the bearing is tight, moves roughly or shows any visual damage, the bearing must be replaced. To replace the bearing, first remove the clip or snap ring from each side of the bearing. Then support the shock in a press and press the bearing out of the shock eye. When supporting the shock, support it with a hollow driver placed against the shock eye. Clean the shock eye while also inspecting it for cracks and other damage. To install the bearing, first place a new clip or snap ring in one of the grooves in the shock eye, then support the shock in a press as before with the installed clip or snap ring facing down. Align and press the new bearing into the shock eye until it contacts the clip or snap ring, then install the other clip or snap ring. Check that both clips or snap rings are fully seated in their grooves. Pivot the bearing to make sure it wasn't damaged when installing it **(see illustration 2.23)**.

26   On standard shocks, install the bushings and collar **(see illustration 2.22b)**. Make sure the bushings seat flush against the shock eye.

27   On Walker Evans gas-oil damper shocks, lubricate the spherical bearing, collars and O-rings with grease **(see illustration 2.23)**. Then install the O-rings and collars, making sure to wipe off any excess grease from the outside of the shock eye.

Spring replacement

28   The springs on both the oil damper and gas-oil damper shocks can be removed for inspection or replacement.

Oil damper shocks

29   While these shock absorbers cannot be rebuilt internally, the external parts can be removed for cleaning or replacement.

30   Because the spring is under high tension, a shock spring tool must be used when removing and installing the spring. Use the Polaris Shock Spring Compressor Tool (part No. 2870623), the Motion Pro Shock Spring Compressor (part No. 08-0608) or an equivalent aftermarket shock tool. If you do not have the proper tool, refer the service to a dealer service department or suspension specialist.

WARNING:

Do not attempt to remove or install the spring without the proper tool as the spring retainer and spring can fly loose under sufficient force

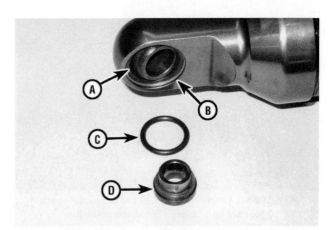

2.23 Spherical bearing details (typical bearing assembly)

A	Spherical bearing	C	O-ring
B	Clip or snap ring	D	Collar

2.24 The rust and corrosion found on this pivot bolt and collar set is typical of what you find on suspension fasteners - clean both before reinstalling them

2.31 Turn the spring adjuster until it settles in its softest position (arrow)

and cause injury. Wear a face shield when compressing the spring.

31   Record the spring preload setting, then turn the spring adjuster to its softest position with a spanner wrench **(see illustration)**.

32   Identify the end of the spring that fits into the spring

2.37 Position the spring retainer so that its notch (arrow) is 180 degrees opposite the end of the spring (not visible in this photograph)

retainer. This ensures the spring will be installed correctly during assembly.

33   Following the manufacturer's instructions, mount the spring compressor onto the shock absorber. If the spring compressor is equipped with a safety pin, make sure to position and use it as described in the instructions. If the spring compressor is designed to be mounted in a vise, clamp it down tightly.

34   Operate the spring compressor to compress the spring. When the spring is compressed and the upper spring seat is free, carefully remove it from the shock shaft. Then slowly release tension from the spring. When there is no tension on the spring, remove the spring compressor from the shock absorber. Then remove the spring and the adjusting cam.

35   Clean and inspect the parts. Replace any damaged part before reassembling the shock absorber. If replacing the shock spring, consult with a dealer parts department on the correct replacement spring to use.

36   Install the adjusting cam over the shock body with the spring retainer side facing up, then install the spring. If the spring was marked, install it facing in its original position.

37   Install the spring retainer over the top of the shock and position it so that its notch is 180 degrees opposite the end of the spring (see illustration).

38   The remainder of assembly is the reverse of removal, noting the following:

39   Mount the spring compressor onto the shock absorber and compress the spring as before. Place the spring retainer on top of the spring and slowly release tension from the spring, making sure it centers itself against the retainer and the retainer centers against the upper shock mount. When the spring and spring retainer are correctly positioned, release all tension from the spring.

40   Remove the spring compressor from the shock absorber, and adjust the spring preload (see Steps 2 through 6).

Walker Evans gas-oil damper shocks

41   While these shocks can be rebuilt, a number of special tools are required. Refer shock overhaul to a dealer service department or suspension specialist.

42   Always work on one shock at a time so you can refer to the assembled shock to help confirm the alignment of parts.

43   Record the spring preload setting before loosening the adjuster and removing the spring. See Step 13.

44   Clean the threads on the shock body so the preload adjuster will turn freely without damaging the threads. These are fine threads that can be damaged if the preload adjuster is forced to turn against sand and hardened mud trapped in the threads.

WARNING:

If the preload adjuster is loosened all the way and there is still tension against the spring, you will have to use a spring compressor to compress the spring so you can safely remove the retainer. Do not attempt to remove the spring retainer when the shock is under tension as severe personal injury may result. Wear a face shield when compressing the spring.

45   Support the shock in a vise with soft jaws and with the preload adjuster facing down and turn it until the spring is no longer under tension and the retainer can be removed off the spring and past the damper rod by hand.

46   Clean and inspect the parts. Replace any damaged part before reassembling the shock absorber. If replacing the shock spring, consult with a dealer parts department on the correct replacement spring to use.

47   Assembly is otherwise the reverse of disassembly. When the shock is assembled, adjust the spring preload (see Step 13 and Step 14).

Installation

48   Installation is the reverse of removal. Install the bolts and new Nyloc nuts. If you are reusing the nuts, clean the nut and bolt threads, and apply a threadlock onto the bolt threads. Hold the bolts and tighten the nuts to the torque listed in this Chapter's Specifications.

3   FRONT CONTROL ARMS AND BALLJOINTS - REMOVAL, INSPECTION, BALLJOINT REPLACEMENT AND INSTALLATION

1   These models use upper and lower control arms. Each control arm is equipped with a replaceable balljoint.

Removal

2   Remove the front wheel for the side being serviced (see Chapter 10).

3   Support the lower control arm with a jack to prevent it

11

3.4a Before removing an upper control arm, note how the brake hose (A) is routed from the brake caliper to the master cylinder. On 2010 models, the speed sensor wiring harness (B) is mounted on the right side and routed with the brake hose

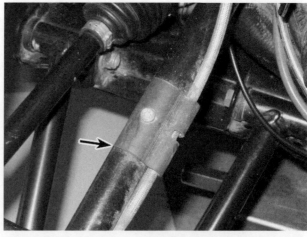

3.5 Brake hose clamp (arrow) and brake hose position at the upper control arm (left side shown)

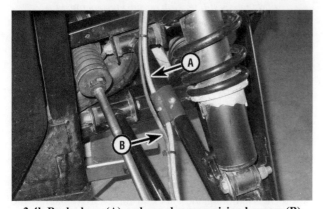

3.4b Brake hose (A) and speed sensor wiring harness (B) routing (2010 models)

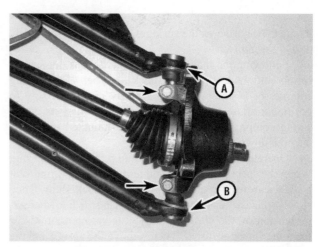

3.7a Upper (A) and lower (B) control arms and pinch bolts (arrows) - knuckle attachment

from dropping when disconnecting the shock absorber.

4   Before servicing the front control arms, note how each front brake hose is routed from its brake caliper to the master cylinder. On 2010 models, also note how the wheel speed sensor wiring harness is routed beside the front right side brake hose **(see illustrations)**. Then remove the brake caliper mounting bolts and pass the brake caliper through the upper control arm without disconnecting the brake hose from the caliper. When the caliper and brake hose are free, support the caliper with a wire hook so it is clear of the upper control arm. By removing the brake caliper while it is attached to its hose, you shouldn't have to bleed the brake system during installation.

5   Remove the screw and the brake hose clamp from the upper control arm **(see illustration)**.

6   Remove the nut and bolt securing the shock absorber to the upper control arm **(see illustration 2.18)**. The control arm and the steering knuckle assembly should now be supported on the jack.

7   Remove the nut and pinch bolt securing the upper control arm balljoint to the steering knuckle **(see illustration)**. Reposition the jack as required, then hold the upper arm and strike the knuckle with a hammer to release the upper control arm ball joint from the knuckle **(see illustration)**. Be careful not to damage the balljoint boot.

3.7b Striking the knuckle will help free it from the balljoint

3.9a Upper (A) and lower (B) control arms and pivot bolts - frame attachment

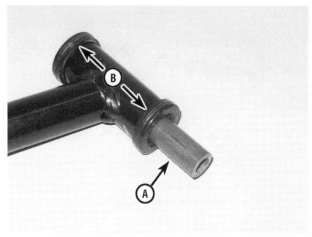

3.11b Remove the pivot tube (A) and bushings (B) from each side of the control arm

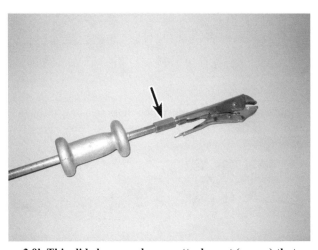

3.9b This slide hammer has an attachment (arrow) that allows a pair of locking pliers to be mounted on the end of the tool's threaded shaft; tools like this one can be found at discount tool stores

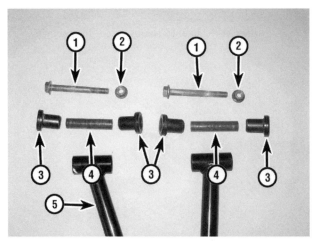

3.11a Control arm details

1 Pivot bolts	4 Pivot tubes
2 Nuts	5 Control arm
3 Bushings	

8   Before loosening the two control arm pivot bolts, pivot the control arm up-and-down. While the control arm should should move under tension, there should be no binding or roughness. Then try to move the control arm from side-to-side. If any excessive side-to-side looseness is felt, the bushings are worn and must be replaced. If you are unsure, compare the side-to-side movement against that of another control arm.

9   Remove the nut from each pivot bolt, then remove the pivot bolts and the upper control arm **(see illustration)**. If a pivot bolt is difficult to remove, it is probably corroded and seized in place. To remove a seized bolt, first spray both ends of the bolt with an aerosol penetrating fluid and allow sufficient time for the liquid to soak between the bolt and the pivot tube positioned inside the control arm. If there is room, try to drive the bolt out from behind with a drift. If there is not enough room, switch ends and use a pair of locking pliers mounted on a slide hammer **(see illustration)**. Close and lock the locking pliers across two flats on the bolt head. Operate the slide hammer to shock the bolt and begin removing it. If the pliers slip off, repeat until the bolt head has pulled away from the frame far enough to where you can lock the pliers across the shoulder on the bolt head for a better grip.

10   Repeat the steps necessary to remove the lower control arm **(see illustration 3.9a)**.

Inspection

11   Remove the pivot tubes and bushings from the control arm **(see illustrations)**. If you noted a problem when checking the control arm in Step 8, isolate each pivot set so you can inspect them separately to help determine the cause of the problem, or to help with further inspection and troubleshooting. The bushings are installed with a snug fit, but you should be able to remove them by hand. If a bushing is stuck, grab its shoulder and twist it loose. If necessary, drive the bushing out with a drift inserted through the opposite end of the control arm. Then clean

11

3.12 Inspect the control arm for any impact damage as well as for weak or damaged welded joints

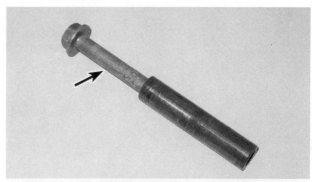

3.14b Slide each pivot bolt through its pivot tube to check for binding

3.14a Inspect each pivot set for for excessive wear and damage

3.14c Check that each pivot tube slides smoothly through its bushings

and dry all of the parts.

12   Inspect all welded joints and brackets on the control arm for cracks, bending and other damage **(see illustration)**. Inspect the tubes for impact damage. If damage is evident, replace the control arm. Don't attempt to straighten or repair it.

13   Inspect the welded brackets on the frame for cracks and bending. If the paint is cracked in any of these areas, inspect it carefully. If necessary, refer further inspection to a dealer service department.

14   Inspect the bushings for cracks, excessive wear and other visual damage, such as surface tearing. Always replace bushings in sets of two. Check the pivot tube for wear and damage. Because the pivot tube operates against the bushings, its outer wear should be minimal, though inner wear can be severe if the pivot bolt is bent or corroded, or if there is rust present on the parts. If necessary, clean these parts with a wire wheel mounted in a drill, then inspect their contact surfaces for excessive wear, cracks and other damage **(see illustrations)**.

15   Inspect the balljoint for a damaged boot or stud **(see illustration)**. Then grasp the shaft and swivel it in all directions, including vertically. Check for roughness, binding and excessive play. If wear or damage is noted, replace the ball joint using one of the two procedures described in Steps 17 through 34.

16   Install a bushing into each side of the control arm, then install and center the pivot tube between the bushings **(see illustration)**.

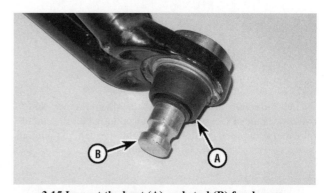

3.15 Inspect the boot (A) and stud (B) for damage

3.16 Install the bushings and pivot tube into each side of the control arm

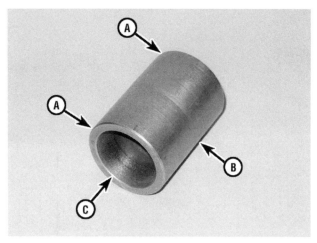

3.18 Driver dimensions

A   *Minimum length: 3.0 in. (76.2 mm)*
B   *Outside diameter: 1.75 in. (44.5 mm)*
C   *Inside diameter: 1.375 in. (34.9 mm)*

3.21 Remove the snap ring before pressing the balljoint out of the control arm

Balljoint replacement

17 The balljoints can be replaced with the control arm removed from the vehicle or with the control arm installed on the vehicle. Special tools are required for both procedures.

Control arm removed from vehicle

18 Special tools: A press and driver are required to replace the balljoints after the control arm has been removed from the frame. Because of the balljoint design and how it must be pressed out of the control arm, it may be necessary to have a driver fabricated at a machine shop if you do not have access to a lathe. The critical dimensions are 3.0 in./76.2 mm (minimum length) x 1.75 in./44.5 mm (outside diameter) x 1.375 in./34.9 mm (inside diameter) **(see illustration)**.

3.22 Support the control arm on the driver (A) that has an inside diameter large enough for the balljoint to pass through; place a suitable size socket or bearing driver on the balljoint shoulder (B). Then press the balljoint out of the control arm and into the driver (A)

19 The control arm balljoint is installed with a press fit and a snap ring. Before starting work, read this procedure through. If you do not have tools required to replace the balljoint, refer the service to a dealer service department or other qualified shop. Do not attempt to replace the balljoint by driving it out of or into the control arm, as you may damage the control arm and the new balljoint.
20 Remove the control arm from the vehicle (see Steps 2 through 10).
21 Remove the snap ring from the groove in the balljoint and discard it **(see illustration)**. The snap ring is stiff, so use one hand to guide and prevent it from flying off once it's released from the balljoint. If you can't open the snap ring with your pliers, the balljoint may have moved and is causing the snap ring to bind against the control arm. If necessary, place the control arm in a press with the snap ring facing down, and press carefully against the balljoint to see if it moves slightly.
22 Support the control arm on the driver described in Step 18, making sure it has an inside diameter large enough to accept the balljoint as it is being pressed out, while also having an outside diameter wide enough to support the control arm while under pressure. When the control arm is supported in the press, the boot on the balljoint must be facing up. Then place a socket or bearing driver on the balljoint shoulder and press the balljoint out of the control arm **(see illustration)**.
23 After removing the balljoint, clean and inspect the end of the control arm. Carefully remove any burrs from the balljoint bore while checking it for cracks and other damage. If any damage is noted, replace the control arm.
24 Support the control arm in the press so the balljoint will be installed from its correct side, then center the balljoint into the control arm with its boot side facing down. Place

11

the driver on top of the ball joint, and press the ball joint into the control until it bottoms **(see illustration)**.

25 Install a new snap ring into the ball joint groove with its flat side facing away from the ball joint **(see illustration 3.21)**. Make sure the snap ring seats in the groove completely.

Control arm installed on vehicle

26 Special tool: A balljoint hand press tool is required to remove and install the balljoint while the control arm is mounted on the vehicle. Use the Polaris balljoint tool (part No. PU-50506) **(see illustration)**, the OTC Balljoint Service Kit (part No. 4964) or a similar tool. The hand press slides over the control arm and balljoint, and as pressure is applied with its pressure screw, the balljoint is removed or installed without damaging the control arm. Steps 27 through 34 describe how to use the Polaris balljoint tool. If using a different tool, follow the manufacturer's instructions.

27 Remove the wheel from the side of the vehicle being serviced (see Chapter 10).

28 Separate the control arm from the steering knuckle (see Steps 2 through 7).

29 Remove the snap ring from the balljoint(see Step 21). If the snap ring will not open, mount the hand press in its installation position (see Step 33) and tighten the pressure screw to see if you can move the balljoint to release pressure against the snap ring.

30 Before removing the balljoint, identify the terms used to describe the hand press assembly and its adapters **(see illustration 3.26)** and the parts of the balljoint **(see illustration)**.

31 Place the seat adapter on top of the balljoint face. Then slide the removal adapter over the balljoint shaft and center it against the balljoint. While holding the removal adapter in place, slide the hand press over the seat adapter and the removal adapter. Tighten the pressure screw until it contacts the removal adapter, then check that the opening in the hand press is contacting the seat adapter and not the balljoint face. When the hand press is correctly positioned, tighten the pressure screw and press the balljoint out of the control arm.

32 Perform Step 23 to clean and inspect the balljoint bore.

33 Center the new balljoint into the control arm and place the installation adapter on top of the balljoint face. Slide the seat adapter over the balljoint shaft and rest it against the control arm. Install the hand press over the control arm and balljoint and tighten the pressure screw to center it against the installation adapter, then continue tightening the pressure screw until the seat adapter is centered and held between the control arm and the hand press. When the tool alignment is correct, tighten the pressure screw and press the balljoint into the control arm until it bottoms and its snap ring groove is visible **(see illustration 3.30)**. Remove the hand press and its adapters from the control arm.

34 Perform Step 25 to install a new snap ring into the balljoint groove.

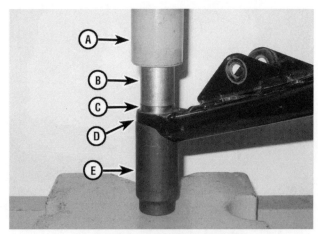

3.24 Ball joint installation details

A	*Press*	D	*Control arm*
B	*Driver or socket*	E	*Driver*
C	*Balljoint (installed)*		

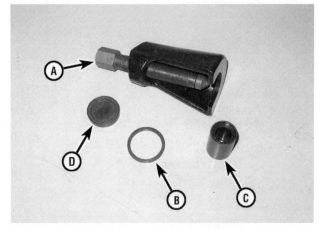

3.26 Polaris balljoint tool details

A *Hand press - when removing the balljoint, the pressure screw faces toward the balljoint shaft; when installing the balljoint, the pressure screw faces toward the balljoint face*
B *Seat adapter*
C *Removal adapter*
D *Installation adapter*

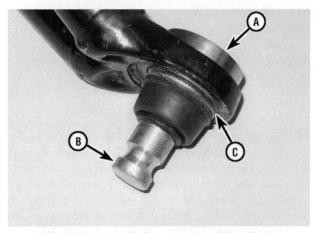

3.30 Balljoint details for removal and installation

A	*Balljoint face*	C	*Snap ring groove*
B	*Balljoint shaft*		

4.3 With the front wheel pointing forward, make sure the bottom steering wheel spoke is centered (arrow) with the vehicle

4.4 Pry the cover (arrow) from the center of the steering wheel to access the steering wheel nut

4.5 Steering wheel nut (arrow)

Installation

35   Installation is the reverse of the removal steps, noting the following:

a) *Lubricate the pivot bolts with grease and install them through the control arms, facing in their original direction. With the pivot bolts installed, pivot each control arm to make sure there is no binding or roughness. Then remove any exposed grease from the bolt threads with contact cleaner and allow to dry. Install new Nyloc nuts and thread them onto the pivot bolts until they stop. If you are reusing the original Nyloc nuts, clean the nut and bolt threads, and apply a threadlock onto*

the bolt threads before installing and tightening the nut.

b) *Slip the upper or lower control arm balljoint shaft into the steering knuckle. Then align the notch in the ball joint shaft with the hole in the knuckle and install the pinch bolt and a new nylock nut and thread into place by hand until it stops. If the pinch bolt is difficult to install, the balljoint shaft is not fully installed in the steering knuckle. The bolt should slip into place as it passes by the notch machined in the shaft. Do not drive the bolt into place as this will damage the balljoint shaft. Repeat for the other control arm, if removed.*

c) *With the upper and lower balljoints installed into the steering knuckle, hold the pinch bolt and tighten the nut to the torque listed in this Chapter's Specifications. Repeat for the other pinch bolt and nut, if removed.*

d) *Reconnect the shock absorber onto the upper control arm with the bolt and a new Nyloc nut. Hold the bolt and tighten the nut to the torque listed in this Chapter's Specifications.*

e) *Hold the control arm pivot bolts and tighten the nuts to the torque listed in this Chapter's Specifications. Repeat for the other control arm, if removed.*

4   STEERING WHEEL - REMOVAL AND INSTALLATION

1   When the front wheels are pointing straight ahead, the steering wheel's bottom spoke should be centered and positioned at the bottom. If the bottom spoke is incorrectly aligned, do not remove the steering wheel to realign it without first checking the steering system. Check that the tie-rods are not damaged and that the steering column and steering gearbox mounting bolts are tight. If these items are okay, check the toe adjustment (see Chapter 2). Only after checking these items and correcting any problems should the steering wheel be readjusted.

2   Refer to illustrations 5.1b or 5.1c for a breakdown of the steering wheel and the alignment of the washers and spacer installed directly underneath it.

Manual steering models

3   Turn the steering wheel so the front wheels are pointing straight ahead. Then check that the steering wheel's bottom spoke is centered and positioned squarely at the bottom **(see illustration)**.

4   Using a small flat-tipped screwdriver, pry the steering wheel cover off the steering wheel **(see illustration)**.

5   Loosen the steering wheel nut and back it off several turns **(see illustration)**. Do not remove it completely.

6   While wearing gloves, use one hand to push the steering wheel up while using your other hand to tap the steering wheel nut with a hammer to help shock the steering wheel loose. When the steering wheel loosens and hits against the

11

nut, remove the nut and steering wheel.

7   If the steering wheel will not break free of its splines, remove steering shaft with the steering wheel attached to it (see Section 5). With the steering shaft removed from the vehicle, rest the steering wheel on a vise with the steering shaft hanging down through the jaws on the vise. Do not lock the steering shaft in the vise as it must be free to move. Use a brass or bronze drift and strike the steering nut to free the shaft from the steering wheel. When the steering wheel is free, remove its nut and the steering wheel.

8   On 2010 models, note the two wave washers and spacer installed on the steering shaft below the steering wheel.

9   On 2011 and later models, note the thick washer, thin washer and spacer installed on the steering shaft below the steering wheel.

10   Installation is the reverse of removal, noting the following:

a) *Clean the splines on the steering wheel and steering shaft, making sure to remove rust and corrosion from all surfaces, including the nut. If the nut cannot be thoroughly cleaned, replace it.*

b) *Make sure the front wheels are pointing straight ahead, then install the steering wheel. The bottom spoke should be centered and positioned at the bottom. Install the steering wheel nut and tighten to the torque listed in this Chapter's Specifications.*

c) *Drive the vehicle slowly on a straight level surface and make sure the steering wheel points straight ahead when you're driving in a straight line and not turning the steering wheel. Readjust the steering wheel mounting position, if necessary.*

Electric power steering models

CAUTION:

Do not strike the steering wheel when trying to remove it, as the force may permanently damage the EPS unit and set a power steering fault code.

11   Do not remove the steering wheel when the upper steering shaft is mounted on the vehicle. Attempting to do so may damage the power steering unit. The upper steering shaft must be removed with the steering wheel attached, then the steering wheel must be removed separately.

12   Remove the upper steering shaft with the steering wheel attached (see Section 5).

13   Pry the cover from the center of the steering wheel **(see illustration 4.4)**. Then hold the steering wheel and loosen the steering wheel nut until the outer end of the nut is flush with the end of the steering shaft. Do not remove the nut.

14   Rest the steering wheel on a vise with the upper steering shaft assembly hanging down through the jaws on the vise. Do not lock the upper steering shaft in the vise as it must be free to move. A taper is used to secure the steering wheel to the steering shaft. Use a brass or bronze

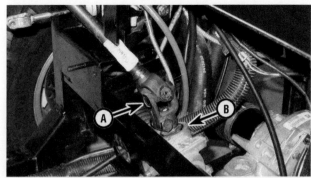

5.1a The lower steering shaft (A) is secured to the steering gearbox shaft (B) with a bolt and nut (2010 model shown)

drift and strike the steering nut to free the shaft from the steering wheel - have an assistant catch the shaft and EPS unit (if installed on the shaft) once the shaft is free of the steering wheel. When the steering wheel is free, remove its nut and the steering wheel.

15   On 2010 models, note the two wave washers and spacer installed on the steering shaft below the steering wheel.

16   On 2011 and later models, note the thick washer, thin washer and spacer installed on the steering shaft below the steering wheel.

17   Installation is the reverse of removal, noting the following:

a) *Before installing the steering wheel, first install the upper steering shaft onto the power steering unit (see Section 5).*

b) *When the steering shaft is in place and the wheels are pointing forward, install the parts described in Steps 15 or 16 onto the steering shaft if they were removed. Then install the steering wheel and tighten its nut (see Step 10).*

c) *Drive the vehicle slowly on a straight level surface and make sure the steering wheel points straight ahead when you're driving in a straight line and not turning the steering wheel. Readjust the steering wheel mounting position, if necessary.*

5   STEERING SHAFTS AND POWER STEERING UNIT - REMOVAL, BUSHING/BEARING REPLACEMENT AND INSTALLATION

Manual steering models

1   2010 models are equipped with separate upper and lower steering shafts. On 2011 and later models, the upper and lower steering shafts are permanently attached. Universal joints are used at the bottom of the lower steering shaft, and where the upper and lower steering shafts attach to each other. The steering shaft pivots on bushings (2010 models) or ball bearings (2011 and later models) installed in a pivot tube mounted on the frame. Models are also equipped with a tilt steering wheel damper **(see illustrations)**.

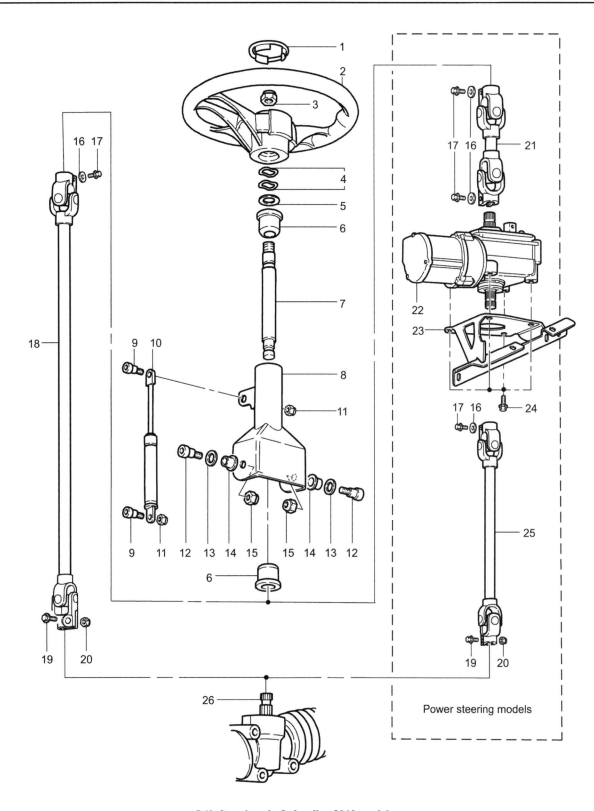

5.1b Steering shaft details - 2010 models

1	Cover	8	Pivot tube	14	Bushings	21	Middle steering shaft
2	Steering wheel	9	Shoulder bolt	15	Nuts	22	Power steering untit
3	Nut	10	Steering wheel	16	Washer	23	Mounting bracket
4	Wave washers		tilt damper	17	Screw	24	Screws
5	Spacer	11	Nut	18	Lower steering shaft	25	Lower steering shaft
6	Bushings	12	Shoulder bolts	19	Bolt	26	Steering gearbox
7	Upper steering shaft	13	Washers	20	Nut		shaft

Power steering models

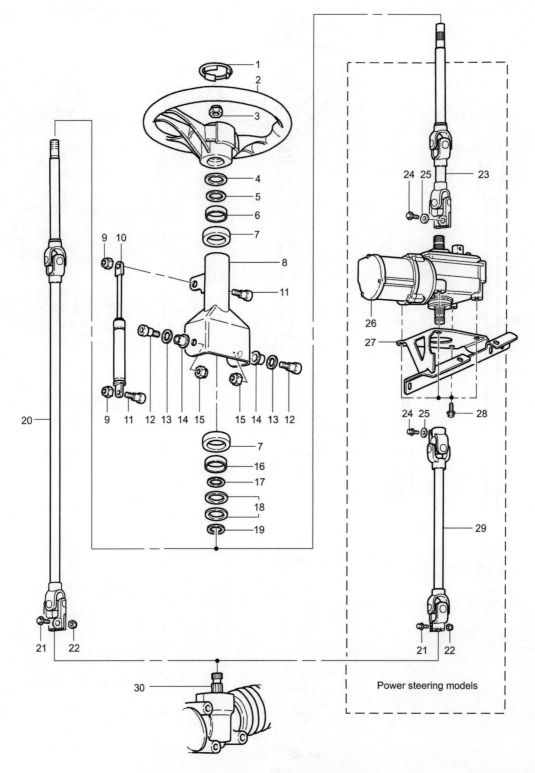

5.1c Steering shaft details - 2011 and later models

1	Cover	9	Nuts	16	Spacer	24	Screw
2	Steering wheel	10	Steering wheel tilt	17	Thin washer	25	Washer
3	Nut		damper	18	Thick washers	26	Power steering unit
4	Thick washer	11	Shoulder bolt	19	Thin washer	27	Mounting bracket
5	Thin washer	12	Shoulder bolts	20	Steering shaft	28	Screws
6	Spacer	13	Washers	21	Bolt	29	Lower steering shaft
7	Bearing	14	Bushings	22	Nut	30	Steering gearbox
8	Pivot tube	15	Nuts	23	Upper power		shaft
					steering shaft		

5.5 Scribe an alignment mark across the steering gearbox shaft and the lower steering shaft universal joint

5.7a Remove the nut and bolt (arrow) . . .

5.6a Hold the bolt and remove the nut (arrow) located at the bottom of the lower steering shaft

5.7b . . . and lower the steering wheel tilt damper and pivot tube

5.6b Tap a screwdriver into the slot in the universal joint . . .

5.6c . . . and slide the bolt out of the hole

Removal

2   Clean the steering gear and steering assembly parts that are accessible underneath the front of the vehicle.
3   Park the vehicle on a level surface and apply the parking brake. Loosen, but do not remove, the wheel nuts on both front wheels. Block the rear wheels to prevent the vehicle from rolling off the jackstands. Raise the front of the vehicle and secure it with jackstands, then remove the front wheels (see Chapter 10).
4   Remove the floor (front floor on Crew Models) (see Chapter 14).
5   Using a paint marker, scribe an alignment mark across the steering gearbox shaft and universal joint mounted on the lower steering shaft to help align the parts during installation **(see illustration)**.
6   Use a wrench to hold the bolt that secures the universal joint (lower steering shaft) to the steering gearbox shaft and remove its nut **(see illustration)**. If the bolt is tight and won't slide out, take a small wide-blade screwdriver and tap it into the slot in the universal joint to widen the offset hole until the bolt loosens, then slide it out. Leave the screwdriver in place to make it easier to slide the universal joint off of the steering shaft when removing the lower steering shaft **(see illustrations)**.
7   Remove the nut and bolt that secures the steering wheel tilt damper to the pivot tube, then carefully lower the tilt damper and pivot tube **(see illustration)**.

11

8   Raise and support the pivot tube assembly to access its fasteners. Remove the nuts, pivot tube mounting bolts, washers and bushings that secure the pivot tube to the frame, then lift and remove the pivot tube, steering shaft and steering wheel (if attached) as an assembly (see illustration). During removal, the universal joint on the lower steering shaft will release from the shaft on the steering gearbox. On some models it may be necessary to have an assistant spread the upper dash panel by hand to provide additional room when removing the steering shaft assembly.

Bushing replacement (2010 models)

9   The pivot tube is equipped with upper and lower bushings (see illustration 5.1b). Both bushings are the same.
10 Remove the steering wheel from the upper steering shaft (see Section 4). Then remove the two wave washers and spacer installed at the top of the upper steering shaft. Slide the upper steering shaft down and out of the bushings, and remove it with the attached lower steering shaft (see illustration 5.1b).
11 If a knock puller and a suitable size collet are available, slide the collet through the upper bushing, then expand and lock it against the bushing. Operate the slide hammer and remove the bushing from the pivot tube bore. If a puller is not available, use a thick wooden dowel and drive the bushing out by working from the opposite end of the pivot tube. Alternately work around the bushing to prevent it from binding. Repeat to remove the opposite bushing. Discard both bushings as they must not be reused (see illustration).
12 If it is necessary to separate the upper and lower steering shafts, use a paint marker and scribe an alignment mark across the upper steering shaft and the universal joint mounted on the lower steering shaft to help align the parts during installation. Remove the screw and washer from the universal joint, then separate the two steering shafts (see illustration 5.1b). After completing any necessary service, assemble the two steering shafts by aligning the marks, then install the steering shaft screw and washer and tighten to the torque listed in this Chapter's Specifications.
13 Clean and dry the steering shaft, and the upper two wave washers and spacer of all grease and dirt.
14 Inspect the upper steering shaft at the point where the two bushings operate for any heat damage (bluing), scoring and other damage. This surface must be smooth; otherwise, it may be difficult for the shaft to pass through the two new bushings while any surface roughness may cause rapid bushing wear. Then inspect the wave washers and spacer for damage.
15 Clean and dry the pivot tube bore to remove all traces of grease and dirt. Then inspect the bushing bores for cracks, gouge marks made when removing the bushings, and other damage. Any surface roughness must be removed, or it may be difficult to align and install the new bushings.
16 Support the pivot tube and either press or drive the new

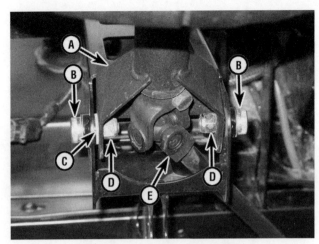

5.8 Pivot tube assembly details

A   Pivot tube
B   Pivot tube mounting bolts
C   Bushing and washer - bushings are installed through the frame mounting holes
D   Locknuts
E   Steering shaft assembly

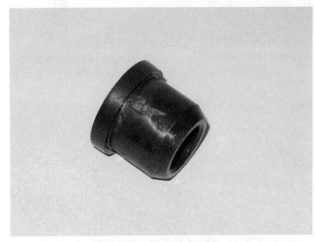

5.11 Steering shaft bushing

bushings into place until their shoulders bottom against the top of their respective bores. Whatever installation method is used, make sure each bushing is aligned squarely with its bore when installing it.
17 Slide the upper steering shaft through the bushings, making sure it pivots freely.
18 Install the spacer and the two wave washers over the upper steering shaft (see illustration 5.1b).
19 Install the steering wheel and tighten the nut hand-tight. Don't worry about aligning the steering wheel with the steering shaft at this time, as you will align the steering wheel when the steering shaft assembly is installed on the vehicle. The steering shaft assembly is now ready to be installed on the vehicle.

5.21 New pivot tube with installed bearings

5.27a Secure the pivot tube in a vise with soft jaws and remove the bearings with a knock puller. Here is the upper bearing (arrow)

5.27b . . . and the lower bearing (arrow)

5.27c Pivot tube with bearings removed

Bearing replacement (2011 and later models)

20 The pivot tube is equipped with an upper and lower bearing (see illustration 5.1c). Both bearings are the same.

21 When replacing the steering bearings, there are two options to consider. First, replacement bearings are available that can be installed in the original pivot tube installed on your vehicle. Second, OEM replacement pivot tubes are available with upper and lower bearings installed (see illustration). It may be worthwhile to compare the cost of the new bearings and the time required to replace them with the purchase of a new pivot tube and installed bearings.

22 With the pivot tube removed from the vehicle, remove the steering wheel from the steering shaft (see Section 4).

23 Remove the thick washer, thin washer and spacer installed at the top of the steering shaft.

24 Slide the steering shaft assembly out of the pivot tube, noting that the upper and lower steering shafts are permanently attached. Then remove the spacer, the upper thin washer, the two thick washers and the lower thin washer from the steering shaft. Note that the upper and lower thin washers are identical.

25 Clean and dry the steering shafts, and the upper and lower washer assemblies of all grease and dirt. Clean the upper and lower washer assemblies separately to prevent intermixing the parts.

26 Inspect the upper steering shaft at the point where the two bearings operate for any heat damage (bluing), scoring and other damage. This surface must be smooth for the shaft to pass through the two new bearings. Then inspect the individual parts that make up the upper and lower washer assemblies for damage.

NOTE:

A strong threadlock was applied to the bearing races when they were originally installed. If the bearings are difficult to remove, heat the pivot tube to help soften the threadlock, then try removing the bearings.

27 If a knock puller and a suitable size collet are available, slide the collet through the upper bearing, and expand it to lock it against the bearing. Operate the slide hammer and remove the bearing from the pivot tube bore. If a puller is not available, use a suitable drift and drive the bearing out by working from the opposite end of the pivot tube. Alternately work around the bearing to prevent it from binding. Repeat to remove the opposite bearing. Discard both bearings as they must not be reused (see illustrations).

28 Clean and dry the pivot tube to remove all traces of grease, dirt and threadlock from the bearing bore surfaces. Then inspect the bore surfaces for cracks and gouge marks made when removing the bearings, or other

11

damage **(see illustration)**. Any surface roughness must be removed, or it may be difficult to align and install the new bearings.

29   Install the lower thin washer, two thick washers, the upper thin washer and the spacer onto the steering shaft **(see illustration 5.1c)**. Note that the two thin washers are identical, and the two thick washers are identical.

NOTE:

When you install the new bearings in Step 30, you are simply sliding them onto the steering shaft at this time. Do not drive the bearings into their bores at this point in the assembly. The bearings will be seated after the pivot tube is installed in the vehicle and when you are tightening the steering wheel nut. This way, you are using the steering shaft to align the bearings with their bores in the pivot tube.

30   Install the new lower bearing onto the steering shaft. Apply Loctite 271 to the bearing's outer race, making sure not to allow any of the Loctite to enter the bearing. Then align and slide the steering shaft up through the pivot tube so the lower bearing race centers against its bore. Repeat and apply Loctite onto the upper bearing's outer race and slide the bearing over the steering shaft and allow it to center itself against its bore.

31   Install the spacer, the thin washer and the thick washer over the steering shaft and allow them to seat against the bearing.

32   Temporarily install the steering wheel and tighten the nut hand-tight. You will align the steering wheel after the steering shaft is installed on the vehicle.

33   Complete bearing installation by performing Steps 34 through 39.

Installation

34   Several Nyloc nuts are used to secure components in the steering shaft assembly. Because these nuts are critical to steering operation, and some are difficult to check and access when the steering assembly and all of the body components are installed on the vehicle, always install new Nyloc nuts during installation. If you will reuse the original nuts, clean and dry the threads on the nuts and bolts before reinstalling them. As you assemble and install the steering shaft, apply a threadlock onto the bolt threads before installing and tightening the nuts.

35   Install the lower steering shaft by sliding it over the steering gearbox shaft, while at the same time aligning the marks previously made during removal **(see illustration 5.5)**. Tap a screwdriver into the gap in the universal joint to widen the gap as described in Step 6, then install the bolt and a new Nyloc nut. Remove the screwdriver to close the gap. Do not tighten the nut at this time.

36   Install a bushing through the outside of each hole in the pivot tube frame mounting holes as shown in **illustration 5.1b or 5.1c**. Raise the pivot tube and align the bushings with

5.28 Before installing the new bearings, inspect the pivot tube bores for any scoring and other damage, and smooth surfaces as necessary

the holes in the frame, then install the pivot tube mounting bolts, washers and new Nyloc nuts **(see illustration 5.8)**. Hold the pivot tube mounting bolts and tighten the nuts to the torque listed in this this Chapter's Specifications.

37   Raise the steering wheel and install the bolt and a new Nyloc nut that secures the steering wheel tilt damper to the pivot tube **(see illustration 5.7a)**. Then hold the bolt and tighten the nut to the torque listed in this Chapter's Specifications.

38   Turn the steering so the front hubs are pointing straight ahead. Then check the steering wheel alignment to see if its bottom spoke is pointing straight ahead **(see illustration 4.3)**. If not, remove the nut and steering wheel and realign it as necessary. Then install the nut and tighten to the torque listed in this Chapter's Specifications. If you installed new bearings in the pivot tube, make sure both bearings are pressed squarely in their bores as you tighten the steering wheel nut. When the front wheels are pointing straight ahead and the steering wheel alignment is correct, push the steering wheel cover firmly into the steering wheel.

39   If you installed new bearings in the pivot tube, check underneath the pivot tube and along the steering shaft and wipe up any excess threadlock that was forced out past the bearings with a rag.

40   Hold the bolt and tighten the nut securing the lower steering shaft to the steering gearbox shaft **(see illustration 5.6a)** to the torque listed in this Chapter's Specifications.

41   Install the front wheels (see Chapter 10). Turn the steering wheel so the wheels are pointing straight and recheck the steering wheel alignment **(see illustration 4.3)**.

42   Install the floor and any other body components previously removed (see Chapter 14).

43   Drive the vehicle slowly on a straight level surface and make sure the steering wheel points straight ahead when driving in a straight line. Readjust the steering wheel mounting position, if necessary.

Electric power steering (EPS) models

44 On these models the power steering unit is installed between upper and lower steering shaft assemblies. 2010 models are equipped with an upper steering shaft, a middle steering shaft and a lower steering shaft. 2011 and later models are equipped with upper and lower steering shafts. The upper steering shaft pivots on either bushings (2010 models) or ball bearings (2011 and later models) **(see illustrations 5.1b or 5.1c)**.

45 To remove the power steering unit, it is necessary to remove the pivot tube along with the upper steering shaft assembly. The lower steering shaft can be left in place after it is disconnected from the power steering unit.

46 This section removes the steering shafts and the power steering unit.

Removal

47 Clean the steering gear and steering assembly parts that are accessible underneath the front of the vehicle.

48 Park the vehicle on a level surface and apply the parking brake. Loosen, but do not remove, the wheel nuts on both front wheels. Block the rear wheels to prevent the vehicle from rolling off the jackstands. Raise the front of the vehicle and secure it with jackstands, then remove the front wheels (see Chapter 10).

49 Remove the lower dash panel and other body components as required to access the steering shafts and the power steering unit (see Chapter 14).

50 Before removing the steering shaft bolts, turn the steering wheel so the front hubs are pointing straight ahead. Then check that the steering wheel's bottom spoke is centered and positioned squarely at the bottom **(see illustration 4.3)**.

51 On 2010 models, remove the screws and washers that secure the middle steering shaft to the power steering unit **(see illustration 5.1b)**.

52 On 2011 and later models, remove the screw and washer that secure the upper steering shaft to the power steering unit **(see illustration 5.1c)**.

53 Remove the nut and bolt that secure the steering wheel tilt damper to the pivot tube, then carefully lower the tilt damper and pivot tube **(see illustration 5.7a and 5.7b)**.

54 Raise and support the pivot tube assembly to access the pivot tube fasteners. Remove the nuts, pivot tube mounting bolts, washers and bushings that secure the pivot tube to the frame, and remove the pivot tube, steering shaft(s) and steering wheel as an assembly.

55 If you are performing this procedure just to remove the steering wheel, you can remove it now as described in Section 4. If you are performing this procedure to replace the bearings in the pivot tube, it will be necessary to remove the steering wheel before you reinstall the pivot tube back onto the vehicle.

56 Trace the two wiring harnesses from the power steering unit, noting their routing alignment, and disconnect their wiring harness connectors.

57 Remove the screw and washer securing the lower steering shaft universal joint to the power steering unit. Remove the screws that secure the power steering unit to its mounting bracket and remove it from the vehicle.

58 Perform Steps 5 and 6 to remove the nut and bolt that secure the lower steering shaft universal joint to the steering gearbox shaft.

59 If necessary, remove the screws securing the power steering unit mounting bracket to the frame and remove the mounting bracket.

Bearing replacement

60 If you will be replacing the steering bearings in the original pivot tube, perform Steps 20 through 33 to remove them.

Installation

NOTE:

Power steering units are programmed for specific vehicles. If you are replacing the original unit on your vehicle and considering the purchase of a used unit, make sure it will work on your year Ranger model. See a dealer parts department for additional information and to confirm part numbers.

NOTE:

When tightening a steering shaft fastener identified in the following Steps, first identify the fastener as to either a screw, or a bolt and nut. Then refer to the appropriate steering shaft fastener torque listed in this Chapter's Specifications.

61 Note the information in Step 34 on the use of Nyloc nuts when installing the steering shaft assembly in the following steps.

62 Install the lower steering shaft by sliding it over the steering gear shaft, while aligning the marks previously made during removal **(see illustration 5.5)**. Tap a screwdriver into the gap in the universal joint to widen the gap as described in Step 6, then install the pinch bolt and nut. Remove the screwdriver to close the gap. Do not tighten the nut at this time.

63 If the mounting bracket was removed from the power steering unit, reinstall the mounting bracket and tighten its mounting screws securely.

64 Install the power steering unit by aligning the skip-tooth spline on the power steering unit shaft with the slot in the top of the lower steering shaft universal joint. Pivot the power steering unit in place against its mounting bracket and install the mounting screws and tighten to the torque listed in this Chapter's Specifications.

65 Install the bolt and washer that secure the lower steering shaft to the power steering unit and tighten to the

11

torque listed in this Chapter's Specifications.

66 Reconnect the power steering unit 2-pin and 8-pin connectors, making sure the wiring harnesses are properly routed.

67 Make sure the front hubs are pointing straight ahead. If it is difficult to determine this alignment, reinstall the front wheels and use them as a visual reference.

68 Lift the pivot tube with the steering wheel and upper steering shaft attached and position it in the frame. On 2010 models, the middle steering shaft must be attached to the upper steering shaft when installing the steering assembly into the frame. Install the middle steering shaft (2010 models) or the upper steering shaft (2011 and later models) by aligning the slot in the steering shaft with the skip-tooth spline on the power steering unit shaft. At the same time, make sure the center spoke on the steering wheel is at the bottom and facing forward. Do not install the screw at this time.

69 Perform Steps 34, 36 and 37 to install and tighten the pivot tube and steering wheel tilt damper fasteners.

70 On 2010 models, if the steering wheel was removed, install the bushing and the two wave washers over the upper steering shaft.

71 On 2011 and later models, if the steering wheel was removed, install the spacer, thin washer and thick washer over the upper steering shaft.

72 Perform Step 38 to install the steering wheel and seat the steering bearings in the pivot tube - required on 2011 and later models if the original bearings were replaced.

73 On 2011 and later models, if the original bearings were replaced, check underneath the pivot tube and remove any excess Loctite with a rag.

74 Hold the bolt and tighten the nut securing the lower steering shaft to the steering gearbox shaft **(see illustration 5.6a)** to the torque listed in this Chapter's Specifications.

75 If removed, install the front wheels (see Chapter 10). Turn the steering wheel so the wheels are pointing straight and check the steering wheel alignment.

76 Perform Step 42.

77 Drive the vehicle slowly on a straight, level surface and make sure the steering wheel points straight ahead when driving in a straight line. Readjust the steering wheel mounting position, if necessary.

6 TIE-ROD BOOTS, TIE-ROD ENDS AND GEARBOX BOOTS - REMOVAL AND INSTALLATION

1 The tie-rod boots, tie-rod ends and the steering gearbox boots can be replaced separately. Replacement tie-rods are not available from Polaris.

Removal

2 Remove the front wheel for the side being worked on (see Chapter 10).

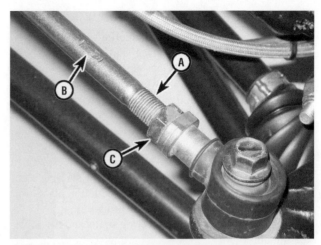

6.3 Measure the length of the exposed threads (A) on the tie-rod, then hold the tie-rod with a wrench across its flats (B) and loosen the locknut (C)

6.4 Tie-rod mounting details

A Bolt   D Nut
B Tie-rod   E Cotter pin
C Washers

Tie-rod boots and tie-rod ends

NOTE:
If you're only replacing the tie-rod boot, it is not necessary to loosen the tie-rod locknut in Step 3.

3 If the tie-rod end will be removed, measure the length of the exposed tie-rod threads, starting at the locknut. This dimension will be used to approximately reposition the tie-rod end during assembly. Then hold the tie-rod with a wrench across its flats and loosen the tie-rod locknut **(see illustration)**.

4 Remove the cotter pin at the bottom of the tie-rod, then hold the bolt and remove the nut. Remove the bolt and the two washers and pivot the tie-rod away from the steering knuckle **(see illustration)**. Discard the cotter pin.

6.5 With the tie-rod free from the steering knuckle, remove the boot

6.10c Before cutting the plastic tie that secures the inner boot end, note where the boot end seats over the steering gearbox (arrow). Then spread the boot end to expose the plastic tie and cut it with a pair of cutters. Save this plastic-tie so you can measure its width to match a new one if you're not purching an OEM replacement

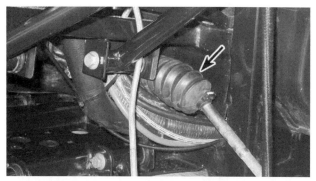

6.8 The left-side boot (arrow) is more difficult to replace due to the cables and hoses routed next to it

6.10d Release the outer boot end from the groove in the tie-rod and and slide the boot (arrow) off the tie-rod

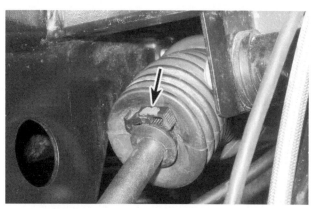

6.10a Lift the locking arm (arrow) on the outer clamp . . .

5   If it is only necessary to replace the boot, remove it from the tie-rod end **(see illustration)**.

6   If you're replacing the tie-rod end, turn the tie-rod end and remove it **(see illustration 6.3)**.

Gearbox boots

7   Remove the tie-rod end from the side the boot will be replaced on (see Steps 3 through 6).

8   Remove components or remove and reroute any cables or hoses to access the gearbox boots **(see illustration)**.

NOTE:

If you cannot obtain enough access to replace the left-side boot, remove the steering gearbox assembly, then replace the boot (see Section 7).

9   Because the tie-rod joint will be exposed once you have removed the boot, first clean the boot and the area around the boot to prevent sand and dirt from falling onto and contaminating the grease on the tie-rod joint. If necessary, wrap dirty and contaminated areas with plastic sheets (large garbage bags work well for this).

10   Remove the clamp at each end of the boot, and slide the boot off the tie-rod **(see illustrations)**.

6.10b . . . and remove the clamp from the groove in the boot

11 Inspect the tie-rod joint for any damage that may have been caused by sand and dirt that entered the damaged boot. Clean the tie-rod joint thoroughly and lubricate the exposed parts with grease **(see illustration)**.

12 If you will not be immediately installing the new boot, wrap the tie-rod joint with plastic to prevent sand and dirt from contaminating grease and exposed operating surfaces.

Installation

13 Clean the tie-rod, tie-rod end and locknut threads.

14 If installing a new steering gearbox boot, slide it over the tie-rod and seat its outer end into the groove in the tie-rod **(see illustration)**. Then seat the boot's inner end onto the steering gearbox in the same position as the original boot. Make sure the boot is not twisted and install the plastic-tie onto the inner boot end shoulder. Spin the boot around the steering gearbox to make sure the plastic-tie is completely seated in the shoulder in the end of the boot. If the plastic-tie is not properly installed, water and debris will enter the tie-rod joint. When selecting a plastic-tie for the inner boot end shoulder, make sure its width is the same as the original so that it can seat in the boot shoulder **(see illustration 6.10c)**. When the boot is properly seated, install the clamp into the boot's outer groove and lock it in place. Then make a final check that the boot is not twisted.

15 Install the locknut, then install and turn the tie-rod end onto the tie-rod to the dimensions recorded in Step 3. Do not tighten the locknut as this is an approximate position only.

16 If installing a new tie-rod end boot, slide it over the tie-rod end and center the hole in the boot with the hole in the tie-rod end **(see illustration 6.5)**.

17 Wipe off the tie-rod boot and clean its bore in the knuckle of all dirt and corrosion. Install the tie-rod and secure it to the steering knuckle with the bolt, two washers and nut. On all models, the tie-rod end is installed on top of the steering knuckle. The washers fit on each side of the steering knuckle **(see illustration 6.4)**. Hold the bolt and tighten the nut to the torque listed in this Chapter's Specifications. Install a new cotter pin through the hole in the bolt and bend the ends over to lock it in place.

18 Install the front wheels (see Chapter 10).

19 Check and adjust the toe-in (see Chapter 2). After adjusting the toe-in, hold the tie-rod and tighten the tie-rod end locknuts to the torque listed in this Chapter's Specifications.

7   STEERING GEARBOX - REMOVAL AND INSTALLATION

1 Replacement parts to overhaul the steering gearbox, other than boots and clamps, are not available from the manufacturer. If the steering gearbox is damaged, it will be necessary to replace the complete unit.

6.11 The exposed tie-rod joint assembly - this area must be kept clean

6.14 Seat the outer boot end into this groove (arrow) in the tie-rod. Here the boot has been slid rearward along the tie-rod to identify the groove

CAUTION:
Work carefully around the brake lines and coolant hoses when performing the service in this section.

Removal

2 Remove both front wheels (see Chapter 10).

3 Remove the floor (front floor on Crew models) to expose the steering gearbox mounting nuts (see Chapter 14).

4 Check the position of the intake air duct and how it passes by the steering gearbox **(see illustration)**, and reposition or remove it if it will interfere with removal of the steering gearbox (see Chapter 7).

5 Disconnect the tie-rods at the steering knuckles (see Section 6).

6 Note how the cables, wiring harnesses and brake

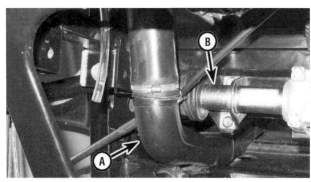

7.4 Note how the intake air duct (A) passes by the steering gearbox (B) and release or remove it if necessary

8.3c Check that the spring clip remained in the axle groove

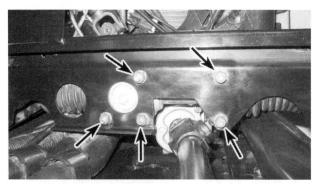

7.8 Remove the steering gearbox nuts (arrows) and bolts

8.3a Grab the front axle and pull it sharply . . .

8.3b . . . to remove it from the front gearcase

hoses are routed next to the steering gearbox to help with alignment during installation.

7   Scribe an alignment mark across the steering gear shaft and universal joint, then remove the nut and bolt from the universal joint as described in Section 5. Leave the screwdriver in the universal joint to help the lower steering shaft slide off the steering gearbox shaft in Step 8.

8   Remove the nuts and bolts securing the steering gearbox to the frame, then lower the steering gearbox to disconnect it from the universal joint mounted on the lower steering shaft **(see illustration)**.

Installation

9   Installation is the reverse of removal, noting the following:

   a) *Tighten the steering gearbox mounting fasteners to the torque listed in this Chapter's Specifications.*
   b) *Hold the bolt and tighten the nut securing the lower steering shaft to the steering gearbox shaft to the torque listed in this Chapter's Specifications.*
   c) *Check toe-in and adjust if necessary (see Chapter 2).*

8   FRONT AXLE - REMOVAL, INSPECTION, BOOT REPLACEMENT AND INSTALLATION

Removal

1   Clean both sides of the front gearcase to prevent dirt from entering when removing the front axle.

2   Remove the steering knuckle from the front axle (see Chapter 10). Note that the steering knuckle can be removed from the vehicle, or left attached to the lower control arm.

3   Grab the front axle with both hands and jerk the axle (not the outboard joint) sharply to disconnect it from the front gearcase **(see illustrations)**. The spring clip on the inboard side of the front axle will cause some resistance when removing the axle. After removing the axle, check that the spring clip remained on the axle and not fall inside the gearcase **(see illustration)**.

4   Cover or plug the axle opening in the front gearcase to prevent dirt from entering.

11

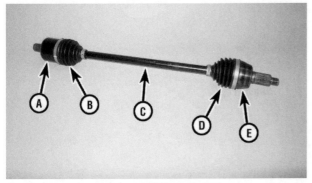

8.5a Front axle details

A	Inner CV joint	D	Outer boot
B	Inner boot and clamps		and clamps
C	Axle	E	Outer CV joint

Inspection

5   Clean the axle, boots and splines on both ends of the axle **(see illustration)**. Do not submerge the axle boots in solvent as the CV joints (inside the boots) are packed with grease and may become contaminated. Also clean the splines in the front gearcase so the splines and clip groove can be inspected **(see illustration)**.

6   Inspect the boots for tearing, cracks and other damage. Check that the clamps are tight and have not slipped off either boot. A loose or torn boot will allow dirt and moisture to enter the CV joint. If necessary, replace damaged boots (see Chapter 12) **(see illustrations)**.

7   Inspect the threads on the outer CV joint for stripped or damaged threads. Check also that the cotter pin hole in the axle is not cracked or damaged **(see illustration 8.6a)**.

8   Inspect the clip groove on the inner CV joint for cracks and other damage **(see illustration 8.6b)**. If the clip and clip groove are damaged, check the clip groove inside the front gearcase for the same conditions **(see illustration 8.5b)**.

9   Inspect for worn, distorted and broken splines on both CV joints **(see illustrations 8.6a and 8.6b)**. If damage is noted, check the splines inside the front hub and gearcase for the same conditions.

10   Clamp the axle in a vise with soft jaws. Then pivot each CV joint and check for roughness or play in the joint. If damage or excessive play is evident, disassemble the axle and inspect the parts (see Chapter 12). If roughness or play remains after cleaning and lubrication, replace the worn or damaged parts, or the complete axle if necessary.

11   Use a straightedge to check the axle for straightness. If the axle is bent, it must be replaced as its operation will damage the bearings in the steering knuckle and front gearcase and cause vibration problems with the steering assembly.

Boot replacement

12   The front and rear axles are very similar in design and are disassembled and reassembled in the same way (see Chapter 12).

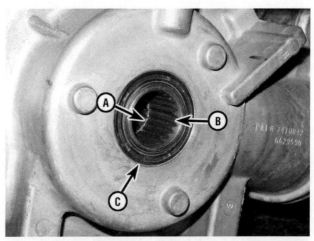

8.5b Front gearcase details

A	Clip groove	C	Oil seal
B	Output hub splines		

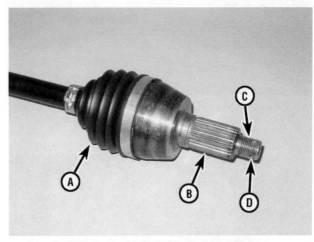

8.6a Outer CV joint inspection points

A	Axle boot and clamps	C	Axle threads
B	Axle splines	D	Cotter pin hole

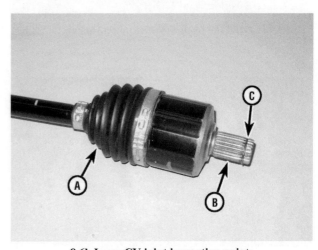

8.6b Inner CV joint inspection points

A	Axle boot and clamps	C	Clip groove
B	Splines		

8.14 To install the new spring clip, start one end in the groove and continue to work the clip over the shaft end, into the groove

8.15 With the new spring clip installed in the groove, lubricate the splines with anti-seize

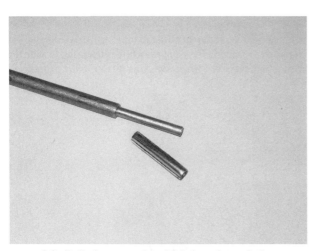

9.2a Roll pin removal tool fabricated on a lathe, and a roll pin

Installation

13 Carefully wipe the gearcase oil seal with a rag to remove all old grease, then lubricate the gearcase splines with an anti-seize compound **(see illustration 8.5b)**.

14 Use a small screwdriver or awl to pry the old spring clip from the groove in the inner end of the axle and discard it. Then install a new spring clip into the groove **(see illustration)**. Don't distort the new clip when installing it, as it will make it more difficult to compress the clip when trying to install the axle into the output hub splines inside the front gearcase.

15 Lubricate the inboard axle splines with an anti-seize compound **(see illustration)**.

16 Align the inboard axle splines with the gearcase splines and push the axle sharply into the gearcase. If the axle does not enter the gearcase, check the spring clip for damage and replace if necessary. Repeat until the spring clip compresses as it passes through the gearcase splines and seats inside the clip groove. Then lightly pull on the axle to make sure it is locked in place.

17 Installation is otherwise the reverse of removal.

NOTE:

If the axle was rebuilt, make several test drives and then stop and check the axle for any grease that may have leaked out of the boots. Wipe off the axle and then repeat the checks to make sure no more grease leaks out. Usually, grease that is trapped along the edge of a boot will leak or squeeze out one or two times, and then stop after the boot is completely seated. If grease continues to leak out, check the clamps for tightness.

9   DRIVESHAFT - REMOVAL AND INSTALLATION

Standard Ranger models

1 The single piece driveshaft is equipped with two universal joints and a grease nipple mounted on the rear yoke. Grease should be applied at the specified intervals to lubricate the yoke and transmission snorkel shaft (see Chapter 2). The two U-joints are sealed units and cannot be lubricated. A roll pin secures the driveshaft universal joint to the front gearcase pinion shaft.

2 Special tools: A long punch is needed to reach and remove the roll pin that secures the driveshaft to the front gearcase. Use the Polaris Roll Pin Removal Tool (part No. 2872608) or a suitable punch. The removal tool used in this procedure is a length of 3/8 inch diameter steel rod, with a shoulder machined (using a lathe) on one end and sized to pass through the holes in the universal joint and gearcase pinion shaft when driving the roll pin out **(see illustration)**. A second tool to consider, and especially if you have access to a lathe, is a roll pin holding tool. Because of how far you have to reach in to access the

11

roll pin holes in the universal joint/front gearcase shaft, aligning and starting the roll pin into the universal joint can be difficult to do, and especially when working alone in the shop. A holding tool was made by drilling a hole into the end of a long round shaft, with an inside diameter slightly larger than the roll pin and to a maximum depth half the length of the roll pin **(see illustration)**. You then install the roll pin into the holding tool, align the roll pin with the hole in the universal joint, and drive the roll pin into position until the tool bottoms. You finish by driving the roll pin into place with the same tool used to remove it. Purchase a new roll pin from a dealer parts department and measure it to determine the actual dimensions required when fabricating one or both tools.

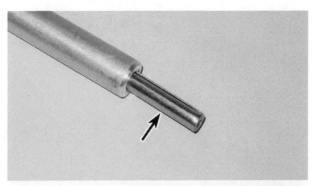

9.2b Roll pin holding tool with a roll pin (arrow) installed in one end

Removal

> NOTE:
>
> *After disconnecting the driveshaft from the gearcase and transmission, the manufacturer states to pull the driveshaft toward the left side of the vehicle, and then remove it by sliding it out rearward in front of the clutch housing. However, due to the length of the driveshaft, we were unable to remove the driveshaft following this path* **(see illustration)**. *If you want to give this method a try, make sure to work carefully so you don't damage any components when attempting to maneuver the driveshaft into position. We found it easier to remove the front gearcase first, then the driveshaft.*

3   Remove the floor panel (see Chapter 14).
4   Before disconnecting the driveshaft from the gearcase pinion shaft, check the exposed part of the transmission snorkel shaft for dirt, sand, rust and corrosion **(see illustration)**. Because it is necessary to slide the driveshaft rearward along the snorkel shaft during this procedure, any debris on the shaft will make it difficult to move the driveshaft. If necessary, spray the snorkel shaft where it enters the universal joint with a penetrating oil, and allow sufficient time for the oil to soak in between the two parts. You can also use sandpaper or a small wire wheel mounted on a hand grinder to clean the snorkel shaft.
5   Roll the vehicle on a level surface until the roll pin used to secure the driveshaft universal joint to the front gearcase pinion shaft is accessible on the right side of the vehicle **(see illustration)**.
6   Shift the transmission into NEUTRAL and apply the parking brake. Then support the vehicle on jackstands so both front wheels are off the ground. Remove the front, right side axle (see Section 8).

> WARNING:
>
> *When driving the roll pin out of the driveshaft, safety glasses or goggles must be worn to prevent debris released from the punch from injuring your eyes.*

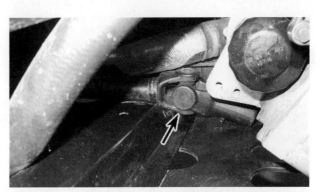

9.2c In attempting to remove the driveshaft by passing it out the left, rear side of the vehicle, we could not turn and move the driveshaft rearward past the point shown here (arrow)

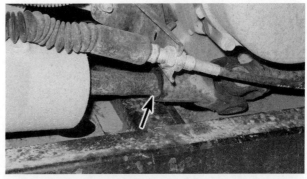

9.4 Note that a buildup of rust and other debris on the snorkel shaft (arrow) should be removed before attempting to slide the driveshaft rearward when removing it later in the procedure

9.5 Here is the roll pin (arrow) used to secure the driveshaft universal joint to the front gearcase pinion shaft

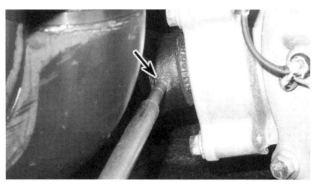

9.7a Remove the roll pin with a punch and hammer . . .

9.8b . . . to release the universal joint (A) from the front gearcase pinion shaft (B)

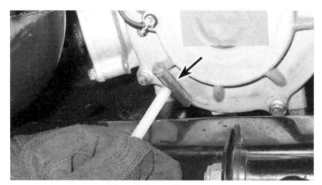

9.7b . . . roll pin removed from driveshaft

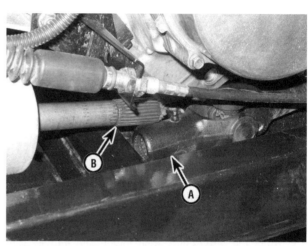

9.9 Slide the drive shaft forward to disconnect its universal joint (A) from the snorkel shaft (B)

9.7c Before removing the driveshaft, use a stiff brush to clean the mating holes in the universal joint and front gearcase pinion shaft of any rust and corrosion

7   Use a punch (see Step 2) and drive the roll pin out of the universal joint and front gearcase pinion shaft **(see illustrations)**. If it is difficult to start the roll pin moving, spray a penetrating oil at the top the universal joint and also through its two openings and allow sufficient time for the oil to soak in.

8   Working through the floor panel opening, slide the driveshaft rearward toward the transmission while allowing the universal joint to slide off the front gearcase pinion shaft **(see illustrations)**.

9   With the front part of the driveshaft free, grasp the driveshaft and slide it forward to disconnect its universal joint from the snorkel shaft on the transmission **(see illustration)**.

10   Remove the front gearcase (see Section 11).

9.8a Slide the driveshaft rearward toward the transmission until it stops . . .

9.11 Remove the driveshaft (arrow) through the front of the vehicle

9.12 Remove the O-ring (arrow) installed in the rear universal joint

11   Maneuver the driveshaft as required and remove it through the front of the vehicle **(see illustration)**.
12   Remove and discard the O-ring installed in the rear universal joint **(see illustration)**.

Inspection

13   Thoroughly clean the universal joint and remove all grease and dirt from the splines in the universal joints.
14   Inspect the splines in each end of the driveshaft for twisting, cracks and other damage. If damage is noted, check the mating splines on the front gearcase pinion shaft and the transmission snorkel shaft for the same conditions.
15   Hold the driveshaft, then pivot and move each universal joint by hand **(see illustration)**. Each joint must move smoothly throughout its full range of motion. Then check for any visual damage or any signs of grease leaking from the bearings. If necessary, overhaul the universal joint (see Section 10).
16   Clean the roll pin hole in the front universal joint with a brush, then check the hole for cracks, grooves and other damage **(see illustration)**. Clean and check the mating hole in the front gearcase pinion shaft for the same conditions.

Installation

17   Installation is otherwise the reverse of removal, noting the following:

   a) *Lubricate a new O-ring with grease and install it into the groove in the rear universal joint (see Step 12).*
   b) *Install the drive shaft by aligning the holes in its front universal joint with the hole in the front gearcase pinion shaft.*
   c) *Use a new roll pin to secure the driveshaft universal joint to the front gearcase pinion shaft.*

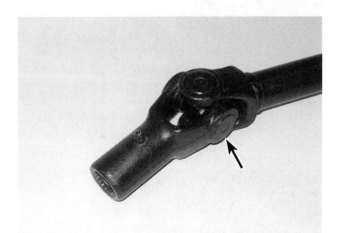

9.15 Check the universal joint for any binding, roughness or signs of grease leaking from the bearings (arrow)

9.16 When inspecting the driveshaft assembly don't overlook the roll pin hole in the front universal joint. Clean the hole while checking it for cracks and other damage

d) *If possible, use the roll pin holding tool to align and initially start the roll pin into the universal joint (see Step 2).*

e) *After installing the driveshaft onto the vehicle, inject grease through the grease fitting mounted on the driveshaft's rear yoke (see Chapter 2).*

Crew models

18   Because of this vehicle's long wheelbase, two separate driveshafts, joined together with splines, are used. The front driveshaft is equipped with two universal joints, where the front part is installed over the front gearcase pinion shaft and the rear part is installed over the splines on the rear driveshaft. The rear driveshaft is supported on its front end with a separate bearing mounted on the frame, and is equipped with a universal joint that is installed over the transmission snorkel shaft. A roll pin secures the front drive shaft universal joint to the front gearcase pinion shaft.

Removal

19   Remove the roll pin from the front drive shaft (see Step 7). Note that this step is only necessary when removing the front drive shaft. If you are only servicing the rear drive shaft or support bearing, the roll pin and front drive shaft can be left in place.

20   Remove the front seat base and the storage container mounted underneath it (see Chapter 14).

21   Working through the access opening (centered between the two front seats), remove the nuts and bolts on each side of the bearing housing.

22   Before separating the front and rear driveshafts, draw an alignment mark across each shaft where they mate. An index spline is used on each shaft, and the shafts will only mesh when these splines are aligned. These alignment marks will help you locate the index splines when assembling the two shafts together.

23   Slide the rear driveshaft rearward along the snorkel shaft, then pivot both driveshafts toward the left side of the vehicle to disconnect them.

24   If you are removing the front driveshaft, slide it rearward to disconnect it from the front gearcase pinion shaft and remove it from the vehicle.

25   If you are removing the rear driveshaft, remove the driveshaft bearing support bracket nuts and bolts from the bearing, then remove the support bracket. Slide the rear driveshaft forward to disconnect it from the transmission snorkel shaft, then maneuver it so that its rear end is positioned towards the left, rear side of the vehicle. When the driveshaft is free, slide it past the clutch outer cover and remove it from the vehicle.

26   Remove and discard the O-ring installed in the rear universal joint of both drive shafts (see Step 12).

Inspection

27   Refer to Steps 13 through 16.

Driveshaft bearing replacement

28   Provided that the driveshaft bearing has not seized against the rear driveshaft, the bearing can be replaced with the rear driveshaft mounted in the vehicle.

29   If used, remove the snap ring from the front side of the bearing and discard it.

NOTE:

Before removing the set screws in Step 30, make sure the hex recess in each screw is clean and free of sand and dirt. If necessary, use a small pick to clean them. This step will help the Allen wrench to grip the screws fully, instead of slipping and possibly damaging them to the point where you have to drill them out.

30   Loosen the two set screws to free the bearing, then slide the bearing off the shaft. If the bearing has seized to the shaft, remove the rear driveshaft from the vehicle (see Steps 19 through 25). Then use a press to separate the bearing and shaft.

31   Clean the driveshaft and inspect the bearing surface for any scoring and other surface roughness. Smooth these areas with a file before installing the new bearing.

32   Slide the new bearing onto the driveshaft.

33   If the driveshaft was originally equipped with a snap ring, install a new snap ring into the groove in the driveshaft. Apply Loctite 242 to the set screw threads and thread them partway into the bearing. Slide the bearing along the driveshaft and seat it firmly against the snap ring, then tighten the two screws to the torque listed in this Chapter's Specifications.

34   Align the staked spline on the rear driveshaft with the wide spline on the front driveshaft and mesh the shafts together.

35   If the driveshaft was not equipped with a snap ring, install the support bracket and secure in place with the bolts and nuts and tighten the nuts finger-tight. Slide the rear driveshaft as required until the correct spline engagement is achieved and tighten the bearing set screws to the torque listed in this Chapter's Specifications. Then tighten the driveshaft bearing support bracket nuts to the torque listed in this Chapter's Specifications.

36   On driveshafts with the snap ring, install the support bracket and secure in place with the bolts and nuts and tighten to the torque listed in this Chapter's Specifications.

37   Snap a grease gun onto the grease nipple on each driveshaft and lubricate the driveshaft yokes (see Chapter 2).

Installation

38   Installation is the reverse of removal, noting the following:

a) *Clean all of the splines before installing the driveshaft. This includes the splines in both ends of each drive shaft and the external splines on the front gearcase pinion shaft and the transmission snorkel shaft. Then lubricate the splines with grease.*

11

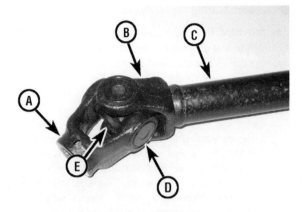

10.2 Universal joint details

A	Slip yoke	D	Bearing cap
B	Solid yoke		(bearing assembly)
C	Driveshaft	E	Spider

b) *Lubricate two new O-rings with grease and in-stall an O-ring into the groove in the rear universal joint in each driveshaft.*

c) *Align the staked spline on the rear driveshaft with the wide spline on the front driveshaft and mesh the shafts together.*

d) *Tighten the driveshaft bearing support bracket nuts to the torque listed in this Chapter's Specifications.*

e) *Install the front drive shaft by aligning the holes in its universal joint with the hole in the front gearcase pinion shaft.*

f) *Use a new roll pin to secure the front driveshaft universal joint to the front gearcase pinion shaft.*

g) *Snap a grease gun onto the grease nipple on each driveshaft and lubricate the driveshaft yokes (see Chapter 2).*

10 DRIVESHAFT UNIVERSAL JOINT - OVERHAUL

1   Remove the driveshaft(s). See Section 9.

NOTE:

A new bearing set (spider, bearings and lock rings) must be installed whenever the slip yoke is removed from the driveshaft. Do not reinstall the old parts.

2   Mark the slip yoke, solid yoke and the spider so the spider and slip yoke can be reassembled facing in the same direction/position on the driveshaft **(see illustration)**.

3   Support the drive shaft in a vise with soft jaws so you have access to the universal joint. Locate the inner lock rings that secure the bearing caps in place and drive them out of the bearing cap grooves with a punch and hammer **(see illustration)**.

4   Select a socket that is slightly smaller than the bearing cap's outside diameter. Then place the socket on a vise and

10.3 Remove each lock ring with a punch and hammer

10.4 With the lower bearing cap supported on a socket (A), drive the solid yoke down to press the upper bearing cap assembly (B) out of the slip yoke

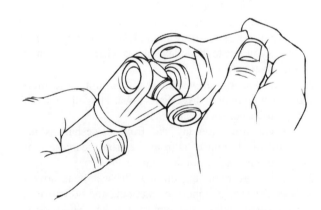

10.5 When the bearings have been removed, remove the slip yoke from the spider

center one of the slip yoke bearing caps onto the socket. Support the driveshaft so that it is parallel with the floor, and drive the solid yoke down with a hammer to press the upper bearing cap up and out of the slip yoke **(see illustration)**.

5   Turn the drive shaft over and repeat by driving against the spider to remove the opposite bearing cap assembly, then remove the slip yoke from the spider **(see illustration)**.

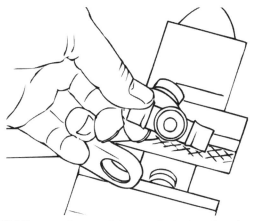

10.6 Remove the remaining two lock rings, bearings and spider

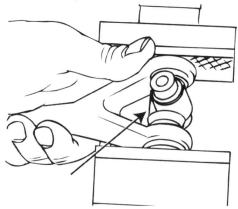

10.10 With the bearing caps partially installed in the solid yoke, fit the spider in place

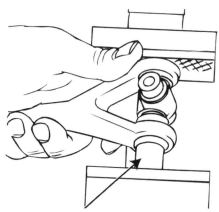

10.11 Place a large socket (arrow) against the solid yoke (to prevent the bearing it is protecting from moving) and press the exposed bearing into the yoke

6   Repeat to remove the remaining two lock rings, bearings and the spider **(see illustration)**.

7   Discard the spider and bearing assembly.

8   Clean and dry all parts.

9   Inspect the slip yoke and solid yoke bearing surfaces for cracks, scoring and other damage. Remove burrs with a fine-cut file. Replace damaged parts as required.

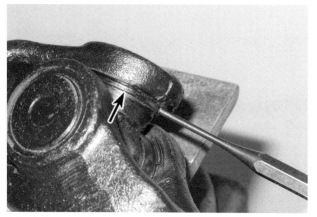

10.14 With the final two bearings and the slip yoke installed, install the remaining two stop rings

10   Begin assembly by installing new bearing caps into the solid yoke, then fit the spider in place and in the two bearings while making sure not to dislodge any bearings from the bearing caps **(see illustration)**. At the same time, position the spider with the grease fitting (if one is used) facing the center of the driveshaft. If the spider does not have a grease fitting, refer to the marks on the original spider and install the new spider facing in the same direction.

11   Select a socket with an inside diameter large enough to fit against the solid yoke without contacting the bearing caps. Then place the assembly in a vise, with the socket placed against one jaw and the exposed bearing positioned against the other jaw. Make sure the socket and bearing are seating squarely against the vise jaws. If you cannot square these parts in the vise, you may want to use a press. Turn the vise handle to tighten the jaws and press the exposed bearing cap into the yoke. Stop frequently to check and make sure the bearing cap is entering the yoke bore squarely and is not binding the spider. This is probably the most important part of the procedure, as you can damage the bearing bore if the bearing is cocked to one side **(see illustration)**. Before the bearing is fully installed, stop and check the stop ring groove position in the spider in relation to the inside part of the yoke that the stop ring will rest against when it is installed. You must make sure the bearing is installed to its correct depth so the spider will be correctly positioned for installation of the stop rings.

12   Turn the driveshaft over in the vise while placing the socket against the side of the yoke where the bearing was just installed, then press the opposite bearing into the yoke, again stopping to make sure the bearing cap is entering the bore squarely and is not binding the spider.

13   Once the first set of bearings are installed, install new lock rings by driving them into the spider grooves and against the yoke. If a lock ring will not slide into its groove, you will have to adjust the spider's position. Make sure both lock rings are installed and locked fully in place. Pivot the spider to make sure there is no roughness or binding.

14   Perform Steps 10 through 13 to install the slip yoke **(see illustration 10.5)** and the remaining two bearings and stop rings **(see illustration)**.

11

10.15 With the universal joint resting on a vise, tap each side to seat the bearings against the stop rings

15   With the bearings and stop rings installed, place the universal joint on a vise and tap each side to help the bearings against the stop rings **(see illustration)**.

16   Move the universal joint throughout its full range of motion. The slip yoke must move smoothly without binding. If necessary, tap the yoke slightly to center the spider until the joint moves freely in all directions.

11   FRONT GEARCASE - REMOVAL, INSPECTION, RING GEAR BACKLASH SCREW ADJUSTMENT AND INSTALLATION

Removal

1   Park the vehicle on a level surface and apply the parking brake. Block the rear wheels to prevent the vehicle from rolling off the jackstands.

2   Remove the front cover (see Chapter 14).

3   Remove the wheel panels (see Chapter 14).

4   Remove the front axles (see Section 8).

5   Disconnect the driveshaft from the front gearcase pinion shaft (see Section 9).

6   Open the clamp and disconnect the breather hose from its fitting on top of the front gearcase **(see illustration)**. Plug the hose fitting to prevent dirt from entering the gearcase and oil from leaking out if the gearcase is turned over when removing it.

7   Trace the wiring harness from the front gearcase to its connector, then disconnect the connector and remove the wiring harness from the upper and lower clamps **(see illustrations)**.

8   Remove the screws securing the front gearcase to the frame and remove it through the front of the frame **(see illustrations)**.

9   When handling the gearcase, do not turn the backlash adjust screw **(see illustration)**. This screw has been preset at the factory and adjustment is unnecessary unless the front cover has been replaced or the screw was loosened. If the screw is loose, adjust it as described in Steps 13 through 17.

11.6 Disconnect the breather hose from the fitting on top of the front gearcase

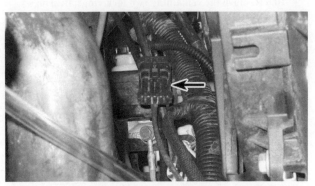

11.7 Disconnect the front gearcase wiring harness connector and free its wiring harness from the clamps

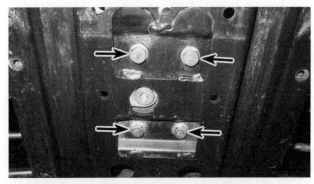

11.8a Remove the front gearcase mounting screws . .

11.8b . . . then left, turn and remove the gearcase through the front frame tubes

11.9 Do not turn the backlash adjust screw (arrow)

11.11a Axle seal

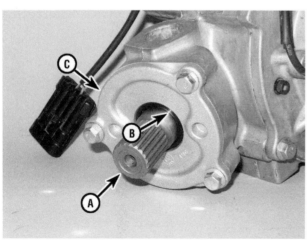

11.11b Pinion shaft seal details

A	*Pinion shaft*	*C*	*Front cover*
B	*Pinion shaft seal*		*and screws*

Inspection

10   Plug the breather vent hose and axle openings and clean the gearcase housing.

11   Inspect the axle and pinion shaft oil seals for oil leaks and damage. To replace the axle seals **(see illustration)**, refer to the seal information in the General Information chapter at the front of this manual. To replace the pinion shaft oil seal, remove the screws and the front cover from the gearcase housing **(see illustration)**. Note the O-ring installed behind the cover and remove it. Then press the oil seal out of the cover. Clean the seal bore and press the new seal into the bore from the outside with its flat side facing out. Lubricate a new O-ring with gear oil and install it onto the gear housing cover. Install the front cover and tighten the screws to the torque listed in this Chapter's Specifications.

12   Inspect the gearcase housing for oil leaks and damage. Then turn the pinion shaft to check the ring and pinion gears for roughness, noise, play and binding. The bearings should turn smoothly and quietly. If bearing rotation is rough or noisy, or the gearcase housing is damaged, refer service to a dealer service department.

Ring gear backlash screw adjustment

13   Ring gear backlash is controlled by an external screw **(see illustration 11.9)** installed in the output cover. The ring gear does not require periodic adjustment. However, it is important to note that adjustment is required whenever the screw is loosened or becomes loose, and after replacing the output cover. Threadlock applied to the screw threads prevents the screw from loosening under operating conditions.

CAUTION:

Because a strong threadlock was applied to the adjust screw threads during gearcase assembly, you must heat the screw before turning it; otherwise, the threadlock bond formed between the two sets of threads could pull the threads out of the cover as the screw is being turned. Heating the screw softens the threadlock to prevent this type of thread damage.

14   Heat the screw to loosen the threadlock.

15   Turn the screw counterclockwise 3-4 turns to back it out of the housing without removing it. Clean the exposed parts on the screw, then apply Loctite 262 to the exposed lower threads.

16   Turn the screw clockwise until it lightly seats, then back it out 1/4 turn.

17   Turn the pinion shaft four turns to rotate the ring gear one full turn. If you did not feel any tightness when turning the shaft, the backlash adjustment is complete. If you felt some tightness, back the screw out an additional 1/8 turn, then turn the shaft four turns once again while checking for tightness. Repeat this sequence until you can turn the shaft four turns without any detectable tightness.

11

Installation

18 Installation is the reverse of removal, noting the following:

a) *Before installing the front gearcase, clean the frame and gearcase mounting surfaces.*

b) *The manufacturer recommends installing new front gearcase mounting screws. This is because the screws are pre-treated with a dry-film lock-ing compound. If you are installing the original screws, clean the screws and apply a thread-lock onto the screw threads before installing them. Install the screws and tighten in a cross-ing pattern to the torque listed in this Chapter's Specifications.*

c) *If the front gearcase oil was drained, fill the gearcase with the recommended type and amount of oil (see Chapter 2).*

SPECIFICATIONS

Front suspension

Front suspension type	Independent dual A-arm
Travel	9.6 in. (244 mm)

Walker Evans shock absorber adjustment specifications

Compression adjustment positions	
Standard	8 clicks out from fully counterclockwise position
Softest.	Adjuster turned fully counterclockwise
Hardest	Adjuster turned fully clockwise
Spring preload stock settings	
Front	10.75 inches (273 mm)
Rear	10.5 inches (267 mm)

Torque specifications	Ft-lbs	In.-lb	Nm

NOTE

One foot-pound (ft-lb) of torque is equivalent to 12 inch-pounds (in-lbs) of torque. Torque values below approximately 15 ft-lbs are expressed in inch-pounds, because most foot-pound torque wrenches are not ac-curate at these smaller values.

	Ft-lbs	In.-lb	Nm
Balljoint pinch bolt nuts* (at steering knuckle)			
2010 models	17	--	23
2011 and later models.	23	--	31
Control arm pivot bolt nuts*	30	--	41
Driveshaft bearing			
Crew models			
Set screws			
2010 models.	--	65-75	7.3-8.5
2011 and later models	--	30-35	3.4-4.0
Support bracket nuts*	30-36	--	41-49
Front gearcase front cover mounting screws.	7-11	--	10-15
Front gearcase mounting screws**	40	--	54

Torque specifications (continued)	Ft-lbs	In.-lb	Nm

NOTE

One foot-pound (ft-lb) of torque is equivalent to 12 inch-pounds (in-lbs) of torque. Torque values below approximately 15 ft-lbs are expressed in inch-pounds, because most foot-pound torque wrenches are not accurate at these smaller values.

	Ft-lbs	In.-lb	Nm
Power steering unit mounting screws	20-24	--	27-33
Pivot tube mounting bolt nuts*	23	--	31
Shock absorber mounting bolt nuts*	30	--	41
Steering gearbox mounting fasteners*	17	--	23
Steering shaft fasteners			
Bolt nuts*	30	--	41
Screws	15-19	--	20-26
Steering wheel nut	25-31	--	34-42
Steering wheel tilt damper bolt nuts*			
2010 models	12	--	16
2011 and later models			
Upper	7	--	10
Lower	12	--	16
Tie-rod end locknut	12-14	--	16-19
Tie-rod bolt nuts*	40	--	54

Replace all nylock nuts with new ones.
**Replace screws with new ones.*

NOTES

CHAPTER TWELVE

REAR SUSPENSION AND REAR GEARCASE

CONTENTS

1 GENERAL INFORMATION

1 The rear suspension consists of an upper and lower control arm and shock absorber installed on each side of the vehicle. Each control arm is secured to a knuckle with a pivot bolt and nut. All models are equipped with a stabilizer bar, mounted between the frame and upper control arm. The rear axles are mounted between the knuckles, wheel hubs and transmission.

NOTE:

After working on the rear suspension, test ride the vehicle slowly at first to make sure that each system is working correctly before putting the vehicle into hard or severe service.

2 REAR SHOCK ABSORBERS - ADJUSTMENT, REMOVAL, INSPECTION, SPRING REPLACEMENT AND INSTALLATION

WARNING:

Do not attempt to disassemble the shock absorbers. The oil damper shocks (no reservoir) are not designed to be rebuilt. The gas-oil damper shocks (with reservoir) are nitrogen charged and under high pressure. While these shocks are designed to be rebuilt, service should be referred to a dealer service department or suspension specialist. Severe personal injury can occur from mishandling these shocks when trying to disassemble them.

2.1 Rear Nivomat shock absorber

2.2 Rear shock adjustment position details

A   *Inside position - softer*
B   *Outside position - stiffer*

Adjustment

1   Unless indicated below, procedures required to adjust the rear shock absorbers are the same as for the front shock absorber (see Chapter 11). See Chapter 11 Specifications for shock adjustment specifications. Note there is no external adjust mechanism available on the rear Nivomat shock absorbers used on some models **(see illustration)**.

Shock mounting adjustment position (all models)

2   To increase or reduce suspension stiffness, the frame has two upper shock mounting positions for each wheel - the inside position is softer and the outside position is stiffer **(see illustration)**. Refer to Step 3, 4, 6 and 10 for information on how to reposition the upper shock mounts when making this adjustment.

Removal

3   Support the vehicle with both rear wheels off the ground. Block the front wheels to prevent the vehicle from rolling off the jackstands.
4   Place wooden blocks underneath the rear wheels to prevent them from falling when the shock absorber mounting bolts are removed. This will also help to remove tension from the bolts when removing them. If the wheels are removed from the vehicle, place the wooden blocks underneath the rear knuckles.
5   Remove the nut, bolt, spacer and linkage rod from the lower shock absorber/upper control arm mounting bracket and reposition the linkage rod away from the shock absorber **(see illustration)**.
6   Remove the upper shock absorber nut and bolt and remove the shock absorber **(see illustration)**.
7   If split bushings are installed in the ends of the shock absorbers, make sure they didn't fall off.

2.5 Shock absorber lower mounting detail

1	*Nut*	4	*Linkage rod*
2	*Shock absorber*	5	*Shock absorber*
3	*Spacer*		*mounting bolt*

2.6 Upper shock absorber nut and bolt

3.1 One or both rear control arms can be removed without having to separate or remove the rear hubs, brake calipers and rear knuckles (arrows) - right side shown

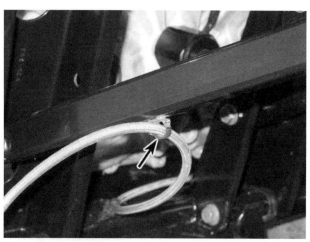

3.6 A brake hose clamp is installed underneath each upper control arm (right side shown)

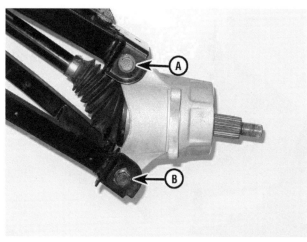

3.7 Upper (A) and lower (B) control arm pivot bolts at the rear knuckle (right side shown)

Inspection

8   Inspection is the same as for the front shock absorbers (see Chapter 11).

Spring Replacement

9   Spring replacement is the same as for the front shock absorbers (see Chapter 11).

Installation

10   Installation is the reverse of removal. Install the bolts and new nylock nuts. If you are reusing the nuts, clean the nut and bolt threads, and apply a threadlock onto the bolt threads. Hold the bolts and tighten the nuts to the torque listed in this Chapter's Specifications. Make sure to align the linkage rod and spacer with the shock absorber when installing the lower shock mount **(see illustration 2.5).**

3   REAR CONTROL ARMS - REMOVAL, INSPECTION AND INSTALLATION

1   When servicing the rear control arms, there are different ways to approach the job, depending on whether you will also be servicing the rear hub and rear knuckle. If you're only servicing the control arms, you can leave the rear hub, brake caliper and rear knuckle assembled together on the axle **(see illustration)**. Just make sure to support the knuckle assembly with a jack to prevent from placing any stress on the brake hose when handling the parts. If you're also servicing the rear hub and/or rear knuckle, remove these parts first, then the control arms.

Removal

2   Remove the rear wheel for the side being worked on (see Chapter 10).
3   Support the lower control arm with a jack.
4   If additional work is required and the rear hub will be removed, remove it now (see Chapter 10). Likewise, if servicing the rear knuckle, remove it also (see Chapter 10).
5   If removing the upper control arm, remove the nut and bolt securing the lower shock absorber mount and stabilizer bar linkage to the upper control arm (see Section 2).
6   If removing the upper control arm, open the clamp and disconnect the brake hose from underneath the control arm **(see illustration)**.
7   If both control arms will be removed, remove the upper and lower pivot bolts at the knuckle. If you're only removing one control arm, remove its nut and pivot bolt at the knuckle **(see illustration)**.
8   Before loosening the two control arm pivot bolts, pivot the control arm up-and-down. While the control arm should should move under tension, there should be no binding or roughness. Then try to move the control arm from side-to-side. If any excessive side-to-side looseness is felt, the bushings are worn and must be replaced. If you are unsure,

3.9a Upper control arm pivot bolts and nuts (arrows)

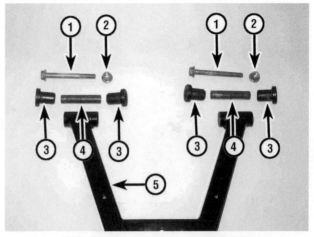

3.10a Upper/lower control arm details

1	Pivot bolts	4	Pivot tubes
2	Nuts	5	Control arm
3	Bushings		

3.10b Remove the bushing sets (A) and pivot tube (B) from each side of the control arm

3.9b Lower control arm pivot bolts and nuts (arrows)

compare the side-to-side movement against that of another control arm.

9   Remove the nuts and pivot bolts securing the upper or lower control arm to the frame **(see illustrations)**. If a pivot bolt is difficult to remove, it is probably corroded and seized in place. For tips on removing a stuck pivot bolt, refer to the information in Chapter 11, Section 3.

Inspection

10   Remove the pivot tubes and bushings from the control arm **(see illustrations)**. If you noted a problem when checking the control arm in Step 8, isolate each pivot set so you can inspect them separately to help determine the cause of the problem, or to help with further inspection and troubleshooting. The bushings are installed with a snug fit, but you should be able to remove them by hand. If a bushing is stuck, grab its shoulder and twist it loose. If necessary, drive the bushing out with a drift inserted through the opposite end of the control arm. Then clean and dry all of the parts.

11   Inspect all welded joints and brackets on the control arm for cracks, bending and other damage **(see illustration)**.

3.11 Inspect the control arm for any impact damage as well as for weak or damaged welded joints

3.12a Typical pivot set includes pivot bolt, pivot tube and bushings

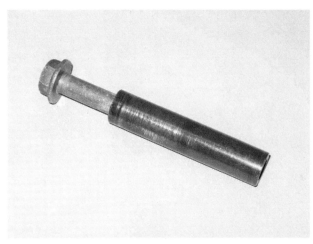

3.12b When the parts are clean, make sure each pivot bolt slides smoothly through its pivot tube. You should not detect any binding or roughness

3.12c Check that each pivot tube slides smoothly through its bushings

Inspect the tubes for impact damage. If damage is evident, replace the control arm. Don't attempt to straighten or repair it.

12 Inspect the bushings for cracks, excessive wear and other visual damage, such as surface tearing. Always replace bushings in sets of two. Check the pivot tube for wear and damage. Because the pivot tube operates against the bushings, its outer wear should be minimal, though inner wear can be severe if the pivot bolt is bent or corroded, or if there is rust present on the parts. If necessary, clean these parts with a wire wheel mounted in a drill, then inspect their contact surfaces for excessive wear, cracks and other damage **(see illustrations)**.

13 To service the pivot bolts, pivot collars and bushings installed in the rear knuckle, see Chapter 10.

Installation

14 Installation is the reverse of the removal, noting the following:

a) *Make sure to route the rear brake hose and secure it with the clamp on the upper control arm (see Step 6). Replace the clamp if damaged or if it will not lock in place.*

b) *Lubricate the pivot bolts with grease and install them through the control arms, facing in their original direction. With the pivot bolts installed, pivot each control arm to make sure there is no binding or roughness. With the pivot bolts fully installed and before installing the nuts, remove any exposed grease from the bolt threads with contact cleaner or solvent. Repeat to install the pivot bolts through the rear knuckle.*

c) *Install a new nut on each control arm pivot bolt. However, if you are reusing the original nuts, clean and dry the threads on the nuts and pivot bolts, then apply a threadlock onto the control arm pivot bolt threads and install the nuts. Hold the control arm pivot bolts and tighten the nuts to the torque listed in this Chapter's Specifications.*

d) *Install a new nut on each knuckle pivot bolt. However, if you are reusing the original nuts, clean and dry the threads on the nuts and pinch bolts, then apply a threadlock onto the knuckle pivot bolt threads and install the nuts. Hold the knuckle pivot bolts and tighten the nuts to the torque listed in this Chapter's Specifications.*

e) *Reconnect the shock absorber and stabilizer bar onto the upper control arm (see Section 2).*

**4   REAR STABILIZER BAR ASSEMBLY
- REMOVAL, INSPECTION AND
INSTALLATION**

1 All models are equipped with a rear stabilizer bar assembly. The stabilizer bar is attached to the frame with mounting brackets and split bushings. The outer ends of

12

4.1 Rear stabilizer bar details (right side)

1	*Shock mounting bolt and nut*	*5*	*Bushing nut*
2	*Spacer*	*6*	*Mounting bracket, bolts and nuts*
3	*Linkage rod*	*7*	*Split bushings*
4	*Stabilizer bar*		

4.3 To disconnect the stabilizer bar ends, remove the bushing nut (arrow) from the top of each linkage rod

4.4a Mounting bracket and bushing details

1	*Stabilizer bar*	*4*	*Mounting bolts and nuts*
2	*Mounting bracket*		
3	*Split bushings*		

the stabilizer bar are attached to the upper control arms with linkage rods **(see illustration)**.

Removal

2   Park the vehicle on level ground, then raise and support it securely with its rear wheels off the ground. Block the front wheels to prevent the vehicle from rolling.

3   Loosen and remove the left and right bushing nuts that secure the stabilizer bar to the two linkage rods **(see illustration)**.

4   Remove the nuts and bolts securing the stabilizer bar mounting brackets to the frame and remove the stabilizer bar from the vehicle **(see illustration)**. Separate and remove the split bushings from the stabilizer bar **(see illustration)**.

5   If the linkage rod will be disconnected from the upper control arm, support the rear knuckle with a jack to prevent the suspension assembly/rear wheel from dropping to the ground. Then remove the nut, bolt, spacer and linkage rod from the shock absorber/upper control arm mounting bracket and remove the linkage rod **(see illustration 2.5)**.

Inspection

6   Clean and dry all parts. If a grease nipple is used on the stabilizer bar mounting brackets, remove old grease from all surfaces.

NOTE:

The stabilizer bar mounting brackets were not originally equipped with grease nipples. When working on an unfamiliar model, you may find where a previous owner installed grease nipples in the mounting brackets.

7   Inspect the stabilizer bar for cracks, bending and

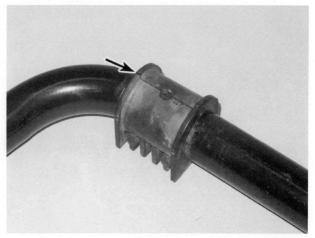

4.4b Remove the split bushings from each side of the stabilizer bar

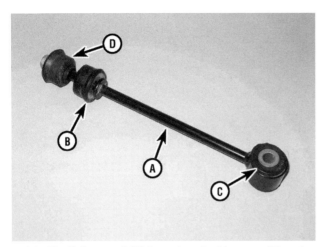

4.8a The linkage rod (A) is equipped with upper (B) and lower (C) bushings that cannot be replaced separately. The bushing nut (D) can be replaced separately. Inspect the linkage rod for cracks at its welded joint and bending. Inspect the bushings for cracks and tears

4.8b Make sure the collar (arrow) is a tight fit in the lower linkage rod bushing

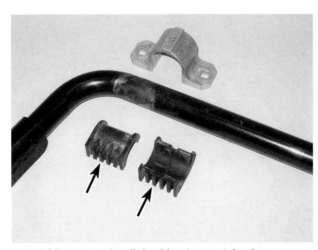

4.9 Inspect each split bushing (arrows) for damage

5.2 The axle can be removed with the knuckle (arrow) attached to the lower control arm

other damage, especially where the bushings are installed against the bar. Replace the stabilizer bar if damaged. Do not attempt to straighten or repair it.

8   Inspect the linkage rods for bending and other damage. Then inspect the two bushings integral with each linkage rod for cracks, deterioration and other damage. If one or both bushings are damaged, it will be necessary to replace the linkage rod as an assembly. The bushing nuts can be replaced separately. Inspect these for the same wear and damage conditions (see illustrations).

9   Check the split bushings for cracks, deterioration and tears (see illustration). Replace the bushings in sets of two (each side).

Installation

10   Installation is the reverse of removal, noting the following:

   a) First install the stabilizer bar and linkage rods in position and tighten all of the fasteners finger-tight. Then tighten the fasteners as described below.
   b) Tighten the stabilizer bar mounting bracket nuts to the torque listed in this Chapter's Specifications.
   c) Reconnect the shock absorber and stabilizer bar onto the upper control arm (see Section 2).
   d) Tighten the stabilizer bar bushing nuts that secure the stabilizer bar to the linkage rods to the torque listed in this Chapter's Specifications.

5   REAR AXLE - REMOVAL, INSPECTION AND INSTALLATION

Removal

1   Clean both sides of the transmission housing to prevent dirt from entering the housing when removing the rear axles.

2   Partially remove the knuckle (see Chapter 10, Section 7). Note that the knuckle can be removed from the vehicle, or left attached to the lower control arm (see illustration).

5.3a Grab the rear axle and pull it sharply . . .

5.3c Check that the spring clip (arrow) remained in the axle groove

5.3b . . . to remove it from the transmission

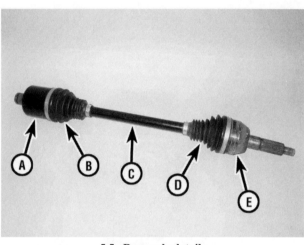

5.5a Rear axle details

A   Inner CV joint
B   Inner boot
    and clamps
C   Axle

D   Outer boot
    and clamps
E   Outer CV joint

3   Grab the rear axle with both hands and jerk the axle (not the outboard joint) sharply to disconnect it from the transmission **(see illustrations)**. The spring clip on the inboard side of the axle will cause some resistance when removing the axle. After removing the axle, check that the spring clip ring remained on the axle and did not fall inside the transmission **(see illustration)**.

4   Plug the axle opening to prevent dirt from entering the transmission.

Inspection

5   Clean the axle, boots and splines on both ends of the axle **(see illustration)**. Do not submerge the axle boots in solvent as the CV joints (inside the boots) are packed with grease and may become contaminated. Also clean the splines in the transmission so the splines and clip groove can be inspected **(see illustration)**.

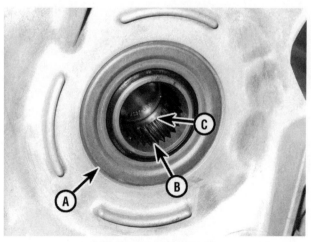

5.5b Transmission details

A   Oil seal
B   Transmission splines

C   Clip groove

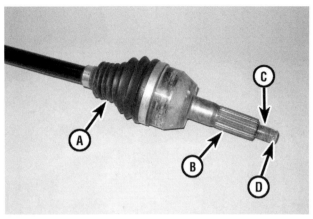

5.6a Outer CV joint inspection points

A   Axle boot and clamps   C   Axle threads
B   Axle splines   D   Cotter pin hole

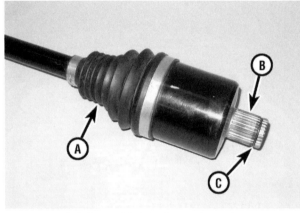

5.6b Inner CV joint inspection points

A   Axle boot and clamps   C   Clip groove
B   Splines

**5.13 To install the new spring clip, start one end in the
groove and continue to work the clip over the shaft end, into
the groove**

6   Inspect the boots for tearing, cracks and other damage.
Check that the clamps are tight and have not slipped off
either boot. A loose or torn boot will allow dirt and moisture
to enter the CV joint. If necessary, replace damaged boots
(see Section 6) **(see illustrations)**.

**5.14 With the new spring clip installed in the groove,
lubricate the splines with anti-seize**

7   Inspect the threads on the outer CV joint for stripped
or damaged threads. Check also that the cotter pin hole in
the axle is not cracked or damaged **(see illustration 5.6a)**.
8   Inspect the clip groove on the inner CV joint for
cracks and other damage **(see illustration 5.6b)**. If the
clip and clip groove are damaged, check the clip groove
inside the transmission for the same conditions **(see
illustration 5.5b)**.
9   Inspect for worn, distorted and broken splines on both
CV joints **(see illustration 5.6a and 5.6b)**. If damage is
noted, check the splines inside the rear hub and transmission
for the same conditions.
10   Clamp the axle in a vise with soft jaws. Then pivot
each CV joint and check for roughness or play in the joint.
If damage is evident, disassemble the axle and inspect the
parts (see Section 6). If roughness or play remains after
cleaning and lubrication, replace the worn or damaged
parts, or the complete axle if necessary.
11   Use a straightedge to check the axle for straightness.
If the axle is bent, it must be replaced as its operation will
damage the bearings in the rear knuckle and transmission
and cause vibration problems.

Installation

12   Lubricate the transmission splines with anti-seize
compound **(see illustration 5.5b)**.
13   Pry the old spring clip from the groove in the inner end
of the axle with a small screwdriver or awl. Then install a
new spring clip into the groove **(see illustration)**.
14   Lubricate the inboard axle splines with an anti-seize
compound **(see illustration)**.
15   Align the inboard axle splines with the transmission
splines and push the axle sharply into the transmission.
If the axle does not enter the transmission, check the
spring clip for damage and replace if necessary. Repeat
until the spring clip compresses as it passes through the
transmission splines and seats inside the clip groove.
Then lightly pull on the axle to make sure it is locked in
place.

12

16   Installation is otherwise the reverse of removal.

NOTE:

If the axle was rebuilt, make several test drives and then stop and check the axle for any grease that may have leaked out of the boots. Wipe off the axle and then repeat the checks to make sure no more grease leaks out. Usually, grease that is trapped along the edge of a boot will leak or squeeze out one or two times, and then stop after the boot is completely seated. If grease continues to leak out, check the clamps for tightness.

6   AXLES - BOOT REPLACEMENT

1   Special tool: When installing and tightening the axle boot clamps, a special type of boot clamp pliers is required. The RV Service Tools (www.rvservicetools.com) CV Boot Clamp Pliers (part No. 900723) is used in this procedure **(see illustration)**.

2   The inboard and outboard CV joints on both the front and rear axles are similar in design. The following procedure can be used to replace the axle boots on both the front and rear axles **(see illustration)**.

3   Remove the axle from the vehicle (see Section 5 in this Chapter or Chapter 11).

4   Purchase replacement boot repair kits for the axle **(see illustration)**. If servicing both sides of the axle, purchase the correct kit for each side. Consult with a dealer parts department on the parts included in the kit to make sure you will have everything you will need for the job. Note that some parts can only be purchased with a complete boot kit.

5   After removing the axle, clean and dry it to prevent dirt from entering the CV joints when removing the boots. If the boots are leaking or damaged and the grease in the CV joint has been contaminated, it may be necessary to replace the CV joint.

6   Mount the axle securely in a vise. The jaws of the vise must be lined with wood or rags to avoid damage to the axle. Aluminum jaw inserts can also be used and work well.

7   **Follow the accompanying illustrations, beginning with 6.7a to remove the CV joint and boot from the axle.** Be sure to stay in order and read the caption under each illustration.

8   With the CV joint removed, clean the joint with new solvent, if possible. Then dry the joint thoroughly to prevent any solvent from contaminating the grease during assembly **(see illustration)**.

9   Tilt the bearing and inspect the balls and cage for pitting, scoring marks, cracks and other signs of wear and damage. Also check for excessive play between the balls and cage. If damage or excessive play is evident, replace the CV joint.

10   Remove the spring clip from the end of the axle and discard it **(see illustration 6.7e)**.

6.1 When installing the OEM boot clamps, you'll need a pair of special boot clamp pliers

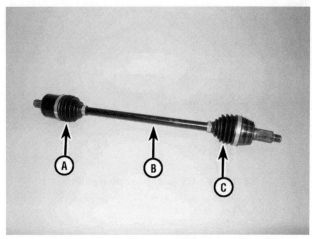

6.2 Axle details

A   Inboard CV joint
B   Axle

C   Outboard CV joint

6.4 Replacement boot kit for outboard joint on the rear axle; kit includes everything to replace boot and lubricate CV joint

6.7a Cut the clamp on the end of each boot and discard them

6.7d Place a brass drift against the inner part of the CV joint where it mates (arrow) against the axle and not against the bearing balls . . .

6.7b Break the boot loose on the CV joint and slide it inward on the axle. Before removing the old grease, inspect it for water and dirt contamination. If contamination is apparent and inspection shows the bearings are scratched and worn, the CV joint should be replaced. Then use a clean rag to remove as much of the old grease from the CV joint as possible; discard the grease as it will not be reused

6.7e . . . and drive the CV joint over the spring clip (arrow) and off the axle (be careful not to let the joint fall). Then slide the old boot and the inner clamp off the axle

6.7c The CV joint (A) is held onto the end of the axle (B) with a spring clip that cannot be seen at this stage of disassembly

6.8 Clean the CV joint with solvent and dry thoroughly

12

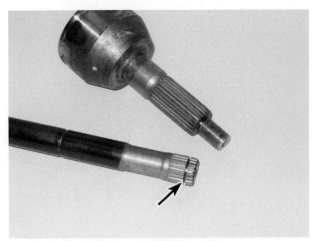

6.11 The axle and CV joint splines, and the spring clip groove (arrow), must be in good condition

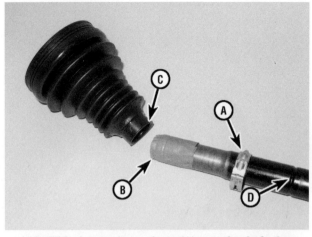

6.13a Slide the new inner clamp (A) onto the shaft, then wrap the splines with tape (B) to protect the boot when installing it. Slide the boot (C) onto the shaft (narrow end first) and past the groove (D) in the axle. Remove the tape from the axle

6.12 Here is the spring clip groove (arrow) inside the CV joint; this groove must show no sign of wear or damage

6.13b Mount the axle in a vise similar to the way you secured it during disassembly. Install the new clip (arrow) in the axle groove - start one end in the groove and continue to work the clip over the shaft end, into the groove

11   Inspect the axle splines, CV joint splines and the spring clip groove in the axle for damage **(see illustration)**. The axle spines that operate inside the CV joint should show little wear.

12   Inspect the spring clip groove inside the CV joint for cracks and damage **(see illustration)**. The sides of the groove must be straight with no signs of rounding, wear or damage.

13   **Follow the accompanying illustrations, starting with 6.13a**, to lubricate and install the CV joint onto the axle. Be sure to stay in order and read the caption accompanying each illustration.

NOTE:

It is important to clamp the large boot end first, then the small boot end.

6.13c Pack the CV joint assembly with the grease supplied in the boot kit. Make sure to fill the area behind the bearing and the spline hole . . .

6.13d . . . then fill the outer part until the outer face of the CV joint is flush with grease. If you didn't use all of the grease, save it to smear inside the boot just before you clamp the boot in place

6.13e With the axle mounted securely in a vise, align the splines inside the CV joint with the axle splines (arrow) and drive the CV joint into place with a soft faced hammer until the spring clip on the axle seats into the groove in the CV joint

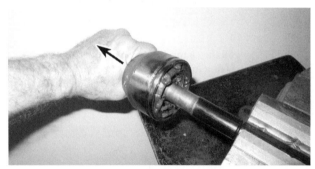

6.13f With the axle secured in the vise, tug on the CV joint to make sure it is locked on the axle

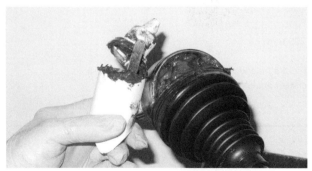

6.13g Before clamping the boot in place, cut the grease container open and dip out any remaining grease and smear it inside the boot - wipe off any grease from inside the boot lip where it seats against the CV joint

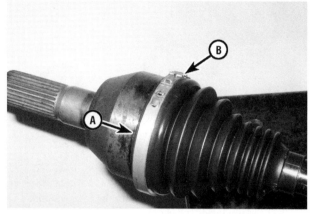

6.14a Slide the boot (A) over the CV joint and seat it into the groove, then center the clamp (B) in the boot groove . . .

6.14b ... and hook the boot clamp pliers over the stationary arm on the clamp (A) and pull the movable clamp arm (B)...

6.14c . . . to pull the clamp (arrow) over the fixed locking tab. With the clamp in place, release the pliers to lock the clamp in place

14   Before clamping the large boot end, wipe off the CV joint and the inner seat surface inside the boot, then slide the boot into place and seat it into the groove in the CV joint. Place the clamp in the boot groove, position the pliers across the clamp and pull the clamp to lock it in place (see illustrations).

12

6.15a When the boot is aligned with the axle, equalize the pressure inside the boot by inserting a small, dull screwdriver between the boot and the axle, while at the same time making sure the end of the boot seats into the groove in the axle, then remove the screwdriver

6.15b Center the clamp in the boot groove and use the boot clamp pliers...

6.15c ... to pull the clamp (arrow) over the fixed locking tab. With the clamp in place, release the pliers to lock the clamp in place

15   Before clamping the small boot end, make sure the boot is aligned squarely with the axle and is not twisted. If necessary, turn the boot to align it. Then insert a small, dull screwdriver between the small boot end and axle to create a gap and equalize the air pressure in the boot. Don't damage the boot when inserting the screwdriver. Remove the screwdriver, making sure the end of the boot seats in the groove in the axle. Place the clamp in the boot groove, position the pliers across the clamp and pull the clamp to lock it in place **(see illustrations)**.

7   REAR GEARCASE - REMOVAL, INSPECTION AND INSTALLATION

1   The rear gearcase is integral with the transmission. Refer to Chapter 6 to service the transmission.

SPECIFICATIONS

Rear suspension

Travel
    2011 and 2012 Ranger HD 800 models . . . . 7.5 in. (191 mm)
    All other models . . . . 9 in. (229 mm)
Type
    2011 and 2012 Ranger HD 800 models . . . . Self leveling independent dual A-arm
    All other models . . . . Independent dual A-arm

Torque specifications	**Ft-lbs**	**Nm**
Rear control arm pivot bolt nuts*		
(at frame and rear knuckle).	30	41
Shock absorber bolt nuts*	30	41
Stabilizer bar mounting bracket bolt nuts*	17	23
Stabilizer bar bushing nuts*.	17	23

Replace all nylock nuts with new ones

CHAPTER THIRTEEN

BRAKES

CONTENTS

1 GENERAL INFORMATION

1   This chapter covers the front and rear disc brake system consisting of the brake pads, brake calipers, master cylinder, brake discs, brake pedal, brake lines and brake light switch. A separate brake line is attached between each front brake caliper and master cylinder. A brake line that supplies brake fluid to the rear brake calipers is attached between the master cylinder and a junction block, and from there a separate brake line is attached between each rear brake caliper. On 2010 models, the brake light switch is mounted on the junction block. On 2011 and later models, the brake light switch is mounted on the master cylinder. The brake light switch is serviced in Chapter 8. The front calipers are a twin piston design. The rear calipers on standard Ranger models are a single piston design and on Crew models a twin piston design. Each caliper operates on a sliding caliper mounting bracket. The brake discs are mounted respectively on the front and rear wheel hubs. When the brake pedal is operated, hydraulic pressure moves the caliper pistons outward, applying pressure to the brake pads, and from there the pads apply pressure against the brake discs. Brake maintenance intervals and routine inspection and adjustment procedures are found in Chapter 2.

2   In addition to the main hydraulic brake system described in Step 1, all models are equipped with a mechanical parking brake caliper mounted on the transmission. This system includes a hand-operated brake lever, brake cable and brake caliper assembly. The parking brake system is described in Section 9.

WARNING:

Do not drive the vehicle until the front and rear brakes are operating correctly.

WARNING:

Only use DOT 4 brake fluid. Do not use brake fluid labeled DOT 5. This is a silicone-based brake fluid that is not compatible with glycol-based DOT 3, DOT 4 or DOT 5.1. Do not intermix two different types of brake fluid as it can cause brake component damage and lead to brake system failure.

13

WARNING:

Never reuse brake fluid expelled during brake bleeding. Contaminated brake fluid can cause brake failure. Dispose of brake fluid properly.

WARNING:

Whenever working on the brake system, do not inhale brake dust. Do not use compressed air to blow off brake parts as it may contain asbestos, which can cause lung injury and cancer. Wear a face mask that meets OSHA requirements for trapping asbestos particles, and wash hands and forearms thoroughly after completing the work. Before working on a brake component spray it with brake cleaner to wet the dust. Secure and dispose of all brake dust and cleaning materials properly.

CAUTION:

When working on the brake system, cover all parts that could become contaminated by the accidental spilling of brake fluid. Wash any spilled brake fluid from any surface immediately as it will damage the finish. Use soapy water and rinse completely.

3   When adding brake fluid, use DOT 4 brake fluid from a sealed container. However, because DOT 4 brake fluid is glycol-based and draws moisture, purchase brake fluid in small containers and discard any small leftover quantities. Do not store brake fluid that has been opened for reuse later on.

4   The brake system transmits hydraulic pressure from the master cylinder to the brake calipers. This pressure is transmitted from the calipers to the brake pads, which grip both sides of the brake discs and slows the vehicle. As the pads wear, the pistons move out of the caliper bores to automatically compensate for wear. As this occurs, the fluid level in the master cylinder reservoir goes down. This must be compensated for by occasionally adding fluid.

5   Proper brake operation depends on routine inspection, a supply of clean DOT 4 brake fluid and a clean work environment when any service is performed. Any debris that enters the system or contaminates the pads or brake discs can damage the components and cause poor brake performance.

6   Perform brake service procedures carefully. Do not use any sharp tools inside the calipers or on the pistons. Damage to these components could cause a loss of hydraulic pressure. If there is any doubt about your ability to correctly and safely service the brake system, have a professional technician perform the task.

7   Always keep the master cylinder reservoir closed to prevent dust or moisture from entering. This contaminates

the brake fluid and can cause brake failure.

8   Clean parts with an aerosol brake parts cleaner. Never use petroleum-based solvents on internal brake system components or any rubber part. They will cause the seals to swell and distort.

9   When servicing the vehicle do not allow any grease or oil to contact the brake pads.

10   When cleaning the brake components, wear rubber gloves to keep brake fluid off skin.

11   If the hydraulic system has been opened or whenever the pedal feels soft, bleed each brake caliper separately to remove air from the system (see Section 8).

2   BRAKE PADS - REPLACEMENT

WARNING:

The dust created by the brake system may be harmful to your health. Before removing the brake pads, place paper towels underneath the caliper and spray the caliper with brake cleaner to wet the dust and prevent it from becoming airborne.

1   Read Section 1 before replacing the brake pads.

2   Replace the brake pads in sets on both sides (front or rear) of the vehicle. Never replace the pads on only one wheel.

3   There is no recommended time interval for changing the brake pads as pad wear depends greatly on trail conditions, driving habits, brake pad compound and the condition of the brake system.

4   The caliper bracket should be serviced when replacing the brake pads to allow the fixed pins and their bores inside the caliper to be cleaned and lubricated, and the rubber boots replaced if damaged.

5   Work on one caliper at a time. Do not operate the brake pedal while the pads are out of the caliper.

Twin piston calipers

NOTE:

The following steps and illustrations show the brake pads replaced on a front twin piston brake caliper. Procedures required to service the brake pads on a rear twin piston caliper are similar.

6   Before removing the brake caliper, check the brake fluid level in the master cylinder reservoir. If the fluid level is at the top, use a syringe to remove and discard some of the fluid from the reservoir to prevent the master cylinder reservoir from overflowing when compressing the caliper pistons. Do not drain the entire reservoir or air will enter the system.

7   Remove the front or rear wheel from the side being worked on (see Chapter 10).

2.8 Brake pad adjust screw position

2.10 Push the pistons into the caliper bores so the brake pads and caliper bracket can be removed

2.9a Loosen and remove the two brake caliper mounting screws . . .

2.9b . . . then slide the brake caliper off the brake disc

8   Turn the brake pad adjust screw 2-3 turns to loosen it (see illustration). Because you will readjust the screw after installing the brake pads, it is okay if the screw backs out all the way.

CAUTION:

Do not damage the tie-rod rubber boot when loosening the upper brake caliper mounting bolt. On some models it will be necessary to leave the bolt in the steering knuckle.

NOTE:

Note the brake hose routing before removing the brake caliper.

9   Remove the upper and lower brake caliper mounting screws and slide the caliper off the brake disc (see illustrations).

CAUTION:

In Step 10, excessive force should not be required when pushing the pistons into their bores. If there is any binding or tightness, release the C-clamp and inspect the parts to determine which part is stuck or binding.

10   Mount a large C-clamp between the caliper housing and brake pads, then tighten it and alternately push each each piston into its bore. This must be done before the brake pads and caliper bracket can be removed from the caliper (see illustration).
11   If there is the possibility the brake pads will be reused, mark the shim on the outer pad to identify it as used brake pads must be installed in their original mounting positions. Then push the caliper bracket into the caliper by hand and

13

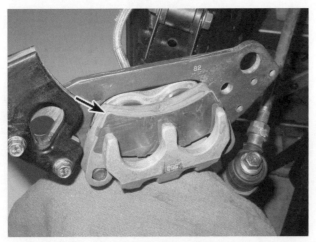

2.11a With the caliper bracket pushed into the caliper,
remove the outer brake pad . . .

2.11b . . . and the inner pad

remove the outer and inner brake pads and their shims **(see illustrations)**.

12 Slide the caliper bracket out of the caliper, noting that the short boot may come off attached to the caliper bracket **(see illustration)**. The longer boot is installed with an interference fit and will remain inside the caliper housing. Because the longer boot is difficult to remove, do not remove it unless it is going to be replaced.

13 The friction surface on both brake pads must be inspected carefully for several conditions **(see illustration)**. First check the friction surface for brake fluid, shock oil and grease, and replace the pads if contaminated. Do not attempt to clean or degrease them. Then run a finger across the friction surface and check for dirt contamination and glazing. The friction surface will have a smooth and shiny appearance if glazed. Remove light dirt and glazing by running a fine wire brush, that is free of oil and grease, across the friction surface. However, if the friction surface is scored or grooved, the pads must be replaced as these conditions will wear grooves in the brake disc. Hold both pads and inspect them for any uneven wear. If the outer pad is worn more than the inner pad, the caliper pins and their bores inside the caliper housing may be corroded, which can hold the caliper in place and prevent it from properly sliding on the pins. If the inner pad is worn more, the caliper pistons may be stuck or slow to retract when the brake pedal is released. If the wear on a pad surface is tapered, where one side is worn more than the other, the caliper bracket may be stuck on one side, causing the caliper to move at an angle when the brakes are applied. If the friction surface on both pads are in good condition, measure the thickness to make sure each pad is within specification (see Chapter 2). Remove the shim from the back of each pad and check the pad plate for any cracks and other damage. Finally, spray each pad with an aerosol brake cleaner to remove any dust. Clean the shims, and when dry, reinstall onto the back of the pads.

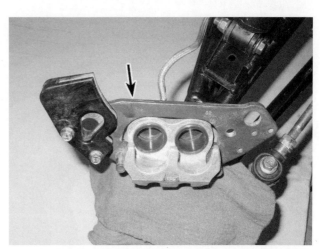

2.12 Slide the caliper bracket (arrow) out of the caliper

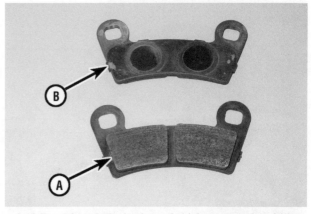

2.13 Even though the brake pad thickness may be within specification, inspect the pad material (A) for any sign of damage such as cracks and uneven wear and for any brake fluid or oil contamination-make sure a shim (B) is fixed securely to the back of each pad

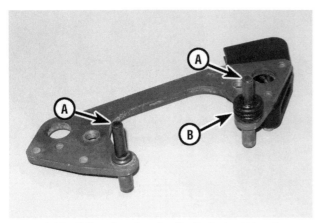

2.15a Caliper bracket details: Pad pins (A) and short boot (B)

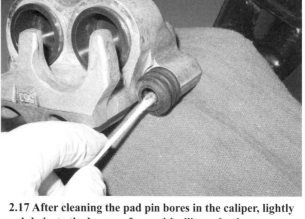

2.17 After cleaning the pad pin bores in the caliper, lightly lubricate the bore surfaces with silicone brake grease

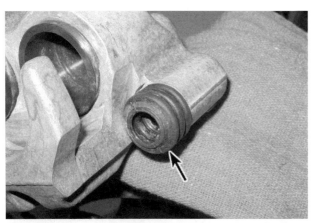

2.15b The long rubber boot (arrow) is installed in the caliper and should not be removed unless damaged

2.19 Slide the caliper bracket back and forth several times to distribute the grease, then bottom it against the caliper to help seat the boots onto the caliper and caliper bracket shoulders. When the boots are seated, slowly slide the caliper bracket outward to make sure the boot ends remain seated. Each boot must be seated on both ends to prevent water and other debris from entering them and contaminating the pins and caliper pin bores

2.16 Clean the brake disc before installing new brake pads

14   Inspect the area around the pistons for any sign of brake fluid. If any leaks are found, overhaul the caliper (see Section 3).

15   Inspect the pad pins for excessive wear, corrosion or damage. Remove corrosion and dirt from the pad pin surfaces. Dirty or damaged pad pins prevent the brake pads and caliper from sliding properly and results in uneven brake pad wear, brake drag and overheating of the brake disc. Then inspect the boots for cracks, tearing, softness or other damage and replace if necessary (see illustrations).

16   Check the condition of the brake disc (see Section 4). If the brake disc is in good condition, use brake cleaner and a fine-grade emery cloth to remove debris and brake pad residue from the both sides of the disc (see illustration).

17   Clean the pad pin bores in the caliper with brake cleaner and dry thoroughly. Then lightly lubricate the bore surfaces and the inside of both boots with silicone brake grease (see illustration).

18   Lightly lubricate the caliper bracket pad pins with silicone brake grease. Then install the short boot onto the caliper bracket by seating it fully onto the bracket shoulder (see illustration 2.15a).

19   Install the caliper bracket into the caliper and slide it back and forth to help distribute the grease and to seat both ends of each boot (see illustration).

20 Install the inner pad and its shim by sliding it over the two pad pins on the caliper bracket and seating it against the piston **(see illustration 2.11b)**. Make sure the friction material faces toward the disc. Then install the outer pad and its shim **(see illustration 2.11a)**.

CAUTION:

When installing the brake caliper over the brake disc, make sure the brake hose is routed correctly and is not twisted out of its normal position, as any stress placed on the hose will damage it. Hold the brake caliper and if it feels like it is under pressure the hose is probably twisted.

21 Spread the pads so there is clearance to fit the caliper over the brake disc. Then position the caliper over the brake disc and slide it across the disc and into place against the steering knuckle **(see illustration 2.9b)**. Apply a medium strength threadlock onto the caliper mounting screw threads. Then install the screws **(see illustration 2.9a)** and tighten to the torque listed in this Chapter's Specifications.

NOTE:

The adjust screw threads were originally equipped with a nylon coating that serves as a threadlock to hold the screw in position once it is adjusted. If you can turn the screw by hand, or if it otherwise feels loose, clean the screw and apply a threadlock onto the screw threads before adjusting the screw in Step 22.

22 Loosely install the adjust screw if it was removed, or loosen it one or two turns if it was left in place **(see illustration 2.8)**. Apply the brake pedal several times to seat the brake pads against the brake disc and center them on the caliper bracket. With the brake pedal released move the outer brake pad by hand, noting that it should have some side play that can be seen and felt **(see illustration)**. If not, the adjust screw is too tight and should be loosened. When the outer pad has some play, turn the adjust screw clockwise until the outer brake pad contacts the brake disc. Check by visually inspecting the pad and disc and by trying to move the pad by hand. Now loosen the adjust screw 1/2 turn to remove pressure from the brake pad so that it is not forced against the brake disc, which will cause brake drag **(see illustration)**. When the adjustment seems correct, turn the front hub by hand to check for brake drag. Repeat the check several times, and if there is any brake drag loosen the adjust screw and repeat the step.
23 Repeat for the opposite side.
24 Make a final check by turning each front hub to make sure there is no brake drag.
25 Install the front wheels (see Chapter 10).
26 Operate the brake pedal to seat the pads against the disc, then check the brake fluid level in the reservoir. Add new DOT 4 brake fluid to bring the level to the MAX mark on the reservoir (see Chapter 2, Section 3).

2.22a Before tighening the brake pad adjust screw, check for clearance (arrow) between the outer brake pad and the brake disc . . .

2.22b . . . then tighten the adjust screw until the outer brake pad touches the brake disc (arrow) - complete the adjustment by loosening the adjust screw 1/2 turn to prevent the pad from dragging on the disc

27 To break in OEM brake pads, drive in a flat, safe area while increasing vehicle speed to 30 mph, then slowly apply the brake to slow and stop the vehicle. Repeat this sequence 10 times, though do not slow/stop the vehicle more than three times within one mile (unless necessary for driver and vehicle safety). Immediate hard application glazes the pads and reduces their effectiveness while causing the disc to become hot and possibly warp. To prevent the brake pads and brake discs from overheating, allow them to cool as required. When installing aftermarket brake pads, follow the manufacturer's instructions for pad break-in.

WARNING:

Do not drive the vehicle until the front and rear brakes and the rear brake light work properly.

2.30 Rear caliper brake pad adjust screw position

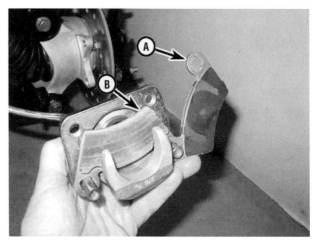

2.33 Remove the outer (A) and inner (B) brake pads

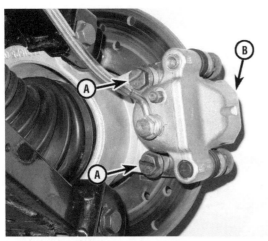

2.31 Loosen and remove the two brake caliper mounting
screws (A) and slide the brake caliper (B) off the brake disc

2.32 Push the piston into the caliper bore to reposition the
caliper bracket so the brake pads can be removed

Single piston calipers

28   Before removing the brake caliper, check the brake
fluid level in the master cylinder reservoir. If the fluid level
is at the top, use a syringe to remove and discard some of
the fluid from the reservoir to prevent the master cylinder
reservoir from overflowing when compressing the caliper
piston. Do not drain the entire reservoir or air will enter the
system.

29   Remove the rear wheel from the side being worked on
(see Chapter 10).

30   Turn the brake pad adjust screw 2-3 turns to loosen
it **(see illustration)**. Because you will readjust the screw
after installing the brake pads, it is okay if the screw backs
out all the way.

NOTE:
*Note the brake hose routing before removing
the rear brake caliper.*

31   Remove the upper and lower brake caliper mounting
screws and slide the caliper off the brake disc **(see
illustration)**.

NOTE:
*In Step 32, excessive force should not be re-
quired when pushing the piston into its bore.
If there is any binding or tightness, release
the C-clamp and inspect the piston for corrosion and the brake pads for damage.*

32   Use a large C-clamp and push the piston into its bore.
This must be done before the brake pads and caliper bracket
can be removed from the caliper **(see illustration)**.

33   If there is a possibility the brake pads will be reused,
mark the shim on the outer pad to identify it as used brake
pads must be installed in their original mounting positions.
Then push the caliper bracket into the caliper and remove
the outer and inner brake pads and their shims **(see
illustration)**.

13

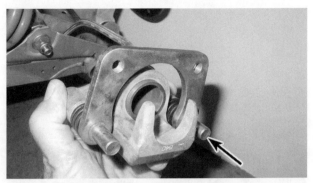

2.34 Slide the caliper bracket out of the caliper

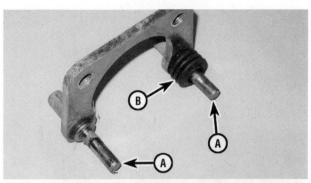

2.37a Caliper bracket details: Pad pins (A) and short boot (B)

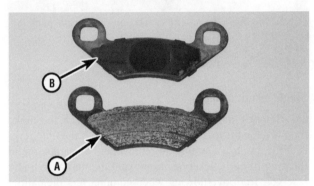

2.35 Even though the brake pad thickness may be within specification, inspect the pad material (A) for any signs of damage such as cracks and uneven wear and for any brake fluid or oil contamination - make sure a shim (B) is fixed securely to the back of each pad

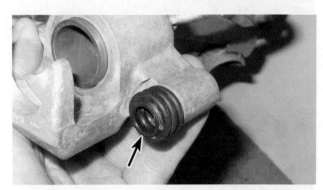

2.37b The long rubber boot is installed in the caliper and should not be removed unless damaged.

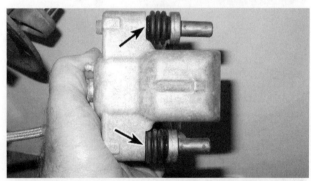

2.41 Slide the caliper bracket back and forth several times to distribute the grease, then bottom it against the caliper to help seat the boots onto the caliper and caliper bracket shoulders. When the boots are seated, slowly slide the caliper bracket outward to make sure the boot ends remain seated. Each boot must be seated on both ends to prevent water and other debris from entering them and contaminating the pins and caliper pin bores

34   Slide the caliper bracket out of the caliper, noting that the short boot may come off attached to the caliper bracket. The longer boot is installed with an interference fit and will remain inside the caliper housing. Because the longer boot is difficult to remove, do not remove it unless it is going to be replaced **(see illustration)**.

35   Refer to Step 13 to inspect the brake pads **(see illustration)**.

36   Inspect the area around the piston for any sign of brake fluid. If a leak is found, overhaul the caliper (see Section 3).

37   Inspect the pad pins for excessive wear, corrosion or damage. Remove corrosion and dirt from the pad pin surfaces. Dirty or damaged pad pins prevent the brake pads from sliding properly and results in uneven brake pad wear, brake drag and overheating of the brake disc. Then inspect the boots for cracks, tearing, softness or other damage and replace if necessary **(see illustrations)**.

38   Check the condition of the brake disc (see Section 4). If the brake disc is in good condition, use brake cleaner and a fine-grade emery cloth to remove debris and brake pad residue from the both sides of the disc.

39   Clean the pad pin bores in the caliper with brake cleaner and dry thoroughly. Then lightly lubricate the bore surfaces and the inside of both boots with silicone brake grease **(see illustration 2.17)**.

40   Lightly lubricate the caliper bracket pad pins with silicone brake grease. Then install the short boot onto the caliper bracket by seating it fully onto the bracket shoulder **(see illustration 2.37a)**.

41   Install the caliper bracket into the caliper and slide it back and forth to help distribute the grease and to seat both ends of each boot **(see illustration)**.

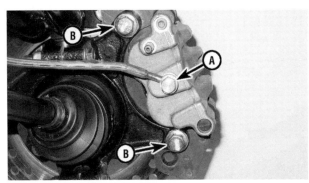

3.6a Front brake caliper details

A   Brake hose banjo bolt
B   Brake caliper mounting screws

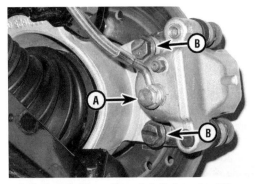

3.6b Rear brake caliper details (standard Ranger shown)

A   Brake hose banjo bolt
B   Brake caliper mounting screws

42   Install the inner pad and its shim by sliding it over the two pad pins on the caliper bracket and seating it against the piston. Make sure the friction material faces toward the disc. Then install the outer pad and its shim **(see illustration 2.33)**.

CAUTION:

When installing the brake caliper over the brake disc, make sure the brake hose is routed correctly and is not twisted out of its normal position, as any stress placed on the hose will damage it. Hold the brake caliper and if it feels like it is under pressure the hose is probably twisted.

43   Spread the pads so there is clearance to fit the caliper over the brake disc. Then position the caliper over the brake disc and slide it into place against the bearing carrier. Apply a threadlock onto the caliper mounting screw threads. Then install the screws **(see illustration 2.31)** and tighten to the torque listed in this Chapter's Specifications.

NOTE:

The adjust screw threads were originally equipped with a nylon coating that serves as a threadlock to hold the screw in position once it is adjusted. If the screw can be turned by hand or otherwise feels loose, clean the

screw and apply a threadlock onto the screw threads when adjusting the screw.

44   Install and tighten the adjust screw (see Step 22).
45   Repeat for the opposite side.
46   Make a final check by turning each rear hub to make sure there is no brake drag.
47   Install the rear wheels (see Chapter 10).
48   Operate the brake pedal to seat the pads against the disc, then check the brake fluid level in the reservoir. Add new DOT 4 brake fluid to bring the level to the MAX mark on the reservoir (see Chapter 2, Section 3).
49   If new OEM brake pads were installed, see Step 27 for information on how to break them in. If aftermarket brake pads were installed, follow the manufacturer's instructions for pad break-in.

WARNING:

Do not drive the vehicle until the front and rear brakes and the rear brake light work properly.

3   BRAKE CALIPER - REMOVAL, INSTALLATION AND OVERHAUL

1   This section covers the front and rear brake calipers. Read the general information in Section 1 before servicing the brake calipers. Note that it is only necessary to disconnect the brake hose if the caliper is being removed from the vehicle. Otherwise, the brake hose can remain attached to the caliper if you are just removing the caliper for pad replacement or when removing it to service the steering or suspension units.
2   Work on one caliper at a time. Do not operate the brake pedal while the caliper has been removed from the brake disc.

Removal

3   Remove the front or rear wheel(s). See Chapter 10.
4   Before loosening the banjo bolt, and because there is no brake hose alignment guide on the caliper, note the angle of the brake hose banjo union with the caliper. This will help you reinstall the hose so that it is aligned in its same approximate position. Then note the hose routing through the suspension assembly so that it can be returned to its original path.
5   On 2010 models, remove the speed sensor from the front right caliper (see Chapter 8). Note the routing of the speed sensor wiring harness and its mounting angle at the caliper and how the speed sensor wiring harness is secured to the right brake hose. Unless it is necessary to do so, do not cut the plastic ties securing the speed sensor wiring harness to the brake hose.
6   Loosen and then hand-tighten the brake hose banjo bolt at the caliper to prevent it from leaking **(see illustrations)**. It will be easier and create less brake fluid loss if the brake

13

hose is disconnected after the caliper is removed from the vehicle.

7   Remove the two brake caliper mounting screws and slide the caliper off the brake disc **(see illustrations 3.6a or 3.6b)**.

8   If necessary, remove the brake pads from the caliper (see Section 2). If the brake pads are not going to be removed, insert a spacer block between the pads to prevent the pistons from being forced out of the caliper if the brake pedal is applied with the caliper removed. If the caliper will remain attached to its brake hose, support the brake caliper with a wire hook to protect the brake hose from any damage.

9   Remove the brake hose banjo bolt (loosened in Step 6) and disconnect the hose at the caliper **(see illustration 3.6a or 3.6b)**. Remove and discard the two crush washers. Plug the hose to keep contaminants out of the brake system and to prevent brake fluid from spilling out and contacting other parts.

Installation

10   If removed, install the brake caliper bracket and brake pads onto the caliper (see Section 2). Then spread the pads so there is clearance to slide the caliper over the brake disc. If you did not remove the brake pads and there is not enough clearance between the brake pads to slide them over brake disc, loosen the brake pad adjust screw **(see illustration 2.8 or 2.30)**. If the brake hose was not disconnected, make sure it follows its original path and is not twisted. When the brake caliper is in place, install and tighten the mounting screws to the torque listed in this Chapter's Specifications. If removed, connect the brake hose to the caliper using a new crush washer on each side of the brake hose. Align the hose correctly and tighten the banjo bolt to the torque listed in this Chapter's Specifications.

11   On 2010 models, reinstall the speed sensor onto the front right caliper, if removed (see Chapter 8).

12   If necessary, bleed the brake system (see Section 8).

13   Operate the brake pedal several times to seat the pads.

14   If the brake pad adjust screw was loosened, adjust it so the brake pads will have adequate clearance when the brake is released (see Section 2).

15   Turn the front or rear hub by hand to make sure there is no brake drag and the brake operates properly.

16   Have an assistant apply the brake pedal and hold it in position while you visually check the banjo bolt(s) for leaks. Thoroughly check the operation of the brakes before driving the vehicle.

17   The remainder of installation is the reverse of removal.

Overhaul

18   These procedures apply to the front and rear brake calipers.

19   Remove the brake pads, caliper bracket and the brake

3.22a Use compressed air to remove the piston(s) while using rags and/or a wooden block to control piston movement and prevent damage

pad adjust screw (see Section 2).

20   Clean the caliper body with denatured alcohol or a brake system cleaner. Do not use a petroleum-based solvent.

21   Before removing the pistons from dual piston calipers, mark the inside of each piston so they can be installed in their original bores.

WARNING:

Wear eye protection when using compressed air to remove the pistons and keep your fingers away from the pistons to prevent serious injury.

CAUTION:

Do not pry a piston out of its bore or attempt to turn the outside of a piston and slide it outward with pliers. Either method could damage the piston and/or its cylinder bore.

NOTE:

Step 22 describes how to remove the piston(s) with compressed air. If servicing a rear caliper on standard Ranger models, the piston can be removed by inserting a brass rod through the banjo bolt hole in the caliper body and driving the piston out. Because there is no access hole in line with the pistons in dual piston calipers, this technique cannot be used.

22   Close the bleed valve so air cannot escape. Cushion the caliper piston(s) with a shop rag and/or a wooden block and position the caliper with the piston bore(s) facing down. Be sure to keep hands away from the piston(s) and apply compressed air through the brake hose port to pop the piston(s) out **(see illustration)**. Use only low air

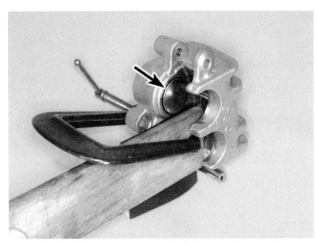

3.22b If you're working on a dual piston caliper and only one piston came out, block off the bore opening with a piece of thick rubber, a block of wood and a clamp. Then reapply compressed air to the caliper and remove the remaining piston (make sure to block the piston as before, though to better show the tool setup, a rag and wooden block are not shown being used)

3.23 Carefully remove the dust (outer) and piston (inner) seals from the caliper bore - single piston caliper shown

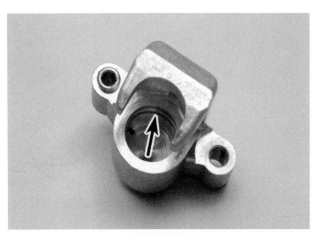

3.26 Carefully clean the seal grooves to prevent damaging them or the caliper bore - hardened debris stuck in the grooves can be difficult to remove

pressure to remove the pistons. If servicing a dual piston brake caliper and only one piston came out, block the vacant bore opening with a piece of thick rubber (old inner tube), wooden block and clamp **(see illustration)**. Apply compressed air again to remove the remaining piston.

CAUTION:
Do not damage the caliper bore grooves when removing the seals.

23 Carefully remove the dust (outer) and piston (inner) seals from the caliper bore grooves and discard them **(see illustration)**. When using a metal tool to remove the seals, work carefully to prevent from scratching the caliper bore and grooves.
24 Remove the bleed valve from the caliper.
25 Use only DOT 4 brake fluid, denatured alcohol or an aerosol brake cleaner to clean the caliper parts. Never use a petroleum based product to clean the rubber parts in a brake system as they will cause the rubber parts to swell and require their replacement.
26 Clean the dust and piston seal grooves carefully to prevent from damaging the caliper bore(s) **(see illustration)**. Use a small pick or brush to clean the grooves. If a hard varnish residue has built up in the grooves, soak the caliper housing in solvent to help soften the residue before trying to remove it. Then wash the caliper in soapy water and rinse completely to remove all of the solvent residue.
27 Check each cylinder bore for corrosion, pitting and other damage. If any surface defects are present, replace the caliper.
28 Inspect the pistons for pitting, corrosion, cracks and plating wear. You may be able to remove light surface corrosion that has not penetrated the piston surface with fine emery cloth. However, if the piston surface is pitted or corroded and you can feel the damage, the piston must be replaced as any roughness will cut the caliper seals and cause the caliper to leak brake fluid.
29 Measure the piston outside diameter and the caliper bore inside diameter. If either measurement exceeds the limit listed in this Chapter's Specifications, replace the the piston(s) and caliper as an assembly.
30 Clean the bleed valve and banjo bolt with compressed air. Replace the bleed valve if there is any damage to its hex shoulder or if its tapered end is not smooth. Replace the banjo bolt if its bore is corroded and cannot be thoroughly cleaned.
31 Install the bleed valve into the caliper and tighten finger-tight.
32 Soak the new piston and dust seals in DOT 4 brake fluid.
33 The dust (outer) and piston (inner) seals installed in the front calipers are identical. The seals installed in the rear calipers are different - the piston (inner) seals are thicker than the dust (outer) seals. After identifying the seals, install them into caliper bore grooves, making sure each seal seats squarely in its groove. To prevent any confusion when installing seals in a rear caliper, have the dealer parts

13

department identify the seals when you purchase them.

34   Lubricate the cylinder bore(s) and piston(s) with DOT 4 brake fluid.

35   Install a piston into its caliper bore with its open side facing out **(see illustration)**. To prevent the piston from damaging the seals, turn the piston into the bore by hand until it bottoms. Repeat if working on a dual piston caliper.

36   Install the rubber boots and lubricate the caliper bracket shafts (see Section 2).

37   Install the caliper bracket, brake pads and brake caliper (see Section 2).

4   BRAKE DISC - INSPECTION, REMOVAL AND INSTALLATION

Inspection

1   Park the vehicle on a level surface and apply the parking brake. Block the wheels since you may be releasing the parking brake.

2   Remove the wheel for the brake disc you will be servicing (see Chapter 10). When inspecting a rear brake disc, release the parking brake and shift the transmission into NEUTRAL.

3   Remove the brake caliper, noting it isn't necessary to disconnect the brake hose unless you will be removing the caliper from the vehicle (see Section 3). After removing the caliper, suspend the caliper out of the way with a stiff piece of wire.

4   Visually inspect the disc surface for score marks and other damage. Light scratches and shallow grooves are normal after use and won't affect brake operation, but deep grooves and heavy score marks will reduce braking efficiency and accelerate pad wear. If the discs are badly grooved they must be replaced.

5   To check disc runout, clean both sides of the disc with brake cleaner and allow to dry. If checking a front disc, turn the steering wheel to one side and lock it in place with a tie-down to prevent the steering assembly from moving and causing a reading error when measuring runout. Place a dial indicator at a point near the outer edge of the disc where it can't contact the holes in the disc **(see illustration)** and secure it in place with a magnetic stand. Set the indicator to zero and slowly turn the hub. The indicator runout reading should not exceed the service limit listed in this Chapter's Specifications. If the runout limit is greater than allowed, check for loose brake disc mounting screws, then for a damaged hub, especially where the disc seats against the hub. If everything is okay, check the wheel bearing (installed in the knuckle) for excessive wear or damage (see Chapter 10). If the bearing is worn, replace it and repeat this check. If the disc runout is still excessive after making these checks and not finding a problem, the disc is warped and will have to be replaced.

6   Measure the disc thickness with a micrometer at eight different spots around the disc - do not measure across the outer rim of the disc **(see illustration)**. If the disc thickness

3.35 Install the piston(s) with their open side facing out

4.5 Set up a dial indicator with its tip contacting the brake disc, then slowly turn the hub to measure runout

4.6 Measure the disc thickness with a micrometer at eight different points around the disc

4.7 Brake disc details

4.9a Disc with countersunk screws - loosen screws in a crossing pattern

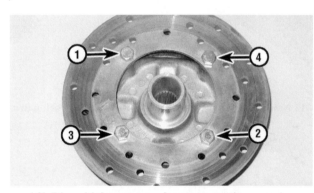

4.9b Disc with hex screws - loosen screws in a crossing pattern

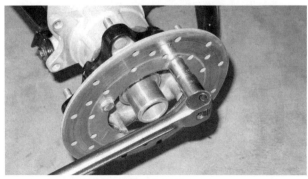

4.9c To help hold the brake disc when loosening and tightening its mounting screws, mount the hub on its axle with the disc facing out, if possible

4.10 Clean the brake disc mating surfaces and the threads inside the hub to ensure proper disc installation

is less than the service limit listed in this Chapter's Specifications, the disc must be replaced.

Removal and installation

7   The brake discs are secured to the hubs with with either countersunk screws or hex screws **(see illustrations)**.

8   Remove the hub with the brake disc attached (see Chapter 10). If the disc will be reused, mark it in relationship to the hub and on its outside so it can be installed in the same position. If countersunk screws are used to secure the brake disc to the hub, the disc can only be installed one way.

9   The brake disc mounting screws are secured with a threadlock and may be difficult to loosen. Before loosening countersunk screws, use a small pick to clean the recess in each screw of all dirt and other debris. This will help your Torx bit to grip the screw fully so that it doesn't slip and damage the screw splines. Support the hub and loosen the disc mounting screws in several steps and in a crossing pattern, then remove the screws and disc **(see illustrations)**. If it is difficult to hold the hub, mount it on its axle with the disc side facing out, if possible **(see illustration)**. If the screws don't loosen with moderate effort, apply heat to the hub from a heat gun (not a torch), then try loosening them again.

10   Clean the hub and disc mating surfaces **(see illustration)**. If these surfaces are not clean the disc will not sit flat, and probably operate with excessive runout. This will cause uneven brake pad wear, brake grab and overheating of the brake disc. Remove all threadlock residue from the threaded holes in the hub and inspect the threads for any damage. If necessary, use a thread chaser to loosen and remove the threadlock from the threads in the hub.

11   Install the disc onto the hub. If countersunk screws are used, position the disc with the tapered screw hole

13

side facing out **(see illustration)**. If you're reinstalling the original disc, align the previously applied matchmarks (see Step 8).

12 Replacement OEM brake disc screws have a preapplied threadlock patch **(see illustration)** and the manufacturer specifies to install new screws when installing the disc. If it is necessary to use the original screws, clean them thoroughly and apply Loctite 272 or a similar threadlock to the screw threads. Install the brake disc mounting screws and tighten in a crossing pattern **(see illustration 4.9a or 4.9b)** to the torque listed in this Chapter's specifications.

13 The remainder of installation is the reverse of removal. With the hub installed on the vehicle, operate the brake pedal several times to bring the pads into contact with the disc. Check the operation of the brakes carefully before driving the vehicle. If there is any vibration when applying the brakes during vehicle operation, stop and check the brake discs for loose mounting screws or incorrect installation.

5   MASTER CYLINDER - REMOVAL, INSPECTION AND INSTALLATION

1 A single master cylinder is mounted inside the front, left side of vehicle and secured to the frame with two bolts and nuts. A pushrod mounted on the brake pedal contacts the piston assembly installed inside the master cylinder. On 2011 and later models, the brake light switch is threaded into the master cylinder, and also serves as a banjo bolt for two of the brake hoses. Read the general information in Section 1 before servicing the master cylinder.

2 If the brake pedal does not produce a firm feel when the brake is applied and the brake hoses are in good condition and there is no sign of leaking along the hoses or at their fittings, bleed the brake system (see Section 8). If bleeding the system doesn't help and no other problem can be found in the brake system, master cylinder replacement is recommended. The master cylinder should also be replaced when it is leaking from its bore at the pushrod. Replacement parts to overhaul the master cylinder are not available from the manufacturer.

Removal

3 Park the vehicle on a level surface and apply the parking brake.

4 Remove the left wheel panel (see Chapter 14).

NOTE:

If necessary, hose off the master cylinder and the area around it to prevent dirt from contaminating the brake hoses and master cylinder (if it will be reinstalled).

5 On 2011 and later models, disconnect the brake light switch wiring harness connector at the switch where it is mounted on master cylinder **(see illustration)**.

4.11 Countersunk screw and mating hole in disc

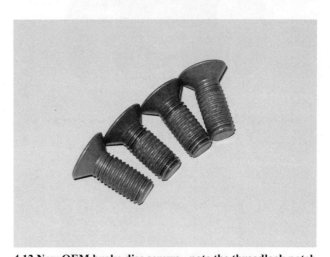

4.12 New OEM brake disc screws - note the threadlock patch on the screw threads

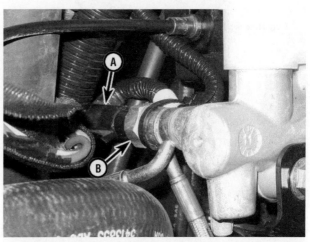

5.5 Brake light switch wiring harness connector (A) and switch (B) - 2011 and later models

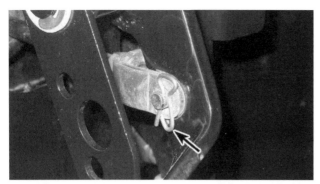

5.6a Remove the clip (arrow) . . .

5.11b . . . then withdraw the bolts (arrows) and remove the master cylinder

5.6b . . . and withdraw the clevis pin (arrow) from the brake pedal and master cylinder

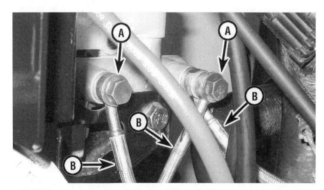

5.10 Remove the banjo bolts (A) and disconnect the brake hoses (B) - 2010 model shown. On 2011 and later models, remove the brake light switch, then disconnect the brake hoses

5.11a Remove the nuts (arrows) . . .

6   Remove the clip and clevis pin securing the brake pedal to the pushrod on the master cylinder (see illustrations).

NOTE:

Perform Step 7 if it is necessary to remove the throttle cable mounting bracket and its large plastic cover to access the banjo bolts and brake hoses on the right side of the master cylinder.

7   Remove the throttle cable mounting bracket and its large plastic cover at the front of the vehicle, beside the master cylinder (see Chapter 7, Section 18). With these parts removed, the right side of the master cylinder is now accessible.

8   Remove the cap from the master cylinder and remove as much brake fluid as possible from the reservoir with a syringe or vacuum pump, then reinstall the cap.

9   Place a plastic sheet underneath the master cylinder to prevent brake fluid from contacting other parts once the brake hoses are disconnected.

10   Before disconnecting the brake hoses, identify the routing position of each hose at the master cylinder. Some hose ends are angled so that the hose end is not placed under any stress when mounted on the master cylinder. Then identify each hose as to left front brake hose, right front brake hose and supply brake hose. Loosen and remove the banjo bolts and their crush washers from the master cylinder (see illustration). On 2011 and later models, the brake light switch is also used as a banjo fitting - remove the switch and disconnect the brake hoses mounted on it. Discard the crush washers as new ones must be installed. When the hose ends are free, cover them with a clean rag or place the open end of each hose in a separate container to prevent further leakage and contamination of the hoses. If necessary, use plastic ties to secure the brake hoses with their hose ends facing upward to prevent further spillage. See Section 6 for additional information.

11   Remove the nuts and and bolts securing the master cylinder to the mounting bracket (see illustrations). Slide the master cylinder forward while holding a rag underneath it, and remove it from its mounting bracket.

13

Inspection

12 Visually inspect the master cylinder for any leakage between the reservoir and the body and at the pushrod. If there is any leakage, replace the master cylinder.

13 While there are no OEM parts available to rebuild the master cylinder internally, a repair kit is available that contains a new external pushrod seal, clevis, locknuts and cap.

Installation

14 Installation is the reverse of removal, noting the following:

   a) *Tighten the master cylinder mounting fasteners to the torque listed in this Chapter's Specifications.*
   b) *Route the brake hoses and align them with the master cylinder as noted during removal.*
   c) *Install new crush washers on each side of the brake hose banjo unions, and tighten the banjo bolts and the brake light switch used on 2011 and later models to the torque listed in this Chapter's Specifications.*
   d) *Install a new clip when securing the clevis pin to the clevis and brake pedal. Make sure the clip is fully installed and locked in place.*
   e) *Fill the master cylinder reservoir with DOT 4 brake fluid and bleed the brake system (see Section 8).*
   f) *Have someone apply and hold the brake pedal while you check the brake hose banjo unions for leakage.*
   g) *Turn the ignition switch ON and make sure the rear brake light comes on when operating the brake pedal.*
   h) *Check the brake pedal operation to make sure there is no binding and there is a small amount of free play when the pedal is initially depressed (see Section 7).*
   i) *Slowly drive the vehicle in a safe area to make sure the brakes operate correctly. If the brake pedal is spongy or its travel is excessive, bleed the brake system again.*

6 BRAKE HOSES - INSPECTION AND REPLACEMENT

1 Brake hose condition should be checked regularly and after the vehicle is involved in a crash or roll-over (see Chapter 2).

2 The brake system is equipped with five separate brake hoses - two front brake hoses, a supply brake hose and two rear brake hoses. A separate front brake hose is connected between each front brake caliper and the master cylinder using banjo bolts and washers. The supply brake hose is connected between the master cylinder and the brake hose joint mounted at the rear of the clutch cover, and a separate

6.2a Brake hose joint (A) and brake light switch (B) -
2010 models

6.2b Brake hose joint (arrow) - 2011 and later models

rear brake hose is connected between the brake hose joint and each rear brake caliper. The supply hose and both rear brake hoses are equipped with a banjo union on one end and a preformed metal brake line and flare nut on the other. Note that all five brake hoses are different, so make sure to purchase and install the identical replacement hose(s). On 2010 models, the brake light switch is mounted on the brake hose joint **(see illustrations)**.

Inspection

3 When working on an unfamiliar vehicle, make sure the brake hoses are correctly routed **(see illustration)**. If not, check the hoses for damage and replace if necessary.

4 Braided brake lines are used on all models and are harder to inspect than other brake hose designs where the rubber and steel material is visible. In a braided brake line, a flexible brake hose is enclosed in a woven mesh of long, thin steel strips. Run a white cloth along the hose and see if

6.3 Note how this brake hose is incorrectly routed underneath the front axle

6.8a These brake hose guides are used to route a brake hose around one side of the transmission

6.8b Note how brake hose ends are angled and positioned so you can correctly reinstall them during assembly

it picks up any brake fluid that may be leaking from inside the steel strips. Also check for wet spots and seeping fluid. A buildup of moist dirt on the hose may be a sign that the hose is leaking at that spot. Check extra carefully where the hoses are connected to their banjo fittings and metal brake lines (where used) as these areas are less flexible and are common areas for hose failure. If there is a problem with the brakes and they will not release after you release the pedal, check for a crushed brake hose.

5   Check the guides and plastic ties that route and secure the brake hoses for any looseness or damage.

6   Check the banjo bolts and the brake line fittings for looseness. Then have someone apply and hold the brake pedal while you visually inspect each hose end and its fitting for leakage.

Replacement

7   Remove the floor and other body components as necessary to access the brake hoses (see Chapter 14).

8   Clean the hose fittings before disconnecting them to prevent dirt from entering the brake component. Then note how the brake hose is routed and any guides it may pass through **(see illustrations)**.

9   Surround the areas around the brake hose fittings with a sheet of plastic to prevent brake fluid from contacting other components on the vehicle. Unscrew the banjo bolt or flare nut on either end of the brake hose. To prevent from rounding off the flats on the flare nuts, use a flare-nut wrench, which wraps around the fitting on the nut. Note the crush washers used on the banjo bolts and discard them as new washers must be installed during assembly.

10   Position the new hose in place following its original path and through its original guides. Install the banjo bolts, using new crush washers on both sides of the banjo union. When installing the front brake hoses onto the master cylinder, note that three washers are required - one on the outside of each banjo union and one where the banjo unions are installed next to each other. Carefully thread the flare nuts into the brake hose joint **(see illustration 6.2a or illustration 6.2b)**. After checking the hose alignment, tighten the banjo bolts and the flare nuts to the torque listed in this Chapter's Specifications.

11   Refill the master cylinder reservoir with new DOT 4 brake fluid, then flush the old brake fluid and bleed air from the system (see Section 8). Check the operation of the brakes carefully before driving the vehicle.

7   BRAKE PEDAL - INSPECTION, REMOVAL AND INSTALLATION

Inspection

1   Park the vehicle on a level surface and apply the parking brake.

2   Operate the brake pedal to make sure it travels freely a short distance before the brakes take hold. This movement is brake pedal free play, and note that a free

13

play specification is not listed for these models. If the brake pedal free play seems excessive, bleed the brake system (see Section 8). If there is not enough free play, remove the brake pedal assembly and check it for damage (see Step 4 through Step 7). Check that the locknut securing the clevis to the brake rod is tight (**see illustration**). Also check for any obstruction around the brake pedal linkage that could lock or bind the brake pedal as well as checking the master cylinder pushrod for damage. If the problem hasn't been found, a crushed brake hose could cause this problem by preventing the brake pedal from returning to its at-rest position (see Section 6). If the brake pedal movement is incorrect after you have installed the brake pedal assembly, check for missing or incorrectly installed parts.

3   If the brake pedal does not pivot squarely on its shaft when you apply the brakes, remove the brake pedal and check the brake pedal bore, shaft and bushings for excessive wear and damage (see Step 4 through Step 7).

Removal

4   Block the wheels and apply the parking brake.

5   Remove the clip and clevis pin securing the brake rod to the brake pedal. Then remove the E-clip securing the brake pedal to its pivot shaft and remove the brake pedal and its two bushings (**see illustration**).

6   Inspect the nylon brake pedal bushings for excessive wear and damage. Replace these bushings in sets of two.

7   Inspect the brake pedal bore and its pivot shaft for excessive wear. Also check the pivot shaft for cracks, bending and other damage. The E-clip groove on the end of the pivot shaft must have sharp edges and be in good condition to prevent the E-clip from releasing. The bore and pivot shaft surfaces must be smooth.

Installation

8   Installation is the reverse of these steps, plus the following:

   a) *Install the two bushings and the brake pedal onto the pivot shaft. Install a new E-clip into the shaft groove, making sure it is fully seated. Then move the brake pedal from side-to-side by hand to make sure the E-clip does not pop out of its groove. Pivot the brake pedal to make sure there is no binding or roughness.*

   b) *Install a new clip when securing the clevis pin to the clevis and brake pedal. Make sure the clip is fully installed and locked in place.*

   c) *Check the brake pedal operation (see Step 2).*

8   BRAKE BLEEDING

1   Air in the brake system increases brake pedal travel while causing it to feel spongy and less responsive. Bleeding the brake system is a process of removing air from the system. Bleeding is necessary when a banjo bolt

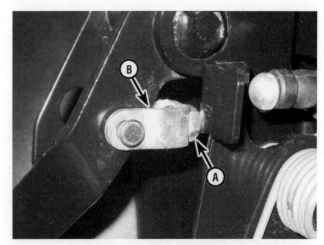

7.2 Make sure the locknut (A) securing the clevis (B) to the brake rod is tight

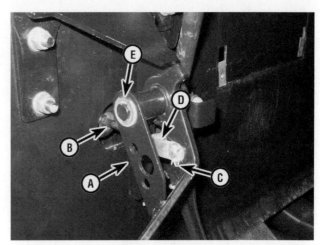

7.5 Brake pedal details

A	Brake pedal	D	Clevis
B	Brake rod	E	E-clip
C	Clip and clevis pin		

or brake hose has been loosened or disconnected, when a component or hose is replaced, when a leak occurs in the system or when the brake fluid level drops so low that the ports in the bottom of the master cylinder reservoir are uncovered and exposed to air. This final condition can be caused by excessive brake pad wear or a leak in the brake system.

2   Read Section 1 before bleeding the brake system.

Bleeding Tips

CAUTION:

Cover all parts that could become contaminated by the accidental spilling of brake fluid. Wash any spilled brake fluid from any surface immediately, as it damages the finish. Use soapy water and rinse completely.

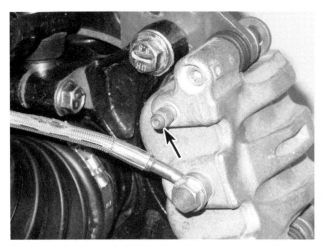

8.6 The holes through the bleed valves (arrow) must be clear to allow brake fluid to flow through when bleeding the system

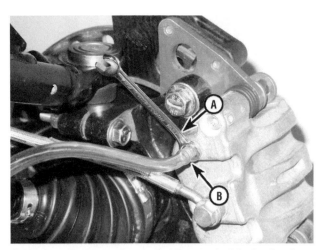

8.10a Install a box-end wrench (A) onto the bleed valve first, then connect the hose (B)

8.10b The Motion Pro 8 mm Mini Bleeder (arrow) is a combination wrench/bleed tool that fits tightly onto a caliper bleed valve. The clear hose is sized to fit tightly onto the bleed valve, which helps prevent fluid and air from leaking between the hose and valve. A check valve installed inside the tool prevents fluid from leaking past the hose when it is disconnected from the bleed valve. When flushing the system, the check valve also allows brake fluid to drain continuously through the caliper when the wrench is left open

6   Clean the bleed valves and the area around the valves of all dirt, sand and other debris (see illustration). Because the bleed valves are not equipped with covers, make sure the holes in the valves are not plugged with dirt or sand. If necessary, and when the valves are closed, use a piece of stiff wire and compressed air to clean the holes.

7   To prevent damaging the bleed valves use a box-end wrench to open and close them.

8   Replace bleed valves with damaged hex-shoulders as they are difficult to loosen and cannot be tightened fully.

9   If a bleed valve will not loosen after applying pressure with a wrench, stop and tap the wrench with a hammer to shock it. Then attempt to loosen it with a 6-point socket. Bleed valves are often over-tightened and thus damaged.

10   Install a box-end wrench on the bleed valve before installing the catch hose (see illustrations). This will allow you to open and close the bleed valve without having to disconnect the hose.

11   Use a clear catch hose to allow visual inspection of the brake fluid as it leaves the caliper.

12   Depending on the play of the bleed valve when it is loosened, it is common to see air exiting through the catch hose even through there may be no air in the brake system. A loose or damaged catch hose can also cause air to leak into the catch hose. In both cases, air is being introduced into the catch hose at the bleed valve threads and/or catch hose connection, and not from within the brake system itself. This condition can be misleading and cause excessive brake bleeding when there is no air in the system.

13   Open the bleed valve just enough to allow fluid to pass through the valve and into the catch bottle. The farther the bleed valve is opened, the looser the valve becomes. This

3   Always start the bleeding procedure at the caliper farthest away from the master cylinder. Bleed the brake system in the following order, using the brake pedal as described:

    a) Right rear
    b) Left rear
    c) Right front
    d) Left front

4   When bleeding the brake system make sure the vehicle is parked on a level surface so the master cylinder is positioned higher than the brake calipers. The brakes can be bled without having to remove the calipers from their mounting positions on the vehicle.

5   Before bleeding the brake system check that all banjo bolts and flare nuts are tightened to the torque listed in this Chapter's Specifications. At the same time visually inspect the brake lines for any leakage and other damage.

13

may allow air to be drawn into the system from around the valve threads.

14 If the system is difficult to bleed, tap the brake lines on the master cylinder a few times to remove air bubbles trapped in the hose connection where the brake fluid exits the master cylinder. Also tap the banjo bolt and line connection points at the calipers and other brake units.

15 When bleeding the brakes, check the fluid level in the master cylinder frequently to prevent it from running dry, especially when using a vacuum pump. Maintain the brake fluid level so that it is above the low mark on the reservoir when bleeding the brake system. If the fluid level drops too low and uncovers the ports in the bottom of the reservoir, air will enter the system and the brakes must be rebled.

16 Before removing the cap from the master cylinder reservoir, clean the cap and the area around and above the cap to prevent dirt from falling into the reservoir.

17 Before bleeding the system, have an assistant apply and release the brake pedal slowly while you check for bubbles coming from the holes in the bottom of the reservoir. If bubbles are produced, continue to slowly apply and release the brake pedal until they stop.

18 After bleeding the system, have someone apply and hold the brake pedal down while you check each caliper bleed valve for leakage.

19 The brake system can be bled manually (Steps 20 through 31) or with a vacuum pump (Steps 32 through 44).

Manual bleeding

20 This procedure describes how to bleed the brake system with a bottle partially filled with DOT 4 brake fluid, length of clear hose that fits tightly onto the bleed valve and a wrench **(see illustration)**. Two people will be required to perform the procedure. One person can open and close the bleed valve while the other person operates the brake pedal.

21 Read Steps 3 through 19 in this section.

22 Begin bleeding the brake system by starting at the caliper the farthest away from the master cylinder (see Step 3).

23 Remove the wheel at the caliper being bled (see Chapter 10).

24 Connect the catch hose to the bleed valve on the brake caliper **(see illustration)**. Submerge the other end of the hose into the bottle partially filled with DOT 4 brake fluid to prevent air from being drawn into the catch hose and back into the brake system when the brake pedal is released.

25 Apply the brake pedal firmly (do not pump) until it stops and hold in position, then open the bleed valve. This will force air and brake fluid from the system and the pedal will travel downward. When the pedal can move no farther, hold it and close the bleed valve, then slowly release the pedal to its rest position. Do not release the pedal when the bleed valve is open as this will allow air to be drawn back into the system.

26 Check the fluid level in the reservoir and replenish, if necessary. Do not allow the fluid level to drop below the

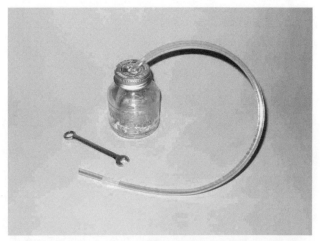

8.20 A bottle, clear hose and 8 mm wrench used for bleeding the brake system

8.24 Set-up for bleeding the brakes manually. Connect one end of the bleed hose onto the bleed valve (arrow) and submerge its open end into a bottle partially filled with DOT 4 brake fluid

lower mark on the reservoir during the bleeding process.

27 Repeat until clear fluid is seen leaving the tube, then tighten the bleed valve to the torque listed in this Chapter's Specifications. Perform the same procedure on the other wheels in order (see Step 3).

NOTE:

If all four calipers have been bled but the pedal is still not firm when applying it, small bubbles may be present in the system. With the bleed valves closed, tap all of the banjo bolts with a plastic hammer and allow the system to stand undisturbed for a few hours before bleeding the system again. The system should stabilize as the small bubbles group and shape into large bubbles.

28 The bleeding procedure is completed when the pedal feels solid when applied. If the pedal sinks or feels soft,

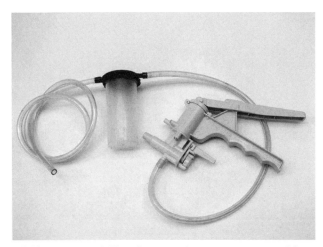

8.32 A commercial hand-operated vacuum pump used for bleeding the brake system

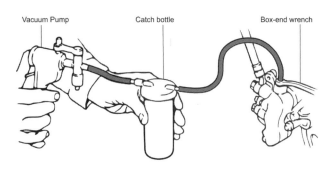

8.36 Set-up for bleeding the brakes with a hand-operated vacuum pump

there is still air in the system and the entire process must be repeated.

29   Check the brake fluid reservoir and fill the reservoir to the upper level as described in Chapter 2, Section 3.

30   Reinstall the wheel(s). See Chapter 10.

31   Test drive the vehicle slowly at first to make sure the brakes are operating correctly.

Pressure bleeding

32   This procedure describes how to use a hand-operated vacuum pump with a catch bottle and two hoses. These can be purchased as a kit that includes both the vacuum pump, catch bottle and hoses **(see illustration)**. An assistant is not required when bleeding the brakes with a vacuum pump.

33   Read Steps 3 through 19 in this section.

34   Begin bleeding the brake system by starting at the

caliper the farthest away from the master cylinder (see Step 3).

35   Remove the wheel at the caliper being bled (see Chapter 10).

36   Connect the catch hose between the bleed valve and catch bottle. Connect the other hose between the catch bottle and vacuum pump. The hose inside the catch bottle must be connected to the hose attached to the bleed valve. If necessary, refer to the tool manufacturer's instructions for additional information. Then secure the vacuum pump to the vehicle with a length of stiff wire so you can leave the pump in place when refilling the master cylinder and operating the brake pedal **(see illustration)**.

37   Pump the handle on the vacuum pump to create a vacuum in the catch hose. Then open the bleed valve with a wrench to allow air and brake fluid to be drawn through the master cylinder, brake hoses and lines. Close the bleed valve before the brake fluid stops flowing from the system (no more vacuum in line) or before the gauge on the vacuum pump (if so equipped) reads zero.

38   Check the fluid level in the reservoir and replenish, if necessary.

39   Repeat until clear fluid is seen leaving the tube, then tighten the bleed valve to the torque listed in this Chapter's Specifications. Perform the same procedure on the other wheels in order (see Step 3).

NOTE:

If all four calipers have been bled but the pedal is still not firm when applying it, small bubbles may be present in the system. With the bleed valves closed, tap all of the banjo bolts with a plastic hammer and allow the system to stand undisturbed for a few hours before bleeding the system again. The system should stabilize as the small bubbles group and shape into large bubbles.

40   The bleeding procedure is completed when the pedal feels solid when applied. If the pedal sinks or feels soft, there is still air in the system and the entire process must be repeated.

41   Check the brake fluid reservoir and fill the reservoir to the upper level as described in Chapter 2, Section 3.

42   Reinstall the wheel(s). See Chapter 10.

43   Test drive the vehicle slowly at first to make sure the brakes are operating correctly.

9   PARKING BRAKE CALIPER AND BRAKE PADS - REMOVAL, BRAKE PAD SERVICE/ GAP ADJUSTMENT AND INSTALLATION

1   All models are equipped with a mechanical hand-operated parking brake assembly. The assembly consists of a parking brake lever and switch, cable, parking brake caliper and a parking brake disc mounted on the transmission output shaft. Lowering the lever applies the parking brake and unlocking/raising the lever releases the parking brake.

13

9.1 Parking brake caliper (2010 model shown)

9.6a Loosen the parking brake cable inner (A) and outer (B) locknuts . . .

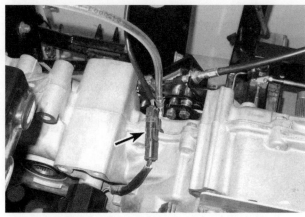

9.5 Disconnect the rear differential solenoid wiring harness connector (arrow)

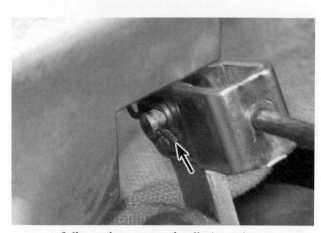

9.6b . . . then remove the clip (arrow) . . .

The parking brake should be applied whenever the vehicle is parked **(see illustration)**.

2   Before removing and servicing the parking brake caliper in this section, refer to Step 11 (2010 through 2012 models) or Step 30 (2013 and later models) for repair information on the brake pads and caliper assembly.

Removal

3   Park the vehicle on a level surface and shift the transmission into gear. Block the wheels to prevent the vehicle from rolling.

4   Raise the cargo bed (see Chapter 14).

5   Disconnect the rear differential solenoid wiring harness connector - routed over the transmission and parking brake caliper **(see illustration)**.

6   To disconnect the parking brake cable at the caliper, first release the parking brake lever located beside the steering wheel. Locate the cable at the parking brake caliper and loosen the inner and outer cable locknuts. Then place a rag underneath the linkage assembly to catch any dropped parts, and remove the clip and clevis pin securing the parking brake cable to the brake lever mounted on the

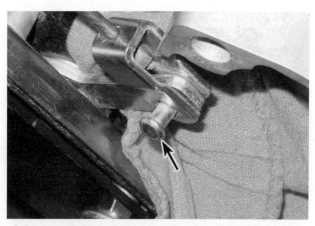

9.6c . . . and clevis pin (arrow) securing the parking brake cable to the brake lever on the caliper

caliper. When the cable end is free, disconnect the two cable locknuts from the mounting bracket and set the cable aside **(see illustrations)**.

7   Identify the mounting bracket and the brake caliper **(see illustration)**. Both are removed as an assembly.

8   If the brake caliper will be disassembled, loosen, but

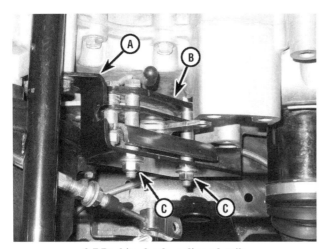

9.7 Parking brake caliper details

A   Mounting bracket
B   Parking brake caliper
C   Parking brake caliper mounting bracket bolts and nuts -
these fasteners secure the caliper to the mounting bracket

9.9c As shown here, a flex socket's (arrow) overall length is shorter than a universal joint and socket, and its use in this step will provide easier access to the front lower mounting screw

9.9a Remove the upper parking brake caliper mounting screw (arrow) . . .

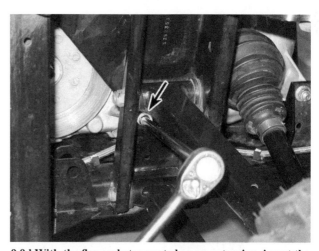

9.9d With the flex socket mounted on an extension, insert the socket through the opening below the rear suspension arm to access the mounting screw

9.9b . . . and the two lower screws (arrows) - if the clutch housing is mounted on the engine/transmission, the front screw is more difficult to access

do not remove, the parking brake caliper mounting bracket nuts **(see illustration 9.7)**.

9   Remove the upper and lower parking brake caliper mounting screws, noting that these screws secure the parking brake caliper mounting bracket to the transmission **(see illustrations)**. If the clutch housing is mounted on the vehicle, the front lower mounting screw is obstructed and cannot be reached straight on. To remove this screw with the clutch housing in place, you will need a flex socket and a long extension **(see illustrations)**.

10   With the mounting screws removed, lift the parking brake caliper assembly off the brake disc, position it as required to clear the transmission and remove it **(see illustrations)**.

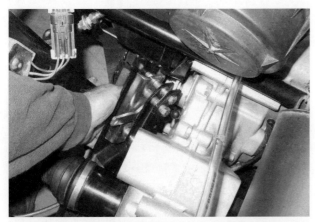

9.10a Lift the parking brake caliper assembly off the brake disc . . .

9.12a Remove the nuts and washers securing the mounting bracket (arrow) to the brake caliper . . .

9.10b . . . then maneuver the assembly as required to clear the transmission and remove it from the vehicle

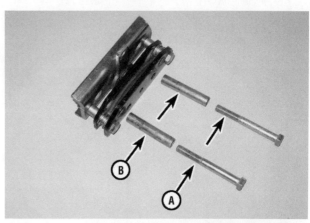

9.12b . . . then remove the bolts (A) and collars (B) from the opposite side

Brake pad service/gap adjustment

2010 through 2012 models

11   On 2010 through 2012 models, the parking brake pads can be replaced and several different parking brake repair kits are available from the manufacturer. After removing the brake pads and inspecting the caliper parts, purchase the kit that will provide the necessary parts for complete repair and assembly. See a dealer parts department for information on the repair kits.

Disassembly

12   Remove the parking brake caliper mounting bracket nuts and washers and slide the bracket off the bolts. Then remove the bolts and collars **(see illustrations)**. Note that the nuts should have been loosened in Step 8. If not, lock the mounting bracket in a vise, then loosen the nuts.

NOTE:

When removing the parking brake caliper assembly nuts and bolts and separating the caliper assembly in Step 13, three steel balls will fall out from between the brake plate and brake lever. Make sure to retrieve them to prevent their loss.

9.13 Lock one of the parking brake caliper assembly bolts in a vise, then loosen its mating nut. Repeat to loosen the other nut, noting not to remove the nuts (arrows) at this time or the assembly will separate and three steel balls will fall out

13   Secure one of the parking brake caliper assembly bolt heads in a vise. Then loosen, but do not remove, the mating nut **(see illustration)**. Repeat for the other nut. When both nuts are loose, remove the caliper assembly and place it on a workbench.

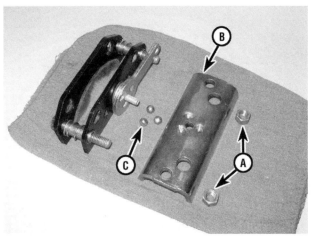

9.14 Unscrew the nuts (A) and slide off the brake plate (B), then retrieve the three steel balls (C)

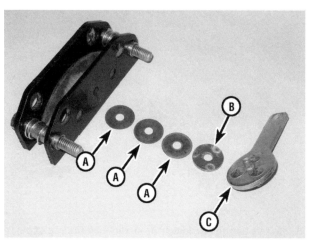

9.15b Here is the shim pack (A) and thrust washer (B) installed on the brake lever (C). Because the shims are used to adjust the clearance between the brake pads, the number of shims shown here may differ from the number of shims found on the caliper you are working on

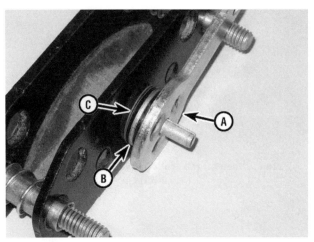

9.15a Brake lever (A), thrust washer (B) and shim pack (C) alignment

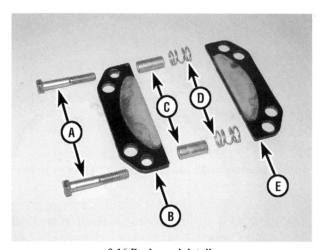

9.16 Brake pad details

A   Assembly bolts   D   Springs
B   Outer brake pad   E   Inner brake pad
C   Collars

13

14   Remove the nuts, brake plate and the three steel balls from the caliper assembly (see illustration). The three steel balls will fall out when tension is removed from them.

15   Remove the brake lever, thrust washer and shim pack (see illustrations).

NOTE:

The outer and inner brake pads are different. When performing Step 16, identify one of the brake pads so both can be installed in their original mounting position.

16   Remove the outer and inner brake pads from the assembly bolts, springs and collars (see illustration).

Inspection

17   Inspect the steel balls for flat spots, cracks and other damage. Then inspect the ball detents in the brake lever and brake plate for excessive wear, cracks and other damage. Replace worn or damaged parts as required.

18   Before measuring the brake pads, inspect the lining surface for contamination and other damage. If the contamination is minor, resurface the lining with sandpaper. However, if oil or grease has penetrated the lining material, or the lining is damaged, replace the brake pads as a set.

19   Before measuring the brake pads, note that the outer and inner brake pads are different – the outer brake pad backing plate is thicker. Measure the total thickness of each pad with a vernier caliper - lining material and backing

9.19a Note how the backing plate on the outer brake pad (A) is thicker than the backing plate used on the inner brake pad (B)

9.22a Assemble the caliper without the springs and shims . . .

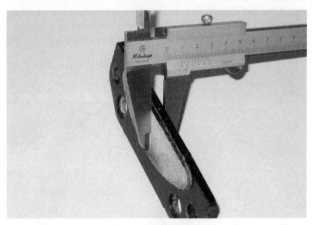

9.19b Measuring brake pad thickness with a vernier caliper

9.22b . . . then lift the brake pads and measure the gap between them

plate. If the thickness of either pad is less than the limit listed in this Chapter's Specifications, replace both brake pads as a set **(see illustrations)**.

20   Perform the brake pad gap measurement adjustment (see Steps 21 through 24).

Brake pad gap adjustment

21   Brake pad gap is the distance between the brake pad lining surfaces when the pads are installed in the caliper. This gap is important because it determines the brake pad-to-disc clearance when the caliper is installed over the disc. Shims placed between the brake lever and the inner brake pad are used to adjust the gap. Whenever the caliper is disassembled, or when it becomes difficult to adjust the parking brake cable, measure the brake pad gap and adjust if necessary. Before measuring the brake pad gap, make sure the thickness of both brake pads are within specification (see Step 19).

22   Assemble the brake caliper using all of the parts except the springs and shims **(see illustration)**. When installing the brake pads, the pad friction surfaces must face each other. With the caliper assembled, push the brake pads apart until they bottom and measure the gap between the pads with a vernier caliper **(see illustration)**. Compare the

9.23 If the brake pad gap is incorrect, determine the correct number of shims to use - shim thickness is 0.010 in. (0.254 mm)

recorded brake pad gap measurement to the value listed in this Chapter's Specifications. If necessary, refer to Steps 25 through 28 on how to assemble the brake caliper assembly.

23   Using the gap determined in Step 22, select the correct number of shims required to set the brake pad gap at its correct distance **(see illustration)**. Note that the thickness of each shim is 0.10 in. (0.254 mm).

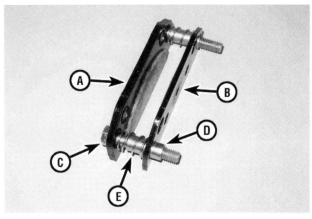

9.25 Brake pad assembly details

A   Outer brake pad (thicker pad)
B   Inner brake pad (thinner pad)
C   Assembly bolts
D   Collars
E   Springs

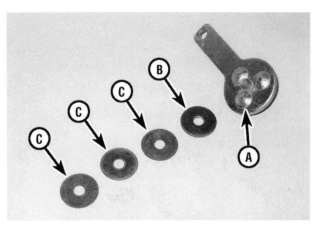

9.26a Brake lever assembly details

A   Brake lever (convex side up)
B   Thrust washer
C   Shims (number can vary)

24   Disassemble the caliper and then reassemble it with the correct number of shims to make sure the brake pad gap is correct. If the gap is still incorrect, repeat the procedure. When the gap is correct, disassemble the brake caliper and lay out the parts for final assembly.

Assembly

25   Assemble the brake pads using the parking brake caliper assembly bolts, collars and springs. Make sure to install the outer and inner brake pads facing in their correct position **(see illustration)**.
26   Position the brake lever on the workbench with the three convex ramps facing up, then install the thrust washer and shims onto the pin in their correct order **(see illustration)**. Hold the shim pack in place and install the brake lever by inserting its pin into the hole in the inner brake pad **(see illustrations)**.

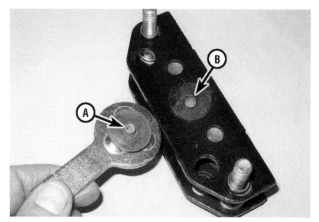

9.26b Align the pin (A) in the brake lever with the hole (B) in the inner brake pad . . .

9.26c . . . and install the brake lever, making sure the shims and washer did not fall off

9.27a Install the balls in the brake lever indents (A), then align and install the brake plate so that its indents (B) align with the three balls . . .

27   Install a ball in each of the concave indents in the brake lever. Then align and install the brake plate over the assembly bolts, making sure mating concave indents in the plate engage with the three balls. When the alignment is correct, install the two parking brake caliper assembly nuts and tighten finger-tight to hold the caliper assembly in place **(see illustrations)**.

13

9.27b . . . and install the parking brake caliper assembly nuts (arrows) to hold the assembly in place

9.28a Hold the parking brake caliper assembly bolts in a vise (one at a time) and tighten the nuts to the specified torque

28   Secure one of the parking brake caliper assembly bolt heads in a vise and tighten its nut to the torque listed in this Chapter's Specifications **(see illustration)**. Repeat for the other bolt and nut. With both bolts and nuts tightened, and the caliper assembly secured in a vise, operate the brake lever to ensure the pads lock and unlock correctly **(see illustration)**.

29   Install the mounting bracket by installing the collars onto the parking brake caliper mounting bracket bolts and passing the collars through the holes in the inner brake pad **(see illustration 9.12b)**. Then install the mounting bracket and secure with the washers and nuts **(see illustration 9.12a)**. Tighten the nuts finger-tight. Final tightening of the bolt nuts will take place after the caliper assembly has been installed on the transmission.

9.28b Operate the brake lever by hand to check brake pad operation

2013 and later models

30   On 2013 and later models, replacement parking brake pads and caliper parts are not available from the manufacturer. If the pads are excessively worn, or the caliper is damaged, the manufacturer specifies to replace the parking brake caliper as an assembly.

Inspection

31   Secure the brake caliper in a vise. Then operate the brake lever by hand to make sure it locks the inner brake pad in both open and closed positions **(see illustration 9.28b)**. If the brake lever moves easily and doesn't remain locked in either position, the index balls and/or the ball seats in the brake plate and brake lever are severely worn or damaged. This condition will require replacement of the brake caliper assembly.

32   Measure the brake pad lining thickness (do not include the backing plate) and compare to the value listed in this Chapter's Specifications. If the lining thickness on any pad less than the service limit, replace the brake caliper as an assembly **(see illustration)**.

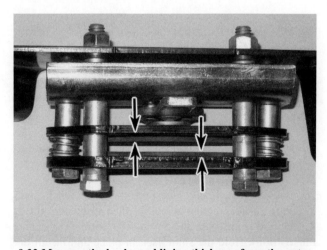

9.32 Measure the brake pad lining thickness from the outer friction surface to the metal backing plate

10.3 Inspect both sides of the parking brake disc (arrow) for deep score marks or grooves, cracks and oil

10.4 Measure the parking brake disc thickness with a micrometer

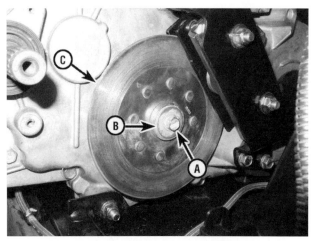

10.7 Parking brake disc details

A   *Mounting screw*   C   *Parking brake disc*
B   *Washer*

Installation

33   Position the brake caliper over the brake disc and install the brake caliper mounting screws finger-tight (**see illustrations 9.9a and 9.9b**).

34   Tighten the parking brake caliper mounting bracket bolt nuts to the torque listed in this Chapter's Specifications (**see illustration 9.7**).

35   Tighten the parking brake caliper mounting screws to the torque listed in this Chapter's Specifications (**see illustrations 9.9a and 9.9b**).

36   The remainder of installation is the reverse of removal, noting the following:

  a) *After securing the brake cable to the brake lever with the clevis pin, install a new clip through the clevis pin, making sure it is fully installed and locked in place. See Step 6.*

  b) *Adjust the parking brake cable and test drive the vehicle to make sure there is no brake drag on the parking brake disc (see Chapter 2).*

10   PARKING BRAKE DISC - INSPECTION, REMOVAL AND INSTALLATION

1   Park the vehicle on a level surface and shift the transmission into gear. Block the wheels to prevent the vehicle from rolling.

2   Raise the cargo bed (see Chapter 14).

Inspection

3   The parking brake disc is mounted on the transmission output shaft. Inspect the disc surface for any visual damage, score marks, cracks and other damage (**see illustration**). Also make sure there is no oil on the disc surface. If there is oil on the disc, check for the source of the oil leak and repair it. Because this disc is used just for the parking brake, wear and scratches on the disc surface should be minimal, though sand, dirt and mud caught between the disc and the brake pads will cause wear to these parts. If the disc surface is severely worn or damaged, there could be a problem with the parking brake caliper. Remove the parking brake caliper and inspect the brake pads for excessive wear and the caliper parts for damage (see Section 9). If the disc is damaged, it must be replaced (see Step 5 through Step 15). Maintain the disc by keeping it clean and corrosion-free. Clean the disc with an aerosol brake parts cleaner and a lint-free cloth.

4   If the disc surface is okay, measure its thickness with a micrometer at several locations around its perimeter and compare to the service limit in this Chapter's Specifications. If the disc thickness is less than the minimum allowable, replace it as described in Step 5 through Step 15 (**see illustration**).

Removal

5   Remove the clutch inner cover (see Chapter 5).

6   Shift the transmission into gear and apply the parking brake.

7   Loosen the parking brake disc mounting screw (**see illustration**).

13

8   Release the parking brake.

9   Remove the parking brake caliper (see Section 9).

10   Remove the screw, washer and parking brake disc **(see illustration 10.7)**.

Installation

11   Remove all threadlock residue from the mounting screw threads and also from the threads inside the output shaft. Then clean and dry the screw, washer and the output shaft threads. At the same time clean both sides of the disc and its mating surfaces on the output shaft. Use an aerosol brake parts cleaner to clean these parts, and allow them to dry before installing them.

12   Slide the parking brake disc onto the transmission output shaft. Install the washer onto the mounting screw, then temporarily install the screw and tighten finger-tight to hold the brake disc in place.

13   Install the parking brake caliper (see Section 9).

14   Remove the brake disc screw and washer and apply Loctite 262 to the screw threads, then reinstall the screw and washer and tighten finger-tight. Apply the parking brake to prevent the disc from turning and tighten the screw to the torque listed in this Chapter's Specifications.

15   The remainder of installation is the reverse of removal. Check the parking brake adjustment (see Chapter 2).

11   PARKING BRAKE CABLE REPLACEMENT

1   Park the vehicle on a level surface and shift the transmission into gear. Block the wheels to prevent the vehicle from rolling.

2   Remove the fasteners securing the dash assembly to the frame, then slide the dash assembly up the side cab tubes and secure it in place (see Chapter 14).

3   On standard Ranger models, remove the floor cover, seat and kickboard (see Chapter 14).

4   On Crew models, remove the front and rear floors. Remove any additional components as necessary to access the parking brake cable. See Chapter 14.

5   Release the parking brake lever.

6   Note the parking brake cable routing from the parking brake lever to the caliper. Also note the use of any cable ties and remove them **(see illustrations)**.

NOTE:

The front and rear clevis pins used to secure the parking brake cable ends in place are different. Identify and store each pin separately so they can be correctly installed. The clips used to secure the clevis pins are identical.

7   Disconnect the parking brake cable at the parking brake caliper (see Section 9).

8   Remove the clip and clevis pin securing the parking brake cable to the lever assembly **(see illustration)**.

9   Hold the parking brake cable and loosen the cable

11.6a Parking brake cable routing underneath the floor (2010 Ranger shown)

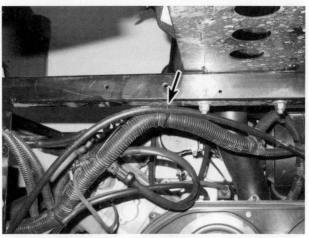

11.6b Parking brake routing on the left side of the vehicle, over the clutch housing (2010 Ranger shown)

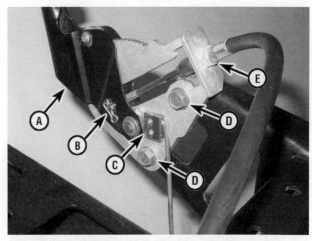

11.8 Parking brake lever details

A	Parking brake lever assembly	C	Parking brake switch
B	Cable clip/clevis pin	D	Mounting bolts/nuts
		E	Parking brake cable

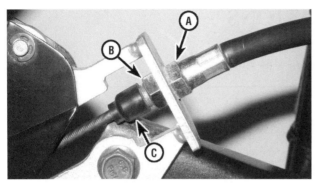

11.9 Hold the cable (A) and loosen the locknut (B); if necessary, slide the rubber cover (C) down the cable to provide additional room to loosen the locknut

12.4a Remove the screws securing the parking brake switch . . .

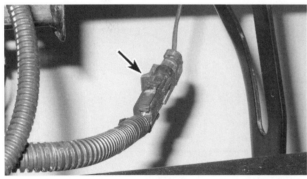

12.4b . . . or disconnect the parking brake switch wiring harness connector

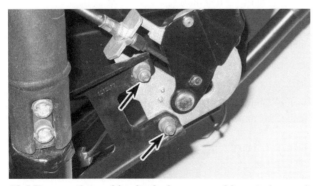

12.6 Remove the parking brake lever assembly nuts (arrows) and bolts

locknut **(see illustration)**. Then disconnect the cable end from the lever and slide the cable out of the lever assembly.

10   When the cable is free at both ends and all cable ties have been removed, remove the cable from the vehicle.

11   Installation is the reverse of these steps, plus the following:

a) *Compare the old and new cables to make sure the length and the end fittings are the same.*

b) *Install the new cable into the vehicle, making sure it follows the same path as the original cable. Secure the cable in place with plastic ties placed in their original positions.*

c) *Secure the front and rear cable ends with new clips. Make sure the clips are locked in place.*

d) *Adjust the parking brake cable (see Chapter 2).*

12   PARKING BRAKE LEVER - REMOVAL AND INSTALLATION

1   Park the vehicle on a level surface and shift the transmission into gear. Block the wheels to prevent the vehicle from rolling.

2   Remove the fasteners securing the dash assembly to the frame, then slide the dash assembly up the side cab tubes and secure it in place (see Chapter 14).

3   Release the parking brake.

4   Depending on whether you will be removing the parking brake lever from the vehicle or setting it aside, either remove the parking brake switch or disconnect its wiring harness connector **(see illustrations)**.

5   If the parking brake lever will be removed from the vehicle, disconnect the parking brake cable from the lever (see Section 11).

6   Remove the nuts and bolts securing the parking brake lever assembly to the frame **(see illustration and illustration 11.8)**.

7   Depending on the service required, either remove the parking brake lever assembly from the vehicle, or set it aside by resting it onto the frame, making sure not to damage the parking brake cable if it is still attached.

8   Clean the parking brake lever assembly and then inspect it for damage. Because the lever is an assembled unit, if damaged, a new one must be installed.

9   Installation is the reverse of removal, noting the following:

a) *Tighten the parking brake lever assembly bolts and nuts securely.*

b) *Check and adjust the parking brake cable adjustment (see Chapter 2).*

13

SPECIFICATIONS

Front and rear brakes

Brake caliper bore inside diameter
    Twin-piston caliper
        New . . . .   1.373 inch (34.87 mm)
        Service limit . . . .   1.375 inch (34.93 mm)
    Rear
        Single piston caliper
            New . . . .   1.505 inch (38.23 mm)
            Service limit. . . . .   1.507 inch (38.28 mm)
        Twin-piston caliper
            New . . . .   1.192 inch (30.28 mm)
            Service limit. . . . .   1.194 inch (30.33 mm)
Brake caliper piston outside diameter
    Front
        New . . . .   1.370 inch (34.80 mm)
        Service limit . . . .   1.368 inch (34.75 mm)
    Rear
        Single piston caliper
            New . . . .   1.500 inch (38.10 mm)
            Service limit. . . . .   1.498 inch (38.05 mm)
        Twin piston caliper
            New . . . .   1.186 inch (30.12 mm)
            Service limit. . . . .   1.184 inch (30.07 mm)
Brake disc
    Runout limit . . . .   0.010 inch (0.254 mm)
    Thickness
        Front and rear
            New . . . .   0.188 inch (4.78 mm)
            Service limit. . . . .   0.170 inch (4.32 mm)
    Maximum allowable difference between any two disc
    thickness measurements . . . .   0.002 inch (0.051 mm)
Brake fluid . . . .   DOT 4
Brake pad thickness . . . .   See Chapter Two
Brake pedal travel . . . .   Not specified

Parking brake

Brake pad gap
    2010 through 2012 models . . . .   0.203-0.193 inches (5.16-4.90 mm)
    2013 and later models. . . . .   Not applicable
Brake disc thickness
    New . . . .   0.164-0.173 inch (4.17-4.39 mm)
        Service limit
            2010 models. . . . .   0.140 inch (3.56 mm)
            2011 and later models . . . .   0.150 inch (3.81 mm)
Brake pad thickness
    2010 through 2012 models
        Outer brake pad
            New . . . .   0.360 inch (9.14 mm)
            Service limit. . . . .   0.310 inch (7.87 mm)
        Inner brake pad
            New . . . .   0.304 inch (7.72 mm)
            Service limit. . . . .   0.240 inch (6.1 mm)
    2013 and later models. . . . .   Not applicable
Brake pad lining thickness service limit
    2010 through 2012 models . . . .   Not applicable
    2013 and later models. . . . .   0.40 inch (1 mm)

Torque specifications	Ft-lbs	In.-lb	Nm

NOTE

One foot-pound (ft-lb) of torque is equivalent to 12 inch-pounds (in-lbs) of torque. Torque values below approximately 15 ft-lbs are expressed in inch-pounds, because most foot-pound torque wrenches are not accurate at these smaller values.

	Ft-lbs	In.-lb	Nm
Banjo bolts	15		20
Bleed valves	--	47	5.3
Brake line flare nuts	12-15		16-20
Brake light switch	12-15		16-20
Front brake caliper mounting screws	30		41
Front brake disc mounting screws	18		24
Master cylinder mounting bolt nuts	15		20
Parking brake caliper assembly bolt nuts			
2010 models	25		34
2011 and 2012 models	35		47
2013 and later models	--		
Parking brake caliper mounting bracket bolt nuts	18		24
Parking brake disc mounting screw			
2010 models	15-18		20-24
2011 and later models	10-15		14-20
Parking brake lever mounting bolts	13		18
Parking brake caliper mounting screws	40		54
Rear brake caliper mounting screws	30		41
Rear brake disc mounting screws	28		38

13

NOTES

CHAPTER FOURTEEN

BODY

CONTENTS

1 GENERAL INFORMATION

1   This Chapter covers the procedures necessary to remove and install the body panels and other body parts. Since many service and repair operations on these vehicles require removal of the panels and/or other body parts, the procedures are grouped here and referred to from other Chapters.

2   In the case of damage to the panels or other body parts, it is usually necessary to remove the broken component and either attempt to repair it or replace it with a new (or used) one. There are several aftermarket companies providing kits designed to repair plastic body panels.

NOTE:

When attempting to remove any body panel, first study the panel closely, noting any fasteners and associated fittings, to be sure of returning everything to its correct place on installation. In some cases, the aid of an assistant will be required when removing pan-

els, to help avoid damaging the surface. Once the visible fasteners have been removed, try to lift off the panel as described but DO NOT FORCE the panel - if it will not release, check that all fasteners have been removed and try again. Where a panel engages another by means of tabs and slots, be careful not to break the tabs or to damage the bodywork. Remember that a few moments of patience at this stage will save you a lot of money in replacing broken panels!

2 PLASTIC RIVETS

1   Plastic rivets are used to position and secure many of the plastic panels and other components on the vehicle. The rivets are a two-piece design, consisting of an outer rivet body and an inner rivet head. A set of multi-function pliers designed to remove the rivets is available from

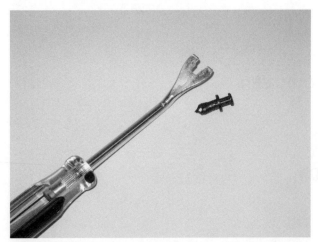

2.1a Automotive type door upholstery removal tool and rivet

2.1b Using pressure, slide the tool fully between the rivet head and the rivet body . . .

2.1c . . . then pry the tool upward to release the rivet head . . .

2.1d . . . and remove the rivet

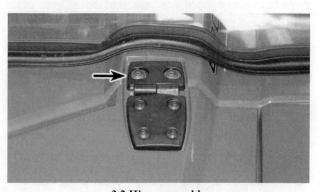

3.2 Hinge assembly

the manufacturer (part No. 2876389). Otherwise, the easiest way to remove a rivet is with an automotive door upholstery removal tool **(see illustration)**. Insert the tool between the rivet head and rivet body, then pry the tool to pull the rivet head upward, and remove the rivet **(see illustrations)**. Note that when using the correct tool, some rivets can still be difficult to remove due to damage, dirt and the misalignment between body panels and alignment holes. Before installing a rivet, inspect it for damage and replace if necessary.

2   To install a rivet, release the rivet head from the rivet body. Install the rivet into the body hole, then push the rivet head to lock it in place. If a rivet is difficult to install, check for any misalignment between the two parts. When installing a body panel that uses a number of rivets, it may be helpful to install all of the rivets first without locking them. This way, if there is any misalignment with the body panel, some movement may be possible to help align it. When the body panel is in place, properly aligned and all of the rivets are installed, lock the rivets in place.

3   If the rivet head cannot be pushed fully into the rivet, the plastic body components and frame member (if used) that the rivet is installed through are not aligned or the rivet is damaged.

3   HOOD - REMOVAL AND INSTALLATION

1   The hood pivots on left and right hinges, and locks in place using a striker and latch assembly.

2   Remove the two screws securing each hinge to the frame. Or you can remove the four screws securing each hinge to the hood **(see illustration)**.

3   Slide the latch lever to unlock the hood, then lift remove the hood from the dash **(see illustrations)**.

4   Installation is the reverse of removal. When closing the hood, make sure the striker mounted underneath the hood locks into the latch mounted on the frame.

3.3a Slide the latch lever to unlock the hood . . .

3.3b . . . then lift off and remove the hood (arrow)

4.1 Hood latch details (2010 and 2011 model shown). On 2012 and later models, the spring seat and the screw and washer (arrows) are not used

4.4a Right side screw and washer (arrow) - 2010 and 2011 models shown

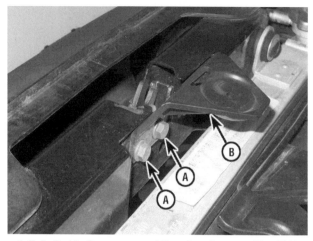

4.4b Left side flange screws (A) and spring seat (B) - 2010 and 2011 models shown

4.5 Remove the hood latch through opening in the frame

4   HOOD LATCH AND STRIKER - REMOVAL AND INSTALLATION

1   The hood latch is an assembled unit **(see illustration)**. Do not disassemble it.

2   Release the latch lever, then raise and pivot the hood rearward until it stops **(see illustration 3.3a).**

3   Remove the front cover (see Section 6).

4   On 2010 and 2011 models, the hood latch is secured to the frame with a screw and washer on the right side, and two flange screws on the left side. Remove these screws and the spring seat **(see illustrations)**. On 2012 and later models, remove the two screws securing the hood latch to the frame

5   Slide the hood latch through the opening in the frame and remove it **(see illustration)**.

6   To remove the striker, remove screws from underneath

14

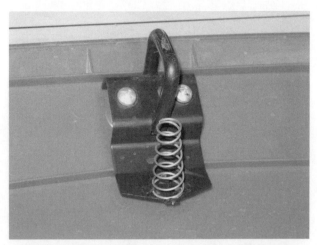

4.6 The striker assembly is secured to the hood with two screws (2010 and 2011 model shown). On 2012 and later models, the spring is not used

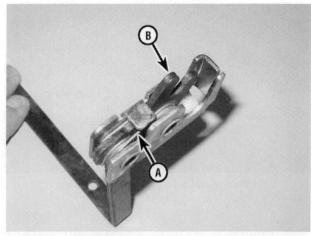

4.7 Inspect the spring (A) and latch lever (B) for damage

the hood. On 2010 and 2011 models, it is not necessary to remove the spring unless you are going to replace it **(see illustration)**.

7   Clean the hood latch of all dirt and sand so the mechanism opens and closes without any binding. Then inspect the return spring inside the hood latch to make sure it is not broken or otherwise damaged **(see illustration)**. Also inspect the latch lever for cracks or other damage. If any damage is found, replace the hood latch as an assembly.

8   Installation is the reverse of removal. Apply a threadlock onto the two flange screw threads and tighten securely. When closing the hood, make sure it locks in place.

5   FRONT BUMPER - REMOVAL AND INSTALLATION

1   Park the vehicle on a level surface and apply the parking brake.

2   Remove the screws and the lower grill mounted on the front bumper **(see illustration)**.

3   If aftermarket lights are mounted on the front bumper, either remove the lights or leave them in place and disconnect their wiring harness connectors so they don't interfere with front bumper removal.

4   Remove the upper bolts and nut and the lower screws securing the front bumper to the frame and remove it **(see illustration)**.

5   Installation is the reverse of removal. Tighten the upper nuts and the lower screws securely. If aftermarket lights are mounted on the front bumper, turn the ignition switch ON, then turn the light switch ON and make sure the lights work correctly.

5.2 Upper grill (A) mounted on front cover. Lower grill (B) mounted on front bumper

5.4 Front bumper (A) and front cover (B). The lights and shield mounted on the front bumper are aftermarket parts

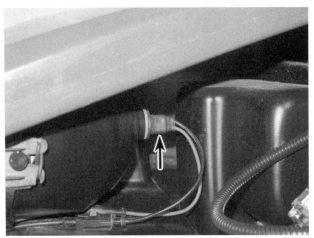

6.5 Remove the headlight bulb holders (arrow) before removing the front cover

7.1 Seat base (A) and seat back (B)

6.6a The front cover is secured with left and right screws and washers (arrow) on the top side . . .

6.6b . . . and left and right screws (arrows) on the front side

6   FRONT COVER AND GRILL - REMOVAL AND INSTALLATION

1   The front cover (see illustration 5.4) is mounted behind the front bumper and houses the left and right headlight housings.
2   Park the vehicle on a level surface and apply the parking brake.
3   Open the hood.
4   Remove the screws securing the upper grill to the front cover (see illustration 5.2).
5   Turn the bulb holders 90 degrees counterclockwise and remove them from the left and right headlight housings mounted inside the front cover (see illustration). Wrap the bulbs with clean paper towels and set aside to protect them from damage when removing the front cover.
6   Remove the screws and washers securing the front cover to the frame (see illustrations). Then lift the front cover and remove it from the vehicle.
7   Installation is the reverse of these steps. After reinstalling the headlight bulb holders, turn the ignition switch ON and make sure both headlights work properly.

7   SEAT AND HEADREST ASSEMBLY - REMOVAL AND INSTALLATION

1   The seat assembly consists of a seat base and seat back, and each can be removed separately (see illustration). Also note that the rear seat assembly used on Crew models is removed and installed in the same way as for the front seat assembly.
2   Park the vehicle on a level surface and apply the parking brake.

14

7.3a Lift the seat to release its left and right pins (A) from the grommets (B) . . .

7.3c . . . and remove the seat base

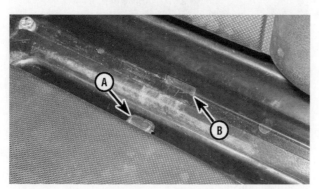

7.3b . . . then slide the seat base forward to release its tabs (A) from the frame slots (B) . . .

7.4 Heat foil mounted underneath the seat base (2010 standard Ranger model shown)

Seat base

3   Grab the seat at one of its corners and pull it upward to release its pin from the grommet mounted inside the frame. Then repeat on the opposite side of the seat. When both sides of the seat are free, slide it forward to release its rear tabs from the slots in the frame and remove it from the vehicle **(see illustrations)**.

4   Before installing the seat base, check the seat pins, tabs and grommets for damage. Also make sure the heat foil mounted on the bottom of the seat base is in place and in good condition and is not torn or missing **(see illustration)**. The heat foil protects the part of the seat base positioned directly over the exhaust system from heat damage. On Crew models, the heat foil is mounted on the rear seat base. Replacement heat foil sheets can be purchased through a dealer parts department.

5   When installing the seat, insert the left and right tabs into the mating frame slots, then push both sides of the seat down until the pins underneath the seal lock into the two grommets. Then grasp the seat and try to roll it forward, making sure it doesn't move and is locked in place.

Seat back

6   Remove the clutch air baffle box (see Chapter 5, Section 2).

7.7 Remove the seat back mounting screws and remove the seat back (three of eight screws shown)

7   Remove the left and right side screws securing the seat back to the cab rail, and remove the seat back **(see illustration)**.

8   Installation is the reverse of removal.

Headrest

9   Remove the screws securing the headrest to the cross brace and remove the headrest **(see illustration)**.

10   Installation is the reverse of removal.

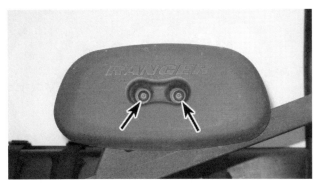

7.9 The headrest is secured to the cross brace with two screws

8.3b The retractor housing is secured to the frame with a nut and bolt (arrow)

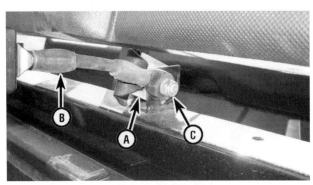

8.2 The lap belts (A) and buckle housings (B) are secured to the frame with a nut and bolt (C)

8.3a The retractor belt is secured to the side cab with a nut and bolt (arrow)

3   Remove one retractor housing at a time, while leaving the other housing installed to be used as a reference. Remove the upper and lower retractor housing fasteners and remove the retractor housing assembly **(see illustrations)**.

4   Replace the seat belt assembly if any part is damaged or the reel will not return the belt when released.

5   Installation is the reverse of removal, noting the following:

   a) *Replace damaged fasteners with OEM fasteners. Install new Nyloc nuts during installation.*

   b) *Tighten the seat belt fasteners to the torque listed in this Chapter's Specifications.*

   c) *Check the seat belt operation. Push the latch plate into the buckle until it clicks, indicating the belt assembly is locked in place. If there was no click, the latch plate is not locked and the buckle housing may be damaged. Release the button on the buckle housing to release the latch plate. The latch plate should release freely. Pull the latch plate to expose the seat belt and check it for cuts, fraying, stiffness and other damage. Make sure the belt moves smoothly and returns under spring tension into the retractor housing. Periodically flush the buckle housings and retractor housings with water from a garden hose to clean them of dirt and other debris. Replace any buckle housing or retractor housing if it does not operate as described or if other damage is present. If necessary, have the seat belt assembly inspected by a dealer service department.*

8   SEAT BELTS - REMOVAL AND INSTALLATION

WARNING:
The seat belts are critical to driver and passenger safety when riding in the vehicle. Inspect the seat belts before each use and replace damaged seat belt assemblies.

1   Remove the seat base (see Section 7).

2   Remove the nut and bolt and the lap belt and buckle housing **(see illustration)**.

9   STORAGE BOX - REMOVAL AND INSTALLATION

1   On standard Ranger models, a storage box is mounted underneath the seat base, on the left side. On Crew models, a storage box is installed underneath the length of the front seat base, and a smaller storage box is mounted underneath the rear seat base, on the left side.

2   Remove the seat base (see Section 7).

14

9.3a Storage box and position used on standard Ranger models. The same size storage box is used on Crew models and located underneath the rear seat base, on the left side

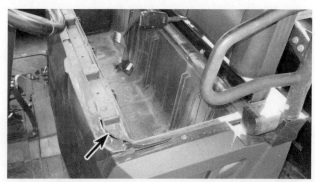

9.3b Front storage box (arrow) used on Crew models

10.2 Left side wheel panel (removed for clarity)

3   Remove the contents stored in the storage box, then lift out and remove the storage box **(see illustrations)**. When removing the front storage box on Crew models, it may be helpful to have someone help you.

4   Installation is the reverse of removal.

10   WHEEL PANELS - REMOVAL AND INSTALLATION

1   Park the vehicle on a level surface and apply the parking brake.

2   Remove the rivets securing either the left or right wheel panel to the frame, then remove the wheel panel **(see illustration)**.

3   Installation is the reverse of removal.

11   DASH - REMOVAL AND INSTALLATION

1   The dash covers the front part of the vehicle, is installed over the side cab tubes and extends into the driver's compartment **(see illustration)**. The dash can be partially removed to service components that are installed underneath it and difficult to access, or it can be completely removed (requiring partial removal or removal of the cab assembly, depending on model).

2   Remove the hood (see Section 3).

3   Disconnect the negative battery cable at the battery (see Chapter 8).

4   Remove the front bumper (see Section 5).

5   Remove the two screws (one each side) securing the dash to the electrical box assembly that sits underneath the dash **(see illustration)**.

6   Remove the screws and rivets securing the rocker panel to the dash. It is not necessary to remove the rivets

11.1 Dash assembly (arrow)

11.5 With the front bumper removed, remove the left and right screws (arrows)

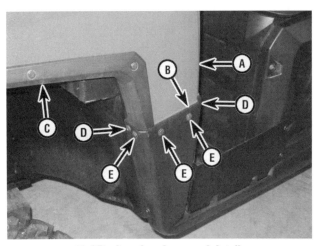

11.6 Dash and rocker panel details

A   Dash
B   Rocker panel
C   Trim panel
D   Screws (one hidden)
E   Rivets

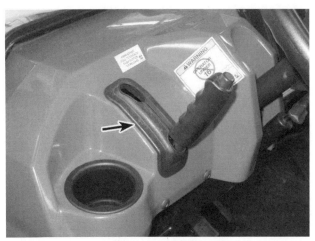

11.7a Parking brake boot (arrow)

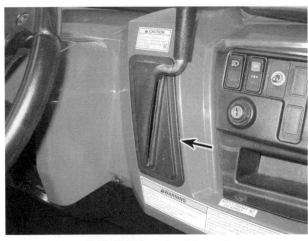

11.7b Shift lever boot (arrow)

11.8 Remove the instrument panel rivets (arrows) and carefully position the instrument panel inside the dash

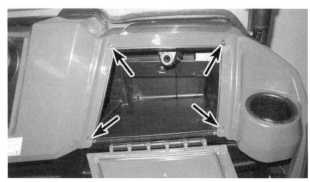

11.9 Remove the screws securing the dash to the glove box (arrows)

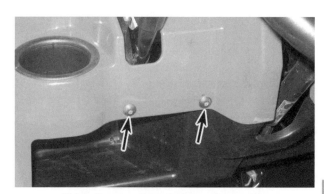

11.10a Remove these dash panel mounting screws (arrows) . . .

14

that secure the trim panel to the dash (see illustration).

7   Remove the parking brake and shift lever boots from the dash (see illustrations).

8   Remove the two rivets securing the instrument panel to the dash, and carefully turn and install the instrument panel inside the dash. This way, you don't have to disconnect any of the electrical connectors (see illustration).

9   Open the glove box and remove the screws located around the glove box opening (see illustration).

10   Remove the screws securing the dash panel to the frame (see illustrations).

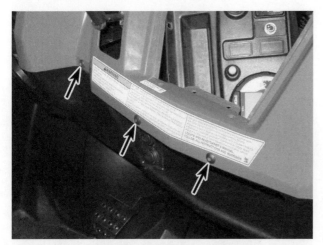

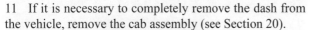

11.10b . . . and these screws

11.12 Here the dash has been partially removed and slid up the side cab tubes to access components installed underneath it

11   If it is necessary to completely remove the dash from the vehicle, remove the cab assembly (see Section 20).

12   If it is only necessary to partially remove the dash, slide it up the side cab tubes, then secure it in place with bungee cords or tie-downs **(see illustration)**. If the steering wheel interferes with dash movement, remove the nut and bolt that secures the steering wheel tilt damper to the pivot tube, then carefully lower the tilt damper and pivot tube (see Chapter 11, Section 5). This will prevent the dash from contacting the steering wheel and allow you to slide the dash higher up the side cab tubes.

13   Installation is the reverse of removal, plus the following:

   a) *If the pivot tube was lowered, install the steering wheel tilt damper and pivot and tighten their fasteners as described in Chapter 11, Section 5*

   b) *Once installation is complete, start the engine and check that the headlights and all electrical components operate correctly.*

12.2a Rocker panel assembly (A). The boot guard (B) is an aftermarket part

12   ROCKER PANELS - REMOVAL AND INSTALLATION

NOTE:

Procedures required to remove the left and right rocker panels are similar for both standard Ranger and Crew models.

1   Park the vehicle on a level surface and apply the parking brake.

2   Remove the screws and rivets securing the rocker panel to the side of the vehicle, and remove it from the vehicle **(see illustrations)**. When working on the right side, reinstall and tighten the fuel cap after removing the rocker panel.

3   Installation is the reverse of removal. When working on the right side, install and tighten the fuel cap after sliding the rocker panel into place.

12.2b Rocker panel assembly

13.1a Floor panel (arrow) mounted on floor and secured in place with mounting screws

14.5a Remove the screws securing the kickboard to the frame, then lift the kickboard (arrow) and remove it from the vehicle

13.1b Note how the hooks (arrows) on the bottom, front side of the floor panel fit underneath the lip in the floor opening

14.5b Hooks (arrow) on the bottom of the kickboard help hold the kickboard in place against the floor

a) Make sure no tools or other parts were left in the area below where the floor panel is installed.
b) Install the floor panel by inserting the hooks on the bottom of the panel into the lip in the floor opening.
c) Tighten the screws securely.

14 KICKBOARD - REMOVAL AND INSTALLATION

NOTE:

Procedures required to remove the front and rear kickboards used on Crew models are similar to the procedures described in Steps 1 through 6 for standard Rangers.

1   Remove the seat base (see Section 7).
2   Remove the storage box (see Section 9).
3   Remove the ECU from the kickboard (see Chapter 7). On Crew models, the ECU is mounted on the rear kickboard.
4   Remove the screws securing the left and right rocker panels to the kickboard (**see illustration**).
5   Remove the screws at the bottom of the kickboard, then lift and remove the kickboard from the vehicle (**see illustrations**).

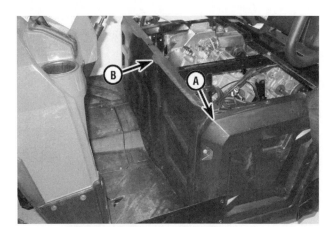

14.4 Rocker panel (A) and kickboard (B)

13 FLOOR PANEL - REMOVAL AND INSTALLATION

1   Remove the screws and slide the floor panel rearward to disconnect it from the floor (**see illustrations**).
2   Installation is the reverse of removal, noting the following:

14

15.1 Storage panel removed from vehicle

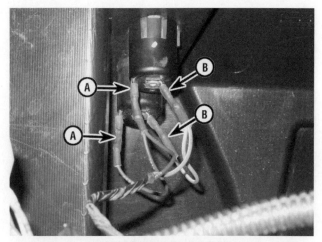

15.5 Disconnect the negative (A) and positive (B) wiring harness connectors at the 12-volt accessory outlets

6   Installation is the reverse of removal. When installing the kickboard, insert its hooks (see Step 5) over the shoulder on the floor while also hooking the top of the kickboard over the frame.

15 STORAGE PANEL - REMOVAL AND INSTALLATION

1   The storage panel is installed lengthwise between the dash and floor (see illustration). The instrument panel, glove box and two 12-volt accessory outlets are installed in the storage panel.
2   Park the vehicle on a level surface and apply the parking brake.
3   Disconnect the negative battery cable at the battery (see Chapter 8).
4   Raise and secure the dash (see Section 11).
5   Working at the front of the storage panel, locate the 12-volt accessory outlets and disconnect their wiring harness connectors (see illustration).
6   Open the glove box and remove the inner and outer screws holding the storage panel in place, then lower and remove it from the vehicle (see illustrations).
7   Installation is the reverse of removal. After reconnecting all of the wiring, make sure the 12-volt accessory outlets work correctly.

15.6a Remove the storage panel mounting screws . . .

16 FLOOR - REMOVAL AND INSTALLATION

Standard Ranger models

1   The floor is a one-piece assembly that begins at the bottom of the storage panel and ends at the kickboard.
2   Park the vehicle on a level surface and apply the parking brake.
3   Remove the seat base (see Section 7).
4   Remove the rocker panels (see Section 12).
5   Remove the floor panel (see Section 13).

15.6b . . . and the storage panel (arrow)

16.9a Uppper mounting screw (left side)

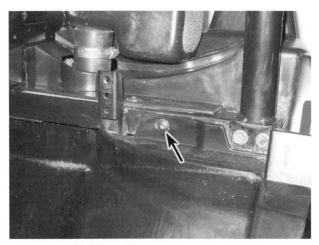

16.9b Upper mounting screw (right side)

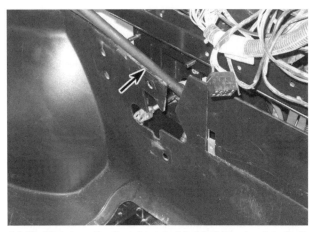

16.10a Note how the floor is routed behind the steering shaft
and over the brake/throttle pedal mounting bracket studs,
then remove the floor at this spot so that it is free of the studs
and positioned in front of the steering shaft (arrow)

16.10b Turn the floor upward from its mounting position...

16.10c . . . and slide it out of the driver's compartment

6   Remove the kickboard (see Section 14).

NOTE:

*Because the upper floor mounting screws
are mounted behind the storage panel, it is
necessary to either reposition or remove the
storage panel. Step 7 instructs to remove the
storage panel mounting screws so you can
reposition the storage panel without removing it. However, if you cannot reposition the
storage panel far enough to access the floor's
upper mounting screws, it will be necessary
to partially remove or completely remove the
storage panel.*

7   Remove the storage panel mounting screws (see
Section 15).
8   Remove the brake and throttle pedal mounting bracket
(see Section 17).
9   Remove the upper mounting screws securing the floor
to the frame **(see illustrations)**. Reposition or remove the
storage panel to access these screws (see Step 7).
10   Remove the remaining screws securing the floor to
the frame. Carefully work the floor off of the brake/throttle
pedal mounting bracket studs and past the steering shaft.
Then turn the floor upward and remove it from the vehicle
(see illustrations).
11   Installation is the reverse of removal. Check the
throttle cable/pedal operation before driving the vehicle.

14

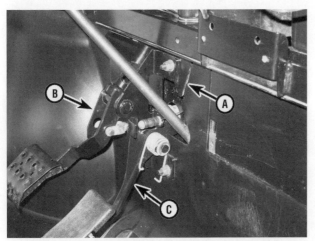

17.1 Brake/throttle pedal mounting bracket (A), brake pedal (B) and throttle pedal (C)

17.3b . . . and withdraw the clevis pin (arrow) to disconnect the brake rod from the brake pedal

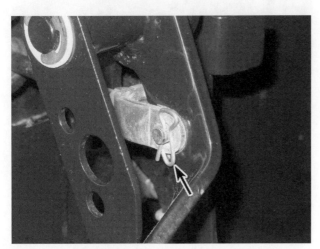

17.3a Remove the clip (arrow) . . .

17.5a Remove the right side mounting bracket nuts (A), noting that it may be necessary to pry the spring (B) away from the lower nut when removing it

Crew models

Front floor

12 Procedures required to remove the front floor are similar to the procedures described in Steps 1 through 11.

Rear floor assembly

13 The rear floor consists of front (vertical) and rear (horizontal) panels.

14 Perform Step 2.

15 Remove the rear seat base (see Section 7).

16 Remove the rear kickboard (see Section 14).

17 Remove the fasteners securing the front (vertical) and rear (horizontal) panels in place, and remove the panels.

18 Installation is the reverse of removal.

17 BRAKE/THROTTLE PEDAL MOUNTING BRACKET - REMOVAL AND INSTALLATION

1 This section describes how to remove the brake/throttle pedal mounting bracket with both pedals installed on the bracket **(see illustration)**. If it is only necessary to remove the throttle pedal, see Chapter 7. If it is only necessary to remove the brake pedal, see Chapter 13.

2 Park the vehicle on a level surface, block the wheels and apply the parking brake.

3 Remove the clip and clevis pin securing the brake rod to the brake pedal **(see illustrations)**.

4 Disconnect the throttle cable at the throttle pedal (see Chapter 7).

5 Remove the nuts securing the brake/throttle pedal mounting bracket to the studs, and remove the mounting bracket as an assembly **(see illustrations)**.

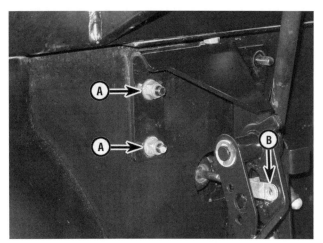

17.5b Remove the left side nuts (A), then remove the mounting bracket while allowing the brake rod to disconnect from the brake pedal (B)

17.7 Route the throttle cable (A) through the opening in the floor, and make sure the clevis locknut (B) is tight

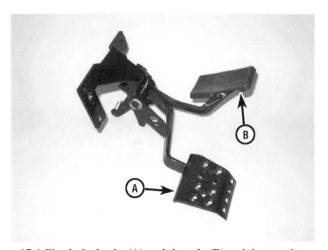

17.6 Check the brake (A) and throttle (B) pedal operation and for any missing or damaged parts

17.8 Installed position of the throttle pedal return spring (arrow)

6   Check each pedal for binding, tightness and other problems **(see illustration)**. If necessary, remove and service the pedals and their separate parts (see Chapters 7 and 13).

7   Before installing the mounting bracket, make sure the throttle cable is routed through the opening in the floor so that it will align with the throttle pedal. Also, while you have access to the brake rod, hold the clevis and make sure its locknut is tight **(see illustration)**.

8   Make sure the throttle pedal return spring is properly installed on the pedal mounting bracket **(see illustration)**.

9   Installation is the reverse of removal, noting the following:

a) *Tighten the brake/throttle pedal locknuts securely.*

b) *Install a new clip when securing the clevis pin to the clevis and brake pedal. Make sure the clip is fully installed and locked in place (see Step 3).*

c) *Check the throttle pedal operation (see Chapter 7).*

d) *Check the brake pedal operation (see Chapter 13).*

18   SKID PLATE - REMOVAL AND INSTALLATION

CAUTION:

Do not operate the vehicle without the skid plate(s) installed, as any contact with the ground can damage the frame and other components.

1   Park the vehicle on a level surface, block the wheels and apply the parking brake.

2   On standard Ranger models, a single skid plate is used. On Crew models, two separate skid plates are used.

14

18.4a Screw and washer set used to secure the skid plate(s) in place

18.4b Use a small jack to support the skid plate during its removal and installation

3   Before removing the skid plate, mark its bottom front side to help align it with the vehicle during installation. On Crew models, do this for both skid plates.
4   Remove the screws and washers securing the skid plate to the bottom of the frame and remove the skid plate **(see illustrations)**.
5   Inspect and replace any damaged or missing screws or washers.
6   Installation is the reverse of removal. Tighten the skid plate mounting screws to the torque listed in this Chapter's Specifications.

19   CARGO BOX AND DAMPER - REMOVAL AND INSTALLATION

WARNING:

Before dumping the cargo box, make sure the load is distributed evenly (front to rear) or toward the front of the cargo box. If the majority of the weight is positioned at the rear, do not release the cargo box as this could cause the load to fall abruptly and possibly injure anyone standing nearby.

1   Remove objects or dump materials located in the cargo box.
2   Park the vehicle on a level surface and apply the parking brake.
3   When the cargo box is empty, pull the release lever and raise the cargo box to its dump position.
4   Locate and disconnect the taillight wiring harness connector **(see illustration)**.

WARNING:

When supporting the cargo box in its raised position in Step 5, make sure the box cannot fall on you when you disconnect the damper in Step 6. From this point on, the cargo box will not be as stable as when it is attached to the damper.

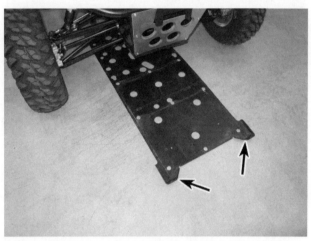

18.4c Skid plate (standard Ranger model shown) - note how the shoulders on the front of the skid plate face upward. On Crew models, the rear skid plate is not equipped with these shoulders

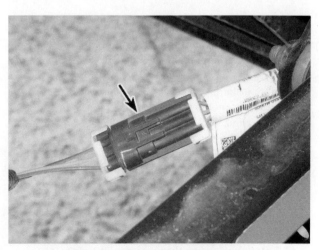

19.4 Disconnect the taillight connector (arrow)

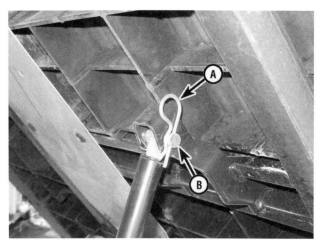

19.6 Remove the clip (A) and pin (B) securing the damper to the cargo bed

19.10b . . . and right hinge pins (2011 and later models)

19.7 Remove the clip (A) and pin (B) securing the damper (C) to the frame and remove the damper

5   With the cargo box in its dump position, support the cargo box with sturdy wooden boards or use a hoist to stabilize it before disconnecting the damper and removing the hinge pins in the following Steps.

6   Remove the clip and push the pin out of the damper and cargo box **(see illustration)**.

7   If it is necessary to remove the damper from the vehicle, remove the lower clip and pin and the damper **(see illustration)**.

8   With the help of one or more assistants (as required), remove the wooden boards or disconnect the hoist used to prop the cargo box in its dump position and lower the cargo bed.

9   On 2010 models, remove the screw that secures each hinge pin in place, then remove the left and right hinge pins that secure the cargo bed to the frame.

10 On 2011 and later models, note the direction the hinge pins are installed through the frame - they should be reinstalled facing in the same direction **(see illustrations)**. Then remove the nuts and both hinge pins from the cargo bed and frame.

11 With the help of one or more assistants (as required), remove the cargo bed from the vehicle.

12 Inspect the hinge pins and the damper pins for cracks and other damage and replace if necessary.

13 On 2011 and later models, inspect the bushings and collars installed in the frame for cracks, severe wear and other damage. Replace if necessary.

14 Installation is the reverse of removal, noting the following:

   a) On 2010 models, install the left and right hinge pins. Then turn each hinge pin as required and secure it in place with its locking screw.

   b) On 2011 and later models, install the left and right hinge pins from their original side. Install new Nyloc nuts or apply a threadlock onto the threads on the hinge pins. Hold the hinge pins and tighten the nuts to the torque listed in this Chapter's Specifications.

19.10a After loosening and removing the nuts, remove the left . . .

14

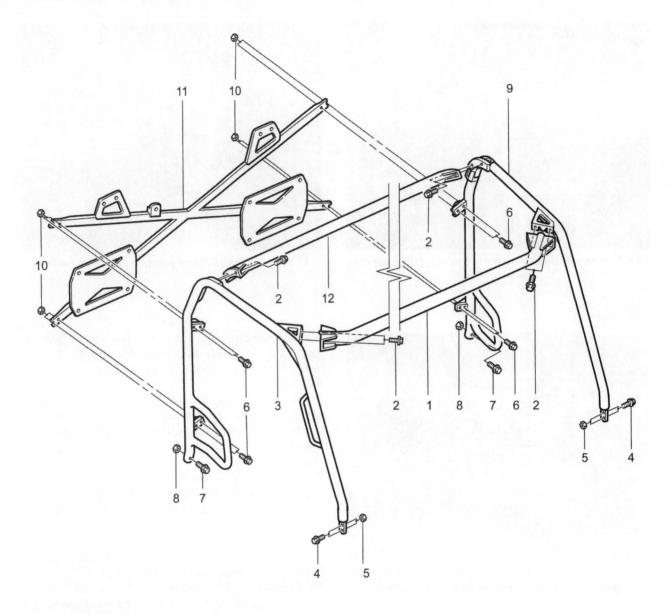

20.3 Cab details (standard Ranger models)	1	Front brace	4	3/8 in. bolts	7	5/16 in. bolts
	2	10 mm screws	5	3/8 in. nuts	8	5/16 in. nuts
	3	Side cab (right)	6	8 mm bolts	9	Side cab (left)

c) *Make sure the damper is installed in place and secured with the pins and clips.*

d) *Close the cargo bed, making sure both sides of the latch locks the cargo bed in place.*

e) *After completing installation, turn the ignition switch on and check the brake light and taillight operation.*

20   CAB ASSEMBLY - REMOVAL AND INSTALLATION

1   Refer to the appropriate owner's manual for information on the side safety nets and how to install and service them.

2   Different size and length fasteners are used to assemble the cab together and to the vehicle's frame. When removing the cab, identify the fasteners and either store them in boxes with divided compartments, or reinstall them onto the cab components in their original mounting positions.

Standard Ranger models

3   When removing the cab assembly, **refer to the illustration** to identify the components and fasteners.

Removal

4   The cab assembly consists of left and right side cabs, front brace, rear brace and rear cross brace. Each part is secured in place with threaded fasteners.

5 Park the vehicle on a level surface and apply the parking brake.

6 Remove the seat base and seat back (see Section 7).

7 Remove the left and right headrest assemblies (see Section 7).

8 Remove the clutch air intake box (see Chapter 5).

9 Loosen, but do not remove all of the fasteners that secure the cab assembly together and to the frame.

10 Remove the nuts and bolts securing the cross brace to the side cabs, and remove the cross brace.

11 Remove the screws securing the front brace to the side cabs, and remove the front brace.

12 Remove the screws securing the rear brace to the side cabs, and remove the rear brace.

13 Remove the nuts and bolts securing one of the side cabs to the frame, then lift and remove the side cab. Repeat for the other side cab assembly.

Installation

14 Before installing original cab components, inspect them for creasing, cracks and other damage. Inspect all welded joints for cracks and damage. If any damage is noted, do not attempt to straighten or repair them, but instead install new components.

15 Inspect all of the fasteners for bending, cracks and damaged threads. When damage is noted, replace the fastener with an OEM fastener.

16 Clean all of the fasteners and threaded holes before installing them.

17 Install new Nyloc nuts during installation.

NOTE:

When installing the cab assembly, tighten the fasteners finger-tight at first. The fasteners will be tightened to their final torque specification and in a specified order after all of the cab components have been installed and assembled together.

18 Lift and install a side cab over its mounting position on the frame. Install a 5/16 in. bolt through the rear mounting hole, and two 3/8 in. bolts through the front mounting holes. Install a nut on each bolt and tighten finger-tight. Repeat for the other side cab.

19 Align and mount the front brace to the side cabs with 10 mm screws. Tighten the screws finger-tight. Repeat for the rear brace.

20 Align the the cross brace with the headrest mounting brackets facing forward, and assemble onto the side cabs with 8 mm bolts and nuts. Tighten the nuts finger-tight.

21 Tighten the front brace 10 mm mounting screws to the torque listed in this Chapter's Specifications.

22 Tighten the rear brace 10 mm mounting screws to the torque listed in this Chapter's Specifications.

23 Tighten the left and right side cab 5/16 in. nuts to the torque listed in this Chapter's Specifications.

24 Tighten the left and right side cab 3/8 in. nuts to the torque listed in this Chapter's Specifications.

25 Tighten the cross brace 8 mm nuts in a crossing pattern to the torque listed in this Chapter's Specifications.

26 The remainder of installation is the reverse of removal.

Crew models

27 When removing the cab assembly, **refer to the illustration** on the following page to identify the components and fasteners.

Removal

28 The cab assembly consists of a front brace, middle brace, rear brace, four side cabs, front cross brace and a rear cross brace. Each part is secured in place with threaded fasteners.

29 Park the vehicle on a level surface and apply the parking brake.

30 Remove the front and rear seat base and seat back assemblies (see Section 7).

31 Remove the front and rear headrest assemblies (see Section 7).

32 Remove the clutch air intake box (see Chapter 5).

33 Loosen, but do not remove all of the fasteners that secure the cab assembly together and to the frame.

34 Remove the nuts and bolts securing the rear cross brace to the rear side cabs, and remove the rear cross brace.

35 Remove the screws securing the rear brace to the side cabs, and remove the rear brace.

36 Working at the top of the cab assembly, remove the nuts and bolts securing one of the rear side cabs to its mating front side cab. Then remove the nut and bolt securing the rear side cab to the frame, and remove the rear side cab. Repeat for the other rear side cab.

37 Remove the nuts and bolts securing the front cross brace to the front side cabs, and remove the front cross brace.

38 Remove the screws securing the middle brace to the front side cabs, then remove the middle brace.

39 Remove the screws securing the front brace to the front side cabs, then remove the front brace.

40 Remove the nuts and bolts securing one of the side cabs to the frame, then lift and remove the side cab. Repeat for the other side cab assembly.

Installation

41 Perform Steps 14 through 17.

NOTE:

When installing the cab/frame assembly, tighten the fasteners finger-tight at first. The fasteners will be tightened to their final torque specification and in a specified order after all of the cab/frame components have been installed and assembled together.

42 Lift and install a front side cab over its mounting

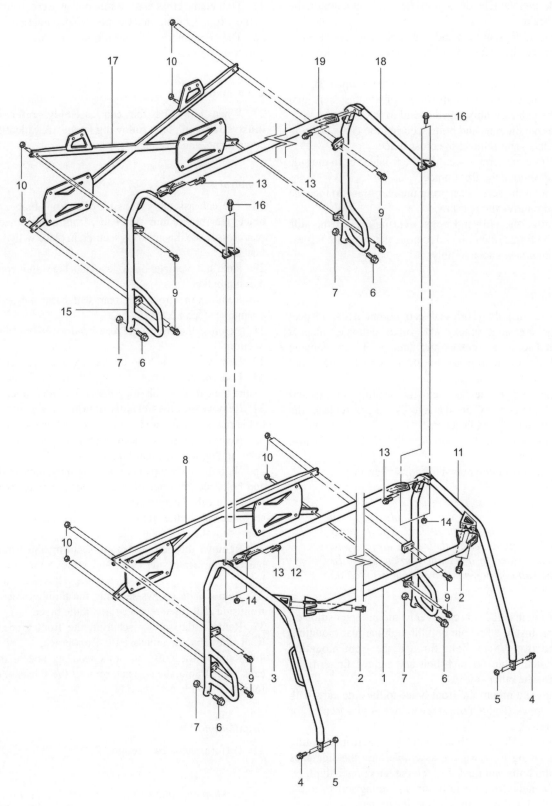

10	8 mm nuts				
11	Cross brace				
12	Rear brace	1	Front brace	6	5/16 in. bolts

20.27 Cab details (Crew models)

1	Front brace
2	10 mm screws
3	Front side cab (right)
4	3/8 in. bolts
5	3/8 in. nuts

6	5/16 in. bolts
7	5/16 nuts
8	Front cross brace
9	8 mm bolts
10	8 mm nuts

11	Front side cab (left)
12	Middle brace
13	10 mm screws
14	10 mm screws
15	Rear side cab (right)

position on the frame. Install a 5/16 in. bolt through the rear mounting hole, and two 3/8 in. bolts through the front mounting holes. Install a nut on each bolt and tighten finger-tight. Repeat for the other front side cab.

43 Align and mount the front brace to the front side cabs with 10 mm screws. Tighten the screws finger-tight. Repeat for middle brace.

44 Align the front cross brace with the headrest mounting brackets facing forward, and assemble onto the front side cabs with 8 mm bolts and nuts. Tighten the nuts finger-tight.

45 Tighten the front brace 10 mm mounting screws to the torque listed in this Chapter's Specifications.

46 Tighten the middle brace 10 mm mounting screws to the torque listed in this Chapter's Specifications.

47 Tighten the front left and front right side cab 5/16 in. nuts to the torque listed in this Chapter's Specifications.

48 Tighten the front left and front right side cab 3/8 in. nuts to the torque listed in this Chapter's Specifications.

49 Tighten the front cross brace nuts in a crossing pattern to the torque listed in this Chapter's Specifications.

50 Lift and install a rear side cab over its mounting position on the frame. Install a 5/16 in. bolt through the lower mounting hole, then install the nut and tighten finger-tight. Align the rear side cab with the front side cab and install two 10 mm bolts through the mounting holes. Then install a nut on each bolt and tighten finger-tight. Repeat for the other rear side cab.

51 Align and mount the rear brace to the rear side cabs with 10 mm screws. Tighten the screws finger-tight.

52 Align the rear cross brace with the headrest mounting brackets facing forward, and assemble onto the rear side cabs with 8 mm bolts and nuts. Tighten the nuts finger-tight.

53 Tighten the rear side cabs left and right side 5/16 in. nuts to the torque listed in this Chapter's Specifications.

54 Tighten the rear side cab-to-front side cab left and right side 10 mm nuts to the torque listed in this Chapter's Specifications.

55 Tighten the rear brace 10 mm mounting screws to the torque listed in this Chapter's Specifications.

56 Tighten the rear cross brace 8 mm nuts in a crossing pattern to the torque listed in this Chapter's Specifications.

57 The remainder of installation is the reverse of removal.

14

SPECIFICATIONS

Torque specifications	Ft-lbs	Nm
Cargo bed hinge pin nuts		
2011 and later models............................	30	41
Cab/frame		
Standard Ranger models		
Cross brace 8 mm nuts	16-18	20-24
Front brace 10 mm screws	25-28	34-38
Rear brace 10 mm screws	25-28	34-38
Side cab 5/16 in. nuts	16-18	20-24
Side cab 3/8 in. nuts	25-28	34-38
Crew model		
Front and rear cross brace 8 mm nuts	16-18	20-24
Front brace 10 mm screws	25-28	34-38
Front side cabs		
5/16 in. nuts	16-18	20-24
3/8 nuts..................................	25-28	34-38
Middle brace 10 mm screws	25-28	34-38
Rear brace 10 mm screws	25-28	34-38
Rear side cabs		
5/16 in. nuts	16-18	20-24
Rear side cab-to-front side cab 10 mm nuts......	25-28	34-38
Seat belt		
Side cab frame fasteners		
2010 through 2012 models	35-40	47-54
2013 and later models	36-44	49-60
Seat base fasteners	36-44	49-60
Skid plate mounting screws........................	6-8	8-10

CHAPTER FIFTEEN

INDEX

15

15

15

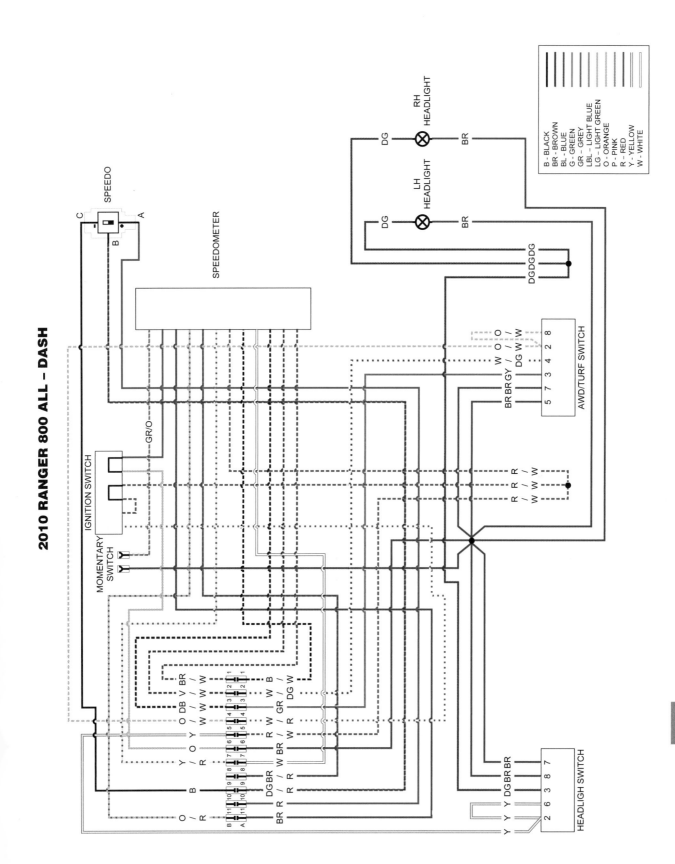

2010 RANGER 800 ALL – DASH

16

2010 RANGER 800 XP, CREW & 6X6 (1 OF 2)

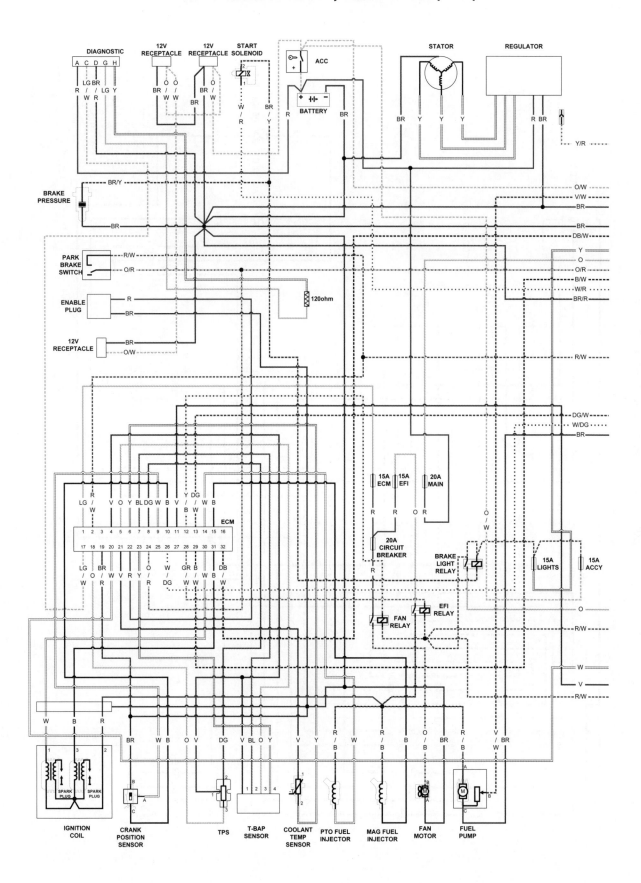

2010 RANGER 800 XP, CREW & 6X6 (2 of 2)

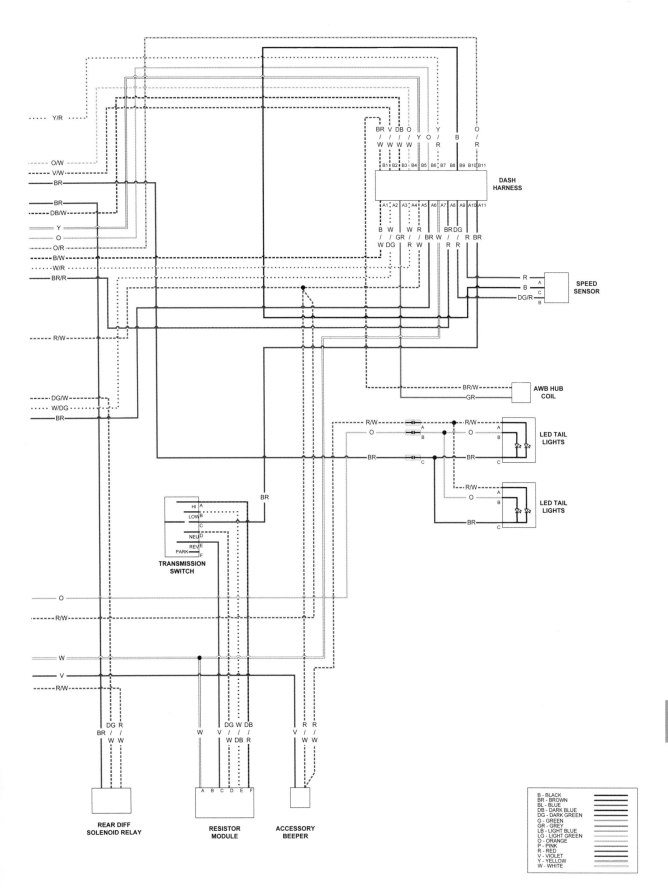

16

2010 RANGER 800 HD 4X4 (1 OF 2)

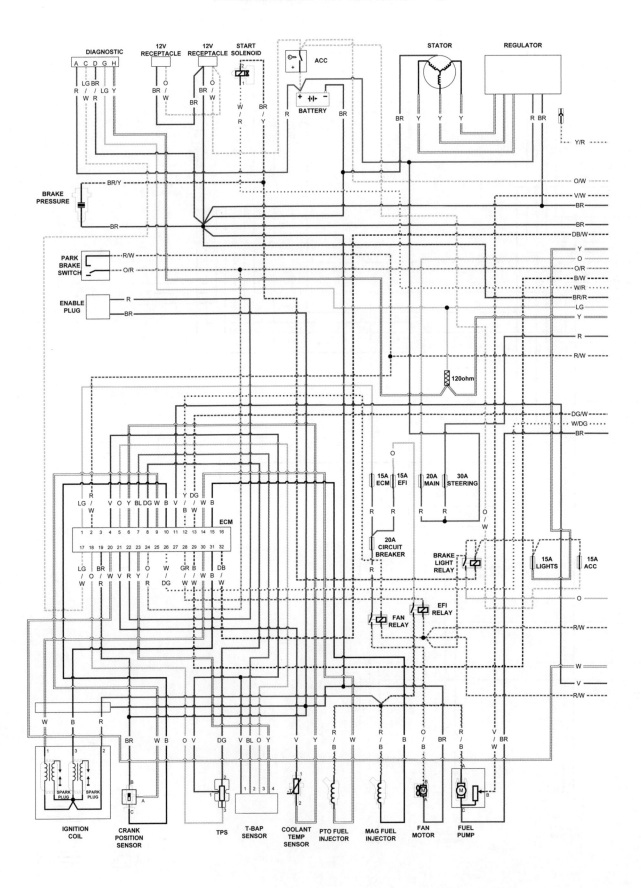

2010 RANGER 800 HD 4X4 (2 of 2)

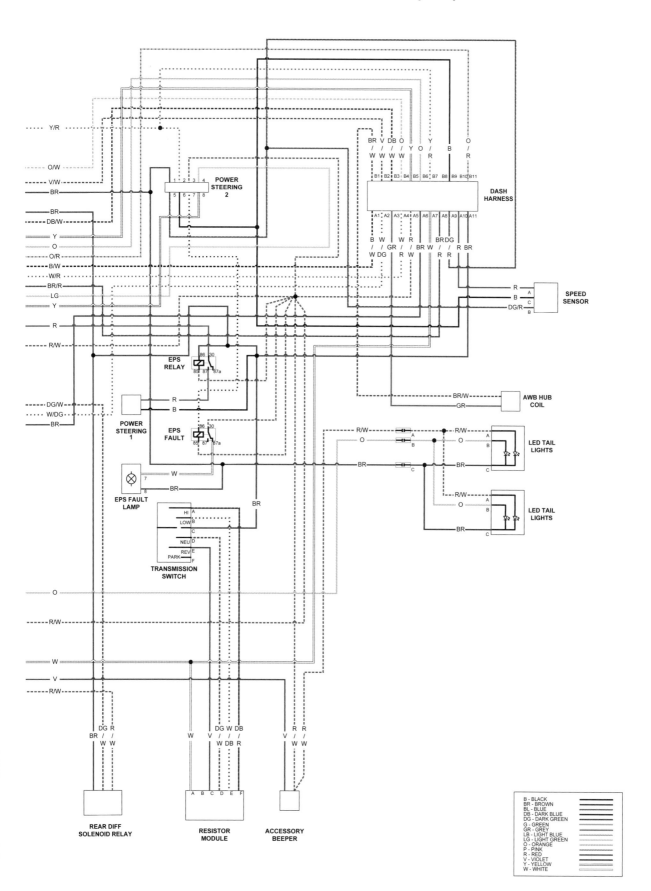

2010 RANGER 800 HD 4X4 – ELECTRONIC POWER STEERING (EPS)

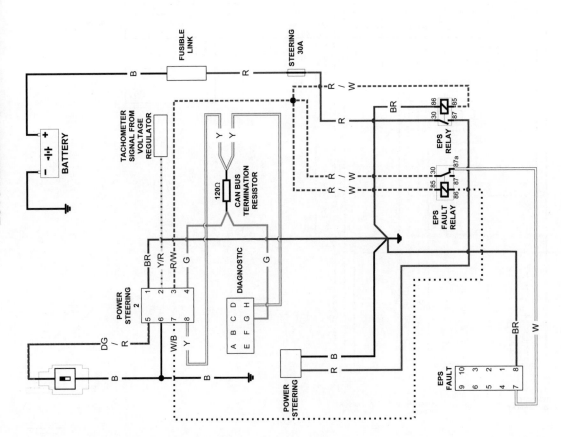

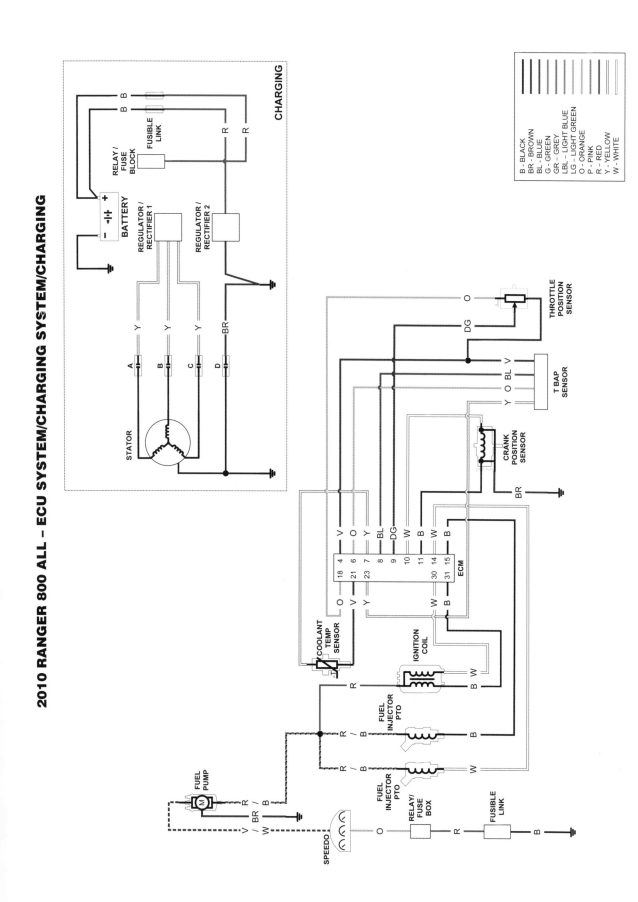

2010 RANGER 800 ALL – ECU SYSTEM/CHARGING SYSTEM/CHARGING

B - BLACK
BR - BROWN
BL - BLUE
G - GREEN
GR - GREY
LBL – LIGHT BLUE
LG – LIGHT GREEN
O - ORANGE
P - PINK
R - RED
Y - YELLOW
W - WHITE

2011 RANGER 4X4 HD, 800 (1 of 2)

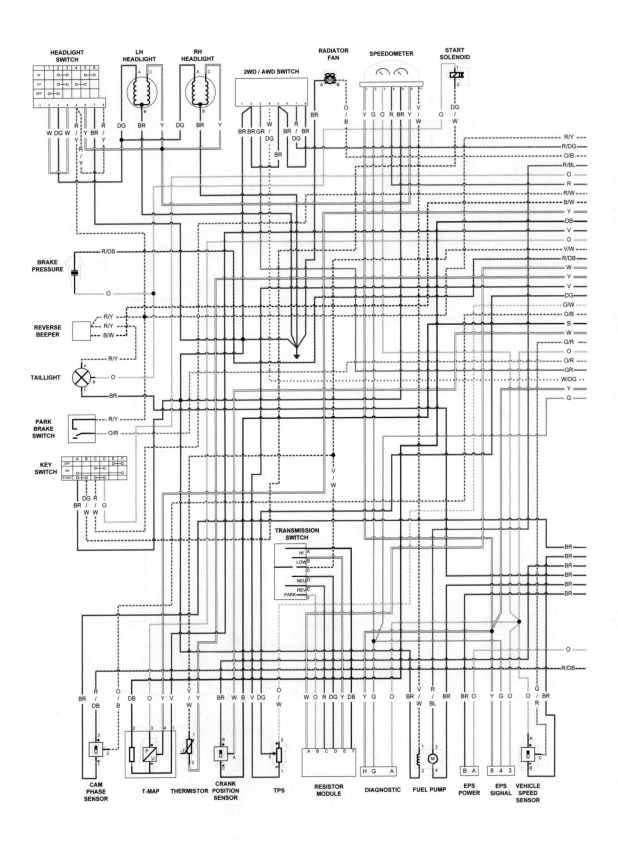

2011 RANGER 4X4 HD, 800 (2 of 2)

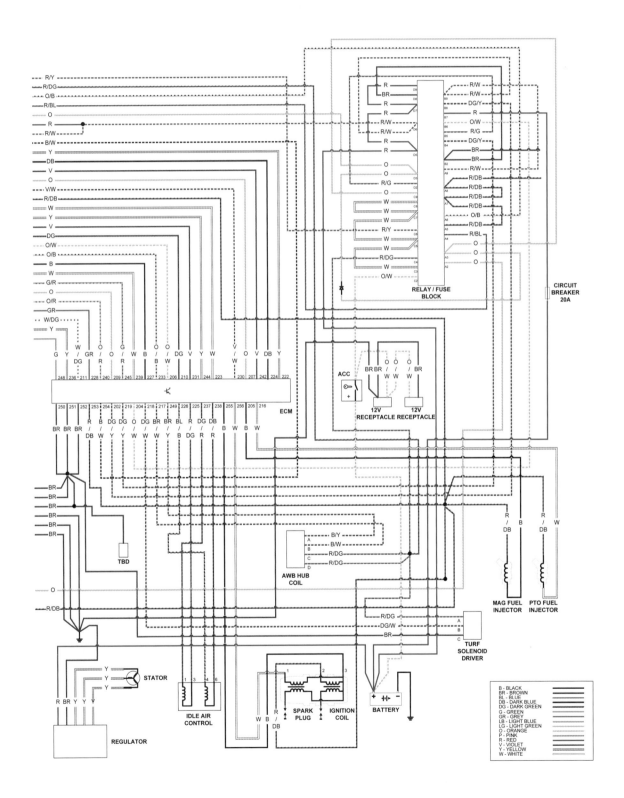

2011 RANGER CREW 800 AND CREW 800 EPS (1 of 2)

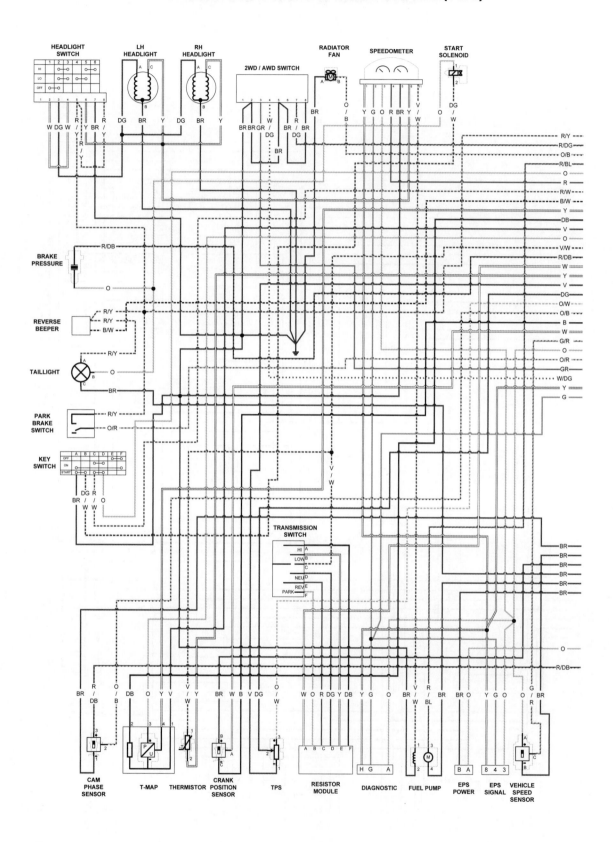

2011 RANGER CREW 800 AND CREW 800 EPS (2 of 2)

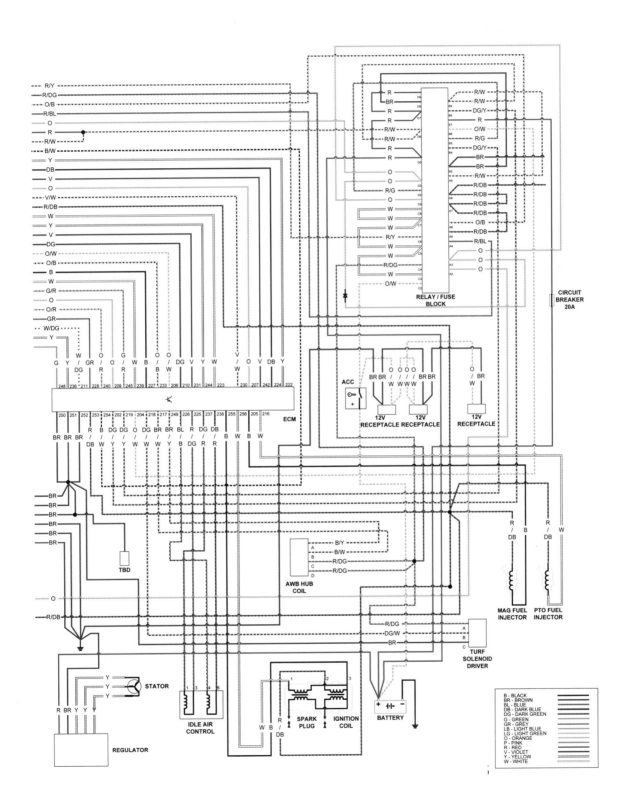

2012 RANGER 800 XP/HD/EPS (1 of 2)

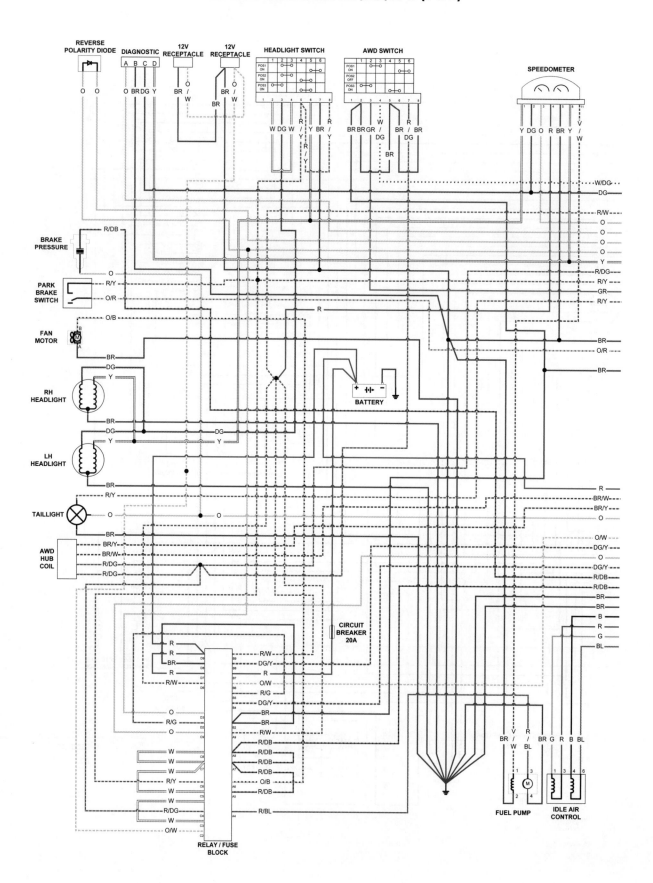

2012 RANGER 800 XP/HD/EPS (2 of 2)

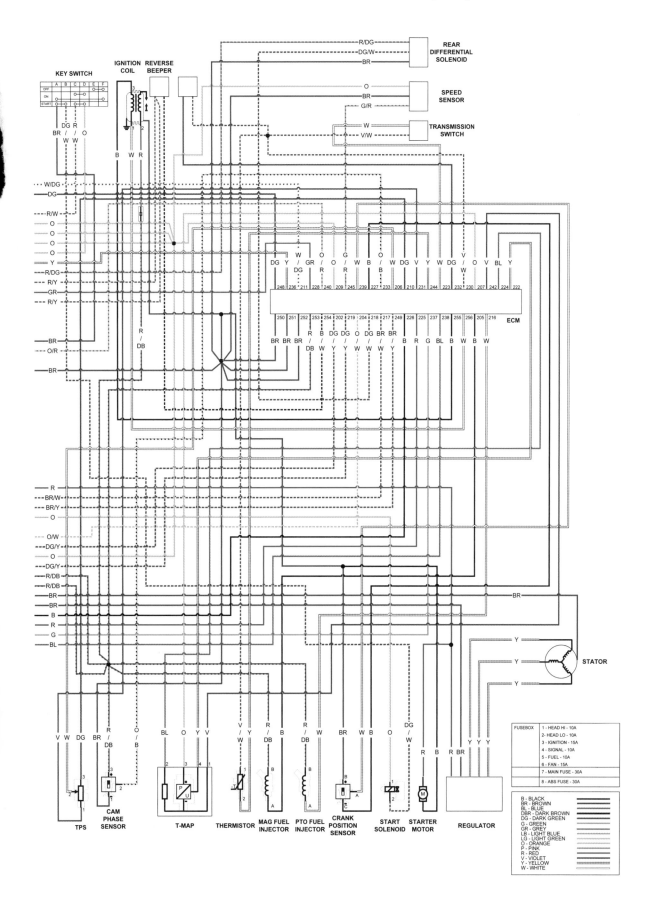

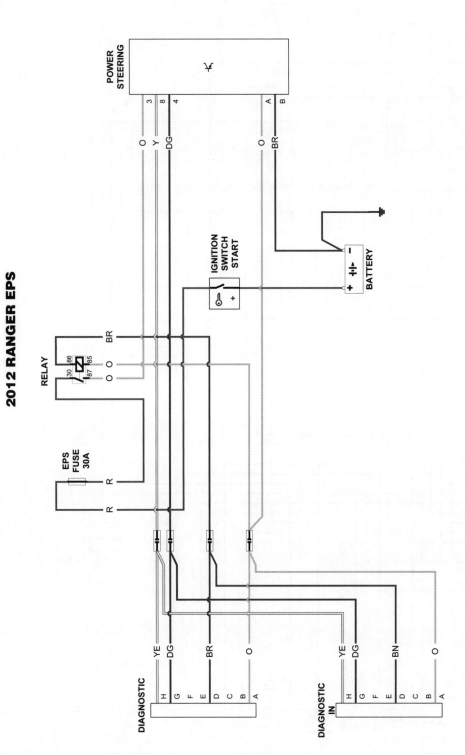

2012 RANGER EPS

B - BLACK
BR - BROWN
BL - BLUE
GR – GREY
LBL – LIGHT BLUE
LG – LIGHT GREEN
O - ORANGE
P - PINK
R – RED
Y - YELLOW
W - WHITE

2012 RANGER 1X1 AND 2014 RANGER – CARGO BOX

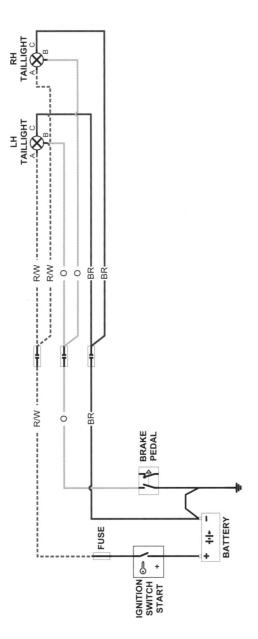

RH TAILLIGHT

LH TAILLIGHT

R/W

O

BR

BRAKE PEDAL

FUSE

BATTERY

IGNITION SWITCH START

16

Check out *clymer.com* for our full line of powersport repair manuals.

BMW

M308	500 & 600cc Twins, 55-69
M502-3	BMW R50/5-R100GS PD, 70-96
M500-3	BMW K-Series, 85-97
M501-3	K1200RS, GT & LT, 98-10
M503-3	R850, R1100, R1150 & R1200C, 93-05
M309	F650, 1994-2000

HARLEY-DAVIDSON

M419	Sportsters, 59-85
M429-5	XL/XLH Sportster, 86-03
M427-3	XL Sportster, 04-11
M418	Panheads, 48-65
M420	Shovelheads,66-84
M421-3	FLS/FXS Evolution,84-99
M423-2	FLS/FXS Twin Cam, 00-05
M250	FLS/FXS/FXC Softail, 06-09
M422-3	FLH/FLT/FXR Evolution, 84-98
M430-4	FLH/FLT Twin Cam, 99-05
M252	FLH/FLT, 06-09
M426	VRSC Series, 02-07
M424-2	FXD Evolution, 91-98
M425-3	FXD Twin Cam, 99-05

HONDA

ATVs

M316	Odyssey FL250, 77-84
M311	ATC, TRX & Fourtrax 70-125, 70-87
M433	Fourtrax 90, 93-00
M326	ATC185 & 200, 80-86
M347	ATC200X & Fourtrax 200SX, 86-88
M455	ATC250 & Fourtrax 200/250, 84-87
M342	ATC250R, 81-84
M348	TRX250R/Fourtrax 250R & ATC250R, 85-89
M456-4	TRX250X 87-92; TRX300EX 93-06
M446-3	TRX250 Recon & Recon ES, 97-07
M215	TRX250EX, 01-05
M346-3	TRX300/Fourtrax 300 & TRX300FW/Fourtrax 4x4,88-00
M200-2	TRX350 Rancher, 00-06
M459-3	TRX400 Foreman 95-03
M454-4	TRX400EX 99-07
M201	TRX450R & TRX450ER, 04-09
M205	TRX450 Foreman, 98-04
M210	TRX500 Rubicon, 01-04
M206	TRX500 Foreman, 05-11

Singles

M310-13	50-110cc OHC Singles, 65-99
M315	100-350cc OHC, 69-82
M317	125-250cc Elsinore, 73-80
M442	CR60-125R Pro-Link, 81-88
M431-2	CR80R, 89-95, CR125R, 89-91
M435	CR80R &CR80RB, 96-02
M457-2	CR125R, 92-97; CR250R, 92-96
M464	CR125R, 1998-2002
M443	CR250R-500R Pro-Link, 81-87
M432-3	CR250R, 88-91 & CR500R, 88-01
M437	CR250R, 97-01
M352	CRF250R, CRF250X, CRF450R & CRF450X, 02-05
M319-3	XR50R, CRF50F, XR70R & CRF70F, 97-09
M312-14	XL/XR75-100, 75-91
M222	XR80R, CRF80F, XR100R, & CRF100F, 92-09
M318-4	XL/XR/TLR 125-200, 79-03
M328-4	XL/XR250, 78-00; XL/XR350R 83-85; XR200R, 84-85; XR250L, 91-96
M320-2	XR400R, 96-04
M221	XR600R, 91-07; XR650L, 93-07
M339-8	XL/XR 500-600, 79-90
M225	XR650R, 00-07

Twins

M321	125-200cc Twins, 65-78
M322	250-350cc Twins, 64-74
M323	250-360cc Twins, 74-77
M324-5	Twinstar, Rebel 250 & Nighthawk 250, 78-03
M334	400-450cc Twins, 78-87
M333	450 & 500cc Twins, 65-76
M335	CX & GL500/650, 78-83
M344	VT500, 83-88
M313	VT700 & 750, 83-87
M314-3	VT750 Shadow Chain Drive, 98-06
M440	VT1100C Shadow, 85-96
M460-4	VT1100 Series, 95-07
M230	VTX1800 Series, 02-08
M231	VTX1300 Series, 03-09

Fours

M332	CB350-550, SOHC, 71-78
M345	CB550 & 650, 83-85
M336	CB650,79-82
M341	CB750 SOHC, 69-78
M337	CB750 DOHC, 79-82
M436	CB750 Nighthawk, 91-93 & 95-99
M325	CB900, 1000 & 1100, 80-83
M439	600 Hurricane, 87-90
M441-2	CBR600F2 & F3, 91-98
M445-2	CBR600F4, 99-06
M220	CBR600RR, 03-06
M434-2	CBR900RR Fireblade, 93-99
M329	500cc V-Fours, 84-86
M349	700-1000cc Interceptor, 83-85
M458-2	VFR700F-750F, 86-97
M438	VFR800FI Interceptor, 98-00
M327	700-1100cc V-Fours, 82-88
M508	ST1100/Pan European, 90-02
M340	GL1000 & 1100, 75-83
M504	GL1200, 84-87

Sixes

M505	GL1500 Gold Wing, 88-92
M506-2	GL1500 Gold Wing, 93-00
M507-3	GL1800 Gold Wing, 01-10
M462-2	GL1500C Valkyrie, 97-03

KAWASAKI

ATVs

M465-3	Bayou KLF220 & KLF250, 88-10
M466-4	Bayou KLF300, 86-04
M467	Bayou KLF400, 93-99
M470	Lakota KEF300, 95-99
M385-2	Mojave KSF250, 87-04

Singles

M350-9	80-350cc Rotary Valve, 66-01
M444-2	KX60, 83-02; KX80 83-90
M448-2	KX80, 91-00; KX85, 01-10 & KX100, 89-09
M351	KDX200, 83-88
M447-3	KX125 & KX250, 82-91; KX500, 83-04
M472-2	KX125, 92-00
M473-2	KX250, 92-00
M474-3	KLR650, 87-07
M240-2	KLR650, 08-12

Twins

M355	KZ400, KZ/Z440, EN450 & EN500, 74-95
M360-3	EX500, GPZ500S, & Ninja 500R, 87-02
M356-5	Vulcan 700 & 750, 85-06
M354-3	Vulcan 800 & Vulcan 800 Classic, 95-05
M357-2	Vulcan 1500, 87-99
M471-3	Vulcan 1500 Series, 96-08
M245	Vulcan 1600 Series, 03-08

Fours

M449	KZ500/550 & ZX550, 79-85
M450	KZ, Z & KZ750, 80-85
M358	KZ650, 77-83
M359-3	Z & KZ 900-1000cc, 73-81
M451-3	KZ, ZX & ZN 1000 &1100cc, 81-02
M452-3	ZX500 & Ninja ZX600, 85-97
M468-2	Ninja ZX-6, 90-04
M469	Ninja ZX-7, ZX7R & ZX7RR, 91-98
M453-3	Ninja ZX900, ZX1000 & ZX1100, 84-01
M409	Concours, 86-04

POLARIS

ATVs

M496	3-, 4- and 6-Wheel Models w/250-425cc Engines, 85-95
M362-2	Magnum & Big Boss, 96-99
M363	Scrambler 500 4X4, 97-00
M365-4	Sportsman/Xplorer, 96-10
M366	Sportsman 600/700/800 Twins, 02-10
M367	Predator 500, 03-07

SUZUKI

ATVs

M381	ALT/LT 125 & 185, 83-87
M475	LT230 & LT250, 85-90
M380-2	LT250R Quad Racer, 85-92
M483-2	LT-4WD, LT-F4WDX & LT-F250, 87-98
M270-2	LT-Z400, 03-08
M343-2	LT-F500F Quadrunner, 98-02

Singles

M369	125-400cc, 64-81
M371	RM50-400 Twin Shock, 75-81
M379	RM125-500 Single Shock, 81-88
M386	RM80-250, 89-95
M400	RM125, 96-00
M401	RM250, 96-02
M476	DR250-350, 90-94
M477-3	DR-Z400E, S & SM, 00-09
M384-4	LS650 Savage/S40, 86-07

Twins

M372	GS400-450 Chain Drive, 77-87
M484-3	GS500E Twins, 89-02
M361	SV650, 1999-2002
M481-5	VS700-800 Intruder/S50, 85-07
M261-2	1500 Intruder/C90, 98-09
M260-2	Volusia/Boulevard C50, 01-08
M482-3	VS1400 Intruder/S83, 87-07

Triple

M368	GT380, 550 & 750, 72-77

Fours

M373	GS550, 77-86
M364	GS650, 81-83
M370	GS750, 77-82
M376	GS850-1100 Shaft Drive, 79-84
M378	GS1100 Chain Drive, 80-81
M383-3	Katana 600, 88-96 GSX-R750-1100, 86-87
M331	GSX-R600, 97-00
M264	GSX-R600, 01-05
M478-2	GSX-R750, 88-92; GSX750F Katana, 89-96
M485	GSX-R750, 96-99
M377	GSX-R1000, 01-04
M266	GSX-R1000, 05-06
M265	GSX1300R Hayabusa, 99-07
M338	Bandit 600, 95-00
M353	GSF1200 Bandit, 96-03

YAMAHA

ATVs

M499-2	YFM80 Moto-4, Badger & Raptor, 85-08
M394	YTM200, 225 & YFM200, 83-86
M488-5	Blaster, 88-05
M489-2	Timberwolf, 89-00
M487-5	Warrior, 87-04
M486-6	Banshee, 87-06
M490-3	Moto-4 & Big Bear, 87-04
M493	Kodiak, 93-98
M287	YFZ450, 04-09
M285-2	Grizzly 660, 02-08
M280-2	Raptor 660R, 01-05
M290	Raptor 700R, 06-09

Singles

M492-2	PW50 & 80 Y-Zinger & BW80 Big Wheel 80, 81-02
M410	80-175 Piston Port, 68-76
M415	250-400 Piston Port, 68-76
M412	DT & MX Series, 77-83
M414	IT125-490, 76-86
M393	YZ50-80 Monoshock, 78-90
M413	YZ100-490 Monoshock, 76-84
M390	YZ125-250, 85-87 YZ490, 85-90
M391	YZ125-250, 88-93 & WR250Z, 91-93
M497-2	YZ125, 94-01
M498	YZ250, 94-98; WR250Z, 94-97
M406	YZ250F & WR250F, 01-03
M491-2	YZ400F, 98-99 & 426F, 00-02; WR400F, 98-00 & 426F, 00-01
M417	XT125-250, 80-84
M480-3	XT350, 85-00; TT350, 86-87
M405	XT/TT 500, 76-81
M416	XT/TT 600, 83-89

Twins

M403	650cc Twins, 70-82
M395-10	XV535-1100 Virago, 81-03
M495-6	V-Star 650, 98-09
M281-4	V-Star 1100, 99-09
M283	V-Star 1300, 07-10
M282-2	Road Star, 99-07

Triple

M404	XS750 & XS850, 77-81

Fours

M387	XJ550, XJ600 & FJ600, 81-92
M494	XJ600 Seca II/Diversion, 92-98
M388	YX600 Radian & FZ600, 86-90
M396	FZR600, 89-93
M392	FZ700-750 & Fazer, 85-87
M411	XS1100, 78-81
M461	YZF-R6, 99-04
M398	YZF-R1, 98-03
M399	FZ1, 01-05
M397	FJ1100 & 1200, 84-93
M375	V-Max, 85-03
M374-2	Royal Star, 96-10

VINTAGE MOTORCYCLES

Clymer® Collection Series

M330	Vintage British Street Bikes, BSA 500-650cc Unit Twins; Norton 750 & 850cc Commandos; Triumph 500-750cc Twins
M300	Vintage Dirt Bikes, V. 1 Bultaco, 125-370cc Singles; Montesa, 123-360cc Singles; Ossa, 125-250cc Singles
M305	Vintage Japanese Street Bikes Honda, 250 & 305cc Twins; Kawasaki, 250-750cc Triples; Kawasaki, 900 & 1000cc Fours